INDEX

Acknowledgments

————

Index of Subjects

————

Index of Names

————

Index of Places

————

Index of Scripture

————

Index of Textual References
for Primary Sources in Inner Margins

————

Bibliography

A three-volume series

FRANCIS OF ASSISI: EARLY DOCUMENTS

INDEX

Acknowledgments
Index of Subjects
Index of Names
Index of Places
Index of Scripture
Index of Textual References
for Primary Sources in Inner Margins
Bibliography

Index of:
Francis of Assisi: Early Documents

Edited by
Regis J. Armstrong, O.F.M. Cap.
J. A. Wayne Hellmann, O.F.M. Conv.
William J. Short, O.F.M.

New City Press
New York   London   Manila

Published in the United States, Great Britain, and the Philippines by
New City Press, 202 Cardinal Rd., Hyde Park, New York 12538
New City, 57 Twyford Ave., London W3 9PZ and
New City Publications, 4800 Valenzuela St. Sta Mesa, 1016 Manila

Cover design by Nick Cianfarani

Library of Congress Cataloging-in-Publication Data:
Francis of Assisi : early documents / edited by Regis J. Armstrong, J. A.
    Wayne Hellmann, William J. Short.
            p.   cm.
        Includes bibliographical references and index.
        Contents: v. 1. The saint.
        ISBN 1-56548-172-0 (Index : hardcover). -- ISBN 1-56548-171-2 (Index
: pbk.)
        1. Francis, of Assisi, Saint, 1182-1226.   2. Christian saints-
-Italy--Assisi--Biography--Early works to 1800.   3. Franciscans-
-History--Sources.   I. Francis, of Assisi, Saint, 1182-1226.
Works.   English.   1999.   II. Armstrong, Regis J.   III. Hellmann, J.
Wayne.   IV. Short, William J.
BX4700.F6F722   1999
271'.302--dc21
[b]   99-18776
                                                                CIP
Printed in Canada

Editors:

Regis J. Armstrong, O.F.M. Cap.

J. A. Wayne Hellmann, O.F.M. Conv.

William J. Short, O.F.M.

Compilers:

John and Vicki Chiment

Jay Hammond III, Ph.D.

Daniel Michaels, Ph.D. (Cand.)

Donald Patten, Ph.D (Cand.)

Michael Dolan

Sande Burr

Contributors:

Anthony Basso

Jonathan Barlow

Arnold Dearing, O.F.M. Conv.

Contents

Acknowledgments 9

Index of Subjects. 12

Index of Names. 145

Index of Places 167

Index of Scripture 176

Index of Textual References
for Primary Sources in Inner Margins. 215

Bibliography 228

Acknowledgments

While working on the index for these volumes, a colophon in many medieval manuscripts came to our attention: "As travelers rejoice to see their homeland, so do those who toiled in these volumes rejoice at its conclusion." Eleven years is a long time to await the completion of a project of this magnitude. As we come to the end of this journey of *Francis of Assisi: Early Documents,* we want to acknowledge all those who throughout these years patiently supported us financially, gave us their talents and gifts unstintingly, encouraged us enthusiastically, offered us hospitality graciously, or prayed for us unceasingly. They journeyed with us and we are indebted to them.

Robert Karris and Anthony Carrozzo provided us with resources that sustained our initial efforts. They obtained the financial help of the Franciscan Provinces of the Most Holy Name, the Sacred Heart, the Immaculate Conception, Christ the King, St. John the Baptist, the Assumption, St. Barbara, Our Lady of Guadalupe, the Provinces of Ireland, England, and Malta, the Vice Province of the Most Holy Savior, the Custody of Saint Mary of the Angels, the Commissary of the Holy Land, and the Conventual Province of Our Lady of Consolation. From their limited resources, four monasteries of Saint Clare—those in New Orleans, St. Louis, Cleveland, and Evansville—contributed, as did the National Fraternity of the Secular Franciscan Order. Saint Louis University through its funding of graduate research assistants, as well as other individual lay supporters, provided important financial assistance.

Impressive as this financial generosity may have been, it was that of the translators, scholars, and technicians that continually amazed us. At the outset, we consulted friars from each of our traditions who could critique the directions we had chosen: Oktavian Schmucki, Lorenzo DiFonzo, and Conrad Harkins. Their years of scholarship and in-depth knowledge of the early texts concerning Francis of Assisi provided us an ideal starting place. Canisius Connors personified the dedicated translator: working long, hidden hours, struggling with words and their meanings, continually striving to make the efforts of the author shine authentically and significantly. Friars from all branches of the First Order: Claude Jarmak, Peter Nickles, Gregory Shanahan, and Paul Barrett joined him in producing translations that were accurate, readable, and poetic, and never asked any reimbursement. Professors Serge Hughes and Ewert H. Cousins gave permission for us to use their earlier translations, and Professors Timothy Noone, Timothy Johnson, Jaime Vidal, and Stephen Cordova provided us with new translations of classic texts. The contributions of these men enabled us to study the texts in a chronological way and to rework the translations accordingly.

It is difficult for us to categorize the contribution of Dominic Monti. His role was twofold: as both an excellent translator and a thorough and objective scholar. In both capacities, Dominic added to each volume documents that paralleled the hagiographical texts. Working quietly and unassumingly, Dominic was unabashedly enthusiastic about each volume and was always ready to make a contribution.

The translators were bolstered by a large number of scholars from across the globe. From Europe, help came to us from Servus Gieben and Philippe Yates. From Australia, Cistercian Michael Casey was an email away when questions about monasticism and its Cistercian expression arose. In the United States, Joseph Chinnici and Cyprian Rosen were always available, as were Michael Cusato, Bernard McGinn, William L. Burton, Timothy Johnson, Jay Hammond III, and Daniel Van Slyke. Keith Warner and John Isom spontaneously volunteered to use their expertise in geography and cartography in researching the maps and the gazetteer found in each volume.

As in the case of Dominic Monti, it is difficult to determine the place of John and Vicki Chiment. In addition to proofreading each volume, they did not hesitate to devote long hours in the Cornell University library or to consult their colleagues in its Agriculture or Veterinary Schools about obscure references that, in their judgment, were worthy of explanation. The final, refined edition of the Index is largely their work.

In addition to the Chiments, Ingrid Peterson, Eileen Haugh, Blaine Burkey, Peter Nickles, and William H. Winters were extraordinary in the tedious, time-consuming task of proof reading; Daniel Michaels and Donald Patten were heroic in assisting with the index. And throughout the years, Noel Riggs of the Franciscan Institute was always available to offer advice, run to the library stacks, or do whatever was needed to expedite our project.

Everywhere we encountered a hospitality that proved we were, in Francis's words, "members of the same family." One after another, our brothers—and truly they showed themselves to be such—encouraged us, inquired about our progress, and patiently listened as we responded. They cleaned or straightened the libraries or conference rooms that we overwhelmed. The Conventuals of Prior Lake, Mount St. Francis, and St. Louis; the Capuchins of Wilmington, Interlaken, and Berkeley; the Friars Minor of Danville, Berkeley, Phoenix, Quincy, as well as those of Munich, Germany, and Glasgow, Scotland. We are grateful to all our brothers for providing us enjoyable and conducive environments in which we found inspiration and encouragement to complete this project.

As publication drew near the expanding English-speaking Franciscan Family embraced our work and did what was necessary to promote it. The General Minister of the Capuchins, John Corriveau, insured that every English-speaking Capuchin throughout the world would have his own set. The Franciscan International Study Centre in Canterbury, England, sponsored successful book launches for both *The Saint* and *The Prophet*. The Franciscan School of Theology in Berkeley, California, celebrated the publication of *The Founder* with a special symposium, as did the Washington Theological Union.

The Franciscan Institute of Saint Bonaventure University in New York sponsored a session at the annual Medieval Conference at Western Michigan University, Kalamazoo, Michigan. All of these initiatives have enhanced the years of unstinting generosity and work that have gone into *Francis of Assisi: Early Documents.*

A special word of thanks must go to Patrick Markey, our unflagging helmsman. He steered our course patiently and gently and, when the currents were turbulent, calmly sustained us. His commitment to deepening the bonds of unity enhanced our desire to work together and enabled us to rejoice as more and more followers and would-be followers of the universal saint, Francis of Assisi, became involved in our efforts.

Finally, we owe our greatest debt of thanks to God Who, through divine inspiration, called us to the Gospel life and gave us Francis of Assisi as our model and guide. This has been for us a journey of discovery. Each crevice or detail offered us new insights into the wonder of the Franciscan tradition and made us tremulous at our role in making it available to contemporary and future admirers of the saint, followers of the founder, and emulators of the prophet. With gratitude we pray that those who contributed to the success of *Francis of Assisi: Early Documents,* and all those into whose hands it will fall, will, like us, be more eager to perpetuate in deed—as well as in word—the heritage the Lord has left us in Francis. And so we exclaim with many other manuscripts: "The end of these volumes: thanks be to God!"

Index of Subjects

of texts in *The Saint* (I), *The Founder* (II), and *The Prophet* (III)
(not including introductions and footnotes)

A

Abandonment. See also Resignation: III 721
Abode. See also Dwelling: I 408, 452, 501,
517, 529; II 120, 729, 819; III 83, 101, 220,
372, 749, 778
Abomination: I 140; II 569, 736
Absence: I 226, 239, 285, 381, 404, 419, 468,
553; II 110, 478, 489; III 67, 400, 446, 484,
507, 511, 524, 561–62, 751, 756, 862
Absolution: I 77; II 420, 656, 804; III 554
Abstinence: I 133, 198, 321, 392; II 77,
149–50, 165, 182, 561, 570; III 234,
278–79, 346, 502–03, 529, 579, 617, 649
Abundance
  alms: II 199
  birds: III 175
  blessing: II 282, 531, 684
  dish: I 552
  flower: I 251
  food: I 392
  fruit: II 260
  God's house: II 392
  good thing: III 551, 597
  grace: I 271; II 179, 644, 688, 716; III
  354, 458, 467, 542, 590, 656
  grain: II 375
  heaven: I 534; III 524
  humility: II 569
  mercy: I 120; III 220, 372, 531, 651
  merit: II 350
  milk II 463, 679
  peace: II 518
  piety: II 697
  possession: I 548; III 33, 551, 628, 708,
  749
  poverty: I 416; II 152, 512, 555; III 235,
  279
  rain: II 719; III 101, 733
  tear: II 655; III 473
  wisdom: II 644
Abuse: I 75, 142, 145, 186, 219, 440, 478,
548, 564; II 79, 82, 144, 210, 365, 687,
698; III 96, 99, 308, 316, 325, 450, 580,
731, 757, 777–78
Acceptance: II 144, 347, 588, 639; III 295,
753, 775, 779
Access: I 575; II 106, 261, 779; III 192, 395,
401, 415, 760–61

Accidie. See Acedia
Accumulation: II 622; III 394, 732, 780
Accusation: I 135, 741; III 136, 326, 489,
722, 785
Accuse: I 182–83, 213, 234, 396; II 35, 412,
537, 589, 624, 733, 817; III 48, 165, 244,
281, 306–07, 329, 439, 447, 451, 570, 578,
605, 608, 693, 798, 804, 829, 846
Acedia. See also Sloth: I 438–39; II 329–31,
718; III 49, 342
Acolyte: I 84
Acquire: I 71, 92, 132, 155, 190, 214, 543,
551; II 194, 300, 368, 512, 518, 678, 732,
816; III 182, 215, 265, 269, 273, 283, 321,
342, 389, 545, 637, 748, 753, 778–79,
787–88, 833
Acquisition: I 447; III 186, 381, 465, 777
Activity: I 42, 44, 49, 75, 105, 127, 303, 364;
II 459, 550, 597, 610, 613, 635, 724, 813;
III 117, 150, 181, 184–85, 386, 397, 412,
689, 758
Address: I 320, 322, 404, 491, 503; II 203,
325, 511, 622, 718, 744, 795; III 92, 175,
199, 203, 218, 328, 370, 860, 884
Administration: I 47, 77, 90; III 766
Administrator: I 580; III 463
Admiration: I 181, 183, 231, 450, 487, 549,
603; II 511, 527, 603, 613, 686, 698, 718,
750, 810; III 148, 356, 437, 445, 449, 519,
562, 616, 681, 792, 813
Admire: I 290, 518, 584; II 390, 406, 415,
418, 477, 540, 570, 722, 726, 749; III 389,
457, 486, 724
Admission: I 457; III 60, 90
Admonish: I 48, 66–67, 94, 101–02, 105,
119, 472, 565; II 52, 101, 214, 339, 341,
572; III 245, 321, 638
Admonition: I 45, 67, 79, 105, 127–28, 205,
252, 491; II 52–53, 85, 209, 331, 643; III
179, 317, 343, 357, 383, 401, 406, 488,
619, 711, 726, 743–44, 772
Adolescence: I 183
Adoration: I 46–47, 78, 80, 85, 88, 91, 116,
124, 151, 222, 388, 475, 509, 536; II 42,
90, 449, 671, 773; III 619, 652, 798
Adulation: II 705
Adultery: I 73, 79, 440

12

Advantage: II 45, 87, 92, 164, 370, 747, 787; III 39, 242, 302, 402, 747
Advent: I 514; III 381, 820
Adversary: I 155, 331; II 407, 603, 787, 796, 800; III 56, 539, 876
Adversity: I 199, 374, 440, 447, 465, 530, 542; II 45, 178, 512, 523, 741; III 160, 476, 530, 648, 650
Advisor: III 714, 773
Affable: I 183, 252, 370, 430, 544; II 531; III 81, 835
Affection: I 84, 193, 214; III 50
    angel: II 373
    Bethlehem: I 256
    brother: I 380–81, 419, 505; II 52, 95, 100–01, 126, 276, 358, 366, 370, 386, 393, 437, 439, 466, 617, 643, 666, 668, 715, 775; III 67, 226, 232, 255, 326, 355, 415, 425, 561, 697, 702, 741, 753, 774, 834
    Cardinal Leo: II 575
    Conrad: III 522
    creature: I 235, 248–50; II 592, 715; III 175, 357, 856
    flesh: III 538
    Francis: I 245; II 388, 403, 476, 582, 593; III 833–34
    God: I 320; II 310, 373, 391, 477, 612, 669; III 362, 365, 401, 446, 470, 651, 869, 875
    Hugolino: I 247, 270
    John of Greccio: II 228
    Leo: II 575
    one another: I 217–18; II 751; III 38–39, 61, 447, 548
    poor: II 302, 589, 697; III 850
    Poor Ladies: II 128, 378; III 229, 516, 624, 794
    Portiuncula: II 258
    priest: III 856
    sick: III 794
    Tau: II 556, 693
Afflict: I 154; II 76, 177, 704, 711; III 118, 233, 395, 504, 506, 618–19, 666, 691
Affliction: II 522, 524; III 450, 581
    brother: I 465; II 467, 491, 628, 740; III 354, 400, 413, 547
    Elias: II 489
    Francis: I 184, 262, 346–47, 509, 511; II 522, 524, 531, 561, 631, 740; III 232, 334, 346–47, 478, 599, 731, 852
    healing: I 240–42, 257, 298, 303, 324–25, 343, 487, 494; II 432–33, 458, 461, 467, 479, 589, 628, 674, 678, 704; III 69, 71
Age: I 50, 129, 147, 182, 215, 263, 272, 284, 293, 331, 347, 401, 410, 479, 493, 514, 517, 550; II 99, 120, 201, 249, 351, 360, 387, 390, 401, 406, 463, 477, 514, 553, 649–50, 679, 711; III 147–49, 158, 176,

187, 191, 216, 220, 274, 415, 426, 548, 679, 816, 840, 849
    Clare: I 197
    Francis: I 187, 319; II 99, 384, 463, 530, 679, 684, 715
    old age: I 100, 183, 187, 189, 197, 215, 260, 277, 294, 319, 373, 385, 446, 457, 519; II 76, 99, 307, 384, 423, 428, 432, 441, 463, 530, 536, 580, 626, 656, 669, 679, 684, 686, 715; III 48, 54–55, 150, 529, 603, 741, 770, 802
    San Damiano: I 189, 373; II 76, 536, 686
Agitation: III 105
Agreement: I 223, 293, 312, 546; II 383, 432, 468, 594, 664, 733; III 41, 546, 555, 766
Air: I 114, 225, 234, 241, 251, 296, 322, 390, 396, 410, 434, 447, 450, 470, 484, 489, 492, 502, 535, 599; II 132, 147, 159, 285, 372, 401–02, 412, 473, 478, 557, 578, 624, 628, 632, 638, 650, 674, 700, 709, 762, 786, 800, 813, 815; III 92, 102, 124, 203, 254, 262, 315, 368, 418, 455, 462–63, 470, 478, 494, 499, 512–13, 525, 527, 535, 588, 593–94, 609, 636, 653, 713, 780, 860, 874
All Saints: I 66, 101; III 772
Allegory: I 459
Alleluia: I 83, 138, 257, 347, 349, 351–53; III 151, 372
Alliance: I 440
Almond confection: II 32, 122; III 222, 360
Alms
    Basilica of St. Francis: I 564
    brother: I 47, 61, 69–71, 91–92, 94, 103, 125, 565, 572–73, 575, 584, 586, 598; II 41, 47, 88–89, 94, 150–52, 161, 173, 176, 189, 199, 201–02, 208, 256, 287, 291, 295, 297–98, 466, 582, 589, 656, 776, 779, 794, 809; III 39, 59, 156, 169, 215–19, 234–35, 240, 250, 264–65, 269–76, 310, 338, 386, 450, 461, 525, 580, 585–87, 610, 696, 745, 748, 750, 752–55, 760, 766, 774, 776–77, 781, 785, 827
    Francis: I 195, 377, 598; II 34–35, 69, 71–74, 81–82, 130, 150–51, 195–96, 198–202, 208, 256, 273, 287, 292, 295–99, 306, 455, 531, 534, 539, 581–83, 585, 596, 601, 674, 685, 688, 707, 792; III 38, 57, 81, 100, 123, 174, 214–17, 234, 265, 269–76, 280–81, 284, 286, 307, 310, 321, 338, 385–86, 450, 461, 496, 580, 585–87, 610, 695, 800, 820, 846, 849
    others: I 195, 248, 377; II 34, 44, 91, 138, 165, 183, 195–96, 221, 304, 306, 455, 466, 583, 589, 674, 802; III 59, 275, 280, 286, 495–96, 610, 846
    Poor Ladies: I 115

Rule: I 61, 69–71, 94, 103; II 776; III 747, 750, 752–53, 774, 776–77, 785

Testament: I 125

Alps: I 76, 499; II 56, 105, 122, 740–41; III 222, 559

Altar: II 327; III 304, 463, 481, 522, 527, 588, 600, 636, 638, 792, 848, 865
  appointment: I 56; II 534, 590
  Basilica of St. Francis: II 428, 661
  Blessed Virgin: II 291–92, 555, 579, 591, 692; III 57, 91, 590
  cross: I 46
  eucharistic: I 47, 52, 56–57, 118–19, 128–29, 325, 419, 562; II 109, 163, 215, 478, 534, 573; III 67, 83, 241, 301, 480, 543, 656–57
  Francis: I 257, 262, 407, 409, 509, 567; II 73, 86, 163, 168, 247, 291–92, 328, 375–76, 423, 428, 452, 534, 573, 579, 590–91, 631, 658, 660, 676–77; III 70, 72, 241, 301, 304, 463, 480–81, 588, 804, 811, 848, 865
  incense: II 760
  other churches: II 73, 86, 168, 247, 376, 455, 573, 631; III 620
  Portiuncula: II 47, 291–92, 579, 591; III 811

Altar cloth: II 376, 423, 658

Ambition: I 439; II 327, 330, 340, 343; III 156, 700

Ancestor: II 263; III 160

Angel: I 83, 118, 158, 449, 499, 529, 534, 538, 549, 567; II 268, 358, 364, 519, 622, 724, 734, 746, 754, 756, 812; III 160, 386, 391, 440, 449, 481, 522, 531, 547–48, 567, 571, 580, 611, 645, 650, 715, 804
  brother: I 542; II 208, 258, 476, 647, 722, 814; III 298, 320, 381, 442–44, 524, 527, 529, 531, 535–37, 542–43, 549, 555, 573, 600, 645–46, 648, 653–54, 656–57, 689–90, 697, 706
  Francis: I 251, 279–80, 284, 286–87, 289, 349, 554; II 526–27, 544, 628, 638, 714, 721, 735, 764; III 100, 117–18, 125, 149, 152, 156, 181, 188, 191, 308, 324, 373, 393–96, 435, 442–43, 453–54, 460, 464, 474–75, 490, 494, 505, 509, 512, 540, 551, 557, 567, 578, 582, 585, 588, 595, 598, 600, 605, 609, 615, 618, 628, 647, 666, 687, 717, 719, 727, 744, 762, 811–12, 814–16, 867, 869–70
  Gabriel: I 46; II 760
  God: II 628; III 393, 440, 443, 500, 547–48, 571, 573–74, 618, 642
  Jacob: II 753–54
  Matthew: III 690
  Michael: II 226, 373
  peace: II 526; III 829
  Philadelphia: III 156
  robber: III 497–500, 611–13
  Satan: I 569, 576; II 751

sixth seal: II 496; III 149, 152, 156, 188, 191, 816

Zechariah: II 760

Anger: I 136, 438, 440, 538, 554; II 509, 517, 756, 764; III 44, 524
  brother: I 48, 67, 72, 91–92, 94, 96, 104, 133; II 52, 102, 134, 143, 347, 359; III 118, 125, 178, 203, 252, 295–96, 394, 442, 489, 524, 573, 693
  Francis: I 184, 253, 479, 506; II 52, 102, 146, 359, 367, 451, 678; III 203, 252, 288, 571, 582, 865
  God: I 133; II 178, 452, 519, 677, 748, 779; III 147, 318, 764, 767, 783, 790
  greed: I 545, 548
  other: II 188, 453, 464, 752; III 350, 607
  Pietro Bernadone: I 190, 193, 375, 443, 447; II 78, 80, 537, 687
  Rule: I 67, 92, 104; II 359; III 288
  Satan: III 411

Anguish: I 43, 51, 75, 79, 87, 90, 285, 287, 431; II 172, 324, 499, 657, 669; III 43, 393, 539, 612, 615, 650

Animal: II 178, 216, 283, 455, 462, 464; III 70, 454, 613

Anthony: III 520–21, 632–33
  Christmas: I 256–57, 599; II 411, 802; III 230, 363
  Francis: I 234, 248, 256–57, 396–97, 401, 501, 599; II 130, 269, 279, 321, 354, 411, 414, 518–19, 590–91, 594, 611, 628, 634, 697, 706, 708, 711, 727, 772, 798; III 104, 176, 230, 245, 363, 449, 482–85, 498, 580, 601–04, 669, 733, 838, 851
  obedience: I 165
  possession: I 73, 583

Announcement: I 57, 59, 74, 89–90, 95, 98, 176, 225, 298, 320, 381, 394, 461, 464, 591; II 37, 43, 52, 90, 102, 192, 205, 356, 391, 413, 490, 594, 602; III 67, 94, 119, 125, 168, 259, 276, 324, 396–97, 421, 464, 476, 536, 542, 547, 588, 642, 653, 699, 719, 808, 835, 843, 863
  death of Francis: I 296; II 403, 477; III 835
  exhortation: I 78, 90
  Gregory IX: I 296, 298, 461; II 391, 477; III 67, 259
  peace: I 381, 461; II 43, 52, 90, 102, 543; III 44, 276; III 119
  Saracen: I 74, 95, 394; II 602
  word of God: I 74, 89, 95, 320, 394

Ant: I 206, 586; II 413, 473, 593

Antichrist: I 582, 585; III 136, 424, 816, 879

Anxiety: I 50, 69, 71, 79–80, 88, 137, 182, 224, 244, 273, 371, 440, 570–71; II 75, 489, 510, 554, 618, 701, 775, 816; III 151, 502, 596, 657, 742, 761, 769, 813, 864

Apostasy: II 265; III 135, 192, 721

Apostle: I 83, 129, 259, 287, 369, 539–40, 554, 594; II 46, 53, 98, 135, 348, 400, 457, 540, 542, 689, 755, 764; III 42, 85, 148, 192, 195–98, 201, 386, 392, 404, 423, 453, 588, 631, 693, 740, 789–90
  Andrew: III 683
  James: I 72, 77; III 654, 686, 689
  John: I 89; II 527; III 555, 640, 687
  Judas: I 117; III 34
  Paul: I 69–70, 73, 83, 91, 106, 117, 132, 295, 561–62, 565, 567; II 272, 477, 560, 575, 598, 731, 757, 760, 764, 779, 815, 817; III 41–42, 175, 399, 450, 542, 561–62, 581, 588, 611, 694, 718, 724, 764, 767, 783, 786, 790, 850, 867
  Peter: I 83, 106, 292, 295, 384, 561–62, 565; II 73, 247, 477, 534, 540, 547, 598, 620, 688, 749, 756, 779; III 41–42, 588, 684, 701, 718–19, 764, 767, 783, 790
  Philip: III 689
  Simon: III 691–92
  sixth age: III 148, 156–57
  Thaddeus: III 692
  Thomas: III 687
Apostleship: I 259, 558, 580, 582, 589, 593; II 94, 399, 477; III 192, 195–98, 201, 244, 336, 381, 435, 566, 680–83, 686, 689, 690–92, 699, 701, 719, 740, 789, 824
  Francis: I 259, 271, 287, 329, 413; II 53, 107, 248, 390, 477, 513, 586, 598, 682, 688–89, 765; III 33–34, 148, 157, 174, 244, 336, 381, 435, 453, 566, 568, 589, 680, 683, 687, 699, 701, 719, 732
  sixth age: III 148, 156–57
Apostolate: III 566
Apparition: II 402, 635, 638, 651, 711; III 79–80, 87, 117, 191, 194, 400, 595, 698, 717, 874
Appeal: II 254
Appearance: I 193, 214, 265, 569; II 119, 267, 349; III 863, 867
  angel: I 252, 277; III 117, 393, 395
  Bernard: III 426, 567
  brother: I 216, 547; II 148, 264, 294, 300, 618, 772; III 41, 134, 393, 399, 425, 779, 781
  Christ: II 632; III 79, 534, 543, 589, 619, 840–41, 866
  deed: I 225
  Francis: I 193, 252–53, 340, 416, 503, 505; II 97, 143, 250, 340, 490, 620, 644, 743, 808; III 173, 188, 288, 728, 840–41, 865–66
  lust: I 440
  piety: I 543
  virtue: II 721, 581
Applause: I 273, 404; II 334, 455, 571; III 177
Application: I 457; II 696

Appointment: I 56, 468; II 109, 534, 590, 697
Approval: I 267, 443; II 37, 49, 69, 145, 240, 337, 365, 529, 542, 722, 753, 777; III 53, 59, 79, 88, 188, 326, 418, 680–81, 740, 760
April: I 565; II 34, 472, 498
Archangel: I 76, 108, 138, 141, 301; II 593, 598, 709, 711; III 527, 636–37
Archbishop: I 558–59, 565, 576, 606, 608; III 35, 58, 63, 770
Archdeacon: I 558, 565, 576
Architect: II 569
Ardor: I 582, 588; II 108, 392, 547, 552, 599, 601, 631–32, 697, 709–10, 790, 795, 798; III 147, 202, 333, 530, 540–41, 649, 883
Argument: I 89, 95, 359, 395, 413, 433, 545, 606, 608; II 62, 406, 817; III 79, 119, 194, 390, 497, 561–63
Ark: I 599; III 398, 470, 519, 593, 631
Arm: I 149, 193, 253, 276, 375; II 40, 80, 129, 187, 200, 204, 228, 418, 421, 426, 430, 432, 441, 444, 454, 460–61, 480, 489, 538, 610, 657, 659, 662, 670, 675, 807; III 70, 74, 216, 219, 229, 274, 304, 340, 345, 350, 357, 381, 426, 430, 447, 455, 457, 463, 472, 475, 501, 528, 544, 548, 577, 592, 595, 600, 635, 637, 645, 695–96, 728, 874
  cross: I 87, 281, 536; II 39, 319, 336, 371, 402, 516, 545, 557, 578, 643, 650, 692, 699, 715, 744, 795; III 438, 529, 532, 569, 649, 651, 657
  faith: III 501
  God: III 410
  seraph: I 263, 410; III 117, 393
  sky: III 87
  statue: II 301; III 486–87, 723–24
  weapon: I 186, 358, 372, 436, 463–64, 554; II 35, 41, 70, 89, 271, 532, 637–38, 685, 744–45; III 46, 63, 87, 478, 597, 722, 778, 781
Armed: I 186, 316, 371, 470; II 271, 407, 425, 607, 614; III 133, 176, 343, 454, 471, 482, 601, 609
Armor: I 191; II 70, 78, 245, 404, 560, 615, 650, 655, 703, 744; III 161
Army: I 216, 371, 385, 389, 440, 485, 541, 550, 581, 584, 607, 608–09; II 141, 265–66, 365, 399, 401, 541, 560, 614, 652, 720, 760, 800; III 94, 176, 325, 489, 527, 552, 596, 604, 636, 653, 846, 864, 888
Aroma: I 552; II 354; III 715
Arrest: II 437–39, 481, 667; III 804
Arrogance: I 182, 253, 273, 437, 554, 601; II 178, 338, 570, 789; III 353, 389, 722, 840
Arrow: I 269, 304, 443; II 404, 467–68, 654–55, 797; III 182, 343, 500, 615, 669
Art: I 448, 465, 497, 509, 511; II 353, 405, 747; III 63, 828, 892
Ascension: I 147–50; II 744; III 421, 732

Ascent: I 430, 532, 549, 589; II 77; III 81, 155, 381

Ash: I 227, 278, 392, 415, 514; II 77, 122, 182, 209, 287, 370, 372, 380, 418, 437, 475, 522, 561, 694, 794; III 136, 222, 258, 305, 360, 578, 707, 801, 835, 852, 868

Asia: III 150, 152, 687

Ass: I 221, 255, 387, 474, 506, 566; II 94, 130, 332, 610, 783, 793; III 101–02, 153, 363, 520, 562, 632

    Brother Ass: II 130, 325, 562, 564, 795, 807; III 230

Assault: I 71, 244; II 607; III 194, 446, 487, 724, 733, 826, 853

Assembly: I 142, 203, 238, 271, 293–95, 358, 418, 469; II 268; III 476–77, 490–91, 597, 854

Assumption: II 226, 374, 598, 808; III 544, 656, 658, 810

Athlete: I 190; II 537, 715; III 670, 888

Attachment: II 510; III 85, 164, 191, 401

Attraction: II 814

August: I 297, 419; II 32, 68, 478, 648; III 151, 764

Austerity: I 356, 505; II 76, 85, 102, 149, 358, 529, 561, 564, 570, 599, 631, 712; III 62, 96, 118, 150, 152–53, 395, 495, 575, 691

Authentication: III 191, 151

Authority: I 273, 470; II 364; III 834, 857

    apostolic: I 221, 385, 565; II 83, 99, 109; III 32, 36, 41, 684, 748, 758, 762–63, 769–70, 845, 855

    Apostolic See: I 99; II 106, 514, 550, 629, 690–91; III 79, 180, 391, 755

    Bonaventure: III 31, 698

    brother: I 67, 273, 571–72, 574; II 45, 93, 133, 213, 341; III 47, 116, 127, 154, 158, 173, 258, 265, 297, 399, 419, 423, 698, 707, 749, 773, 828

    Church: I 569; III 154, 424

    civil: III 747, 780

    Francis: I 221, 385, 414, 492; II 45, 93, 99, 240, 256, 629, 665, 691, 695; III 38, 41, 91, 157–58, 185, 203, 845, 855

    God: II 788, 813; III 203, 842

    Gregory IX: I 270, 419, 499; II 83, 109; III 67, 802

    Honorius III: I 561–64; III 38

    Innocent III: I 583; II 51, 106; III 391

    other: I 100; II 603; III 447, 526, 684, 805

    priest: II 133, 341, 376, 468, 695

    procurator: III 766–67

    Scripture: III 789–90

    simplicity: II 368

Authorization: I 574; II 777, 809; III 185, 755, 794–95

Availability: I 545; II 136, 144, 174, 288, 365; III 45, 259, 325, 708, 752

Avarice: I 137, 370, 375, 438–40; II 134, 192, 279, 319, 722, 745

Aversion: I 440, 548; III 480

Awe: I 189, 263, 338, 462–63, 468, 478, 499; II 41, 86, 104, 311, 402, 419, 457, 489, 513, 764–65, 811; III 816, 866

Axe: I 435, 440, 514; II 159, 440; III 238, 261

B

Baby. See also Infant: I 255, 302; II 374, 440, 443, 463, 669, 679–680; III 155, 158, 466, 531, 800

Babylonian: II 180, 246, 602, 698; III 151, 383, 398, 490, 605, 798

Backbiter: II 364

Badge: II 338

Baggage: I 567, 587; II 269; III 132, 550

Ball: I 224, 389, 476; II 325, 457, 691, 745, 795; III 845

Bandage: I 305; II 102, 467, 481, 514, 539, 653, 688, 750; III 513

Bandit. See also Brigand, Robber, Thief: I 194

Banner: I 247–48, 355, 438, 463, 473, 484–85, 495; II 651; III 91, 594

Banquet: I 551, 567; II 427–28; III 577

Baptism: I 488; II 241; III 366, 491–92, 606–07

Baptize: I 74, 95, 495, 564; II 443; III 119, 381, 490, 493

Barefoot: I 356, 428, 594, 597–98; II 37, 40, 88, 809, 817, 819; III 497, 611–12, 884–85

Barn: I 336, 396; II 400, 466, 679; III 780, 891

Baron: II 35, 69, 109; III 476, 532, 596–97, 652

Barrel: II 762; III 479–80

Basabove: II 196, 196a, 410–11, 634, 711, 727

Basilica

    Lateran: II 256, 548, 690; III 88, 682

    Portiuncula: III 66

    St. Francis: I 419; II 478, 648, 661

Basket: I 206, 484, 569; II 40, 88, 155, 171, 174, 276, 417, 784; III 51, 120, 228, 236, 298, 359–60

Bastard: III 203

Bath, Bathing: I 300, 303; II 267, 375, 411, 418, 456–57, 610, 617, 680; III 651

Battle

    physical: I 138, 186, 231, 395, 587; II 209, 265–66, 614; III 94, 186, 257, 482, 707, 758, 856, 864

    spiritual: I 138, 263, 272, 355, 358, 436, 441, 463, 465, 514, 599; II 260, 326, 353, 373, 401, 404, 406, 650–51, 655, 811; III 43, 79, 84, 102, 161, 190, 425, 564, 576, 618, 838

Beam: I 221, 386; II 99, 229, 423, 427, 429, 449, 481, 658, 662, 671; III 233, 342

Beard: I 253, 453, 505, 598; II 348; III 534, 728, 865

Beast
 animal: I 165, 255, 322, 338, 397–98,
  400, 406, 474, 488, 492, 501, 507; II
  174, 229, 321, 354, 412, 590, 595; III
  104, 146, 175, 177, 344, 484, 490,
  521, 602–03, 816, 838, 851
 body: II 229; III 344
 human: I 584; II 428; III 146, 177,
  816–17
 Satan: III 152, 177, 490, 605, 817
Beating: I 192–93, 447; II 153, 326, 464, 512,
 537, 602, 750, 796, 805; III 302, 354, 398,
 451, 493, 610, 834, 842, 856
Beatitude: I 530
Beauty: I 185; II 353, 596; III 173
 angel: I 264, 410; II 473; III 443, 574
 brother: I 206, 564; II 255, 348,
  370–71; III 62, 635
 church: II 789–90
 creation: I 185, 212, 251, 472; II 98,
  354, 389, 408, 566, 817; III 365, 559,
  583, 648
 cross: III 512, 624
 dwelling: II 159, 224; III 38, 238, 261
 fire: I 114; II 355, 408; III 368, 455
 Francis: I 185, 278, 280, 282, 371, 489;
  II 50, 67, 70, 72, 97, 108, 159, 171,
  224, 255, 301, 317, 338, 353, 389,
  422, 456, 490, 596, 646, 693, 789,
  804; III 62, 66, 173, 188, 238, 261,
  366, 426, 455, 457, 476, 499, 560,
  596, 606, 614, 620, 627, 640, 668–69,
  720, 723–24, 728, 798, 811, 870, 875
 God: I 42, 49, 109, 188, 339; II 354,
  794; III 367, 695, 866
 heaven: I 294, 331; II 35, 168, 389,
  723; III 304, 487
 Innocent III: I 212; II 98
 Mary: III 53
 moon: I 114, 278; III 367
 other persons: I 458, 537; II 70, 72,
  141, 322, 440, 444, 610, 669; III 46,
  62, 334, 391, 491, 606, 528
 other things: I 220, 551, 568; II 62,
  171, 192, 215, 245, 265, 276, 376,
  389, 417, 422, 425, 440, 464, 573,
  668, 804; III 66, 245, 309, 359, 366,
  457, 470, 474, 486, 526, 534, 557,
  587, 593, 600–01, 606, 616, 647
 queen: II 141, 323; III 46, 88, 334
 saint: I 588; III 392
 seraph: I 264, 410; II 473; III 443, 574
 statue: III 486
 sun: I 113; II 186
 Tau: II 317
 Virgin Mary: III 53
 virtue: I 272, 534–35; II 141, 284, 322,
  378, 581; III 173, 334, 489, 726
Bed: I 586–87, 594; II 135–36, 288–90, 423,
 817; III 259
 contemplation: I 587
 death: I 349, 494; II 76, 204, 407, 420

flower: II 192; III 366
Francis: I 227, 321, 392, 435, 453, 456,
 462, 493, 598; II 35, 76, 126, 146,
 204, 211, 313, 367, 417, 561, 635,
 694; III 62, 97, 153, 171, 188, 218,
 226, 288, 317, 355, 370, 414, 436–37,
 447, 474, 491, 497, 525, 549, 567,
 578, 606, 611, 634, 711, 834, 852
 marriage: II 142, 323; III 188, 334
 other: I 240, 302–03, 405, 494, 568; II
 149, 197, 274, 407, 419–20, 423, 426,
 429, 431–33, 446, 461, 615, 653–54,
 656, 658, 662; III 56, 58, 73, 475–76,
 525, 539, 596, 626, 645, 706–07, 793,
 800
Bee: I 250, 400, 568; II 202, 297, 354, 356,
 414, 798; III 217, 275
Beech tree: III 455, 530, 650
Beggar: I 70, 91, 306, 440, 456–57; II 47, 74,
 82, 235, 276, 287, 299, 417, 450, 458,
 523–24, 534, 539, 582, 673, 784, 791, 793;
 III 71, 81, 100, 311
Begging: I 44, 51, 56, 58, 60–61, 70–71, 75,
 80–81, 83, 86, 88–89, 91, 94, 96, 115, 117,
 119, 125, 189, 240, 248, 254, 384, 412,
 448, 500, 531, 534, 536, 543, 550, 553–54,
 565, 575, 587–88, 599; II 34, 38, 45, 47,
 58, 69, 76, 83, 94, 100, 106, 126, 129, 140,
 146, 172–73, 198–99, 240, 252–53, 258,
 261, 272, 278, 291, 295, 297–98, 303–05,
 307, 332, 343–44, 351, 359, 361, 367, 375,
 446, 455, 468, 533, 541, 582, 589, 653,
 679, 690, 773, 779; III 100, 127, 129, 162,
 190, 215, 273, 280–81, 288, 295, 352, 355,
 363, 397, 464, 479, 481, 485, 509, 521,
 527, 531, 545, 547, 549, 553–54, 580, 582,
 587, 599–600, 604, 620, 630, 636, 638,
 650, 662, 696, 719, 745, 800–01, 811, 878
 brother: I 70, 103, 125, 248, 384; II 41,
 89, 150–51, 201–02, 296–97, 589; III
 215–16, 268–69, 273–74, 405, 462,
 468, 760, 778, 780
 Francis: I 195–96, 384, 500; II 72–73,
 82, 199, 202, 295–96, 540, 582–83,
 688, 794; III 214–15, 268–69,
 272–73, 495, 849
 other: I 298, 301; II 94, 138, 479; III 62
 Rule: I 70, 103; III 462
 Testament: I 125
Beginning: I 258, 541; II 135, 189, 213, 283,
 300, 330, 352, 387, 440, 450, 513, 652,
 672, 721, 735, 764; III 41, 244, 327, 557,
 717, 770, 849
 church: II 124, 515; III 149, 224, 291,
 381, 816
 conversion: I 530, 544; II 107, 123,
 137, 150, 160, 189, 211, 229, 290,
 401, 562, 639, 643, 650, 682, 694,
 723, 742; III 131, 221, 223, 233–34,
 239, 263, 279, 290, 316, 338, 385,
 465, 468, 695, 841, 873

creation: I 82, 86, 140–41, 150, 160–61,
    401, 537, 552; II 590, 724; III 382,
    393, 423, 542, 562
division: III 410
Francis: I 203, 288, 380, 417, 549–50;
    II 247–48, 285, 371, 386, 439, 477,
    529, 561, 577, 639–40, 643, 650, 682,
    693–94, 696, 714, 723, 742, 783; III
    66, 255, 855
Poor Ladies: I 197; II 83; III 842
Portiuncula: I 201; II 176, 257
prayer: II 213; III 329
preaching: I 380, 529; II 84, 738, 748,
    812
religion: I 206, 246; II 34, 123, 149,
    189, 195, 201, 205, 211, 257, 371,
    386, 399, 477, 553, 696, 783, 809; III
    66, 90, 132, 217, 219, 223, 275–76,
    284, 290, 388, 394–95, 412–13, 444,
    450, 486, 538, 566, 571, 575, 581,
    589, 633, 697, 723, 845
Rule: I 571; II 206; III 257, 742
sixth *status*: III 149, 424, 816
Third Order: III 64
Behavior: I 135, 252, 254; II 144, 215, 347,
    358, 365, 367, 391, 402, 477, 663; III 32,
    36, 56, 79–80, 92, 118, 133, 148, 155, 245,
    295, 309, 325, 343, 486, 523, 546, 552,
    554, 629, 724, 729, 793, 865
Belief: I 390, 492; II 95, 457, 463; III 559
Bell: II 356, 407, 413, 427, 594, 661, 797; III
    854
Belt: I 201–02, 218, 239, 355, 379, 381, 449,
    460, 494, 583, 589; II 37, 72, 84, 259, 542,
    628, 689, 733, 792; III 40, 803, 824, 833
Benediction: I 99, 349, 558–60, 563–65, 570,
    576; II 530
Benefactor: II 72; III 596, 749, 770
Benefit: I 105, 189, 261, 266, 370, 381, 384,
    512, 519, 568, 587; II 48, 95, 105, 165, 208,
    216–17, 240, 261, 263, 277, 325, 350, 411,
    420, 568, 630, 648, 706, 717, 775–76, 783;
    III 102, 155, 178, 219, 246–47, 264, 308,
    310, 321, 346, 387, 392, 405, 470, 503,
    593, 741, 747, 754–55, 759, 784, 787, 809,
    845, 848–49, 859, 862
Benevolence: II 708; III 188, 887
Betrayal: III 693
Bible. See Scripture
Bird: I 138, 482, 492, 504, 532, 535; II 130,
    267, 279, 299, 375, 416, 592, 594,
    799–800, 813; III 46, 105, 175, 230,
    362–63, 390, 449, 470, 478, 485, 540, 548,
    580, 604, 635, 645, 698, 780, 838, 851
bible: I 535; II 159, 578, 815; III 262
Francis's preaching: I 234, 321, 338,
    343, 353, 396–97, 488–89, 491, 599;
    II 411–12, 624, 706, 760, 783, 789,
    798; III 469–70, 591, 593–94, 826,
    835, 839, 860
taming: II 355, 412, 592

Birth or Birthday
Christ: I 42, 49, 82, 156, 254, 256, 360,
    506, 535; II 123, 269, 542, 610, 689,
    800, 803, 815; III 223, 331, 361, 639
figurative: I 203, 330, 346, 547; II 97,
    145, 208, 318, 352, 359, 366, 399,
    546, 587, 697; III 158, 175, 321, 397,
    706, 721
Francis: I 185, 228, 448, 569; II 68,
    245, 418, 528, 670; III 80, 681, 683,
    697b, 800, 838
literal: I 239, 404–05, 494, 507; I 321,
    439–41, 443–44, 590, 628, 668–70,
    783; III 158
status: I 185, 209, 226, 228, 390, 597; II
    204, 276, 419, 532, 685, 736, 792–93;
    III 56, 255, 458, 523
time: I 306; II 406, 450, 627, 673
Bishop: I 60, 100, 104, 166, 294, 558; II 57,
    160; III 63, 78, 126, 154, 170, 218, 239,
    251, 263, 289, 294, 297, 384, 476, 487,
    516, 596, 624, 724, 758, 770, 773, 808,
    829, 859
    Albano: III 31
    Ambrose: II 557
    Anthony: II 342; III 519, 631
    Arezzo: III 370
    Assisi: I 210, 277, 334, 375, 414,
        449–50, 470; II 37, 41, 49, 74, 79–81,
        89, 95–96, 119, 152, 154, 160–61,
        173, 187–88, 202–03, 251, 313, 390,
        474, 538, 608, 643–44, 687, 716, 751,
        782; III 46, 85, 102, 119–20, 165,
        220, 239, 255, 263–64, 297, 349–50,
        352, 358, 360, 369, 437, 471, 502,
        568, 615, 695, 702, 710, 833, 840,
        842, 869
    brother: I 99, 104, 166, 243, 270, 470,
        499, 501, 513, 560, 562–63, 570, 576;
        II 49, 57, 95, 134, 154, 160–61, 176,
        261, 574; III 63, 78, 119, 126, 251,
        263–64, 289, 294, 297, 384, 476, 487,
        770, 773, 834
    Clare: III 624, 794
    Clement: III 769
    Fondi: II 348
    Francis: I 99, 192–93, 212, 240, 243,
        245–47, 249, 267, 277, 300, 334, 375,
        383, 399, 403, 413–414, 449–50, 500;
        II 37, 41, 74, 79–80, 89, 119, 124,
        138, 148, 152, 154, 173, 184, 187–89,
        197, 200–03, 216, 224, 251, 274, 296,
        304, 306, 313, 339, 342, 348, 352,
        390, 405, 461, 474, 538, 574, 582,
        608, 627, 643–44, 655, 687, 751, 763,
        770, 782, 789, 797; III 46, 85, 102,
        119–20, 154–55, 165, 170, 196,
        215–18, 220, 224, 239, 246, 255, 259,
        273–74, 291, 309–10, 349–50, 352,
        358, 360, 369–70, 390, 437, 460, 471,
        502, 519, 568, 615, 631, 695, 702,
        808, 824, 833, 840, 842, 857

Gregory IX: I 199, 243, 245–46, 267, 270, 294, 413, 499–500, 513, 564–65, 570, 576, 603; II 55–57, 83, 104, 148, 176, 184, 189, 200–01, 216, 224, 261, 274, 296, 342, 582, 660, 763, 797, 814; III 155, 215–17, 246, 259, 273–74, 309–10, 390, 794, 824, 834, 859, 861, 864–65
Hereford: III 53–54
Honorius III: I 99, 558, 560, 562–63
Imola: II 342, 574; III 154, 839, 857
Innocent III: II 690
James of Tivoli: III 805
John: III 784
Marsi: II 138, 304
Narni: III 300
Nicholas: III 739
Potenza: II 405
Rieti: II 197, 274, 306, 416; III 862
Rule: I 100, 104, 210; II 56; III 390, 758
Sabina: III 196, 390
Siena: III 460, 584
Spoleto: III 36
stigmata: II 655, 770
Terni: III 224, 291
Tivoli: II 438, 667
Bitterness: I 43, 72, 205, 220, 231, 264, 271, 499, 531, 540; II 76, 91, 105, 250, 320, 324, 379, 407, 445, 457, 517, 537, 545, 564, 570, 681, 690, 694, 712, 744, 762; III 228, 335, 397, 534, 843
   prophetic vision: I 206; II 783
   separation: I 218, 226, 285–86; II 128, 164, 387, 423, 443, 658
   sweetness: I 50, 124, 195, 276, 541, 588; II 40, 74, 82, 180, 243, 248–49, 253, 791, 794
Blasphemy: I 76, 79, 90, 132, 145, 608; II 42, 90, 162, 404, 421–22, 437, 451–52, 457, 656, 733, 804; III 422
Blessing: I 270, 293, 295, 307, 411, 550, 605; II 37, 240, 750; III 447, 547, 577, 609
   bird: I 396; II 355, 412; III 593, 604, 860
   bishop: II 161; III 264
   brother: II 53, 102, 144, 174, 277, 336, 361, 557, 588, 700, 748; III 201, 295, 421, 874
   cardinal: III 404
   Clare: II 128; III 357
   Francis: I 225, 240, 270, 297, 346, 390, 396, 468, 515; II 53, 82, 102, 126, 126b, 128, 144, 162, 174, 185, 251, 272, 277, 336, 347, 475, 530–31, 557, 625, 700, 702, 705, 784; III 65, 99, 201, 295, 323, 335, 357, 404, 407–08, 420, 426, 447, 465, 546, 609, 714–15, 855, 874
   God: I 101, 127, 158, 224, 235–36, 261, 282; II 151, 160, 475, 531, 545, 684, 719; III 65, 159, 263, 269, 383–84, 386, 388, 390, 457, 538, 598, 633, 697

hare: II 414
healing: II 462, 480
peace: I 296; II 478
pope: I 471, 599; II 98; III 88
praise: I 49, 76, 78, 90, 113, 141, 161–62, 296, 298, 301, 308; II 40, 173; III 367, 303
zealot: III 323, 715
Blindness
   cure: I 240, 290, 301, 323–24, 353–54, 420, 494, 518, 595; II 410, 447, 449–50, 452, 627, 649, 670–72, 783; III 50, 57, 71–72, 150, 185, 580, 804, 834
   figurative: I 43, 283, 328, 349, 416, 476; II 100, 143, 186, 258, 270, 340, 448, 523, 541, 716, 732, 745; III 86, 136, 198, 226, 287, 316, 320, 335, 367, 585, 650, 688, 711
   Francis: I 445; II 126, 715; III 439, 446, 570
Blood: I 219, 228, 302, 305, 307, 325, 469, 478–79, 492, 503, 513, 554, 585; II 118, 137, 164, 167, 293, 345, 349, 407, 428, 430, 444, 452–54, 588, 662, 675, 677, 750, 808; III 40, 90, 119, 174, 267, 293, 302, 634, 723
   Christ: I 41, 43, 46–47, 50, 52–54, 56–58, 60, 77–78, 82, 116–17, 125, 128–29, 136, 147, 540; II 34, 214, 250, 536, 586, 599, 622, 686, 697, 803; III 60, 175, 187, 189, 382, 393, 651, 656, 801
   covenant: I 46, 117, 129, 548
   Francis: I 166, 264, 274, 280–81, 357, 359, 410, 416, 432, 486, 517, 600–01; II 76, 108, 161, 335, 351, 388, 403, 473, 476, 514, 601, 633, 637, 710, 719, 770–71, 792; III 73, 240, 334, 509, 513, 866, 882
   leper: III 243, 303
Blood of Christ. See also Body of Christ: I 41, 43, 46–47, 50, 52–54, 56–58, 60, 77–78, 82, 116–17, 125, 128–29, 136, 147, 540; II 34, 214, 250, 536, 586, 599, 622, 686, 697, 803; III 60, 175, 187, 189, 382, 393, 651, 656, 801
Boat: I 206, 235–36, 397; II 355, 412–13, 434–35, 592, 625, 664–65, 705, 805; III 185, 448, 578
Body
   absence: III 90, 388, 845
   bird: I 234; II 267, 355, 411–12, 592; III 470
   Christ: I 41–43, 46–47, 49–50, 52–54, 56–58, 60, 74, 77–78, 84, 89, 95, 187, 283, 285, 450, 488, 540; II 52, 101, 214, 221, 308, 375, 449, 476, 591, 598, 671, 719–20, 746, 773, 803; III 250, 309, 386, 675, 745
   Clare: I 197

conversion: I 187; II 182, 282, 562
cross: I 147, 157, 260, 279, 355, 517,
    536; II 401, 535, 560, 607, 631, 638,
    640, 650–51, 699, 714, 719, 727, 738;
    III 42, 181
death: I 259, 272, 278, 284, 286, 291,
    296, 323–24, 412, 414, 417, 420, 565,
    602; II 58, 73, 93, 109, 119, 121, 123,
    129, 202, 204, 388, 418, 423–24, 445,
    452–53, 458–59, 475–78, 529, 641,
    645, 647–48, 673–74, 677, 703,
    714–15, 737, 746, 806; III 292–93,
    819
demon: I 43, 50–51, 242, 488, 495; II
    167–68, 228, 267, 274, 289, 324–25,
    328, 352, 423, 426, 562–63, 750,
    795–96; III 847
faithful: II 531; III 531
Francis: I 187, 371, 404, 432; II 152,
    184, 229, 308, 382, 605, 734; III 90,
    102, 194, 247, 249, 267–68, 278, 304,
    306–07, 312, 331, 339, 341, 344–45,
    356, 364, 369, 371, 388, 462, 583,
    587, 691, 847, 852–53, 861, 869, 877
heart: I 42, 46, 49, 224, 228, 262, 538,
    604; II 249, 308, 343, 515, 562, 564,
    606, 626, 632, 650, 695, 699; III 181,
    190, 388, 542, 649, 657, 877
Innocent III: I 579, 598
John: III 333, 657
Masseo: III 587
minister: I 104, 293
miracle: I 290–91, 298–99, 301, 305,
    307, 324; II 423–26, 428, 430,
    433–34, 445–46, 452, 454, 457, 479,
    555, 566, 627–28, 635, 656–58, 660,
    662, 664, 673–75, 692, 865, 691; III
    706
needs: I 64; II 137, 149–50, 152, 158,
    183–84, 189, 193, 201, 218, 225, 229,
    259, 293, 331, 382–83, 560–61, 565,
    590; III 306, 312, 344–45, 356, 371,
    391, 426, 462, 477, 596–97, 811
peace: I 134, 324; II 127, 153, 229; III
    227, 341, 356, 426
poverty: I 133, 165, 466; II 150,
    220–21, 400, 550; III 234, 279, 344
preaching: I 498
renunciation: I 130, 132, 207, 228, 266,
    390, 413; II 538, 782
seraph: I 263, 279, 283, 340, 410, 509;
    II 108, 226, 402, 473, 632, 635, 709,
    816
servant: II 584
sin: I 41, 43, 48, 50, 79, 87, 132, 183,
    227, 282, 449; II 511, 732, 740–41,
    804, 817
soul: I 43–44, 50–51, 72, 84, 90, 224,
    257, 296, 353, 431, 449–50, 465–66,
    477; II 93, 121, 124, 127, 140, 149,
    153, 167, 180, 201, 204, 215, 267,
    298, 301, 305, 308, 311, 332–33, 388,

    475, 511, 562, 565, 588, 599, 607,
    609, 660, 694, 740, 750, 818; III 118,
    216, 224, 274, 291, 356, 391, 393,
    853
spirit: I 224, 227; II 109, 127, 153, 165,
    175, 220, 309, 332, 490, 551–52, 566,
    605, 662, 714; III 249, 302, 343, 356,
    370
stigmata: I 108, 260, 267, 279, 281,
    318, 340–41, 346–47, 355, 357, 359,
    416–17, 466, 517, 536, 604; II 76,
    108, 240, 250, 335–36, 401, 403, 476,
    490, 499, 513–16, 528, 629, 635, 637,
    645, 651, 654, 682, 719–20, 722, 727,
    734, 738–39, 742–43, 780–81, 784,
    816; III 152, 346, 792, 866, 868, 875,
    877
suffering: I 45, 50, 75, 90, 95, 184, 191,
    228, 257, 262, 266–67, 272–74, 303,
    304, 319, 323, 353, 371, 403–04, 409,
    414, 432, 486, 513; II 53, 76, 78, 121,
    123, 127, 149–50, 152, 167, 169, 177,
    180–82, 184, 190, 193, 218, 221,
    228–30, 258, 274, 289, 330, 332, 354,
    366, 382–83, 400, 408, 433–34, 444,
    446, 454, 457, 474, 490, 532, 535,
    540, 566–67, 631, 640–41, 662, 664,
    673, 675, 685, 687–88, 692; III 304,
    331, 339, 364, 691, 852–53, 867
veneration of Francis's: I 280, 299,
    565; II 479, 673, 806; III 357–58,
    361, 474, 835–36, 870–71, 886
virtue: I 46, 142, 165, 197, 219, 501,
    505; II 93, 145, 149, 298, 323, 343,
    345, 352, 524, 540, 564, 571, 615,
    694–95, 702, 751, 789
Body of Christ. See also Blood of Christ: I
    41–43, 46–47, 49–50, 52–54, 56–58, 60,
    74, 77–78, 84, 89, 95, 187, 283, 285, 450,
    488, 540; II 52, 101, 214, 221, 308, 375,
    449, 476, 591, 598, 671, 719–20, 746, 773,
    803; III 250, 309, 386, 675, 745
Bone: I 146, 173, 276, 420, 518; II 198, 274,
    376, 424, 437, 462, 573, 615, 627, 641,
    649, 673–74, 702, 714, 764; III 35, 95,
    408, 497, 538, 544, 644, 795
Book
    Francis: I 262, 278, 339, 405, 409–10,
        509, 516, 539; II 38, 85–86, 254, 306,
        314, 372, 380, 387, 467, 475, 544,
        590, 612, 631, 643, 697, 773, 813; III
        45, 255–59, 314, 316, 319, 450, 702,
        704–10, 819
    Gospel: II 38a, 254, 288, 631; III 196,
        258, 815, 865
    Gregory IX: I 199
    life: II 146, 380; III 323, 382, 549, 715
    money: I 69
    Mystical Theology: III 815
    Rule: II 146, 380; III 255–59, 323, 581,
        704, 747
    scarcity: II 508, 551

scripture: I 262, 339, 405, 409–10, 509, 516, 539; II 85–86, 306, 314, 387, 509–10, 519, 522–23, 544, 612, 643, 723, 726, 728–29, 731–32, 734–36, 740, 742–46, 749, 751, 754–56, 764, 773, 775, 813, 815
  text divisions: I 180, 239, 257–58, 278, 287; II 262, 468
  use: I 65–66, 69, 573; II 46, 54, 94, 102, 136, 145, 147, 204, 206–07, 209–10, 288, 362, 365, 372, 551, 597, 777; III 54, 118, 130, 325, 394, 405–06, 413, 706, 748, 752, 755, 785
Boredom. See Acedia
Bowel: I 540; II 348, 445–46, 452, 677
Bowl: I 551; II 82, 167, 253, 287, 444, 464; III 217, 243, 303, 305, 463, 803
Box: III 776, 819
Boxer: II 363
Boy
  brother: I 590; II 147, 273, 381; III 323, 474, 594
  Francis: I 195, 202, 416–17, 429–30, 597; II 389, 476–77, 647; III 33, 80, 696, 800
  healing: I 239–40, 298–300, 302–03, 306–07, 324, 403; II 421–22, 424, 426–28, 431, 442–43, 445, 449–50, 454, 456, 461, 463, 467, 479–81, 528, 627, 657–58, 660–61, 669, 671, 673, 675, 680, 783–84, 805
  witness: II 419
Branch: I 238, 260, 270, 284, 296, 322, 402, 417, 485, 566–67; II 129, 154, 157, 159, 217, 260, 400, 476, 478, 647, 676, 746; III 557, 647
Brawl. See also Fight: II 431
Bread: I 73, 89, 201, 238, 322, 356, 379, 384, 472, 539, 547, 551–52, 554, 583, 587, 589; II 35, 43, 73, 77, 84, 91, 99, 156, 171, 176, 193, 200–01, 221–22, 276, 283, 289, 295–96, 299, 307, 323, 375, 387, 416–17, 420, 462, 565, 628, 733, 756, 802–03; III 50, 91, 197, 271, 359, 715, 787, 796
  alms: II 200–01, 299; III 121, 216, 274, 282, 299, 310–11, 359, 846, 878
  angel: II 582; III 100, 386
  beg: I 588; II 295; III 100, 130, 216, 274, 495, 509, 587, 878
  break: II 122b, 794; III 336–37, 831
  Christ: I 46, 117–18, 128; III 650
  crumb: II 381, 555, 558, 692; III 91, 196
  daily: I 159, 475
  Eucharist: III 675
  fasting: II 449, 558, 671; III 93, 197, 611
  Francis: I 405, 803; II 135, 411; III 51, 244, 336–37, 448, 463, 578–79, 587, 610, 803
  idleness: III 793

lack: I 99, 220
life: III 388
living: I 336, 416
rye grass: II 227, 289a; III 345
tears: II 531
wheat: II 200, 807; III 216, 274
word: I 588
Breast: I 142, 239, 302, 441, 453, 459, 463; II 182, 301, 309, 374, 420, 429, 461, 463, 466, 607, 662, 679, 699, 772, 798; III 43, 445, 528, 532–33, 539, 555, 582, 651–52, 639, 695, 835
Breastplate: I 435, 462; II 150, 259; III 398
Breviary: I 101, 319; II 196, 209, 306, 773, 775; III 130, 258, 286, 451, 581, 665b, 707, 747, 819
Bride: I 187–88, 535; II 70, 72, 142, 245, 295, 301, 323, 581; III 147, 151, 331, 334, 515, 859, 882
Bridegroom. See also Groom: I 291, 294; II 309, 527, 596, 608, 742; III 175
Bridge: I 454
Brigand. See also Bandit, Robber, Thief: I 376; II 720
Bronze: III 117–18, 393, 486–88, 723
Broom: I 437; II 162–63; III 240–41, 300–01
Brotherhood: I 116, 573–74, 587, 603; II 777; III 384, 759, 843
Building: I 193, 419, 458–59, 547; II 158, 161, 285–86, 378, 421, 429, 481, 541, 657, 688, 785; III 33, 86, 237, 240, 259, 262, 264, 384, 389, 403, 405, 752, 781, 778
  charity: I 217
  Church of St. Francis: III 68, 184
  spiritual: II 300, 337, 377, 579
Bull. See also Seal
  animal: II 761
  Minos: I 512
Burden: I 46, 218, 347, 405, 446, 452, 532, 537, 546; II 145, 148, 211, 269, 351, 366; III 171, 317, 461, 586, 711, 757, 783
  Christ: III 389, 627
  cross: I 281
  disease: I 290
  habit: III 480
  honor: I 442
  ministry: III 325–26
  money: II 603
  poverty: I 461
  sin: II 814
  title: II 725
  tribulation: III 421
Burial: I 601; II 121, 418–19, 424, 430, 557, 663, 805; III 162, 178, 405, 421, 473–74
Business: I 187, 192, 372, 383, 419, 543, 574; II 34–35, 69, 72, 261, 308, 310, 323, 431, 478, 530, 533, 564, 684–86, 809; III 67, 82, 100, 156, 402, 417, 442, 573, 610, 751, 801, 833
Businessman: I 319, 370; II 344

C

Cake: I 241; II 461; III 359–60

Camel: II 722

Camp: I 19, 263, 272, 322, 462, 487, 568, 581, 584, 606–08; III 602

Candelabra: II 157, 361; III 49, 122, 237, 300

Candle: I 255, 284, 305, 406, 506, 601; II 123, 191, 353, 418, 423, 431, 437, 443, 453, 653, 647, 667, 798; III 223, 361, 365, 543, 882

Canon: I 582; II 154, 274, 404, 551, 615, 664, 702, 743, 765, 770; III 54, 59, 95, 119–20, 297, 305, 501, 529, 649, 740, 813, 820, 828, 862

Canonical: I 98, 100; II 311, 551, 592, 609, 779; III 135, 515, 522, 722

Canonization: I 293, 418–19, 602; II 109, 391, 477, 529; III 80

Capon: II 298, 802; III 50, 846

Captain: I 338, 343, 428, 462–63; III 412

Capuche. See also Habit, Hood, Tunic: II 45, 47, 94, 130, 189, 228, 434, 799, 809; III 202–03, 230, 232, 362, 444, 450, 461, 480, 503, 575, 581, 586, 592, 600, 616

Cardinal: II 49, 51, 133, 462, 718, 763, 777, 789, 817; III 125, 312, 402–03, 475–76, 595, 710, 741, 756, 830, 839, 859

   bishop: I 383

   Bonaventure: III 31, 738

   church: II 718, 777

   Hugolino: II 55, 104; III 478, 598, 794

   John of Murrovale: III 830

   John of St. Paul: II 49, 55, 96, 103–04, 547

   legate: I 608

   Leo: II 326, 796; III 230–31, 311

   lord: I 98; II 132, 316, 326; III 404–05, 479

   Ostia: II 56–57, 261, 814; III 124, 273, 275, 289, 794–95

   priest: III 698

   protector: III 127, 478, 598–99, 737–38

   Ranieri: I 295; III 698

   Raynald: II 779

   Riccardo: III 804

   Sabina: II 96

   Santa Croce: II 326, 796

   Thomas: III 698

Care: I 202, 320, 381, 384, 395–96, 413, 447, 476; II 170, 214, 275, 306, 325, 361, 363, 369, 376, 415; III 103, 326, 445, 571, 759, 819, 877

   animal: I 249, 400; II 357, 412–13, 624, 591, 679

   anxiety: I 58, 80, 88, 105, 356, 529; II 34; III 489, 596, 726, 786

   Bishop of Ostia: III 834

   body: I 412; II 382, 592; III 227, 356, 391, 477, 596

   Body of Christ: II 214; III 309

   brother: I 57, 66, 71, 92, 103, 273, 279, 591; II 46, 93, 106, 142, 144–45, 154, 211, 340, 365–66, 393, 601; III 119, 171, 287–88, 316–17, 325, 414, 597, 711

   business: II 69

   chastity: II 562, 694

   church: I 581; II 163; III 241, 766, 857–59

   corpse: III 293

   doctor: I 412

   door: III 461

   Francis: I 271, 412–14; II 127, 190, 416, 464, 583–84, 636; III 227, 337, 457, 627

   freedom: II 533

   garden: II 192; III 366

   God: I 565; III 530, 649

   governing: II 557

   heart: I 379; II 84

   heaven: I 584

   household: III 49

   image of cross: II 250

   kitchen: III 795

   knowledge: II 207; III 168, 257, 319–20

   leper: I 456; II 524, 750, 782; III 493, 527, 636

   Lord: I 191, 207; II 546, 605; III 476–77, 715, 800

   monastery: III 700

   mother: I 306

   neighbor: I 273, 576; II 107, 445, 587, 697, 751, 753–55, 759; III 178

   Order: III 834

   parish: II 788

   poor: II 276, 291, 417, 530, 685; III 819

   Poor Ladies: II 378–79

   Portiuncula: I 201; II 156, 540; III 121, 300

   poverty: II 532

   religion: I 269

   self: I 413

   sick: II 193, 423, 776–77, 814; III 282, 747, 756–57, 772

   son and daughter: II 563

   spiritual exercise: I 546

   tree: II 466

   vessel: I 119

   world: II 34

Carnival: III 578

Carpet: III 798

Castle: I 583; II 466, 659; III 230, 304, 363, 453–54, 523–25, 830

Catalogue of saints: I 161, 295, 325, 601; II 477, 780; III 836, 871

Cathedral: II 551; III 59, 305, 778

Cauterization: I 271, 413; II 189–90, 354, 360, 408, 566, 655, 704; III 97, 363–64, 861

Cavalry: III 877

Cave. See also Grotto, Pit: I 177, 187, 218, 372, 453, 472; II 74, 687, 782; III 127–28, 397

Celebration: I 119, 254, 406, 420; II 163, 455, 671; III 67–68, 70, 78, 241, 301, 452–53, 828

Celibacy. See Chastity

Cell: I 61, 219, 226, 285, 287, 374, 516, 598; II 152, 159, 161, 268–70, 350, 356–57, 402, 413–14, 438, 462–63, 562–63, 593, 597, 608, 618–19, 667–68, 675, 700–01, 796, 798; III 45, 49, 97, 102, 105, 169, 200, 231, 238–40, 245, 258, 261–62, 264, 270, 309, 313, 329, 341, 345–47, 365, 393, 416–17, 454–55, 457, 478, 506, 514, 518, 535, 538, 547, 594, 598, 619, 623, 625, 633, 642, 653, 667, 688, 696, 708, 795, 797–98, 808, 810, 812, 864

Cellar: I 566; II 400; III 778, 780

Cement: III 260

Cemetery: III 749, 785

Ceremony: II 648

Chain: I 126, 192, 319, 325, 374, 447–48, 477; II 79, 216, 243–44, 319, 436–39, 481, 537, 539, 602, 665–67, 687, 698, 804; III 78, 245, 393, 398, 833, 842

Champion: I 339; III 164, 888

Chancellor: II 728

Change: I 184, 259, 289, 292, 370–72; II 45, 72, 167, 246, 249, 302, 367, 419, 458, 462, 479, 511, 531, 629, 790

Chapel: I 442; II 159, 410, 678; III 85–86, 90, 238

Chaplain: II 200, 296; III 215, 273

Chapter: I 225, 249, 477, 501, 807; II 51, 53, 55, 57, 142, 341
  Anthony of Pauda: I 225, 477; II 557
  general chapter: I 104, 419, 570; II 67, 132, 146, 239, 331, 367, 370, 478, 528, 557; III 51, 124, 171, 260, 288, 313, 317, 321, 414–15, 475, 595–96, 676, 709, 714, 741, 760, 765, 782–84, 798, 804–05, 813, 819, 825, 828–29
  Mats: II 132; III 124, 313, 596, 709, 819
  Pentecost: I 67, 76, 104, 547; II 51, 55, 104, 778; III 760
  Portiuncula: I 249; II 51, 125, 208, 285, 288, 557, 700; III 124, 225, 260, 271, 313
  provincial chapter: I 104, 390, 477; III 641
  room: I 551
  Rule: I 98, 311, 573; II 206, 778; III 167, 256, 406, 704, 758, 820
  Saint Michael: II 51

Character: I 182, 430, 441, 505, 513; II 513; III 31, 45, 63, 81, 190, 192, 334, 780, 838, 865

Charge: I 68, 207, 227; II 71, 96, 448, 671, 739; III 88, 92, 480, 586, 722, 751, 756, 760, 768, 783, 803, 805, 829

Chariot: I 224, 321, 389, 476; II 526, 552, 620, 691, 743, 761, 783; III 90, 388, 421, 423, 815, 838, 845–46, 890

Charioteer: I 389; II 552, 692

Charism: I 542; II 243, 577, 681; III 503, 513, 539, 862, 865

Charity. See also Love: I 40, 47, 71, 92, 94, 104, 109–10, 133, 136, 164–65, 191, 194, 206, 217, 239, 248, 283, 440, 544, 553, 568, 588; II 80, 147–50, 172, 188–89, 198, 209, 222, 259, 282, 288, 314, 342, 358, 362–63, 372, 385, 458, 562, 565, 587, 599–600, 681; III 47, 51, 78–79, 125, 135, 161, 175, 185–86, 201, 203, 250–52, 258, 278, 282, 286, 289, 311, 315, 325, 333, 388, 392, 397, 400, 404, 407, 411, 425–26, 462, 464, 466, 469, 486, 488, 510, 522, 524, 551, 562, 571, 576, 586, 588, 590, 592, 628, 635, 639, 652, 707, 719, 724–25, 730, 770, 786
  act: I 71, 92, 94; II 259; III 397, 476, 596, 786
  bond: I 198, 223; II 93, 189, 261, 343; III 41, 161, 324, 338, 369, 395, 401
  Christ: I 254, 349, 358, 599; III 153–54, 161, 163, 384, 386, 395, 403, 423–25, 655–57, 855
  cold: I 546, 566, 576; III 118, 135, 186, 389, 394–95, 408, 410, 425
  fire: I 93, 217, 260, 540, 596; II 596, 600–01, 637, 698; III 38, 147, 152, 173, 176, 391, 410, 526, 540, 636, 638, 678, 730
  Francis: I 40, 390; II 149–50, 172, 191, 193, 196, 248, 332, 362, 458, 565, 587, 599–601, 637, 681, 698, 712; III 278, 282, 469, 571, 592, 730
  fraternal: II 252, 259; III 39, 336, 369, 476, 652, 869
  fruit: III 388
  gift: III 496
  God: I 109; III 525, 555, 655
  kiss: III 528
  law: III 381
  love: I 119, 390
  neighbor: I 283
  order: II 282
  Poor Ladies: I 223; II 188
  practice: III 400
  rebuke: III 407, 638
  reward: I 47
  title: I 598; III 79
  seraphic: III 410
  Spirit: I 67; III 201

Charm: I 120, 332

Chastity: I 63, 100, 198, 292, 355, 458, 554, 572, 585; II 172, 562, 581, 694, 723; III 62,

81, 334, 392, 457, 476, 481, 596, 601, 742–43, 770–71, 834, 877
celibacy: II 553
Chatter: I 322, 397, 438, 491; II 322, 412, 625, 798–99; III 105, 835
Cheek: I 73, 89, 306, 505; II 540, 671
Cheerful: I 69, 91, 253, 469, 487, 505, 542, 551; II 70, 151, 165, 331, 383, 427, 661; III 98, 230, 235, 269, 279, 326, 338, 346, 444, 481, 515, 536, 623, 653–54, 728, 842, 865
Cheese: II 222; III 250, 311, 477, 597, 795
Cherry tree: II 466, 678
Cherub: II 722; III 54, 83, 147, 412, 420–21, 529, 539, 649, 883
Chest: I 264, 299, 324, 761; II 317, 407–08, 456–57, 680, 693; III 69, 117, 203, 393, 486–87, 575, 723–24, 801
Chicken: I 228, 392, 427, 478; III 485, 604, 800
Child: 50, 64, 84, 129, 138, 145, 153, 182, 238, 246, 249, 400, 443, 531, 541–42, 548, 553, 565, 589, 603; II 73, 93, 97, 102, 147, 177, 208, 263, 272, 279, 302, 381, 399–400, 418, 422, 426, 457, 480, 489, 517, 544, 552, 587, 657, 660, 668, 717; III 44, 74, 177, 180, 444, 459–60, 470, 507, 529, 531, 561, 575, 584, 620, 696, 721, 800, 803, 851, 875
  Adam: II 491
  Belial: I 542; III 164
  brother: I 353, 530; II 255, 260, 294, 343, 352, 393, 415, 546, 548, 587, 601; III 88, 90, 117, 160, 194, 321, 324, 335, 706, 712
  church: I 294; III 147
  cured: I 353, 494; II 422–23, 434, 457, 463, 481, 627, 657, 679, 717, 805
  death: II 283, 423, 440, 669; III 117
  devil: I 43, 50, 78, 91
  flesh: III 182
  foolish: I 182–83, 547–48; II 530
  Francis: I 241, 262, 269, 411, 490, 610; III 80, 695–96
  God: I 41, 48, 117, 133–34, 138, 251, 591; II 324, 392
  grace: I 193; II 241, 538
  Israel: I 276; III 129, 318
  Jesus: I 156, 256, 406, 506; II 123, 269, 374, 411, 610; III 223, 361, 528
  light: III 383
  peace: I 203, 320; II 133, 341; III 297, 857
  sinful: I 182–83, 547–48; II 530
  unbelief: I 554
  world: II 168, 284, 330; III 186
  wrath: II 241
Childbirth: I 238, 493, 507; II 439–41, 444, 463, 668–70, 716–17
Childhood: I 182–3, 280, 597; II 646, 685; III 81, 870
Children. See Child

Chirping: I 235, 600; II 217, 357, 414, 593, 801; III 860
Choice: I 183, 253, 262, 443; II 259, 449, 466, 603, 671; III 103, 680, 782, 865
  free choice: I 334; II 189
  poverty: I 524
Choir: I 83, 287; II 168, 328, 373, 591, 597; III 180, 304, 323, 499, 531, 534, 541–42, 613, 650, 656, 662, 885
Christian: I 183, 314, 465, 564, 584, 606–07; II 120, 130, 589, 726, 728, 745, 751, 759
  brother: II 166–67
  faith: I 212, 229, 395, 608; II 600, 603, 755, 757, 814
  religion: II 520
Christmas. See also Nativity: II 175; III 270
Church, Local. See also Parish
  abandonment: I 244; II 39, 42, 87, 249, 376, 606, 688; III 102, 181, 243, 302, 304, 479, 833
  adornment: II 73, 76; III 192
  cleaning: II 162–63; III 240–41, 300
  parish: I 561–62, 597–98, 600
  Peter: I 291, 434, 470; II 73, 247, 540; III 464, 588, 719
  possession: I 126; II 777
  poverty: III 172, 239, 263–65, 752, 781
  priest: III 44, 83
  privilege: III 114, 133, 722
  rebuilding or repairing: I 36, 189, 196, 201, 250, 314, 335, 373, 377–79, 441; II 36, 38, 81, 84–85, 251–53, 425, 443, 536, 540–41, 659, 686, 688–89, 749, 782, 792; III 79, 85, 103, 195, 202, 370, 416, 424, 438, 569, 682, 827, 838, 843–44, 874
  Saint Francis: III 35, 62, 69–70, 72–73, 184, 474, 515–16, 626, 836
  visit: I 47, 125; II 36, 38, 87, 91, 476, 606, 699; III 239, 264
Church, Universal: I 55–56, 65, 75, 119, 270, 292, 330, 346, 348; II 37, 84, 90, 96, 344, 370, 406–07, 423, 425, 431, 591, 654, 659, 773, 780, 785, 787, 789–90, 809; III 36, 51, 59, 65, 74, 78, 86, 89, 91–92, 126, 154–55, 159–60, 166, 189, 196, 221, 224, 236, 246, 251, 263, 266, 286, 290–91, 294, 299, 336, 339, 341, 352, 354, 386–87, 395, 402–03, 405, 423, 441, 463, 467, 479, 487, 503, 507, 527, 542, 544, 572, 588, 591, 616, 620, 630, 636, 642, 681, 684, 697, 715, 755, 770, 776, 792–93, 802, 804, 811, 818, 826, 859, 890
  Apostolic: II 46; III 192, 194, 740
  Christ: I 278, 292, 294, 488; II 690; III 488, 725, 816
  defense: III 37, 890
  faith: I 100, 124, 238, 313, 388; II 96, 160, 551, 643; III 37, 89, 192, 263, 385, 746, 842, 856
  fifth *status:* III 146–47

final age: I 124; II 514; III 147, 192, 224, 291, 387, 514
future: III 116, 129, 419, 721, 864, 873
God: I 212, 269, 291, 568; II 90, 92, 103, 106, 120, 124, 189, 343, 724, 743, 764; III 192, 221, 224, 229, 275, 289–91, 338, 402
grace: I 348; III 542, 656
growth: I 330; II 352, 587, 620; III 152
heaven: II 378; III 150, 387, 422, 616
last days: III 397, 424–25
law: III 775
Militant: I 569, 780; II 418, 811; III 53, 557, 647, 740–41, 769, 811, 864
mission: III 370
Mother: I 48, 55; II 95, 154, 160; III 240, 336, 425, 476, 596, 695, 724, 844
needs: II 478, 514
primitive: I 579–80, 582; II 46, 148, 342, 399; III 185, 289
reform: III 701
Roman: I 101, 106, 125, 136, 181, 238, 270, 295, 327, 388, 558–59, 573, 599, 775, 777; II 48, 95, 105, 260, 262, 477, 551, 643; III 31, 42, 78, 135, 180, 324, 385, 387, 425, 721, 748–49, 766–67, 772, 777, 785–88, 808, 819, 830, 839, 855–56, 859
sacrament: I 100; III 385, 494, 609
sixth age: III 149, 156, 679, 816
status: II 148, 343; II 802; III 118, 129, 152, 289, 394, 557, 647, 816
tribulation: III 199, 721
Triumphant: I 569, 780; II 418, 811
unspiritual: III 151
Virgin: I 163, 201, 387; II 100, 155, 257–58, 542, 689, 749; III 57, 121, 236, 299, 397
work: I 80, 83; II 280
Circumstance: I 189, 191, 221, 290, 573; II 138, 293, 512, 617, 776; III 54, 61, 411, 729, 750–52, 756–57
Cistercian: II 122, 761; III 61–62, 222, 795
Clay: 146, 344; II 356, 414, 512, 694, 734; III 117, 393, 395, 486, 488, 723, 725
Cleaning
    church: III 242, 492
    leper: III 242, 492
Clemency: I 431, 476, 608; II 607, 690; III 97, 181, 645, 730, 855
Clergy: I 45, 47–48, 53, 56, 60, 95, 136, 238, 284, 594–95, 600, 606; II 129, 133, 154, 341, 419, 423, 446, 481, 656, 658, 775; III 47, 114, 119, 133, 156, 229, 297, 357, 409, 424, 521, 722, 829, 854, 857, 871
Clerk: I 581
Cliff: II 430, 635, 666
Climate: I 102; III 32, 102, 747, 757
Cloak: I 73, 89, 248–49, 461, 502, 539, 582–83; II 37, 39, 87, 94, 138, 140, 304–05, 473, 531, 538, 782; III 58, 64, 156,

280–82, 284, 382, 384, 393, 682, 799, 840, 850
Cloister. See also Enclosure: I 195, 249, 399, 454, 471, 524, 575, 585; II 122, 187, 364, 779; III 222, 349, 361, 662, 760, 795, 871
Cloth: I 186, 189, 301, 323, 371, 373; II 34, 69, 122, 275, 416, 515, 536, 658, 809; III 45, 64, 72, 118, 222–23, 250, 267–68, 280, 283–84, 310, 360–61, 538, 587, 600–01, 710, 752, 774, 793, 840, 886
Clothing: I 64, 69–70, 91, 102, 137, 235, 238, 253, 277, 379, 401, 443, 453, 542–43, 545, 549, 598; II 36–37, 40, 47, 70, 80, 90, 92, 94, 105, 130, 218, 244, 247–48, 287, 293, 364, 369, 406, 411, 430, 434, 455, 464, 664, 674, 740, 776, 800, 805, 808; III 425, 470, 481, 550, 627, 639–40, 653, 747, 757, 776
    expensive: I 65, 269, 296, 376, 451, 546; II 68, 70–71, 80, 293, 532, 791; III 362, 470
    poor: I 101, 198, 253, 339, 450, 462, 586, 588, 597; II 36, 44, 82, 88, 130, 138, 194, 210, 218, 285, 478, 561, 635, 694, 808, 810; III 45, 64, 118, 153, 170, 247, 267, 279, 283, 316, 413, 482, 593, 601, 729, 772, 818, 834
    religious: II 164, 177; III 242, 267, 302, 567
    removal: I 193, 322, 375, 449, 454, 531–32; II 37, 73–74, 80, 325, 422, 534, 685, 687, 782, 795
    secular: I 195; II 248, 406; III 115, 136, 351, 436, 722
Cloud: I 143, 223, 271, 278, 295, 323, 389, 413, 416, 431, 483–84, 503, 510, 518, 533, 535, 568, 583, 604; II 107, 261, 388, 475, 520, 526, 607, 644, 651, 699, 711, 716, 729, 746; III 102, 181, 324, 368, 392, 717, 732, 815, 869, 887
Coal: I 204; II 322, 562, 596, 635; III 34, 96, 141, 176, 435, 488, 534, 539–40, 567, 634–35, 689, 725
Coat: I 454
Cold: I 102, 166, 218, 250, 339, 400, 432, 452–3, 503, 505, 510; II 43, 82, 118, 137, 139, 150, 182–84, 194–95, 218, 224, 251, 304, 379, 561–62, 570, 635, 694, 792, 795, 798; III 61, 90, 118, 168, 234, 237, 267–68, 279–80, 284, 306–07, 311, 315, 319, 394, 408, 425, 449–50, 524, 544, 579–80, 657, 678, 705, 721, 723, 731, 747, 757, 795, 798, 801, 850, 852, 883
Coldness: III 410, 487, 725
Collection: II 378, 558
Color: I 114, 280, 452, 494, 504; II 77, 108, 122, 138, 293, 296, 317, 388, 402, 476, 556, 693, 723, 758; III 222, 230, 267, 360–62, 368, 470, 588, 687, 774, 793, 875

Column: II 744

Comfort: I 220, 285, 287, 292, 474, 812; II
  121, 250, 267, 354, 360, 408, 482, 489,
  605, 692, 740, 757; III 73, 89, 217, 239,
  263, 306, 340, 344, 364, 371, 639, 645,
  711, 800, 819, 884

Command. See also Obedience: I 129, 510,
  558–59, 564, 571, 576, 587; II 46, 67, 118,
  239, 346, 412, 571, 603, 625, 676; III 100
  church I 56; II 254
  divine: I 40, 70, 538; II 245, 248, 250,
    319, 536, 540, 624, 686, 688, 705,
    772, 785, 812; III 397, 405, 411, 416,
    419, 604
  Francis: I 73, 86, 102, 105–06, 242–43,
    404, 491, 493, 495–96, 599; II 122,
    127, 137, 215, 290, 356–57, 410, 567,
    592–93, 665, 672, 680, 697, 745, 795,
    798; III 97, 128, 137, 153, 157, 222,
    227, 229, 234, 266, 355, 361, 406,
    420, 437, 440–41, 451, 456, 459, 465,
    469, 568, 570–71, 577, 582, 584–85,
    589, 592, 596–97, 602, 610–11, 620,
    629, 684, 733, 743–44, 793, 862
  heart: III 81
  minister: I 67, 105; II 157, 309; III
    157–58, 294, 309
  obedience: I 68, 126, 206–07, 228, 242,
    404, 564, 587; II 93, 118, 215, 346,
    376, 381, 456, 546, 580, 627, 642,
    812; III 128, 293–94, 386, 416, 440,
    451, 459, 495, 507, 571, 582, 584,
    597, 610, 620, 762, 805
  Pope: I 86; II 812; III 31, 37, 624,
    755–56, 762–63, 781
  rash: II 118, 346; III 294
  Rule: I 67, 105; II 157, 309; III 116,
    158, 386, 419–20, 744, 762

Commander: I 463, 465, 469, 608; II 801; III
  143, 877

Commandment: I 58, 215, 543, 546, 589; II
  34, 37, 42, 89–90, 211, 378, 385, 512, 735,
  739; III 171, 317, 414, 508, 531, 621, 632

Commemoration: II 670; III 534

Commerce: I 214; II 686

Common: I 289, 401, 461; II 253, 260, 533;
  III 40, 89
  agreement: II 664
  custom: III 424
  good: I 289
  legend: III 214
  Lent: III 497, 611
  life: II 177; III 58a
  ownership: I 272; II 46, 94, 131, 371,
    373, 386, 566, 642, 772, 777; III 39,
    123, 157, 259, 700, 708–09, 744, 748,
    777–78, 786, 816, 842
  people: II 271; III 596
  profession: II 146, 380; III 323, 715
  saying: III 123
  sense: II 404; III 125, 333

state: III 160
thing: III 96

Communication: II 690; III 421, 844

Communion
  Eucharist: I 129; II 375, 598; III 229,
    357, 515–16, 626
  faithful: II 514
  give: II 341
  saints: I 587

Community: I 575, 579; II 243; III 714, 778,
  804

Companionship: I 158; II 742; III 456, 548

Company: I 273, 279, 437, 581; II 67, 75,
  244, 268, 413, 509, 653, 728, 743, 812; III
  161, 553, 629, 892
  angelic: I 331–32, 568
  brotherly: I 332, 344, 380; II 40–41,
    150, 348–49; III 55, 66, 83, 196, 241,
    268, 301, 329, 346, 400, 551, 578,
    606, 628; III 192, 499, 524, 654
  demonic: III 524

Compassion. See also Piety, Tenderness: I
  195, 352, 368, 470, 511, 536, 565; II 180,
  182, 184, 190, 223, 227, 386; III 159, 175
  Christ: II 142, 249, 266, 359, 436, 515,
    586, 669, 671, 686, 697, 712, 792
  other: II 52, 107, 374, 379, 534,
    589–90, 666, 735, 793, 795; III 44,
    59, 232, 249, 278, 285, 305–06, 310,
    338–39, 346, 351, 364, 407, 441, 572,
    794, 800, 838, 840, 849–51, 861, 864,
    875

Competition: I 322; II 332, 430; III 389

Compilation: III 678, 837

Complaint: I 289, 438, 546; II 79, 134, 161,
  289, 319, 351, 458, 464, 681; III 125, 264,
  295, 483, 788

Compline: I 61, 66, 101, 139; II 89, 167, 407,
  797; III 304, 345, 474, 594, 696

Compunction: I 437; II 570, 583, 626, 701,
  712; III 95, 501, 608, 621, 855

Conceit: I 331, 338; III 157, 178, 182, 186

Concentration: I 119; II 292, 534, 685, 721;
  III 181, 596

Conception: II 544

Concession: I 561–62; II 333; III 82, 417,
  420, 770, 809

Conclusion: I 258, 426, 541; II 57, 623; III
  581

Concubine: II 787–88

Condescension. See also Self–emptying: I
  565–66; II 375, 547, 565, 567, 586, 598,
  708

Condition: I 248, 303, 305–06, 374, 453, 537,
  582; II 37, 305, 446, 552, 716, 734, 759,
  793, 818; III 84, 155, 281, 354, 503, 654,
  695, 746, 757–58, 763, 781, 850
  human: I 266, 759; III 90, 92, 95, 411,
    503

illness: I 241; II 122, 453, 457, 463; III 73, 222, 360, 363, 447
original: II 665
Confession: I 136, 228, 234, 283, 476, 553, 792; II 147, 264–65, 323, 329, 406–07, 410, 420, 439, 448, 563, 594, 652, 695, 703, 800, 804; III 94, 151, 231, 233, 312, 323, 342, 350, 506, 525, 546–47, 562–63, 608, 619, 642, 811
Confessor: II 441, 738, 780–81; III 35, 47–48, 56, 92, 134, 202, 318, 662, 686, 694, 730, 740–42, 747, 761, 769, 773, 776, 797, 799, 808, 871
Christ: I 366, 369, 390, 393, 571; II 419, 557, 647, 700; III 92, 740
Confidence: I 103, 184, 409, 472, 564; II 42, 77–78, 80, 89, 99, 439, 539, 550, 660, 668, 690, 781; III 60, 87, 174, 187, 386, 413, 426, 456, 482, 505, 527, 547, 601, 636, 640, 645, 747, 777, 843, 856
Confinement: I 182, 221, 303, 334, 356, 386, 442; II 70, 79, 216, 243, 309, 433, 436–38, 453, 457, 666–67, 681, 803; III 38, 310, 331, 527
Confirmation
blessing: I 127, 415
contemplation: II 606
Dominic's *Rule:* II 785–86
faith: III 50
Francis's death: I 203
Francis's *Rule:* I 63, 99, 106, 210, 321, 383–84, 418, 571, 580, 583, 593, 598–99; II 56–57, 83, 95, 98, 105–06, 381, 513, 529, 550, 558–59, 629, 690, 742, 772, 779, 783, 792; III 89, 93, 115, 387, 390, 680, 720, 740
Gospel: I 539; II 626, 691; III 680
humility: II 751
miracle: II 435, 444, 447–48, 567, 610, 648, 727
mission: I 373
plan: II 86, 544
prophecy: II 617, 672
stigmata: II 427, 513–14, 636–38
successor: III 93
Conformity
brothers' ways: I 269; II 331
Christ: I 288, 375, 441, 567, 586; II 77, 401, 525, 527, 631, 642–43, 650, 710, 721, 738–39, 756, 764; III 879b
Divine Will: II 71, 631, 760; III 188, 195
eternal law: II 724; III 186
Good: I 430
Gospel: II 542, 561, 689
poor: I 369
simplicity: II 369
Testament: I 571
Confrontation: I 409, 582; II 86, 240; III 154, 199, 203, 483

Confusion: I 142, 145, 312, 389, 543, 560, 570; II 115, 230, 268, 428, 455, 528, 661, 701, 741, 788; III 70, 102, 320–21, 342, 381, 422, 583, 650; III 70, 102, 320–21, 342, 381, 422, 583, 650
Conquest: I 231, 331; III 193
Conscience: I 42, 49, 228, 393, 545, 559, 571–72; II 46, 93, 128, 265, 329, 337, 382, 445, 518, 552, 556, 614, 617, 691, 782, 817; III 167, 228, 256, 356, 406, 457, 462, 493, 496, 533, 596, 610, 621, 704, 741–42, 744, 751–52, 754, 772, 864
Consecration: I 52, 54, 101, 163, 257, 271, 294, 329, 406, 465, 517, 579; II 240, 300, 406, 428, 661, 676, 723; III 176, 189, 381, 397, 417, 534, 543–44, 656–57, 809, 824, 879
Consent
cardinal: I 569
church: III 749
Francis: II 157; III 47, 260, 819
God: II 440, 669; III 618
Lady Poverty: I 534
Pope: I 267, 384; II 785
Consideration: I 337, 398; II 96, 622, 696, 811; III 200, 247, 250, 268, 305, 750, 759, 768, 782, 788
Consignment: I 357, 480; II 143, 340, 720; III 159, 187–88, 287
Consolation: I 256, 285, 324, 380, 476, 534, 550, 569; II 121–23, 127, 129, 158, 164, 169, 175, 180–81, 186, 194, 201, 209, 211, 227, 239, 272, 312, 386, 418, 489, 536, 686, 719, 742, 761; III 171, 237, 242, 257, 302, 410, 426, 510, 518, 528, 531, 534, 540, 555, 614, 616, 619, 625, 637, 643, 651, 655, 707
Bernard: III 356
Clare: III 466–67, 478, 590–91
Conrad: III 694–95
Francis: I 255, 287; II 129, 169; III 216, 221, 227, 242, 272, 283, 302, 347, 369–70, 414, 502, 588–89, 811, 869
God: I 262; III 451–52, 582
music: II 330
Lady Jacoba: III 222–23, 360, 473
Poor Ladies: II 129, 188; III 229, 337, 516, 626
Spirit: I 225; III 464
Constancy: I 375, 554; II 690; III 102, 884
Bernard: III 575
Divine service: II 85
faith: II 96; III 490, 605
Francis: III 436, 490, 605, 856
mind: I 322, 374, 409; II 626
preach: II 408
Construction: I 406, 419–20, 589, 603; II 198, 212, 414, 429–30, 478, 642, 648, 662; III 68, 85, 127, 260–61, 752
Consultation
cardinal: I 109

Christ: III 123, 266, 709
Clare: II 623
doctor: II 189, 441
Francis: II 617; III 862
Lord: I 333; II 52, 75, 131
Pope: I 471, 498
Contagion
dust: I 243: II 565
human: I 414
miraculous: I 494, 507; II 108, 797
Contamination: I 440; II 321, 363, 563
Contemplation. See also Leisure *[vacatio]*,
Rest *[quies]*
Bernard: III 439, 503, 504a, 569–70,
616–17, 684
Body of Christ: III 616, 657
brother: I 597; III 49, 586
Clare: III 591
church: III 192–93, 387
Francis: I 261, 284, 375, 380, 508; II
141, 191, 312, 414, 699, 722, 728,
742; III 148, 174–77, 181, 296, 441,
453, 456, 579, 717, 815, 838, 847,
855, 865–66
Giles: II 544; III 125, 184, 333, 447,
578, 685
God: II 121
Innocent III: II 690
Jesus: III 195
Leo: III 456
Masseo: III 515, 691
place: I 579; II 277–78, 356, 402, 409,
584, 705, 709; III 49, 177, 181, 453,
461, 548, 578–79, 645, 861
Poor Ladies: I 199
poverty: III 884
Rachel: III 87
Rufino: III 507, 511, 620, 622
Simon: III 538
sixth *status:* III 192–93, 387
stigmata: III 148
Contempt: I 68, 185; II 443, 457, 670, 676,
736
body: I 48, 68
brother: I 217, 534–35; II 256, 290, 602
Christ: II 802
church: I 568
disciple: I 547
Francis: I 566; II 37
God: II 616
habit: II 37
Lady Poverty: I 548
money: III 260
poor: I 547
priesthood: II 787
religion: II 619
Rule: II 291
self: I 228, 241, 335, 377, 416; II 82,
750
world: I 207, 381, 434, 572, 582–83; II
317, 688; III 382, 426, 436, 476, 490,
508, 605, 688, 818, 843

Contest: I 460; III 440, 452, 582, 737, 853
Continence: I 100; II 732, 793; III 730
Contradiction: I 218, 441, 543; II 182, 260,
514, 804; III 39, 98, 189, 303, 305, 313,
389, 418, 781, 789
Contrition: I 136, 283, 546; II 229, 380, 817;
III 137, 233, 342, 608, 811
Control: I 67, 292, 438, 452; II 454, 575, 694,
740; III 543, 751, 787, 858
Contuition: II 532, 545, 596, 614, 624, 692
Convent: II 670; III 132, 480, 552, 559–60,
600, 714, 773, 777, 780
Conversion. See also Penance
brother: I 554, 583; II 317, 319; III 117,
242, 268, 301, 338, 684, 690
Clare: III 228–29
Francis: I 184, 258, 269, 288, 314, 322,
377–78, 394–95, 412, 418, 530; II 63,
66, 77, 120–21, 123, 125, 240–41,
340, 401, 410, 415, 446, 509, 536,
541, 568, 600, 602, 638–39, 641–43,
650, 682, 684, 694, 713, 715, 717,
723, 742, 754–56; III 33, 66, 86, 131,
160, 171, 173, 221, 223, 225, 233–34,
239, 263, 279, 287, 290, 306, 316,
339, 385, 414, 468, 591, 682, 695,
711, 727, 815–16, 824, 826, 833, 835,
852, 871, 873
sinner: I 382; II 587, 618; III 49, 251,
408, 521–22, 611, 646, 697
Corpse: II 312, 345, 425, 571, 606, 660, 740,
803, 805; III 293, 847
Correction: I 67, 95, 105, 135, 209, 271–72;
II 143, 240, 290, 340, 358, 518, 620, 794;
III 287, 404, 440, 571, 701, 777, 886
Corruption: I 48, 92, 183, 446, 470, 543, 545,
547, 561; II 144, 332, 365, 723; III 117,
135, 157, 165, 180, 186, 194, 325, 382,
563, 739, 815, 866
Cough: II 164, 308, 369; III 242, 302
Council
church: II 205, 370, 811; III 519, 540,
635, 741, 799, 828
war: I 355
Counsel: I 72, 89, 102, 261, 283, 372, 437,
470, 559; II 41, 71, 254, 323
bishop: III 239, 263
brother: II 55, 154; III 120, 297, 564,
782
Christ: III 393, 421, 568, 814
Francis: III 64, 358
God: II 38, 44, 531; III 357
Gospel: I 196; III 198, 241–42, 301–02,
335
Mother of God: III 53
perfection: III 198
Rule: III 744, 773–74, 782, 788
Count
cause: II 183
consideration: II 523
numerical: I 409; II 272; III 63, 174

person: II 35–36, 69–70, 419, 463; III 802
Countess: II 439, 668
Courage: I 450, 465, 479, 486, 497; II 140, 305, 426, 428, 552, 600, 603, 637, 661, 812; III 78, 202, 281, 481, 507, 601, 731, 741, 884
Court: I 539, 591; II 97, 255, 327, 575; III 56, 174, 720–21, 751, 765–66, 777, 779, 786, 788, 884
    heavenly: I 554; II 348, 588, 800; III 192
    papal: I 512, 570; III 352, 476, 595–96, 819
    Sultan: I 395, 606; III 798
Courtesy: I 461, 503–04, 534; II 199, 307; III 125, 214, 272–73, 551–52, 628, 892
Cowardice: II 252, 537
Crazy: I 333, 440, 588; III 389, 436, 507, 575, 620
Creation: I 433, 537; II 567, 729, 763, 813; III 174, 457, 520, 562
Creative: I 489; II 813
Creator: I 74, 78, 85–86, 158, 251, 301, 438, 538, 601; II 101, 124, 316, 353, 414–15, 585, 705, 719, 746; III 39, 163, 364, 456, 655, 799
    goodness: I 119, 250, 704
    likeness: I 538
    love: I 216, 234, 321–22, 396; II 40, 43, 90, 411–13, 798; III 541
    praise: I 194, 234, 250, 396, 453; II 164, 353, 411–14, 431, 492–93; 514, 539; III 79, 224, 291, 347, 353, 452, 470, 520, 593, 632–33, 826, 835
Creature: I 49, 95, 113–14, 234, 236, 248, 321–22, 396, 455, 489, 502–03, 516; II 124, 176, 186, 353, 411, 499, 665, 726, 762, 798; III 224, 366, 439–40, 457, 459, 512, 541, 563, 570–71, 583, 603, 633, 640, 733, 826, 851
    brother or sister: I 503; II 121, 358, 696; III 221, 346, 367, 371, 851
    contemplation: I 250, 537; III 366
    feeling: II 783; III 79, 362, 367, 870
    God: III 242, 302, 371, 387, 483
    human: II 48, 74, 808; III 47, 119, 271, 882
    invitation: II 188, 250, 798, 803; III 79, 337, 366–68, 831, 840, 868
    irrational: I 235, 396, 492; II 164, 186, 190, 321, 353–56, 408, 411, 586; III 51, 79, 347, 349, 364–65, 367, 521
    obedience: I 131, 236, 328; II 411, 625, 629, 708, 717; III 51, 79, 97, 104, 185, 364, 839
Creed: I 66
Crib: I 507; II 610
Cricket: II 217–18, 357, 414, 593, 798
Crime: I 48, 184, 438, 446–47, 457, 547; II 274, 299, 379, 407, 439, 528, 555, 665,

668; III 95, 390, 416, 422, 483, 493, 495–96, 526, 553
Crippled: I 240, 274, 299, 323–24, 420, 518; II 458–62, 480, 615, 627, 649, 753, 784; III 69–70, 150, 580
Crisis: I 432
Criticism: II 42, 147, 240, 341, 350, 358, 362, 581, 599, 696; III 164, 322, 757
Cross. See also Crucifix
    altar: I 46
    armor: II 560
    book: II 551
    carry: I 64, 131, 471, 518, 582; II 383, 534–35, 544, 560, 566–67, 631, 639–40, 686, 756, 761, 816; III 83, 176, 195, 422, 438, 444, 529, 541, 550, 568
    Christ: I 260–61, 360, 448, 536, 587, 600; II 82, 172, 358, 360, 599, 684, 719–21; III 84, 89, 366, 423, 513, 535, 652, 687, 821, 842, 874, 884
    conformity: I 375, II 738, 745; III 380, 877
    death: I 536; II 522, 643, 715, 745–46; III 382, 392
    devotion: II 90, 377, 758; III 84, 191, 799
    discipleship: III 445, 516, 576, 624, 876
    enemy: I 269; III 862
    feast: II 108, 632, 709, 743; III 457
    foolishness: III 403
    Francis: I 261, 280, 283, 358, 390, 477; II 532, 685, III 870, 873
    Francis's death: II 643, 715, 745–46
    Francis's stigmata: I 225, 260, 280, 287, 323, 345, 355, 357; II 320, 402, 620, 640, 650–51, 712, 714, 719, 727–30, 738, 761; III 175, 188, 421, 448, 667, 670, 826, 835
    glory: I 281, 328, 346; II 377, 682, 758; III 422, 450, 581, 667
    golden: I 325, 419; II 109, 319, 478, 623, 692, 795; III 87, 438, 468, 569, 592, 874
    healing: I 475
    life: III 399
    love: II 758; III 83, 792, 798
    meditation: III 874
    mission: II 546
    Monaldo: I 225, 390; II 402, 557, 620, 638, 700, 783
    mystery: I 46, 82, 131, 260, 281, 287, 360, 601; II 172, 401–02, 650–51, 681–82, 713, 719, 722–30
    nakedness: I 375, 582; II 82, 538, 642, 687; III 383, 550, 627, 842
    offering: II 137, 290; III 195, 266
    Pacifico: II 317, 402, 556, 638, 693
    painting: III 189, 639
    pattern: III 420, 470, 577
    power: II 650, 682, 717; III 50

prayer: I 125, 222, 388; II 90, 168, 328, 361, 551, 607, 699; III 49, 181, 305, 426, 670
preach: I 601; II 402, 545, 638, 682; III 403, 470, 575, 594, 694
relic: I 325, 419; II 109, 551; III 67
seal: I 323, 355, 436
seraph: I 263–64, 340, 410, 509; II 108, 402, 473, 632, 709, 783; III 835, 866
sign: I 188, 222, 234, 240, 262, 287, 300, 302, 373, 396, 403, 409, 495; II 77, 175, 274, 328, 355, 408, 410, 420, 447, 450, 454–55, 461, 467, 536, 615, 619, 624, 627, 638, 674, 702, 704, 796, 799; III 50, 74, 85, 92, 94–95, 97, 364, 422, 437, 470, 480, 482, 502, 516–17, 544, 568, 575, 592–94, 601–02, 616, 624, 657, 835, 847, 861–62, 865
sign of virtues: II 722–27; III 153, 161, 332, 384, 397, 410, 464, 517, 588, 665, 719
staff: II 717, 742
standard: II 651, 681, 685, 693, 712; III 873
stigmata: I 225, 260, 280, 287, 323, 345, 355, 357; II 320, 402, 620, 640, 650–51, 712, 714, 719, 727–30, 738, 761; III 175, 188, 421, 448, 667, 670, 826, 835
suffering: I 131, 360; III 152, 392, 692, 884
sword: I 441; II 317, 638, 693, 798; III 792, 874
Sylvester: II 38–9, 87, 319, 401–02, 544–45, 623, 638, 692–93, 795
tunic: I 202, 460; II 401, 527, 538; III 196, 444, 684, 692
vision: I 225, 390, 463; II 638, 685, 783; III 51, 83, 87, 92, 102, 383, 438, 468, 512, 569, 592, 668, 838, 874
voice from: II 249–50, 378, 401, 536, 540, 638, 686, 688; III 79, 84
way: II 95; III 125, 315, 323, 333, 335, 393, 420, 715
Crowd: I 206, 244–45, 255, 261, 293–94, 306, 385, 409, 416, 442, 487, 491, 518, 544, 562, 600; II 90, 109, 178, 183, 246–47, 252, 268, 288, 291, 309, 317, 333, 349, 381, 388–89, 400, 403, 417–18, 422, 426, 430, 446, 476, 478, 481, 509, 558, 606, 625, 630, 647, 657, 660, 676, 705, 797, 808; III 34, 66, 74, 89, 101, 176–78, 185, 199, 263, 306, 331, 353, 459, 500, 508, 528, 564, 596, 614, 640, 846–47, 854, 870
Crown: I 479, 497, 535; II 267, 324, 743; III 248, 327, 446, 666, 718, 726, 885
empire: I 221
glory: I 294; III 578
gold: I 339, 346; II 743
life: II 119, 268, 349; III 134, 316, 723
martyrdom: I 479; III 37, 323, 400, 856

merit: I 270; III 577
poverty: III 489, 726
righteousness: I 568; II 386
royal: II 746
stars: III 499, 614
thorns: I 360
Crucifix. See also Cross: II 168, 249, 551, 760; III 527, 636, 792, 841
Crumb: I 529; II 227, 279, 555, 692; III 91, 93, 160, 196
Rule: II 558, 381; III 93, 196
Cry. See also Town Crier: I 50, 142–43, 151, 193, 209, 221, 223, 228, 249, 265, 278, 285–87, 298, 344, 400, 478, 488, 516, 533; II 76–77, 83, 125, 142, 173, 180, 258, 265, 353, 403, 424, 426, 438, 443–44, 446, 449, 458–59, 474, 476, 520, 522, 537, 541, 575, 584, 614, 658, 660, 667–68, 670–71, 705, 772, 795, 797–98, 816–17; III 56, 59, 69, 74, 175, 225, 250, 301–02, 310, 318, 339–40, 352, 387, 390, 426, 474, 483, 509, 531, 541, 543, 580, 602–03, 616, 640, 644, 648, 651, 655, 657, 835
　Francis: II 122, 125; III 222, 241, 361
　heart: II 311
　joy: I 151, 275, 294; II 142; III 340, 623
　pain: I 265, 502; II 403, 474; III 424
　strength: III 152
　tears: I 287; II 122, 142, 541; III 222, 340, 361, 450
Crypt: I 218; III 40
Cultivation: I 223, 563, 565; II 192, 521, 765; III 41, 47, 153, 366, 408, 780
Cup: I 46; II 311, 353, 414, 434, 609, 664, 779; III 158–59, 597, 803
　praise: I 338
　salvation 732
　suffering: I 540; III 159
Cupidity: I 381, 435; III 722, 755, 816–17, 842
Cure: I 431, 443, 493, 511, 513; II 53, 407, 431; III 54, 94, 179, 317, 711, 839
　animal: II 196, 196a, 611, 722; III 669
　basabove: II 196, 196a
　blindness: I 301; II 671; III 72, 185
　cripple: I 299–300, 304; II 457, 459, 462, 479–80, 620; III 60, 69–71, 95, 185
　deformity: II 454
　dropsy: I 303; II 432; III 73
　Francis's eyes: III 336, 339, 364
　leprosy: I 305–06; III 494, 608–09
　loss of limb: I 304, 323, 402
　mute: I 307; II 451–3; III 72–73, 185
　rupture: II 446; III 74
　serious injury: I 303, 323, 402; II 654–5; III 44
　swelling: I 302
　tumor: III 50, 55
　ulcer: I 305; II 467, 481

various diseases: I 238, 323, 402; II 197, 408, 628, 675, 692, 702; III 91, 97, 280, 835, 839, 862
women in labor: II 628
Curia
Perugia: I 579; III 709
Rieti: II 197
Roman: I 126, 210, 267, 413, 470, 579–80; II 49, 55, 96, 105–06, 197, 216, 514, 547, 648, 660; III 62, 64, 127, 310, 386, 405, 420, 532, 554, 761, 813, 830
Curiosity: I 183, 587; II 147, 282, 336; III 555
knowledge: II 147, 368, 372; III 314, 706
those in charge: I 227
Curse: I 43, 46, 50–51, 58, 68, 117, 191, 248, 447, 536, 538–39; II 37, 82, 92, 140, 162, 251, 279, 305, 319, 321, 348, 440, 443, 588, 590, 669, 815; III 99, 199, 281, 336, 383, 397, 407–08, 421, 447, 451, 477, 493, 577, 580–82, 597, 606, 706, 795, 851, 874
Curtain: II 435
Custodian: I 56–57, 60, 62, 98, 102, 104, 109–10, 120, 126, 560, 570, 573–74; II 777–78; III 393, 402, 697, 747, 750, 756–57, 760, 765–66, 772, 775, 780, 858
Custody: I 104; II 438, 679; III 528, 535, 540, 542, 555, 635, 637, 639, 653, 750, 766, 780
Custom: I 182, 185, 553; II 405, 751; III 32, 424, 441, 600, 755, 774
brother: I 602; II 143, 347, 700; III 132, 295
church: III 385
cleric: I 65
Francis: I 195, 246, 261, 396, 456; II 162, 175, 194, 213–14, 279, 355–56, 402, 413, 551, 630–31, 615, 619, 691; III 59, 245–46, 268, 295, 308, 600, 793, 795, 831, 855, 867
teacher: III 559

D

Damnation: I 355, 438, 477; II 348, 367, 522, 615, 703; III 451, 603, 612, 617–18, 629–30, 638, 642–43, 650
Danger: I 239, 279, 292, 371, 377, 394, 405, 536, 571, 595 II 139, 217, 304, 341, 360, 363, 383, 432–33, 435, 443, 450, 462, 467, 481, 544, 565, 584–85, 602, 625, 657, 663, 665, 672, 716; III 73, 87, 116–17, 135, 150, 197, 247, 280, 308, 404, 413, 419, 482, 550, 554, 574, 618, 627, 630, 712, 761, 851, 888
Darkness: I 40, 46, 191, 205, 215, 282, 289, 323, 374, 380, 385, 389, 431, 482, 503, 534, 541, 570, 584; II 35, 78, 143, 281, 283, 316, 320, 343, 347–49, 353, 407, 489, 526, 568, 635, 677, 684, 707, 711, 734, 743, 772, 811; III 90, 159, 295, 321, 381, 383,

390, 397, 404, 411, 491, 505, 520, 524, 618, 650, 678
Daughter: I 567; II 54, 58, 109, 124, 129, 272, 317, 323, 325, 333, 405, 423, 426, 432, 441, 443, 446, 450, 463, 563, 571, 652, 656, 669, 679, 793, 795, 805; III 117, 180, 224, 229, 291, 422, 680–81, 689–90, 712
churches: II 749
Clare: II 554; III 467, 517, 591, 624, 879
grace: II 367
Mary: I 241
obedience: III 467, 517, 591, 624
Orders: II 750
Pharaoh: II 752
Poor Ladies: I 285, 417, 501, 603; II 379, 476; III 67, 136, 516, 626
Sion: I 534
Dawn: I 143, 435, 506; II 35, 158, 167, 186, 215, 227, 254, 275, 327–28, 356, 370, 413, 416, 449, 457, 490, 594, 671; III 186, 245, 304, 309, 367, 452, 499, 527, 542, 636, 678
Day
approval: I 479
battle: II 265, 614; III 864
crucifixion: II 720; III 513
death: I 58, 295, 325, 420; II 107, 109, 120–21, 180, 183–84, 187, 203–04, 207, 211–12, 262, 474, 477, 641, 649, 735, 802; III 166, 168, 171, 218, 221–22, 255, 257, 313, 317, 339, 358, 360, 367, 369, 372, 414, 548, 702, 711–12, 840, 861, 869
distress: I 152–53
final: I 276, 299, 323, 414; II 474, 499; III 59, 527, 549, 636, 868
human approval: I 479
judgment: I 44, 53, 55, 59, 67, 95; II 143, 564, 719–20; III 125, 287, 324, 549
Lord: I 479; III 103, 270
Nativity: II 411, 783; III 363
Passover: I 516
reckoning: I 446; II 147; III 314, 706
wrath: I 538
Deacon: I 256b; II 389; III 66
Dead body: I 291, 412; II 345, 400, 571, 640, 714; III 293, 544, 562, 657, 838
Deaf: I 191, 202, 290, 306, 320, 324, 374, 420, 489, 518, 545; II 78, 246, 450, 453, 530, 537, 649, 673, 685, 687, 716; III 73, 150, 185, 436, 449, 567, 580
Death
Adam: I 455, 538
bed: I 349, 494; II 76; III 182, 803
Bernard: III 33, 447, 501, 577–78
body: I 272; II 93; 383; III 371, 423, 606, 653, 730
Christ: I 82, 288, 360, 475, 510, 517–18, 536, 589; II 77, 522, 643,

654, 697, 726, 800, 802, 814; III 89,
    118, 382, 384, 392, 394, 421, 423,
    680, 693–94, 821
Clare: II 128–29; III 228–29, 357
Conrad of Offida: III 522, 638
day: I 58; II 280, 618, 733, 735
devil: III 381
dust: I 146
Elias: III 631
eternity: III 381, 392, 397, 423, 524,
    537
Eve: I 488
faith: II 268; III 423
fear: II 203, 602, 818; III 370
Francis: I 180, 254, 274–75, 277, 279,
    284–85, 295, 325, 407, 414–15, 419,
    446, 513–17, 600; II 58, 76, 108–09,
    120, 123, 125–28, 135, 138, 143, 147,
    155, 159–60, 162, 171, 180, 183–84,
    187, 192, 194–95, 202–05, 207, 212,
    217, 220, 226, 230, 280–81, 283, 285,
    293, 336, 340, 344, 373, 379, 386,
    403, 417–20, 467, 474–75, 477, 490,
    519, 528, 531, 541, 577, 610, 635–37,
    641, 643, 645, 648, 651, 685, 696,
    715–16, 746, 758, 765, 773, 784, 793,
    797, 810, 816; III 56, 66, 86, 91, 121,
    166–68, 171–72, 217–18, 221, 223,
    225–28, 231, 233, 236, 238–40, 244,
    249, 255, 257, 262, 265, 267, 283–84,
    287, 292, 299, 313, 315, 317, 324,
    328, 335–36, 339, 346, 355–57,
    360–62, 366–67, 369–71, 385,
    415–14, 425–26, 446–47, 471–73,
    475, 491, 512, 537, 577, 595, 643,
    682, 687, 702–03, 711–12, 730, 732,
    807, 821, 831, 835, 840, 846, 861,
    863, 871, 874
Francis's teaching: I 43, 50, 52, 54, 58,
    79, 82, 87, 89, 95, 164; III 171, 218,
    471–72, 604, 798
general minister: I 574; II 778
Giles: III 799
hand: I 242
Honorius III: II 107, 814
hypothermia: II 325, 563, 795
James: III 536, 654
John: III 151, 242
Leo: III 809
letter of law: I 132; III 423
life: I 52, 54, 238, 449, 479, 487, 497,
    514–15, 540, 586; II 58, 108, 110,
    121, 123, 202, 220, 490, 519, 564; III
    185, 217, 221, 223, 249, 292, 371,
    412, 446, 485, 522, 577, 636, 638, 753
martyrdom: I 79, 87, 275, 479, 485,
    607–08; II 601, 726, 741; III 136,
    195, 257, 382, 398, 401, 491, 606,
    667, 707, 856
minister: I 574; II 778
mourning: II 440, 669; III 525
Pellegrino: III 615

persecution: I 89, 95, 607–08; II 209;
    III 79, 115, 384, 422, 490
personified: I 285, 479; II 385; III 840,
    868, 884
Peter: III 225
phoenix: I 512
preparation: II 615, 703, 715; III 94,
    548, 609, 645
prudence: III 399
punishment: II 34, 270, 279, 321,
    590–91, 702; III 136, 483, 723
religion: III 392
resurrection: I 497, 519; II 816
Rule: III 194
salvation: I 324, 394; II 407, 421–22,
    424, 427–28, 431, 435, 441, 443–44,
    446, 462, 528, 590, 657, 661–63, 669,
    671, 707, 717, 805; III 80, 150, 485,
    490, 497, 604, 835
separation: II 173
shadow: I 534, 587; II 373, 489, 526,
    602, 707, 772
sickness: I 303; II 161, 423, 426,
    430–31, 440, 443, 446, 448, 465, 628,
    656, 662, 669–71, 681, 692, 802–03;
    III 172, 369, 407, 548, 645
sin: I 468; II 34, 178, 816–17; III 317,
    711
sister: I, 114; II 121, 204, 388, 803; III
    219, 221, 368, 370–71, 831, 868
sleep: I 154
soul: I 221, 386; II 172, 563; III 41, 51,
    222, 343, 368, 423
starvation: I 483; II 149, 222, 259, 283,
    332, 463, 585, 727
stigmata: I 249, 428, 518; II 401,
    635–37, 650–51, 746, 770; III 176,
    840, 856, 866, 871, 874
teaching: I 43, 50, 52, 54, 58, 79, 82,
    87, 89, 95, 164; III 171, 218, 471–72,
    604, 798
threat: I 231, 607–08; II 601–02, 741;
    III 95, 490, 878
vice: I 221, 386, 438; III 97, 317, 397,
    711
violence: II 282, 407–08, 425, 662
Debt: I 80, 299, 406, 475; II 313, 436–37,
    458, 608, 666, 690, 715; III 95, 131
Debtor: II 190, 436, 666; III 337, 850
Deceased: I 65–66; II 423, 427, 486, 587,
    656; III 61, 494, 755, 835
Deceiver: II 739; III 811
Deception: I 242, 302, 445; II 264, 618, 793,
    800; III 180, 411
Decision: I 214, 377, 465, 561; II 445; III
    491, 615, 761, 768, 833
Decline: III 149, 177, 179, 389, 723
Decorum: II 156; III 121, 237, 299
Decree: I 65, 86, 101, 106, 117, 295, 356,
    561–62, 569, 573; II 169, 270, 375, 402,
    418, 477, 779

Dedication: I 296, 460; II 47, 100–03, 346, 372, 468, 402; III 151, 181, 506–07, 513, 548, 619
Deed
  ancestor: II 263
  Anthony: III 63
  apostle: I 540; III 33
  bishop: III 460
  canon: III 55
  Christ: I 254, 259, 497; III 117, 152, 384, 421, 667, 712
  commandment: II 42
  evil: I 225, 368, 546; II 222, 292, 321, 348, 588, 790, 793; III 251, 311, 408, 451, 524, 610, 863
  example: I 260; II 160, 200; III 263, 317, 396, 712, 818
  faith: I 77
  Francis: I 180, 185–86, 188, 220, 229, 257–58, 260, 263, 272, 287, 369, 373, 479, 568; II 34, 52, 55, 58, 67, 75, 80, 89, 96, 101–02, 108, 200–01, 207, 239–40, 251, 254–55, 258, 263, 278, 301, 317, 319, 358, 392, 489, 640, 691, 714, 780; III 32, 50, 137, 168, 216, 257, 396, 403, 406, 420–21, 435, 444, 460, 494, 585, 678, 685, 704, 730, 806, 839
  fruit: III 722
  God: I 135, 137; II 407, 660, 730
  good: I 117, 542–43, 550, 552; II 173, 278, 458, 681
  Gregory IX: III 698
  heart: II 726
  humility: I 321; II 534, 801
  hypocritical: II 206; III 705
  knight: III 94
  lesser brother: I 75, 77, 90, 135, 224, 274, 321, 540, 579; II 34, 52, 55, 58, 89, 102, 143–44, 160, 200, 222, 347–48, 588, 783; III 239, 256, 263, 274, 295, 390, 394, 397, 405, 408, 425, 428, 444–45, 511, 575, 704, 791, 818
  love: I 72, 132, 229; II 726
  minister: I 67
  Monaldo: II 402
  poor: I 401
  preaching: I 75, 90, 95, 117, 552; II 201
  reward: II 521–22
  Riccerio: I 390
  saint: II 209, 406
  simplicity: I 321; II 534, 801
  vanity: I 185–86, 443
  virtue: III 258, 315, 342
  word: I 72, 75, 77, 90, 117, 135, 220, 263, 331, 401; II 52, 89, 96, 101, 144, 239–40, 251, 254, 258, 263, 317, 347, 588, 637, 691; III 41, 343, 381, 383, 389, 392–93, 399, 401, 403, 420, 422–24, 692, 834, 837, 846, 867

Defeat: I 331, 457, 460; III 91, 188, 342, 412, 876–77, 890
Defect: II 341, 518; III 188–89, 297, 388, 547, 626, 800, 848, 853, 857
Defender: I 109–10, 608; III 56, 103, 445, 576
Defense: I 144, 358, 460; II 425, 514, 667–68; III 37, 396, 877, 890
Deformed: I 299–300; II 75, 167, 447, 456, 459–60; III 69–70, 243, 303, 557, 648
Deformity: I 298; II 75, 167, 458, 479; III 69, 157
Delegate: I 574; II 778; III 776
Delegation: I 203; II 91
Delight: I 75, 90; II 75, 145, 191, 365, 383, 393, 518, 760; III 39, 157, 233, 242, 326, 342, 356, 426, 453, 463, 470, 487, 549, 667, 724, 772, 885
  pleasure: I 85, 89, 135, 185, 214, 217, 251, 262, 328, 416, 435, 488, 539, 547; II 45, 75, 93, 128, 137, 248, 293, 330, 392, 418, 509, 567, 582, 607, 644; III 66, 98, 186, 193, 276, 334, 343, 364, 389, 455, 542, 543, 593, 595, 596, 645, 649, 653, 655, 769, 882
Delivery: I 256; II 441, 443, 669
Demand: II 92, 290, 531, 630; III 50, 63, 127, 505, 750–53, 766, 788, 859
Demon. See also Devil
  Arezzo: II 215–16, 318–19, 574–75, 795
  evil spirit: I 131, 343, 402, 455, 462, 469; II 215, 318, 328, 343, 352, 455, 561, 575–76, 628, 716, 783, 791, 808; III 96, 115, 129, 134–36, 157, 176, 180, 185, 231, 245, 318, 382, 392, 396, 405, 411–12, 416, 423–24, 449, 487–89, 497, 509, 524, 557, 577, 580, 585, 600–01, 604, 611, 617–19, 634, 721–22, 724–25, 739, 838–39, 843, 847–48, 862
  police of God: II 326, 796; III 231, 312
  possession: I 241–42, 301–02, 324, 369, 403–04, 495–96; II 320, 426, 432, 454, 456, 627, 674, 701, 716; III 43, 407, 528, 607, 637, 846
  tormentor: I 403; II 167, 224–25, 227, 326, 328, 575, 607, 674, 699, 796; III 102, 181, 232, 243, 304, 312, 346, 478, 576, 617, 642, 695, 731, 847
Demonstration: II 436, 698
Denial: I 207; II 259, 546, 732, 756–57; III 198
Depression: I 93, 271, 298, 439; II 56, 70, 230, 331, 458, 479; III 69, 233, 342
Deprivation: III 397, 762
Depth: I 158, 368, 449; II 329, 423, 426, 445, 513, 540, 656, 660; III 158, 164, 179, 182, 354, 384, 404, 443, 456, 514, 542, 550, 559, 567, 648, 818, 855, 870, 882
Derision: I 447; II 512; III 135

Description: I 506, 575
Desert: I 260, 564, 568; II 97, 255, 383, 518, 526, 583, 597, 682, 717, 742, 744, 752; III 117, 129–30, 262, 318, 381, 391, 411, 415, 712, 720, 818
Desire: I 74, 76, 80, 85, 90, 99, 125, 152, 180, 183, 202, 212, 230, 254, 263, 270, 274, 319, 335, 342, 358, 373, 395, 409, 449, 457, 466, 500, 534, 571, 576, 579; II 49, 52, 86, 98, 102, 108, 121, 172, 209, 213, 254, 280–81, 292, 362, 429, 441, 475, 499, 509–10, 519–20, 523, 528, 547–48, 556, 578, 588, 601, 618, 631–32, 646, 662, 689, 693, 709, 717, 723–24, 732, 734, 737, 740–41, 746, 754, 763, 775; III 90, 94, 347, 364, 382, 401, 453, 516, 534, 570, 641, 646–47, 650, 652, 740, 748, 828, 837, 845, 860, 865, 887
 blessing: I 270, 276; II 174–45, 277, 280, 475, 619; III 464, 719
 death: I 72, 91, 94, 479; II 34, 146, 336, 359, 601–02, 741, 764; III 56, 159, 288, 336, 392
 devotion: II 596; III 804
 discipleship of Christ: I 42, 49, 243, 267, 590; II 509–11, 554, 720, 726, 741; III 125, 159, 175, 181, 322, 333, 336, 372, 380, 392, 417, 464–65, 531, 547, 575, 588, 629, 639, 650–51, 719, 854–55
 discipleship of Francis: II 67; III 90, 229, 328, 401, 404, 583, 589, 718, 803, 861
 Divine Love: I 76, 90, 197; II 149, 360, 754–55
 eternal life: I 529, 547; II 315, 533, 631, 709, 762; III 643, 646
 Eucharist: III 534, 650, 652
 fear of God: I 76, 90; II 520
 flesh: I 43, 50, 75, 437, 439, 567, 590, 598; II 46, 74, 93, 182, 197, 274, 560, 605, 615, 669, 687, 694, 702, 720, 723–24, 741, 754, 762–63; III 133, 181, 202, 288, 306, 392, 613, 624, 722, 776, 862
 food: II 135, 356, 413; III 244, 336, 466, 590
 freedom: I 243, 267; III 392, 818
 friendliness: II 227; III 232
 God: I 76, 84, 261–62; II 121, 525, 554, 605, 728, 763; III 221, 371, 657, 797
 God's word: I 254, 460; II 542, 547, 618, 689, 701; III 235, 855
 Gospel: II 757; III 383, 546, 843
 heal: II 258, 446, 450–51, 453, 541; III 72, 74, 364, 733
 heart: I 80, 88, 152, 202, 358, 459; II 281, 542, 689, 724, 726, 740–41; III 529, 535, 551, 628, 649

heaven: I 367, 506, 547, 597; II 533, 631, 709; III 394, 417, 480, 508, 546, 621, 641, 646, 650
holiness: I 75, 90, 262, 269, 459, 525, 554; III 391
hope: II 525
humility: I 135, 273; II 523–24, 640, 714, 725, 738; III 290, 321, 514–15, 623
joy: III 342, 515
learn: II 207; III 130, 168, 257, 319, 705, 707
life: II 34; III 390
Lord's honour: II 737, 746; III 797
Lord's will: I 71, 91, 96, 120, 262, 275, 409; II 97, 146, 360, 525; III 288, 383, 592, 865
martyrdom: I 229–31, 339; II 415, 529, 599–602, 604, 698; III 119, 174, 293, 323, 383, 490, 501, 605, 855–56, 864
meditation: I 198; III 535
mercy: II 149, 360, 754–55; III 234, 278
money: I 70, 125, 165, 543, 546; II 39, 47, 71, 87, 94, 221, 303, 510, 722, 815; III 130, 249, 258, 285, 707, 750, 755
music: II 567
peace: III 843
penance: III 412, 529, 649, 843
perfection: II 554, 623; III 198, 372, 464, 719, 745
pilgrimage: III 818
Portiuncula: III 120
position: I 48, 273; II 71; III 156, 258, 285, 707
possessions: I 70, 125, 165, 543, 546; II 39, 47, 71, 87, 94, 221, 303, 510, 722, 815; III 130, 249, 258, 285, 707, 750, 755
poverty: I 162, 165, 379, 405, 523, 572; II 47, 74, 94, 581, 686, 722, 745; III 162, 290, 463–64, 589, 705, 719, 849
prayer: I 381; II 605; III 245, 329, 383, 453, 465, 705–06
response to God's word: I 254, 460; II 542, 547, 689; III 235, 855
re–unite: I 207, 209, 218, 255, 530; II 49, 546, 749; III 39, 741
salvation: I 266, 580; II 520, 588, 735; III 55, 152, 173, 412, 759, 849
solitude: I 261; II 634; III 175, 453
spirit: I 105
spread the Gospel: II 757; III 383, 546, 843
tribulation: II 185, 741; III 347, 547, 575
truth: I 262
vain–glory: I 247, 265; II 70, 366, 739; III 408, 867
virtue: III 868
vocation: III 412, 628–29, 741

wisdom: I 76, 90, 190; II 725, 728, 751; III 646–47

work: I 125, 193, 372; II 52, 102

Despair: I 226, 302, 368, 405, 438, 587; II 145, 153, 329, 365, 425, 428, 432, 441, 444–45, 450, 481, 555, 659, 661, 672; III 59, 325, 335, 354, 436, 502

Desperation: II 429, 435, 446, 450, 628, 661, 665, 672; III 502, 615

Despicable: I 144, 183; II 45, 341, 519, 726, 752–53

Destination: I 284

Destitution: I 456; II 512, 579–80, 585; III 161, 165

Destruction: I 292; II 270, 318, 510, 545, 692, 722; III 87, 101, 189, 423, 700

Detraction: I 72, 105, 438, 542; II 588; III 165, 788

Detractor: I 72, 499; II 108, 588; III 750, 762–63

Development: II 515, 603, 749; III 118, 165, 186, 195–96, 385, 394

Devil. See also Demon

    Arezzo: II 215, 574

    children: I 43, 50, 78, 91

    evil spirit: I 43, 50–51, 65, 67, 69–70, 73, 79, 87, 92, 129, 214, 230, 244, 408, 438, 463, 495, 541; II 53, 75, 79, 102, 127, 137, 153, 185, 229–30, 248, 280, 289–90, 292, 297, 319, 323–24, 328–29, 423, 427, 481, 510, 551, 564, 575, 580, 619, 626, 691, 701, 720, 733–34, 761, 791, 793, 795, 800–01; III 44, 54, 59, 100, 157, 199, 227, 233, 266, 342–43, 345, 347, 354, 382, 417, 424, 460–61, 481, 489–90, 493, 505–06, 539, 585, 618, 622, 688, 794, 798

    police of God: II 225; III 230–31, 312

    possession: I 241, 323, 495; II 127, 225–28, 248, 269, 280, 289, 299, 325, 328, 426, 454–55, 562, 607, 619, 627, 674, 700, 793, 795–96; III 70, 232, 312–13, 345–46, 354, 356, 446, 480, 504, 509, 511, 622, 688

Devotion

    alms: II 199–201, 792; III 215–16, 274

    Anthony: III 62

    archangel: II 374, 598; III 527, 636

    Bernard: III 443

    brother: I 102, 203, 213, 217–18, 222, 230, 293, 417, 445, 559, 652, 673, II 55, 92, 94, 174, 307, 427, 440, 458, 669, 672, 681, 777; III 236–37, 247, 300, 351, 396, 467, 476, 595–97, 621, 647, 709, 756–57, 765, 770, 785, 793

    Christ: I 199, 244, 323, 406; II 42, 90, 101, 214, 249, 374–75, 377, 449–50, 527, 554, 586, 591, 597–99, 610, 637, 648, 666, 669, 671, 678, 758, 783; III 83, 194, 426, 621, 656, 680, 799, 839

church: II 260; III 324

Clare: III 446, 467, 515–16, 624

confession: I 234, 420; II 420

creation of animals: I 234; II 192, 353, 591–92, 596

Curia: I 413; II 55, 170, 261

Divine Office: I 119, 462, 562; II 156, 229, 311, 609; III 341

Dominic: II 148–49, 334, 342; III 47, 289, 597

Elias: III 553, 630

Eucharist: II 101, 375, 381, 449, 558, 589, 591, 671; III 245, 309, 517, 534, 656

Euphemia: III 54

faith: II 624; III 606

Francis: I 185, 201, 203, 207, 209, 220, 222, 235–6, 238, 262, 265, 286, 288, 290, 293, 298, 304, 306–7, 323, 326, 332, 400, 402–03, 405, 413, 417, 484, 496, 501, 545, 565, 569; II 39, 55, 98, 105, 149, 152, 170, 172, 174, 179, 183, 188, 192–94, 199–201, 204, 217, 222, 259, 275, 281, 288, 296, 298, 312, 314, 322–23, 353, 357, 363, 373–77, 407–08, 411, 413, 420, 422, 427, 435, 437, 439–40, 447, 449, 456–58, 461–62, 468, 534, 540, 566, 583–84, 586, 593, 596, 599, 606–08, 614, 624–25, 627, 652–53, 655–58, 663–64, 666–669, 672, 674, 676–78, 681, 690, 698, 702, 705, 727, 733–34, 750, 760, 773, 791, 804–05, 808; III 50, 78, 83, 97, 102, 176, 184, 194, 215–16, 219, 232, 235, 247, 273–74, 280, 283, 306, 308, 311, 346, 350, 352, 366, 401, 437, 448, 452, 455, 464, 467–68, 471–72, 474–75, 484, 513, 550–52, 560, 567, 571–72, 578–79, 584, 588, 593, 595, 603, 605, 628–29, 698, 719, 730, 798, 802, 832, 839, 846–47, 854, 874

Giles: II 39; III 564, 625

God: I 206, 271–72; II 122, 152, 156, 204, 207, 222–23, 256–57, 266, 271, 376, 552, 574, 586, 616–17, 652, 659, 693, 695, 701–02, 734, 744, 760; III 222, 408, 765, 844

heart: II 228–29, 314, 736; III 232–33, 342, 513, 621, 645

Honorius III: I 270, 579

Hugolino: I 271, 293, 413, 500; II 201, 296, 572, 651, 667; III 275–76, 595–96

Innocent III: II 256, 548, 690

judgment: I 441

Lady Jacoba: II 121–22; III 66, 222, 360–61, 472, 474

Leo: III 455, 513, 550

Leo of Santa Croce: II 224

leper: I 218, 377; II 539, 792

listen: I 499; II 52, 101, 156, 162, 187, 542
Mary: I 201, 378, 462, 475; II 374, 540, 782; III 57, 66, 466, 645, 843
Masseo: III 464, 691
Michael Archangel: II 374, 598; III 527, 636
minister general: II 144, 365; III 325–26
miracle: II 457, 610, 624, 651, 712; III 484, 603
neglect: I 370; II 207, 228–29, 311, 353, 695; III 168, 233, 316, 319, 342, 394, 405, 408, 648, 705, 711, 798, 853
obedience: I 203; II 50, 52, 98, 239, 319, 344, 462, 464
Pacifico: III 792
Paul: II 598
people: I 357; II 87, 307, 361, 418, 639, 661, 703, 727, 729, 738, 744; III 50, 446, 508, 517, 519, 804, 813
Peter: II 534, 540, 598
poor: II 94, 420, 615
Poor Ladies: I 199, 286
Portiuncula: II 155; III 120–21, 236, 298–99, 561
prayer: I 102, 107, 219, 244, 261–62, 380, 385, 409, 502, 567; II 42, 44–46, 85, 91–92, 96, 156, 179, 192, 208, 228, 254, 328, 402, 404–05, 422, 481, 548, 612, 656, 665, 730; III 342, 346, 464, 508, 539, 547, 552, 567, 588, 630, 719, 757, 874
preach: I 202, 225, 266, 491, 551, 576, 597, 599; II 105, 261, 332; III 176, 519, 593
priest: I 189; II 77; III 856
Ranieri: I 295; III 402
read: I 180; II 239, 393, 528
relic: II 199, 376; III 215, 273
saint: I 262
suffer: II 451, 678
sultan: II 603, 698; III 490–91, 605
Sylvester: III 592
tears: I 293; II 122, 152, 695; III 57, 62, 176, 235, 501, 513, 553, 588, 596, 621, 630, 657
write: I 180; II 239, 393, 528
Dialect: II 454, 789; III 443
Dictation: I 469; II 122, 558; III 127, 186, 222, 349, 360, 500
Dignity: I 118, 215, 231, 281, 388, 413, 458, 534–35, 586, 609; II 106, 148, 199, 201, 242, 261, 342, 582, 651, 679; III 44, 47, 56, 63, 78, 99, 155, 214–16, 272–74, 289, 385, 397, 421, 728, 845, 857–58
Diligence: I 409, 544, 583; II 512, 711, 772; III 36, 59, 550, 730–31
Disappointment: I 239, 435
Discernment *[discretio]*: I 137, 272; II 229, 259a, 564, 810; III 98, 199–200a, 269, 279,
338, 344, 393, 459–60, 502, 583, 615, 642, 730, 892
  alms: I 115; II 189
  care of body: II 229, 259, 331, 564–65
  Eucharist: II 52, 54
  Francis: I 125, 227, 231, 243, 251, 366, 390, 395, 473, 489; II 473, 597, 686; III 31–32, 44, 83, 149, 182, 259, 278–79, 346, 362, 383, 477, 511, 541, 564–65, 585, 597
  minister: I 74–75; II 145, 365–66; III 199, 326
  recognition: I 125, 243, 251, 359, 390; II 145, 337, 366, 473, 735; III 44, 58, 63, 121, 224, 234, 291, 300, 334–35, 362, 478, 497, 511, 541, 573, 648, 848
Discipline: I 117, 120, 135, 182–83, 219, 221, 412, 581; II 99, 145, 240, 257, 314, 325, 366, 371, 382, 445, 489, 524, 532, 560, 562, 564, 619, 622, 678, 694, 701, 815; III 32, 43, 153, 326, 488, 522, 615, 725, 731, 834, 843, 855, 877
Discouragement: I 205, 526; II 202, 277; III 217, 388, 570, 856
Discourse: I 338, 487, 498, 604; III 147, 415, 666
Discovery: I 193, 402, 404
Discreet: I 383, 573; II 775, 778
Discretio. See Discernment
Discretion: I 461, 543–44, 573, 590; II 777; III 399, 458, 759, 766, 768, 796, 829, 877
Disease: I 188, 238–39, 256, 267, 290, 323, 325, 398, 403, 405, 407, 431, 510, 514; II 363, 382, 410, 465, 540, 628, 805; III 97–98, 827, 862
  acedia: II 330; III 49
  animal: II 196–97, 196a, 410–11, 634, 711, 727; III 733
  eye: I 267, 274; II 120, 159, 168, 170–71, 180–81, 184–85, 189–90, 228, 289, 306, 311, 354, 408, 474, 609, 634; III 220, 232, 238, 262, 282, 339, 345–46, 352, 359, 363, 372, 598
  leprosy: II 540, 675; III 85
  self–will: II 360
  stomach: II 161; III 334
Disgrace: I 142–43, 148, 191, 195, 246, 370; II 82, 179, 270, 456, 680, 734, 789–90; III 199, 264, 354, 401, 414, 842
Disgusting: I 48, 79, 87, 377, 438; II 327; III 600
Disobedience: I 576; II 269, 593, 619, 700; III 135, 393, 400, 402, 423–25, 511, 622, 768, 876
Disorder: I 592; II 724, 731, 789; III 178
Dispensation: II 170; III 158, 353, 417, 420, 801, 865
Disposition: I 252, 306; II 531; III 343, 787

Dispute: I 72, 74, 89, 95, 213, 525; II 41, 89, 343; III 46, 119, 133, 782–83, 789
Disrepute: I 388, 592; III 444
Dissipation: I 370, 546; III 858
Dissolution: I 412; III 326, 638
Distinction: I 489; II 318; III 149, 384, 739, 741, 752, 882
Distraction: I 218, 508; II 127, 311, 554, 607, 609, 622, 681, 699; III 151, 227, 394, 780
Distribution: II 300, 557, 622
Disturbance: I 104, 136, 223, 261; II 349, 724; III 598
Divinity. See also Father, Godhead, Son, Spirit, Trinity: I 161, 475; II 744, 813; III 95, 153, 190, 192, 532, 541, 563, 652
Division: II 54; III 116, 135, 419, 488, 725, 787
Dizziness: III 459, 584
Doctor: I 188, 267, 276, 303–06, 339, 412, 431–32, 460, 511, 513; II 53, 102, 121, 127, 166, 171, 189–93, 203–04, 276, 306–08, 355, 357, 388, 407, 409, 413, 416–17, 421, 431–33, 440–41, 446–47, 458, 465–67, 513, 555, 565, 583–84, 669, 675, 695, 704, 737; III 44, 74, 85, 87, 91, 97, 101, 218, 227–28, 242, 282, 303, 356, 359, 363–64, 370–71, 420, 478, 495, 598, 610, 652, 669, 862
   Jesus: I 431–32; III 87, 645
   law: III 407, 575
   Mary: III 549, 645
   theology: II 140, 315, 352, 358, 613; III 54, 63, 92, 132, 149, 164–65, 198, 296, 385, 680, 698–99, 763, 828–30
Doctrine: I 331, 446, 461, 469, 471, 530, 600; II 120, 513, 517, 728; III 87–88, 92, 96, 220, 372, 769, 842
Dog: I 146, 580, 585; II 143, 340, 732; III 226, 287, 483–84, 602–03, 740
Dominion: I 573; II 586, 688, 800; III 457, 747, 766, 786–87, 876
Donation: I 419; II 140, 305, 776; III 67, 748, 781
Donkey: I 267, 474; II 99, 137, 143, 174, 195, 266–67, 278, 290, 312, 332, 339, 347, 409, 584, 617, 635, 679, 681, 705, 805, 807; III 266, 284, 295, 477, 597
Doubt: I 154, 537; II 189–90, 250, 377, 404, 429, 463, 465, 617, 622–23, 633, 647, 651–52, 654–55, 680, 710, 724, 760; III 54, 64, 88, 90, 93, 149, 152, 190, 197, 465, 492, 502, 534, 555, 574, 640, 645, 778, 784, 790, 882
   conscience: I 559
   Elias: III 537
   Francis: III 468, 592
   Gospel mandate: I 571; III 742, 782
   interpretation of vision: II 307
   mandate: I 571; III 742, 782
   Mary's virginity: III 564

ownership: III 748, 779
poverty: III 88
relationship: I 477
removal: I 509, 601; II 514, 636, 646, 797; III 54, 149, 152, 190
Rule: I 471; II 513, 775; III 164, 741, 757, 760, 763, 769–72
stigmata: II 108, 514, 646; III 187–89
Testament: III 761
truthfulness: I 180
virginity: III 564
Dove: I 74, 234, 321, 396, 458, 533, 570, 583; II 105, 260, 574, 613, 692, 696, 728, 798; III 36, 44, 451, 474, 485, 511, 513, 515, 581, 604, 623, 826
Dowry: II 294
Dragon: I 355, 462; II 544–45, 692–93; III 87, 421, 482, 498, 524, 642
Drawer: II 473, 771
Dread: I 241, 285, 302, 455, 477, 483, 502–03, 515; II 75, 415, 454, 482, 489, 644, 677; III 103, 176, 335, 770, 876
Dream. See also Sight, Vision: I 464; II 127, 245, 410, 463, 468, 815; III 60, 71, 130, 227, 356, 889
   brother: II 327
   communication: I 389; III 723, 863
   cross: II 39, 87, 319, 795
   delusion: I 325; III 56
   dragon: II 544–45, 692–93
   foreboding: I 438
   Francis: I 225, 300, 304; II 447–48, 454, 460, 468, 480, 651, 670, 672, 782; III 58, 486, 840
   home: II 421
   lady: II 440, 669
   Lord: II 70
   palace: II 245
   paradise: II 725
   Pope: II 651; III 88, 390
   Roman Basilica: II 548, 690, 785; III 390
   Rule: II 381
   weapon: II 782
   woman: II 440, 669
Drink: I 47, 73, 101, 219, 244, 307, 392, 400, 405, 439, 473, 531, 539, 546, 583, 597; II 52, 76, 127, 150, 278–79, 356, 392, 409, 414, 438, 453, 563, 584–85, 597, 667, 678, 694, 704–05, 707, 815; III 40, 101, 135, 162, 165, 227, 356, 463, 470, 477, 596–97, 610, 876
   Christ's blood 47, 78, 129;: II 454; III 665
   delight: II 392
   demon: I 302
   fast: II 76, 150, 597; III 73, 234, 279, 346, 448, 579
   Gospel: I 582
   judgment: I 47, 129
   medicine: II 383

Spirit: III 388, 557, 647
vinegar: I 146
water: I 227, 239, 301, 321, 392; II 278,
    409–10, 561, 628, 678, 694; III 593,
    852, 861, 876
wine: I 227, 392, 552, 589; II 567, 704,
    807; III 117, 712, 852
wisdom: I 408; III 388
Drone: I 202, 297
Dropsy: I 303, 324, 518; II 194, 198, 203, 432;
    III 73, 218, 272, 283, 370
Drunkenness: I 71, 228, 439; II 40, 88, 246,
    252, 524, 538, 598, 687, 783; III 160, 649,
    656, 876, 878
Dung. See also Manure: I 231, 529, 543–44,
    549, 588; II 40, 48, 88, 94, 130, 137, 143,
    270, 290–91, 347; III 54, 161, 230, 266,
    295, 362, 491, 503, 582, 616
Dust: I 70, 94, 96, 190, 193, 243, 261, 278,
    373, 409, 508, 543; II 78, 89, 329, 376, 522,
    537, 574, 622, 630, 687–88, 715, 732, 738,
    788, 792, 801; III 701
    death: I 146
    flesh: II 639
    worldly things: II 283, 526
Duty: I 130, 217, 293, 519, 607; II 145, 200,
    352, 365, 367, 374, 433, 521, 532, 576,
    587, 592, 598, 735, 794; III 56, 59, 216,
    274, 325, 407, 586, 647, 661–62, 746,
    749–50, 783, 858
Dwelling. See also Abode, House: I 41, 48,
    80, 88, 126, 163, 243, 329, 342, 386, 442,
    535, 561, 588, 597; II 39, 74, 100, 210, 212,
    327, 420, 489, 691, 703; III 89, 95, 579,
    752
    brother: I 386, 597; II 54, 135, 327,
        691; III 45, 101, 172, 259–60, 265,
        313, 316, 413, 499, 709–10, 749, 812
    Christ: I 535; II 58; III 330, 383–84,
        396, 421
    city: I 600; II 54
    God: I 158, 275, 529; III 330, 842
    heaven: I 271, 342, 587; II 310, 615,
        734; III 125, 333
    heavenly spirit: I 258
    Jacob: I 544
    leper: II 312, 606; III 847
    mountain: I 532
    Nazareth: III 397
    peace: I 443; II 489
    poverty: I 532
    scripture: II 737
    spirit: I 217, 258; III 413
    town: I 600; II 54
    wood: II 135, 285; III 45, 259

E

Eagle: II 745; III 436, 470, 527, 636
    Bonaventure: III 698
    Church: I 593

poverty: I 532
theology: II 141, 315, 613; III 296
Ear
    birds: I 343, 491
    corn: I 336
    Francis: I 459; II 190, 355, 409, 704; III
        97, 364, 861
    general minister: II 366
    heart: I 116
    Lord: I 142,152
    Pietro Mancanella: II 432; III 74
    reader: III 198
Earth
    Adam: I 539
    captivity: I 447; II 440
    Christ: III 331, 398, 436
    creation: III 678, 884
    creature: I 49, 547, 586; II 130, 813; III
        230, 362, 583
    divinity: III 685
    end: I 71, 381; II 260, 811; III 329, 382,
        438, 468, 523, 592, 651, 826, 843,
        854
    glory: I 538; II 478, 818
    heaven: I 56, 109, 434, 534, 537, 553;
        II 40, 90, 108, 477, 513; III 125, 161,
        269, 273, 333, 366, 385, 391, 451,
        457, 582, 588, 733, 811
    humility: II 148, 519, 521–22, 734
    medicine: I 267
    mother: III 368
    nakedness: I 552
    people: II 720; III 63, 115, 136
    prince: II 301, 477
    ruler: I 81; II 772
    salt: I 585
    shame: I 364
    Sister Earth: III 368
    thing: I 193, 436, 438, 529, 537, 539; II
        364; III 46, 382, 470, 478, 487, 580,
        598, 684, 691, 724
Earthquake
    foretell: II 814
East: I 289; III 470, 569, 594
Easter
    fast before: I 66
    Greccio: II 287, 582
    Office: I 148
Edict
    Sultan: II 602
Egg: II 222; III 250, 311, 604, 787, 795
Election
    Celestine: III 816
    first minister: II 104–05
    Francis: III 174
    general minister: I 104, 574; II 778; III
        760, 782, 788
    Gregory IX: II 814
    Honorius III: I 579
    provincial minister: III 782–83
    vocation: I 368; II 735–36, 755; III 388,
        422

Elevation
  host: II 449, 671; III 536
  spiritual: II 544, 699; III 513, 538, 619, 633, 649, 688
Eloquence
  Bonaventure of Iseo: III 829
  brother: II 53, 102; III 31, 118, 327, 394, 405, 717
  door: I 225
  Francis: I 231, 245, 389, 395, 497; II 556, 582, 626, 693; III 855, 865
  God: II 539
  Hugolino: I 246
  Masseo: III 125, 333
  rhetoric: II 520, 755
  Rule: III 834
Emotion
  flesh: III 838
  Francis: I 430; III 131, 174, 407
  human: I 514–15; III 178
  John: III 534
  Pope: I 599
Emperor: II 129, 185, 317, 375, 556, 720; III 56, 92, 230, 347, 363, 692, 802, 808, 829, 888
  Charles: II 209; III 257, 70
  Constantine: I II 720
  Frederick: III 693
  Greek: III 829
  Jean: III 55
  Lord John: III 56, 63
  Oliver: II 209; III 257, 707
  Otto: I 221, 386; III 41
  Roland: II 209; III 257, 707
  Roman: III 56
Empire
  Christ: I 307
  earth: I 221; III 41, 56
  France: I 579
  Roman: III 802
  spiritual: III 135
  whole: II 285; III 347
Emptying
  self: II 586, 589, 622
Emulation: II 712
Enclosure. See also Cloister: I 61–62, 552; III 45, 64, 448, 696, 760
Encouragement
  Francis: I 252, 470; II 690; III 323, 466, 496, 716, 835
  Gospel: II 509
  Rule: II 146, 380
  spouse: III 95
Endurance
  Francis: I 514
  saint: III 392
  wine press: I 566
Enemy
  another: I 132, 272, 437; II 407, 653, 662, 794
  body: II 168, 328, 796; III 304, 847
  city: III 483, 602
  cross: III 862

devil: I 263, 272, 358, 461, 545, 554, 568, 573; II 75, 289, 295, 323, 325, 329, 386, 404, 429, 545, 562, 564, 607, 640, 642, 662, 694, 714, 778, 791, 795; III 504–06, 619, 740
  flesh: I 72, 91, 94, 96; II 146, 334, 359
  Francis: I 445; III 425
  idleness: I 69, 102–03; II 46, 93
  instigation: I 98
  lash: II 794
  Order: III 388
  public: III 164
  Saracen: I 581; II 266
  soul: III 288, 757
  subject: II 518; III 195, 342, 489, 519, 618, 876–77
Energy
  adolescent: I 18
  expend: II 207; III 152, 168, 319
  spiritual: II 246
  weakness: I 514; III 176, 705, 815
Enjoyment
  empty: II 329
  Francis: III 801
  God: I 158; II 746
  heaven: I 467
  longevity: I 493
Enmity
  Assisi and Perugia: II 178; III 353
  men: II 406
  world: III 818
Enslavement
  pleasure: I 567
  sin: I 567; II 511, 732, 740; III 80
Enthusiasm
  brother: II 448, 671; III 235
  Francis: I 212; II 73, 108; III 299
  people: I 403
  prudent: I 560
Entry
  city: I 512
  death: III 97
  Francis: II 437, 667
  house: I 461
  Kingdom of God: III 381
  Order: I 583; III 54, 87, 890
  point: I 486
  ship: I 394
  vice: I 576
Envy
  absence: I 220
  avoidance: I 105, 132, 346, 512
  comrade: I 438
  conquering: I 440
  devil: III 342, 416
  effect: I 438
  enemy: III 80
  origin: I 79, 541, 547 II 230, 556, 794
  poverty: III 849
  Roman: I 292
  sin: III 423
Epilepsy: II 783

Epiphany
  fast after: I 66, 101
  Office: I 148, 150, 156–57
  retreat: II 597
Error
  absence: II 511, 516, 819
  correction: II 240; III 424
  darkness: II 811; III 321, 381, 410, 425
  friend: I 445
  heresy: II 667; III 135, 198, 816
  law: III 802
  result: I 473, 480
  trap: III 422
  worst: I 447
Erudition: II 629
Escape: I 114, 140, 145, 230, 323, 376, 389, 436, 445, 453, 495, 535; II 121, 178, 196, 274, 291, 385, 437–38, 463, 615–16, 665, 667, 702–03, 705, 789, 804; III 95, 135, 177, 221, 368, 371, 381, 482, 490, 509, 598, 605, 856, 862
Espousal
  heaven: I 356
  Lord: I 553
  Poverty: II 284, 577, 696
Eternity
  cellar: I 566
  exchange: I 289
  Gehenna: III 484
  God: III 541, 769
  hidden: III 158
  home: II 645
  life: II 121, 324; III 221
  merit: III 747
  ordination: III 381
  poverty: I 536, 550; II 47
  riches: I 332; III 452, 459
  storehouse: I 568
  thing: I 433; II 301; III 470, 814
Eucharist. See Blood of Christ, Body of Christ, Mass
Evangelist: I 83; III 475, 595
  Francis: I 259; II 318
  John: I 83; II 527; III 149–50, 555, 567, 639, 686, 692
  Luke: I 535
  Mark: III 177, 697
  Matthew: I 369; III 690
Exaltation: III 290, 372
  boast: II 521; III 48
  Cross: II 108, 632, 709, 743; III 457
  promise: II 752; III 396
Examination: I 221, 574, 603; II 778; III 32, 41, 770
Example
  Apostle: I 250, 558
  bad: I 67, 92, 95, 130; II 322, 340, 347; III 103, 153, 165, 240, 248–49, 264, 287, 327, 389, 408, 442, 472, 717–18
  brother: I 213, 218, 357, 544, 583; II 92, 96, 347, 772; III 46, 239, 263–64,

289, 316, 325, 336, 390, 393, 465, 572, 636, 857
  Christ: I 46, 329; II 287, 522; III 51, 159, 177, 269, 381–83, 448, 462, 495, 502, 553, 579, 587, 630, 740, 758
  Clare: I 197
  creature: III 230, 362
  Dominic: II 772
  evangelical: III 577
  faith: II 728
  Father: III 424
  Francis: I 184, 221, 228, 260, 266, 273, 282, 321, 380, 388, 406, 446, 568, 600; II 123, 246, 253, 287, 293, 295, 298, 322–23, 326, 358, 525, 527, 543, 662, 689, 693, 697, 715, 735, 748; III 32, 50, 82, 126, 171, 175, 182, 215–16, 234, 246–48, 262, 267–68, 273–74, 279, 297, 306–08, 313, 316–17, 321, 335, 396, 406, 411, 413–14, 447, 464, 711–12, 718–19, 813, 821, 842, 849
  God: III 238
  good: II 294, 315; III 46, 57, 147, 154, 169–72, 174, 217, 225, 231, 238, 240, 264, 317, 413, 566, 579, 621, 641, 644, 710, 759, 850
  humility: I 209, 293, 597; II 123, 517; III 40, 155, 271, 328
  Innocent III: I 418
  Martin: III 840
  obedience: III 462, 587
  other: I 49, 125; II 240, 300, 315, 525, 527; III 63, 326
  pilgrim: II 287
  poverty: II 123, 285, 293; III 45, 237, 261, 263, 271, 328
  punishment: II 441
  religion: III 122, 237, 260–61, 300, 308, 399, 408
  statue: III 486, 723
  temptation: II 740
  virtue: III 800
  women: II 322–23
  word: III 224, 252, 266, 291, 294, 317, 319, 321, 343, 398, 694, 712, 740, 744, 769, 780, 818, 820
  work: I 125, 132, 266, 307, 428; II 42, 92, 96, 296, 341–42, 526, 587, 772; III 219, 223, 240, 261, 361, 385
Excellence
  creation: I 131
  Divine Majesty: III 568
  Francis's life: I 243; III 152, 730
  heavenly vision: II 635
  kingdom: I 438
  perfection: III 404
  virtue: II 634
Exception: I 575; II 259, 336; III 78, 186, 343, 746, 760, 795, 802–03, 859
Excess: I 137, 182, 392, 406, 568; II 53, 326, 448, 670; III 82, 202, 781

austerity: II 76, 82, 149–51, 182, 565, 599
bitterness: I 540
concern: II 147, 372
contemplation: II 630; III 843
desire: I 94; III 749
example: II 599
familiarity: II 323
fervour,: I 549, 688
joy: II 537
love: II 709; III 541
marvel: II 406
meekness: II 145, 366
self–love: II 739
vice: I 431, 457, 477; II 796; III 271
Exchange: I 202, 279, 289, 357, 533, 573, 583, 603; II 73, 151, 156, 185, 285, 294, 330, 363, 474, 567, 686, 777, 792; III 118, 164, 174, 269, 347, 394, 405, 601, 753, 755, 766, 785–86, 849, 881
Excommunication: I 564; III 554, 631, 762–63
Excuse
noun: I 550, 587; II 91, 138, 190, 207, 213, 229, 293, 295, 575, 619, 637, 700; III 118, 168, 170, 172, 216, 233, 244, 249, 257, 267, 274, 316–17, 328–29, 390, 396, 414, 416, 620
verb: I 135, 223, 389, 429, 538, 561; II 106, 201, 206, 210–12, 220, 717; III 40, 167, 170–71, 248, 256, 316–17, 328, 344, 355, 413–14
Exercise
noun: I 93, 319, 546; II 240, 350–51, 372, 447, 561, 612, 622, 700; III 178, 181, 215–16, 321, 577, 757, 852
verb: I 68, 93, 386, 564, 575; II 163, 199–200, 328, 352, 367, 465; III 241, 309, 847
Exhortation: I 78, 90, 127, 390, 419, 579, 585, 599; II 706; III 386, 447, 470, 510, 521, 743–44, 772, 820
Exile
body: II 699
earthly: I 344, 375, 446, 452, 456, 515, 529, 539; II 136, 352; III 85, 159
grace: I 335
Lady Jacoba: II 417
pilgrimage: II 353, 522; III 259, 396
song: II 136, 287
Exodus
Book: II 723, 742; III 188–89
leader: II 731
Exorcist: I 84
Expense
basilica: I 419
birds: II 279
friend: II 71, 246
monastery: I 603
payment: II 190; III 45, 68, 104, 164, 282, 337, 445, 576

poor: II 193, 291, 306, 554
Experience: I 187, 275, 292, 390; II 155, 190, 248–49, 265, 310, 463, 512, 514, 606, 669, 694, 700; III 181, 418, 695, 742, 761, 780, 786, 814
action: I 191, 219, 225–26, 265, 285, 290, 389, 405, 411; II 45, 53, 57, 102, 128, 246, 312, 317, 377, 409, 436, 445, 447, 449, 465, 512, 528, 601, 631, 651, 691, 699, 706, 709, 717, 756, 760–62, 783, 795; III 103, 364, 371, 398, 422, 528, 573, 620, 797
Christ: II 180
death: II 422
kindness: I 493
lack: III 196
learn from: I 534; II 475, 575; III 115, 685
past: I 472
perfection: I 385
personal: I 234, 397, 492; II 561, 648, 678, 795; III 329, 343, 364, 506
time: I 537
Expression: I 216, 241, 256, 305; II 124, 310, 341, 346, 373, 435, 453–55, 462, 515, 528, 572, 674; III 132, 157, 160, 203, 224, 291, 343, 397, 417, 536, 551, 574–75, 628, 651, 654, 691, 743, 771
Extinction
charity: I 546, 600
fire: II 191; III 365–66
hatred: III 628
heresy: III 689
joy: III 342
lamp: II 805
Spirit: I 102, 107; II 137, 293; III 45, 267
Exultation
celebration: I 406
heavenly: I 554; III 93
state: I 477
time: I 255
Eyes: I 97, 219, 240, 253, 271, 277, 280, 293–95, 301, 323–24, 359, 403, 411, 413, 450, 462, 472, 477–79, 485, 494, 496, 512–13, 538, 549, 583–84, 588; II 126, 139, 141–42, 146, 188, 196, 201, 250, 296, 304, 308, 310–12, 322–23, 331, 335, 338, 340, 355, 363, 379–80, 403–05, 410, 412, 419–20, 463, 513–14, 521, 524, 536, 563, 570, 588, 591–92, 609, 615, 631, 636, 646, 648, 651, 671, 680, 686, 702–03, 710, 715, 721, 736, 780, 789, 796, 800; III 41, 47, 92, 117–18, 136, 159, 176, 178, 188, 199, 217, 226, 275, 280, 286–87, 292, 323, 394, 401, 406, 412, 437, 467, 490, 501, 503, 510, 515, 534, 539, 560, 567, 591, 593, 616, 623, 635, 686, 688, 716, 728, 792, 804, 864, 867, 870, 885, 887–88
blindness: I 301, 328, 353; II 450, 452, 627; III 54, 71, 472, 598, 805

blood: II 76, 430, 662
chaste: II 141–42, 323; III 334
Christ: I 283; II 597
covenant: II 694
disease: I 267, 412, 510–11; II 159, 168, 170–71, 185, 190, 192, 197, 228, 311, 432, 443, 447, 452, 461, 562, 609, 670, 798; III 72, 74, 232, 238, 262, 282, 339, 346, 352, 359, 478, 861
faith: I 281; III 513, 541
God: II 201, 332, 524, 574, 721, 813; III 91, 216, 274, 323, 458, 560, 583
heal: II 189, 276, 307, 330, 386, 416, 627; III 36, 363
healthy: I 271
hidden: I 411, 532; II 473; III 509
learned: III 712
Leo: III 131, 455
light: I 154, 476, 541; II 186, 431, 489; III 89, 157, 335, 367, 392, 396
majesty: I 187; II 147, 381
mind: I 435, 499; II 686, 773; III 542, 549
mocker: I 187; II 72
open: I 302; II 449, 552, 657, 671; III 393, 405
paternal: III 335
physical: I 129, 225, 255, 276, 390, 596; II 317, 402, 474, 557, 695; III 90, 173, 486, 510, 686
pierce: II 141, 322; III 334
poverty: I 466
pupil: I 505
remove: II 734; III 540, 635, 804–05
Rule: III 183–84, 188, 398
saintly: II 515
shameless: II 141, 322; III 334
sign: I 240; II 403
soul: II 565
spiritual: I 129; III 90, 136
wash: II 410, 678, 695
watchful: II 336
weakness: I 414; II 392, 515, 798; III 478, 863
world: II 201; III 164, 216, 781
Eyesight
loss: I 413; II 184; III 339
recovery: II 429, 448, 661, 672
weak: II 269, III 97, 863

F

Fable: II 781
Face: I 143, 145, 188, 265, 302, 333, 353, 390; II 35, 175, 179, 295, 307, 423, 425, 431, 607, 635, 637, 695, 701, 789; III 220, 372, 548, 560, 632
angelic: III 157, 443, 870
Bernard: III 445, 503, 578, 617
Christ: I 70, 91, 94, 536, 548, 582–83; II 303; III 190, 531, 651, 728
church: II 790

earth: I 71; II 519; III 115
flint: I 70, 91, 94
Francis: I 253, 280, 484, 600; II 74, 132, 244, 296, 309, 323, 346, 348, 361, 386, 418, 444, 537, 553, 556, 570, 572, 642, 651, 670, 678, 693, 695, 715, 808; III 124, 131, 175, 221, 254, 305, 371, 437, 442, 455, 463, 472, 512, 573, 583, 588, 713, 728, 796, 870
God: I 112, 147, 153–54, 230; II 319, 575, 647; III 128, 131, 221, 371, 689
James: III 536, 653
John: III 530, 650–51
joyful: II 296, 439, 572, 688; III 343
Lady Poverty: I 537
Masseo: III 514–15, 584, 623
nobility: III 551
Pope: III 418
sad: I 240, 443; II 50, 331, 461; III 343
statue: III 486, 723
Sylvester: III 689
Tau: II 556, 693
twisted: I 242, 403, 496, 546
women: II 322, 563, 790; III 153, 491, 822
Faction: I 439; II 808; III 412, 488, 725, 808
Faith: I 473, 480, 493; II 166, 223, 271, 377, 468, 521, 624, 735–36; III 129, 151, 160, 387, 392, 397–98, 401, 422–25, 449, 490, 513, 541, 605, 689, 739, 842, 856
Abraham: III 422
arms: II 614; III 501
article: I 488
brother: I 563–64; II 294, 348
Catholic: I 77, 84, 100, 106, 238, 291, 322, 327, 388, 402; II 56, 96, 104, 248, 551, 643; III 192, 385, 490, 521, 633, 741, 746, 790, 855–56
Christ: I 395; II 160, 209, 603, 610, 726, 757, 814; III 37, 257, 382, 384, 400, 580, 605–07, 632–33, 707
Christian: I 212, 229, 395; II 600, 603, 755, 757, 759, 814
church: I 124
clergy: I 125, 136; II 77, 160
conversion: I 166, 563
defender: I 291
Elias: III 553, 630–31
eye: I 281, 579
foundation: I 578
Francis: I 238, 307, 567; II 96, 122, 188, 226, 324, 386, 421, 438, 440–41, 454, 540, 584, 638, 642, 656–57, 660, 663, 665, 667–68, 671, 675, 712, 780, 787, 814; III 43, 231, 346, 468, 477, 482, 585, 597
gospel: III 398
humility: III 727
inheritance: I 549
Lady Jacoba: II 122; III 222, 361
Lady Poverty: II 642

light: I 529; III 421, 632
little: II 171, 190; III 359, 364
minister: III 89, 351, 564, 839
Most High: I 40, 109–10; III 263, 422,
 471, 799
obedience: III 89, 388
one: I 223, 542; II 358; III 41
Order: III 318
orthodox: III 789
Paul: II 757
podesta: III 350
poverty: III 125, 165, 333
Rufino: III 618, 688
salvation: I 448, 548; II 406
shield: I 191, 355, 441, 462
stigmata: II 108, 514, 646, 648
strength: I 298, 322, 326, 343; II 348,
 668, 671, 712; III 521, 633
Sultan: II 603, 757; III 79, 383, 398,
 490–92, 605, 798
Sylvester: II 215; III 246
Trinity: II 601
truth: I 188; III 50, 56, 386, 520, 857
war: II 614
word: III 95
Falsehood: II 364; III 96, 136, 320–21, 404,
 422, 789
Fame
 anonymous: I 415; II 388
 brother: I 278; II 155; III 120, 298
 church: III 788
 Francis: I 195, 209, 214–17, 327, 382,
  428, 442, 600; II 109, 241–42, 337,
  339, 440, 475, 539, 668, 778; III 92,
  694, 843, 845, 869
 Giacomo: II 445
 Lady Jacoba: II 417
 Lady Poverty: II 301
 nobleman: II 70
 Poor Ladies: II 83
 Portiuncula: III 331
 praise: II 570
 well–educated: I 215
Familiarity
 anyone: II 473
 excessive: II 323; III 625
 forgotten: I 447
 Francis: I 569
 great: I 544; III 387
 reception: I 105; III 420, 485
 women: II 321–22
Family: I 241, 590; II 58, 148, 164, 174, 405,
 420, 652, 659, 663, 667, 680; III 121, 237,
 300, 322, 404, 510, 528, 621, 629, 858–59
 brother: II 148, 156, 219, 351, 364–65;
  III 266, 522, 553, 637–38, 643, 709,
  717, 885, 891
 Brother Fly: II 579
 business: I 192, 374
 Lady Jacoba: II 147
 Lord: I 270; II 42, 90, 131, 142, 144,
  219; III 123, 248, 287, 325, 327, 701

member: I 103
 poor: II 73, 139; III 281, 302
 possessions: I 538
 Soffiano: III 537, 644
Famine. See also Shortage
 death: I 483
 foretell: II 282–83, 793; III 498, 512,
  612
Farmer
 call: I 84
 cloak: II 538
 example: II 521
 report: II 807
Fast: I 47, 65, 483, 587; II 334, 432, 437, 571,
 667; III 60, 193, 611, 772, 817, 877
 day: II 359; III 527
 forty–day: III 262, 448, 454–55, 457,
  579
 Lenten: III 448, 527, 578
 penitent: I 47
 Rule: I 65, 101; III 775
 season: I 101; II 374, 598–99, 593, 631,
  709
Fasting: I 478, 515; II 449; III 525
 Bonaventure: III 731
 brother: I 219; II 153, 156, 259, 565; III
  40, 93, 121, 237, 299, 354
 Christ: III 381, 397
 Francis: I 191, 374, 567; II 57, 76–78,
  151, 323, 540, 599, 688, 740, 807; III
  174, 197, 199, 269, 415, 851
 Gunther of Brabant: III 60
 Masseo: III 623
 penitent: II 177
 Peter of Monticello: III 636
 Rufino: III 618
 Rule: I 65, 101; II 147, 381; III 197,
  323, 775
 season: I 101; II 597–98
 virtue: II 364, 524
Father. See also Divinity, Godhead, Son,
 Spirit, Trinity: I 64, 80, 88, 246, 277, 298,
 332, 413, 448, 456, 476, 480; II 54, 93,
 144, 276, 342–43, 360, 365, 399, 414, 417,
 458, 510, 574, 750; III 60, 134, 178, 218,
 370, 531, 649, 695, 857
 Francis: I 180, 202–03, 205, 209,
  213–14, 216, 220–226, 229, 234–36,
  238, 241–42, 247–50, 254, 257–58,
  260–61, 267, 270–72, 274, 276–80,
  283–85, 287–88, 295, 298–300, 302,
  305, 307–08, 319, 324, 329–30, 336,
  338–39, 342, 344, 347, 355, 357,
  380–81, 388–90, 400, 403, 405,
  407–08, 412, 414–18, 464, 501, 514,
  519, 589, 592, 602; II 34, 53, 55, 67,
  79, 95, 99, 102, 104, 110, 120–23,
  126, 128, 134, 138–39, 140–42, 144,
  147, 150, 152–53, 160, 162, 166–72,
  175, 177–78, 180, 190, 199, 201, 204,
  209–10, 213–15, 239–41, 254,
  258–60, 263–65, 270–72, 274–77,

289, 300–01, 304–07, 310, 315–17,
319–25, 328, 330, 332, 335–36, 340,
345–46, 351, 354–55, 357–58, 360,
364, 366–68, 371–72, 374, 376,
378–83, 385, 387–93, 399, 403, 405,
408–09, 412–16, 418, 420, 429–30,
432, 434, 442–43, 445–49, 451,
453–54, 456, 458–461–463, 467–68,
475–79, 489–91, 528, 543, 546,
551–52, 554–57, 562, 568, 573, 575,
589, 592–93, 610, 613, 617–19,
627–28, 644, 646–48, 650, 652–54,
656–58, 664–65, 669–71, 674–75,
677, 679, 681, 690, 692–93, 700–01,
711–12, 716–17, 722, 750, 772–73,
792–93, 795–96, 802–04, 813; III 32,
35, 38, 41, 44, 66–67, 70, 78, 89, 92,
98, 120, 126–29, 131–33, 136, 150,
152, 157, 165–66, 170, 179, 182–86,
189–91, 193, 199, 203, 217, 221–23,
226, 228, 234–35, 237–40, 243,
245–46, 251, 255, 257, 259, 262–63,
267, 279–81, 287, 292–96, 303, 305,
308, 313, 316, 319, 323, 325, 329,
331–33, 335–37, 339, 342–44, 353,
355, 357–61, 369–71, 384, 393, 400,
406, 411, 413, 417, 435, 440–41,
444–47, 449–53, 455–56, 459–63,
465–67, 469–72, 475, 478–79, 482,
485, 489–92, 494–95, 502, 509,
512–14, 518, 520, 522–23, 525, 529,
555, 560, 571–72, 576–77, 580–82,
584, 586–87, 590–91, 593, 596–97,
599, 605, 609–11, 618–21, 624, 626,
628–30, 638–39, 641, 653–54, 670,
678–79, 682, 699, 702, 707–08, 710,
715, 720, 727, 731, 744, 748, 769,
774, 787, 792, 794, 797, 799, 801–05,
807, 809, 811–12, 814–15, 824, 831,
834, 837, 840, 843–44, 846, 850, 852,
856, 858, 861–64, 867, 869–71, 885
God: I 42–43, 45–47, 49–51, 63, 65–66,
74, 76, 78, 80–82, 86, 88–91, 95,
109–10, 116, 119, 120, 125, 127–29,
140–48, 150, 156, 158, 160–61, 163,
182, 187, 222, 224, 257, 288, 295,
262, 278, 280, 282–84, 287, 339, 347,
355, 368, 388, 449–50, 475, 516, 520,
531, 534–35, 539, 554, 564; II 38, 42,
52, 75, 80, 102, 120, 122–23, 160,
185, 199, 204–05, 213, 294, 309, 330,
350, 354, 368–69, 393, 477, 551, 513,
569, 583, 587–88, 607, 684, 699, 717,
728, 738, 744, 754, 762, 765, 813,
815; III 119, 130, 158–59, 166, 193,
195, 198, 202, 214, 220, 244–45, 272,
276, 329–30, 347, 372, 381–82, 384,
387, 421, 423, 426, 447–48, 451, 572,
577–78, 582, 649, 652, 655, 689, 702,
712, 717, 730, 739–40, 765, 769, 800,
844, 851

Gregory IX: I 270, 327, 419, 429, 470,
472, 480, 499; II 57–58, 103–04, 107,
262; III 834, 859, 865
other: I 213, 239–40, 246, 267, 271,
298–99, 305, 592; II 53, 55, 58, 66,
93, 102–03, 203, 267, 279, 343, 346,
357, 362, 418, 421–24, 427–28, 430,
444–46, 448–49, 451, 453, 459, 468,
480–81, 544, 656–58, 661, 663,
671–72, 736, 772, 804–05; III 34–35,
47, 53, 63–64, 71, 74, 88, 92, 102,
158, 165, 184–85, 241, 301, 392, 401,
404, 418, 422, 424, 564, 577, 681,
690, 695, 758, 800, 802–03
Pietro di Bernardone: I 190–93, 196,
319, 333–34, 370, 374–376, 430,
442–43, 445, 447–450, 452, 455; II
37, 68, 73, 77–82, 160, 164, 251, 284,
510, 531, 537–38, 577, 684, 687, 696,
782, 792, 809; III 33, 79–80, 84, 239,
618, 683–84, 833, 838, 842, 884
prayer: I 47, 65–66, 80, 88, 101, 125,
158, 222, 224, 388; II 80, 152, 213,
251, 329, 350, 491, 551, 738; III 130,
244–45, 329, 354, 441, 522–23, 525,
572, 638–39
Favor: I 465, 526; III 60, 94, 116, 534
Christ: III 94, 184, 384–85, 765, 797,
811, 844
church: II 260; III 324, 749
Clare: III 466, 590
divine: I 213, 225–26, 332, 342, 380,
390, 471; II 216, 282, 546, 584, 617,
678
Francis: I 226, 299, 305, 307, 477; II
78, 312, 390, 437, 448, 451, 459, 462,
464, 466, 477, 657; III 305, 407, 409,
483, 554, 590, 714, 860
general minister: II 144
God: III 94, 184, 384–85, 765, 797, 811,
844
gratitude: II 546
healing: I 299, 305; II 459
human: I 265, 393, 540; II 312, 336,
364, 390, 608, 747, 753, 810
Lady Jacoba: II 122; III 222, 860
Pope: I 325, 470, 479, 526, 558, 560,
598; II 648, 690; III 88, 198, 554
Riccerio: I 226, 390, 477; II 276–77
Rivo Torto: I 386
Tau: II 402
worldly: I 219; II 569
Fear: I 438, 496, 529, 534, 536, 547, 568; II
142, 239, 265, 290, 334, 367, 438–39, 441,
447, 455, 463, 467, 615, 633, 662, 666–67,
675, 736, 748, 791, 817; III 70, 88, 94, 319,
326, 334, 468, 484, 559, 600, 728, 878
animal: III 454
bad example: II 162
Bernard: I 203; III 445
bird: II 706

brother: II 105–06, 131, 207, 554; III 266, 336, 388, 780
carnal: I 165; II 142, 323, 334
charity: I 136; II 600
cross: II 378
death: II 818
Divine: I 76, 90
female: II 322
Francis: I 215, 228, 262, 276, 320, 376, 409–10, 415, 432, 568, 581; II 40, 75, 78, 87, 90, 137, 167, 207, 265, 322, 328, 359, 378, 475, 626, 643, 807; III 243, 337, 443, 446, 573, 576, 845, 852, 877
Francis's parents: I 190, 319, 373; II 78, 537, 686, 792; III 833
freedom: I 192, 219, 228, 320, 376, 409, 581; II 548, 554, 706; III 408, 446, 549, 799
future: I 372; III 484
God: I 78, 90, 116, 118, 137–38, 151, 161, 193, 205, 276, 283, 368, 415, 437; II 39–40, 43, 87–88, 90, 92, 265, 271, 274, 442, 475, 520, 643, 656, 670, 702, 735, 794, 807; III 39, 496, 559, 610, 569
Hugo: I 245
humility: III 566
hunchbacked woman: II 75
ingratitude: II 528
John: III 650, 656
joy: I 410
leper: II 688
motive: I 117, 305
obedience: II 292; III 136
Orland dei Caetani: III 803
other: I 75, 144, 549
Pietro: III 555, 640
playing lute: II 139, 193, 304
possessions: II 816
poverty: I 573
reverence: I 262, 409; III 200, 303, 336
Riccerio: I 390
rock: II 192
Rule: II 131; III 123–24, 127, 253–54, 713
servant: I 436
sin: III 770
stigmata: II 710
wolf: III 601, 603
woman: II 75, 139, 193, 330; III 280, 282
Feast, Liturgical. See All Saints, Assumption, Christmas, Francis, Nativity, etc.
Feather
    animal: III 137
    bed: III 58, 345, 606, 852
    bird: I 234, 396; II 130, 411, 624, 800; III 362, 498, 860
    pillow: II 227–28, 289–90, 562; III 232, 345
    wing: I 283; III 613

Feeling: I 84, 279, 300, 456, 473, 540; II 147, 223, 264, 350, 352, 355, 372, 392, 408, 421, 428, 455, 675, 678, 712, 749, 794, 810, 816–17; III 61, 322, 388, 391, 421, 461, 492, 513, 525, 589, 646
    Clare: III 591
    compassion: I 247; III 539, 849
    creature: I 234–35; 492; II 191
    Francis: I 189, 205, 235, 247, 339, 372, 435, 447; II 126, 169, 174, 191, 207, 249, 252, 600, 651; III 49, 85, 98, 168, 226, 249, 285, 351, 364, 439, 591, 851
    Francis's mother: II 79
    James of Massa: III 647
    John: III 530, 532, 542–43, 652, 657
    Poor Ladies: I 198
    prayer: I 224, 372; II 169, 249
    presence of God: III 543, 656
    Simon: III 540, 635
Feet: I 202, 245, 269, 293, 320, 379, 440, 456, 460, 496, 508, 583, 589–90; II 46, 84, 197–98, 265, 289, 303, 317, 335, 437–38, 455, 457, 461, 467, 489, 531, 542, 556, 563, 614, 622, 627–28, 652, 693, 702, 709, 733, 744, 761–62, 792–93; III 49, 70, 92, 131, 388, 440, 455–56, 459–60, 488, 501, 531, 584, 668, 726, 729, 801, 830, 874
    church: I 106
    clay: III 117, 393, 395, 486, 488, 723, 725
    condition: I 240–41, 253, 274, 302, 304, 505; II 105, 260, 431, 433; III 642
    cover: III 509, 866–67
    crucifix: III 527, 636
    embrace: II 143, 347; III 513, 533
    iron: III 117, 393, 395, 486, 488, 723, 725
    kiss: I 51, 86, 117, 248, 280, 401; II 339, 458, 540, 805; III 47, 85, 295, 455, 473, 513, 532–33, 651, 681
    position at: I 130, 240, 247, 319, 381, 402, 442, 500, 502, 534; II 124, 168, 174, 188, 197, 221, 267, 269, 320, 339, 359, 361, 424, 461–62, 589, 617, 619, 751, 795; III 43, 151, 154, 224, 249, 285, 291, 305, 350, 401, 439, 474, 483, 521, 525, 530–33, 570, 602, 629–30, 633, 650–51, 769, 801, 864
    position under: I 135, 254; II 94, 354, 723; III 440, 475, 682
    print: I 536; III 457, 473, 532, 584, 652, 866
    seraph: I 263, 410, 509; II 108, 402, 473, 632; III 835, 866
    trap: I 143
    wash: I 68, 130, 335, 411, 539, 633, 688, 711, 727, 750–51; III 78, 469, 473, 551, 592, 628, 733
    wound: I 146, 264, 280, 287–88, 323, 344–45, 359, 410, 416, 510, 517, 536,

589, 596, 600–01; II 108, 197,
335–36, 388, 402–03, 406, 473–74,
476, 490, 514, 633, 636, 640, 645–46,
652, 710, 714, 743, 758, 780, 784,
796, 798, 806, 816; III 131, 176, 272,
457, 509, 681, 826, 866, 870–71
Female. See also Lady, Woman: II 272, 279
  fear: II 322
Ferocity
  anger: I 438
  thief: I 453
  wolf: III 104
Fervor
  Bentivoglia of San Severino: III 636
  Bernard: III 438, 569
  brother: I 470, 537; II 265, 333; III 91,
    260, 389, 391, 394, 500, 552, 635
  chastity: I 585
  Christ: II 108; III 152
  Divine: II 78; III 463, 588
  encouragement: I 58
  Francis: I 191, 193, 234, 236, 245, 254,
    266–67, 375, 409, 459, 462, 471; II
    80, 83, 87, 119, 121, 123, 216, 264,
    375, 534, 538, 551, 553, 557, 562–63,
    598, 603, 609, 623, 642, 688, 690–91,
    698, 715; III 103, 173–74, 176, 196,
    220–21, 246, 276, 301, 310, 314, 323,
    336, 341, 343, 371, 398, 406, 417,
    458, 463, 465, 469, 476, 491, 507,
    567, 583, 589, 592–93, 596, 606, 620,
    629, 710, 815, 819, 853
  Giles: III 625
  John: III 241, 542–43, 651, 655–56
  John of Parma: III 150
  John the Simple: II 163
  Masseo: III 459, 463, 514, 583, 623
  Pellegrino: III 615
  poverty: III 159, 223
  Rinieri: III 615
  Simon: III 540
  unnamed woman: II 172; III 491
Fetus
  dead: II 440, 669
  imprisoned: II 494
Fever: I 239, 303, 431–32, 443, 478, 484, 518;
  II 225, 326, 570; III 56, 73, 131, 312, 499,
  547, 614, 642
  cure: I 239, 354; II 405, 411, 431, 447,
    453, 655, 664; III 50
  figurative: I 395
  quartan: II 181–82, 181a, 185a; III
    305–06
Fidelity
  brother: III 400
  Francis: II 733; III 396
  poverty: III 161
  truth: II 99
Field: I 147, 149, 156, 248, 251, 372, 420,
  432, 454, 473, 488, 492, 501, 518, 531,
  543, 547, 583, 600; II 156, 163, 177–79,
  205, 249, 270, 339, 368, 414, 416, 426,

478, 536, 594, 602, 660, 676, 686, 706,
760, 807, 810, 813, 817
battle: II 353; III 890
beauty: I 185, 251; III 38, 46, 67, 121,
  219, 237, 241, 276, 299, 301, 354,
  469, 474, 476, 593, 596, 780, 835,
  841, 860, 885
Church Militant: III 769
flower: II 67; III 366
freedom: I 274
Gospel: II 578, 636
heart: I 216; II 511
Lord: I 333, 372
ministry: III 756
painted: III 520
poverty: I 329, 331; II 88; III 164
preach: I 587
Reeds: III 476
untilled: I 216
Fig tree: II 217, 357, 414, 593, 798
Fight. See also Brawl
  banner: I 463
  Christ: I 479
  clergy: II 133, 341; III 47, 297, 788, 857
  Damietta: I 485
  demon or devil: III 481, 601
  father: I 448
  God: II 266
  habit: III 196
  martyr: II 209; III 707
  prayer: III 94
  serpent: I 462, 699
  sin: I 441, 462–63; II 326, 699
  war: I 144, 263, 465, 485; II 209; III
    257, 460, 584–85, 799
  world: I 506; III 890
Figure
  Christ: I 441–2; II 744, 746; III 84, 191
  crucified: II 633; III 193
  Francis: II 638
  justice: II 366
  New Testament: III 161
  seraph: III 835
  speech: I 188
  sun: III 90
  Tau: II 458, 681, 805
Finger
  cure: I 494; II 442, 676–77
  Francis: I 253, 505, 510; II 217, 335,
    711, 743; III 509, 729
  God: I 436; II 559, 634, 711; III 417,
    833
  John: III 544, 657
  leper: II 167; III 243, 303
  oblivion: II 780
  Ralph: III 54
  Rufino: III 510, 688
  sign: I 496; II 223, 272, 335, 351, 381,
    558, 636, 780, 793; III 351
Fire: I 191, 202, 250–51, 263, 300, 322, 431,
  435, 438, 443, 454, 473, 484, 486, 506,
  515, 566; II 176, 185, 191, 209, 215, 271,

311, 346, 354–55, 370, 373, 375, 408–09, 439, 455, 463, 522, 553, 563, 566, 568, 576, 596, 598, 600, 603, 609, 625, 631–32, 668, 674, 704, 707, 709–10, 740, 754, 757, 798–99; III 97–98, 153, 173, 190, 258, 271, 346, 364–67, 380, 392, 398, 455–57, 467, 484, 488, 490–91, 493, 497–98, 524, 551, 561, 591, 605–06, 612, 619, 628, 649, 652, 678, 689, 707, 725, 733, 795, 846, 861, 874–75
avarice: II 745; III 289
Brother Fire: I 114; II 186, 189, 190–02, 355, 566, 704, 798; III 364–68, 861
chariot: II 552; III 90
charity: III 147
compassion: I 401
Divine: I 187; II 75, 137, 293, 604, 714; III 267, 467
everlasting: I 78, 82, 91; II 815; III 524, 603
fervor: III 398
greed: II 148, 342
heart: III 90, 875
illumination: III 814
love: I 245, 247, 275, 358, 456, 463, 567; II 46, 489, 515, 526, 600, 635, 637, 686, 698, 714, 734; III 190, 330, 398, 530, 541, 591, 730, 846
lust: II 563
martyrdom: III 398
patience: II 740
penance: II 740
possessiveness: II 745
seduction: I 460
soul: III 174
spirit: I 120, 224, 245, 252; III 383, 398, 469
stone: I 288
tribulation: III 488, 725
vision: III 191
Firmament: I 400, 603; II 723, 811; III 679
Firstborn
Bernard: III 571, 577
Francis: II 543
God: I 156
Peter: II 646
Fish
brother: III 520, 632
exchange: II 155; III 120, 236, 298–99, 359
feeling toward: I 235–36, 397–98, 492; II 413, 417, 592; III 449, 520–21, 580, 632–33
figurative: I 206, 484, 489, 504; II 40, 88
food: II 171, 173–74, 247, 276, 298–99; III 50, 175, 360, 390, 520, 838, 846
obedience: II 583; III 520–21, 632–33
Fisherman
love: II 746
poor: I 535

Fitness: III 759
Flame
actual: II 191, 346, 653, 576, 799; III 49, 365, 887
figurative: I 187, 217, 339, 357, 460, 476, 479, 511, 519; II 75, 270, 318–19, 361, 533, 561–62, 569, 600, 631, 685, 694, 698, 709, 714, 727, 754; III 89, 97, 455–56, 463, 484, 496, 529, 588, 603, 649–51, 668, 846, 855, 887
Flattery: I 221, 321, 479; II 326, 344, 523, 571; III 41, 43, 99, 855
avoidance: I 215; II 99; III 90
Flesh: I 67, 103, 128, 133, 193–94, 253, 264, 266, 273, 279, 320, 340, 353, 359, 412, 416, 429, 443, 450, 460, 486, 488, 540, 567; II 102, 125, 160, 165, 172, 202, 218, 251, 273, 293, 297, 300, 357, 364, 377, 384, 389, 408, 449, 451, 453, 538, 560, 562, 564, 655, 694, 736, 750; III 47, 72–73, 97, 196, 203, 239, 267, 388, 393, 422, 459, 529, 533, 544, 550, 627, 649, 657, 666, 729, 850, 867
animal: I 228, 392, 478
blood: II 118, 137, 164, 293, 345, 349; III 119, 242, 267, 293, 302, 315, 723
brother: I 542; II 251; III 159
chastisement: II 524, 740–41, 807; III 43
Christ: I 46–47, 78, 129, 323; II 108, 744; III 188, 420, 733, 769
concupiscence: III 488, 725
corruption: II 723; III 153, 189, 853
death: I 281; II 654; III 423
desire: I 43, 50, 72, 91, 94, 96, 219, 221, 321, 386, 430, 433, 437, 541, 567, 597–98; II 53, 88, 102, 110, 137, 182, 197, 274, 530, 615, 684, 702, 720, 724, 815; III 40, 96, 202, 306, 411, 525, 730, 838, 862, 882
devil: II 481
disease: I 302; II 447–48, 467, 653, 670–71; III 608, 795
dust: II 639
enemy: I 43, 50; II 334
Francis: I 258, 266–67, 274, 276–77, 280, 321, 323, 336, 356, 412, 416, 428, 486, 505, 569; II 76, 82, 128, 355, 358, 409, 475, 566–67, 570, 600, 604, 641, 644, 694, 697, 704, 714, 716, 726, 784, 799, 816; III 97, 162, 181, 188, 190, 225, 228, 356, 398, 665, 667–68, 811, 835, 854, 861–62, 865
freedom: I 72, 91, 94, 274, 416, 569, 601; II 146, 359; III 288, 513, 869
friend: II 283
grass: II 817
harshness: III 730
heart: III 505, 619
holiness: II 332, 645; III 153

integrity: III 48
interpretation: I 129; II 245
living: I 67, 79, 87, 180, 250, 274, 276,
    278, 289; II 168, 182, 186, 362, 430,
    435, 444, 461–62, 467, 474, 647, 770;
    III 36, 58, 184, 188, 207, 275,
    305–06, 347, 410, 792, 871
love: II 165, 300, 579; III 267
lust: II 88, 110, 283, 561, 724, 734, 741
martyrdom: II 632, 709
mind: II 138, 293; II 267
mortal: I 389; III 191
modesty: I 440
nobility: I 254
obedience: III 853
pride: II 357, 414, 688; III 459
prison: I 258, 569; III 549, 645
prompt: I 199, 221; II 320; III 43
prudence: I 90; III 182, 203, 388, 393, 410
rant: I 469
rest: I 412
sin: I 344, 358; II 741
son of: III 394, 410, 425
spirit: I 75, 90, 266, 276, 466; II 173,
    245, 250, 280, 325, 429, 499, 618,
    640, 701, 724; III 97, 352, 388, 482,
    839, 842
stigmata: I 264, 410, 416, 510, 517–18;
    II 108, 249, 383, 388, 403, 473, 476,
    514, 633–34, 645–46, 710–11, 758,
    770, 780; III 35, 187–88, 420,
    668–69, 866, 870, 875
temptation: I 221, 386; II 53, 562–63,
    723, 732, 740–41, 795; III 43, 96,
    634, 853
tribulation: II 329
untainted: III 48
urge: I 321, 386; II 53, 325; III 539
virgin: III 47–48, 99, 730
wall: I 194, 273, 375; II 308, 605, 715
war: III 97
way: II 419, 656, 804; III 182
weakness: II 328, 565, 641; III 848
whore: II 788
wisdom: I 48, 75, 90; III 406
Flight
    birds: I 234; II 260, 411, 624; III 860
    deer: II 813
    demon: I 131, 355; II 427, 545, 574,
        694, 707, 716, 791; III 862
    description: II 73; III 613, 745, 866
    evil–doer: I 148
    figurative: I 403, 455; II 411, 545, 573,
        693; III 50, 99, 528, 881
    Philistine: I 566
    temptation: II 801; III 43
    vice: I 136–37, 479, 587; II 819
    wing: I 263, 410; II 108, 402, 473, 632, 709
Flock
    birds: I 397, 488; II 129–30, 592, 624,
        644, 706, 810, 813; III 362, 469–70,
        635, 835

bishop: II 160; III 239, 263
Christ: I 192, 376; II 219; III 327, 519
Francis: I 285, 321, 334, 336–37, 340,
    343, 356–57, 380–82, 396, 412, 568;
    II 42, 144, 204–05, 259–61, 359, 365,
    392, 533, 690; III 92, 166, 276, 325,
    391, 399–400, 489–90, 596, 605, 702,
    886
goats: I 248, 399, 501
Hebrew: II 620
listener: I 492; III 476
Pope: I 518, 569, 601
sheep: II 414, 591, 634, 742
shepherd: I 291
Flower: I 114, 216, 251, 260, 472–73,
    498–99, 504; II 320, 354, 553–54, 817–18;
    III 173, 366, 368, 491, 559
    Brother Flower: III 366
    chastity: III 81
    companion: II 67
    nobility: III 63
    perfection: I 216
    virtue: I 342
    way of life: I 564; III 511
    world: III 500
    youth: I 259; III 529
Fly: II 198, 298, 311, 566, 583, 609, 798; III
    272
    Brother Fly: II 165, 201, 297, 300, 564,
        579; III 217, 275
Flying
    birds: I 234; II 355, 412, 783, 800; III
        230, 362, 498–99, 613, 860
    brother: I 533; III 504, 617
    eagle: I 532; II 358
    fever: I 354
    fortune: I 446
    Francis: II 384
    wing: I 509
    word: II 452
    world: I 446
Follower
    brother: II 48; III 402, 416, 878–79
    Christ: II 508, 527, 548, 570, 694, 696,
        756; III 587, 716, 833
    Dominic: II 785
    Francis: I 209, 221, 265, 278, 320, 394,
        462, 477; II 107, 137, 144, 240, 254,
        257, 290, 295, 364, 384, 404, 572,
        644; III 32, 66, 86, 93, 162, 325, 411,
        425, 464, 468, 588–89, 679, 719, 740,
        813
    perfection: III 174
    poverty: I 103, 218
    Rule: III 769
    Sultan: I 584
Folly
    knight: II 804
    penance: II 88
    praise: II 753
Food: I 91, 117, 213, 230, 430, 483, 513, 531,
    545, 584, 591, 607; II 49, 145, 150, 183,

229, 239, 253, 259, 276, 282, 311, 364,
417, 432, 550, 555, 557, 585, 627, 667,
707–08, 733, 747, 757, 794, 815; III 50, 96,
233–34, 278, 303, 326, 341, 363, 386, 466,
470, 480, 520, 539, 632
  animal: II 279, 321, 591, 727, 798; III
    602, 851, 860
  beg: II 99, 253, 814; III 100
  bring: I 229, 350; II 224, 227, 253, 438,
    585, 600; III 104, 597, 856
  brother: I 198, 594, 597; II 88, 99, 150,
    259, 565; III 40, 46, 120, 234, 278,
    290, 463, 495, 524, 550, 617, 634
  cheap: I 392; II 150, 276, 417, 564; III
    279
  Christ: I 146; II 584; III 521, 579, 610,
    656
  Clare: III 467, 591
  cross: III 667
  delicate: I 392; II 77, 246; III 96, 834
  eternal life: I 270
  excess: I 47, 219; II 73, 150, 201; III
    216, 628
  Francis: I 190, 227, 230, 274, 283, 321,
    323, 356, 392, 454, 479, 514–15, 598;
    II 50, 76–78, 81–82, 149, 165,
    181–84, 193, 229, 277, 333, 365, 411,
    415, 561, 609, 615, 694, 703, 707,
    727, 741; III 50, 101, 153, 165, 176,
    234, 282, 306–07, 312, 448, 467, 469,
    492, 539, 549, 551, 591, 627, 667,
    801, 852, 856
  Gospel: I 66
  lack: I 230, 394, 482–83, 515, 597; II
    218, 301, 550, 597; III 234, 247, 279,
    346, 503, 646
  love: I 430
  poor: I 392; II 150, 276, 417, 564; III
    279
  rich: I 392; II 77, 246; III 96, 834
  Rule: I 70–71, 101–02; II 123; III 223, 747
  salvation: I 291, 585
  Scripture: I 356
  seeking: I 213–14, 376, 394; II 298,
    583, 678
  solid: II 737, 763
  Spirit: III 519
  uncooked: II 556
Footprint
  apostle: I 259; II 107, 390, 477
  Christ: I 254; II 110, 545, 682, 697,
    715, 802; III 33, 67, 148, 182, 188,
    289, 339, 380, 383, 394, 426, 492,
    596, 701, 765, 855
  church: III 324
  Francis: I 307, 320, 418; II 67, 99, 110,
    145, 366, 554, 792; III 32, 83, 155,
    288, 400–01, 499, 701, 831, 891
  passer–by: I 250
  predecessor: III 771
Forehead
  Francis: I 253, 505; III 728

  Jesus: III 728
  Tau: II 317, 328, 402, 527, 556, 693,
    714, 720–21, 735; III 189, 502, 616
Foresight
  discretion: I 543
  greed: I 545
  evil: I 389
Forest: I 194, 235, 255, 376, 453; II 191, 221,
  309, 364, 539, 607, 610, 699; III 310, 365,
  591–92, 811
  beast: I 397
Forgetfulness
  Christ: I 406; II 516
  God: I 215; II 702
  good: I 543
  heaven: I 541
  past: I 582
  piety: II 687
  self: II 309
  stigmata: III 188–89, 410, 669
Form: II 745; III 185, 562, 743, 746, 757,
  763, 789, 859
  angel: III 117–18, 394, 443, 573–74
  beauty: I 458
  bread: I 128; III 657
  brother: I 603; III 838
  Christ: I 359; II 541, 688; III 393, 465,
    589, 618, 688, 870, 875
  church: I 579, 582, 602
  cross: I 280, 495; II 168, 328, 361, 607,
    632, 638, 643, 699, 715, 745, 783,
    798; III 49, 92, 181, 196, 305, 383,
    420, 426, 470, 692, 792
  death: I 522
  flower: I 251
  follower: I 394
  Francis: III 89, 247, 268
  God: II 732
  Gospel: II 44, 49, 86, 96, 151, 542; III
    79, 83, 235, 270, 326, 328, 404
  habit: III 773
  Lady Poverty: II 301
  Lawrence: III 534
  life: I 210, 216, 243, 356, 582; II 88,
    149, 218, 344, 370, 517, 547, 749,
    815, ; III 93, 149, 177, 196, 290, 314,
    381, 710
  money: I 102; II 750, 775–76, 820
  obedience: III 157, 293
  ownership: III 787
  Rule: I 210, 216; II 558; III 196, 744,
    769, 771–72
  seraph: I 283; II 108, 498, 515, 713,
    742, 783; III 79, 194, 457
  servant: I 586; II 732, 751; III 765
  soul: III 562, 892
  stigmata: II 513
  sun: I 389, 416; II 784, 803; III 732
  virtue: I 353; II 756; III 326, 381
  women: II 307, 563
  word: I 307
  world: II 815

Formula
  prayer: II 551
  profession: III 743
Fornication: I 73, 79, 440; II 741; III 48
Fortitude
  assurance: I 193
  love: I 84
Foundation: I 457; III 195, 260
  apostolic: III 201
  Basilica: I 325; II 478; III 67, 836
  church: III 192
  Clare: I 197; III 842
  Dominic: III 136
  Francis: III 136
  Gospel: III 196–97
  Order: II 66, 211, 257, 547, 578; III
    149, 164, 170, 194, 316, 394, 413,
    517, 595, 681, 711, 801, 823, 850
  perseverance: I 217
  religion: II 66, 211, 257, 547, 578; III
    149, 164, 170, 194, 316, 394, 413,
    517, 595, 681, 711, 801, 823, 850
  religious life: I 582; II 579
  San Damiano: I 196
  testimony: II 681
  virtue: I 529; II 569; III 290, 319, 334,
    397, 489, 726
  world: II 735
Founder
  apostle: III 740
  brother: I 469, 584, 597, 602; II 243,
    645; III 228, 357, 380, 387, 393,
    401–02, 410–11, 413, 420, 425,
    756–57, 815, 825, 840
  Christ: III 411, 744
  final state: III 388
  Poor Ladies: II 128
Fountain
  construction: II 429
  drink: I 301; II 454, 674; III 532, 652
  Gospel: I 582
  grace: III 530, 650
  life: II 645; III 487, 724
  mercy: I 368
  paradise: III 398
  religion: I 513
Fox
  cunning: I 542; III 178
  den: I 535; II 159, 285, 578, 815; III
    262
  fur: II 183, 332; III 307
Fragrance:III 559, 648
  Christ: III 547, 643, 652
  Divine: III 532, 651
  flower: I 251; III 769
  fullness: III 295
  life: III 220, 392, 412
  Mary: III 549, 645–46
  prayer: I 554, 567
  reputation: II 141, 315, 556; III 50,
    296, 298, 324, 408

virtue: I 198, 203, 206, 260, 296; II
    120, 143, 258, 261, 319, 347, 361,
    392, 554, 587, 648; III 372, 426
  world: III 532
Frailty: I 458; III 118, 395, 848
  human: III 180, 200, 437, 568, 686
  Christ: I 46; III 745
Fraternity. See also Brotherhood: I 67, 77,
    104–05, 217, 542; III 149
Fraud
  contrivance: II 618; III 783, 803, 876,
    881
  follower: II 404
  Francis: I 478; II 564–65
  merchant: I 448
  origin: I 439
  vision: I 477
Freedom
  abuse: II 367
  creature: I 397; II 355, 412, 625
  desire: III 818
  empty: I 274
  enjoyment: I 193; II 79; III 214, 324
  evangelical: III 573
  father: I 196
  figurative: I 446–47; III 469, 593
  gift: II 437–38, 462, 677
  God: I 251; II 260
  Gospel: III 442
  heart: I 333
  poverty: I 466–67, 480, 489, 514; II 199
  privilege: II 340, 750; III 116, 287, 419
  sin: III 396
  spirit: I 375
Friend: I 43, 50–51, 69, 75, 91, 95, 132, 140,
    265, 272, 438, 442, 445, 448, 494; II
    422–23, 428, 430, 440, 446, 465, 480, 518,
    566, 601, 617, 656–57, 663, 668, 737–46;
    III 80, 178, 195, 435, 438, 450, 453, 481,
    524–25, 530, 600, 747, 799
  authentic: I 87
  belly: II 297
  betrayer: I 79, 87
  bridegroom: I 291; II 527, 596; III 173
  brother: II 138, 153, 183, 268, 304,
    343, 407, 427; III 280, 750, 776
  Christ: II 87, 284, 358, 361, 375, 383, 474,
    599, 604, 623, 697–99, 709, 742–43; III
    103, 174, 188, 452, 530, 581
  Dominic: III 813
  flesh: II 283
  fool: II 291, 509
  Francis: I 188, 195, 204, 245, 249, 301,
    334, 376, 400, 411, 442, 456, 461,
    476, 515–16, 569; II 55, 68, 71, 247,
    250, 418, 435, 447, 519, 539, 610,
    760; III 94, 102–03, 484, 579,
    679–80, 854
  Giles: III 18
  God: I 235, 265, 323, 600; II 39, 137,
    169, 174, 241, 290, 309, 414, 473,
    607, 620, 645, 700, 744, 746; III 266,

445, 514, 567, 569, 576, 622–23, 653, 846, 866, 891
goodness: II 439, 668
Hugolino: II 55, 751
integrity: II 242
John: III 643
leper: II 74
light: II 415, 644
Masseo: III 808
mercy: II 455
peace: I 335
Pietro Bernardone: I 190, 374; II 78
poverty: I 533, 537, 547–49; II 542; III 161
prayer: II 144, 365; III 325
simplicity: I 290
spiritual: I 102, 573; III 776
Friendship: I 376, 390, 544; II 435, 452, 462, 482, 509, 655, 784; III 349
    brother: II 405; III 401, 858, 864
    Christ: II 740, 742–43; III 730
    concept: II 738
    falcon: II 356, 593
    Francis: I 246, 301, 376, 390, 499, 571; II 153, 356, 435, 452, 462, 482, 593, 655, 740, 742–43, 784
    Giles: III 625
    God: III 424, 512
    Hugolino: I 246, 499, 571; II 751
Frivolity
    Francis: II 68–69
    laity: III 389
Frugality: I 466; III 162
Fruit: I 114, 135, 230, 246, 285, 329, 394, 464–65, 501, 566, 579, 600, 608; II 148, 210, 245, 260, 297, 320, 343, 375, 441, 466, 519, 521, 553, 556, 572, 578, 678, 718–19, 736, 746; III 34, 92, 252, 259, 368, 557, 559, 606, 647–48, 678, 708, 825, 857, 889
    absence: I 80; III 849
    bitterness: I 206, 465
    charity: III 388
    contemplation: I 409, 599
    evil: III 173
    first: I 480; II 297, 422
    honor: I 216
    humility: II 519–21; III 320
    kindness: III 94
    labor: I 68; II 190, 208, 300; III 320, 337, 678, 706, 722
    martyrdom: II 601
    ministry: I 576
    obedience: II 344, 571; III 849
    patience: I 80, 88
    penance: I 41, 47, 78, 91; II 270, 594, 706; III 388, 480, 599
    prayer: I 319; II 314
    preaching: I 402–03
    production: III 53, 289, 396, 444, 491, 494, 521, 526, 532, 575, 604, 609, 636, 652, 875
    respectability: I 216
    salvation: III 320, 404

    soul: III 444, 575, 592, 633
    wisdom: III 398
    womb: I 475; II 670
Fulfilment
    attainment: II 764; III 88
    Divine counsel: II 44
    Gospel: I 262
    grace: III 383
    need: II 581–85
    perfection: II 763
    promise: III 546
    wish: II 415
Fullness
    authority: III 762, 766, 815
    birth: III 158
    charity: I 553; III 770
    end: III 424
    faith: III 160
    God: I 85
    Gospel: III 195
    grace: I 163; III 381, 683
    heart: I 283; II 261
    knowledge: II 682
    life: II 501
    Order: I 584
    piety: II 697
    sea: I 156
    Spirit: II 552
    virtue: I 377; III 372, 534
    wisdom: II 682
Funeral
    arrangement: II 426, 430; III 778
    dream: II 422
    Francis: I 324, 417, 515–18; II 138, 293; III 66
    Innocent III: I 579
    Martin: III 93
    mourning: II 421; III 50
    procession: I 284
    rite: II 423, 804
    tunic: II 427; III 267
Fur
    cap: II 119; III 220
    clothing: I 247–48, 305; II 333, 467; III 58, 64, 307, 850
    fox: II 183; III 307
Furnace: III 497, 535, 541, 612, 652, 655
    Daniel: I 250; II 754
    fornication: I 440
    heart: III 173
    love: II 697; III 670
    poverty: II 736, 756–57
    seraph: II 635
    trial: III 489, 726
Fury
    Bonaventure: III 648
    brother: III 400
    demon: III 136
    father: I 334, 375, 449
    persecutor: III 163
    tyrant: II 515
    wolf: III 482

Future: I 49, 287, 334, 371, 376, 384, 449,
     464, 469, 472, 475, 485, 509, 545, 553,
     583; II 50–51, 69, 70, 75, 82, 95, 107, 118,
     150, 157, 201, 212, 239, 247, 258, 317,
     351, 359, 377, 423, 438, 475, 518, 531,
     604, 645, 656, 688, 691, 698, 762, 792; III
     80, 135, 156, 159, 173, 176, 187, 199–200,
     203, 216, 260, 264–65, 274, 278, 335, 382,
     386, 391, 408, 415, 419, 421, 458, 470,
     484, 489, 517, 542, 603, 681–82, 692, 703,
     720, 726, 748–49, 754, 758, 770, 785,
     787–88, 802, 831, 868
  contemplation: I 380
  fear: I 372; III 56
  foretaste: I 530
  knowledge: I 206, 225, 292, 330, 380;
     II 294, 617, 638, 643, 813; III 34,
     95–96, 129, 387–88, 408, 422, 556,
     646, 834, 839, 863–64, 867
  omen: II 35; III 405, 864
  prediction: I 389, 464; II 283, 692, 700,
     728, 809, 814; III 81, 116, 129, 176,
     182, 449, 580, 681, 695, 721, 839,
     863–64, 869
  status: III 156
  view: I 205, 226, 336, 357; II 207,
     260–61, 533, 541, 545, 614, 616–20,
     690; III 159, 168, 319, 687, 705

                                G

Gain: I 71, 92, 196, 203, 216, 225, 285, 337,
     339, 342, 348, 357, 395, 436, 440, 477,
     563; II 145–46, 245, 261, 307, 312, 338,
     365, 381, 430, 663, 575, 810; III 163, 180,
     325, 400–01, 445, 576, 588, 606, 616, 787,
     857
  bees: III 217, 275
  conversion: I 486; II 208, 365, 630
  death: II 601
  Francis: I 512
  ill–gotten: II 251
  loss: I 443
  money: I 70, 430, 435–36, 439, 452; II
     20
  neighbor: I 385; III 169, 319
  work: III 217, 275, 746
Game
  checkers: III 57
  devil: II 423
  Francis: I 370; II 83
  Gineldo: II 451–52
Garden
  brother: III 238, 262
  care: II 192, 354
  Christ: III 769, 889
  church: III 890
  contemplation: III 656
  flower: II 192, 354; III 366
  Francis's cell: III 810, 812
  God: I 270
  hedge: II 217
  knowledge: I 552
  mortification: II 325
  Poor Ladies: III 834
  possession: II 160
  praise: I 251, 504
  presence: II 422, 466, 551, 563, 737,
     743, 804; III 529, 649
  scripture: II 737
  search: II 281
  spring: II 649
  Virgin's womb: III 740
Gardener
  absence: I 552
  benefit: II 466
  Francis: I 459
  Gregory IX: I 418
  instruction: II 192, 354; III 366
  Ranieri: II 217
Garment: I 65, 146, 294, 456, 583, 594, 598,
     603; II 69, 301; III 57, 406, 489, 508, 774
  birds: III 469
  Francis: I 183, 269, 450, 456, 460, 493,
     598; II 84, 247, 386, 463, 531–32,
     642, 675, 685; III 83, 682, 811
  innocence: I 539
  sackcloth: I 598; II 386, 642
  silk: I 607
  skin: I 539
  stigmata: II 734
Gem
  cross: I 325; II 109; III 67
  desire: I 449
  Francis: I 519
  humility: I 198; II 338; III 848
  possession: II 753
  robe: III 481
  stigmata: II 417, 419, 476, 514, 516
  stone: III 479
Generosity
  beg: III 214, 273
  Bernard: II 319
  Christ: II 247
  conformity: III 186
  divinity: II 516, 550
  Francis: I 185; II 73, 246, 333, 531
  Lady Jacoba: II 405
  servant of God: II 199
  unknown man: II 300
Gentleman
  knight: III 627
  Rufino: III 567
Gentleness
  absence: I 444
  brother: I 272; II 53, 102; III 456, 656
  Christ: II 697
  Francis: I 351, 489; II 53, 531, 534,
     595, 660, 685, 712
  heal: II 408
  humanity: II 736
  movement: II 408, 426, 517–18
  Spirit: III 634

Sultan: I 584; III 398
virtue: III 44, 476, 692, 857
German: I 206; III 36, 36a, 697–98, 837
Gesture
   accusation: I 547
   birds: II 412; III 860
   confession: II 264, 618
   education: I 182
   expression: II 318, 338, 363
   imitation: II 164, 369
   lamb: II 591
   pilgrim: III 385
   rhetoric: I 498
Gift: I 296, 390, 436–37, 449, 545, 588; II
   123, 319, 374, 379, 427, 558, 580, 594,
   661, 672, 698; III 33, 36, 91, 423, 461–62,
   504, 514, 516, 546, 585–86, 622, 633, 649,
   685, 829
   alms: II 47; III 754
   bread: III 39
   charism: II 577
   charity: III 496
   Christ or God: I 186, 206, 212–13, 224,
     249, 256, 261, 337, 342, 459, 472,
     475, 488, 552, 565, 567; II 124–25,
     134, 225, 230, 247, 270–71, 275, 278,
     312, 349, 359, 361, 370, 410–11, 416,
     420, 510, 514, 526, 545, 550, 577,
     588, 622, 631, 655, 678, 695–96, 709,
     721, 772, 781; III 33, 50, 56, 103,
     125, 159, 193, 224, 291, 295, 342,
     347, 383, 388, 391, 393, 426, 516,
     581, 585–86, 622, 650, 666, 843
   Christ Child: III 223, 361
   Clare: III 516
   confession: II 420
   contemplation: III 503–04, 548, 617
   donor: III 753
   ecstasy: III 564
   Eucharist: I 346–47, 350, 352
   forgiveness: III 231, 312
   Francis: I 216, 224, 226, 260, 288–89,
     308, 333, 389, 400; II 140, 149, 247,
     276, 299, 305, 313, 344, 381, 390,
     618, 678–79
   grace: II 46, 524, 526, 530, 729; III 396,
     472, 505, 513, 532
   Gregory IX: I 429; II 109
   haste: III 690
   heal: III 36, 862
   heaven: I 186, 308, 330, 346, 542; II
     530, 622, 631
   holiness: II 543
   Holy Spirit: I 567; II 510, 618, 729,
     787; III 392, 450, 524, 540, 581
   hospitality: II 449, 673
   humility: II 337
   Innocent III: I 384
   kindness: II 696
   king: III 223, 361
   Lady Jacoba: II 123
   La Verna: III 802

   learning: II 144, 365; III 325
   light: II 566
   nature: II 523
   non–believer: III 291, 224
   patience: III 36
   perseverance: III 393
   preaching: III 586
   prophesy: II 808; III 892
   Rule: II 381
   simplicity: II 369
   solitude: III 565
   speech: II 453; III 439, 488, 725
   stigmata: I 281, 354; II 655; III 668
   Sultan: I 231, 395, 487; II 603; III 605
   thanksgiving: I 296; II 478
   time: II 147, 351; III 322
   virtue: III 867
   word: III 459, 461, 507, 524, 526
   work: II 240
Giver
   donor: III 754
   generosity: II 319
   God: I 186, 261; II 577, 704; III 347
   provocation: II 312, 608
Gladness. See Happiness, Joy
Glass
   drinking: II 175, 287, 793
Globe
   light: I 446, 476; II 552, 783
Glorification
   Christ: III 421
   Francis: II 648, 650; III 150, 194, 687
   self: I 594
Glorify, Glory: I 105, 143, 146–47, 185–86,
   247, 265, 273, 281, 284, 294, 328, 336,
   342, 346, 371, 386, 416–17, 437, 446, 467,
   489, 534, 538, 544, 588; II 37, 70, 124,
   188, 209, 328, 332–33, 336, 340, 359, 370,
   384, 477, 521, 524, 573, 588, 724, 739,
   744, 754–55, 814; III 37, 338, 448, 481,
   511, 535, 578, 639, 853, 888
   brother: II 340; III 481, 499, 600–01
   Christ: I 74, 82, 288, 307, 339, 347,
     520, 535; II 404, 522, 545, 650, 655;
     III 385, 397, 421–23, 566, 655, 666,
     680, 683, 732, 866
   conscience: I 272
   cross: I 328, 346; II 377, 400, 545, 650,
     682, 758; III 332, 422–23, 581
   emperor: I 221; III 41
   eternity: I 588; II 415, 521, 746; III
     382, 395
   Francis: I 42, 49, 246, 281, 288, 351,
     355, 529; II 109–10, 143, 298, 333,
     361, 392–93, 410, 440, 445, 449, 468,
     490, 526, 581, 642, 644–45, 649, 668,
     673, 675, 677–78, 681–82, 711, 714,
     717, 738, 746, 748, 750, 780; III 66,
     130, 152, 288, 499, 529, 555, 640,
     649, 666, 732, 866
   God: I 74, 81, 85, 89, 113, 143, 148–49,
     153–56, 159, 182, 184, 241, 279, 295,

308, 326, 328, 332, 339, 368, 370,
400, 420, 520, 534, 536, 538; II 38,
48, 58, 67, 95, 125, 282, 334, 339,
351–52, 404, 412, 477, 490, 571, 587,
673, 683, 733, 739–40, 743, 747, 751,
759, 772, 780; III 192, 383, 418, 450,
460, 494, 534, 584, 608, 730, 759,
848, 856
Gregory IX: I 294
heaven: I 357, 467; II 50, 328, 386, 402,
521–22, 573, 715–16, 723, 738, 742,
746, 796; III 46, 150, 182, 184–85,
192, 387, 392, 396, 481, 720, 868
infinitity: II 370; III 476, 596, 852
knighthood: II 246, 533
light: III 846
Lucifer: I 455; III 84
martyrdom: I 600; II 814; III 856
obedience: III 670
paradise: II 522; III 472, 481, 523–24,
526, 600–01
poverty: I 535; II 260, 301; III 324, 335,
384
praise: III 435, 440, 447, 449, 459, 461,
471, 475, 490–92, 512–18, 521, 523,
538, 542, 544, 550, 559, 564–65, 571
prayer: I 66, 86, 89, 140–41, 148, 150,
155–56, 160–61, 346, 351; III 89,
220, 372, 376, 358, 382–84, 583
promise: I 553, III 46, 323, 382–83,
392, 395, 715, 720, 868, 870
punishment: I 105; II 37, 370; III 476,
596, 747
queen: III 528
religion: III 338, 487, 724
Rule: III 323, 381, 715
saint: I 131, 251, 588; II 209, 343, 780;
III 707
Spirit: I 339, 520
stigmata: III 535, 653, 870
throne: I 287, 351; II 328, 796; III 848
verb: I 49, 57, 76, 81, 85, 90, 138, 147,
149, 151, 161–62, 180, 250, 278, 282,
284, 286, 289, 291, 304, 306; II 52,
87, 108, 120, 125, 377, 388, 400, 403,
426, 476, 520, 648, 682, 752, 758,
780, 796, 810; III 220, 372, 452, 582,
730
vestment: I 419; III 555
world: I 370, 442, 446, 579; II 316, 332,
535, 545, 555; III 117, 291, 408, 410,
608, 707, 816–17, 849
Gloss: I 385
Gospel: I 459; II 517, 520; III 692, 831
Ordinaria: II 520
Rule: I 127, 571; II 132, 132a; III 124,
200, 254, 315a, 386, 420, 713–14
Glutton: I 228, 392, 439, 478; II 259, 297,
351, 570; III 155
Goat: I 248, 399, 501
Goatskin: I 514; III 392
Godfather: I 106; II 744; III 497, 612

Godhead. See also Divinity: I 161, 475, 813,
818; II 744; III 95, 153, 532, 652
Godmother: III 496, 612
Gold: I 419, 473, 494, 497, 607–08; II 301,
434; III 49, 96, 273, 347, 457, 487, 514
charity: III 118, 294–95, 486, 488, 687,
724–25
Christ: II 515
cross: I 325, 419, 463; II 109, 319, 402,
478, 545, 692, 795; III 67, 87, 438,
468, 569, 592, 874
crown: I 339, 346; II 743
earth: III 479, 598
Francis: II 756
Gregory IX: I 294
head: III 117–18, 393–94, 486, 488,
723, 726
palace: III 503, 616
Sultan: I 607–08; II 602
tree: III 557, 559, 647–48
test: III 489, 502, 726
virtue: I 196, 201, 379, 448–49, 459,
520, 537, 539–40, 583; II 37, 47, 84,
185, 284, 301, 384, 512, 542, 577,
689, 696, 756–57; III 196, 394, 457,
849
vision: III 117, 393, 438, 468, 592, 874
Goodness: I 433, 457; II 404, 439, 515, 518,
668, 760; III 63, 641
brother: I 572; II 211; III 171, 317, 414,
711
Christ: III 173, 403
creation: I 353–54, 597
Francis: I 279, 306; II 515, 716; III 605,
886
God: I 229, 291, 400, 449, 472, 476; II
34, 87, 109, 125, 415, 513, 545, 575,
597, 600, 616, 655, 716; III 101, 224,
291, 362, 372, 456–57, 541, 650,
654–55, 801, 844
humanity: II 518
love: II 814
Mary: III 843
poverty: I 535
Goods
administration: III 766, 776, 788
Apostolic See: III 777, 788
dominion: III 789
entrant: I 100–01; II 291; III 773
eternal: I 588; II 38, 282; III 81, 384,
488, 725, 747
immovable: III 766, 778
material: I 100–01, 356, 436, 438, 529,
544, 597, 608; II 38, 85, 89, 97, 270,
282, 523, 594, 733, 752, 756, 814–16
III 82, 405, 628, 721, 773–74, 780,
786
movable: III 759, 785–87
ownership: III 786
relative: II 300, 579
renunciation: I 100–01, 285, 336, 448,
529, 540–42, 544–45, 567, 573, 578,

586, 597, 608; II 89, 126, 165, 300, 579, 686, 733, 752, 815; III 84, 227, 355, 438

spiritual: I 588; II 38, 282; III 81, 384, 488, 725, 747

synagogue: III 423

Goodwill: III 95, 788

Gospel: I 46, 65, 68–69, 106, 125, 202–03, 254, 328, 392, 462, 567, 597; II 94–96, 101, 151–52, 159, 188, 254, 261, 284–85, 300, 387, 508–09, 539, 561, 571–73, 578–79, 581–82, 621, 643, 685–86, 696, 728, 750, 755–56, 815; III 197, 235, 398, 406, 423, 471, 496, 568, 685–87, 690, 692, 696, 721, 728, 750, 755–56, 815, 819, 846

book: II 38a, 85, 254, 288, 631; III 169, 815

Christ: I 63, 89, 100, 106, 394, 563, 572; II 38, 168, 207; III 197, 350, 471, 510, 568, 578, 610, 621, 681, 701, 704, 742–43, 745

counsel: I 196, 203, 572; II 84, 91, 163–65, 579, 755; III 91, 241–42, 301–02, 393, 743–44, 771–72

example: II 561, III 326, 328, 447, 740

form: II 44, 49, 86, 115, 542, 756; III 79, 83, 86, 235, 270, 326, 328, 404, 743

Francis: III 60, 709, 739

freedom: III 442

humility: I 106, 572; II 520, 755, 815; III 53, 197, 328, 423, 770

life: I 63, 68, 81, 89; II 542, 621, 756; III 96, 135, 194–96, 201, 384, 405, 739, 744

marrow: II 146, 380; III 323, 715

Mass: I 201, 366; II 56, 191, 542, 689, 773, 783; III 86, 365, 709, 843

mercy: III 611

observance: II 47, 95, 206, 261, 298, 387, 547, 579, 643, 755, 775; III 50, 53, 79, 83, 116, 135, 150, 152, 154, 157, 167–68, 179–80, 196, 198, 235, 257, 315, 323, 326, 405, 438, 569, 704, 714, 742–43, 770, 852, 855, 869

opening: II 209, 254, 631; III 169, 196, 258, 568, 708, 815, 839

pattern: I 125; II 92

perfection: I 210, 366; II 49, 91, 95–96, 98, 101, 126, 146, 151, 188, 206, 254, 261, 300, 387, 508, 520, 526, 535, 547, 561, 564, 579, 581, 639, 643, 645, 733, 755; III 148, 167–68, 179, 185, 198, 227, 257, 328, 355, 357, 426, 704, 715, 844, 850

poverty: I 106, 572, 597; II 91, 285, 303, 387, 578–79, 581, 815; III 53, 160, 164, 197, 328, 406, 438, 447, 526, 681, 701, 742, 745, 770, 869

preach: I 202, 227, 230, 322, 366, 584, 597, 600; II 348, 511, 526, 541–42, 594, 597, 600; II 348, 511, 526,

541–42, 594, 602, 610, 626, 629, 783; III 53, 392, 398, 423, 568, 727, 739, 770, 850

precept: III 198, 743, 771–72

prohibition: I 572; II 775; III 406, 704, 743–44

purity: II 261; III 269, 324

read: I 506, 516; II 254; III 74, 86, 833

Rule: I 65–67, 94–95, 100, 210, 321, 383, 582, 597; II 52, 54, 97, 101, 205–07, 300, 348, 380–81, 547, 558, 564, 613, 775; III 60, 93, 116, 132, 150, 167–68, 195–98, 201, 256, 326, 384, 406, 442, 448, 573, 680, 704, 714, 725, 740, 771, 815, 831

saying: III 238, 346, 425, 510, 578, 621, 702, 715, 800

sin: I 43, 48, 50, 79, 87; III 198, 610

status: III 148

stigmata: II 719

Sultan: III 799

Gossip: I 72, 191, 438; II 258, 366; III 186, 326

Gout: I 290; III 547, 642

Government: III 710, 756

Governor

cardinal protector: I 106, 573; II 56, 777; III 741

Francis: I 58

Poor Ladies: III 690

Grace: I 94, 97, 102, 117, 240, 261, 307, 329, 332, 335, 374, 390, 537, 548, 552, 568; II 35, 46, 93, 185, 293, 299, 312, 322, 326, 377, 419, 443, 468, 521, 588, 599, 633, 701–02, 738, 746, 818; III 37, 285, 297, 540, 562, 602, 621, 739, 859

beg: III 269

brother: I 212, 270, 272, 274–75, 554; II 48, 94, 102, 110, 157, 210, 222, 260, 387, 320, 643, 690; III 37, 438, 444, 446, 455, 457–58, 461, 467–68, 501, 505–07, 511, 515, 527–29, 533, 542–43, 545–49, 551, 569–70, 575, 583, 586, 589, 606, 616–17, 620–23, 633, 636, 638, 641–42, 645, 651, 656, 686, 693, 797

Christ: I 258, 291, 298, 341, 346, 391, 553; II 48, 53, 94, 102, 268, 277–78, 320, 536, 682, 684; III 86, 409, 421, 464, 473, 531–33, 546, 588–89, 598, 606, 609, 623, 626, 650–51, 683, 719, 769, 855, 888

Clare: I 197; II 128; III 467, 590

Francis: I 186, 193, 195, 197, 205–06, 216, 225–26, 230–31, 234, 244, 253, 259, 265, 272, 301, 321, 323–24, 331, 338, 342, 379, 400, 410, 414, 459, 531; II 35–36, 44, 69, 73–74, 79, 84, 89, 125, 179, 195, 203, 228, 241, 243, 248, 310, 344, 364, 411, 415, 461, 473, 490, 524–26, 530–31, 536, 538, 544–45, 550, 553, 571, 588, 606, 608,

642, 644–45, 649, 672, 684–85, 688,
690–91, 695, 701, 704, 721, 726, 813;
III 33–34, 50, 78, 128, 130, 153, 158,
180, 292, 354, 387, 401, 403, 422,
451, 455, 465, 467, 473, 479, 494,
513, 567, 582, 590, 617, 619, 628,
666, 683, 846–47, 849, 855–56, 867
friend: II 738, 742
God: I 71–72, 85, 94, 102, 120–21, 158,
166, 184, 186, 195, 197, 206, 213,
230, 236, 244–45, 256, 259, 270, 275,
301, 304, 321, 332, 342, 377, 435,
459, 531, 537, 553, 566, 569; II
36–37, 53, 66, 68–69, 73–74, 79, 87,
91, 96, 110, 122, 125, 128, 153, 157,
172, 177, 179, 195, 197, 203, 210,
222, 225, 228, 274, 277, 387, 411,
415, 475, 480, 525, 643, 684, 726,
729, 736, 742, 750, 754, 757, 816; III
115, 170, 218, 228, 231–32, 251,
311–12, 316, 329, 345, 354–55, 357,
360, 369–70, 386, 413, 419, 436, 438,
457–58, 465, 472, 475, 479, 503, 505,
513, 515, 527, 529, 532, 542–44,
566–67, 569, 575, 582–83, 595, 598,
602, 606, 616–19, 626, 628, 633, 636,
638, 642, 649, 656, 685, 710, 714,
797, 807, 841, 846, 849–50
Gregory IX: I 293
heal: I 166; II 443, 445, 461, 529, 622;
III 50, 79
love: I 71; II 94
martyrdom: I 280, 322
Mary: I 138; II 520, 542, 715, 760; III
48, 53, 528, 548–49, 637, 656
poor: II 35, 69, 195, 299, 415; III 285,
438, 503, 616, 850
Portiuncula: I 275; II 642; III 621
poverty: II 110, 381, 457; III 384, 503
prayer: II 605, 622; III 390, 455, 461,
586, 622, 645, 686
Rule: I 158, 321; III 381, 396
salvation: I 225, 275, 335, 338; III 33,
45, 116, 150, 153, 188, 194, 382–83,
423–24, 863
sin: I 184, 369–70; III 267, 389, 397,
423, 491
Spirit: I 163, 205, 224, 271, 321, 385; II
41, 51, 89, 137, 203, 520, 618, 626,
729, 762; III 128, 369–70
stigmata: I 265, 395; II 406, 473
virtue: I 71–72, 198, 234; II 44, 46, 91,
243, 344, 367, 393, 519, 649, 695, 730,
753, 757, 813; III 36–37, 44, 57, 514
work: I 102; III 390, 757
Grain: II 465–66, 679; III 158
birds: II 129, 375; III 230, 362–63
collection: III 778, 891
Francis: I 336, 416
measure: III 498, 612
Grape
blood: III189

despoil: II 170–71; III 352–53, 479–80,
598–99
gift: II 276, 417; III 359
press: II 424
sickness: II 152, 360; III 235, 279
Grass
cut: II 426, 660
flower: I 498, 551
humanity: II 817
rye: II 227; III 345
table: I 551
Gratitude. See also Thanksgiving: I 214,
565; II 274, 354, 411, 616; III 372, 797
Grave: II 440, 480, 669, 674; III 82, 94, 694
Greatness: II 448, 457, 680
Francis: I 188, 290, 416; II 180, 242,
791
Lord: I 149, 151, 153, 155, 456, 496; III
456
world: III 583
Greed: I 79, 105, 455, 486, 543–46; II 88,
148, 342, 764; III 264, 289, 382, 389, 410
fifth age: III 147
Francis: I 183, 430; II 38–39, 86–87,
279, 319, 530, 576, 583, 603, 684,
764
Pietro Bernardone: I 193, 449; II 538;
III 833
poverty: I 137, 165, 543–46, 548; II
756; III 397
Rule: I 69, 79
Sylvester: II 38–39, 86–87, 319; III 438,
569
Grief: I 305, 330, 469, 476, 545; II 423,
427–28, 523, 656, 661, 669, 804; III 74,
321
brother: I 223, 280, 595; II 40, 121,
407, 646; III 221, 370–71, 522
Clare: I 174, 286, 417; II 129; III 229,
357
day: III 335
Francis: I 174, 280, 286, 417, 482, 515;
II 40, 121, 212, 332, 473, 805; III
130, 172, 265, 306, 395, 408, 415,
703
John: III 530, 650
Passion: III 508
poverty: I 547–48
Grille: II 129; III 299, 357
Groom. See also Bridegroom: III 692, 885
Grotto. See also Cave, Pit
Francis: I 187, 190–91, 356, 372, 374,
436, 453; II 74–75, 78, 537, 660, 687,
782; III 82
misery: II 664
Growth
church: III 152
Order: I 583; II 552; III 149, 441c
presumption: I 368
subject: I 273
tree: III 648

vegetation: I 322; II 426, 660
virtue: I 213
Grudge: II 331
Guarantee: II 706
 poverty: II 284
Guard: I 69, 75, 80, 88, 90, 120, 127, 137,
 221, 408, 415, 447, 471, 583, 587; II 284,
 462, 519, 547, 562, 801; III 51, 395, 405,
 754
 demon: III 405
 Francis: II 466
 humility: II 695
 palace: III 369
 security: II 202, 424–25, 437–38, 659,
 667
Guardian
 Angelo: III 495, 609
 brother: III 482, 499, 527, 543–44,
 561–63, 571, 601, 610, 614, 675
 Christ: III 683
 Francis: I 484; III 225, 282–84, 292,
 307, 365, 797
 God: I 80, 88
 humility: II 337, 569, 801
 Leo: III 797
 meaning: I 90a; III 858
 ministry or office: I 98, 126; II 52, 101,
 125, 148, 183, 193, 195, 275–76,
 306–07, 332, 344–45, 351, 386, 416,
 571, 642, 799; III 36, 133, 546, 642,
 780
 poverty: I 529
 robber: III 495, 610
 Servado: III 527, 636
 silence: II 564
 Virgin: III 36
Guide: I 187, 250, 323, 341, 445, 467; II 35,
 105, 132, 143, 340, 353, 448, 452, 526,
 541, 587, 629, 671, 680, 705, 725, 754; III
 72
 angel: III 381, 500
 blind: III 226, 287
 brother: II 587; III 497–98, 612–13
 Christ: I 549; III 384
 church: II 105
 Francis: I 180, 342, 370, 464, 484; II
 254, 353, 489, 526, 647; III 335, 400
 God: I 341, 372; II 361, 754, 759
 truth: I 293
Guilt: I 445, 471, 494, 497, 538, 778; II 147,
 268, 321, 381, 519, 547; III 93, 228, 252
 blasphemy: II 547
 Judas: I 117
 Rule: II 147, 381
 sin: I 43, 133; II 788, 817; III 252, 343

H

Habit. See also Capuche, Hood, Tunic
 bad: II 200; III 216, 274
 behavior: I 266, 269, 466, 597; II 311,
 406, 511, 609; III 481, 853

brother: I 299, 583; II 58, 459, 479,
 653, 751, 783; III 56, 70, 78, 480,
 500, 529, 843
 cruciform: II 527; III 196, 649, 684,
 692
 Francis: III 491, 503, 529, 607, 616,
 630, 649
 frugality: I 466
 garb: I 73, 166, 376, 378, 380, 385, 563,
 582, 586, 598; II 37, 43, 85–86, 90,
 94, 145, 267, 335–36, 365, 386, 517,
 543, 588–89, 642, 690, 738, 808–10;
 III 47, 55, 57, 66, 92, 118, 129–30,
 202–03, 283, 318, 325, 384, 393, 410,
 425, 444, 481, 496, 554, 575, 600,
 620–21, 631, 681, 692–93, 726,
 773–74, 793–94, 803, 845, 854, 858,
 861, 879
 good: I 430; II 164
 hermit: I 379; II 81, 84, 86, 782; III 66
 humility: III 396
 novice: III 773
 Order: I 561; II 109; III 315, 838
 penance: I 560
 penitent: II 401, 650
 pilgrim: III 135
 poverty: III 396
 religion: I 402, 542; II 54, 57, 103, 107,
 462; III 156, 539, 553, 725
Hail: I 458, 485; II 177, 269–70, 411, 594,
 634–35, 706, 711; III 733
Hair: I 145, 253, 433, 453, 504, 508, 594, 598;
 II 229, 323, 423, 428, 439, 524, 564, 584,
 668, 809; III 78, 91, 233–34, 331, 342,
 558, 728–29, 840
Hair-shirt: I 299, 415, 454, 510, 590; II 80,
 150, 251, 438, 459, 555, 692, 792; III 279,
 473, 842, 865
Halter: I 460, 468
Hammer: I 448; II 385, 633, 642, 710, 770
Hand: I 97, 101, 118, 147, 196, 213, 293,
 299–300, 307, 331, 412, 448, 495, 501,
 506, 510, 568, 586; II 45–46, 100, 187–88,
 193, 198, 215, 228, 267, 274, 279, 281,
 283, 303, 307, 328, 351, 355, 380, 407–08,
 419–20, 425, 428, 437, 440, 457, 460, 463,
 533, 550, 555, 560, 580, 592, 659, 666–67,
 669, 675–76, 680, 687, 692, 702, 718, 733,
 739, 745, 751, 797–98; III 55, 92, 100,
 124, 178, 188, 309, 314, 409, 467, 480–81,
 525, 544, 547, 591, 600, 695
 beg: I 240, 305, 587; II 72, 82
 Bernard: III 443, 445
 bless: I 225, 240, 276, 320, 323, 390; II
 126, 135, 387, 474–75, 643, 700, 715,
 803
 charity: I 440
 Christ: I 53–54, 146, 271, 482, 536; II
 74; III 381, 531–33, 651, 657, 668,
 688, 728; 801

coin: II 39, 73–74, 76, 87, 92, 137, 247,
   249, 290, 319, 533, 801; III 45, 266,
   438, 569, 753
death: I 242; II 407, 475, 697
demon: III 612, 642, 819, 828
Dominic: II 149, 344
Elias: I 276; II 475
emptiness: II 72, 147, 195, 372, 531,
   583, 815; III 134, 284, 314, 320, 409,
   706, 821
enemy: II 428, 510, 662; III 485, 489
entrust: I 50–51, 53–54, 193, 276, 356,
   375, 455, 529; II 126–27, 145, 216,
   222, 257, 366, 475; III 288, 290, 356
evil: III 604–05
executioner: I 275, 414
fate: I 494
Father: I 146, 148–49, 155, 284
fight: I 244, 292, 408, 453, 485; II 118,
   326, 346, 407, 436, 699; III 181, 281
Francis: I 125, 195, 201–02, 212, 225,
   227, 238–40, 253, 271, 276, 283, 286,
   323, 349, 356, 379, 383, 390, 392,
   405, 414, 458, 460, 477, 489, 494,
   505, 568; II 39, 71, 76, 84, 87, 126,
   135, 139–40, 142, 146–47, 149, 164,
   168, 175–76, 192, 197, 204, 209,
   217–18, 246, 278, 280, 285, 287,
   304–05, 309, 312, 317, 319, 325, 331,
   335–36, 340, 344, 348, 351, 353, 355,
   357, 359, 367, 369, 381, 386, 408–09,
   411–12, 414, 426, 429, 436, 444, 458,
   461, 480, 538, 556, 584, 589, 593,
   607, 618, 625, 627, 635, 642–43,
   653–54, 660–62, 666, 681, 693, 697,
   699–701, 705, 711–12, 715, 727, 742,
   754, 761, 783, 793, 798, 801, 805; III
   71, 127, 130, 165, 226, 244, 258, 270,
   280, 287, 301–02, 305, 318, 336, 340,
   345, 355, 366, 370, 417, 438, 454,
   456, 469, 483, 493, 525, 557, 569,
   577, 602, 608, 707, 710, 714, 729,
   733, 795, 808, 811, 815, 824, 852,
   865, 868
general minister: I 126–27
generosity: I 253, 545; II 300–02
Giles: III 564
God: I 67, 149, 155, 184, 236, 246, 259,
   288, 319–20, 332, 370, 436, 565; II
   178, 270, 317, 353, 418, 421, 519,
   521, 531, 556, 596, 607, 624, 641,
   685, 693, 695, 729, 754, 762; III 176,
   396, 409, 477, 552, 563, 792
Gregory IX: I 295; II 56, 132, 261, 391,
   477, 648
head: I 276; II 126, 474; III 117, 127,
   130, 226, 294, 336, 355, 410, 446–47,
   577, 714, 831, 868
heal: I 240, 299, 302–03, 324, 403, 494;
   II 431–33, 442, 459–61, 479, 627,
   654–55, 676–77, 712, 784, 797; III 74
heart: III 81

help: I 565; II 294, 814
John: III 555, 642–43
kiss: I 189, 271, 280, 286, 373, 417; II
   52, 74, 77, 101, 248–49, 335–36, 376,
   458, 476, 533–34, 681, 788–92, 803,
   805; III 47, 532, 651, 841
leper: II 74, 248–49, 533–34, 792; III
   841
madman: II 118, 346; III 294
Mary: II 312; III 549, 645
Masseo: III 469, 619
mercy: I 195, 377; II 178
money: II 39, 73–74, 76, 87, 92, 137,
   247, 249, 290, 319, 533, 801; III 45,
   266, 438, 569, 753
persecution: I 191; II 93, 319, 537
poor: III 284
prayer: II 100, 142, 187, 258, 278, 309,
   312, 340, 348, 359, 369, 386, 409,
   477, 541, 584, 607, 642, 705; III 70,
   302, 318, 350, 398, 467, 469, 481,
   869
priest: I 118, 128–30, 189, 373; II 52,
   77, 101, 376, 788, 803; III 657, 856
right: I 146, 148, 184, 236; II 228, 331,
   661, 754; III 117; 340, 355, 410, 563,
   577, 714
Rufino: I 264–65, 411; III 510
Rule: II 147, 381; III 127, 323, 398, 409,
   445, 575
shoulder: III 57
sin: I 386; II 45, 522, 788
stigmata: I 264, 280, 283, 286–88, 323,
   340, 342, 344, 426, 436, 509–10, 596,
   600–01; II 108, 197, 335–36, 386,
   388, 402–06, 418–19, 473–74, 476,
   490, 514, 632–34, 636, 642, 645–46,
   652, 709–10, 715, 719, 743–44, 770,
   780, 784, 796, 806; III 174, 410, 509,
   513, 560, 804, 826, 866–67, 870–71,
   874, 835
thief: I 455, 466
vengeance: II 270, 283, 421, 657
wash: I 551; II 192, 335, 411, 634, 680,
   711, 727, 751; III 366, 385, 493, 608,
   733
work: I 101, 125, 204, 218, 229, 260,
   457–58, 504, 537, 553, 578, 580,
   586–87; II 46, 50, 93, 147, 208, 215,
   222, 285, 351, 358, 365, 433, 521,
   596, 670, 678, 695, 751, 814; III 40,
   63, 71, 219, 276, 251, 281, 284, 311,
   321, 385, 400, 420, 485, 743, 792,
   803, 815, 852
write: II 126, 280, 403, 618, 701, 801;
   III 165, 226, 355, 642
Handmaid: II 380; III 161, 887
   Christ: I 292; II 379
   God: I 531; II 750
   Mary: II 520
Hanging
   cord: I 460; II 430, 663

cross: I 448; III 382, 512
curls of Christ: III 728
eye: II 672; III 189
God: III 691
Judas: III 34
lamb: I 249, 400
sack: III 57
self: II 445
Happiness. See also Gladness, Joy: I 99, 294, 299, 306, 402, 452, 495, 513, 516; II 141, 149, 322, 344, 651, 662, 775, 780; III 388, 580
   brother: I 276, 415, 472, 501, 551; II 83, 87, 94, 121, 147, 151, 164, 171, 201–02, 348, 357, 362, 387, 414, 475, 593, 643; III 465, 653
   eternal: I 339, 565, 589; III 173, 221, 492, 849
   Francis: I 180, 187–88, 191, 256, 263–64, 278, 331, 335, 370, 372, 417, 443, 455, 458, 470, 491, 520, 537; II 70–71, 75, 78, 87, 108, 150, 171, 201, 203, 211, 217, 227, 243, 251, 255, 285, 353, 357, 361, 384, 413–14, 477, 593, 716, 793; III 465
   God: I 46, 110, 158, 446, 537
   Gregory IX: II 224, 226
   penance: I 41
   Poor Ladies: I 197
   poverty: I 537, 588; II 171, 201–02
Harassment: I 333; III 150, 504
Hare: I 235, 397, 491, 586–87; II 414, 592, 783
Harmony: I 119–20, 220, 223, 266, 275, 412, 542; II 102, 173, 187–88, 279, 330, 332, 567, 640
Harp: I 143, 489; II 169; III 98
Harvest: I 331, 418, 563, 586; II 424, 601, 658; III 81, 263, 480, 599, 770, 778, 857, 885, 891
Hat: I 583; II 72, 119, 175–76, 287, 386; III 270
Hate: I 64, 74, 81, 87, 132, 140, 143, 145, 203, 320, 430, 438, 477, 480, 530, 535; II 136, 140, 178, 187, 215, 287, 305, 343, 351, 363, 425, 438, 443, 510, 588, 756; III 281, 510
   bishop: II 187; III 349
   body: I 41, 48, 79; II 53, 74, 102
   brother: III 397, 425
   podesta: II 187; III 349
Haughty: I 437, 508; II 343, 519, 730; III 81, 203, 885
Hay: I 255–57, 406, 506–07; II 375, 411, 610, 783, 817
Head: I 144–45, 234, 240–41, 271, 282, 293–94, 298, 306, 392, 403, 413, 429–30, 432, 445, 452–53, 535, 541, 552, 583, 606–07; II 45, 48, 52, 61, 101, 126–27, 135, 141, 153, 159, 182, 189, 223, 227, 264, 285, 287, 290, 301, 307, 313, 317,
342, 361, 380, 386–87, 411, 414, 418, 420, 427, 439, 458, 474, 479–80, 515, 524, 527, 556, 561–62, 591, 602, 608, 624, 627–28, 660, 668, 693–94, 702, 741, 746, 748, 761, 793, 798, 802, 810, 815; III 49, 69–70, 151, 274, 334, 351, 422, 480, 497, 581, 611, 635, 645, 799, 816
   angel: III 393
   ashes: II 209, 370; III 258, 707
   Basilica of St. Francis: II 109
   Bernard: III 227, 355–56, 426, 441, 446–47, 572, 577
   birds: III 454
   bishop: III 102
   Christ: I 118, 360; II 404, 655; III 131, 382, 693
   Dominic: III 475, 595
   dragon: I 355, 468
   Elias: I 276; II 474; III 446–47, 577
   Francis: I 253, 504, 581; III 58, 92, 118, 136, 203, 232, 258, 341, 345, 394, 421, 454–55, 469, 476, 596, 707, 728, 852, 857, 874, 878
   general minister: I 63; II 144, 365; III 325
   Giles: III 226, 355
   gold: II 301; III 117–18, 393–94, 486–88, 723, 726
   hand: I 276; II 126, 135, 474; III 117, 131, 134, 226, 244, 336, 355, 410, 426, 446–47, 577, 714
   John Capella: III 693
   Mary: II 257
   Masseo: III 461, 515, 584, 586
   minister: I 63; II 144, 365; III 325
   Peter of Catanio: III 684
   Pope: I 270, 500, 518
   Portiuncula: II 154; III 120, 236, 298, 328
   seraph: I 263, 410, 509; II 108, 402, 473, 632, 709; III 866
   serpent: I 355, 468
   statue: III 486–87, 723, 726
Health: I 58, 99, 122–23, 213, 558–59, 565; III 189, 220, 406, 418, 524, 733
   brother: II 258, 359, 557
   Francis: I 271, 185, 315, 398, 413; II 184, 208, 556, 561, 567, 570, 694, 704; III 169, 339, 579
   healing: I 238–40, 256, 299, 303–04, 306, 324, 403, 405–06, 496; II 258, 274, 404, 407, 410–11, 426, 429–34, 440, 442–46, 454–55, 457–61, 464–66, 540–41, 555, 615, 626–28, 635, 653–54, 657–58, 662–64, 669–70, 674–75, 681, 692, 711–12, 716, 783, 803, 805; III 30, 55, 69–70, 73–74, 86, 91, 313, 406, 418, 624, 669, 862
Hearing: I 189, 274, 284, 308, 383, 407, 429, 438, 442, 487, 537, 548–49, 607; II 87, 96, 132, 139, 141, 198, 270, 304, 315, 330,

421, 430, 468, 622, 654, 678, 719, 724, 757; III 49, 109, 412, 475, 809
brother: I 119, 220, 401; II 54, 92, 96, 106, 127, 161, 213–14, 219, 222, 225, 255, 264, 275, 301, 311, 313, 326, 349, 361, 389, 416, 573, 575, 582, 588, 592, 618, 644, 719, 799; III 167, 218, 256, 281, 329, 369, 406, 461, 528, 546–47, 564, 569, 571, 573, 592, 625, 640, 653, 704, 715, 869
Christ: I 116, 283; II 77, 84, 108, 609, 715; III 847
confession: I 573; II 134, 420, 511, 656, 778
evil: I 76; 90; II 363
Francis: I 215, 228, 236, 240, 242, 246, 261, 344, 374, 381, 393–94, 401, 403, 435, 443, 484, 487, 548, 606–07; II 50, 53, 72, 97, 99, 102, 121, 127, 132, 163, 166, 181, 202–03, 206, 214, 225, 271, 301, 313, 315, 322, 326, 330, 338, 341, 370, 373, 412, 461, 531, 539, 542–45, 548, 567, 569–70, 572, 624–26, 648, 682, 687, 689, 752, 789, 792, 799, 802; III 84, 117, 124, 200, 237, 241, 248, 284, 352–53, 357, 408, 410, 456, 458, 462, 551, 568, 576, 583, 586, 714, 824, 846–47
God: I 152–54, 548; II 44, 191, 271, 373, 510–11, 531, 737; III 128
God's Word: I 79–80; II 129, 191, 264, 379, 412, 511, 517, 624, 689, 719, 759, 792, 810; III 824, 830
heal: I 290, 306–07, 324, 518; II 432, 450–51, 453, 455, 673–74, 716; III 73–74, 449, 580
minister: II 206; III 128, 167, 237, 256, 406, 704
Mass: II 44, 52, 101, 119, 162, 191, 375, 542, 773; III 437
Office: II 91
petition or prayer: I 381, 599; II 44, 330, 420, 539, 548, 567, 730, 748, 758
Heart: I 137, 146, 187–88, 193, 196, 202, 213, 221, 224, 226, 228–29, 244, 249, 255–56, 262, 264–65, 281, 290, 295, 305, 320, 335, 337, 358–59, 373, 381, 389, 409, 432–33, 449, 457, 463, 475, 477, 483, 489, 499, 504–06, 519, 531, 533, 541, 544–46, 548, 550, 556, 571, 579, 587, 598, 604–05; II 50, 54–55, 57–58, 69, 73, 77, 79, 86, 107–08, 145, 168, 177, 179, 215, 246–47, 249, 270, 273–74, 282–84, 288, 303–04, 314, 328, 355, 358, 361, 370–71, 380, 384, 388, 393, 399, 404–06, 408–09, 424, 434, 440, 463, 476, 489, 510, 512, 515, 518, 521–22, 531, 552, 564, 570, 580, 583, 592, 601, 604, 606, 610, 617, 625–26, 629, 632, 659, 664, 668, 689, 691–92, 699, 714, 718–19, 745–46, 751–52, 787, 791–92, 796, 811, 814, 816–17; III 58–59, 154,

157, 162, 198, 203, 369, 388, 393, 474, 499, 529, 542–43, 559, 563, 617, 781, 867, 888
admiration: II 73
adultery: I 73
altar: I 567; II 375
anxiety: I 571
aridity: I 546
arrogant: II 178; III 353, 440, 443
beat: I 443
beg: I 189
bitter: II 690; III 397, 571
broken: I 519; III 178, 521, 606, 633, 657
burn: III 190, 173, 588
caring: I 379
carry: I 42, 49, 85, 135, 265; II 57, 473
charity: II 288
Christ: I 283, 325, 509; II 465, 663, 726; III 55, 381, 418, 501, 770, 855, 875, 878
Christ's passion: I 510, 540; II 108, 249, 401; III 83, 188, 394, 867
Christ's wounds: I 604; II 76
clean: I 46, 80, 88, 105, 120, 134, 223, 252, 322; II 50, 230, 510, 563–65, 695, 738–41; III 153, 233, 342, 397, 401, 408, 720, 793
cold: II 726
compassion: II 374; III 446
compunction: III 95, 621
concern: II 473
contrition: I 262, 409; II 54, 677, 754, 817; III 514, 525, 530, 808
convert: I 480; II 45, 798; III 95, 117, 154–55, 282
cross: I 345, 358, 518; II 383, 535, 650, 686
crushed: I 432
darkness: I 40, 509
death: I 406, 485, 546
depth: III 479, 494, 536, 870
desire: I 80, 88, 152, 202; II 281, 542, 689, 724; III 535, 551, 628, 649
devotion: I 238; II 736; III 513
dictate: I 457
direction: II 214
divided: II 343; III 41
doubt: II 651–52
drowsy: I 71; II 263
drunkenness: I 228
duplicity: I 223
ear: I 116
enlightenment: I 275
ensnare: I 80, 88
enthusiasm: II 108
evil: I 48, 50, 79, 87, 439
expansion: III 724
exultant: II 169; III 457
eye: I 570
faint: II 190
faithful: I 437

fearful: I 205; II 137, 290, 292
fervor: I 254; III 196
field: I 216; II 511
fierce: II 555
filled: II 530, 685
forgive: II 45, 92
freedom: I 333, 337, 381, 514; II 251, 425
full: I 283; II 72, 261, 697
gentle: I 608
glad: I 264, 410, 469; II 642, 726; III 481
glory: I 551
goodness: I 441; II 203; III 252, 369
grace: II 195; III 285
grieve: I 142, 357, 515, 545; II 311, 523; III 399
hard: I 129, 137, 435, 476, 599–600; II 265, 291, 513, 614, 616, 701, 746; III 505, 618
hide: I 389, 605; II 404
Holy Spirit: III 218, 252, 437, 848
human: I 43, 537; III 541
humble: I 347, 542; II 187, 272, 498, 508, 516–17, 519–21, 524, 574, 688, 739, 751, 817; III 384, 424, 730, 818
idle: II 148, 351; III 322
implant: II 530, 685
imprint: II 726, 757
innocent: II 728
instruction: I 461
integrity: III 342
joy: I 154, 205, 214, 263, 275, 279, 324, 416, 452, 464, 514, 537; II 82, 85, 151, 193, 228–29, 329, 341, 386, 476, 658; III 233, 342, 401, 623
languid: I 439
law: I 335, 341, 346, 349
listening: I 116
loving: I 41, 46, 84, 159, 198, 282–84, 443, 536, 542, 685, 726–27; II 46, 49, 55, 57, 107, 250, 759, 762; III 551, 877
lust: II 562
marrow: I 379; II 84, 310, 543, 689
meditation: II 280, 301
meek: III 157, 739
mercy: I 104, 137; II 365
move: I 245, 402, 499; II 106, 186, 192, 303, 531, 581, 795; III 159, 544
mystery: III 686
naked: II 302
open: II 748, 759
passion: I 506; III 175
paternal: III 173
peace: I 220, 320; II 52, 102, 526; III 38, 44
penetration: II 103
pierce: II 317, 320, 370, 676; III 151, 669
piety: III 175, 325

pious: II 564, 589, 592, 599, 697; III 850
plant: I 79, 260, 351; II 722
poison: III 489
pour out: I 118, 163, 351; II 762, 814
prayer: III 181
pure: I 46, 80, 88, 105, 120, 134, 223, 252, 322; II 50, 230, 738–41, 510, 563–65, 695; III 153, 233, 342, 397, 401, 408, 720, 793
purgation: I 433
purpose: I 383; II 72; III 81, 308, 567
raise: III 136
ready: I 143; III 739
reception: I 46, 118
recess: I 224–26, 321, 473; II 534, 578, 686
remembrance: II 155
resolute: I 457; II 35, 42, 69, 90; III 567
restless: I 370
room: I 437
Rule: III 445
sacrifice: III 744
secret: I 251, 390, 479, 600; II 263, 333, 375, 570, 578, 614, 617–18, 700, 728, 800; III 397, 459–60
serious: I 542
sigh: I 432
silence: III 393
sincere: I 262, 290; II 512
softness: I 440, 506; II 702, 616
sorrow: I 154, 190, 248, 264, 285; II 78, 219, 402, 476, 499; III 417, 717
speak: III 99, 585, 605, 625, 847
still: I 436
string: II 373, 596; III 846
sweet: I 358
teacher: I 613
think: III 99, 585, 605, 625, 847
tongue: II 453
touch: I 245, 249
transparency: III 131
turning: I 80, 88
unbelieving: II 405, 655
united: III 528, 637, 639
vice: I 48, 50, 79, 87, 439
vow: I 304, 307; II 451, 453; III 73
whole: III 161, 165, 372, 383–84, 394, 479, 516–17, 529, 531, 589, 613–14, 645, 651, 666, 720, 833, 865; wide I 386
wisdom: II 308; III 518
word: I 79–80, 117, 265, 411; II 50, 474, 536
wounded: I 229; II 76, 404, 655, 758
Heat
    charity: III 176, 655
    cold: III 883
    fever: I 432
    fire: II 190–91, 408–10, 566, 568, 704; III 97, 153, 364–65, 733
    heaven: II 729

iron: III 839, 862
pain: II 404
passion: I 589; II 310, 319, 355, 762
stigmata: II 635, 655, 797
sun: II 464
temptation: III 635
thirst: III 101
vice: I 259; II 562
weather: I 339, 386, 431–32, 472, 503, 505, 510; II 180, 678
youth: I 184; III 833
Heaven: I 45, 49, 65, 75, 85, 103, 114, 117, 119, 127, 131, 134, 137–38, 146, 155, 161, 180, 184, 186, 198, 210, 219–20, 288–89, 294, 330, 333, 342, 433–34, 436–37, 446, 448, 463–65, 467, 475, 479, 504, 506, 538, 544; II 47, 50, 80, 94, 102, 121, 123, 132, 142, 165, 244, 251, 265–67, 270, 278, 280, 283–84, 407, 720, 744–45, 762; III 87, 183, 191, 215, 223, 367, 382, 389, 455, 457, 464, 480, 484, 512, 525, 535, 537, 545, 582, 609, 641, 644, 652, 719, 825
  angel: I 85, 115, 119, 127, 141, 158, 251, 286, 342, 529, 537, 553–54, 569, 588; II 52, 288, 348, 369, 376, 389, 554, 588, 647–48, 650, 721, 724, 726, 764, 780, 805, 811; III 152, 436, 464, 501, 507, 511, 538, 567, 588, 622, 644, 654, 719, 856
  Beatrice: III 882
  birds: I 138; II 130; III 362
  characteristic: II 721–30
  Christ: I 148, 180, 282, 536; II 226, 521–22, 553, 593, 682, 720, 744, 746, 751, 754; III 150, 381, 386, 396, 422, 447, 464, 471, 706, 719–20, 732, 821
  citizen: I 286, 342, 554
  Clare: II 554, 647
  contemplation: I 464, 597; II 100, 142, 258, 278, 283–84, 312, 340, 359, 369, 379, 381, 386, 391, 401, 409, 420, 477, 541, 558, 584, 592, 606, 615, 642, 649, 703, 705; III 200–01, 230, 246, 254, 287, 290, 302, 340, 367, 387, 417, 437, 442, 447, 455, 467, 480, 503, 508, 514, 530, 539, 567, 573, 583, 591, 603, 617, 621, 623, 635, 688, 691, 847, 868
  cross: II 39, 87, 319, 545, 692, 720, 795; III 438, 468
  earth: I 147, 149, 156, 158, 161, 210, 215, 219, 276, 322, 347, 433–34, 438, 446, 450, 465, 475, 534, 536, 553, 565; II 40, 43, 58, 90, 108, 151, 192, 199, 226, 359, 369, 400, 475, 521, 626, 644, 717, 721, 744–45; III 269, 273, 333, 366, 385, 391
  exultation: I 118, 143, 147–49, 156, 270
  fire: III 435
  Francis: I 188, 202, 215, 260, 263, 267, 271, 274, 278, 281, 288, 295, 319,

322–23, 336, 339, 349, 353, 416, 418, 436, 450, 459, 499; II 146, 168, 252, 260, 348, 359, 369, 381, 386, 388–89, 391, 308–09, 312, 318, 322, 331, 340, 400, 402, 409, 412, 420, 473, 477, 491, 553, 584, 606, 615, 624, 626, 630, 642, 644, 648–49, 650, 677, 682; III 157, 242, 254, 287, 302, 396–98, 417, 442, 458, 573, 583, 606, 713, 798, 826, 840, 866, 868, 869–71
  gate: I 474, 544
God I 42, 46–47, 49, 80–81, 88, 109–10, 140–41, 143, 147–48, 154, 156, 158, 163, 276, 282, 347, 450, 534, 553; II 40, 43, 90, 475, 490, 513, 538, 548; III 158, 451, 457, 695
  key: III 423
  kingdom: I 70, 74, 78, 91, 103, 105, 133, 188, 203, 274–75, 319, 465, 529–30, 535–36, 541; II 89, 295, 512, 517–18, 537, 582, 588, 596, 722, 736; III 159, 163, 329, 381–82, 386, 392, 508, 536, 545, 577, 621
  Lady Poverty: I 533, 537; III 162
  light: I 260, 538; II 100, 258, 435, 541, 665; III 635
  Lucifer: III 422
  manna: I 568; III 548
  peace: I 45, 117
  Poor Ladies: I 115
  power: I 56, 141, 333, 534, 536; II 623–24, 629, 631, 700, 707, 718–20
  prayer: I 464, 597; II 100, 142, 258, 278, 283–84, 312, 340, 359, 369, 379, 381, 386, 391, 401, 409, 420, 477, 541, 558, 584, 592, 606, 615, 642, 649, 703, 705; III 200–01, 230, 246, 254, 287, 290, 302, 340, 367, 387, 417, 437, 442, 447, 455, 467, 480, 503, 508, 514, 530, 539, 567, 573, 583, 591, 603, 617, 621, 623, 635, 688, 691, 847, 868
  purgatory: III 715
  Queen: III 637, 811
  revelation: I 263; II 548, 551, 669, 691–92, 711; III 147, 157, 192, 194, 196, 198, 201, 399–400, 408, 416, 422, 682, 692, 809, 835, 841, 849, 858
  reward: I 64, 75, 115, 127, 137, 146, 186, 198, 203, 270, 276, 281, 295, 330, 346, 418, 435, 459, 467, 499, 537, 588; II 50, 58, 86, 121, 168, 244, 266, 275, 328, 381, 416, 435, 475, 477, 521, 544, 550, 573, 608, 622, 645, 721, 752, 796; III 151, 221, 371, 384, 447, 455, 534, 545, 797, 815
  saint: I 85, 115, 119, 127, 141, 158, 251, 286, 342, 529, 537, 553–54, 569, 588; II 52, 288, 348, 369, 376, 389, 554, 588, 647–48, 650, 721, 724, 726, 764, 780, 805, 811; III 152, 436, 464,

501, 507, 511, 538, 567, 588, 622, 644, 654, 719, 856
sign: I 56
third: III 435
throne: II 168, 328, 573, 721, 752, 796; III 99, 152, 304–05, 692, 838, 848
treasure: I 64; II 38, 86
voice: I 538; II 61, 381, 558, 676; III 201, 416, 418, 474, 479, 514, 598, 623, 715
weapon: I 333
wine: I 518
Hebrew
people: II 400, 583
synagogue: I 455
Hedge
biblical: I 184
plant: I 222; II 161, 217; III 239, 264, 810
Heir
Christ: I 449
king: II 255, 548; III 239, 264, 810
kingdom: I 103, 336; II 295–96, 582, 736; III 386, 391, 886, 889
legacy: III 753, 755, 766, 777–78, 803
Hell
another: I 446
citizen: III 383
flame: III 603
mouth: III 603
pain: III 496, 526, 610–11
pit: III 411, 484
prey: III 423
sentence: I 44, 51, 58, 79, 87; II 750, 817–18; III 451, 460, 508, 524, 563, 621
slave: II 452, 677
worthy: III 493, 514, 581, 583, 608, 623
Help: I 159, 283, 285, 299, 306, 405, 446, 456, 546; II 95, 197, 216, 383, 421, 431, 434, 524, 625, 705, 753; III 81, 310, 859, 878, 884
brother: I 67, 92, 269, 532, 586; II 133, 156, 160, 166, 260, 268, 341, 378, 411, 427, 491; III 235, 279, 317, 328, 337, 421, 464, 495, 640, 718
Christ: I 568; II 94, 358; III 124, 153, 200, 254, 418, 532, 650–51, 713–14
cleric: II 52, 102, 341, 534; III 47, 297, 857
Divine: I 304, 475; II 266, 435, 447
Elias: III 630
Francis: I 243, 247–48, 267, 289, 332, 374–75, 394, 412–13, 450, 495, 503, 505, 565, 569, 602; II 37, 83, 95, 132, 152, 163, 184–85, 190–91, 193, 216, 220, 251–52, 299, 306, 314, 382, 424, 426, 428, 432, 435–36, 446, 449–50, 455, 457–58, 463, 465, 491, 616, 657–58, 660, 662, 664–66, 668–69, 671–72, 678–81, 688, 712, 798, 805; III 301, 346–47, 364–65, 402, 418,

421, 459, 464, 522, 554, 568, 638, 711, 850
Frederick: III 553, 630
God: I 98, 140, 144, 148, 152–53, 156, 203, 226, 254, 285, 339, 418, 475, 566, 569; II 74, 80, 123, 185, 203, 207, 213, 438, 540, 698, 718, 738, 744, 754, 814; III 50, 56, 168, 218, 223, 257, 290, 452, 495, 498, 530, 568, 704, 718–19, 741, 800, 843
grace: I 117; II 94, 736
Holy Spirit: III 370
lack: I 142, 303–04, 413; II 421, 424, 431, 433, 435–36, 440, 445, 447, 450, 458, 462–63, 540, 627, 658, 663, 666, 669, 672, 679, 804
Mary: II 465
neighbor: I 283, 306, 383; II 260, 547
Roman Church: III 324
Rule: II 132; III 168, 254, 257, 418, 713–14, 747, 859
spiritual: I 67, 92; II 314
Helper: II 635
bishop: II 80
brother: II 491
Christ: II 358, 547
Francis: I 194–95; II 436, 440, 449, 666, 668, 671
God: I 153, 541
Hen: II 105, 260; III 824
Herald: I 488; II 352
Anthony: II 557
Bonaventure: III 32
Elias: III 381
Francis: I 194, 289, 334, 376, 453, 478; II 109, 382, 437, 526, 539, 553, 594, 614, 623, 626, 628–29, 645, 687, 691, 717, 782, 792; III 32, 51, 80, 423
Order: I 469
Sylvester: II 574
Heresy
accusation: II 438, 481, 667
Anthony: III 521
development: I 480; II 515; III 147, 425
Ebionites: III 689
excommunication: I 564
overcome: I 354; II 515; III 879
renunciation: II 667
Hermit
Anthony: II 728
habit: I 379; II 84, 86, 782; III 66
soul: II 215; III 245, 309
Hermitage: I 470–71, 579; II 158, 194, 182–83, 209, 215, 222, 224–25, 278, 295, 355, 361–62, 409, 413, 444, 584; III 238, 251, 261, 309, 311–12, 707, 835, 861
body: III 245, 309
Fonte Colombo: II 171, 189, 196–97, 226, 276, 410–11, 416, 583, 634, 711; III 232, 359, 363, 416

Greccio: II 174–75, 177, 227, 287, 289, 355, 412, 592, 594, 619, 793; III 345
La Verna: I 238, 262–63, 404, 409–10; II 226, 402, 473, 593; III 866
Monte Casale: II 221
Poggio Bustone: II 333
Rieti: II 410, 634, 711; III 101
Rocca di Brizio: II 220
Rule for: I 61–62
Saint Francis: II 196
San Sepolcro: III 250
Sant'Eleuterio: II 218; III 268
Sant'Urbano: I 236, 398; II 410, 567, 704, 706, 783, 799; III 862
Sarteano: II 286, 324, 562
Spain: III 49
Holiness. See also Sanctity: I 542, 544, 547; II 173, 364, 400, 514, 547, 610; III 50, 115, 136, 185, 224, 296, 394, 404, 407, 489–91, 701, 726
Anthony: II 448, 671, 811; III 519, 632
apostle: I 554
brother: I 219; II 53, 104, 144, 156–57, 204, 208, 287, 341, 347, 362, 410, 448, 550, 555–56, 636, 671, 752, 811; III 31, 36, 121, 169, 237, 255, 295, 300, 320, 351, 380, 389, 401–02, 435–36, 468, 510, 517, 526, 537–38, 546, 548, 557, 566–67, 571, 579, 583, 592, 596, 601, 604–06, 615, 617, 625, 629, 633, 636, 641, 643–46, 649, 689, 694, 697, 706, 792, 799
Clare: I 285; III 516, 624
description: II 511, 748–49, 759
devotion: I 262
false: II 264–65, 267–68, 364, 618; III 408
Francis: I 203, 238, 240–41, 260, 269; II 123–24, 141, 149, 153, 171, 174, 178, 188, 222–24, 263, 276, 315, 338–39, 341, 344, 392, 417, 514–15, 528, 543, 563, 569–70, 572, 629, 640, 645, 647–48, 717, 730–31, 751–53, 787–88; III 66, 222–23, 251, 290–91, 359, 401, 438, 471, 482, 569, 594, 603, 669, 680, 848, 853–54, 875
Lady Jacoba: II 417
miracle: I 243
Pope: I 213; II 67–68, 106; III 809
Portiuncula: II 156; III 122, 299
religion: I 75, 90
Rule: I 582, 592; II 550
sign: I 294; II 265
spirit: I 75, 90, 266
virtue: II 729
Holocaust
biblical: I 567; II 272
Francis: II 310, 599; III 174
Rule: I 572
Home: I 239–40, 256, 299, 301, 304, 307, 374–75, 403, 458; II 39, 43, 80, 85, 87, 172–73, 177, 193, 272–73, 279, 300, 307,

316, 319, 351, 357, 410, 413, 421, 428, 432, 436–37, 441, 445, 447–49, 452–53, 459–61, 464, 480, 616, 627, 657, 662, 666–67, 671–73, 678–79, 702, 793, 804; III 51, 61, 70–74, 101, 134, 282, 445, 551, 579, 584, 793, 870
ancestral: I 493, 517
animal: I 234; III 520, 632, 860
Bernard: III 436, 444
body: III 181
brother: I 533; II 200, 202, 278, 284; III 92, 96, 216, 276, 454, 642
church: III 841
destruction: II 481, 518
evil: I 80
Francis: I 188, 192, 334, 435, 445, 468, 492; II 36, 72–73, 75, 79, 246, 289, 309, 533, 537, 561, 579, 645, 687
God: I 41, 48, 80, 88; III 841
heaven: I 449; II 533, 561, 645; III 184
hospitality: II 43–44, 91, 420, 448, 614–15, 672
Orlando: III 453
peace: I 474; II 43, 90; III 89
penance: III 91
Sylvester: III 438, 569
wisdom: II 322
world: I 446
Homeland: I 210, 445, 603; II 286, 419, 578; III 59
angel: III 574
Francis: III 79, 84
heaven: I 278, 336, 344, 416, 535, 566; II 250, 254, 310, 403; III 496, 501, 535
pilgrim: III 818
Honesty
companion: III 326
confession: II 524
endowment: II 145, 366
example: III 449
figurative: I 479
life: I 243; II 407
other: I 265
pinnacle: I 498
request: I 475, 495
work: I 125, 218
Honey
bees: I 250, 400 II 354, 798
food: II 122, 171, 276, 297, 417; III 222, 359–60
Francis: III 877
goodness: I 449
Jesus' name: I 322; II 299, 374, 609
love: III 190, 534
manna: I 520
milk: I 539
poison: II 321
voice: I 204, 225, 256, 295, 322, 338, 406, 519, 537; II 51, 148, 342, 391, 477; III 34, 289, 479, 519, 689

word: I 204, 225, 256, 295, 322, 338, 406, 519, 537; II 51, 148, 342, 391, 477; III 34, 289, 479, 519, 689
Honeycomb
  contemplation: II 356, 414, 763
  Jesus' name: II 374
Honor: I 216, 231, 254–55, 329, 429, 449, 473, 501, 504; II 164, 370, 417, 448, 491, 553, 573, 576, 746, 750, 791; III 37, 99, 147, 585, 791
  ancestor: II 263
  apostle: II 73
  archangel: II 226, 374, 593, 631, 709; III 454
  Bernard: III 227, 355, 426, 445
  brother: I 69, 91, 93, 118, 131, 335, 473; II 151, 296–97, 345, 363, 366, 448, 553, 571, 576, 772, 798, 806; III 44, 269, 538, 770
  Christ: I 49, 57, 59, 70, 92, 94, 117–18, 125, 307, 506, 554; II 101, 123, 201, 250, 609; III 89, 174, 180, 382–84, 576, 665
  church: I 295; II 339, 477; III 67, 74, 788
  Clare: III 91
  cross: II 402, 651
  Damian: I 189, 373; II 36
  false: I 247, 273, 433, 441, 486, 544, 547; II 70, 145, 209, 292, 341, 343, 365–66, 524, 575, 739; III 257, 576, 707
  Francis: I 180, 210, 228, 231, 236, 257, 261, 265, 281, 284, 288–89, 292, 325, 327, 331, 333, 335, 349, 395, 407, 413, 416, 442, 448, 478, 500, 504, 506–07, 513, 518–19; II 70, 95, 109, 123–24, 217, 245–47, 252, 263, 295, 339, 410, 422, 425, 429, 440, 442, 446, 448, 478, 480, 491, 521, 531, 570, 573, 581, 604, 636, 648, 656, 668, 670, 673, 676–78, 694, 698, 733, 746, 783, 788, 802; III 50, 67, 74, 184, 223, 247, 308, 335, 361, 460, 474, 584–85, 627, 668, 846
  general minister: II 127, 145, 365–66; III 270, 326
  God: I 76, 78, 80, 85, 88, 90, 113, 118, 138, 141, 147, 149, 161–62, 236, 261, 275, 296, 308, 339, 420; II 34, 124–25, 164, 177, 200, 226, 270, 296, 520, 582, 594, 649–50, 717, 719, 724, 737, 750, 755, 759, 761, 788; III 103, 186, 224, 291, 302, 367, 395, 459, 494, 527, 583, 608, 633, 665, 730, 781, 811
  Gregory IX: I 429; II 572
  Honorius III: I 498
  Lady Poverty: I 536
  Mary: I 118, 378; II 124, 258, 374, 598, 670; III 372

  Michael Archangel: II 226, 374, 593, 631, 709; III 454
  parent: II 510
  Portiuncula: I 265, 415; II 475; III 330
  prelate: I 125, 136, 238, 321, 544; II 52, 101, 160, 200, 247, 296, 344, 376, 551, 557, 582; III 216, 239, 263, 385
  priest: I 125, 136, 238, 321, 544; II 52, 101, 160, 200, 247, 296, 344, 376, 551, 557, 582; III 216, 239, 263, 385
  soul: II 518
  synagogue: III 423
  theologian: I 125, 321; II 207, 352; III 168, 705
  vain: I 247, 273, 433, 441, 486, 544, 547; II 70, 145, 209, 292, 341, 343, 365–66, 524, 575, 739; III 257, 576, 707
Hood. See also Capuche, Habit, Tunic
  burn: II 346, 576
  Francis: II 311, 386, 609, 793
  stigmata: II 636
  tunic: I 64–65, 101, 583, 598; II 267, 386
Hope: I 476–77; II 354, 439; III 178, 539, 766, 780, 795, 797
  Christ: I 272, 553; II 96, 98, 131, 525, 640, 714; III 123, 266, 384, 397, 470, 482, 502, 709
  Francis: I 273, 332, 455; II 400, 530, 640, 684, 696, 714, 726, 814; III 469, 611
  God: I 109–10, 142–43, 147, 152, 472; II 78, 439; III 568, 611, 628, 655, 715, 800
  holiness: I 273
  lack: I 299, 303–05, 432, 453, 494, 587; II 118, 346, 418, 423, 426, 428–32, 438, 447, 449, 457–58, 466–67, 482, 537, 653, 662, 677–78, 681, 819
  mercy: I 154, 268, 369, 551
  salvation: II 146, 380; III 323, 541, 643, 715
  stigmata: I 637
  Trinity: I 86
  virtue: I 40, 355, 441, 449, 542
Horror
  building: III 184
  everlasting: I 587
  leper: II 248, 533; III 83
  martyrdom: I 280
  prison: I 447
  softness: II 561
Horse: II 52, 101, 173, 178–79, 271, 308, 313, 417, 608
  forbidden: I 73; III 284
  Francis: I 188–89, 239, 373, 404–05, 441, 482; II 36, 55, 74, 77, 104, 195, 229, 248–49, 311, 444, 533, 536, 552, 628; III 82, 233, 284, 341, 841
  Lord of Ostia: III 709
  stigmata: II 746

Horseback: II 52, 101, 173; III 55, 132, 352, 772
  brother: I 73, 102
  Francis: I 238; II 120, 189, 228, 298, 311, 444, 628; III 220
Hospice. See also Hospital
  leper: II 74
  reception: II 215; III 71
  staff: I 299; II 459
  temptation: II 327–28
  woman: I 579
Hospital. See also Hospice: III 580
  Bovara: II 167
  Città di Castello: II 462
  leper: II 166–67, 291; III 243, 303–04, 607
  Portiuncula: II 120, 555, 692; III 220, 371, 472
Hospitality
  Arezzo: II 318, 574
  Bevagna: II 450
  brother: I 94, 241, 584; II 43–44, 103, 425, 448–49, 659, 672–73; III 39
  Francis: I 227; II 289, 318, 450, 455, 574, 615, 627, 659, 807; III 50, 407, 793, 852
  monk: II 807
  people: I 584; II 103
  reception: I 227, 241
  recompense: II 615
  Rome: II 659
  San Gemini: II 455, 627
  stranger: II 289
  Zancato: II 448–49, 672–73
Hours, Liturgy of. See also Office, Divine: I 101, 149, 161, 224; II 54, 551; III 522
  birds: II 592–93; 799
  book: II 102, 551
  celebration: II 102, 104, 154, 158, 228–29, 311, 592–93, 799; III 119, 261, 297
  church: II 154
  Clare: III 515
  Francis: II 228–29, 311, 592, 609; III 232–33, 341
  matins: I 61; II 562; III 696
  Our Father: I 66
  recitation: II 102, 104, 154, 158, 228–29, 311, 592–93, 799; III 119, 261, 297
House. See also Abode, Dwelling: I 36, 68, 70, 93, 239–41, 251, 437, 442, 495, 501, 588, 594; II 59, 71, 83, 91, 172, 198, 201, 407, 420, 423, 427, 431, 510, 584, 615, 628, 658, 661, 732, 752; III 94, 159, 178, 216, 488, 500, 551–52, 576, 578, 598, 626–28, 800, 826
  appropriation: I 103, 573, 583; II 777; III 386, 744, 749, 826
  arms: I 186, 371
  beam: I 221, 386
  Bernard: II 85

birds: II 279, 415, 644; III 229, 362
bishop: I 449; II 200, 224, 296; III 165, 216, 259, 274, 284, 286
brother: I 474; II 43–44, 56, 91–92, 154, 161, 175–76, 198, 212–13, 225, 249, 279, 306, 578; III 259–61, 264, 270, 312, 329, 448, 826, 831, 854
canon: II 274, 616, 765; III 862
church: I 479; II 76
Clare: III 467
commune: II 154, 285–86; III 260
departure: I 534, 567
destruction: II 76, 249, 401, 536, 644; III 84
devil: II 328
door: I 225, 390
dream: I 186
enclosure: I 319
fiery chariot: I 224, 389; II 552, 743
foundation: I 529
Francis: I 185–86, 190, 195, 218, 242, 319, 374, 403–04, 408, 432, 435, 442, 452, 568; II 83, 129, 152, 155, 157, 159, 167–70, 183, 185, 194–98, 210, 217, 249, 252, 281, 285, 287, 295, 298, 415, 456, 582, 644; III 117, 170, 230, 258–62, 270, 272–73, 284, 306, 312, 347, 352, 463, 467, 491, 606, 708, 854
God: I 567; II 58, 392
heaven: II 378; III 579
king: I 65, 587; II 142, 323; III 334
legacy: III 754–55
leper: I 456; II 74, 123, 534; III 223, 290
light: I 569
Marco: II 306
mice: II 185; III 347
peace: I 73, 102, 461
Pietro Bernardone: II 78–79, 81; III 695
pillar: I 272
pit: I 190
poverty: I 227, 392, 529, 551, 578; II 123, 136, 154, 157, 159–61, 212, 258, 285–87; III 45, 165, 163–64, 172, 238, 259–62, 264, 297, 407, 463, 587
rebuilding: I 196, 442; II 76, 249, 378, 401, 536, 686; III 84
religion: II 123; III 33, 117, 223, 298, 712
Rivo Torto: I 220–21
use: I 573; II 287, 777; III 749; 386–87
vineyard: II 170
vision: I 225, 371, 390
wolf: III 603
Household: I 239, 452; II 164, 443, 448, 460, 465, 480, 654, 665, 672
  brother: I 246; II 104, 361
  church: II 358
  destruction: II 510–518
  God: I 286, 564; II 733, 747

Hovel. See also Hut
    Rivo Torto: I 386, 474
Humanity: II 817
    bile: II 364
    creation: II 724
    downfall: II 751
    enlightenment: I 351
    flesh: I 46
    gentleness: II 736
    Jesus: I 128, 201, 351; II 534, 744, 746, 813
    poverty: I 553
    understanding: I 401
Humiliation
    presence: II 522
    proud: II 755
Humility: I 209, 229, 293, 597, 601; II 570; III 40, 53, 57, 150, 220, 223, 311, 325, 328, 350, 560, 647, 650
    apostle: III 464, 566, 719
    building: III 262, 264
    Christ: I 70, 91, 118, 248; II 180–81, 540, 569, 572, 688, 800, 815; III 153, 223, 271, 274, 290, 339, 405, 423
    church: I 582
    Clare: I 197
    clothing: I 586; III 385
    corpse: II 345, 571
    crib: I 255; III 381
    cross: II 726
    demon: II 575
    Dominic: II 148–49, 342, 344; III 289
    Eucharist: I 78, 118; III 543, 657
    express: I 106, 271, 584; II 522, 619; III 514–15, 849
    foundation: I 217, 225; II 46, 124, 569, 695–96, 732, 748–49
    Francis: I 229, 273, 381, 404; II 37, 125, 142, 168, 519–20, 572–3, 626, 725–26, 732, 739, 748–49, 796–97, 800–01, 815; III 44–45, 47, 98, 120, 126, 152, 276, 298–99, 301, 305, 307–08, 314–15, 452, 458–59, 476, 500, 512, 570–71, 583–84, 592, 608, 691, 730, 815, 818, 834, 838, 848, 886
    fruit: II 519–21
    God: I 109, 114, 118, 262, 368; II 725, 728, 732; III 876
    grace: I 292
    Incarnation: I 254; III 543, 657, 855
    Job: II 749
    learn: III 313, 319
    leper: I 195; II 74, 123, 534, 539, 675, 688, 719, 732; III 290
    Mary: II 257
    Moses: III 424
    Order: I 217, 321, 594, 602; II 204, 572, 725; III 601, 615, 702, 727, 740, 781, 818
    papal teaching: I 572; III 740, 781, 826
    path: II 522–24

patience: I 48, 76, 90, 105, 133, 135–36, 171, 218; II 42, 90
persistence: II 574; III 292
Poor Ladies: I 198, 458
Portiuncula: II 155, 257
poverty: I 70, 91, 100, 103, 106, 164, 255, 572, 582, 586, 601; II 37, 123–24, 126, 159, 161, 176, 204, 212, 257, 260, 393, 534, 578, 645, 688, 696, 756–57, 759, 772; III 324, 361, 383–84, 386, 389, 394–97, 400, 405, 408, 413, 425, 601, 702, 740, 777, 781, 815
prayer: I 244; II 343, 522, 524
prelate: II 188, 571–72; III 293–94
school: I 213
service: I 103, 114; III 368
simplicity: I 255, 587, II 728; III 710
strength: III 133
understand: III 38, 136, 276, 287, 320
virtue: I 47, 133, 135–36, 165, 440; II 44, 103, 800; III 321, 334, 406, 462, 501, 585–86, 588, 615, 622–23
Word: I 51, 262
Humor: II 298
Humors: II 127; III 227
Hunger
    alms: II 297–98, 583
    cause: II 283
    contemplation: II 277; III 503, 514
    death: II 50, 149, 216, 222, 331–32, 354, 259, 548; III 250, 278, 310–11, 512
    discipleship: I 131
    distress: I 454; II 565
    emaciation: I 510
    facing: II 512
    hell: III 524
    mortification: I 567
    prevention: I 472, 483
    sterility: I 547
    suffer: I 585; II 45, 92, 214, 225; III 231, 246, 278, 310–12, 450, 524, 602, 715
    thought: II 374
    wolf: III 482–83
Hunter: I 492
Husband: I 241, 550, 588; II 43–44, 91, 425, 436, 440, 447, 449, 465, 671; III 498, 612, 884
    abusive: II 172–73, 272, 441, 457, 464, 616; III 95
    brother: II 58
    continence: I 100; II 665, 701, 793
    Francis: II 284
    Pietro Bernardone: I 192, 374, 447; II 79, 537
Hut. See also Hovel
    angel: III 498–99
    ascent: I 220
    lake: III 579
    La Verna: III 454

Portiuncula: II 87, 129–30, 157
Rivo Torto: I 220–21; II 99–100, 551, 691; III 38
San Rufino: II 551
temptation: III 810
Hymn
   angel: III 481, 869
   brother: II 156, 568, 707; III 122, 237, 300
   canonization: I 296
   death: I 259, 284, 324, 516; II 129, 476, 647; III 229, 357, 869, 871
   Francis: I 113, 328, 331, 338, 342, 349; II 610; III 698
   Gregory IX: III 698
   Portiuncula: III 331
   Raynerius: III 698
   stigmata: II 636
   Thomas: III 698
Hypocrisy
   accuse: II 333
   avoid: II 181–83
   hunter: I 437
   infection: II 282
   teaching: II 332–33; III 118, 382, 394, 488, 725

I

Ice
   element: I 454–55; III 524
   exposure: I 219, 221, 321, 386; III 90, 853
   suffering: I 166
Ideal: III 100, 744
Idealists: II 13
Idleness
   accusation: I 191
   avoidance 69, 102, 125;: II 46, 93, 213, 351, 564; III 51, 264, 322, 329, 385, 747, 757, 793
   cesspool: II 564
   denunciation: II 327, 350–51
   enemy: I 69, 102; II 46, 93
   numbness: II 119, 349; III 723
Ignominy: I 442
Illiterate: III 308, 325, 800
   counsel: I 105; III 705
   Order: II 371
Illness. See also Infirmity, Sickness
   Bernard: III 356
   brother: II 293, 359; III 288
   Clare: III 515
   consolation: II 202
   cure: I 241, 236, 300, 304, 324, 402–03; II 404, 410, 434, 446, 455, 459, 467, 479, 654–55, 662–64, 678, 692; III 150, 536, 607, 630, 653, 793, 862
   dropsy: II 203; III 370
   eye: I 412; II 192, 410, 562, 565, 678, 695; III 282

Francis: I 184, 230, 266, 274–75, 290, 319, 323, 370, 392, 412–14, 433; II 119, 120–21, 123, 127, 135, 138, 146, 161–62, 169, 180–88, 204, 211, 281, 297, 333, 356, 367, 382, 384, 386, 474, 532, 567, 589, 594, 601, 628, 636, 641–42, 646, 685, 702, 791; III 46, 59, 61, 217, 305–07, 317, 328, 335, 337, 341, 350, 360, 369–70, 471–72, 493, 598–99, 608, 669, 711, 831, 833, 868
   Gedeone: I 197; II 274, 615
   head: II 562
   liver: I 274; II 228
   poor: II 192, 220–21, 303
   Ruggero: II 404, 654–55
   shoe: II 210; III 258, 708
   spleen: II 183, 228, 332
   stomach: I 274; II 183, 228, 332
Illumination: II 607, 699; III 181, 532, 541, 841, 863
Illusion
   devil: II 264, 793; III 243
   ensnarement: II 406
   fear: II 464
   pious: II 797
   vision: I 477; II 430; III 56
Image
   Christ: I 131, 288, 356, 359, 518, 553; II 249, 401, 548, 634, 710, 792, 816; III 180, 669, 815, 867
   Creator: II 599, 751, 812–13, 818
   cross: II 401, 620, 650; III 792, 838
   Crucified: II 76–77, 249–50, 401, 536, 651, 686; III 59–60, 841
   Elijah: III 815
   Francis: I 504–06; II 404–06, 446, 552, 652, 654, 692, 797; III 74, 560
   God: I 82; II 751, 812–13, 818; III 483, 602, 679
   Matthew: III 690
   Order: III 62
   perfection: II 263
   piety: III 325
   reflection: II 517, 727
   seraph: I 263
   stigmata: II 405–06, 652, 710
   wax: I 299, 303, 307; II 436, 453, 459; III 69, 73
   woman: II 563, 719
   wound: I 340, 518
Imagination
   absurdity: II 781; III 644
   bold: II 406
   drive: II 406
Imitation
   act: I 182, 204, 543; II 149, 207
   apostle: I 582
   brother: I 585
   Christ: I 358, 530, 586; II 386, 510, 515, 613, 687, 732–33, 756, 814; III 147, 335–36, 392, 397, 423, 831

church: I 580
evil: I 182–83, 538
Francis: I 330, 346, 461; II 164, 308,
  320, 349, 365, 512, 527–28, 570, 748,
  795; III 744
general minister: II 144
John: II 164, 369
Lady Poverty: I 543, 549; II 207
saint: I 549
Impediment: I 97; II 773
Imperfection
  religion: III 327, 717
  status: III 151
Impiety
  detractor: II 588
  punishment: II 591
  Rule: II 291
Impression: III 774, 875
Imprisonment
  freedom: II 665
  Perugia: I 243
Impulse
  blessed: I 188; II 532, 700
  carnal: II 102; III 634
  divine: II 498; III 380, 541
  evil: I 50, 386, 442; II 333, 421
  imaginary: II 675
Incarnation
  Christ: II 757; III 541, 563
  devotion: II 758; III 839
  herald: III 381
  humility: I 254; III 855
  reason: I 488
  year: I 258, 325, 418, 523; II 34, 107,
    390, 478, 647–48; III 66, 816, 823
Incense
  altar: II 760
  Christmas: I 506
  Francis's death: II 123; III 223, 361
  temple: II 599; III 174
Incredulity
  Francis: II 804; III 425
Indigence
  brother: II 579
  Francis: II 524
  other: III 850
  Poor Ladies: I 603
Indiscretion: III 194
Indulgence
  attitude: II 145, 366
  brother: I 601
  discipline: III 326, 407
  fifth age: III 147, 158
  Gregory IX: III 698, 809
  meat: I 478
  pilgrim: III 520
  Portiuncula: III 693, 806–11
Infant. See also Baby
  Bethlehem: I 255
  vision: II 440, 669
Infidel. See also Non–believer: I 231b

conversion: I 563; III 449, 816
  Francis: I 322; II 814; III 826
Infirmity. See also Illness, Sickness
  cure: I 304; II 432, 445; III 55
  emperor: III 56
  endure: II 114, 187
  Francis: I 404; II 184, 202, 803; III 217,
    307, 341, 369, 479
  patience: I 105; III 349, 368
Inhabitant
  Arezzo: II 444
  Assisi: II 418; III 810
  Bologna: II 808
  Citta' della Pieve: I 239, 405
  Greccio: II 177; III 104
  heaven: I 554; II 389
  La Verna: II 635, 711
  Montefeltro: III 452
Inheritance: I 555; II 255; III 55, 426, 778
  Israel: I 544; II 753
  John: II 163–64; III 241, 301
  poverty: II 151, 715; III 46, 123, 269,
    290, 820
  promise: I 533; II 123, 295, 384, 733;
    III 123, 183, 223, 269, 290, 821
  renunciation: I 193, 534, 597
Injustice: II 794
Innocence: I 183, 272, 368–69; II 321, 333,
  363–64, 407, 436–39, 443, 588, 590–91,
  666–68
  Adam: I 538–39
  brother: I 469; III 400, 424, 474, 545
  Eve: III 423
  Francis: I 228, 280, 283; II 260, 332,
    355, 358, 600, 646, 697, 740; III 153,
    185, 380, 400, 402, 511–13, 870
  heart: II 728
  life: I 223, 252
  primeval: I 538–39; II 409, 436, 679,
    724; III 423
  state: II 586, 697
Innovation
  brother: III 415
Insanity: I 291
  demoniac: I 302, 404; II 454
  Francis: I 191, 374, 442; II 70, 537
  possessed: I 302, 404; II 454
Insignia
  cross: II 532; III 655
  Francis: II 791
  stigmata: III 666, 669
Inspiration
  Divine: I 64, 74, 106, 216, 335, 372, 375,
    379, 565, 567; II 99–100, 345, 432,
    509, 750, 759; III 119, 175, 293, 585
  Francis: I 307, 388; II 508, 516, 600
  preach: II 737
  spirit: I 212; II 96, 123, 199, 222, 310,
    555, 606, 692, 793; III 477, 510
Instigation
  devil: I 73, 98, 103, 573; II 778; III 480,
    600

Instigator: I 548
Instinct
    base: II 138, 293; III 267
    maternal: I 192
Insult
    brother: II 43, 90, 143, 217, 554, 602,
        656, 687; III 575
    Francis: I 374–76, 395, 478; II 37, 217,
        537, 569–70; III 179, 247, 308, 440,
        567, 591
    God: I 117, 145, 401, 536
    Rule: I 94
    saint: II 452
    Saracen: I 231, 395; II 602
    virtue: I 70, 90, 92, 94, 219, 228, 231,
        248, 374–376, 401, 438, 478, 487,
        548; II 43, 145, 217, 365, 452, 554,
        677, 741
Integrity
    desire: II 723; III 342
    feeling: I 198
    fifth age: III 147
    flesh: III 48
    life: I 67, 242, 645; III 401, 486, 724
    modesty: I 272
    moral: I 597; II 810; III 343
    obedience: III 158
    offering: I 572
    Rule: III 752
Intelligence
    Bernard: III 567
    Francis: III 855
    other: I 588, 810
    Ranieri: I 295
    uncreated: III 421
Intention
    agent: II 776; III 765
    brother: I 218, 223, 282–83, 387, 389,
        572; II 96, 99, 368; III 55, 58, 178,
        451, 538, 545, 568, 641, 644, 742–43,
        770, 801
    Francis: I 117, 159, 187, 192, 253–54,
        282, 371, 450, 457, 529, 537; II 67, 79,
        204, 536, 686; III 81, 93, 115, 123,
        165–66, 195, 214, 255, 262, 335, 362,
        380, 386, 396, 401, 409–11, 416, 420,
        426, 697, 701–02, 705, 709, 713–14,
        741, 743, 756–57, 771, 842, 855
    God: II 536, 686; III 195
    miracle: II 536, 686
Intercession
    apostle: II 540
    brother: I 762
    Francis: I 226, 569; II 109, 430, 667,
        716, 805; III 516, 626
    Mary: I 159
    saint: I 475
Intermediary: I 64, 126; II 776; III 386, 420,
    753, 775, 829
Interpretation: I 131–32, 436, 570; II 35,
    240, 301; III 58, 742
    Job: II 749

Rule: I 575; II 206; III 179, 742, 754,
    760, 762–63, 770
    vision: I 186, 509; II 260, 301, 548
Interruption: II 258, 597; III 852
Intervention
    Divine: I 394; III 398
Intimacy
    friend: I 187, 226, 265; II 239, 277
    God: I 261; III 175–76
Investigation
    brother: III 762, 777, 793
    Francis: III 806
    stigmata: II 780
Invitation: I 228, 251, 583; II 43, 47, 171,
    176, 192, 217, 276, 416, 543; III 39, 79,
    247, 308, 359, 366, 752
Invocation: III 72, 400
Irreverence: II 591; III 425
Itch
    ear: II 258
    eyelid: I 510

J

Jail
    brother: I 219
    liberation: II 436–38, 666–67
Jealously
    accusation: II 343
    brother: II 512; III 740
    prelate: II 133, 341; III 47, 297, 847
Jester
    Francis: I 452
Jewel
    cardinal: I 295, 499
    dream: I 435
    heaven: I 520
    poverty: I 531
    stigmata: I 286, 510
    word: I 537
Jeweler
    God: I 294
Jewish: I 204; II 256
Jews: I 225, 390, 447, 599–600; II 422, 481,
    557, 657, 700, 720, 757, 783; III 92, 158,
    382, 851
Joke
    brother: III 476
    children: III 575
    Francis: I 183, 370
    friend: II 75
    knight: II 198
    truth: II 265, 614
Joy. See also Gladness, Happiness
    abuse: II 83
    angel: III 530, 804
    Augustine: II 794
    beg: II 150–51, 199, 202, 297; III 214,
        269, 272
    Bernard: III 438, 443–44, 446–47, 569,
        574–76

birds: II 355, 357, 592–94, 644, 810
birth: I 239, 405
bishop: II 49, 80, 95
blessed: III 500, 649
brother: I 380; II 40, 53, 90, 93, 102,
    122, 195, 298, 331, 448, 473, 476–77,
    572, 646, 673; III 38, 222, 228, 241,
    250, 341–43, 348, 361, 395–96, 401,
    407, 413, 463, 465, 502, 515, 523,
    536, 543, 551, 589, 597, 613, 619,
    623, 639, 641–43, 645, 653–54, 691
canonization: I 293–95
cardinal: II 55, 104, 106
Christ: I 251, 401–02; II 142, 374,
    609–10, 746; III 384, 388, 392, 651
Conrad: III 523
contemplation: III 193
creation: I 433; II 218
crib: I 507
cricket: II 357
cross: I 264, 410, 553
day: I 255, 551
death: II 107, 121, 203–04, 388, 714
demon: II 318, 574
diminish: I 274, 514, 546
Elias: II 490
express: I 69, 79, 81, 91, 96, 135, 151,
    156, 193–94, 202, 204–07, 209, 212,
    217, 245, 262, 275, 291–92, 299, 306,
    324, 343, 372–73, 376, 379, 384, 447,
    464, 484, 489, 501, 537, 551, 553,
    588; II 39–40, III 38, 69, 280, 282,
    340, 550, 826
false: II 332–34
fish: III 521, 633
Francis: I 234, 240, 245, 271, 279–81,
    286, 331, 381, 389–90, 396–97, 399,
    403, 413, 514; II 40, 42, 70–71,
    75–76, 80–81, 85, 107, 139, 164, 177,
    191–93, 200, 218, 222, 246, 249, 277,
    304, 329–30, 361, 402, 408, 533, 537,
    539, 632, 663, 668–69, 686, 690, 695,
    709, 756; III 43, 67, 90, 217–21, 233,
    242, 247, 268, 276, 282, 285, 302,
    340, 346, 358, 364, 369–71, 426, 437,
    446, 454, 458, 472, 478, 485, 577–78,
    587, 593, 598–99, 668, 714–15, 730,
    797, 821, 836, 841, 843, 846, 866
fulfill: I 188, 193
future: I 285, 355, 357, 463, 475, 506,
    554
Giles: III 447, 577
giving: III 272
God: I 109–10, 382
good: I 289
Gospel: II 38, 84
Greccio: I 255–57
heal: I 672; II 427–28, 430, 439,
    445–46, 449, 459, 461
heart: I 214, 416, 537; III 232
hope: I 542
hospitality: II 198; III 272

Hugolino: II 104; III 216, 274
indescribable: I 205, 250, 379; II 84,
    542
infusion: I 390
king: II 97
king's son: II 255; III 720
monk: III 681
mother: II 423–24, 440–41, 443–44,
    461; III 696
newness: I 255, 288, 260
paradise: I 434; III 524
patience: I 220; II 741
peace: I 292
people: I 255, 416; II 40, 43, 45, 230,
    476–77, 646, 654, 658, 711; III 445,
    521, 615, 633, 870–71
perfection: II 764; III 233, 449–50,
    579–81
Pope: II 785
poverty: I 137, 214, 384; II 294, 307,
    386, 580, 722, 736
prayer: I 374, 380; II 229–30, 393
promise: II 384
reject: II 341
Rule: III 117, 714
salvation: I 225, 330; III 49, 343, 531,
    536
seraph: I 410; II 733
share: I 249, 516
solace: I 390, 406
song: I 263, 323, 353, 410, 416
spirit: II 87, 535, 545, 567, 626, 671; III
    39, 548, 552, 629
spiritual: II 40, 45, 186, 229, 329–32,
    557, 687
suffer: II 82, 92, 119, 169, 202, 228,
    355, 512, 754
Sultan: III 491–92, 607
true: I 166–67
unity: I 542
wonderment: I 330
Judge: II 441, 587, 607, 678, 815; III 44, 53,
    445, 576, 804
Judgment: I 147–48, 356, 400, 410, 430,
    433, 438, 441, 460, 487, 540, 574, 588; II
    67, 81, 90, 185, 336, 348, 352, 364, 367,
    517, 618, 622, 753
    Alessandro: II 451, 678
    announcement: II 37
    apostle: I 540
    Babylon: III 151
    church: I 569; II 352
    clergy: I 136; II 341
    day: I 44, 53, 55, 59, 67, 95; 143, 340,
        352, 564, 587, 719–20, 752; III 125,
        287, 324, 549
    Dominic: III 477
    error: I 184
    Francis: I 283, 293, 400, 434; II 53, 90,
        185, 251, 265, 279, 336, 352, 385,
        455, 533, 614, 622; III 852

God: I 94, 136, 148, 152, 158, 226, 283,
    368, 463, 530, 538; II 133, 197–98,
    271, 274, 291, 295, 309, 314, 317,
    341, 352, 441, 443, 452, 457, 513,
    518–19, 587, 620, 641, 702, 764, 802,
    815; III 59, 95, 115, 133, 160, 179,
    320, 408, 421–22, 722, 845
  human: II 468
  just: I 229, 539; II 198, 294
  Lady Poverty: I 550
  liability: I 72
  meekness: II 517–18
  mercy: I 47, 539; II 37
  minister: III 775
  necessity: I 56, 102, 573; II 81
  other: I 71–72, 101–02, 538: II 52, 101,
    364; III 319, 401, 407, 798
  poor: II 220, 302, 764; III 249, 268, 850
  self: I 47, 72, 101, 129, 226–27, 265; II
    46, 93
  stigmata: I 410; II 404
  Sylvester: II 544
Jurisdiction
  exemption: I 419; II 109, 478; III 859
  general minister: II 156; III 299
Justice
  advancement: II 550; III 422
  alms: I 71, 92
  articulation: I 334; II 537
  beauty: II 794
  crown: II 386
  cuirass: I 441
  example II 647
  figure: II 366
  Francis: II 764–65; III 730
  fulfillment: II 695
  general minister: III 326
  genuine: II 800
  God: I 61, 109–10, 149, 152, 194; II 35,
    81, 270, 786, 794; III 95, 188, 190,
    328, 408, 696, 718
  judgment: I 147–48, 152, 550; III 389, 758
  laity: III 701
  longing: I 283
  mission: II 747, 759, 762
  mother: II 367
  neglect: II 794
  norm: I 183; II 145
  path: I 95
  persecution: I 74, 105
  praise: II 362
  proponent: I 214, 384
  punishment: II 576
  rigor: I 386
  rod: I 186
  sun: II 745; III 367, 679
  temperance: II 786
  time: II 272, 616, 702, 793
  weapon: I 462
  work: I 370
  zeal: I 212; II 702
Justification: I 567; III 535

K

King: I 342, 358, 534, 563, 588, 591; II 35,
    69, 97, 475, 578, 746; III 41, 88, 181, 199,
    223, 509, 721, 804
  Ahasuerus: III 189
  Arthur: II 208b
  birds: III 698
  Bonaventure: III 698
  chastity: II 141–42, 322–23; III 334
  Christ: I 331, 358, 360; II 247, 255,
    685, 800; III 88, 152, 177, 216, 633
  David: II 524
  dust: II 801
  earth: I 81, 109–110, 147, 150, 154,
    156, 281, 324, 342, 587; II 537, 664;
    III 457
  emperor: III 63
  England: I 166; III 830
  France: I 166, 290; III 517, 625, 685
  Francis: I 194, 289, 379
  friendship: II 740
  glory: I 529, 534, 536; II 740; III 385
  God: I 141, 261, 343, 354, 416, 537–38,
    540; II 201, 311, 476, 479, 532, 538,
    629, 637, 646, 651; III 632
  heaven: I 81, 109–10, 147, 150, 154,
    156, 281, 324, 342, 587; II 537, 664;
    III 457
  heraldry: I 194, 289, 379; II 352
  Hezekiah: II 762
  Israel: I 138
  Jerusalem: III 55a, 56
  Jews: I 225, 390, 477; II 557, 700, 783;
    III 92
  John: III 830
  locust: I 586
  Louis: III 517–18, 625–26, 685
  mark: I 281, 324, 342; II 629
  mercy: III 665
  name: I 195, 377, 457
  Naples: III 791
  Nebuchadnezzar: III 486, 723
  poor: I 256, 406; II 610
  poor woman: I 591; II 50, 97, 255, 548;
    III 46, 88, 391, 720
  queen: II 141, 375, 322–23, 578
  sacrament: II 634
  Sicily: III 630
  son: II 97, 548; III 46, 88, 100, 391,
    720–21, 750
  verse: II 167, 186, 361, 556; III 92, 304,
    348, 692
  Xerxes: II 800
Kingdom: I 438, 543, 515; II 343, 464; III
    868
  Apulia: II 404, 679
  Castile: I 595; II 407, 466b, 797
  Christ: I 307, 347; II 733; III 818
  coming: I 158, 475
  desire: III 508

eternity: II 546, 548, 740; III 174, 320, 472, 481, 654, 640–41
figurative:: I 534; II 185; III 383
France: I 559, 579
God: I 42, 47, 49, 61, 65, 74, 81, 89, 95, 101, 201, 207, 215, 239, 241, 263, 266, 516; II 99, 185, 205, 209, 455, 489, 546, 553, 722, 733, 736; III 169, 258, 381–82, 389, 409, 533, 545, 696, 708, 696, 814
Gospel: III 398
heaven: I 65, 70, 74, 78, 103, 105, 133, 188, 203, 274–75, 319, 341, 436, 465, 478, 529–30, 535–36, 541, 553, 568, 579, 597; II 89, 310, 512, 517–18, 596, 691, 722, 735, 742, 746; III 159, 162–63, 166, 329, 346, 381–82, 386–87, 392, 397, 501, 577, 621
hell: III 383
inheritance: II 296, 384
key: III 163
Lady Poverty: III 162
Leon: I 595
Miramamolin: I 563
parable: III 391
promise: II 186, 384; III 347, 367, 384, 391, 398, 446, 464, 494, 508, 536, 654, 702, 719, 868
Sicily: III 554
Kiss
  biblical: III 533
  brother: I 217; III 38
  Christ: III 651, 838
  Dominic: II 787
  feet: I 51, 248, 401; II 540; III 85, 295, 455, 513, 532, 455
  feet of Christ: III 651, 838
  footprint: I 404; II 540, 660; III 155
  Francis's body: II 418, 647
  hand: I 271; II 52, 101, 249, 335–36, 376, 788, 803
  image: II 374
  leper: II 248–49, 533, 688; III 492
  nobleman: III 552
  peace: I 551; II 74; III 551
  pillow: I 290
  stigmata: I 281; II 646; III 879
Knee: I 57, 337, 446; II 40, 48, 87, 258, 268, 273, 541, 786, 788; III 468
  miracle: I 299, 324, 459; II 38, 98, 227–28, 289, 335, 457, 460–61, 523, 591, 680; III 69
Knife: I 300, 552; II 195, 448, 464, 671, 679; III 284, 463, 560, 587, 662, 804
Knight. See also Soldier: I 239, 386, 480, 799, 804; II 176, 200, 285, 288, 296, 417, 420, 425, 583, 677, 804; III 50, 481, 552, 600, 627, 629
  Angelo: III 454, 681, 690
  Assisi: II 157, 198, 285, 297–98
  Borgo: II 677
  Celano: II 420, 614

Christ: I 374; II 75, 78, 258, 533, 602, 637; III 57
Cyprus: II 347
death: II 20, 615, 799
desire: I 35, 70: II 401
Francis: I 35, 70; II 401
Gerarado: II 672
Gineldo: II 451
Greccio: II 610
honor: II 245–46, 533
Hospitaller: III 452a
Jerome: II 646
John of Greccio: II 610
Martin: II 244
martyr: II 209
Orlando: III 802
Otto: III 805
Perugia: II 178–79, 271; III 183
poor: I 71, II 244, 532, 685; III 840
pride: II 436, 666, 677, 804
prison: I 70, II 243
Round Table: II 208, 208b; III 320, 320a
spirit: I 411
Templar: II 56, 452a
Teutonic: III 452a
Tuscanella: II 461, 627
vision: II 610
Zancato: II 448, 672
Knowledge: 228, 587; II 47, 133, 209, 213, 263, 719, 812; III 256, 449, 802, 837, 865
  absent: I 224; II 700
  authority: III 265
  Bonaventure: III 31, 78
  brother: II 47; III 173
  cherubim: II 772
  Christ: III 542
  curiosity: II 147, 372; III 314, 706, 821
  discernment: III 135
  distant: I 224; II 700
  energy: III 168, 319, 409, 705
  evil: I 129
  fame: III 63, 487
  Francis: II 511, 528, 530, 612–13, 684, 781, 813–14; III 257, 312, 458, 707, 710, 834, 855, 863
  future: III 556
  God: I 158, 259, 543; II 315; III 193–94, 314, 319, 421, 424, 456, 863
  good: I 129
  higher things: I 274
  holiness: II 207, 528, III 168
  human: III 468
  humility: III 471
  ignorance: I 568; II 511
  inflation: III 118, 258, 387, 394, 408, 415, 707, 710
  James of Massa: III 646
  John La Rochelle: III 63
  John of Parma: III 829
  Lady Poverty: I 548
  love of Christ: III 542

Order: III 487
perfection: I 597; II 247
poor: II 368
reading: II 536, 684
renunciation: III 708
respect for: III 705
saint: III 837
salvation: III 381
Savior: I 543
scripture: III 556, 646, 855
secular: III 117, 712, 814
self: I 216; II 315; III 456, 863
sense: I 40
simplicity: III 124
special: I 131
Spirit: I 460
study: III 182, 747
teacher: II 612
totality: I 131; II 343
trust: III 315, 387, 409, 415
truth: I 400, 585; II 510, 613
vocation: II 207
wisdom: I 43, 51; II 681; III 125

L

Lady. See also Female, Woman: II 43–44, 91,
    272, 405, 425, 436, 440, 592, 616, 656,
    659, 664–65; III 95, 359, 793–94, 809,
    885, 889
  charity: I 164
  Clare: I 197, 285; II 128–29, 476; III
    228–29, 357, 516
  Fonte Colombo: II 171
  Francis' dream: II 301
  Lady Jacoba: II 121–23, 126, 417–19,
    591–92; III 66, 222–23, 226, 360–61,
    471, 473–74, 561, 686, 705, 884, 886
  Maitana: III 809
  Mother of God: I 163; II 302, 540, 783;
    III 528, 548–49, 645–46, 656
  Pica: III 682, 696b, 800
  Poverty: I 164, 531–37, 541, 549–53; II
    88, 91, 162, 294, 307, 386, 580–81,
    642; III 160, 162, 165, 168, 215, 240,
    249, 268, 273, 319, 336, 361, 408
Laity: I 45, 385, 580; II 56; III 64, 389, 424,
    546, 560, 641, 857
Lamb. See also Sheep: I 192, 248–49, 322,
    399, 502; II 259, 321, 360, 429, 590, 662,
    807
  Christ: I 117, 138, 257, 280–81, 343,
    554; II 375, 499, 565, 590, 728, 772;
    III 201, 449, 456, 530, 580, 650, 851
  figurative: I 542; II 79, 489, 724; III
    817
  Francis: III 59
  fraternal: II 321; III 451, 456–57
  Leo: III 580, 582, 686, 699
  wolf: III 178, 483, 602
Lame: I 239, 290, 354, 323, 402, 518, 595; II
    410, 461, 716; III 185, 580

Lament: I 344, 393, 417, 539; II 321, 388,
    418, 421, 427, 449, 456, 476, 511, 523,
    590, 680, 734, 762, 785, 804; III 164–65,
    183, 395, 525, 881
Lamp. See also Lantern: I 269, 278, 332, 428,
    568–69; II 83, 149, 191, 250, 252, 352–53,
    423, 463, 555, 631, 656, 675, 692, 798,
    805; III 90–91, 278, 365, 436–37, 567–68,
    689
Lamp stand: I 569
Language: I 99, 105, 131, 180, 383; III 198,
    882
  angel: III 574
  Anthony: III 519
  French: I 453; II 790
  human: III 518
  miraculous: III 519, 574, 631
  Roman classic: I 426
  Rule: III 747
  oath: III 806
  science: III 198
  Thomas: III 892
  vernacular: III 361
Lantern. See also Lamp: II 353
Lard: II 182–83, 333; III 306
Lark: II 129–30, 375, 415, 644; III 229–30,
    362–63, 362a
Law: I 71, 335, 356, 376, 471, 480, 498, 533,
    546, 548, 584, 606–08; II 129, 255, 291,
    366, 377, 594, 742, 755, 759; III 117, 230,
    363, 698, 758, 881
  canon: III 828
  Christ: II 588; III 117, 712
  Christian: I 231, 608; III 856
  Church: III 775
  civil: II 319, 575; III 831
  common: III 775
  court: III 743
  creature: III 860
  custom: III 755
  Divine: I 321, 388, 418; II 368
  doctor: III 407, 575
  emperor: III 230, 363
  eternal: II 724
  exemption: III 746
  God: I 341, 346, 349, 589; II 441, 725;
    III 423
  Gospel: II 733
  grace: III 381, 422–24
  holiness: I 580
  La Verna: III 802
  lark: III 363
  life: II 489
  matrimony: II 103
  moderation: II 694
  Mohammed: II 603
  Mosaic: I 117, 329; III 93, 424
  nature: I 266; II 514; III 424
  obedience: II 576, 799; III 195, 762
  penance: II 553
  piety: II 594

pilgrim: II 136, 286, 578
property: III 778–79, 787–88
Providence: II 514
public: I 182
Rule: III 93
spirit: I 331; II 688
sword: I 606
wickedness: III 398
youth: I 184
Lawgiver: II 746
Lawsuit: I 579; II 41, 89
Learning: I 212, 457, 588; II 61, 99, 141, 147, 313, 370–72, 512, 517, 612–13, 659, 742, 775, 789; III 132, 246, 296, 394, 407, 583, 789, 821, 890
  Bonaventure: III 380, 698
  brother: III 380, 402–03
  conversion: III 320, 405
  curiosity: III 315
  desire: III 117, 168, 257, 319, 705, 707, 712
  Francis: III 583
  gift: II 144, 365
  human: I 408; II 700
  Julian of Speyer: III 697
  Leo: III 380
  Pietro Stacia: III 697
  praise: III 118, 408, 487, 724
  Spirit: I 215
  supply: II 364
  trial: III 117, 314, 389, 712
  trust: III 117
  way: III 327, 717
Leg: I 166, 253, 274, 298–300, 324, 441, 490, 505, 514; II 105, 191, 198, 260, 457–62, 464, 479–80, 675, 679, 681; III 60, 69, 71, 846
Legacy: I 71, 92; III 754–55, 778
Legal: I 460; II 187; III 201a, 349, 755, 766, 780
Legate: I 246, 499, 608; II 216, 286; III 259
Legend: I 319; II 67–68, 240, 790; III 114, 153–54, 163–64, 174–75, 182, 196, 199, 202, 214, 388, 424, 661, 673, 685–87, 805, 815, 827, 832
Legitimate: II 97; III 183, 188–90, 203, 721, 758, 766, 784
Leisure [*vacatio*]. See also Contemplation, Rest: I 244, 261, 409; II 48, 95, 99, 208, 220, 229, 269, 308a, 324–25, 361, 409, 534, 548, 551, 562, 597, 623
Lent: I 101; II 174, 182–83, 191, 226, 311, 333, 427, 609, 742; III 306, 365, 417, 578–79, 636, 775
Leper: I 70, 91, 94, 124, 195, 290, 305–06, 320, 324, 377, 420, 456, 518; II 74, 100, 123, 166–67, 248–49, 291, 454, 519, 533–34, 539, 640, 649, 675, 688, 714, 716, 750–51, 791–92, 813; III 382
  brother: II 166–67; III 242–43, 303

care: I 456, II 782; III 78, 223, 242–43, 290, 303, 603, 635–36
expense: II 291; III 45
healing: III 492–94, 607–09, 827, 814, 841
horror: I 124; II 248
house: I 218; II 249, 312, 606, 792, 814; III 243, 303–04, 847
kiss: I 195a; II 248, 533; III 838, 841
mercy: I 377
need: I 70
Order: III 693
servant: II 540, 719
service: I 273, 335, 414; II 123, 675, 688, 732, 750; III 184–85, 290, 492
Leprosy: I 305–06, 354; II 381, 453, 558, 675; III 93, 196, 493, 607–08
Letter
  Ahasuerus: III 189
  Anselm: II 802
  Anthony of Padua: I 107; II 352
  Clare: II 128–29; II 229
  custodian: I 56, 60
  Elias: II 490
  faithful: I 41, 45
  Francis: I 320; II 203, 280, 402, 458, 556, 618, 681, 693, 805; III 218, 370, 383
  Gregory: I 419, 569, 571, 576; II 56, 424, 478, 658
  Honorius: I 558–59, 561; II 56
  Hugolino: I 270; II 107; III 478, 598, 865
  Jerome: II 803
  Jerome of Ascoli: III 803–05
  Lady Jacoba: II 122–23, 417–18; III 222–23, 360–61, 473
  learning: I 132, 252, 401, 417, 504, 576; II 203, 477, 515, 620, 647; III 80, 712
  Leo: I 122; III 129
  minister: I 97
  Martin: III 766–67
  Order: I 116
  Roman Curia: I 126, 571; II 57, 105–06; III 133, 154, 386, 761–62, 766–67, 829
  ruler: I 58
  "to the letter": I 576; II 127, 132, 151, 178–79, 188, 199; III 116–17, 763
Liberality: I 603; II 708
Liberty: I 492–93, 516; II 583
Library: III 631
License: I 471, 480; III 759, 788
Lie
  falsehood: I 223, 388, 549; II 273, 619; III 182, 440
  rest: I 194, 227, 303, 334, 376, 403, 416, 450, 453, 466, 518; II 127, 227, 368, 426, 433, 438, 539, 643, 758, 782, 792; III 36, 62, 227, 356, 440, 571, 602, 606, 634

Life: I 42, 44–45, 49, 52, 54, 63–64, 66, 68, 71,
    74, 77, 80–81, 84, 86, 88–89, 92, 95,
    100–01, 115, 125, 128, 130, 140, 142–45,
    148, 180, 182, 184, 188, 194, 228, 230,
    238, 258–59, 264, 269, 277, 293, 302,
    306–08, 320, 336, 342–43, 347, 356–57,
    378, 380, 395, 402, 405, 407, 412, 414,
    416, 419, 428, 430, 432, 434, 436, 442,
    445–46, 448–50, 458–59, 465, 469, 479,
    493, 497, 508, 514, 517, 525, 531, 535,
    540, 542, 548–49, 554, 558, 568–69, 571,
    579, 586, 588, 597, 608; II 41, 49–50, 58,
    66–67, 81–83, 85, 88–89, 93, 96, 104,
    107–08, 120–21, 123, 125, 127, 130, 141,
    144, 146–47, 163, 169, 173, 182–84, 195,
    202, 212, 220, 225, 227, 251, 253, 261,
    264, 272, 300, 315, 318, 320–21, 323, 329,
    336, 351–53, 361, 364, 366, 380–81,
    388–89, 391–92, 402, 420–21, 428, 439,
    445, 467, 477, 489–90, 509–12, 517–18,
    522, 524, 527–28, 534, 543–45, 552, 555,
    564, 569, 590, 595–96, 600, 604, 609,
    617–18, 625–26, 631, 639, 643, 648–49,
    651, 668–69, 682, 689–90, 692–93,
    697–98, 711, 713, 716–17, 725, 730, 735,
    739, 742–46, 749, 756, 760, 764–65, 784,
    793–94, 798, 803, 810, 812–13, 817–18;
    III 92, 94, 125, 147, 160, 217, 225, 227,
    234, 279, 284, 292, 296, 320, 333, 404,
    445, 464, 524, 530, 535, 538, 554, 588,
    594, 601, 615–16, 620, 631, 636, 691, 693,
    697, 753, 761, 797, 801, 828, 831, 863, 869
  active: III 622
  affair: II 509
  allurement: I 401
  angel: II 258, 622; III 151, 578
  apostle: I 259, 554, 580, 582, 593, 598;
    II 107, 390, 477, 765; III 33, 41,
    148–49, 201, 381, 701, 824
  austerity: II 85, 358, 529, 564, 599, 712
  bestial: III 816
  book: I 146, 380; III 323, 382, 715
  bread: III 388
  brightness: I 225; II 141, 315, 645
  brother: III 132, 445, 742, 745, 793
  care: I 43, 50, 69; III 389, 723
  celibate: II 272, 616, 702
  chalice: III 647–48
  chastity: I 292
  Christ: I 120, 358; III 46, 117–18,
    147–49, 151, 153, 195, 202, 391–94,
    396–97, 410, 420–21, 423, 650, 701,
    712
  Christian: III 786
  church: I 582
  Clare: III 689
  common: I 547; II 177; III 58
  conduct: I 203, 213, 267, 293, 542; II
    95; III 389
  contemplative: III 514, 638
  covenant: I 351

crown: I 600; II 119, 268, 349; III 134
depravity: II 587
desperation: II 425, 659
Divine: III 381
earthly: I 369; II 526, 742
eternal: I 64, 71, 74–75, 78–79, 87,
    90–91, 96, 109, 129, 131, 270, 567,
    587; II 146, 252, 315, 360, 384, 513,
    517–18, 656, 765; III 119, 131, 136,
    288, 371, 479, 485, 589, 599, 609,
    614, 617–18, 623, 627, 641, 643,
    654–55, 868
evangelical: I 63; II 547, 621; III 86,
    148, 152, 158, 381, 399, 409, 424,
    569, 768
evil: III 125, 324, 488, 561–62, 725
excellence: I 243
fame: II 83
flesh: III 196
form: I 254, 369, 407, 418, 458; I 67,
    149, 344, 370, 529, 542, 547, 749,
    815; III 93, 149, 196, 221, 290, 314,
    381, 745
fountain: II 645; III 487
Francis: I 569; II 529, 684; III 31–33,
    49–50, 56, 66, 69, 78, 152–53,
    158–59, 214, 223, 335–36, 380, 407,
    410, 426, 446, 473, 503, 566, 568,
    577, 607, 611, 669, 682, 687, 697–69,
    703, 741, 833, 837, 871, 885
future: II 351
gate: III 868
giving: I 128, 132; II 657; III 133, 381,
    390, 410, 423, 548
glory: I 260, 569; II 110; III 152
Gospel: III 135, 195–96, 201, 384
grace: III 856
habit: I 203, 380, 690, 543; II 95; III
    135, 384, 575
heavenly: II 722; III 152, 382, 388,
    548, 769
holiness: III 629, 722
holy: I 267, 293, 583; II 134, 264, 379,
    811; III 36, 86, 126, 251, 294, 306,
    372, 408, 681
honest: II 407, 724
human: I 552
humility: III 394
immortal: II 787
innocence: I 252; II 223, 260
integrity: I 67; II 645
law: II 489
light: II 707; III 471
Martha: I 61; III 696
Mary: I 61; III 696
mendicant: I 524
merit: I 519; II 260, 775; III 759
mirror: I 260; III 87
monastic: I 383; III 60
mortal: I 325, 416; II 385, 390, 477,
    665; III 746, 769, 826

necessity: I 545; II 49, 52, 102, 294, 299, 589, 697, 807; III 60, 391, 720, 746, 780
new: III 888, 890
observance: I 68, 93, 561; III 385, 397, 405, 417, 425
Order: III 58
past: I 432; II 631, 734
peerless: I 462
perfect: II 565
perfection: III 53, 87, 401, 411, 745
philosophy: II 755
physical: II 40, 601
pilgrim: III 115, 117, 136, 641, 722
poverty: II 82, 189, 722; III 64, 338
prayer: III 758
predestined: III 504, 618
present: II 530, 584, 698, 735
pride: II 88
profession: III 408, 681
proof: I 497
religion: II 125, 162, 182, 190, 200, 204, 219, 558; III 216, 248, 276, 306, 327, 336–37
religious: I 524, 582, 586, 592; II 282, 285, 406, 519, 577, 691, 749; III 99, 393, 410, 522, 638, 718, 762, 849
restoration: I 132, 281, 324, 353, 419–20; II 421, 424, 439, 649, 657–58, 805; III 36, 51, 67
revealed: III 390
Rule: I 63, 100–01, 385, 571; II 86, 254, 544, 547; III 91, 114, 116, 132–33, 135, 151, 196–97, 384, 387–88, 396, 418–19, 667, 715–16, 722, 741–43, 770–71
sacred: II 565
secular: II 693
seed: I 230, 239
solitary: II 223; III 351, 453, 845
spirit: I 44–45, 81, 88, 125, 385; II 207, 352, 642; III 202, 385, 396, 423, 557–58, 705
spiritual: II 517; III 646
splendor: II 526
state: III 59–60, 91, 148, 160, 326, 445, 744, 746, 749–50, 754, 763, 770, 779, 781, 788
suffering: III 596, 776
tree: III 398
troubled: I 416
ungodly: II 509
unworthy: I 547
upright: II 223, 405, 514, 652; III 807
way: I 180, 192, 228, 292, 295, 416, 525, 542, 547, 558, 560, 562, 564, 569, 579, 582, 585, 587, 592, 594; II 41, 52, 57, 88, 96, 102, 106, 223, 252, 254, 277, 361–62, 369, 378–79, 391, 405, 445, 462, 477, 535, 544, 547, 553, 690, 692, 751, 811; III 96, 132, 134, 221, 301, 320, 351, 362, 370–71,

382, 395, 397, 399, 409, 423, 745, 774, 778, 815, 823, 826, 829, 879
word: I 553, 600; II 37, 332, 376, 803, 819; III 476, 856
work: III 385
worldly: I 369; II 526, 742
Light: I 46, 128, 154, 224, 255, 289, 342, 380, 389, 443, 458, 463–64, 476, 541, 566, 588; II 35, 76, 100, 143, 149, 258, 263, 283, 349, 361, 385, 413, 423, 435, 449, 463, 489, 526, 541, 552, 568, 607, 647, 656, 665, 668–69, 671–72, 674, 691, 707, 727–29, 744–45, 762, 772, 805, 817; III 182, 331, 392, 481, 524, 535, 541, 559–60, 614, 617, 887
abyss: I 278, 323; II 475, 644, 716
angel: I 569
blindness: I 476
body: II 671
Bonaventure: III 891
brilliant: I 260, 288, 538, 553; II 439, 668, 674, 691, 695, 708, 745; III 147
cherubic: III 883
children: III 383
Christ: I 43, 50, 158, 278, 351; II 449, 740; III 380, 390, 475, 528, 530–31, 535, 549, 637, 650–51
church: II 399
Clare: III 67
consolation: I 569, 576
contemplation: III 183, 456
darkness: I 503; II 35, 526, 568, 613, 684, 707
day: II 185, 189
deprivation: I 323
Divine: II 568, 644, 745; III 410, 549, 648
engulf: I 205; II 78, 545, 690; III 390
eternal: II 283, 314, 353, 385, 612, 618, 700, 716, 740, 794, 798; III 548, 648, 882
example: II 141, 315, 347–48; III 295–96
eye: I 541; II 431, 448, 489; III 335
faith: I 529; III 520, 623
Father: I 344, 541; II 489, 526, 783
fire: I 114; II 185; III 346, 368
Francis: I 215, 323, 325, 339, 425; II 120; III 221, 335, 370–71, 380, 475, 478, 499, 512, 552, 558, 595, 598, 678, 811, 846
friendship 415, 644
fullness: I 282; II 734, 761
gift: I 261; II 566
God: III 515, 623
goodness: III 565
heavenly: II 566, 644, 695, 716
honor: II 250
illumination: II 316, 745
intelligence: III 855
John: III 558
lamp: III 278, 437, 525, 568

life: II 707
love: II 566, 798
mercy: II 258, 514, 684
midday: I 288
mind: I 430
miracle: I 323, 325; II 109, 390, 477
mirror: III 221
moon: III 455
mountain: I 534
new: I 289; II 410, 678
Order: III 318
poverty: I 534, 541
pure: I 353
Satan: II 569
sanctity: III 487, 724
secret: III 465, 809
son: II 407
soul: II 699, 783
spirit: II 201; III 167, 257, 704
spiritual: II 745
splendor: III 465, 809
stigmata: III 499
Sun: I 113; III 367
sweetness: I 205
true: I 277; II 489, 671–72
truth: I 351; II 701
understanding: II 652
unspeakable: I 434
wisdom: I 275; II 613, 620, 684, 700,
    728, 763; III 330, 421, 436, 518, 567,
    652
world: I 585; III 318
Lights: I 260, 282, 284, 293, 419, 511; II 148,
    186, 342, 476, 610, 772, 798, 811; III 136,
    289, 456, 503, 544, 635, 678, 740, 765,
    887–88
Lily: I 198; III 366, 564, 668
Limbs: I 188, 272, 280, 300, 326, 357, 416,
    432, 435–36, 456, 472, 486, 510; II 313,
    325, 374, 427, 476, 480, 490, 608, 640,
    646, 658, 711, 714; III 103, 492, 668, 835,
    846, 870, 885
    heal: I 241, 299, 303, 305, 324, 403,
        494; II 389, 423, 431–32, 441, 453,
        455–57, 459–60, 467, 562, 616,
        627–28, 661, 670, 680, 765, 784; III
        69, 70–73, 449, 497, 611–12
Lion: I 146; II 371, 510, 518; III 482, 536,
    539, 697, 888
Lips: I 204, 253, 256, 265, 271, 283, 296, 338,
    346, 349, 351, 396, 411, 448, 456, 464,
    473, 499, 505, 509, 576; II 57, 203, 223,
    249, 281, 291, 310, 318, 403, 473, 478,
    609, 613, 646, 508, 515, 793; III 34, 45, 85,
    99, 150–51, 199, 218, 351, 369, 435,
    454–55, 473, 501, 518, 528
List: I 463, 519; II 258; III 823–24
Listening: I 115, 118, 135, 151, 202, 206,
    266, 447, 460, 499, 530, 540, 607; II 34, 88,
    90, 141, 156, 222, 240, 289, 323, 361, 419,

548, 687, 689, 701, 705, 725, 737, 749,
    773; III 311, 326, 329, 351, 405, 443
    animal: I 234–35, 599; II 706, 760, 810;
        III 603, 861
    Augustine: II 716
    brother: I 584; II 43, 45, 222; III 396
    Christ: I 460; II 516
    Clare: III 624
    cleric: I 606–08; III 121, 300
    Francis: I 116, 202, 231, 395, 584, 599,
        606–07; II 51, 80, 84, 178, 270, 370,
        603, 690, 708; III 353, 403, 452, 484
    Friar Preacher: III 559
    Giles: II 88; III 561
    God: I 119; II 178, 622, 718–19, 737,
        810
    Gospel: I 335, 598; II 773
    John of Florence: I 225; III 546
    minister: II 223; III 417
    Paul: II 510, 517, 726
    Peter Catanio: III 810
    poor: II 73
    Poverty: I 545, 550
    Praises: II 187, 192, 213; III 350
    preacher: II 282, 705
    saint: II 34
    word: I 578, 599; II 411, 706, 726; III
        520,632, 861
Liver: I 274, 513; II 180, 228, 311, 609; III
    232, 339
Loan: I 247; II 124, 139, 193, 195, 292, 304,
    306–07, 333, 421, 589, 804; III 280, 282,
    750, 850
Lock: I 53–54, 56, 445, 485; II 79, 439, 666,
    804
Locust: I 586–87; II 466, 679
Lodging: I 304, 453, 457, 595; II 43–44, 49,
    54, 90–92, 95, 100, 103, 199, 224, 319,
    390, 416, 554, 568, 635, 702, 707; III 39,
    98, 567, 831, 870
Loquacity: I 360
Loss: I 119, 193, 411, 433, 443, 446, 458, 487,
    512, 515; II 170, 378, 388, 466, 476, 489,
    491, 646
    body: I 130
    brother: III 382
    companionship: III 456
    everything: III 174
    eyesight: I 276, 301, 403, 413; II 126,
        432, 448, 450, 452, 474, 515, 565–66,
        671–72, 695, 744
    grace: I 265, 323
    habit: I 73
    heart: I 80; III 339, 877
    heaven: II 359; III 524–25, 876
    image: I 538
    integrity: III 118, 394
    labor: III 337
    liberty: I 493
    life: I 74, 95, 130, 515

losing: I 47, 79–80, 87–88, 120, 205,
    262, 266, 428, 448, 466, 473, 498,
    587; II 140, 190, 213, 305, 312, 337,
    360, 607, 669, 734, 816; III 118, 157,
    281, 311, 329, 337, 369, 382, 445–56,
    524–25, 576, 877
martyrdom: II 604
merit: III 562
prayer: III 118
produce: II 465
reason: I 439
Rule: II 131, 742
soul: I 43, 50–51, 130; II 140, 222, 305;
    III 311, 857
speech: I 51, 307; II 228, 289, 291, 313,
    389, 416, 451, 453, 455, 608, 644, 803
time: II 322; III 852
vocation: II 207
wine: III 353
wisdom: I 537
world: III 382
Love: I 44–45, 47, 49, 51, 72, 75, 79–80, 83,
    86, 88–89, 110, 115, 117, 130, 140, 195,
    217, 256–57, 283–84, 322, 347, 353, 359,
    430, 440, 462, 484, 509, 529, 532, 534,
    541, 549, 565; II 45–46, 49, 55, 57, 85, 92,
    94, 96–97, 100, 104, 107–08, 118, 123–25,
    127, 134, 160, 162, 188, 250, 283, 345,
    352, 359, 362, 374, 379, 388, 406, 423,
    512, 515, 518, 571, 597–98, 631–32, 646,
    649, 659, 726, 728, 730, 748–49, 758–59,
    762, 765, 772, 784, 812; III 52, 83, 125,
    164, 173, 191, 289, 296, 349, 439, 728,
    882, 884, 887–88
    affection: I 320; III 226
    allurement: I 433
    Bernard: III 439–40, 635
    bond: I 269, 396, 533; III 518, 528, 555,
        625, 639
    boundless: I 209, 273; II 108, 515
    bride: III 147
    brother: I 71, 103; II 51, 145, 150, 366;
        III 227, 240, 278, 288, 405, 425–26,
        447, 534, 561, 596, 858
    charity: I 119
    chastity: I 292
    children: II 263
    Christ: I 74, 79, 87, 95, 134, 140, 148,
        159, 270, 358, 544; II 82, 93, 130,
        140, 144, 188, 199, 244, 256, 282,
        287, 296, 334, 337, 347, 393, 404–05,
        421, 588, 599, 603, 605, 607, 610,
        631, 634, 651, 666, 686–87, 699,
        709–10, 726–27, 737, 814; III 119,
        150, 153, 173–74, 184, 189, 295, 339,
        360, 382, 385–86, 391, 394, 397, 447,
        492, 501, 513, 523–24, 530, 532, 538,
        540, 542, 553–55, 559, 575, 578, 581,
        601, 607, 616, 630, 634, 650, 655–56,
        668, 670, 721, 745, 818, 867, 889
    cold: III 721
    compassion: III 339–40

condescending: II 375
contemplation: III 221
country: I 484, 514
courtesy: III 551
creature: I 250; II 354, 356, 411, 591;
    III 349, 362, 364, 366, 860
cross: II 402, 651, 758; III 535
darkness: I 46
desire: I 197; II 121; III 371, 531, 650
Divine: I 42, 44, 197, 229, 281, 399,
    443; II 81, 91, 530–31, 596, 600, 643,
    685, 715; III 102, 174, 190, 506, 531,
    534, 538, 591, 634, 636, 650–51, 688
Dominic: III 290
earthly treasure: II 733, 745; III 776
enemy: I 48, 79, 87, 97, 105, 132, 159;
    III 195
espouse: III 100
Eucharist: III 543, 652, 656
everlasting: II 219, 284; III 541, 717
fatherly: I 375, 449
fear: I 441, 443; II 88
fervent: III 160, 339, 541, 655–56, 670,
    730, 760, 875
fire: I 245, 275, 456, 463, 567; II 46,
    191, 489, 515, 600, 635, 686, 697,
    727, 734; III 330
flesh: II 165, 300, 579; III 644
font: III 876
Francis: I 270, 306, 391; II 58, 179,
    325, 436–37, 450, 455, 466, 474, 491,
    515, 548, 592, 618, 657, 662, 666,
    673, 804, 814; III 226, 288, 327, 330,
    333, 336, 342, 355, 364, 502, 505,
    628, 692, 730, 821, 844–46, 856, 864,
    875, 877, 884
fraternity: I 542
friendliness: II 153, 187
gift: I 226
Giles: III 625
glue: II 370
goad: II 382, 640
God: I 41, 46, 61, 84, 86, 89, 97, 114,
    118, 132, 135, 158–59, 166, 216, 234,
    248, 251–52, 282–83, 321–22, 352,
    396, 449, 550, 553, 559, 565, 600; II
    39–41, 43–44, 47, 69, 73, 83, 87,
    89–91, 94, 107, 122, 129, 139–40,
    151, 156, 158, 160, 172, 176, 183,
    187, 190, 192–94, 199–201, 207,
    209–10, 218, 222, 229, 244, 275, 287,
    298–99, 304–05, 360, 373, 386,
    411–12, 415–16, 531–32, 555,
    582–83, 596, 600, 674, 685, 734, 736,
    739, 762, 794, 798, 802, 814, 818; III
    39, 46, 103, 118, 121, 130, 168–70,
    173, 214, 216, 221–22, 225–26, 230,
    233, 237, 258, 261, 263, 269, 271–75,
    280–84, 292, 299, 307, 344, 350,
    362–63, 385–86, 409–08, 413, 448,
    450, 501, 512, 522, 544, 561, 587,
    599, 628, 630, 638, 657, 687–88, 696,

705, 708, 715, 721, 730, 739, 745, 748, 759, 799, 838, 846, 856, 860, 868, 878
God's name: I 155, 308, 322
Gospel: II 554
grace: II 468, 685
gratuitous: I 368
greatness: I 188
heartfelt: I 443
heavenly things: I 210; II 533, 745; III 392, 423
holy: I 82, 88; II 314
Holy Spirit: I 93
humanity: I 360, 431; II 92
humility: II 46, 93, 576, 675; III 400, 623
imitation: III 176
imprint: III 189
infinite: III 382
intimacy: I 187; II 397, 618
jealous: III 147
John of La Verna: III 655–56
Lady Poverty: II 88, 162; III 161–162, 240, 336
learning: III 117, 712
Leo: III 580–81
life of brothers: III 248, 327, 335–36, 718
light: II 566, 798
Lord: III 174, 214–17, 224, 250, 291
loving: I 72, 80–81, 85, 88, 91, 96, 117, 125, 322, 358, 390, 536, 591; II 49, 72, 88, 104, 126–27, 146, 160, 190, 219, 240, 255, 271, 277, 349, 515, 734, 737, 746, 750, 794; III 103, 127, 155, 162, 223–26, 239, 288, 291, 296, 335, 342, 349, 353, 364, 371, 396, 426, 531, 587, 614–15, 651, 717, 844
Mary: II 540; III 161
Masseo: III 514
Michael the Archangel: II 598
minister: III 227, 355, 426
money: I 193; III 842
mutual: I 187; II 772
neighbor: I 41, 47, 159; II 41, 89, 737, 739, 814; III 119, 874
obedience: II 643; III 225, 292, 363, 849
Order: II 262, 313, 609
pardon: III 350, 368
parent: II 510
passionate: III 290
perfect: I 158; II 46, 94
persecutor: I 105
personify: I 109, 158; II 194, 520, 726, 763, 794
Philip: III 689
piety: I 322
poor: III 644
Pope: III 127, 401
Portiuncula: III 86

poverty: I 531–32; II 247, 529, 535, 577, 581, 690, 696, 722; III 125, 192, 223, 333, 384, 389, 397, 400, 588, 596, 718–19, 820, 884–86
power: II 358, 515, 734; III 190, 670
prayer: III 190
priest: III 239, 263, 385
purity: II 785
religion: II 106, 216
Riccerio: III 502, 864
righteousness: II 818
Rinieri: III 616
Rufino: III 618, 687–88
Rule: III 396, 776
saint: III 723
Savior: I 308; II 515, 540, 755, 757, 759; III 84, 535, 875
self: I 228; II 789; III 393, 408, 410
seraphic: II 404, 640, 655, 704; III 398
service: I 159
sign: I 281; II 515, 727
silence: III 351
Simon: III 539, 635
solicitude: III 333
solitary life: III 351, 565
solitude: II 223
soul: III 155
special: I 210, 261, 281, 396; II 256, 277, 282, 417, 474
spiritual: I 217; III 38
spouse: I 198; II 462, 482, 675
steadfast: I 352
stigmata: III 670, 875
sweetness: I 235, 399; III 193
treasure: II 733, 745; III 776
Trinity: I 76, 90
truth: III 135, 721
unseen: I 282
virtue: III 116, 385, 419
word: I 283; II 42
world: I 434, 541; III 644
worthiness: I 42, 49, 181, 226; II 137, 290, 527; III 266
you: III 129
zeal: II 649
Lover: I 536; II 284, 314, 334, 515, 612, 634, 710; III 190, 501, 855
all: III 398
chastity: II 562
Christ: III 135
cross: III 792
God: I 226; II 356, 413
heavenly things: I 289; III 689
holiness: II 547
humility: I 195, 246; II 539, 573, 688
innocence: II 463, 679; III 511
integrity: III 343
poor: I 300; II 247, 460, 480, 589; III 71
poverty: II 538, 580
sinner: I 254
unity: I 289

Lucifer: I 455, 488; II 168, 351, 751–52; III
    186, 411–12, 422, 425, 304–05, 524, 682
    devil: I 43, 50–51, 67, 69–70, 73, 78–79,
        87, 91–92, 129, 214, 230, 241, 244,
        323, 408, 438, 495, 541; II 53, 75, 79,
        102, 137, 153, 185, 215, 225–26,
        228–30, 248, 267, 289–90, 292, 297,
        299, 319, 323, 325, 329, 423, 426–27,
        454, 481, 510, 551, 562, 564, 574–75,
        580, 607, 619, 627, 691, 700–01, 720,
        733–34, 761, 791, 793, 795–96,
        800–01
    Satan: I 80, 88, 165, 569, 576, 608; II
        326
Lust: I 73, 89, 228, 439, 541; II 88, 110, 274,
    283, 325, 330, 561–63, 615, 723–24, 732,
    734, 740–41, 756, 815; III 96
Luxury: I 65; II 289, 326, 575, 796; III 114,
    271, 692
Lyre: I 489

M

Magpie: I 234a, 446, 446b, 599
Malice
    absence: I 220; II 94
    avoidance: I 69, 79
    brother: III 560
    cleansing: III 493
    criticism: I 438
    goodness: III 423
    growth: I 273
    heretic: II 788; III 857
    John de Capella: III 511
    persecutor: III 424
    Rule: III 762
    sailor: II 434
    Satan: I 80, 88; III 59
    sincerity: I 265
    stubbornness: II 511
    suspicion: I 549
    wicked: II 119, 349; III 316, 390, 723
    world: III 156, 382
Malignancy
    foe: I 339
    spirit 694
Mammon:: II 510, 809
Manger
    child: I 156, 254–57, 406; II 120, 411,
        610, 783; III 161, 230, 363, 381, 397
    hay: I 255–56, 406, 506; II 411, 610
Manna
    desert: III 129, 318
    heaven: I 568; II 757; III 889
    hidden: I 520; II 309–10
Mantle
    bishop: I 193, 375, 450; II 80, 538
    figurative: I 441; II 660, 700; III 401
    Francis: I 400, 473; II 138–39, 304,
        306–07, 309, 333, 589, 807; III 499,
        614
    loan: II 589, 306; III 850

poor: II 138–40, 304, 306–07, 333, 589;
    III 85, 280, 307
    sister: III 64a
    stigmata: III 499, 614
    theft: II 589
    Virgin Mary: III 53
Manure. See also Dung
    grain: II 130; III 230, 362
    money: II 137, 290–91, 347; III 266
    mouth: II 137, 290–91, 347; III 266,
        295
    pile: II 137, 290; III 266
    sack: III 503, 616
    sin: III 491
Marriage: I 84, 185, 547, 554, 583; II 103,
    272, 405–06; III 163, 859
    defile: II 142, 232; III 334
    desire: I 188, 373; II 75
    king: II 97; III 46, 88, 720
    poor woman: II 97; III 46, 88, 720
Marrow
    cross: III 380
    Eucharist: II 375, 598
    Gospel: II 146, 380
    heart: II 84, 310, 543, 689
    rind: II 368
    scripture: III 814
    soul: I 510
Martyr
    apostle: III 392
    choir: III 323
    Christ: III 37, 257, 707
    crown: III 323, 856
    Francis: I 276, 339, 394, 410; II 726,
        814; III 680, 695, 856
    Order: III 816
    pain: III 453
Martyrdom
    abstinence: III 529
    brother: II 147, 381, 400; III 37, 501,
        529
    charity: II 600–01
    crown: III 400
    desire: I 229, 395; II 415, 596, 600; III
        119, 174, 293, 323, 490, 501, 605,
        855
    Francis: I 229, 275, 395, 414, 484, 600;
        II 265, 343, 415, 596, 600–01, 604,
        631, 698, 710, 783, 816; III 119, 174,
        233, 293, 323, 605, 670, 855, 885
    palm: III 392
    Rule: II 147, 381
    stigmata: II 709–10
Mass. See also Body of Christ, Blood of
    Christ
    attitude: II 52, 101, 449, 591, 671; III
        70, 503, 534–35, 536, 616, 652, 654,
        656–57, 797–98
    celebration: I 117, 119, 201, 406, 419;
        II 44, 431, 449, 455; III 437, 463,
        476, 534, 543–44, 568, 595, 689, 709
    chapter: II 56, 104

Christmas: I 256, 406, 506, 610; III
515, 626
Gospel: I 201, 379; II 56, 84, 104, 191,
542, 689; III 86, 365, 709, 773, 843
priority: II 144, 162, 365, 375; III 240,
325, 335, 365, 773
Proper: I 346–52
Massacre: II 243, 266, 614; III 189
Master. See also Ruler: I 77, 84, 105, 126,
136, 166, 222, 294, 351, 460–61, 464,
476–77, 481, 584, 597; II 44, 46, 52, 93,
101, 203, 269, 325, 343, 425, 466, 563,
733, 747, 750–51, 786; III 39, 57, 148, 218,
281, 370, 447, 480, 506, 524, 529, 331,
600, 649, 748, 809, 849
Christ: I 405; III 177, 336, 471, 495,
619
singer: II 167, 186; III 304, 348
theology: III 31, 58–59, 63, 78, 116,
409, 673, 678, 714–15
Matron: I 547; II 405, 591, 652, 680; III 66
Mats
cell: II 153, 184–85; III 346–47
chapter: II 132; III 124, 313, 569, 709,
819
Mattress: I 227; II 228, 289; III 58, 232, 345
Meat: I 227, 392, 478, 585; II 146, 182, 299,
359, 374, 427, 570, 745, 802; III 50, 96,
288, 399a, 442, 573, 708, 838, 846–47,
851–52
Mediator: I 475; II 619, 700; III 193
Medicine: I 72, 91, 96, 267, 271, 303–04,
307, 413, 471, 493; II 146, 152, 181, 259,
359, 383, 447, 453, 555, 670, 692, 794; III
69, 91, 97, 179, 356, 548, 645, 828
Meditation
Christ: I 254, 506; III 555
God: II 127, 521; III 227
heavenly things: II 77, 205, 208, 212,
326, 412, 834, 847; III 167, 169, 172,
255, 265, 320, 415, 703
preach: I 245
rest: I 137, 137a
Meekness
conversion: II 666; III 157
demonstration: I 254; II 144–45, 172,
365, 590, 736; III 325, 424, 476, 557,
632, 729, 740, 865
excessive: II 366
God: I 109–10
lesson: II 517–18
search: I 219
Melancholy: III 504, 617, 619, 635
Melody: I 119, 224, 296, 506; II 142, 169,
186, 330–31, 567–68; III 98, 340, 348
Memory
book: III 314
building: II 377
Christ: II 107, 181, 686
Christ's birth: I 255–56; II 610

Christ's Passion: I 139, 254, 540; II 76,
108, 401, 534, 686
consciousness: I 80, 180, 202, 253, 256,
307, 379, 540, 588; II 84, 181, 240,
442, 717; III 51, 53, 149
Francis: I 180, 202, 253–54, 335, 351,
379, 564, 569; II 162, 181, 314, 445,
490, 530, 773; III 152, 189, 314, 335,
380, 485, 665, 761
Francis's name: II 445, 530
Gregory IX: II 83, 296, 651, 775, 780;
III 65, 742
Gregory X: III 740
holy: II 67, 85; III 53, 57, 515, 714, 770
Innocent III: I 99; III 418
Innocent IV: III 748
manger: II 411
Mary: II 124; III 224
Nicholas: III III 772, 784
remembrance: I 78, 255, 351, 394,
406–07, 564, 569, 571; II 83, 85, 107,
173, 387, 780; III 53, 526
scripture: I 202, 335, 379; II 84, 542,
612
soul: III 563
spiritual building: II 377
wolf: III 485
Mercy: I 47, 65, 97–98, 245, 342, 548; II 38,
97, 149, 157, 168, 180, 196, 202, 225, 292,
328, 360, 380, 515, 532, 573, 651, 736,
753–55, 759, 786, 811, 818
abundant: II 120
beg: II 258, 436, 541, 666
Christ: I 191, 195, 587; II 177, 185,
319, 420, 705, 818; III 147, 187, 300,
318, 420, 498, 544, 588, 651
desire: I 97; II 149, 360, 754; III 234,
278
experience: II 436, 672, 795
fatherly: II 415
flesh: III 217, 275
forgiving: II 753–54, 759
Francis: I 195, 299, 305; II 152,
440–42, 449, 457, 459, 463, 465, 467,
668, 670, 674, 676; III 71, 81, 451,
235, 638, 804
friend: II 455
God: I 47, 84, 143–44, 149, 153–54,
156, 159, 188, 205, 213, 226, 240,
267, 274, 370, 372, 374, 384, 538,
551, 554, 565, 569, 586; II 34, 75,
100, 105, 119, 178, 203, 212, 215,
222, 225, 228, 230, 272, 326, 344,
350, 416, 438, 455, 462, 525, 557,
588, 655, 674, 677, 684, 703, 736,
753–54, 800, 818; III 46, 51, 122,
135, 172, 218, 220, 231–32, 237, 251,
265, 311–12, 314, 318, 322, 343, 368,
370, 372, 415, 422–23, 451–52, 455,
464, 479, 494, 496, 498, 508, 513,
531, 540, 546–48, 553, 555, 582, 586,
588, 598, 608, 611, 613, 630, 643,

650, 665, 703, 710, 719, 721, 823, 833, 844
hand: I 377
heart: I 104, 137; II 145, 365
holy: I 256
judgment: II 37
kindness: I 550
lack: I 47, 97, 117, 195, 374, 548; II 324, 562, 818
manifestation: I 47–48, 98, 124, 195, 279, 360, 377, 550; II 44, 455, 490, 594, 674, 735, 814; III 137, 300, 318
Mary: I 542; II 343, 638; III 85, 549, 637
peace: I 341, 346; II 682
penance: III 605
piety: II 292; III 280, 325, 411
protective: II 753–54, 759
reception: I 47; II 598, 817; III 125, 324–25, 396
salvific: III 155
sign: II 720
speed: II 440, 668
work: III 746
Messenger: I 59, 166, 571, 606; II 79, 141, 269, 322–23, 440, 527, 555, 619, 629, 669, 692, 701, 784; III 66, 90, 334, 397, 524, 889
Metal: I 304, 504; II 385, 467, 642
Metanoia. See Conversion, Penance
Michael, Feast of Saint: I 76; II 51, 226, 634, 711; III 454, 527
Mile: I 195, 539; II 171, 379, 388, 433, 488, 643, 663, 758, 760–61; III 128, 359, 449, 479, 527, 580, 795
Militia: I 338; II 638
Milk: I 225, 539; II 463–64, 679, 723, 772; III 531, 814, 886
Minister: I 97–98, 98a, 488, 501, 516; II 467, 481; III 55–56, 64, 119, 256, 270, 393, 407, 412, 545, 641, 699, 772, 805, 808, 819, 827, 829, 858–59
    action: I 71, 94, 413; II 95, 216, 352, 555, 772; III 83, 168, 246, 705, 850
    Arnald of Sarrant: III 678
    Augustine: II 389, 644, 716
    Bonaventure: III 31, 33, 78, 380, 698
    books: II 206; III 256, 704, 708–09, 785, 819
    brother: I 64, 100–01, 225
    Christ: II 622, 709
    Cresentius: II 61, 66
    cross: II 557
    death: I 104–05, 574; III 790
    demon: II 225; III 231, 312
    election: I 104, 574; II 56, 104; III 760, 782–83, 825
    faith: III 89
    Francis: I 603, 188; II 125, 142, 158, 174–76, 181–82, 189, 193, 196, 206–11, 215, 223, 288, 338, 467, 481,

557, 622, 695, 709; III 123–24, 128, 157, 167, 170–71, 199–200, 219, 225–27, 237, 253–54, 256–58, 266, 270–71, 283, 286–87, 292, 303, 305, 317, 321, 351, 363–64, 367, 340, 402, 406, 414–17, 426, 596, 704, 706–09, 711
    general minister: I 116, 119–20, 126–27, 570–71, 573–74, 602; II 66,125, 127, 184, 189, 193, 196, 223, 239, 772, 778, 800; III 25, 48, 121–22, 169, 225–27, 283, 292, 303, 798, 806, 825, 827–30
Gerardo: II 174
God: II 248; III 840
Gospel: I 188
Gregory: II 489
Haymo: III 53
John de Schiacia: III 706
John of Florence: I 225, 390
Leo: III 169
Lord: II 216; III 246
Matteo: III 647
novice: II 207–10; III 169, 257–58
obedience: I 62, 67, 93, 126–27, 305; II 695; III 363, 696
Pacifico: II 556, 693, 725
Paul: I 248, 399
permission: I 74–75, 77, 89; II 467, 481; III 119, 257, 707
Peter of Calabria: III 37, 37e
Peter of Catanio: II 166, 182, 286–87, 305
Poor Men of Lyon: I 593
Pope: III 741, 766
Portiuncula: II 100, 156, 158; III 121, 237, 299–300
preaching: I 75, 89, 105, 208; III 758–59, 773
prelate: II 572; III 699
procurator: III 766, 788
provincial minister: I 100–06, 127, 570–71, 573–75; II 61, 104, 106, 125, 131–32, 174–76, 206, 364, 366, 740, 775, 777–78; III 25, 227, 270–71, 355, 641, 715, 765, 793, 840, 859
psalter: II 207, 209–10; III 169, 258, 707
quality: II 144–45, 338, 364–66; III 324–26
reception: I 64; III 60, 759, 773–74
recourse: I 67–68, 103, 573; III 115, 420, 714, 773
Riccerio: III 502
Rinieri: III 615
Rule: I 119–20; II 131–32, 206, 215, 776–78; III 116, 123–24, 127–28, 157, 167, 253–54, 256, 309, 406, 413, 416–17, 419–20, 704, 708–09, 713–14, 747, 750, 756–57, 772, 775, 780, 782, 819
sacrament: III 385, 781

Solomon: III 151
spirit: II 371
theologian: I 125; II 352; III 168, 705
Third Order: III 64
vision: III 557–58, 647
William: III 57
Word of God: II 343, 352, 587
Minority: II 517
Minstrel: II 186; III 98
Miracle: I 131, 166, 461; II 515, 553, 780; III 175, 177
  abbot: II 180
  Anthony: III 519, 521, 631–33
  Bartholomew: III 676
  bed of fire: III 606
  Bentivoglia of San Severino: III 527, 636
  Benvenuto: III 37
  Bernard: II 127; III 227, 356
  birds: II 810; III 469, 540, 639
  bishop and mayor: II 188; III 350
  blindness: I 595; II 449, 670–71; III 804
  boat: II 625, 705
  brother: III 91, 635, 695
  canonization: I 295, 298, 595, 603–04; II 57, 109, 390–91,477; III 871
  Clare: III 91, 516–17
  Conrad: III 638
  cross: II 250
  crow: III 635
  deaf: I 306
  death: II 424, 431, 658–59, 712
  disobedient: II 576; III 272
  eyelid: II 448
  fiery chariot: II 691–92
  fire: II 190, 355, 409, 566; III 606, 862
  fish: I 236; III 521, 632–33
  food: III 165
  Francis: I 180, 243, 259–60, 288, 290, 293, 305, 325, 327, 332, 343, 389, 394, 402, 407, 416, 418–20, 491, 497, 569; II 58, 67, 108, 240, 280, 399, 437, 451, 454, 467–68, 482, 487, 513, 529, 610–11, 625, 628–29, 647–51, 675, 678, 681, 692, 730, 746, 764; III 33, 69, 78, 80, 92, 175, 185, 393, 413, 456, 448, 566, 579, 733, 805, 834
  French: II 790
  Friar Preacher: III 559
  fruit tree: II 466
  Giles: III 184
  hail: II 177
  hand: II 676
  hemmorage: II 454, 675
  hernia: II 447
  injury: II 429, 662
  James of Fallerone: III 537, 654
  John of Parma: III 152
  John of Penna: III 36, 36b, 546, 640
  justice: II 765
  Lady Jacoba: II 418

  lame: I 595; II 681
  language: III 521, 632–33
  Leo: III 131
  leper: III 493–94, 608
  limb: II 458, 680
  loaves: III 516–17
  mayor: II 188; III 350
  meat: II 299; III 50, 846–47
  mouth: II 540; III 85
  mute: I 306
  Nicholas: III 36
  Pacifico: III 692
  paper: III 131
  Pelligrino: III 615
  Peter of Calabria: III 37, 37e
  prisoner: II 439, 666
  provision: II 276, 417; III 165, 516–17
  sea: II 665
  Simon: III 36, 540, 635
  sow: II 807
  Stephen: III 37
  stigmata: I 280–82; II 401, 403–04, 406, 419, 468, 473, 487, 490, 514–15, 634, 646, 650–52, 654, 677, 797; III 187, 457, 559, 561, 792, 870
  swallows: II 624; III 469
  sword: II 317, 556, 693
  tomb: I 290, 302; III 51, 871
  vineyard: II 170; III 480, 599
  water: II 278, 410, 678
  water to wine: I 323, 398, 491; III 185, 862
  William: III 62
  wolf: III 484, 601–03
  wound: II 407
Mirror
  brother: II 392; III 370
  Christ: II 221, 303; III 250, 486, 724
  church: III 370
  contempt: I 583
  dignity: III 289
  discipline: II 366
  eternal light: II 618
  Francis: I 260, 344, 450, 519; II 120, 263, 392, 447, 569, 670; III 370
  goodness: II 353
  holiness: II 645; III 47, 633
  light: II 618
  Mary: II 303
  obedience: II 670
  Order: II 257; III 489, 726
  perfection: III 87, 214, 253, 372
  Portiuncula: II 157; III 122, 237, 300
  poverty: II 221, 303; III 250
  religion: III 122, 237, 300
  vanity: I 583
  virtue: I 344
Mission
  beg: III 269
  Christ: I 355; II 54, 84, 722
  diplomacy: III 829
  Francis: I 373; II 242, 248, 527, 629

Greece: III 829
love: III 875
Miramamolin: I 563
Order: II 399, 772
preach: III 175
world: III 190
Model
  Christ: II 509; III 100, 175, 769
  Francis: I 204, 229; II 150, 181, 200,
    214, 218, 245, 369, 509, 511, 543,
    645, 689, 721, 738; III 99, 216, 234,
    246, 274, 279, 308, 848
  ministry: II 366
  Odo Rigaldi: III 64
  Portiuncula: II 157–58, III 237, 260–61
  virtue: I 463; II 764
Moderates: I 19; II 13
Moderation
  brother: I 219
  God: I 109
  law: II 694; III 441
Modesty: I 272, 286, 417, 440, 442; II 562,
  694; III 442, 573, 596
Monastery: I 470; II 179, 379, 539; III 60–61,
  681, 692, 748, 793, 805, 837
  Gubbio: I 195, 195a, 320, 334, 376,
    453, 456
  Monticelli: III 591
  nuns: I 100, 100b, 106, 575; II 779; III
    760
  Poor Ladies: II 83, 128, 188, 252, 317,
    773; III 64, 67, 199, 228, 467,
    516–17, 590–91, 624, 794–95
  San Giustino: II 313, 608
  San Severino: II 556, 693
  San Verecondo: II 590, 807, 851
  Subiaco: II 100, 100a, 154; III 119, 297
Money: I 134, 375, 441, 448–49, 567;: II 436,
  538, 584–85, 596, 666, 733, 804; III 82,
  114, 133, 165, 178
  avoid: I 64, 69–70, 73, 89, 93–94,
    102–03, 201, 337, 356, 594; II 45,
    47–48, 87, 91–92, 290–92, 298, 583;
    III 45, 266, 325, 722, 820, 878
  Bernard: II 38, 86–87, 538; III 438,
    568–69
  burden: II 603
  coin: I 69–70, 102–03, 572; III 405
  corrupter: II 365; III 325
  Crusader vow: I 601
  detest: I 373, 442; II 36, 48, 77–78, 80,
    89, 94, 137, 144, 290, 365, 537, 583,
    684, 687, 782; III 266, 325
  devil: II 580, 801; III 100
  distribute: II 38–39, 72–74, 76–78, 87,
    247–48, 249–50, 292, 319, 533, 537,
    555, 580, 686, 792, 801; III 82, 438,
    841–42
  dust: I 94; II 47, 537
  Francis: I 94, 183, 185, 188–89, 193,
    201, 249, 319, 333, 370, 373, 442,
    457; II 36–37, 39, 68, 72, 80, 89, 251,

530, 538, 684, 782, 792; III 45, 133,
    165, 266, 382, 438, 568–69, 681, 833,
    841–43, 878
  gain: I 400, 435–36, 441, 448–49; II 39,
    538
  Gospel teaching: I 73, 89, 201, 373,
    459, 539, 583, 589; II 37, 84, 538,
    689, 733; III 100, 196, 382, 568, 681,
    833, 843
  Joachim of Fiore: III 681
  lawsuit: III 389
  leper colony: I 70
  love: I 193; II 37, 39, 80, 87, 251, 319,
    538, 782
  manure: II 48, 137, 290; III 54, 266
  papal teaching: I 567, 572, 576; II 776;
    III 746, 750–56, 775–76, 778–79,
    781, 785
  Peter of Catanio: II 39
  Pietro Bernardone: I 190, 193, 373,
    375; II 37, 78, 80, 251, 687, 782, 792,
    842
  purse: II 73, 144, 206, 292, 300–01,
    306, 365, 491, 578–80, 689, 801; III
    382, 406, 438, 681, 745, 843, 878
  reception: III 114, 133, 405
  snake: II 292, 580, 801; III 100
  Sylvester: II 86, 319, 438, 568–69
  teaching: I 73, 89, 201, 373, 459, 539,
    583, 589; II 37, 84, 538, 689, 733; III
    100, 196, 382, 568, 681, 833, 843
  vow: I 601
Moneybag: II 338; III 167, 256, 325, 704
Monk: I 195, 376, 454–55, 582; II 155, 176,
  463, 782, 807; III 60, 62, 120, 236,
  297–99, 681, 748, 793, 820, 837, 841
  Cistercian: II 122; III 61–62, 222, 322,
    795
Moon: I 250, 278, 295, 322, 400, 503–04,
  518, 568, 604; II 107, 388, 475, 491, 720,
  728, 784, 798, 803; III 455, 835
  Sister: I 113; III 367
Moonlight: II 325, 563
Mortification: I 321; II 53, 645, 732; III 769
Mother: I 42, 49, 64, 142, 145, 153, 298–99,
  302–03, 307, 430, 438, 468, 531; II 47, 54,
  94, 97, 103, 196, 208, 243, 255, 260, 268,
  279, 284, 306, 323, 327, 352, 362, 369,
  405, 419, 421–24, 426, 428, 431–33,
  439–41, 443, 446, 452–53, 455, 458–63,
  479, 510, 523, 548, 577, 627, 656–58,
  668–69, 696, 736, 805; III 51, 59–60, 66,
  70–74, 88, 528, 548, 637
  animal: II 279
  Benjamin: III 144, 158–59
  Bonaventure: II 717
  brother: II 306; III 59–60, 286
  Christ: III 651
  church: I 55, 109; II 48, 95, 160, 162;
    III 240, 324, 336, 425, 476, 486, 596,
    695, 844

Church of St. Francis: I 109
Clare: I 285, 417; II 476, 554; III 331, 517, 624, 626
Constantine: II 720
cross: III 161
Dominic: III 889
earth: I 114; III 368
Elias: I 267, 412
example: I 71, 103, 122–23, 246, 249, 381, 400; II 46, 93, 359, 592, 697
Francis: I 192, 334, 374, 429, 447; II 68, 73, 79, 241, 336, 510, 537, 587, 684, 782; III 33, 46, 80, 88, 175, 335, 680, 682–83, 695, 800, 821–22, 833
God: I 163, 201, 203, 378; II 130, 226, 540, 542, 715, 782, 808; III 53, 57, 66, 85, 90, 230, 397, 466, 548–49, 555, 646
goodness: III 843
Jerusalem: I 351
justice: II 367
Lady Poverty: II 581
Lateran Church: III 844
mercy: II 542; III 85
monk: I 61–62, 603
Pacifico: III 792
Pica: III 680, 800
Portiuncula: II 109, 154; III 120, 236, 298, 328, 330
queen: II 578; III 100
religion: III 328
renunciation: III 397
synagogue: III 423
Virgin Mary: I 46, 83, 92, 141, 163, 201, 203, 378, 458, 475, 519; II 130, 151, 154, 196, 214, 226, 257, 292, 303, 374, 465, 540, 542, 553, 577–78, 589, 591, 598, 715, 782, 786, 808; III 53, 120, 157, 161, 193, 195, 230, 246, 298, 309, 330, 381, 397, 493, 555, 564, 566, 607–08, 640, 645, 811–12
Mountain: I 166, 504, 543, 566; II 131, 159, 278, 324, 356, 409–10, 423, 428, 435, 504, 558, 584, 634, 656, 661, 678, 805; III 44, 92, 123, 177, 262, 346, 453–54, 457, 504, 506, 649, 687, 802–03, 861, 890
ascent: I 276, 329, 532–35, 549, 551; II 247, 278, 409, 584, 634, 711, 745; III 93, 101, 253, 454, 686, 713, 861
figurative: I 567; II 166, 261, 324, 552, 623, 711, 742; III 44, 93, 177, 189, 346, 497, 611, 613, 730
man: I 478; III 99
move: I 447; II 166, 261, 324; III 44, 346
Mountainside: II 287, 632, 709
Mourning: I 279–80, 286, 415–16; II 173, 388, 421, 430, 440, 476, 480, 663, 669, 672; III 189
Mouth
   abstinence: III 617

animal: I 239, 405, 502; II 444; III 602–03, 632
Anthony: III 521
bit: III 879
deformity: I 241, 302, 307, 402, 494, 496; II 428, 431–32, 540, 628; III 70, 73–74, 85
eat: I 439, 510; II 374, 679; III 715
Eucharist: I 53–54, 118
face: II 264, 556, 638, 659, 693
Francis: I 184, 227, 322, 392; II 37, 39, 87, 107, 319, 401, 540, 545, 623, 692, 795; III 85, 87, 130, 318, 438, 440, 453, 463, 465, 468, 569, 570–71, 582, 588, 592, 602, 703, 728, 792, 852, 859, 874, 877
God: II 147, 350, 558, 749; III 49, 93,197, 322, 423
Hildegard: I 595
James: III 458
Jesus: I 283, 535; II 401
John: III 532, 652, 829
kiss: II 249, 534, 688; III 85
lamp: III 689
Leo: III 129, 134, 458, 808
manure: I 48, 137, 143, 290, 347; III 295, 618
Masseo: III 469
Pope: III 808
prophet: III 618
Riccerio: III 167
river: III 520, 632
speech: I 146, 151, 153, 180, 219, 245, 256, 283, 334, 341, 349, 353, 544; II 40, 46, 51, 53, 93, 102, 160, 169, 205–07, 338, 352, 363, 421, 434, 445, 582, 648, 664, 817; III 44, 164, 335, 454, 457, 589
taste: I 439, 510; II 374, 679; III 715
trumpet: III 694
Ugolino of Monte Santa Maria: III 458
word: III 168, 239, 381, 452, 582, 703–04, 802
Mud
   cover: I 166, 598; II 406, 422, 652, 657, 752; III 449, 580, 833
   figurative: I 488, 534; II 283; III 82
   place: II 154, 157, 159, 161, 212; III 172, 239, 260, 262, 264–65, 297, 384
   throw: I 191, 320, 324, 374, 444; II 45, 78, 537, 687, 751, 833; III 436, 450, 567
Multiplication: I 380; II 585; III 79, 104
Murder: I 79, 439
Murderer: I 130, 428; II 725, 752, 797; III 495, 602, 609–10
Murmuring: I 93, 105; III 100, 450
Music: II 567; III 31, 91, 504, 600, 626
Mustard seed: II 166, 324; III 43, 158, 346
Mute: I 248, 290, 306, 324, 420, 518; II 450–51, 649, 673, 678, 716; III 72–73, 150, 436, 567, 580, 589

Mystery. See also Sacrament, Secret
[secretum]
  apparition: III 595
  Christ: III 158
  cross: I 601; II 401, 681; III 420, 448
  Divine eloquence: II 539, 685
  doctrine: III 175
  Eucharist: II 376
  Francis's life: I 194, 366; II 80, 581; III
    633, 684, 866
  Gospel: II 348
  grace: I 366
  king: II 209
  Kingdom of God: III 258, 381, 409,
    708, 814
  poverty: III 381
  priesthood: II 376
  redemption: II 646, 780
  revelation: II 292
  Rule: II 381
  stigmata: I 261, 281, 410–11; III 458,
    578, 866, 867, 875–76
  vision: II 381

N

Nails
  Bonaventure: III 558
  Christ: I 360; II 499; III 83, 383
  Clare: II 874–75
  Francis: I 253; II 275; III 729
  stigmata: I 264, 353, 357, 359, 410,
    416, 510, 596; II 108, 388, 402–03,
    406, 438, 473, 476, 490, 499, 514,
    633, 640, 645–46, 652, 667, 710, 714,
    719, 743–45, 758, 770, 806; III 161,
    176, 420, 457, 513, 835, 866, 870
Nakedness: I 283, 446, 456; II 375, 422, 480,
    694; III 320, 328, 434
  Adam: I 538, 552
  bed of fire: III 491, 606
  before bishop: I 193, 334, 375, 375a,
    449–50; II 80, 251, 538, 643, 687,
    751, 782, 792
  Benedict: II 746
  Bernard: III 438, 569
  brother: I 219, 248, 532, 582; II 44, 92,
    139, 156, 221, 371, 379; III 40, 249,
    280
  Christ: I 375, 582; II 82, 371, 538, 687,
    756, 722, 802; III 84, 378, 381–83,
    438, 508, 569, 621, 627, 842
  cold: II 561; III 61, 121, 237, 299
  Francis: I 227, 238, 248, 320, 339, 376,
    452; II 139, 194, 221, 363, 379, 510,
    563, 642–43, 688, 715, 723, 741, 758,
    795, 803; III 43, 84, 97, 280, 305–06,
    438, 491, 507, 606, 621, 834, 842,
    852, 854, 868
  Innocent: I 579
  Job: II 523
  Lady Poverty: I 531–32, 537

poor: II 244, 581; III 249, 794, 840
Rufino: III 507, 620
Rule: III 378, 383
seraph: I 283
snow: I 320; II 325, 563, 723, 741; III
    43, 97, 834
square: II 182, 745, 752; III 305–06
wrestling: I 194; II 642
Nation
  Christian: I 213
  European: I 206
  every: I 57, 84, 93, 143, 146–49, 151,
    156, 351, 380, 599–600; II 37, 42,
    124, 339, 419, 509, 620, 700, 720,
    735, 747, 759, 762; III 65, 161, 180,
    224, 291, 388, 396, 424–25, 631, 836
  idol: III 180
  lady: I 533
  liberation: I 585
  light: III 811
  mission: III 799–800
  Pope: III 812
Native
  Assisi: I 197, 320, 373, 429, 452, 488,
    514; II 95, 809; III 826
  dialect: III 443, 519
  Rome: III 828
  Tuscany: III 833
Nativity. See also Christmas: I 66, 101, 405;:
    II 333, 347, 411, 783; III 79, 230, 363,
    515–16, 540, 626, 655
Nature
  Divine: II 726, 813; III 563, 745
  essential character: I 131, 266, 185, 234,
    322, 357, 398, 429, 504, 513–14, 537;
    II 299, 367, 377, 405, 434, 445, 457,
    514, 560, 591, 599, 655, 664, 697, 724,
    745, 764–65, 813; III 81, 96–97,
    174–75, 187–88, 388, 395, 423–24,
    563, 739, 745, 751–52, 754, 771, 778,
    780, 787, 847, 853, 862–63, 868
  grace: I 234; II 377, 599; III 48, 150,
    188, 422–24, 815
  law: I 266; II 514
  physical: II 105, 225, 260, 406, 694; III
    153, 231, 792
  trait: I 252–53, 329, 506, 514, 519, 538;
    II 50, 68; III 182, 194, 720, 865
Necessity
  alms: III 265
  exemption: III 746
  extreme: I 198; II 194, 282; III 45, 594
  life: III 159
  love of God: III 283
  manifest: I 101, 195, 374, 376, 587; II
    138, 150, 182, 198, 206, 210, 221,
    277, 579, 679; III 167, 170, 258, 267,
    278, 306, 406, 704, 756, 772, 791
  occasion: I 386, 401
  pleasure: III 45, 852
  pretext: I 219; II 291; III 267
  religion: III 265

satisfaction: I 227, 413; II 82, 218, 293, 458, 560, 681, 707
use: III 749, 766
Neck
bird: I 234, 396; II 412, 624, 706, 800, 810; III 470, 835, 860
figurative: I 185, 292, 320, 371, 441, 468, 508; II 269, 291, 334, 571, 619, 663, 701; III 152, 605, 834, 849
Francis: I 228, 253, 392, 478, 505; II 138, 182, 304, 430, 570; III 280, 305–06, 570–71, 728
hang: II 430, 663; III 33a, 566, 662
John of Capella: III 33a, 566, 662
Judas: III 566
miracle: I 298; II 429, 457–58, 479, 482, 662, 680; III 69
Needle: II 722; III 888
Negligence
accusation: I 234, 396; II 412, 624
allowance: I 550
avoid: II 739
brother: I 65–66, 119
expulsion: I 221
fear: I 413
Francis: III 860
Giles: III 564–65
heir: III 766
human: III 188
minister: III 287
perish: II 142, 340, 392, 462
Nest
biblical: I 243, 535; II 159, 285, 578, 815
figurative: II 355, 412
Newness
apostolic: II 399
fervour: III 868
holy: I 260, 273
Order: I 470
stigmata: I 282, 645–46; III 870
taste: II 567
vision: I 264
News
brother: II 361; III 120, 151
Christ: I 599; III 159
death of John: III 151
Francis: III 249, 268, 483, 602, 877
friend: II 737
Joseph: III 144, 158
kingdom: I 239, 241, 266; II 455
Lucifer: III 411
miracle: II 410, 418, 465, 490, 624, 646, 654–55, 672, 678
poverty: II 220; III 249, 268
salvation: II 255
woe: I 513; II 428
wolf: III 483, 602
Word: I 576; II 819
world: II 156, 258; III 121, 299
Night
Christmas: I 255, 406, 506; II 130, 610; III 363, 516, 626

conversation: II 85; III 475, 527, 538, 617
day: I 47, 126, 142, 149, 156,199, 223–24, 579, 585; II 68, 156, 165, 194, 203, 207, 215, 222, 224, 258, 323, 423–25, 551–52, 610; III 89, 98, 153, 168, 283, 299, 319, 341, 345, 347, 350, 369, 455, 506, 511, 548, 615, 617, 619, 688, 834, 845
death: I 284; II 390, 644, 647; III 357, 362, 369
demon: II 185, 224, 227, 326, 575, 796; III 312, 345, 347, 810, 853, 847
despoil: I 579; II 178, 202
figurative: I 215, 435, 438; II 299, 307, 399, 554
fire: I 114; II 185–86; III 98, 331, 366–68, 436, 567
hospitality: II 85; III 40, 436, 524, 567, 578, 584, 862
hunger: II 565; III 278
illness: II 161, III 131, 334, 345, 493, 598, 608
matins: III 31, 453–54, 497, 611, 697
prayer: I 203, 218, 244, 284, 299, 408, 417, 462, 476; II 44, 46, 93, 156, 169, 186, 202, 226–28, 258, 289, 301, 324, 326–28, 330, 350, 390, 419, 459, 476, 511, 552, 562, 567, 594, 606–07, 647, 656, 691, 699, 743, 817; III 51, 69, 96, 102, 121, 217, 345, 437, 474, 504, 523, 525, 528, 533, 572, 594, 619, 637, 691, 747, 797, 810, 853
silence: III 437
sleep: I 598; II 43, 91, 191, 274, 321, 562, 616, 659, 702; III 56, 72, 93, 436, 862
sleepless: I 299; II 71, 135, 149, 158, 161, 167, 185, 190, 225, 227, 259, 289, 326, 384, 443, 458, 565, 635, 712, 723, 789, 796, 816; III 69, 312, 479, 534, 598, 797
temptation: II 165, 563, 723; III 347, 497, 611, 634
vision: I 185–86, 212, 224, 277, 300, 305, 321, 371, 389, 508; II 35–36, 39, 70, 87, 98, 169, 185, 197, 245, 260, 283, 325, 327, 381, 421, 429–30, 437–40, 443, 448, 451, 455, 457, 463–64, 467, 481, 532–33, 552, 558, 562–63, 567, 575, 634, 644, 651–2, 662, 666–69, 671–72, 674, 679–81, 685, 707, 711, 785–87; III 390, 438, 457, 870
watch: III 217, 471
Noise
birds: I 397; II 356, 592, 594, 813; III 105
concern: I 273
contemplation: III 847

disturb: I 243, 307, 487; II 73, 99, 215,
   313, 371, 404, 413, 425, 606, 654,
   659; III 261, 847
Elias: III 573
laborer: III 105
lute: II 169
Masseo: III 463
other: II 158; III 261
ridicule: I 191
Non–believer. See also Infidel
   adversary: III 56
   behavior: I 74
   fear: II 105
   martyrdom: III 323
   mission: I 106, 216, 345, 555, 600–01,
      698; III 134, 136, 246, 722, 839
   obedience: III 119
   preach: III 727
   Saracen: III 56, 323
   similarity: II 124, 333; III 224, 291
Norm
   anchorite: II 362
   elder: II 369
   justice: I 183; II 145
   life: I 217, 598; II 689
   married: III 879
   Portiuncula: II 155–58
   poverty: II 150, 160, 691; III 234, 239,
      263, 279
Nourishment
   bodily: I 598; II 431, 464, 551; III 588
   new: III 886
   sleep: III 810
   spiritual: II 737
Novelty
   Greccio: II 610
   miraculous: II 403, 407; III 484, 603
   three women: II 580
   way of life: III 826
   wolf: III 484, 603
Novice
   goods: II 291, 579
   obedience: II 125, 345, 571; III 225,
      292, 849
   Peter of John Olivi: III 813
   Psalter: II 207, 209–10; III 169, 257,
      707, 819
   temptation: III 546, 642
Novitiate. See Probation
Nun: I 106, 575; II 647, 779, 808; III 136,
   517, 591
   monastery: I 106, 575; II 779; III 760

O

Oath
   brother: II 146, 380
   Francis: III 323, 456, 716
   God: I 471
   other: II 405, 426, 514, 636, 655
   Rule: II 146, 380; III 25, 323, 716, 766
   witness: II 25; III 766, 805–06

Obedience. See also Command
   Adam: I 129
   Bernard: III 570–72
   body: II 382
   brother: I 63, 67, 93, 130, 218, 222; II
      46, 92–93, 448, 546, 554; III 39, 41,
      381, 410, 570–73, 582, 584–86
   Christ: I 48, 68, 93, 97, 116–17; II 125,
      245, 249, 536, 540; III 198, 419, 655,
      730
   church: III 385, 425, 596
   command: I 206–07, 218, 381, 388,
      413, 587; II 138, 386, 448, 546, 617,
      641; III 293, 597, 610, 620, 624, 647,
      694
   companion: I 165; II 695, 750
   conscience: I 48, 66–67, 130, 393; II
      46, 128, 265, 329, 614
   corpse: III 293
   creature: I 234, 236, 328, 488, 599; II
      345, 357, 411, 414, 595, 625, 629,
      708, 717, 801, 839
   death: I 115; III 338
   disregard: II 138, 182, 240, 346, 376,
      573–74, 576; III 294, 416
   Dominic: II 797
   flesh: III 853
   Francis: I 57, 122–23, 126, 236, 435,
      799; II 53, 182, 189, 265, 292, 327,
      340, 344, 386, 447, 512, 540, 542,
      546, 557, 571, 580, 642–43, 671, 695,
      721, 724, 750, 760, 799, 801; III 133,
      135, 158, 216, 225, 243, 287, 292,
      305, 385, 425, 570–73, 582, 584–87
   Francis and Dominic: II 797
   fraternity: I 65, 68, 73, 103; III 133,
      742, 770
   fruits: II 571
   Giles: I 204
   glory: III 670
   God: I 88, 120, 131, 331, 589, 599; II
      248, 540, 724
   Gospel: I 100; II 571, 581; III 198
   harmony: I 130, 266; II 640, 725
   humility: I 48, 164; II 575, 695,
      734–35; III 152, 292, 730
   life: I 63, 100; III 742
   life outside: I 68, 568
   Masseo: III 584
   merit: III 624, 641
   minister: I 65–66, 100, 104–05, 126,
      305, 584; II 50, 57, 189, 239, 340,
      344, 386; III 235, 287, 292, 419, 696
   mission: I 203; III 119
   mortification: II 125, 142, 340; III 287,
      293
   novice: II 125, 345, 571
   observance: III 392
   Pacifico: III 692
   papal teaching: I 561, 564, 572; III
      742–43, 762, 770–71
   perfection: III 293

Pope: I 63, 100, 413; II 50, 98, 812; III 135, 721
poverty: III 157, 597, 601, 706
prelate: I 130, 222; II 46, 125, 200, 211, 269, 344–45; III 384–85, 859
promise: I 65, 117
renunciation: III 397
Rule: II 291, 461, 481; III 116, 126, 128, 157–58, 252, 294, 386, 388, 419–20, 741
simplicity: II 319
spirit: I 165; III 198
strength: II 281
teaching: I 97, 222; II 345
timing: I 218, 252; II 118, 346, 554, 557, 712
true: I 97, 130
vow: I 304
woman: II 462
yoke: II 269, 571, 619, 701; III 627
Obsequy
  Mary: I 468
Observance
  Francis: III 197
  Gospel: I 608; II 95, 206, 261, 298, 387, 547, 579, 643, 755, 759, 775; III 50, 150, 152, 179–80, 196–97, 257, 315, 323–24, 326, 405, 704, 715, 740, 742–43, 770
  heretical: I 593
  life: III 135, 148, 385, 397, 417, 425, 741, 858
  literal: III 420
  obedience: III 392
  Order: III 765
  papal teaching: III 740, 750–51, 762, 765
  perfect: II 755; III 160, 180, 197, 257, 323–34, 405, 420, 715
  piety: II 588
  poverty: II 378; III 165, 255, 385, 397, 596, 820
  precept: III 750
  promise: III 389, 417, 722
  pure: I 516; III 116, 315, 385, 389, 397, 405, 409, 415, 420, 714, 750, 765, 820
  regular: I 561; II 268; III 769, 859
  religious: II 257; III 770
  Rule: I 204; III 115–16, 135, 152, 159, 166, 179, 182–83, 188, 190, 196, 201, 401, 409, 417, 420, 425, 634, 702, 714, 741–42, 751, 762, 769
  state: III 148, 151
  Testament: III 152, 420
  vocation: III 390
Obstacle
  cares: I 273
  cross: I 495
  Francis: I 457
  illness: I 511
  miscellaneous: II 810
  Order: I 582

  other: II 322
  ownership: III 786
  peace: III 576
  reception: III 55
  salvation: I 570; II 406
  self–judgment: II 818–19
  soul: III 406, 588, 644
Occupation: III 757–58
Odor: I 299, 459; III 71, 412, 447
Offense
  another: I 159, 278, 386; II 45, 591
  brother: I 415; II 143–44, 230, 475; III 337, 560, 835
  guilt: III 228, 578
  pardon: III 560, 602, 835
  personal: I 136, 386; II 311, 326, 331, 350, 358, 442–43, 576, 600, 609, 616, 672, 687; III 337, 343, 404, 483, 602
Office
  acceptance: III 825, 827–30
  Anthony: III 694
  apostolic: III 741, 890
  bishop: II 438, 667
  books: I 65
  brother: III 328, 413–14, 718
  church: III 820
  clergy: I 47, 77, 90
  consul: II 465
  corpse: II 345, 571
  demon: II 225; III 231, 312
  doctor of theology: II 358
  Dominic: II 786
  ecclesiastical: III 680
  executor of wills: III 755, 777
  Francis: II 72, 211, 219, 340, 344, 571, 789; III 413–16
  general minister: II 145, 156, 211, 219, 344, 571; III 287
  Gregory IX: I 418, 603; II 296
  guardian: III 36, 133
  humility: II 188; III 293, 350
  leader: II 72
  lector: III 151
  minister: III 415
  ministry: II 208; III 169, 231
  police: II 225; III 231, 312
  Pope: I 293
  preacher: I 75, 105, 574, 576, 587, 598; II 48, 208, 352, 406, 652, 778, 789; III 219, 694, 758–59, 773
  prelate: II 93, 125, 142, 211, 218, 340, 406, 787; III 31, 225, 247, 287–88, 316–17, 321, 326, 711
  priest: II 787
  provincial minister: II 556, 693; III 782–83
  removal: II 341; III 762, 823
  renunciation: III 413–16
  sacredness: I 411
  scandal: I 68, 93

Office, Divine. See also Hours, Liturgy of: I
222, 327, 562; III 341, 581, 747, 772,
819–20
  Bonaventure: III 698
  celebration: I 65, 101, 119, 125–26; II
    311, 761, 773, 775; III 261, 450, 581,
    596, 820
  church: I 101, 222; II 775; III 385, 698
  Clare: III 516, 626
  cleric: I 65, 101, II 775
  Francis: I 157; II 229, 311, 761, 773; III
    31, 698
  Julian: III 697
  Leo: II 773
  matins: I 61, 66, 101, 506; II 44, 91,
    152, 196, 306, 407, 453, 562, 797; III
    130, 235, 270, 286, 450–51, 454, 497,
    499, 515, 542, 547, 581, 611, 614,
    626, 666, 696, 820
  Nativity: III 516, 626
  night: III 31, 697
  Roman Church: I 101, 222; II 775; III
    385, 698
  Rule: I 65, 101, 120, 126; II 773, 775
  San Damiano: III 516, 626
  vigil: II 491
Oil
  apply: I 435; II 439, 668
  cooking: II 182, 555, 692
  gift: II 155
  gladness: II 329
  holy: III 227–28
  jar: III 227–28, 236, 299
  lamp: II 76, 83, 250, 252, 555, 692; III
    91, 121
  preach: I 600
  salvation: I 274
  time: II 360
Oil lamp: II 250, 555, 692; III 91
Ointment
  heavenly: I 298
  medicinal: II 653; III 295
  precious: II 143, 347, 587
Old age
  church: I 457
  personal: I 446; III 48, 603
Omnipotence: III 423, 568
Opinion
  carnal: II 301
  Crescentius: II 240
  difference: III 762, 803
  Francis: III 290, 407, 848
  medical: I 305; III 91
  personal: II 118, 328, 337–38, 346, 569,
    578, 695, 796
  popular: I 442, 476; II 88, 242, 265,
    330, 391, 477
  Rule: III 198
  self: III 848
Opportunity
  expression: I 372; II 240
  flesh: II 750

  freedom: II 582
  hurt: II 260
  merit: II 295
  return: I 538
  various: III 738, 849
Opposition
  authority: III 154
  demon: III 424
  father: I 374
  observance: III 390
  other: I 465
  Rule: III 409
  salvation: III 396
Oppression
  affliction: III 103
  poor: III 136
  refuge: I 192
Orator: II 352
Order
  advocate: II 374
  affection: II 437, 466, 609, 655, 666,
    776; III 472
  Apocalypse: III 191
  apostasy: III 325, 553, 629–30
  approval: I 559, 598–99; III 844
  beginning: I 258, 564, 581, 584; II 66,
    257, 280, 319, 529, 541, 553, 749,
    783; III 125, 149, 333, 440, 447, 450,
    538, 566, 581, 592, 680–81, 690, 701,
    723, 830, 843, 863
  brother: I 197, 267, 582; II 405, 588,
    657, 811; III 240, 336, 607, 647, 742,
    744, 760
  chapter: I 574
  charity: I 282
  church approval: I 559, 598–99; III 844
  Cistercian: III 795
  cleric: II 371; III 856–57
  community: III 714
  contemporary: I 580, 582, 585; II
    783–84, 809, 811; III 823, 840, 843
  corruption: III 179, 203
  Crosier: II 555, 692; III 845
  decline: III 723
  defame: I 577
  depart: I 561; III 34, 124, 254, 325,
    351, 443, 553–54, 573, 600, 642, 693,
    713–14
  desert: II 742
  destruction: III 706, 795
  enter: I 260, 583; II 39, 57, 110, 118,
    349, 381, 445, 450, 627, 652, 672,
    740, 775; III 44, 53–54, 56–60,
    62–63, 261, 290, 301, 323, 333, 336,
    352, 474, 526, 545, 569, 594, 611,
    634, 641, 649, 759
  espouse: III 62
  expansion: I 579; II 529, 557, 690; III
    196, 572, 838, 849
  France: II 752
  Francis: I 73, 99, 104, 119–20, 166,
    217, 269, 304, 473, 500, 562, 583; II

43, 91, 673, 725, 738, 783–84, 806;
III 53, 62–63, 86, 438, 480, 561,
629–30, 635, 699, 794, 823, 825, 830,
840
general minister: II 364
God: I 576; III 88, 437, 523, 568, 741,
850
governance: III 169, 328, 756
habit: I 561; II 369; III 315, 838, 843
head and mother: II 109; III 328
holiness: III 192, 326, 529, 547, 577,
604, 615, 724
house: II 777; III 260–61
humility: II 572; III 154, 727
ideal: III 754
illiterate: II 371
Jacobite: III 826
Joachim: III 681
learned: III 130, 314, 709
mirror: III 489, 726
mother: II 109; III 328
newness: I 260, 356, 469–70, 473–74,
582; III 90, 92
observance: III 758
origin: II 66
Penitent: I 338; II 43, 55, 553; III 64,
91, 469, 593, 879
perfection: I 585
pilgrim: III 492
Poor Ladies: I 338, 377–78; II 83, 378,
447, 476, 747, 779, 782; III 64, 91,
228, 690, 834, 842, 845, 878
Pope: I 559, 564, 576; III 765
possess: II 777; III 164, 477, 748, 756,
765–66
poverty: I 573; II 285; III 597, 726
Preacher: I 582, 591–92, 594, 600; II
344, 785, 809, 811; III 296, 475, 595,
823
prelate: III 133, 848
priest: III 689
privilege: III 324, 789
profession: I 464, 561, 576
prophesy: I 469; II 349; III 61, 125,
129, 134, 182, 194, 196, 318, 721
protector: II 260, 262, 572; III 324, 478,
598, 824, 838–39, 858–59, 741
province: III 647
religious: I 77, 90, 95, 561; II 731; III
193
seal: III 885
stage: III 486–88, 724–25, 758
Testament: III 179, 182
vicar: III 442, 446, 577
work of God: I 576; III 88, 437, 523,
568, 741, 850
Origin
Divine: I 261; II 696, 724
Francis: III 833
land: III 39
nature: I 458; II 531
Order: II 66

Poor Ladies: I 385
problem: III 761
religious life: II 519
soul: I 433
Originality
personal: II 370
Ornament
Basilica: I 419; II 478; III 67
Francis: I 451
heaven: III 99
Outskirts
Arezzo: II 574
Assisi: I 599
Oven
dwelling: I 218; II 43, 91; III 40
Ownership
book: III 755, 785
church: II 777; III 748, 787–88
inheritance: III 778
money: III 753
movable things: III 755, 778
renunciation: I 214; II 160, 257; III
744, 748–49, 767, 777, 781, 812
rights: III 163, 239, 263, 384, 751, 777
use: III 746–49, 753, 781
Ox
biblical: II 761
Brother Ox: III 230
cure: II 464, 679
Greccio: I 255, 406, 506; II 130, 610,
783; III 230, 363
inheritance: II 164, 368; III 301–02
Julian: III 697
Luke: III 697

P

Pact
covenant: III 323, 398, 715, 887
Francis: II 455, 594, 674; III 483–84,
602–03
greed: I 546
revelation: III 555, 639
Rule: II 146, 380
Pagan: II 720
battle: I 231
Sultan: II 741; III 490
writing: I 252; III 78
Pain: I 431, 433, 516; II 306, 489
animal: I 501–02
brother: I 272; II 349; III 612, 642, 650
childbirth: I 238; II 440, 669, 783
discipleship: I 339, 353; II 76, 212, 332,
375, 378, 697, 816
excommunication: III 762, 805
father: II 80, 82
Francis: I 265, 357, 411; II 336, 355,
403, 474, 566, 704; III 97, 172–73,
244, 265, 335–36, 339, 364, 371, 415,
453, 478–79, 493, 513, 534, 598, 703,
861–63
lust: II 723

people: III 870
Poor Ladies: I 286
Rufino: I 265, 411; II 336, 403, 474,
  636
sick: I 275–76, 283, 299, 303–05, 403,
  487, 509–13; II 135, 162, 197, 181,
  189, 197, 316, 330, 355, 359, 384,
  405, 428, 433, 439–42, 445–46, 458,
  460, 463, 466, 482, 641, 647, 655,
  658, 662, 668, 675, 677, 681, 712,
  797, 799, 805; III 69, 70, 95, 608
sin: III 198
Painting
  cross: II 249
  Lord: II 124; III 224, 291
  stigmata: II 65, 405
  Virgin: II 124
Paladin: II 209; III 257, 707, 892
Pall: I 482
Palm
  hand: III 86, 155
  martyrdom: II 400, 706; III 392, 398
  seraph: I 509
  stigmata: I 344, 410, 517; II 404, 601,
    604, 654, 797
  tree: I 604; II 746; III 854, 875
  victory: II 146, 364, 381, 560; III 446
Pants: II 191; III 365
Paper: I 305; II 280, 609, 618, 701, 801; III
  131, 325, 473, 808
Parable
  discernment: II 259; III 169, 258, 708
  lamb: I 399
  modesty: II 141, 322; III 334
  penance: III 409
  Pope: II 254–56, 548; III 46, 88, 391
  poverty: I 549
  sheep: I 249
  unity: II 369–71
Paralysis: I 240, 306, 518; II 432; III 74
Pardon
  brother: II 92, 134, 303, 376; III 200,
    540, 636, 847
  Francis: I 477, 505; II 574, 793, 803; III
    50, 407, 630
  God: I 85, 114; II 187; III 95, 535, 546
  need: I 332, 369, 690, 701, 802, 804
  other: II 140, 240; III 349, 368, 407,
    489, 535, 602
  Portiuncula: III 806–12
  poverty: I 553
Parent: I 301, 303, 305–07, 430, 441, 443; II
  102, 283, 669
  attachment: II 510
  brother: II 164, 174, 266, 369, 617; III
    241, 301–2, 833, 863–64
  children: II 424, 445–46, 452–55, 457,
    461, 627, 656, 669, 675; III 70, 72
  Christ: II 803
  first: I 488

Francis: I 182–83, 190, 319, 370, 373;
  II 68, 73, 174, 242, 266, 537, 617,
  687; III 840
Parish. See also Church, Local
  Le Simon: II 676
  Massa Trabaria: III 411
  Pisa: II 435
  preach: I 125, 597, 600; III 385
  priest: II 787–88; III 65
  San Severino: III 527, 636
Parsley: II 281, 281a
Partisan
  election: III 782
  evil: I 184
Passion
  animal: II 696
  charity: I 254
  Christ: I 46, 159, 260, 262, 409, 510,
    517, 596; II 76, 515, 632, 645, 749,
    757, 814–16, 784; III 148, 161, 181,
    186–88, 190, 194, 339–40, 380, 421,
    508, 531, 541, 552, 555, 621, 628,
    639–43, 651–52, 656, 666–67, 740,
    811, 816, 839, 855, 865–67, 870
  conform: II 77
  cross: I 264, 280; II 172, 249; III 83
  Gospel: I 262, 409; II 631, 784
  greed: I 38; II 86
  likeness: I 645
  love: II 314, 612; III 855
  mark: I 260, 357, 510, 517, 596; II 249,
    401, 722, 734, 743, 749, 780, 816; III
    76, 180, 250, 607
  power: I 159; III 149
  preach: II 261
  righteousness: II 760–61
Pastor
  church: I 576, 595; III 154, 722
  Pope: I 269; III 770
Patience
  affliction: I 413, 445, 452, 511; II 42,
    45, 90, 225–26, 243, 384–85, 640–43,
    714, 740–41; III 231, 268, 313, 344,
    436, 445, 476, 567, 607, 650, 868
  anger: I 440
  another: I 48, 133, 167, 192, 199,
    218–20, 381, 456; II 360; III 36, 125,
    150, 154–55, 231, 333, 436, 440, 484,
    575, 586, 601, 607, 851
  disciple: II 512
  encourage: I 80, 88; II 387, 718; III
    596, 601, 869
  Francis: I 334; II 531, 640–43, 714; III
    730–31, 851, 868
  God: I 109, 152
  helmet: I 441
  poverty: I 549, 553; II 152, 218, 294,
    722
  presence: I 136; III 38, 40, 325
  reward: I 75; II 384
  shield: I 225; II 384
  spirit: I 76, 90, 105

Patrimony
  Honorius: I 579
Payment
  first: II 296, 339; III 395
  goods: I 572; II 776; III 751–52
  lamb: I 249, 501
  Portiuncula: II 155; III 120, 236
  preach: II 186; III 348
  salvation: I 515
  stone: II 39, 87; III 101
  work: I 69, 102; II 148, 351; III 322, 747, 750
  wrongdoing: I 445
Peace: I 156, 269, 300, 309, 324, 341, 346, 443, 474, 496; II 193, 292, 307, 438, 460, 480, 580, 804; III 35, 44, 49, 89, 282, 304, 501, 506, 524, 532, 536, 615, 632, 691, 703, 765, 769, 772, 782, 861, 863
  angel: I 286; II 526; III 829
  animal: I 599; III 483–85, 601–04
  Arezzo: II 215, 575
  Baptist: II 84
  Bernard: II 127, 280; III 356, 884
  birds: I 599; III 483–85, 601–04
  bishop and mayor: II 187–88, 319, 349–50
  blessing: I 112, 114, 203, 296; II 478, 616
  Body of Lord: I 117
  Bonaventure: II 498
  brother: I 203, 207, 215, 219, 320, 381; II 85, 90, 260–61, 341, 343a, 715; III 879
  canonization: I 296; II 478
  care: I 272
  champion: I 339
  child: I 203, 320, 335; II 52, 133, 341
  Christ: I 42, 49, 300; II 317, 499, 556, 803; III 381, 388, 397
  church: II 260–61, 343; III 324
  clergy: II 133, 160, 341; III 47, 263, 296–97, 856–57
  conflict: I 292
  Conrad: III 638
  conversion: I 194, 203; II 52, 85
  covenant: I 542; II 489
  cross: II 682
  delegation: I 292; II 91
  destruction: I 292
  Dominic: II 772
  endure: I 114–15; II 187; III 368
  eternity: III 370, 396, 654
  food for soul: II 229, 311, 609
  Francis: I 324, 339; II 206, 243, 286, 607, 644, 699, 714, 808; III 355, 425, 728
  friend: I 335
  gentleness: II 53, 102
  God: III 596
  good: II 84
  Gospel: I 600; II 526
  heart: I 272; II 46, 52, 102; III 102, 508

humility: II 575
John of St. Paul: II 55
kiss: I 551; II 74; III 551
La Verna: II 498
Lady Poverty: I 534, 541–42, 545, 551
Leo: II 153
mayor: II 187–88, 319, 349–50
meek: II 518
message: I 45, 58, 60, 73, 102, 122–23, 126, 203, 207, 215, 320, 379–81, 461; II 43, 52, 90, 102, 543, 546; III 44, 71, 95, 203, 219, 276–77, 443, 476, 493, 574, 608, 843, 877
mind: I 272; II 46, 52, 102; III 102, 508
minister: III 858
mission: I 207, 215; II 54
negotiation: II 808
obstacle: III 576
Pacifico: II 556
pilgrim: II 286, 578
place: II 616
poverty: II 715
practice: III 40, 502
prayer: III 129
preach: I 215, 380, 599–600; II 543
prelate: II 133, 160, 341; III 47, 263, 296–97, 856–57
promise: III 189
prophet: II 84
quiet: II 229
reconciliation: I 269; III 92
salvation: I 335, 380, 545; II 543
Seraph: II 499
Siena: III 460, 584–85
spirit: I 76, 90; III 426
spiritual: III 60, 193, 227, 233, 256, 341
state: III 181, 520, 522
temptation: II 153
way: II 489, 526, 714
word: II 206
Peacemaker: I 133–34, 269, 534
Pearl
  biblical: I 187, 372; II 72, 284, 533, 621, 686, 696, 746; III 464, 588, 719, 842, 849
  Poor Ladies: I 197
  poverty: II 555, 577
  stigmata: I 265, 286, 411, 418, 473, 476, 647; III 188, 866, 877
Peasant
  entrance: III 301–02
  Francis: III 440
  judge: II 799
  Rivo Torto: I 222, 474; II 99
  thirsty: II 278, 409, 793; III 861
Pen: III 473, 867
Penance. See also Conversion: I 136, 478; II 323, 425, 428, 459, 480, 524, 546, 562, 564, 659, 800; III 39, 469
  Bernard: II 39, 85, 87, 91; III 567

brother: I 120, 125, 380, 384; II 48, 85,
88–89, 94–96, 98, 107, 186, 219, 574,
645; III 157, 169, 228, 249, 251,
278–79, 285, 311, 407, 472
Brothers and Sisters: I 603; II 103, 553;
III 64, 91, 593
chastity: II 741
conversion: II 177, 208, 219, 221–22,
543, 562, 626; III 39, 52, 248, 250,
319–20, 327, 408, 496, 537, 610, 615,
705, 717, 821
death: I 78, 91
fornication: I 73
Francis: I 124, 195, 392; II 166–67,
174, 356, 543, 546, 562–63, 721, 723,
740, 817; III 153, 243, 303, 372, 439,
448, 570, 811, 823
fruit: I 41, 47, 78, 91; II 102; III 388,
480–81, 599
impose: I 72–73, 77, 98
John of La Verna: III 649
John of Penna: III 545, 641
lack: I 43, 50, 82; II 84
Lady Jacoba: III 474
nobleman: III 552, 627–29
practice: I 77, 299, 587; II 42, 47, 52,
54, 87–88, 94, 102–03, 107, 166–67,
177, 186, 219, 543, 562, 594, 817; III
147, 245, 386, 412, 497, 504, 507,
525, 601, 603, 607, 621, 730–31, 769,
810
preach: I 57, 201–02, 207, 379, 381,
384, 392; II 40, 42, 54, 96, 98, 163,
186, 543, 549, 553, 594, 600, 626,
691, 689, 706; III 240, 300, 310, 348,
381–82, 395, 484, 686, 820
purification: II 740–41
remission: I 565; II 40
request: I 323, 564; III 605
Rufino: III 507–08, 617–21
service: I 82
sign: II 317a
sin: I 50; II 40, 42, 88–89, 128, 299,
546, 562, 817; III 482
Stephen: III 795
symbol: III 366
way: III 65, 315, 529
work: I 587; III 489–90, 496
Penetration
heart: I 379; II 543, 586, 689; III 500,
615
inner self: I 386; III 795, 814
mystery: II 314, 612
spirit: II 754
understanding: III 421, 855
Penitence
example: II 689; III 45
preach: III 53
Penitent. See also Third Order: I 48c, 48d,
49b, 84–85, 338; II 136a, 399b, 524, 527;
III 45
Assisi: II 43, 90

habit: II 650
Order: II 55, 750; III 701, 824, 845, 879
Penitentiary: III 795, 805
Pentecost
chapter: I 67, 76, 98, 104, 574; II 51,
55, 101, 778; III 760
Feast: III 151
Octave: I 150
Perfection: I 81, 449; III 38
Bernard: II 127; III 227, 356
bond: III 786
brother: I 385–86, 553, 585; II 40, 66,
144, 210, 240, 497; III 135, 150, 156,
170, 180, 301–02, 402, 404, 411, 424,
705, 779
call: II 509, 511
charity: III 410
Christ: II 554, 565, 759; III 153, 160,
174, 177, 180, 188, 195, 380–81
church: II 399, 497
counsel: III 198
creature: III 655
decline: III 179, 202, 389, 399, 413,
710
flower: I 216
Francis: I 260, 320–21, 338, 393, 408,
589; II 125–26, 147, 164, 206, 240,
256a, 257c, 263, 350, 358, 382, 385,
392, 509, 533, 560–61, 565, 623, 684,
762, 784; III 32, 152, 214–372, 401,
406
Giles: III 125
gospel: I 210, 320, 379; II 49, 57, 84,
206, 393, 520, 526, 535, 543, 547,
581, 581a, 688a, 691, 744, 792; III
148, 159, 167–68, 179–80, 188, 198,
227, 256–57, 335, 355, 357, 372, 391,
424, 438, 704, 816, 831, 842
hermitage: II 362
Humilis: III 537, 643
humility: II 125–26, 578, 688a; III
287–92
Lady Jacoba: II 417
Lady Poverty: I 553; II 284; III 161
life: III 328, 745
Masseo: III 461, 586
master: I 338
mirror: I 260; II 263; III 214–372
money: II 365; III 325
motivation: III 225–26, 715
obedience: III 292–94
Order: I 585; III 387
Pacifico: III 537, 643
Pellegrino: III 501, 615
plan: II 533
Poor Ladies: I 378; II 378
poverty: III 160, 386, 816–17, 831, 842,
849
prayer: I 408
preservation: III 324–25, 334–36
principle: III 149
privilege: I 378a

profession: III 164, 372
purity: II 210; III 316
Rule: II 146, 380
saint: I 260; II 245; III 32, 381, 424
school: II 372
sign: II 264, 618
spirit: II 764; III 412
state: III 156, 285, 323, 372, 413, 690,
    744
summit: I 229, 321
Third Order: I 385
virtue: III 292
way: I 260; II 146, 362, 380, 685, 689,
    730; III 36, 156, 162, 390, 400, 411,
    568, 745, 849
work: II 147, 362; III 575, 745
zeal: III 327, 333–38, 717–18
Permanence
    inheritance: II 295
    Order: III 850
    papal decree: III 754–55
    Rule: II 557–58
    rust: II 330
    use: III 747
    usufruct: III 747
    warrior: II 692
    writing: I 469
Permission
    absolution: III 554
    acceptance of building: III 384
    beg alms: III 235
    birds: I 234; II 355, 412, 592–93, 624,
        798–800; III 485, 593, 606
    book: II 288; III 256–57, 819
    breviary: II 207, 209; III 169, 257–59,
        707–08, 814
    community of women: I 579
    cricket: II 218, 357, 414, 593
    devil: II 153, 329; III 354, 576
    enter monastery: I 106, 575, 779; III
        760–61
    enter Order: I 100; II 57, 579; III 61,
        352, 577
    fish: II 592
    hermitage: II 226; III 232
    hospitality: II 43
    leave Order: III 499, 614, 714
    liturgical change: II 610
    mice: III 347
    missionary life: I 74, 89, 106, 605, 608;
        III 119, 150, 490, 606, 641
    pilgrimage: I 305; II 425, 467
    preach: I 75, 245, 383–84; II 53, 98,
        102, 106, 342, 574, 810; III 154, 404,
        857–58
    Rule: III 116, 419
    travel: II 286; III 545, 552
    use of goods: II 590; III 747, 756, 776,
        785
    visit: II 224, 274–75
Persecution
    avoid: I 376; III 154

bless: I 74, 105; II 537; III 163
discipleship: I 131
endure: I 89, 95, 130; II 39–42, 77–78,
    437, 481, 667; III 115, 135, 152, 187,
    386, 392, 424, 816
patience: I 105, 219
poverty: I 541; III 162–63
prophecy: III 721–23
search: II 554
vulnerability: I 79
Perseverance
    charity: I 217
    Francis: I 212
    prayer: II 534, 605, 685; III 506, 688
    way of life: II 693; III 59, 393
Pharisee
    humility: II 736; III 422
    obedience: III 158
    poverty: I 536
    sheep: I 248, 399, 501
Pheasant: II 356–57, 413–14; III 175
Physician
    cure: I 494, 511, 513
    eye disease: II 354, 416; III 101
    Gospel: II 539
    need: I 67, 93, 98, 305
    witness: II 318
    work: II 458, 653; III 881
Piazza. See also Square
    Assisi: II 85, 181, 187, 570
    Perugia: II 178
    preach: I 60; II 82; III 39, 224, 291,
        305, 353
    presence: I 530; II 43, 72; III 349, 445,
        575, 603, 614
    Terni: II 124
Piety. See also Compassion, Tenderness: II
    534, 586–89, 586b; III 40, 41, 45, 64, 81,
    115, 135, 411, 525, 540
    absence: II 603, 625
    Assisi: III 372
    brother: I 223, 501; II 193, 320, 343,
        364–65, 383, 555, 564, 571, 579, 819;
        III 43, 120, 232, 235, 241, 279–80,
        286, 337, 553
    child: I 374
    Christ: I 255, 540; II 610; III 175, 285,
        720, 722, 730, 756, 785
    church: I 189, 189c, 201, 377
    companion of knowledge: I 437
    creature: I 234–35, 250, 322, 399, 401,
        501, 503; II 191, 590–95, 599; III
        175, 364–65, 851
    empty: I 542–43; II 291–92, 580; III
        165, 386
    everything: II 586, 595
    false: I 542–43; II 291–92, 580; III 165,
        386
    foe: II 588
    Francis: II 80–81, 154, 180, 182, 185,
        190, 227; III 305–06, 346–47, 364
    general minister: III 325

hardened heart: II 616, 616a
law: III 381
leper: II 74
Lord: II 50, 298, 317, 468, 583, 605
minister: II 587; III 325
needy: I 540; II 44, 92, 152, 172, 193,
  196–97, 220, 244, 251, 253, 272, 283,
  292, 300, 302–03, 306, 359, 422, 424,
  481, 531–32, 534, 540, 589–90,
  657–58, 672, 675, 680, 685, 697, 777;
  III 175–76, 282, 285–86, 302, 850
poor: I 540; II 44, 92, 152, 172, 193,
  196–97, 220, 244, 251, 253, 272, 283,
  292, 300, 302–03, 306, 359, 422, 424,
  481, 531–32, 534, 540, 589–90,
  657–58, 672, 675, 680, 685, 697, 777;
  III 175–76, 282, 285–86, 302, 850
Poor Ladies: II 128; III 229, 338, 357
sacrament: I 53–54; III 534
sick: I 540; II 44, 92, 152, 172, 193,
  196–97, 220, 244, 251, 253, 272, 283,
  292, 300, 302–03, 306, 359, 422, 424,
  481, 531–32, 534, 540, 589–90,
  657–58, 672, 675, 680, 685, 697, 777;
  III 175–76, 282, 285–86, 302, 850
sign of conversion: II 110; III 846
soul: II 587–88
suffering: II 76
warring: II 187, 215, 271; III 349
Pilgrim. See also Wayfarer: I 103, 126, 461,
  515; II 54, 102, 123, 136, 160, 176, 212,
  223, 267, 286–87, 418–19, 434, 451, 578,
  582–83, 664, 677; III 85, 135, 270, 351,
  492, 501, 518, 625, 695–96, 800
Pilgrimage: II 136, 136a, 287, 353; III 146,
  259, 396, 818
  Assisi: II 417–18, 676
  Holy Land: II 664
  holy place: III 400, 517–18, 525, 625
  Monte Gargano: I 301; II 390, 450,
    454, 644, 674; III 869
  Rome: II 73, 247
Pillow
  feather: II 227–28, 289, 562; III 232,
    348–49
  stone: I 552, 598; III 476, 596
  veneration: I 290
  wood: I 227; III 476, 596
Pit. See also Cave, Grotto
  biblical: I 142–43, 664; III 321, 410
  figurative: III 114, 133, 326, 399, 460,
    484, 496, 722
  hiding place: I 190–91; II 78, 537
  well: II 660
Pitchfork: III 497, 612
Pity: I 241, 271, 373, 433, 501, 515; II 190,
  276, 303, 317, 360, 416, 424, 438, 457,
  467, 555, 592, 665, 667, 786
  absence: I 192, 687; II 537
  Divine: I 403, 433, 453; III 82, 100
  feeling: II 455, 628; III 81, 85, 281,
    485, 522, 604, 652

moved by: I 240, 247, 300, 397, 403,
  492, 456; II 140, 305, 461; III 83, 85,
  175, 615
  parental: I 432, 447
  request: II 278, 409, 450; III 97, 161
Plague
  Apulia: II 466, 679
  black: III 680
  famine: III 512
  figurative: I 440, 471; II 588; III 153
  Rieti: II 410, 634, 711
Plain
  Assisi: I 220; II 533; III 82, 475, 595
  Campiglia: II 307–08, 580
  figurative: III 497, 612
Plan. See also Proposal, Purpose
  Bernard: II 544
  change: I 436; II 86, 544
  confirme: I 436; II 86, 544
  demonic: III 412
  Divine: I 152, 185, 207, 282, 368, 371;
    II 533, 585, 623; III 421, 460, 490,
    502, 513, 645, 878
  Francis: I 189, 192, 247, 382, 385; II
    36, 71, 75, 79, 85, 245, 401, 533; III
    412
  Masseo: III 514
Plant
  Clare: I 285; II 128, 476; III 228, 357,
    466, 516, 590, 624
  love: II 192
  Poor Ladies: II 158, 189
  religion: II 157; III 122, 237, 300, 409,
    886
Pleasure: I 135, 227, 359, 434, 492, 515–16,
  529, 588; II 366, 370; III 45, 98, 184, 267,
  476, 733, 749–50, 852
  birds: III 454
  bishop: II 574; III 384
  brother: I 92
  carnal: I 439, 566–67, 597; II 137, 293,
    333, 371, 382, 741, 815; III 326, 525
  daily: I 393
  enslave: I 392
  Francis: I 506; II 104, 415, 567
  God: I 120, 261; II 376, 433, 551, 621,
    623, 631, 663, 721; III 90, 387, 393,
    416, 437, 460, 465, 468, 865
  mundane: I 433, 566, 598; II 81, 362,
    530; III 540
  Pope: II 261, 812; III 859
Plow
  biblical: I 65, 101, 537, 566; III 241,
    739
  tool: II 465, 679
Poet
  Henri: I 429
  secular: I 182
Poison
  actual: I 325; II 439, 465, 663; III 829

figurative: I 552, 566; II 143, 319, 321, 329, 347, 363–64, III 295, 411, 489, 605
Police: II 133, 225, 326, 796; III 125, 171, 230–31, 312, 314, 414, 710, 712
Porter: I 84; III 450, 473, 499, 518, 580, 613–14, 625
Portion
  Benjamin: III 158
  dragon: I 355
  Francis: I 287; III 158
  obedience: II 557
  Portiuncula: II 256–57
  prophecy: I 330
  share: I 103, 483–84; II 130, 164, 246, 707, 747; III 158, 230, 241, 265, 301, 363, 384, 386, 587, 743, 820
Portrait
  Christ: II 589, 697
  Francis: I 253, 504; III 681
Position: II 429, 561
  condition: I 217, 298, 486; II 46, 364, 446, 458, 479, 662, 721, 724; III 69, 178, 227, 289, 356, 442, 486, 723
  humility: III 38, 155
  office: I 93, 130, 135, 273, 569; II 289, 367; III 763, 765
  similar: I 48, 98
Possession
  absence: II 37, 50
  arms: II 41, 89; III 46
  bestowal: I 607–08; III 33
  demonic: II 628
  eternal: I 530, 553; III 88, 815
  keep: I 405, 494; II 85, 510, 628, 745–46, 776–77, 815–16; III 98, 159, 163
  poverty: II 715
  question: II 38, 254, 510; III 746, 751, 767, 786
  renounce: I 204, 375, 430, 478, 540, 567, 583, 597, 607; II 38–39, 41, 50, 88, 165, 371, 400, 518, 534, 538, 578, 603, 685–87, 814–15; III 38, 45, 96, 147, 160, 281, 381, 447, 778, 813, 821
  senses: I 495
Poverty: I 529–54, 586, II 123–24, 131, 135–36, 284–308, 554–55, 577–85; III 45–47, 59–60, 167, 255–77, 609, 849
  abandon: II 160, 294; III 46, 133, 389, 394, 722
  apostle: I 94, 539–40; II 94, 764; III 701
  austerity: III 395
  bed: II 136, 150, 256, 288–90; III 259
  beg: II 94, 189, 295, 582
  Blessed Virgin: I 46; II 151,162, 375, 579, 802; III 195
  bless: I 267; III 88, 235, 279
  boast: III 787
  book: I 65; II 136, 204, 206, 209, 288, 362, 697; III 259, 705

bride: II 72; III 877, 884
building: II 136, 158–61,176, 210, 212, 283–88, 709; III 97, 172, 240, 259, 263, 265, 331, 406–07, 777, 781
charity: III 400, 425
chastity: III 601, 743, 877
Christ: I 46, 70, 91, 94, 106, 122–23, 353, 535; II 110, 123, 128, 151, 221, 287, 296, 577, 582, 688, 733, 742, 745, 756, 802–03; III 100, 152, 159, 223, 228, 250, 269, 271, 285, 381, 383–84, 386, 397, 425, 457, 464, 486, 566, 577, 701, 746, 849, 876
church: I 126; II 39, 36, 154, 161, 212, 540, 582; III 148, 172, 265, 324, 342, 724, 781, 786, 816
Clare: I 128; III 228
clothing: I 64, 101, 194, 202, 586, 597; II 74, 123, 194, 204, 210, 247, 293, 386, 401; III 118, 283, 489, 726, 774–75
coin: I 70, 102; II 44, 73, 76, 89, 137, 209, 290, 580, 583, 599, 687, 776, 801
comfort: III 89
communal: I 540, 547; II 46, 94, 131, 362, 371
compassion: II 91, 220–21, 302, 581; III 285
conformity to Christ: I 586; II 37, 255, 579, 756, 815
contempt: I 356, 461, 466, 582; II 121, 126
covenant: I 384, 539
disparage: III 148, 161–62, 164–65, 749
dream: II 301
early church: I 540, 582; II 148, 342
Emperor Jean: III 55–57
enrich: I 336; II 94, 152, 154, 176, 255, 269, 284, 286–88, 294, 298, 400, 581, 645, 688; III 97, 457, 463–64, 587–89, 719
evangelical: II 303, 578; III 33, 136, 159–60, 163–64, 173, 197–98, 386, 438, 447, 486, 477, 569, 577, 597, 627, 638, 685, 701, 719, 724, 742, 770, 781, 816–17
example: II 160–61; III 45, 120, 159, 172, 237, 239, 259, 261, 263, 271, 298, 324, 381, 457, 550, 627, 750, 815–16, 820
exterminate: III 136, 397
food: I 47, 66, 321, 376, 392–93, 454, 479, 482–83, 531, 551–52, 544, 597–98; II 76–77, 82, 88, 99, 150, 165, 175–76, 276, 417, 564, 597, 694; III 279
Francis: I 267, 285, 329, 331, 336, 353, 356, 380, 386, 392, 451, 461, 466–67; II 37, 50, 72–73, 128, 150, 284–85, 525–27, 688; III 165, 173, 223, 228,

236, 283, 290, 292, 435, 464, 587, 621, 701, 730, 815
freedom: I 466
furnace: II 745, 756
glory: III 335
Gospel: II 303, 578; III 33, 136, 159–60, 163–64, 173, 197–98, 386, 438, 447, 486, 477, 569, 577, 597, 627, 638, 685, 701, 719, 724, 742, 770, 781, 816, 817
height: I 103, 292; II 124, 290, 378, 526, 578, 721; III 162
humility: I 70, 91, 100, 103, 164, 255, 572, 582, 586, 601; II 37, 123–24, 126, 159, 161, 176, 204, 212, 257, 393, 534, 645, 688, 696, 756–57, 759, 772; III 47, 166, 172, 197, 223–24, 226, 239, 262–63, 271, 276, 290, 292, 298, 328, 361, 383–84, 386, 394, 396–97, 400, 405, 408, 413, 425, 601, 702, 740, 742, 770
inconsistent: III 163
Jean: III 55–57
joy: I 137
judgment: III 249
keys of kingdom: III 163
labor: III 395
Lady Poverty: I 529–54; III 160–63, 168, 240, 249, 273, 319, 336, 361, 408, 705
law: III 381
Lesser Brother: I 205, 214, 218, 320, 380, 474, 562, 572, 577, 582, 597–98, 601; II 44–48, 91, 94, 110, 150, 152, 269, 276; III 53, 61, 118, 152, 235–36, 271–72, 276, 279, 290, 298, 316, 333, 405, 435, 438, 463, 477, 481, 566, 569, 638, 685, 701, 740
love: II 74, 525, 529, 535, 609; III 83, 125, 160, 165, 192, 221, 333, 336, 371, 588
money: I 70, 102; II 44, 73, 76, 89, 137, 209, 290, 580, 583, 599, 687, 776, 801
norm: II 150, 160, 691; III 234, 239, 263, 279
obedience: III 597, 601, 705, 742, 877
observance: III 159, 165–66, 170, 239, 255–56, 263, 283, 316, 381, 385, 392, 703, 705
other Orders: III 155
papal teaching: I 561–62, 572–73, 576–77; II 776–77
patience: III 601
perfection: III 33, 100, 159–60, 164, 226, 292, 328, 386
poor: III 249–50, 285
Poor Ladies: I 19, 292; II 128, 378; III 64
Portiuncula: II 39, 154, 158, 176, 285–288
preserve: III 239, 397, 819
profession: III 249

promise: I 63, 63c, 100
property: III 779, 786
provision: II 44, 91, 123, 410, 584–85
revenue: III 779
riches: I 132, 165, 319, 442, 451; II 47, 94, 794
rigorous: I 457, 467, 603; II 45, 47, 50; III 32, 166, 255, 395, 702
San Damiano: I 373
serve: I 103; II 123; III 128, 371, 777
shortage: III 395
sign: II 160–61; III 45, 120, 159, 172, 237, 239, 259, 261, 263, 271, 298, 324, 381, 457, 550, 627, 750, 815, 816, 820
simple: II 37, 164, 205, 207, 211, 255, 267, 320, 380, 577, 645, 722, 756–57, 792; III 114, 170, 316, 400, 408, 413, 705, 711
spirit: III 156, 159–60
status: III 156
stifling: III 163
strict: I 457, 467, 603; II 45, 47, 50; III 32, 166, 255, 395, 702
sully: III 163–64
teaching of Francis: I 133, 133a, 205, 329, 331, 380; III 197, 203, 223, 234, 237, 256, 279, 324, 338, 344, 406, 476, 508, 621, 702, 704, 742, 774, 820, 826, 831, 843, 869
title: I 198, 320; II 339
truth: III 394
violate: III 157, 407
virute: III 159–61, 292
voluntary: I 46, 466, 598, 601; II 44, 91, 296, 721, 756, 772; III 508
vow: I 63, 63c, 100; III 743, 877
way of life: I 586, 597–98; II 94, 126, 150, 154, 176, 189, 210, 229, 253, 276, 285, 416, 524, 643, 691, 809; III 269, 381
way of salvation: II 375
zeal: I 386; III 45, 170, 173, 476, 638, 710
Power
   Christ: I 49, 324–24, 351; II 143, 340, 558, 643, 692, 713, 715; III 91, 188–89, 288, 382, 410, 426, 733, 740, 827
   church: II 260; III 766
   confession: I 265, 420
   creature: I 250; II 597
   cross: II 650, 682, 717; III 50
   evil spirit: I 302; II 318, 320, 454–55, 628, 693; III 318, 411, 421, 721
   faith: II 671
   Francis's teaching: I 240, 248, 351, 385, 494, 533, 603; II 35, 99, 137, 143, 155, 243, 263, 278, 313, 315, 318, 358, 380, 403, 406, 408–09, 411, 429, 436, 449, 454–55, 528, 539, 547–48, 557, 609, 616, 625, 634–35,

648–49, 657, 661–62, 665–66, 672,
675–77, 680, 689, 697, 700, 711, 761,
765, 798, 813; III 391, 815
general minister: I 574; III 759, 782
God: I 149, 161, 230, 240, 242, 259,
301, 379, 389, 400, 402, 534, 543,
585, 603; II 99, 320, 400, 402–03,
405–06, 439, 516, 521, 539, 547, 557,
574, 597, 601, 603, 626, 628, 635,
648–49, 652, 676, 678, 687, 690, 700,
704, 707, 716, 740, 755, 813, 816,
870; III 102, 176, 180, 189–90, 200,
230, 312, 392, 457, 467, 469, 483,
490, 558, 733, 862
gift of God: I 351, 533, 603; II 99, 137,
143, 243, 263, 318, 358, 403, 406,
528, 539, 548, 557, 634, 648–49, 662,
672, 689, 697, 700, 813
grace: II 738, 761
humility: II 519
light: I 389; II 691
love: II 358, 515, 734, 740
others: I 93, 798; III 103
over demon: III 43, 50, 862
passion: I 49, 159; III 552
poverty: II 555, 585; III 163
prayer: II 278, 313, 318, 409, 446, 529,
584, 605, 609, 705, 742; III 342, 861
preacher: II 352, 587
priest: I 78; II 52, 101, 788, 803
prophecy: II 616, 620
speech: II 716, 803; III 45, 345
spirit: I 215, 242, 335, 408; II 50, 99,
528, 543, 548, 553, 625–26, 689, 691,
764; III 314, 392, 397, 423, 525, 545,
640, 710
stigmata: II 403, 406, 634–35, 645, 650,
653–54, 711–13, 797
temporal things: II 35, 155, 408, 411,
429, 436, 449, 454–55, 547, 625, 657,
661, 665–66, 672, 675–77, 680, 697,
765; III 104–05, 815
water: II 634, 678, 711
weather: III 50
word: I 385; II 99, 314–15, 318, 321,
380, 536, 540, 553, 556, 693, 698; III
90, 391, 398, 403
Practice
church: I 65, 75; II 56, 104
Francis's word: I 51, 120, 208, 512,
546, 613, 817
Gospel: I 51, 259, 320; III 830
performance: I 43, 50–51, 86, 185, 320,
407, 431, 466, 497, 593–94; III 115,
392, 628, 740, 756, 759, 781
Poor Ladies: I 199; II 83
Rule: I 86
sin: I 43, 50, 185
vice: I 43, 50, 185
virtue: I 407, 431, 466, 510, 512, 544,
609, 622, 640, 694, 696, 714, 741–42;
II 533; III 334, 401, 617, 649, 852

vision: II 465
way of life: I 210
Praise: I 432, 489, 535, 540, 549; II 271, 291,
295, 818; III 31–32, 98, 117–18, 337, 394,
406, 408, 572, 575, 667, 707, 712, 732,
765, 848, 883, 888, 890, 892
alms: III 216, 274
beg: II 201
birds: I 396; II 130, 280, 356, 411, 592,
624, 644, 800, 810, 813; III 362–63,
469–70, 860
brother: I 255, 275, 386, 406; II 55,
102, 152, 173–75, 177, 202, 213, 258,
319, 574–75; III 40, 45, 121, 237,
245, 299–300, 351, 360, 389, 403–04,
446, 576
Canticle of Creatures: III 349, 367
Christ: I 506; II 436; III 63, 89, 384,
435, 440, 444, 446–47, 449–50, 452,
458, 461–62, 465–66, 468, 471, 475,
478, 480, 482, 486, 490, 492, 494,
500–01, 503, 507–12, 514, 516–19,
521, 523, 528, 533–34, 537–38, 540,
542, 544, 548, 550–52, 554, 556, 559,
561, 564–65, 571, 574, 576, 578–79,
581–83, 585–86, 589–91, 594, 598,
600–01, 604–05, 607, 609, 614,
616–17, 620–24, 626–27, 629, 631,
633, 635, 637, 639–40, 643–44, 646,
648, 652–54, 658, 670, 796, 834, 871,
878
Clare: I 458
creature: I 250, 396–97, 401, 504; II
192, 385, 412, 803; III 51, 104, 221,
349, 367
cricket: II 219, 357, 414, 798
cured: I 303, 306; II 274, 423–24, 431,
437, 449, 451, 455, 467, 615, 653,
658, 672, 678, 702, 805; III 70, 73,
280
deer: II 813
Divine Office: I 65, 329, 516; II 186
encourage: I 57, 60, 76, 90
flower: I 251; II 192
Francis: I 194, 261, 289, 293, 295, 321,
324, 334, 338, 376, 393, 417–18, 453,
462, 477–78, 491, 520; II 55, 57, 121,
169, 180, 203, 214, 217, 240, 288,
332–33, 353, 388, 391–92, 436, 519,
551, 566, 569, 594, 704, 719, 812; III
82, 99, 103, 247, 291, 308, 357, 391,
571, 574, 576, 578–79, 581–83,
585–86, 589–91, 594, 598, 600–01,
604–05, 607, 609, 614, 616–17,
620–24, 626–27, 629, 631, 633, 635,
637, 639–40, 643–44, 646, 648,
652–54, 658, 666, 877
God: I 277, 323, 326, 349, 415, 519,
569; II 48, 67, 169, 177, 186, 188,
192, 202, 213, 280, 330, 339, 393,
401, 468, 644, 650; III 78, 89, 98,
104, 121, 176, 216, 221, 237, 245,

274, 280, 300, 308, 329, 330, 347–48,
    350, 358, 360, 362–63, 367, 369,
    371–72, 445, 453–54, 457, 463,
    469–71, 476–77, 479, 502, 508, 516,
    521, 538, 552, 583, 593, 633, 644,
    831, 835, 860, 868
Gregory IX: II 477
hymn: I 259, 324; II 129, 156, 568, 610,
    707
invitation: I 397, 401, 554, 569; II 186,
    356, 374, 490, 551, 566, 597, 704, 737
liturgical: I 329, 334, 338, 349, 351,
    516, 569
other: I 135; II 197, 245, 374, 417
people: I 274, 279, 368–69, 414; II 52,
    102, 654
poor dwelling: III 384
Praises of Lord: III 329, 337, 347–48,
    350, 367, 369, 868
prayer: I 47, 49–50, 76, 78, 85, 113–14,
    117, 138, 141, 143, 147, 151–56,
    161–62; II 121, 187
Rule: II 146; III 59, 323
sacrifice: II 437
Salutation of Virtues: II 368
self: II 209, 264, 333–34, 341, 352, 364,
    523, 569–70, 572, 587, 695, 722, 747,
    780; III 821
sheep: II 591
virtue: I 534–35; II 260, 284, 292, 301,
    362; III 324, 335, 587
Prayer
abandonment: III 169, 219, 389, 394
adoration: I 46–47, 78, 80, 82, 85, 88,
    91, 116, 124, 151, 222, 475, 509, 536;
    II 42, 90, 449, 671, 773; III 619, 652,
    798–99, 817
brother: II 156, 161, 207, 213–14, 264,
    325, 365, 389; III 299, 309, 476,
    645–46, 656, 705–06, 758, 821
cell: I 61, 226, 390; II 152, 215, 226–28,
    268–69, 277, 280, 286, 289, 309, 313,
    324–25, 350, 356, 361, 562, 597, 608,
    618, 700–01, 796; III 49, 102, 169,
    238, 245, 261, 309, 329, 341, 345,
    365, 454–55, 506, 514, 535, 538, 547,
    594, 619, 623, 633, 642, 653, 667,
    696, 797–98, 810
characteristic: I 137a
Christ: II 247
church: I 124–25; II 38, 44, 90, 249,
    254, 401, 536, 544, 551, 573, 686,
    752, 787, 792; III 304, 318, 522, 573,
    588, 636, 848
Clare: III 468, 592
coldness: III 299
confirmation: I 99; II 49, 96, 547, 648
constancy: III 121, 125, 167, 181, 237,
    255, 299, 328–29, 333, 342, 345, 381,
    400, 455, 468, 476, 592, 618, 623,
    703, 865
Conrad: III 638–40

contemplation: I 137b; II 261, 605,
    622; III 177, 181, 579, 586, 758
creature: I 113–14
cross: II 536, 685–86, 709, 792; III 667,
    670
crucifix: I 40
dead: I 101
dedication: I 398; II 97, 152, 179–80,
    254, 310; II 292, 308; III 174, 181,
    446, 455, 461, 477, 489, 502, 504,
    513, 552, 568, 579, 588, 596–97, 610,
    628, 718, 720, 797–98, 810, 834, 843,
    848, 853
deliverance: I 302; II 404–05, 419–22,
    424, 430, 432, 437–38, 442, 445–47,
    460–61, 466–67, 481, 568, 655–58,
    636, 666–67, 669, 671, 678, 692, 783;
    III 51, 69, 70, 73, 91, 318, 502, 535,
    540, 553, 608, 624, 630, 835
devil: II 167–68, 185, 248, 292, 319,
    324, 326, 328, 562, 627, 701, 795–96;
    III 181, 504–07, 509, 617–20, 810,
    853, 862
devotion: I 102a, 107; II 42, 208, 228;
    III 219, 341–42, 477, 576, 637, 706,
    757, 780, 795, 847, 861, 874
distraction: II 311, 609, 699; III 102,
    344, 441, 461, 572–73, 597
Dominic: II 786
ecstasy: I 271; II 142, 168, 179,
    312–13, 403, 536, 544, 573, 598, 609,
    761, 796, 814; III 98–99, 184–85,
    411, 425, 454, 475, 534–35, 537, 550,
    564, 627, 644, 647, 653, 847, 848
edify: II 208; III 321, 705, 821
effort: III 172, 265, 848
Elias: III 553, 630
encouragement: I 49, 169, 180, 319,
    476
end: I 236, 242–43, 398; III 244, 329,
    364, 498, 637, 720, 848
enemy: I 132; II 92
Eucharist: II 773
external: I 133; II 334, 618
fasting: I 65, 443; II 177, 597, 687, 807
forgiveness: II 126, 717; III 226, 292
Francis: II 308–14, 330, 348, 355, 358,
    374, 377, 408, 412, 490, 533, 546,
    548, 552, 555, 557, 566, 573, 580,
    587–88, 597–99, 602, 607–08, 615,
    619, 622, 697, 703, 715, 726, 730,
    742–43, 754, 783, 787, 801, 806; III
    100, 102–03, 129, 228, 325, 341–44,
    464
frustration: III 219, 248, 327, 717
guidance: I 12–21, 214, 380, 385; II 50,
    96, 131, 209, 214, 225–26, 254, 622;
    III 55, 59, 60, 90, 100, 123, 191, 169,
    246, 266, 383, 390, 437, 464, 468,
    568, 588, 592, 708–09, 814
heal: I 302; II 404–05, 419–22, 424,
    430, 432, 437–38, 442, 445–47,

460–61, 466–67, 481, 568, 636, 655–58, 666–67, 669, 671, 678, 692, 783; III 51, 69–70, 73, 91, 318, 502, 535, 540, 553, 608, 624, 630, 835
heart: II 50; II 215, 520
Hours: I 161–62
humility: I 262; II 38, 520, 524; III 320, 509, 719
internal: I 120; II 215, 551, 571
intimacy: I 261
intoxicate: II 598; III 130, 160
John: III 547, 640–43
joy: II 218, 229–30, 330; III 247, 266, 843
La Verna: II 108, 632, 709, 816
Lady Jacoba: II 122
learning: II 207; III 118, 319, 705
liturgical: I 140a, 327
love: III 190–91
Mary Magdalen: II 763
Masseo: III 462, 691
meditate: I 137, 245, 254, 506; II 77, 127, 202, 205, 208, 212, 326, 412, 521, 834; III 167, 172, 255, 265, 320, 356, 415, 555, 703, 797, 834, 847
mental: III 535, 653
ministry: II 144
mortify: III 121
need: III 50, 61
Our Father: I 158–60
Pacifico: III 643–44
Passion: I 139–57
penance: III 618
persevere: I 69, 93, 105, 140, 144, 219, 244, 253, 261, 337, 408, 436, 443; II 44, 46, 57, 91, 93, 95, 107, 156, 205, 208, 220, 222, 227–29, 331, 384, 533–34, 546, 548, 552, 592, 597–98, 605, 612, 685, 699–700; III 181, 299, 344, 437
person: II 177, 303, 654
petition: I 381; II 55, 104, 179–80, 190, 220–21, 269–70, 566, 589, 608, 616, 641, 748, 793
place: I 205, 408, 415, 562; II 72, 99, 108, 137, 159, 165, 191, 224, 226–27, 248, 286, 309, 328, 478, 608, 686, 699; III 169, 261, 570, 572, 583, 628, 635
poor: III 391
Portiuncula: I 415; II 42, 100, 137, 165, 208, 290, 313, 324, 608; III 134, 299, 489, 615
posture: II 167–68; III 181, 232, 318, 344, 552, 592
poverty: III 160, 168, 319, 320, 705
power: I 402; II 179, 278, 292, 313, 319–20, 352, 409, 584, 608, 611, 622, 685, 699, 705, 742; III 36, 73, 90, 93, 95, 101, 104, 169, 320, 464, 493, 522–23, 536, 546, 549, 552–54, 558,

607, 613, 623, 628, 631, 639, 651, 706, 719, 811, 837, 861, 862, 875
praise: I 49–50, 81–86, 109–11, 138, 398, 549; III 244
preach: II 352, 737, 760, 763; III 321
prostration: I 404, 409; II 328; III 513, 570
refuge: I 381; II 268–72; III 181
religion: III 249
revelation: II 168, 212–13, 254, 328, 350, 551, 558, 563, 691; III 66, 127, 247, 266, 305, 312, 441, 464, 588, 619, 630, 639–40, 645–46, 719, 861
reverence: III 341
Rufino: III 504–07, 617–20, 688
safeguard: III 181
secrecy: II 72, 292, 352, 587, 608, 652, 699
silent: I 224; II 99
simplicity: I 124; III 168, 319–20, 705
solitude: I 384; II 159, 327–29, 597; III 320, 439, 720, 847
spirit: I 102, 105, 107; II 558; III 757
Sylvester: III 468, 592, 688
tears: II 46, 93, 587, 744; III 615
tempt: II 325, 328
thanksgiving: I 81
time: III 96, 232, 249, 299, 328, 345, 347, 350, 382, 572, 718, 797, 847
unceasing: I 244a, 261; II 45, 409, 584; III 415
understand: III 231
vigil: I 244, 299, 505; II 46, 228, 301, 324, 381, 607, 691, 743; III 196, 233, 382, 512, 525
vigilance: III 476
Virgin Mary: I 163; II 374, 689
virtuous: III 333
vocal: I 120
weapon: III 94
woods: I 194, 453, 489; II 42, 165, 309, 539, 687, 782; III 102, 439, 441–43, 455, 458, 474, 527–29, 531–32, 535, 538, 540, 570, 572–74, 583, 594, 609, 617, 619–23, 634–37, 649, 651–54, 811
Preacher. See also Preaching
advice: II 210, 352; III 259, 409, 708
anonymous: II 421, 718, 747; III 177, 190, 219
Anthony: II 557, 700; III 694
appropriate: I 75, 89
authorize: II 809; III 391
brother: I 576, 582, 597; II 406, 421, 428, 652, 661; III 155
empty praise: II 352, 587; III 821
Francis: I 496; II 99, 318, 556; III 176
humility: III 321, 409
Islam: I 607
John de La Rochelle: III 63
John of Parma: III 150
manner: II 186, 352; III 348

need: I 480
Odo Rigaldi: III 63
office: I 105; II 406, 652
Order of Preachers: I 563, 592–94,
600–01; II 140, 315, 466, 771–72,
785, 809, 811; III 296, 407, 475,
559–61, 564, 595, 826, 830
Philip the Tall: III 689
power: II 282
prayer: II 208, 352
reception: I 600
standard: II 747–48
truth: III 115, 135, 722
virtue: II 762
William of Bayonne: III 57
Preaching. See also Preacher
against heresy: I 602
birds: I 236, 343, 353, 402, 599; II 412,
625, 783, 798, 810
bishop: I 134, 342
Catholic faith: I 388, 480
church: II 161, 690
creature: I 251, 599, 625
crucified: I 601; II 545, 556, 682–83
diocese: I 104; II 57, 134, 574
flowers: I 251
Gospel: I 202, 227, 230, 248, 259, 335,
597; II 348, 529, 541, 594, 601, 626,
629, 782
lay: I 49a; II 102
parish: I 125
peace: I 215, 335, 600; II 84, 526, 543
penance: I 202, 212, 379, 384; II 84,
163, 526, 543, 546
Perugia: II 271
Pope: I 243, 383, 409, 564, 578, 583,
597, 690; II 106, 342, 625–26
Praises of Lord: II 186
prayer: II 352, 587, 599, 622
pretext: I 126
reign of God: I 403; II 489
Rule: I 574, 629, 778–79
salvation: I 85, 163, 543, 587
stigmata: II 408
study: II 147, 370, 372
Sultan: I 229, 581, 584, 605, 607–08; II
180, 600–02, 698, 810, 814
Word of God: I 235, 578; II 691, 737,
747, 812
Precept: I 218, 260, 480; III 39
Augustine: I 592
Benedict: I 592
Christ: I 54, 80, 88, 546, 571, 589; III
177, 197–98, 382, 742–43
Francis: II 52, 102
obedience: III 293–94
Pope: II 50, 98
Rule: I 572, 582; II 775, 777; III 740,
743–44, 750, 771–75, 785
Precipice
edge: II 436, 666; III 200
humility: II 341, 572

Precursor
Antichrist: III 424
Christ: III 680
Francis: II 84; III 682
Predestination: III 617
Prediction: II 175–79, 187–88, 222–23,
271–72, 418, 692–93; III 176, 182–83,
251, 350–51, 485, 511–12, 544, 622,
862–64
Bernard: II 126–28, III 227, 355–56
canon: III 862
Christ: III 680
Francis: II 242, 465, 703, III 33, 66–67,
681
Order: I 186; II 41, 58, 89–92, 205–06,
552, 783; III 114–17, 135, 166, 276,
313–15, 404–06, 702, 712, 714
Pope: I 500; III 476, 834
religion: I 186; II 41, 58, 89–92,
205–06, 552, 783; III 114–17, 135,
166, 276, 313–15, 404–06, 702, 712,
714
Preference
brother: I 586; III 389, 394, 403
donor: I 57; II 776
each one: I 446, 471
Francis: I 275; II 147, 579, 761; III 236,
314, 706
Lord: II 155
Prefiguration
Francis: I 378, 464; II 533; III 147
Hugolino: I 413
Prelate: I 130, 130a, 166, 222, 273, 294–95,
327, 418, 450, 519, 558–59, 565, 576, 580,
583, 587, 603; II 46, 52, 57, 93–94, 101,
106, 109, 124–25, 133, 142, 146, 148,
160–62, 200, 209, 211–12, 216–17, 220,
229, 269, 332, 338, 340–45, 351, 358, 360,
364, 366–67, 391, 404, 477, 468, 518, 557,
571–72, 648, 695, 789, 797, 812; III 31,
41, 47, 53–54, 64, 78, 85, 133, 151, 154,
158, 171–72, 216, 220, 224–25, 233,
239–40, 247, 249, 251, 258, 263–65,
287–89, 292–93, 297, 308, 310, 316, 336,
344, 401, 414, 636, 699, 701, 703, 711,
755, 788, 816, 848–49, 871
Premonition
birds: II 594
Pica: II 242
Preparation
heaven: III 387, 499
lack: I 245
stigmata: II 713
Prerogative
Bernard: III 227, 355, 426, 436
Christ: I 196, 231, 368
Francis: II 108, 127, 694–98; III 856
owner: III 776
Portiuncula: III 121, 299, 330–31
poverty: I 529
Rufino: III 511

Prescription
  idle talk: III 328
  medicine: II 421
  Rule: I 120
Pretense
  house: II 28, 136; III 259
  lie: II 570; III 183, 405
Pretext
  edification: II 207; III 118, 168, 319,
    394, 408, 705
  good: I 130; III 202
  guilt: I 445
  holiness: II 268
  humility: II 273, 619
  levity: I 561
  necessity: II 291–92; III 58
  observe: III 116, 350–51, 419
  prayer: II 226; III 423–24
  preach: I 126; III 386, 408
  provide for future: III 749
  save soul: III 155, 412
  self–contempt: II 348
  word: III 845
Prevention
  abuse: III 778
  assault: I 447
  bloodshed: I 503
  destruction: III 101
  devotion: II 229; III 233, 342
  disaster: III 173
  donation: II 140, 305
  evil: I 241, 495, 567
  failure: II 360
  Francis: II 635–36, 757; III 398, 416
  good: III 539, 634, 767
  humility: II 260
  joy: II 229; III 233, 342
  judge: II 818–19
  laziness: II 540
  observe *Rule:* III 714
  Pope: I 419; II 478; III 67
  pray: II 228; III 232, 346, 540, 688
  promise land: III 422
  Rule: III 714
  sleep: II 190, 228; III 232, 345
  speak: II 320
  truth: III 442
Price
  cloth: II 119; III 220, 358, 774
  fame: II 337, 352, 364
  fatigue: I 115
  feather: III 362
  goods: I 189; II 536; III 756
  lamb: I 399, 501
  love: II 596
  mantle: II 139–40, 305; III 281, 851
  pearl: II 686
  piety: II 300
  redemption: I 488; II 376, 522, 622,
    689; III 84, 175, 382, 547, 643, 739
  spring: I 567
  stone: II 319

  sweat: II 83, 251
  work: I 319
Pride
  avoid: I 75, 90, 105; II 52, 520, 522,
    576, 800; III 71, 83, 324, 382, 573,
    622
  confound: I 88, 165, 440, 603; II
    260–61, 328, 688, 756, 800; III 157,
    511
  fruit: I 437, 441; II 575, 752–53, 796;
    III 57, 98–99, 114, 133, 156, 184,
    295–96, 305, 442–43, 573, 585, 848
  origin: I 488, 554, 586; II 101, 134,
    168, 178, 183; III 126, 251, 294, 307,
    320, 440, 571
Priest: I 51, 71, 78, 84; 104, 223, 277, 294,
  304, 319, 388, 390, 399, 442, 470, 476,
  500, 536, 593; II 54, 103, 425, 433, 449,
  453, 460, 466, 480, 491, 603, 623, 656,
  671, 674, 676, 679, 692, 733, 762, 787–88,
  804; III 39–40, 65, 71, 117, 156, 175, 187,
  228, 241, 301, 356, 385, 410, 422, 437,
  524, 531, 533–34, 568, 698, 714–15, 780,
  793, 797, 802, 809, 833, 881
  Benedict of Pirato: III 335
  brother: I 104, 116–17, 119, 225, 388,
    573; II 127, 162, 420, 778
  confessor: I 47, 50, 72, 77–78, 98, 104,
    223, 388, 573, 576; II 153, 329, 420,
    465, 534, 663, 778; III 350, 354, 494,
    608
  dignity: I 118, 238
  Eucharist: I 48a, 54a, 55a, 57, 119, 256,
    388; III 245, 568, 654, 798
  faith: I 125
  hand: I 118, 128–29; II 52, 101, 376,
    442
  John of LaVerna: III 543–44, 656–58
  Leo: II 66
  Massa Trabaria: III 411
  Masseo of San Severino: III 636
  Nicosia: III 72
  Pietro of Monticulo: III 555
  poor: I 125, 189, 333, 373; II 73, 77,
    247, 686; III 239, 263, 309
  reverence: I 238, 246, 321, 327, 388; II
    52, 54, 101, 376, 551, 803; III 44, 47,
    83, 89, 154, 856
  Saint Mary: I 201, 379; II 84
  Saint Nicholas: II 38
  San Damiano: I 189–90, 319, 333, 373;
    II 36, 77–78, 81, 250, 253, 537, 686,
    782, 792
  San Fabiano: II 170; III 352–53,
    479–80, 598–99
  secular: I 223; II 170, 319, 795
  Sylvester: II 38–39, 86–87, 319–20,
    544, 795; III 87, 246, 689, 689a
Prince: I 84, 221, 227, 418, 449, 479, 544,
  547, 568, 587; II 35–37, 42, 68, 71, 205,
  246, 266, 276, 391, 437, 477, 561, 746,
  754; III 824, 883

angel: II 226, 374; III 527, 636
apostle: II 73, 247, 540, 620, 688; III
   464, 684, 719
cardinal: I 210, 245
darkness: II 353, 796; III 381–82, 411,
   423, 505, 618, 876
death: II 353, 796; III 381–82, 411,
   423, 505, 618, 876
Pope: I 292, 384; II 73, 338
singer: II 316
Principle
   first: I 487
   perfection: III 149
   poverty: III 781
Prior
   office: I 68, 559–60, 576
   Friars Preacher: III 560
   Greccio: I 376, 454
   Heisterbach: I 594
   Saint Michael: I 580
Privilege
   calling: II 731
   Church: I 593, 599; III 154
   Elizabeth: II 242
   Francis: II 283; III 511
   freedom: II 143, 340; III 287
   generosity: II 405
   grace: I 395; II 419, 721
   Lord: III 126, 294
   love: II 417
   perfection: I 378
   Pope: I 562; II 134; III 126, 251, 294,
      819–20
   poverty: II 577, 581
   religion: II 295
   right: III 163
   spiritual knowledge: II 512
   stigmata: I 411; II 108, 401, 406, 604,
      642, 645, 650, 712; III 148, 666
   transfiguration: I 389
   virtue: II 629, 695, 712, 717, 719
Prize
   heaven: I 357, 565, 567; II 254, 715; III
      94, 877
   victory: I 485; III 191
Probation: I 64, 101, 561; III 742, 770
Procession: I 184, 284, 294, 402, 601; II 55,
   104, 442; III 481, 600
Proclamation
   peace: I 379–80; II 84
   podesta: II 187
Procurator
   curial: II 49, 96; III 51, 756, 777, 785,
      788
Prodigy: I 328; III 867
Profession
   brother: III 125, 171, 214, 240, 248,
      264, 315–17, 321, 323–24, 326–27,
      372, 408, 413, 681, 710–12, 715, 717,
      744, 746–47, 753, 771, 773, 781–82
   Francis: I 217, 385; III 215, 842, 845
   Gospel: III 197, 392–93, 406, 550, 627

poverty: I 553; III 64
religious: I 370, 455, 464, 561; II 68,
   144, 146, 161, 199, 210–11, 219, 256,
   290, 361, 380, 392, 556, 693; III 164,
   178, 743, 746
Profit: I 457–58, 446, 580; II 190, 324, 466,
   509; III 81, 85, 118, 576
   greed: II 583
   humility: II 572
   neighbor: I 206
   obedience: II 344, 577
   prayer: II 622; III 522
   reader: II 528
   sermon: II 719
   settlement: III 777
   soul: II 133, 214, 217, 298, 341, 572,
      633, 789, 794; III 178, 247, 297, 308
   spiritual life: II 517, 530
   temptation: III 619
   virtue: I 588
   work: III 322, 337, 785
Progress: I 549, 581, 588; II 324, 371, 603; III
   49, 83, 388
   brother: II 775; III 43, 414, 452, 533,
      588, 741
   Francis: III 852, 864
   virtue: I 384; II 613, 672; III 63
Prohibition
   another: I 533; III 157
   Francis: II 379; III 743–44
   Gospel: II 206; III 256, 406, 704
   Hugolino: II 216
   Pope: I 561, 564, 572, 575; II 779
   Rule: II 775; III 743–44, 750, 760, 772,
      775–76
Promise: I 43, 48, 63, 68, 100–01, 106, 120,
   188, 306, 371, 373, 529; II 216, 222, 317,
   369–70, 440–41, 449, 457, 462–63, 531,
   603, 608, 668–69, 685; III 57–58, 182,
   397, 422, 440, 544, 623
   amend: II 448, 672
   bishop: I 450; II 95
   brother: I 550, 553; II 50, 52, 98, 381,
      671; III 133, 250, 311, 409, 526, 536,
      610, 654, 743, 771
   chivalry: II 71
   Christ: I 158, 207, 329, 339, 343, 553,
      600; II 50, 349, 742, 752, 764; III
      129, 190, 197, 318, 347, 383, 396,
      410, 496, 546, 599, 641–42, 844, 858
   eternal life: II 384, 389, 476, 595, 735;
      III 868
   fasting: II 450
   Francis: I 457, 495, 502; II 50, 98, 125,
      179, 288, 313, 340, 344, 378, 531,
      706; III 480, 483, 491, 571, 597, 599,
      603, 607, 610, 614
   freedom 437
   fulfillment: I 117, 539, 553; II 444,
      447, 702; III 163
   glory: III 868

God: I 158, 207, 329, 339, 343, 553,
    600; II 50, 349, 742, 752, 764; III
    129, 190, 197, 318, 347, 383, 396,
    410, 496, 546, 599, 641–42, 844, 858
Gospel: II 572, 579, 703
imitation: II 164, 369
Jeremiah: I 539
kingdom: II 186, 682, 736
non–observance: I 50
obedience: I 48, 65, 100–01; II 50, 98,
    101, 125, 142, 340, 344, 571, 695, 750
penance: II 425, 659
piety: II 424, 658, 685
Pope: I 210, 384; II 256, 548, 691
poverty: I 126; II 160, 212, 550, 756; III
    391
rest: II 420, 656
Rule: I 119, 127; III 387
service: II 422, 656
vision: I 383; II 245
wolf: III 483, 603
Property
    accept: III 773
    brother: III 162, 186
    church: III 785
    distribute: III 773–74
    father: I 449
    Francis: I 183, 333, 450; II 286
    immovable: III 779
    loss: II 140, 305; III 281
    other: II 136, 286, 292; III 163, 354
    permission: II 777
    Pope: III 785
    prohibition: I 573, 597; II 253–54, 287,
        368, 371–72
    renunciation: III 744, 771, 845
    rights: II 367; III 748–49
Prophecy
    Conrad: III 130, 134
    fulfilment: II 541, 582; III 120, 236,
        298, 682
    Francis: II 40, 57, 252; III 129–30, 502,
        512, 721–23, 863–64
    Hildegard: II 808
    Hosea: I 184
    John: II 527; III 546, 642
    Poor Ladies: II 252
    Psalmist: I 411, 582
    Sibyl: II 772, 772a
    spirit: I 205–07, 330, 389, 477; II 83,
        216, 263–64, 526, 612–21, 623, 629,
        700–03, 717, 791; III 89–103, 176,
        182, 246, 310, 349–58, 443, 568, 642
Prophet: I 83, 329, 334, 376, 380, 413, 498,
    500; II 84–85, 181, 242–43, 257, 280, 316,
    543, 615–16, 620, 651, 688, 700, 746, 755;
    III 80, 415, 422, 542, 680–81, 695, 739,
    816–17, 879, 889
    Christ: I 535; II 295; III 728
    David: II 597, 620
    Elijah: III 381
    Ezechiel: II 556, 693; III 618

Francis: II 283, 315, 353, 539, 543, 556,
    570, 615, 693, 700, 703; III 156, 185,
    670, 841, 863
Haggai: III 188
Isaiah: I 380; II 534, 570; III 567
Jeremiah: I 117, 589; II 511
Joachim: III 892
Jonah: III 521, 632
Micah: II 522
Nathan: III 892
Psalmist: I 46, 48, 50, 68, 265, 381; II
    46–47, 94, 251, 474, 597; III 39, 55,
    83, 100, 728
Samuel: II 733
Proposal. See also Plan, Purpose
    intention: I 192; II 533; III 64, 91, 540,
        707
    plan: I 385; II 95, 546; III 403, 412
    presentation to bishop: I 212; II 49
    presentation to pope: I 382, 210, 576;
        II 49, 95, 254, 547, 690, 785
    purpose: I 189
Prose
    Bonaventure: III 78, 80
Prosperity
    Divine: III 530, 650
    joy: III 233, 342
    prediction: II 178, 533
    state: II 230, 523
    temperance: III 596
    worldly: I 371, 542; II 71, 270, 730
Prostitute: III 605–07
Prostration
    altar: I 222, 388, 551; III 57, 841
    another: II 93, 339, 425, 589, 795
    church: I 222, 388, 551; III 57, 841
    Francis: I 207, 381, 402, 500; II 168, 328,
        336, 426, 455, 546, 660, 674; III 513
    God: I 116, 222, 262, 404; II 328, 426,
        536, 660
Protection
    arms: II 89; III 482
    church: II 260–61; III 324, 859
    Francis: I 569; II 426, 653, 660
    God: I 144, 365, 530, 684, 754; III 19,
        54, 189, 325, 426, 730
    grace: I 244; III 847
    Hugolino: I 247; II 55, 104, 261
    human: II 364; III 40
    John of St. Paul: II 103
    Mary: III 66
    modesty: III 343
    papal: III 189, 196
    prayer: II 268
    Rule: III 396
Protector
    angel: II 373; III 527, 636
    cardinal: I 106, 127; II 56, 103–04,
        106–07, 572; III 127, 478, 598, 709,
        741, 785, 794, 824
    God: I 109–10, 152–53, 327; II 349, 588
    modesty: I 272

Protest
  bishop: I 595
  brother: I 608; II 725
  corpse: II 345, 571
  minister: III 417
  people: III 353
Providence
  Divine: I 229, 242, 366, 383–84, 409,
    584; II 177, 241, 267, 276, 317, 335,
    415, 514–15, 541, 550, 567, 574, 585,
    602, 620, 623, 630, 632, 707, 736; III
    101, 173, 188, 200, 202, 359–61,
    391–92, 463, 470, 477, 587, 594, 597,
    745, 780, 794, 858–59, 882
  false: III 265
Province. See also Region
  Aquitaine: III 715
  assignment: I 66, 574, 582–83; II 51,
    53, 57, 101–02, 106; III 128, 393, 557
  building: II 212; III 172, 265
  brother: I 248, 583; II 106, 165, 221,
    303, 376; III 249, 285, 400, 417, 543,
    546, 557, 596, 649, 806
  call: I 115
  chapter: I 225, 574
  Cismonte: II 56; III 782–83
  Cologne: III 61
  France: III 462
  government: I 546; III 647, 750, 760,
    766
  Greece: III 782–83
  hermitage: II 402
  Ireland: III 782–83
  Marches: III 502, 526, 535, 542, 544,
    555–56, 635, 639–40, 642–43, 649
  minister: I 573; III 417, 557
  miracle: II 410–11, 442, 449, 451, 573,
    634, 671, 677, 711, 727
  new Order: I 592
  obedience: II 125
  Order: I 592
  Provence: III 545, 641, 830
  reception: II 56, 104, 125; III 225
  Romania: III 782–83
  Santiago: III 830
  travel: II 41, 88, 105; III 260, 418,
    545–46, 598, 828
  Tuscany: III 840
Provision
  condition: II 702; III 745, 747, 750,
    752, 783, 805, 855
  gluttony: I 439
  riches: I 462, 482; III 79, 102, 475–78,
    800
  travel: I 394; II 585, 707
Provocation
  amazement: I 379; III 548
  anger: II 52, 102, 134, 412; III 44, 125,
    296, 318
  another: I 541; II 287, 796
  benefactor: II 312, 608
  hatred: I 393

martyrdom: I 280
  motivation: III 59, 136, 165, 425, 494,
    572
Prudence
  Dominic: II 772
  flesh: I 90; III 182, 203, 388, 393, 410
  Francis: I 321, 506; II 772
  human nature: III 114, 133, 182, 202,
    399, 401, 403, 413, 415, 703, 712,
    722
  serpent: III 44, 389
  spirit: II 335; III 402
Psalm
  comfort: III 328, 718
  creature: I 192; III 366, 533
  David: I 277
  death: I 325, 415, 516; II 475, 643; III
    835, 854
  devotion: II 761
  illumination: II 745
  meekness: II 518
  mercy: II 754
  mortification: II 732
  poverty: II 721
  prayer: II 719; III 51, 654, 728
  preach: I 370; II 763
  stigmata: I 411
Psalter
  brother: II 196
  decease: II 419, 491, 656
  lay brother: I 65; II 372
  possess: II 207, 209–10; III 169–70,
    257–59, 707–09, 814, 819
  praise: I 143
  preach: II 789
  Roman: I 101; II 775; III 19
  virtue: I 567; III 60
Punishment
  eternal: III 59, 388, 411, 476, 563, 596,
    639
  fear: II 438
  Francis: I 209, 447; III 706–07
  freedom: III 523, 654
  impose: I 79, 87, 117, 129, 497, 548; II
    102, 179, 225, 270, 279, 291–92, 321,
    363, 421, 438, 441–42, 522, 570, 590,
    594, 600, 668, 676–78; III 136, 324,
    598, 642, 722, 853
  increase: I 538; III 35
  powerful: I 58
  preach: I 105; II 37; III 747
  remedy: I 184
  rod: II 360; III 288
  teaching: II 258, 370, 460, 576, 588,
    591; III 71, 231
  thought: II 439, 667
  wise: I 58
  withhold: II 283; III 94
Purgatory
  pain: III 51, 396, 522, 638, 652
  state: III 61, 535, 541, 547, 653, 655,
    715

Purification
    day: III 637, 825
    need: III 654
    prayer: II 622
    spirit: II 762
Purity
    air: I 234; II 412, 624; III 860
    body: II 694–95, 723–24, 735; III 529
    character: III 334
    Christ: III 425, 730
    conscience: III 754
    cross: II 724
    encourage: III 476, 596
    Eucharist: I 117
    faith: II 667
    Francis: I 245, 249, 295, 389, 399, 463;
        II 151, 527, 547, 565, 567–68, 620,
        704, 723–24, 740, 762; III 48, 61, 99,
        153, 158, 235, 269, 296, 402, 730, 846
    gift: I 224
    God: I 262
    Gospel: II 261, 756; III 324
    heart: I 120, 223, 252, 322; II 230, 695,
        738–41; III 233, 342
    John the Simple: II 369; III 242, 302
    Leo: III 125, 333, 456, 511
    libido: I 440
    life: I 180; II 391, 477; III 41, 114, 133
    mind: I 245; II 690; III 529
    Order: I 573; III 135, 300, 413, 721,
        770, 779
    perfection: II 210; III 170, 198, 316,
        342, 710
    poverty: I 561; II 721
    prayer: III 342
    preserve: II 156, 562; III 122
    rejoice: II 164
    religion: I 573; III 135, 300, 413, 721,
        770, 779
    Rufino: II 403
    Rule: III 114, 133, 407, 410, 722, 772,
        780
    soul: II 694, 723
    spirit: I 225
    Stephen: III 793
    stray: II 157, 210; III 122, 237
    Sylvester: III 246
    theology: II 141, 315, 613
    vow: III 779
    wisdom: II 700
    word: III 415
    young man: III 475, 641
Purple
    deacon: I 256a; II 389; III 66
    episcopal: I 498–99, 513, 518
    royal: II 345, 571, 743; III 293
    suffering: I 486; II 743
Purpose. See also Plan, Proposal
    brotherhood: I 117, 218, 220; II 95,
        275; III 40–41, 45, 53, 481
    Clare: I 197; II 750
    Divine: I 368, 409

edify: III 556
evil: I 546
Francis: I 187, 189–90, 230, 263,
    371–75, 383–84, 414, 598; II 77, 244,
    601, 689, 698, 790; III 417, 747, 844
improve: III 446
Pope: I 384, 419; II 95, 478, 547; III
    749, 751, 885
poverty: I 594; III 749, 751, 753, 756,
    766, 776, 781, 785
prayer: III 841, 845
preach: I 574; III 857
sermon: II 737
stigmata: II 377
Sultan: I 606
Testament: I 571
Third Order: III 64
Purse
    missionary: I 73, 89, 379, 459, 583,
        589; II 84; III 196, 382, 681, 833,
        843, 878
    money: I 337, 356, 453, 547; II 292,
        306, 580, 801; III 100, 406, 438, 745

Q

Quarrel: I 102, 484; II 517, 772
    among themselves: I 72; II 407; III
        114, 687
    devil: II 324
Queen
    figurative: I 115; II 141, 322–23; III
        334, 486, 724, 811
    France: I 290
    Mary: I 163; III 100, 528, 549, 637
    poverty: I 533–34, 550–51; II 375, 577;
        III 100, 160–61, 165
    wisdom: I 164; II 368
Question: I 563, 617, 622, 625, 652, 684,
    799, 809, 855
    deception: I 302
    identity: III 481
    other: I 207; II 43, 90, 245, 613, 660,
        691, 728, 755, 812; III 129, 160,
        296–97, 411, 442–43, 571–74
    reception: III 132
    Rule: I 572–73; II 778; III 760, 781–82,
        844
    stigmata: II 513
Quies. See Rest

R

Rabbit. See Hare
Race
    athletic: I 553, 582; II 280, 285, 382,
        417, 491; III 863
    human: I 84, 329, 354, 464, 475, 478,
        504, 511, 513, 535, 589; II 75, 186,
        221, 646, 654, 735, 772; III 89, 96,
        250, 347, 535, 549, 645, 769, 816

Rain: I 220, 305, 386, 454, 503, 529; II 224, 719, 729; III 233, 311, 341, 449, 551, 580, 628
Rainbow: I 503; II 526, 726; III 887
Ransom: I 565; II 590; III 84
Reader: II 34, 419, 528; III 177, 198, 202, 873
Reading: I 516, 587; II 196, 207, 306, 316, 365, 684; III 60, 150, 286, 315, 325, 575, 698, 833
Reality: I 433; II 251, 294, 720; III 396, 421, 786, 876
Rebellion: I 292; II 705
Rebuilding. See also Repair: I 201, 378; II 36, 249, 686, 688; III 827
Reception
    brother: I 65, 574; II 92–93, 775; III 55
    Eucharist: I 77–78
    welcome: I 487; II 448
Recommendation: III 334–36, 834
Recompense: I 452; II 521, 615, III 684
Reconciliation: I 117, 280, 412, 564, 566; II 441, 586
Recovery: II 429, 431, 460, 482, 653; III 70
Reed: I 458; II 592; III 476, 562, 596, 598
Refectory: I 551; III 559
Reflection: I 58, 72, 207, 246, 250, 436, 487, 497, 506, 597; II 39, 87, 217, 225, 445, 590, 647, 727, 755, 790
Reform: II 96, 212; III 118, 135, 148, 157, 193, 313–14, 394, 420, 559, 682, 701
Reformation: III 157
Reformer
    Francis: III 147, 158–59, 172
    imitator of Francis: III 152
Refusal: I 53–54, 70, 92, 193, 195, 267, 271, 377, 436, 482, 514, 583; II 35, 131–32, 134, 159, 219, 288, 297, 373, 421, 455, 531, 547, 585, 674, 685, 720, 817; III 154, 415
Region. See also Province: I 206, 465, 495, 533; II 155, 157, 194, 197, 216, 220, 411, 451, 628; III 63, 87, 157, 176, 223, 245–46, 283, 308, 310, 406, 452, 490–91, 494–95, 523, 525, 545, 559, 577, 606, 616, 669, 681, 694, 800, 854
    Ancona: I 501
    animal: II 727
    Apulia: II 451, 805; III 72
    Arezzo: II 444, 670
    beyond Alps: III 222, 246
    bishop: II 342
    Capitanato: II 426
    Celano: II 426
    distant: II 123, 214
    every: I 214–16, 257, 293, 390, 477; II 69, 120, 388, 403, 476, 692
    forest: II 221
    France: II 214; III 309, 587
    Lombardy: III 825
    lower: III 411

Poitiers: II 676
Rocca di Brizio: II 220
Rome: II 440, 668; III 828
Spain: III 572, 826
Spoleto: I 370; III 120, 220, 453
Syria: I 229, 231, 322; II 415, 600; III 826
Tuscany: II 809
Rejoicing
    blessed: I 85; III 192, 481
    brother: I 94, 159, 381, 547; II 45, 48, 95, 275; III 39, 320, 445, 528, 536, 547–50, 858
    Francis: I 248, 273, 276–77, 436, 453, 514, 532, 568; II 202, 251, 772, 791; III 217, 221, 282, 369, 371
    other: I 240, 274, 284, 301, 419, 477; II 121, 418, 427, 452, 461, 593, 647, 658, 772; III 71, 484, 603, 633
Relationship
    clerical: II 133
    natural: I 440
Relative
    association: I 189, 443; II 47, 94, 173, 177, 273, 317, 443, 451, 457, 656; III 352, 501, 525, 546
    Christ: III 692
    death: I 50
    Hugolino: III 215
    persecution: I 41, 89; III 38, 567, 642
    possessions: I 43, 51, 132, 165, 203, 300, 579; III 33
Relaxation: II 622, 794; III 118, 151, 155
Relic
    alms: II 199; III 215, 273
    brother: III 36
    cord: II 440, 669
    Cross: II 721
    garment: I 493
    saint: II 376–77, 573–74; III 793
Religion: I 183, 581, 607; III 95, 103, 520
    annoyance: III 480
    authority: III 116
    begin: II 34, 39, 56, 87, 104, 123, 195, 205, 211, 399, 542–47, 689–91, 696; III 217, 219, 223, 275–76, 284, 290, 388, 413, 575, 589, 711, 740, 769
    blasphemy: II 162
    book: II 204
    branch: I 260
    brother: I 270, 558; II 43, 126–27, 152–53, 158, 162, 190, 196, 200, 204–05, 207, 212, 219–20, 340; III 46, 116, 168, 172, 216, 223, 225–27, 235, 274, 286, 336, 355, 396, 402, 425–26, 487, 504, 662
    cleric: I 77, 121, 702
    commend: II 105–06, 565; III 310
    compare: I 188; II 72, 88
    conduct: I 213; II 223
    creature: III 362–68
    danger: II 363

decline: III 389, 395, 397
depart: II 264–65, 267, 297, 618; III
    408, 718, 801
deviation: I 90, 95; II 219
disfigure: II 348
division: III 135, 411, 419
Dominic: II 811; III 290
edify: II 128
eldest: II 125, 329
enter: I 206–07; II 103, 123, 156–58,
    165, 173, 176–77, 182, 222, 546, 578;
    III 306, 311, 390, 411–12, 849
evil: III 388–89, 405, 408, 412, 415
example: II 214, 219; III 122, 237, 261,
    308, 408
exterior: I 75, 90
formation: I 216–20; II 201
fountain: I 513
Francis: II 142, 146, 365, 367, 692, 811;
    III 33, 47, 63, 162, 290, 323–32, 337,
    395, 402, 410, 480
fulfill: II 54
future: II 128, 205, 349, 588; III 41,
    116, 125, 166–67, 172–73, 216, 276,
    315, 324, 335–36, 388, 390, 395, 402,
    410, 416, 419, 426, 556–57, 647, 703,
    724, 850
general minister: I 63; II 144, 364–66,
    371; III 324–26, 684
good: II 205, 212; III 167, 255, 265,
    387, 403, 414–15, 628, 703
govern: III 402, 711
growth: I 378; II 210, 348, 693; III 170,
    316, 402, 412, 710
habit: I 209, 236, 402, 542; II 54, 57,
    103, 107, 150, 164, 177, 325, 562–63;
    III 165–66, 302, 396, 481, 539,
    553–54, 601, 630, 725
hatred: III 389, 397, 600
Hugolino: I 267; II 56, 107, 261
imperfection: III 405, 717–18
integrity: I 562; III 135, 234, 279, 316,
    324, 413, 721, 740
interest: II 216
interior: I 90, 75
Lady Jacoba: II 121; III 222, 360–61
lesser: III 166, 292
Lord: II 157, 211, 588
love: II 106, 216
Lucifer: III 425
matter: I 385
nature: II 370
novice: II 125; III 225, 292
opposition: II 212, 273, 619
plant: I 269; II 219, 348
Poor Ladies: I 197, 285, 377–78; II 83,
    476; III 337–38
Portiuncula: II 156, 475; III 236–37,
    261, 297–300, 328–33
poverty: II 150, 548, 578; III 162, 164,
    234, 279, 298, 316
priest: I 77, 121, 702

privilege: II 295
profession: I 247, 455
purpose: III 40–41, 118, 255, 394, 702
respect: III 404
return: II 268
serve: II 100
shoot: I 260
status: III 404, 575, 578, 702
sterility: II 400
struggle: III 388, 410, 695
title: II 90, 123; III 223, 274, 276, 290,
    384, 702
violation: II 348, 588
virtue: III 487, 724
Religious
    person: I 48, 56, 77, 84, 90, 95, 130,
        132, 135, 215, 543–44, 546–47, 560,
        587, 594; II 43, 57, 97, 106–07, 118,
        130, 149, 156, 173, 176, 205, 208,
        210, 215, 225, 287, 344–46, 370, 406,
        555, 564, 605, 613, 617, 692, 799; III
        47, 53, 60–61, 91, 114, 133, 135, 156,
        180, 219, 230–31, 245, 252, 259, 271,
        277, 290, 293–94, 301, 307, 309, 312,
        329, 343, 362, 399, 409, 708, 722,
        783, 786, 816–18, 820, 827, 829
    profession: III 753
    quality: I 45, 61, 239, 294, 405, 418,
        549, 561, 579–81, 582–83, 585–86,
        592–93, 596, 601–02; II 49, 98, 119,
        122, 150, 154, 159, 161, 177, 183,
        187, 243, 248, 256–57, 282, 285, 323,
        349, 367, 445–47, 462, 482, 519, 534,
        577, 628, 691, 731, 750, 786, 809; III
        58, 78–79, 99, 102, 119, 134, 178,
        193, 222, 264, 279, 297, 315, 321,
        393–94, 522, 638, 696, 723, 762–63,
        770, 826, 844, 849
Reluctance: III 98, 155
Remembrance
    ancestor: II 263
    apostle: III 42
    Christ: I 58; II 522
    Francis: II 121, 162, 239; III 221, 371,
        806, 808
    God's mercy: II 753
    Gubbio: III 482
    love: I 159
    Portiuncula: II 155; III 121
    Remembrance of the Desire of a Soul: II
        241–393
    stigmata: I 281, 299
    testament: I 127; III 240, 335, 386
    vision: III 542, 874
Remission
    fault: III 87
    penance: I 565
    sin: I 207, 215, 544, 565; II 816; III
        131, 381, 472, 527, 808–09, 843
Remorse
    conscience: III 406, 496, 610, 722
    fear: II 817

feeling: II 712; III 508, 525–26, 586
sigh: I 409
sin: II 817
spectacle: I 393
weep: III 493–94, 525
Removal
temptation: III 539
Renewal: III 160, 193
elect: III 193
health: II 567
life: III 41
mind: II 760
passion: III 188
wound: II 76
Renunciation: III 397, 710–12, 744–50
Repair. See also Rebuilding
church: II 103, 378, 536, 686; III 84,
321, 438, 569, 811, 841–43, 845
humanity: III 395
Order: III 701
other: II 425, 445–47, 451, 491, 659,
678–79, 772
Portiuncula: I 378, 457–59; II 155, 158,
540, 749, 782; III 120, 261, 321, 843
Saint Peter: II 540, 749, 782; III 321,
843
San Damiano: I 196, 222, 373, 377; II
38, 81, 86, 252–53, 319, 536–37, 540,
686, 749, 782, 792; III 321, 843
Reparation: II 326, III 730
Repentance: II 441, 451, 615, 676, 678, 799;
III 691
armor: II 615
call: III 610
deprivation: I 264, 734
feeling: III 608
fruit: II 270, 594, 706
humility: II 576
longing: I 538
model: II 728
preach: I 229, 320, 335; II 526, 546
tears: III 500
water: II 291
Reproach
beyond: II 637
conscience: I 438; II 46, 128, 795; III
228
Divine: I 185; II 750
Francis: I 377, 568; II 579, 626, 688,
741, 810; III 243, 303, 569
justify: I 71, 92
other: I 191–92, 334, 442, 537, 592; II
78, 523, 547, 591; III 99, 384
Reprobate: III 316
Residence
bishop: III 224, 349, 358, 437, 460, 568
brother: II 199, 447; III 157
prelate: I 587; II 124, 187
Resignation. See also Abandonment: II
125–26, 142, 218–20, 340, 344–45, 571,
799
Resistance: I 412, 510; II 725; III 411, 890

Respect
Characteristic: I 231, 261, 368, 373; III
39, 54, 219, 273, 385, 404, 522
deference: I 293, 401, 470, 480, 500,
531, 536, 544; II 46, 52, 54, 93, 103,
118, 122, 205, 207, 261, 342, 346,
351, 354, 436, 523, 553, 564, 575,
603, 662, 798; III 44, 78, 103, 168,
177, 200, 192, 194, 222, 277, 294,
361, 495, 610, 681–82, 756, 834–35,
859, 87
request: I 125, 135–36
Responsibility
Francis: II 199; III 215
govern: III 169
preach: I 57
Rest [quies]. See also Contemplation, Leisure [vacatio]
eternal: I 66, II 107, 420, 649, 656; III
384, 654
figurative: I 80, 466–67, 484, 566, 582,
587; II 407, 763, 718, 740, 763, 816;
III 134, 161, 177, 193, 221, 384, 398,
426, 501, 536, 548, 650, 786
final: I 259, 518, 647, 716, 804; III 52,
62, 522, 654
God: I 109
physical: I 94, 187, 221, 228, 231, 261,
266, 304, 372, 386–87, 412, 453, 479,
515, 531, 535, 539, 552, 586; II 48,
57, 75, 95, 99, 135, 167, 185, 226,
312–13, 351, 425, 562, 565, 575, 630,
659, 733; III 38–39, 244, 261, 304,
312, 336–37, 347, 370, 398, 426, 448,
479, 491, 497, 534, 536, 547, 598–99,
606, 612, 643, 800, 810, 854
state: I 137, 347; II 93, 121, 630; III
177, 193, 221, 384, 398, 426, 501,
548, 650
Restlessness: I 137, 370
crowd: II 630; III 401
world: II 556
Restitution: III 777
Restoration
church: I 196, 240, 329, 458; II 378,
540–41, 688; III 195
figurative: II 734
Francis: II 532, 616, 685
health: I 256, 298–99, 301, 303–04,
323–24, 353, 403, 432; II 274, 421,
430–33, 440–41, 446, 448–52, 455,
457–58, 460–62, 466, 479–80, 555,
608, 615, 627–28, 653, 656–58, 665,
669, 674, 678–79, 692, 711–12,
716–17
human race: I 475; II 491, 764
peace: II 70, 243
Rule: III 199
vineyard: II 170
Restriction: III 742–43, 749–50, 755, 781, 802
Resurrection
Feast: I 101; II 793; III 775

Lord: II 645, 654, 816; III 159, 162, 421, 521, 633, 687, 816
   reward: I 280, 389; II 476, 816; III 194
   Rule: III 194
Revelation: I 212, 263, 282, 389, 410, 414; II 324, 338, 349–50, 402, 452, 562, 578, 629, 685, 691, 698; III 33, 53, 72, 135, 149, 166, 182, 196, 388, 608, 615, 653, 703, 867
   Book of Revelation: II 523, 527, 721, 728, 732, 735, 764
   Divine: I 224, 276, 379, 383, 509; II 84, 263, 511, 541, 545, 558, 604, 626, 691, 728, 742; III 55, 179, 383, 416, 420, 423, 472, 491–92, 572, 604, 606–07, 617–22, 630, 655, 657–58, 721–26, 835, 841, 844, 850, 863–64, 866
   heavenly: II 381, 551, 638, 700; III 408, 858
   holy: II 98
   miraculous: II 623; III 510–11, 517–18, 537
Revenge
   fear: II 421
   God's: II 133, 211, 341; III 47, 297, 414
   inflict: III 137, 171, 317, 395, 489, 605, 712
Reverence
   all: II 240, 576; III 126, 252, 294
   angel: II 540; III 443, 574
   bishop: I 246, 400, 583; II 134
   brother: I 249, 579; II 47, 96; III 396, 404, 438–40, 509, 521, 569, 571, 576–78, 644–45, 651
   canonization: I 294
   Christ: I 116, 401; II 130, 159, 195, 591, 609, 735; III 230, 363, 575, 579, 792
   church: I 189; III 83, 300–01, 425, 507, 596
   Creator: I 216, 491
   Eucharist: I 56, 117; II 214, 375, 591, 787; III 245–46, 309, 480, 600, 620
   father: I 443
   Francis: I 223, 293, 500, 584; II 40, 50, 87, 98, 109, 159, 170, 191, 252, 296, 356–57, 391, 413, 425, 442–43, 466, 531, 608, 647–48, 659, 666, 672–73, 808; III 116, 200, 238, 282, 303, 308, 311, 364, 401, 456, 460, 477, 572, 577, 584, 836
   Francis's miracles: I 293; II 468, 624
   God: I 558, 560, 576; II 191–92, 194, 203–04, 659, 735, 749–51, 773; III 218–19, 283, 365–66, 370, 611, 773, 811
   Gospel: I 202, 262, 409
   Greccio: I 254
   guardian: II 344
   Isola Maggiore: III 448, 579
   minister: II 248
   ministry: II 248, 252

Office: II 609; III 341
   personal: I 142; II 67, 228; III 90
Peter of Catanio: II 142, 340; III 225, 287
poor: II 94
Poor Ladies: I 579
Pope: I 63, 100, 267, 271, 292, 413, 558; II 50, 98, 125; III 135, 326, 516, 624, 721
Portiuncula: I 415; II 155–56, 252; III 121, 236, 299, 330, 561
prayer: III 232
prelate: I 246, 400, 583; II 134
priest: I 388; II 52, 101, 376, 536, 551, 788, 803; III 47, 83, 126, 251, 294, 389, 425, 856, 859
relic: II 376, 573
Rule: III 397
saint: II 598; III 41, 680
stigmata: I 281; II 334
tunic: I 249
Virgin Mary: III 363
vocation: III 387
wax image: I 307
written word: I 504
Reward
   beg: I 71, 92, 94; II 583
   charity: I 282, 500; II 138, 293, 336
   chastity: II 172
   Christian: II 602
   eternal: I 75, 273, 587, 600; II 468, 532, 746; III 523
   evil: I 607
   give alms: I 47, 71, 92, 94; II 81
   glory: III 732, 801, 811
   guise: I 80, 88, 90, 135, 137, 252, 256, 267, 703, 722
   heavenly: I 75, 273, 587, 600; II 468, 532, 746; III 523
   hospitality: II 44, 92, 425, 615
   humility: II 339, 521; III 886
   illness: I 275; II 384
   Lady Jacoba: II 123
   piety: I 81, 94, 101, 223
   poverty: I 534, 553; II 301
   prayer: II 608
   suffer: I 275; II 384
   work: II 133, 206, 208, 341; III 47, 297, 320, 679, 683, 857
   wickedness: I 542; III 133, 165
Rhetoric: II 520, 755
Riches
   absence: II 70, 742
   acquire: I 132, 541, 543; II 816; III 541, 622, 848–49
   body: III 249, 268
   Christ: III 158
   delight: I 456, 531; II 509, 722
   desire: I 165, 193, 371, 534; II 94, 221, 303, 351; III 249, 285
   disposition: I 442, 565, 586; II 285, 302; III 590

false: II 295, 582, 696
glory: III 384
God: I 109–10
grace: III 384
heavenly: I 193, 332, 565; II 121; III 100, 221, 371, 815, 875
judgment: I 588; II 255, 696, 742, 746, 794, 815
knowledge of God: III 421
lure: I 79
merit: II 351
offer: I 231
poverty: II 581
promise: I 439
scorn: II 284
simplicity: II 577, 722
spirit: III 249, 268
wisdom of God: III 421
worldly: I 231, 319, 534, 588; II 270, 722
Rigor
discipline: II 382; III 529
fasting: II 599, 790; III 174
justice: I 386; III 95
life: I 392–93
penance: II 356; III 439
poverty: I 603; III 32
relaxation: I 273
Rule: III 189, 772
self–denial: II 259
spirit: III 200
Ring: II 150, 189, 234, 279, 597, 743, 887, 890
betrothal: II 325; III 43
brother: I 296
Risk
Order: I 580
self: II 382
vanity: I 321
Rite
canonization: I 419
Church: I 65, 75, 101, 119, 125, 136
espousal: III 889
Eucharist: I 119
funeral: I 284, 417, 512–16; II 804
last: II 430
new: I 260
Office: I 101; II 775; III 772, 819
River: I 324, 454–55, 485–86, 493, 501, 504, 506; II 434–35, 664–65, 805; III 50, 83, 98, 130, 137, 440–44, 470, 479, 498, 520, 550–51, 574, 593, 598, 612, 627, 632, 795
biblical: I 567; II 742; III 201
eloquence: I 246
paradise: I 259
Po: II 568, 707
praise: I 138
tears: I 515; II 423
Volturno: II 422, 480, 657
Road: I 122–23, 189, 212, 217, 222, 234, 239, 250–51, 284, 300, 304, 322, 386, 396, 400, 452, 454, 456, 470, 484, 544, 584, 594; II

42, 46, 94, 98, 120, 129, 130, 177, 223, 229, 248, 250, 273, 278, 291–92, 302, 307, 310, 354, 375, 407, 409, 416, 422, 478, 547, 573, 580–81, 623, 635, 705, 707, 750, 793, 798, 803–04, 810; III 34, 39, 45, 100, 130–31, 157, 183, 230, 233, 341, 351, 362–63, 391, 439, 441, 459–60, 469, 472, 490, 511, 545, 572, 584–85, 587, 592–93, 602, 605, 616, 641, 776, 795, 831, 841, 851
Apulia: II 801
Assisi: II 437, 537
Bari: II 579; III 100
biblical: I 72, 532; II 385, 582; III 317, 711
glory: I 336
humility: II 521
Limisiano: II 172
Llerda: II 653
Morocco: II 601
Osimo: I 248
penance: II 553
Po: II 568, 707; III 98
Portiuncula: II 180, 202, 210; III 220, 258, 275–76, 339, 370, 579, 708
salvation: I 570
San Verecondo: II 807
Spoleto Valley: I 213; II 550, 651
time: I 446
Robber. See also Bandit, Brigand, Thief
brother: I 70
figurative: I 437, 439, 460, 587; II 752, 816; III 163, 483
reception: I 69, 91; II 221–22; III 250–51, 310–11, 494–500, 609–14
victim: I 320, 376, 453, 455; II 687, 782, 792
Robin: II 279
Rock: I 251, 356, 429, 506, 587; II 93, 159, 354, 584–85, 635, 705, 707; III 200, 262, 366, 416, 460, 470, 479, 497, 506, 567, 587, 599, 611, 619, 802
biblical: I 243, 586; II 192, 278, 409, 584–85, 705, 757, 798
Christ: II 192, 354, 798; III 33
church: III 194
God: II 192, 354, 798; III 33
humility: I 217; II 123, 155; III 223, 290
poverty: II 155; III 101, 153, 159, 223, 236, 290, 298, 861
Rod
correction: I 136, 272; III 851
iron: II 360
justice: I 186
meekness: II 518
power: II 260, 518, 818; III 324
punishment: II 146, 360; III 288
Roof
another: II 286, 578; III 95
church: III 847

dwelling: I 442, 457; II 129, 274, 328,
    415, 616, 644, 659, 667, 702, 796
La Verna: II 191; III 365
Portiuncula: II 157–58, 285; III 230,
    260, 362–63
Rivo Torto: I 474
temple: III 192
tower: II 326, 425
Room
    Bernard: III 436
    bishop: II 80, 200; III 216, 274, 525
    chapter: I 551
    heaven: II 727
    hermit: II 326
    house: I 437, 447, 462, 518; II 168, 809
    inn: I 535; II 802; III 606
    personal: II 331
    Pope: II 751
    storeroom: II 276
Root
    charity: III 39
    cross: II 320, 383
    evangelical life: III 397
    evil: III 173, 329, 415
    health: I 511
    holiness: II 748–49, 751, 759; III 136
    humility: II 46, 93; III 740
    inheritance: I 544
    Jesse: II 720
    love: II 46, 93
    moral sickness: I 435, 566; II 140, 305,
        343, 360, 511, 515
    obedience: III 397
    Order: I 418; III 557, 559, 647–48
    perfection: II 578
    personal: I 549
    philosophy: III 424
    piety: II 603; III 175
    plant: II 410, 466; III 449
    poverty: III 740
    tree: I 183, 514
    wisdom: II 751
    word: I 79
    zeal: I 495
Rope
    belt: II 426, 430, 433, 435; II 660, 663
    figurative: I 335, 466
    Francis: I 392; II 182; III 305–06
    habit: I 460, 583; II 542, 689, 792; III
        40, 47
    suicide: III 435
Rule
    apostasy: III 158
    apostle: II 542, 544, 689
    appeal: I 206
    Augustine: II 132–33; III 124, 314, 71
    Basil: III 185
    beg: III 587
    Benedict: II 132–33; III 124; 314,
        709–10
    Bernard: II 132–33; III 314, 710
    book: II 204, 206; III 166

Book of Life: II 146, 380
cardinal: III 859
chapter: III 256, 406, 704
Christ: II 105, 132, 541, 688; III 116,
    124, 127–28, 133, 253, 381, 386, 396,
    421, 712–13, 716, 718
Clare: II 623
clothing: III 118, 166, 170, 255–56,
    258, 702, 708
coins: I 96, 571; II 291
composition: I 98, 210, 216–17, 337,
    383; II 48–51, 56–57, 132, 134, 204,
    210, 219–20, 291, 481, 541, 550, 558,
    579, 783; III 34, 128, 167–68,
    181–82, 189, 245, 383, 386, 703–04,
    826, 831, 834, 844
confirmation: I 99, 212, 321, 337, 384,
    418; II 51, 56–57, 105–06, 205, 254,
    371, 513, 547–48, 557, 629, 690, 792;
    III 79, 88–89, 127, 276, 390–91, 680,
    712–13, 826, 838
cross: II 682; III 188, 420, 667
declaration: III 179, 698–99
disregard: III 177, 180, 183, 393
Dominic: II 785
doubt: II 513
Earlier Rule: III 276, 288, 290, 406, 720
Eucharist: II 214–15; III 309
exposition: III 179
flesh: III 388
Fonte Colombo: II 131
fragment: I 92–96
Francis: I 100, 217, 341, 344, 385; II
    550; III 214, 699, 824
gloss: I 127; II 132; III 117, 128, 254,
    386, 420, 714, 767
Gospel: I 210, 321; II 38, 52, 101,
    206–07, 544, 558, 773; III 34, 60,
    132, 150, 168, 187, 384, 442, 445,
    488, 522, 680, 704, 714–15, 815, 817,
    824, 831
hermitage: I 61
host: II 381, 558; III 93
intention: III 123, 166, 255, 697, 701,
    705, 714, 817
interpretation: II 291
Later Rule: III 254
leper: III 290
letter: III 254, 714
life: I 63, 86, 100, 206, 210, 385; II 86,
    254, 544, 547; III 123, 151, 187,
    256–57, 323, 383, 396–97, 425, 722,
    823
martyrdom: II 147, 381; III 323, 398
meat: III 573
minister: II 131, 206; III 256, 704, 713,
    858
obedience: III 126, 157, 159, 166, 252,
    294
observance: I 105, 119, 126–27, 206,
    213, 305, 384; II 48–51, 56–57, 132,
    134, 204, 210, 219–20, 291, 481, 541,

550, 558, 579; III 116–17, 135, 150, 152, 183, 188, 248, 323–24, 327–28, 386, 396, 401, 420, 425, 702, 714
Office: I 119–20, 129; II 773
opposition: II 212; III 170, 393, 713, 725
papal teaching: I 571–75; II 775–79; III 740–43, 770–75, 779–80, 782, 785, 789
Penitents: III 701
Pope: I 99, 212, 321, 337, 384, 418; II 51, 56–57, 105–06, 205, 254, 371, 513, 547–48, 557, 629, 690, 792; III 79, 88–89, 116, 127, 276, 390–91, 680, 712–13, 826, 838, 844
Portiuncula: III 331
poverty: III 166–67, 172, 383, 704
preach: I 598; II 48
privilege: III 114, 126
profession: III 323, 326, 397, 715
protection: II 57, 105
relaxation: III 722
renewal: II 688; III 184
schism: III 695
sick: III 288
statement: I 86, 93–96, 98, 107, 120, 126–27; III 172, 253, 255, 257, 265, 288, 309
stigmata: II 513, 559
Tau: III 189
teaching of Christ: II 105, 541, 688; III 421
Testament: III 150, 152, 179, 386
theologian: II 352
transgression: III 180, 189, 697
tribulation: III 134
voice of Christ: II 132; III 116, 124, 127–28, 133, 253, 381, 386, 396, 712–13, 716, 718
Ruler. See also Master: I 58–60, 67, 205, 251, 475, 531, 579, 581; II 90, 109, 602, 772, 810; III 381, 488, 540, 687, 697, 722, 725, 727, 804
Rust: I 431, 539; II 330; III 487–88, 725

S

Sack: I 201, 439; II 297
Benjamin 144, 158
bread: III 495, 610
flesh: III 669
habit: III 331, 480
manure: III 503, 666
Sackcloth: I 65, 101, 278, 323, 451, 598; II 119, 123, 138, 293, 370, 386, 475, 527, 642, 772, 807; III 118, 220, 267, 358, 361, 393, 481, 486, 723, 798, 835
Sacrament. See also Mystery, Secret [*secretum*]
church: I 100, 119, 802; III 494, 609
music: II 239, 330
priest: II 52, 101; III 787–88, 385

stigmata: II 633
Sacred
altar: I 262
beginning: II 247
book: II 314, 612
bread: I 129
Christ's blood: II 622
Christ's body: II 591; III 651–52
Christ's life: II 565
Christ's Passion: II 249
Christ's wounds: I 264, 281, 288; II 634, 636–37
command: II 239
consistory: I 293
eloquence: I 295; II 582
encouragement: III 466
font: III 887
Francis's blood: I 410, 416; II 108, 473, 633, 771
Francis's body: I 259, 284, 286, 296, 298, 416–17; II 109, 476, 478, 647; III 845–46
Francis's hands: II 627, 635, 653–54
Francis's stigmata: I 287, 308; II 401, 405–06, 408, 515, 630, 636, 641, 650, 709; III 458, 578, 661, 669, 681, 728, 792
Francis's tomb: I 518
Francis's wounds: I 264, 281, 288; II 634, 636–37
gathering: I 294
gift: II 109
inspiration: I 441
mark: I 281; II 635, 652
meditation: III 834
ministry: III 758
miracle: II 399, 651
mystery: I 296; II 478, 573
name: II 609
offering: II 288
office: I 441
palace: II 419
piety: I 306
place: I 252, 286, 472; II 83, 477
possession: I 494
preaching: II 352
precinct: I 447
purpose: III 885
relic: II 573
religion: II 348, 578, 588
scripture: I 248, 252; II 314, 612, 631, 636, 700, 735, 800; III 705, 789, 839
seal: I 344
seraph: II 633
sign: II 405, 634, 646
spirit: II 622
stigmata: I 287, 308; II 401, 405–06, 408, 515, 630, 636, 641, 650, 709; III 458, 578, 661, 669, 681, 728, 792
study: II 399
testimony: II 573

theology: I 107; II 104, 315, 352; III
673, 678, 828, 830
thing: II 246, 375, 403
treasure: II 648
truth: I 460
utterance: II 638
virgin: II 83, 466
vestment: I 295
womb: I 291
word: I 401
Sacrifice: III 180, 189, 234, 278
Bernard: III 447
Christ: I 46–47, 56, 117; III 174, 739,
875
Francis: I 409; II 359, 375, 405, 437,
600, 609, 698; III 174, 398, 875
personal: I 130, 560, 563; II 149, 259,
272, 311, 360, 510, 519, 587, 656,
702, 744, 761
Sadness: I 281, 286, 403, 515, 546; II 243,
330, 332, 357, 405, 414–15, 454, 457, 675,
816; III 164, 342, 504, 524, 530, 619
Safeguard: I 132, 137, 213, 292; II 159, 523;
III 181, 262, 489, 726
Safety: I 493; II 716
Sailor: I 229–30, 323, 394, 482–83; II 415,
433–35, 585, 600–01, 663, 665, 783; III
104, 855
Sale
cloth: I 371
food: II 298, 583
goods: II 38
lamb: I 249; III 777
Salt: I 552, 560; II 259, 564; III 436, 453, 548
water: III 520, 632
Salvation
achievement: I 529, 545, 587
begging: II 295
benefit: I 288, 565
Church: III 856
counsel: II 71, 92, 543
cross: II 538, 681; III 366
depression: II 331
food: I 29
God: I 140, 142, 145
Gospel: II 526
hatred: I 203, 320, 547
joy: I 152; II 330, 764; III 343
life: I 41
Lord Jesus Christ: I 41, 118, 147, 149,
154; II 130, 221, 532, 622, 689, 803;
III 152, 230, 285, 731, 739
loss: I 446, 462, 495, 515; II 85, 295,
543
mission: III 246, 348, 578, 759, 800,
844–45, 857
obstacle: I 570
oil: I 274
one's own: I 167, 273; II 160, 179, 217,
268, 313, 445, 748; III 54, 239, 247,
263, 308, 445, 743, 772

other: I 266, 322, 380, 535, 587, 601; II
89, 93, 133–34, 156, 186, 214, 216,
260, 294, 358, 564, 587, 598–99, 622,
630, 697, 747, 772; III 116, 246, 251,
294, 297, 299, 301, 308, 324, 326,
348, 578, 592, 759, 800, 844–45, 847,
854, 857, 889
peace: I 335, 540; II 526; III 276
perfection: I 448
port: I 445
poverty: II 578
preach: I 380, 540; II 85, 100, 526, 543,
601, 622; III 49, 90, 381, 845, 849
price: II 532, 689
religion: II 268
Rule: II 146; III 116, 323, 715
seed: II 601
seeker: I 320
spirit: I 203
struggle: II 406
Tau: II 681
teach: II 263, 513
time: II 272
way: I 217; II 100, 578; III 60, 65, 320,
745
word: I 202
Samaritan: I 582
Sanctification: I 393; II 695, 732; III 423,
535
Sanctity. See also Holiness: I 331, 356, 376,
407, 592; II 67, 107, 527, 644, 695, 708,
716, 780, 792, 799; III 118, 154, 394, 446,
724, 848
Sanctuary: I 152, 296; II 301; III 516
Sandal: II 689, 733; III 56, 382, 833
Saracen: I 74, 106, 229, 231, 394, 564, 606,
608; II 145, 381, 555, 600, 602, 726; III 37,
94, 119, 323, 383, 494, 605, 815–16,
855–56
Satisfaction: I 43, 50; II 146, 225, 348, 511,
796, 817; III 237, 288, 312, 397, 549, 811
Savior: I 86, 109, 279, 484, 546; II 603, 683,
786; III 531, 746
Christ: II 602, 717; III 187, 383, 447,
547, 643, 683
Creator: I 85–86; III 452
cross: III 799
crucified: I 75
Father: I 158
glory: I 291, 303, 338, 381, 394
grace: I 391; II 277, 525, 684
John: III 531–32, 536, 543, 650–51
John the Evangelist: III 683
knowledge: I 543
Lord: I 523
Mary: III 51, 86, 549, 645, 811–12
name: I 234, 319
Nativity: III 516, 540
place: III 501
presence: II 597
Redeemer: II 780

reverence: I 195
Simeon: III 528, 530, 637
stigmata: III 452
truth: II 98
world: I 600; II 772
worm: I 250
wound: I 244; II 807
Scandal
actual: II 179, 188, 215, 271
avoid: I 219; II 146, 163, 212–13, 264, 300, 359; III 40, 779
generate: I 68, 93, 106, 218, 500; II 52, 102, 144, 161, 206, 364–65, 579, 588; III 116, 154, 240, 255, 264–65, 288, 301, 325, 350, 375, 560, 703, 718, 799, 857
Scar: I 264–65, 357, 359, 410, 428, 435, 510; II 108, 197, 386, 403, 446, 467, 473, 490; III 74, 835
Scarlet: I 188, 194; III 189, 875
Schism: I 480
Rule: III 410
Scholar: II 316, 370, 412, 625; III 49, 104, 182, 264, 500, 712
School
Christ: I 553; II 572
Francis: I 209; II 259
grace: I 338
humility: I 213
Mohammed: I 487
perfection: II 373
Rete: II 431
theology: I 574; II 778
trial: I 338
Science: III 118, 180, 394
Scorn
body: I 48
Christ: I 144
human: I 473, 496, 515; II 39, 41, 81; III 444, 560, 722, 885
money: II 48, 89, 339, 519
world: III 567
Scourge: I 431; II 117, 676, 741, 791, 803; III 43, 484
Scourging
Christ: I 536
Francis: II 804
goad: I 96, 435; III 853
Scribe
Christ: I 399, 501
Scripture: I 204, 225, 248, 278, 280, 328, 341, 356, 368, 390, 399, 498, 538, 545, 588, 602; II 141, 181, 207, 215, 242, 264, 314–16, 322, 372, 425, 511, 524, 529, 590, 612–13, 617, 697, 700, 717, 722, 728–29, 733, 735–37, 746–47, 750, 755, 757, 760, 762, 800, 818; III 34, 182, 296, 367, 423–24; 436, 485, 519, 563, 567, 705, 789–90, 814, 851
Scruple
anxiety: II 775; III 742

brother: II 291; III 120, 533
conscience: II 617; III 533
doubt: II 631, 651–52; III 95, 120
Francis: I 437, 476
Sea
beast: III 816
description: I 504, 567
fish: I 206; III 520–21
millstone: III 164, 179
miracle: II 584, 665, 682; III 856
Order: III 179, 186
praise: I 49, 147, 149, 155–56, 161, 328
river: III 479
Red Sea: III 399
shore: II 703
storm: I 480, 483–84; II 415, 433, 663, 665
travel: I 394, 479, 583; II 265, 600, 810; III 492, 607, 815, 855
Trinity: III 541
wave: III 392
Seal
general minister: III 325
heart: III 817
papal: I 63, 92–95; II 56, 371, 722; III 712
sixth: III 149, 816
Seclusion: I 356; III 151
Secret *[secretum]*. See also Mystery, Sacrament
action: I 542, 593; II 85, 145, 195, 365
God: I 261, 500; II 638; III 804
heart: I 336, 392, 518; II 578, 617, 633, 710; III 437, 686, 781, 834
keeping: I 98, 265, 386; II 455, 633–34, 727
knowledge: I 489
meaning: II 727
place: I 372, 436; II 78, 309, 537, 607
prayer: I 187, 191, 372; II 75, 312, 352, 405, 587, 652
purpose: I 372, 512
reward: I 500
scripture: III 87
share: I 336, 392; II 74, 455
solitude: I 261; II 539
stigmata: II 634, 710
temptation: III 354
thought: I 226, 386; II 617
Sect: I 593; II 787–88; III 828
Secular
clergy: II 154; III 239, 264, 297
clothes: I 377; II 73, 195, 223, 406, 531; III 79, 115, 284, 351, 436, 634, 824
knight: II 297
knowledge: III 712, 814
life: II 693
people: I 579; II 54, 157, 161, 163, 176, 187, 223, 258; III 165, 241, 301, 351
priest: I 223; II 170, 319, 795

Secular Franciscan. See Third Order, Penitent
Seduction
   flesh: I 221, 460; III 811
   world: II 100
Seed
   Abraham: III 394
   blessing: I 236; III 890
   descendent: I 530, 538; III 160, 470, 593
   harvest: I 311, 435, 447, 568, 589; II 521, 718; III 114
   life: I 230, 239
   love: I 217, 534
   mustard: II 166, 324; III 43, 158, 346
   salvation: II 601; III 890
   virtue: II 256
   word: I 79, 88, 266, 394, 558, 576, 600; II 587, 792; III 681, 793, 854
Seedling: I 417; II 475
Self-emptying. See also Condescension: II 586, 622; III 43, 278, 821
Sense
   brother: II 517, 572
   common: I 464; II 404; III 202, 333
   concern: I 248
   heart: II 592
   hidden: II 377, 592
   humility: II 517, 534
   literal: I 459, 589; II 719–20
   meekness: II 517
   perception: I 433–34, 439, 472
   Rule: II 778; III 111, 116, 743
   sacrament: II 377
   scripture: I 589; II 141, 315, 352, 511, 587, 719–20, 725; III 49
   security: II 791
   simplicity: II 368
   spiritual: I 589
   stigmata: II 377; III 174, 192, 380, 453
   taste: II 704
Sensitivity: II 531, 704
Sentence
   judgment: I 498, 539, 564; II 142, 323, 464, 815; III 334, 533, 630, 763
Sentinel
   biblical: II 614
   Saracen: I 606
Separation: I 285; II 818
   sword: II 103
Sequence
   historical: I 180
   liturgical: I 353–60, 636; III 698
Seraph
   burning coal: II 635, 727; III 147
   crucified: I 515, 638, 709, 743, 758, 769; III 79, 668
   form: I 283; II 742, 783
   meaning: II 727
   revelation: III 423
   similitude: II 638, 709, 742–43

utterance: II 633
vision: I 263–64, 410, 509–10, 596; II 108, 227, 402, 475, 498, 632, 638, 709, 743, 758, 783, 796; III 698, 874
wing: I 279, 410, 509; III 187, 457, 874
Seraphim: I 83; II 727, 816; III 420–21, 530, 840
Serenity: I 243, 356, 413; II 153, 612, 695, 700, 738, 742; III 181, 493, 355
Servant
   Anthony: III 519, 632
   blessed: I 132, 134–37
   brother: I 48, 67
   Christ: I 249, 260, 359, 383, 493, 569, 599, 604; II 87, 110, 251, 256, 282, 329, 439, 479, 521, 541, 543, 546, 548, 553, 556, 566, 570, 573, 602–03, 605, 633, 637, 666–67, 683, 699, 709, 731–32, 748–49, 751; III 448, 462, 475, 519, 536, 666
   chosen: II 734, 747, 754
   crucified: I 264, 604
   David: II 752
   emperor: III 347
   evil: II 141, 322; III 334
   faithful: I 270, 350; II 283, 732–33, 739, 747, 786; III 494, 475
   form: II 732, 751
   Francis: I 45, 51, 56, 58, 97, 116, 127, 215, 230, 242, 256, 301–02, 351, 394, 484, 531, 538, 566, 599, 704, 709, 750; II 421, 464, 657; III 350, 353, 360, 372, 392, 415, 418, 447, 631, 667, 811
   girl: II 442
   God: I 133, 190–91, 230, 234, 240, 263, 265, 279, 323, 376, 378, 402–03, 437, 478, 489, 566, 599; II 58, 79, 81, 92–93, 95–98, 119, 123–24, 141, 178, 186, 190, 198–99, 229–30, 241, 251, 256, 282–83, 295, 312, 315, 321, 325–26, 329–31, 350, 415–16, 444, 461, 463, 481, 525, 527–28, 536–38, 540, 544, 548, 557, 567, 575, 581, 590, 593–94, 597, 601, 608, 625, 627, 634, 645, 648, 660, 676, 687, 690, 693, 704–05, 733, 749–50, 788, 791; III 43, 46, 65, 175, 214, 223–24, 233, 272–74, 296, 322, 342–44, 378, 383, 425, 447, 466, 473, 511, 653, 827, 839
   greater: I 48; II 572
   Greek: II 436
   Hugolino: I 271, 413
   humility: I 56, 58, 404; II 749–50, 733, 751, 753, 755, 759; III 321
   Israel: II 753
   Job: II 733, 749–50
   lazy: III 45, 52
   leper: II 74, 719, 750
   Lord: I 36, 58, 71, 97, 134, 150, 215, 245, 264, 279, 388, 522, 533; II 350,

388, 464, 476–77, 517, 523, 537, 583,
  687, 690, 697, 702, 705, 732
Mary: I 163
minister: I 67, 74, 104, 695; III 699
Moses: II 732
priest: II 788
ready: II 300, 733
servant: I 99, 558–60, 562–65, 570,
  576; III 739
snow: II 325, 563
unworthy: II 166; II 734
useless: I 72, 544
wise: II 747
Zerubabel: II 731, 749
Service
  agent: III 751–52
  brother: III 38, 216, 274, 504, 691
  cardinal: II 55
  charity: III 397
  Christ: II 160, 172, 272, 383, 401, 678,
    701; III 263
  creation: II 585; III 153
  Divine: II 81, 85; III 153, 841
  force: III 163
  Francis: I 191; II 79, 81, 85, 661–62,
    681, 781, 805
  God: I 159, 251, 272; II 259, 605, 616,
    731–34, 739, 749; III 98, 115, 424, 628
  Gregory IX: II 781
  idol: I 183, 548
  knighthood: II 533
  leper: II 688, 675, 750
  Poor Ladies: II 379
  preach: II 587
  sacred: I 459
  senses: II 568
  spirit: I 466
  unqualified: I 104
Severity
  abstinence: II 182; III 306, 326
  affliction: I 303
  chastisement: III 763
  intransigence: II 564
  judge: II 720
  love: II 794
  pain: III 369, 852
Shame: I 79, 131, 135, 148, 152, 182, 192,
  195, 599; II 180, 182, 187, 200, 214,
  216–17, 220, 268, 351, 736, 789–90; III
  118, 159, 291, 306, 848
  beg: II 150, 295, 791; III 269, 291
  bishop: III 349
  brother: III 389, 392, 395, 575, 650
  Christian army: II 266, 614
  confession: II 153, 590
  deformity: II 445, 457
  flesh: II 125
  Francis: II 106, 200, 296; III 216, 274,
    339, 349, 371, 459, 494, 575, 885
  heretic: I 328, 566
  learn: III 403
  mayor: III 349

Passion: III 621
poor: II 581, 794; III 268, 395, 840
prelate: I 580
slander: II 364
Sharing
  alms: III 39
  heaven: I 330, 346
  place: III 749
  suffer: I 288; II 306; III 382
Sheep. See also Lamb
  cure: II 601, 634, 711
  flock: II 414, 591
  Francis: I 247–49, 322, 330, 399, 501;
    II 321, 393, 414, 565, 590–91; III
    175, 475, 489–90, 500, 510–11, 531,
    545, 553, 597, 605, 621, 630, 726,
    851, 886
  goat: I 74, 399; II 602; III 392
  Good Shepherd: I 42, 49, 80, 88, 131,
    473; III 67, 90, 453, 458, 477, 479
  Lady Poverty: I 550
  loss: II 145, 365; III 335
  parable: I 249
  wolf: I 74, 399; II 602; III 392
Sheepfold: II 752
Shelter: I 221, 235, 374, 454, 457, 470, 474;
  II 91, 761; III 262, 563, 579
Shepherd
  bishop: I 246
  Christ: III 477, 479, 531, 533, 596–98
  David: II 620
  Elias: I 412; III 203
  evil: III 115
  Francis: I 209, 285, 334, 337, 376, 381;
    II 144, 259, 349, 360, 365, 464, 553,
    557, 565, 588, 690; III 92, 335,
    399–01, 475–76, 489–90, 510–11,
    553, 595, 605, 630, 678, 726, 886
  God: I 80, 131
  Hugo: II 262; III 834
  ideal: III 325, 559
  Moses: II 742, 752–53
  Pope: I 291, 295, 429; II 254, 648, 764;
    III 834
Shield
  cross: III 873
  faith: I 191, 355, 441, 584; III 482
  Francis: I 186, 435, 499; II 35, 70; III 873
  hardship: I 261, 357
  patience: I 225; II 384; III 868
  prayer: III 147, 343
  spirit: I 437
Ship
  Ancona: I 309, 323, 482–85, 707
  figurative: I 434, 471, 585
  miracle: III 104
  other: II 435, 664–65
  Syria: I 229–30, 394; II 415, 600; III
    855
Shipwreck
  actual: II 433–35, 757, 663–65
  figurative: I 483; II 538, 647

Shop
    father: II 34, 69
    work: I 575
Shortage. See also Famine
    food: I 482
Shoulder: I 249, 442, 461, 471, 532; II 228,
    813
    alms: II 202, 297; III 276
    deformity: I 298; II 458, 462, 479, 653,
        657; III 69
    hand on: III 57, 345
Sick: I 70, 84, 432, 439, 469, 491, 493–94,
    496; II 76, 102, 120, 145, 193, 197–98,
    211, 220, 225, 259, 286–87, 356, 359, 522,
    524, 589, 737, 760, 815; III 44, 59, 91, 282,
    285, 344, 441, 493, 495, 517, 536, 572, 706
    needs: I 67, 73, 93, 98, 102–03, 776,
        814; II 198, 229, 776, 814; III 288,
        441, 572, 493
Sickness. See also Illness, Infirmity: I 115,
    273, 435; II 76, 330, 351, 365, 818; III 325
    animal: II 321, 590, 611
    brother: I 69–71, 73, 91, 94, 96, 103,
        136, 241; II 286, 359–60, 555, 628,
        692; III 43, 55, 58, 259, 279, 288–89,
        325–26, 339, 478, 535, 547–49, 597,
        706
    cure: I 166, 236, 239, 302–03, 322, 403,
        405, 511, 783, 803, 813; II 197, 419,
        421–22, 427, 431–32, 434, 447, 465,
        467, 540, 555, 626, 628, 656, 664,
        692, 783, 803, 813; III 74, 85
    Francis: I 45, 493, 773; II 119, 121,
        190, 195, 198, 203–04, 211–12, 225,
        228–29, 274, 281, 289, 316, 356, 413,
        416, 593, 615, 745, 773; III 82, 94,
        97, 170–73, 218, 220–21, 226, 284,
        231–32, 335, 346, 352, 358, 360, 364,
        369–71, 402, 414, 473–74, 702,
        710–11, 863
Siege
    Arezzo: II 575
    Assisi: III 87
    Damietta: I 485, 608
    Francis: III 878
Sight: I 301; II 566, 695; III 669, 732, 801,
    856–57, 874
    church: III 324
    Francis: III 226, 355, 577
    God: III 59, 396
    leper: III 83
    loss: III 54, 57, 226, 355, 577
    restore: III 50, 57–58, 71–72, 185, 449,
        835
Sign: I 235, 260, 330, 478, 496, 540, 547; II
    219, 222–23, 343, 407, 427, 430, 451; III
    41, 55, 59, 63, 90, 179, 216, 274, 405, 606
    Christ: I 401, 517, 553, 596
    cross: I 188, 240, 262, 279, 287, 300,
        302, 323, 357, 359, 373, 396, 403,
        409; II 82, 175, 190, 197, 274, 277,

    328, 401, 408, 410, 412, 420, 447,
    450, 454–55, 461, 467; III 50, 74, 85,
    364, 422, 437, 568, 575, 593–94,
    601–02, 616, 624, 798, 835, 847
    Francis: I 67, 323, 356–57, 359, 402,
        405, 448, 451, 468, 473; III 51, 48,
        174, 188–90, 240, 248, 327, 335, 364,
        420, 424, 584, 618, 667, 670, 815, 876
    God's purpose: I 409; II 227
    heaven: I 56, 372
    humility: II 123, 155, 161, 212; III 120,
        172, 223, 236, 239, 264, 298, 361,
        396, 815
    holiness: I 294; II 265; III 567
    illness: I 274; II 467
    love: I 281
    martyrdom: I 280
    miraculous: I 324, 407; II 378
    new: I 260, 282, 356; II 399
    nobility: II 201
    poverty: II 123, 155, 161, 212; III 120,
        172, 223, 236, 239, 264, 298, 361,
        396, 815
    praise: I 59; III 189
    pretension: II 285
    relation: II 67, 147, 264, 326, 381, 407,
        468, 490
    remembrance: II 162
    reverence: II 52
    signing: I 241, 306, 601; II 167, 197,
        274, 455, 461
    sorrow: II 439
    Spirit: II 137, 293; III 267, 589
    Tau: II 317, 402, 458
Silence: I 35, 180, 186, 226, 407; II 249, 323,
    334, 364, 377, 399, 482, 528, 544, 717,
    722, 792; III 25, 412, 437, 476, 525, 857,
    876
    birds: I 235, 322; II 412, 593, 624–25,
        706, 783, 798–99, 801; III 835
    conscience: II 614
    humility: II 523
    mystery: II 377
    observance: I 61, 72, 206, 263; II 156,
        215, 257, 264, 380, 564, 628; III 40,
        121, 237, 245, 299, 309, 350–51, 393,
        465, 518, 589, 596, 625, 696, 795
    prayer: I 224; II 99, 156, 264, 539; III
        245, 795, 845
    solitude: II 539
    Spirit: I 221, 273; II 99, 328
    stigmata: II 633, 710
    virtue: II 564
Silk: I 607; II 119; III 220, 358, 801
Silver: I 190, 201, 379, 384, 448–49, 459,
    493, 539–40, 583, 607–08; II 37, 47, 84,
    151, 199, 301, 423, 428, 512, 542, 689,
    736; III 117–18, 196, 214, 269, 393,
    486–87, 514, 557, 723–24
Similarity
    Benedict and Francis: II 740
    Christ and Francis: III 34

Simplicity: I 209, 262, 269, 487, 496; II 240, 251, 263, 318, 392, 528, 531, 544, 694, 792; III 81, 325, 682, 697
  animal: I 322; II 591, 692, 724, 798
  Bonaventure: III 380
  brother: I 48, 125, 462, 547, 580, 586, 588; II 42, 85, 144, 341, 352, 365, 370–71, 447, 497, 544, 547, 552, 587, 620, 690, 695, 798; III 41, 92, 114, 117, 133, 168, 170, 192, 316, 319–20, 335, 388, 408, 413, 465, 507, 523, 526, 697, 705, 710, 843, 855
  Clare: I 458
  Emperor Jean: III 57
  faith: II 551
  Francis: I 126, 205, 259, 262, 267, 290, 321, 339, 356, 378, 380–81, 399, 433, 461, 464, 505, 509, 587, 597; II 32–33, 50, 81, 105, 176, 200, 219, 260, 339, 349, 545–47, 572, 588, 622, 690, 697, 701, 721, 726, 788–89, 792; III 44, 48, 87, 124, 192, 216, 242, 247, 271, 274, 302, 308, 327, 335, 381, 395, 403, 411, 465, 589, 710–11, 717, 728, 826, 843, 849, 854
  general minister: III 325
  Honorius III: I 579
  humility: III 315, 319–20, 710
  innocence: II 418
  James: II 166; III 242, 303
  Jean: III 57
  John: II 163, 368–69; III 241, 301–02, 686, 699
  learning: II 365; III 705, 712
  Leo: III 123, 125, 333, 451, 581, 686
  Matteo: III 557
  Pacifico: III 692
  poverty: I 320, 380; II 37, 546, 577, 696, 722, 792; III 316, 413
  Rule: III 817
  Stephen: III 793
  virginity: III 48
  virtue: I 48, 74, 203–05, 210, 269, 272, 274, 335, 339, 390, 440, 503, 547; II 84, 105, 176–77, 217, 240, 319, 365, 367, 370, 457, 574, 587, 696, 728, 756
  word: I 202, 320, 383, 388, 504, 566; II 81, 85, 98, 318, 543, 547, 689, 747; III 196, 817, 855
Sin
  Adam: I 129, 449, 538; II 501
  alms: III 272, 385
  anger: I 104
  avoid: II 124, 474; III 291
  blasphemy: II 677
  body: II 76
  confess: I 78, 91, 119, 393; II 208, 221, 270, 420, 519, 524, 545–46, 594, 615, 656, 673, 703, 706, 778
  disorder: I 323, 731
  disturbance: I 67, 72, 92, 104, 133
  envy: I 132; III 423

  Eucharist: I 52, 54
  excess: II 76, 259
  excuse: I 538
  forgive: I 91, 97–98, 279; II 168, 300, 511; III 343, 491, 500, 605, 608
  fornication: III 48
  Francis: I 124, 184, 187, 195, 202, 259, 271, 336, 377, 380, 393; II 75–76, 509, 511, 519, 545, 603, 690, 734, 749, 754, 757, 761, 783
  Francis's teaching: I 41, 43, 46–52, 54, 67–68, 72, 75, 77–79, 87, 90–92, 97–98, 103–04, 114, 119, 124, 129, 131, 386; II 40, 42, 88–89, 546; III 156, 214, 224, 231, 233, 252, 272, 312, 344, 392, 395, 397, 407, 451, 480, 484, 598, 610, 621, 630, 862
  hatred: I 283
  ingratitude: II 198, 274; III 59
  joy: III 343
  living in: I 289; II 626, 764
  lust: II 723, 741; III 48, 605–06
  mortal: I 51, 114, 573; II 121, 141, 315, 754; III 49, 198, 221, 296, 368, 371, 396, 445, 662, 771
  original: II 725
  past: I 372, 433
  penance: I 301; II 40, 42, 88–89, 177, 208
  Pietro Bernardone: I 193; II 79
  possession: II 199, 298, 510, 583
  priest: I 125, 388; II 788
  private: I 573; II 778
  public: I 573; II 778
  punishment: II 175, 225, 292
  purification: I 347
  recourse: I 68, 103–05, 573; II 778
  remission: I 46, 259, 280–81, 283, 288, 351, 544, 565; II 300, 511, 545
  Rule: III 417, 770–71
  slavery: II 511, 732, 740, 791
  stigmata: III 560
  vanity: II 169
  venial: I 98; II 754; III 198
  weight: I 533; II 518, 522–23
  world: I 183, 331
Sincerity
  Francis: I 290; III 194
  virtue: I 265; II 173, 512, 641; III 60, 772
Singularity: II 253, 265, 351; III 700
Sinner: II 334, 571; III 662, 811
  Elias: I 489, 491; III 553
  forgiveness: II 34, 324, 562, 817–18, 795; III 125, 324
  Francis: II 312, 338, 569, 725, 739, 752; III 47, 96, 305, 451, 458, 848, 878
  Francis's prayer: I 205; II 312, 608
  Jesus: I 205; III 453, 513
  praise: II 334, 571
  Thomas of Celano: I 308

Sister: I 64; II 510, 798
  acedia: I 438
  Agnes: III 591, 690
  avarice: I 438
  birds: II 592–93, 799; III 860
  brother: I 41, 45, 603
  charity: III 551
  Clare: II 128–29, 188–89, 623, 750,
    760; III 467, 469, 516–17, 590–91,
    690
  courtesy: III 551
  creature: I 251, 397; II 590, 696, 798
  cricket: II 217–18, 357, 414, 593, 798
  death: I 114; II 121, 203–04, 803; III
    219, 221, 368, 370–71, 831, 868
  dove: III 485
  earth: I 114; III 368
  gluttony: I 439
  humility: I 164
  lark: II 129–30, 375; III 230, 362–63
  moon: I 113; III 367
  obedience: I 164
  Ortulana: III 517
  pain: II 641, 714
  poverty: I 541; III 165
  simplicity: I 164; II 368
  swallow: I 235, 491; II 412, 624, 801;
    III 861
  virtues: I 440
  water: I 114; III 368
  wisdom: II 367
Situation
  new: II 43
  Order: III 389
  personal: I 465
  similar: I 134; II 305, 355; III 751, 786
Skin: I 302, 511, 539; II 150, 293, 332–33,
    381, 421, 431, 460, 511, 804; III 70
  Francis: I 253, 276, 280; II 80, 138,
    388, 476, 514, 538, 555, 641, 646,
    692, 714, 743; III 91, 234, 267, 279,
    323, 478, 597, 729, 842, 866, 870, 877
Sky: I 250, 339, 476, 482, 484, 489, 491, 532;
    II 635, 711, 723, 802; III 131, 153, 526,
    569, 592, 635
Slander: I 72, 75, 98, 132, 140; II 221,
    363–64; III 249, 285, 785
Sleep: I 61, 154, 220, 435; II 91, 154, 158,
    176, 430, 635, 810, 815; III 119, 271, 297,
    696, 810
  Christ: I 256, 406; II 610, 783
  flesh: I 320
  Francis: I 186, 212, 227, 253, 392; II
    71, 98, 105, 135, 167, 185, 224,
    227–28, 752; III 153, 232, 244, 304,
    312, 336, 345, 436, 567, 729, 852, 865
  Lady Poverty: I 552
  sacrifice: I 219, 253, 542
  sick: I 299, 304, 306; II 407, 410, 423,
    425, 427, 635, 653, 661, 678, 680
  sloth: I 546
  vision: II 71, 98, 105, 752

Slice: I 552; II 450, 672
Slope: I 533; II 108; III 883
Sloth. See also Acedia: I 191, 440, 546, 550;
    III 57
Smile
  creature: II 354; III 860
  Francis: I 185, 228, 371, 393; II 251,
    296, 319, 355, 368, 409; III 794
  God: III 878
  other: II 342, 574, 757; III 536, 857,
    861
Snake
  figurative: II 462
  money: II 292, 580, 801; III 100
Snore: III 567
Snow
  figurative: I 294, 505; II 723; III 450,
    589–91
  Francis: I 386, 376, 453; II 325, 379,
    539, 563, 635, 694, 723, 732, 740–41,
    782, 792; 795; III 43, 97, 450,
    580–81, 834
  weather: I 194, 305, 320–21, 334, 376,
    386, 452–55; II 325, 379, 539, 563,
    635, 694, 723, 740–41, 782, 792, 795;
    III 580, 810
Sobriety: I 440; II 301
Softness: I 416; II 561; III 154
Soldier. See also Knight: I 550, 587–88; II
    351; III 343, 804
  Angelo: III 125, 333, 808
  brother: I 218
  Celano: II 702–03
  Christ: I 189, 214, 374, 410, 428, 585;
    II 406; III 482, 847
  demon: II 326, 575
  Francis: I 186, 231, 263, 272, 281, 355,
    514, 540, 685
  God: I 244
  John: III 63
  Sultan: I 231, 584
Solemnity: I 349, 419, 512; II 375, 391, 432,
    438, 477–78, 591, 610, 658, 667, 689; III
    36, 68, 151, 452, 871
  Nativity: III 515, 626, 655
Solitude: I 409; II 215, 248, 550, 558, 592,
    597, 634, 690, 711; III 117, 184, 197, 245,
    818
  Christ: II 159
  prophecy: III 182
  secret: I 261; II 539, 630; III 181
Son. See also Divinity, Godhead, Father,
  Spirit, Trinity
  Abraham: III 182, 425
  Babylon: II 246
  Belial: II 260, 298; III 324
  Bernard: II 253, 543; III 86, 440–41,
    446–47, 576–77
  biological: I 71, 103, 246, 270, 291; II
    46–47, 173, 188, 242, 343, 403, 439,
    752, 794; III 39, 134, 161, 178, 180,

182–83, 350, 487, 692, 747, 802, 808, 857

brother: I 123, 209, 220, 226, 248, 252, 265, 271, 274–77, 305, 321, 323–34, 336, 380–81, 385, 390, 393, 399, 415; II 133, 135–36, 138, 144, 151, 154, 162, 164, 190, 208, 259–60, 268, 284, 286, 292–93, 316, 325, 339, 347, 361–62, 365–66, 369, 374–76, 382–83, 386–88, 393, 395, 402, 418, 442–43, 467–68, 474–76, 489–90, 511, 518, 546, 551, 570, 573, 588, 646–47, 671, 677, 691, 715, 791, 801, 807, 814–15; III 41, 43, 58–59, 86, 117, 149, 151, 153, 164, 184, 188–92, 203, 267, 269, 288, 295–97, 320, 325, 330, 335–36, 384, 387, 394, 407, 409–10, 425, 465, 481, 485, 489, 492, 495, 499, 502, 506, 529, 539, 546, 572, 577, 596, 600–01, 604, 608–09, 614, 634, 638, 645–46, 680, 706, 712, 740, 769, 780, 803, 846, 856, 859, 869–70

Christ: I 91; II 58, 284, 292, 296, 375, 764, 772, 815; III 153, 180, 505, 528, 646

darkness: II 407, 452, 672, 677

Dominic: III 47, 147

Elias: I 174, 274, 276; II 474; III 275, 446, 577, 720, 741, 765–66

family with son in Order: II 58, 164, 173, 196, 273, 450; III 59, 241–42, 286, 302, 352

Francis: II 124, 325, 333, 563, 571, 795; III 47, 147, 224, 291

God: II 58, 260; III 86, 324, 530

handmaid: I 531; II 750

heal: I 239, 300, 302, 306, 402; II 421, 423, 427–28, 430, 434, 446, 448, 450, 452, 454–55, 457, 461–63, 465, 467, 481, 627, 656–58, 661–62, 664, 672, 674–75, 680, 804; III 51, 70, 72–73

hermitage: I 61–62; III 696

Israel: II 733, 757, 764; III 399, 410, 415

Jacob: III 422, 577, 868

Job: II 749

John: III 536, 641–42

king: I 591; II 50, 97, 548; III 46, 50, 391, 720

Lady Jacoba: II 122; III 473

Leo: I 123; III 130, 797

light: II 407, 452, 672, 677

Lucifer: II 351

men: II 685; III 695, 728

Noah: III 422

perdition: I 582, 585; III 610–11

Pietro and Pica Bernadone: I 190, 228, 374–75, 393, 443, 447, 449; II 68, 78–80, 570, 687, 809; III 440, 505–07, 571, 618, 620, 680, 842, 885

poor woman: I 591; II 50, 97, 548; III 46, 50, 391, 720

prayer for son: II 441, 443, 669

Rechab: I 589; III 712

Riccerio: I 226, 390; II 277, 617; III 502–03, 864

Rinieri: III 615–6

Rufino: II 403; III 505–06

Seth: II 422

Shealthiel: II 731

Song: I 149, 428–29, 506; II 297, 673
    angel: III 812
    birds: II 415, 799, 813
    cricket: II 414, 593
    Francis: II 68, 142, 169, 454, 593; III 454
    French: II 142; III 340
    joy: I 279–80, 294–95, 506, 516; II 357, 414, 593, 673
    lark: II 415, 799, 813
    lute: II 169, 567
    new: I 147, 149, 156, 295
    psalms: I 149, 153, 156, 323
    Solomon: II 744, 746, 757; III 854
    Te Deum: III 812

Sore: I 195, 299, 320, 377, 476; II 166, 459, 539–40, 688, 706, 750; III 97

Sorrow: I 72, 79, 87, 91, 146, 154, 281, 305, 405, 439, 476, 486, 531, 541; II 272, 329, 371, 423, 439, 443, 453, 489, 615, 656, 658, 668, 680, 741, 818; III 43, 51, 103, 161, 320, 389, 524, 870, 883
    book: III 130
    brother: III 287, 334, 370, 413
    compassion: II 632, 638, 709
    Francis: I 190, 223, 228, 245, 248–49, 264, 320; II 77–78, 82, 121, 129, 142, 250, 324, 329, 331, 340, 386, 489, 511, 631, 638, 697, 709, 734, 749; III 130–31, 221, 267, 327, 343, 357, 370, 413, 417, 668, 717, 848, 866
    joy: I 264; II 402, 440, 632, 709
    Rufino: III 504, 618
    tears: I 245; II 817; III 668

Soul: I 159, 431, 433, 437–38, 466, 477, 496; II 137, 517–18, 614, 626, 723–24, 729, 734–36, 740, 744–45, 748, 791, 816
    Augustine: I 389, 644
    body: I 51, 124, 159, 290, 353, 359, 413, 430, 449, 465, 518; II 121, 124, 127, 149, 153, 158, 164, 180, 201, 204, 215–16, 228–29, 305, 334, 410, 562–63, 599, 632, 660, 694, 750, 818
    care: II 305, 315, 366, 445
    Christ: II 510
    cleric: I 341
    commend: II 430, 448, 671
    enemy: I 66–69, 102, 105, 430, 439, 447; II 46, 93, 146, 156, 293, 359, 423, 510; II 551, 691
    faithful: I 42, 49, 291

Francis: I 277–78, 290, 323, 339, 359, 389, 413, 415–16, 428, 430, 433, 437, 450, 460, 464, 476, 486–88, 501, 503, 508, 510, 514–15, 518; II 107, 167, 202, 227, 249, 267, 301–02, 310, 332, 388–89, 401, 473, 475, 491, 534, 565, 597, 620, 641, 644, 660, 686, 695, 699, 709, 716, 738, 783–84, 792, 803
good: I 68, 122, 130, 142, 462, 468, 563; II 48, 50, 95, 121, 123, 127, 133–34, 140–41, 144, 156, 158, 160, 164–65, 169, 201–02, 207–08, 213, 217, 220, 275, 281, 298, 341, 350, 360, 362, 365, 410, 416, 491, 523, 563, 565, 572, 599, 603, 719
hermit: II 215
inner: I 41, 159, 205, 221, 254, 339, 380, 439, 448, 460, 518; II 308
joy: I 220, 224, 251, 372, 477; II 76, 121, 172, 281, 671, 737, 742, 748, 755, 759
Lord: II 79, 160, 226
loss: I 43, 50–51, 130, 221; II 222
love: I 247, 530, 542; II 108, 140, 153, 227, 250, 358, 399, 401, 534, 545, 589, 686, 754, 792
movement: I 187–88, 209, 224–25, 264, 495, 571; II 75, 272
necessity: I 123
personal: I 122–23, 143, 151, 154–55, 167, 571; II 35
redemption: I 47, 66, 147, 151, 155, 167, 202, 214, 224, 263, 266, 273–74, 277, 283, 473, 547–48, 563, 579–80, 582, 606–07; II 54, 93, 133, 145, 156, 160, 163, 172, 179, 208, 214, 217, 222, 358, 365, 372, 313, 341, 561, 586, 599, 603, 608, 690, 772
refreshment: I 283, 308, 347
salvation: I 47, 66, 147, 151, 155, 167, 202, 214, 224, 263, 266, 273–74, 277, 283, 473, 547–48, 563, 579–80, 582, 606–07; II 54, 93, 133, 145, 156, 160, 163, 172, 179, 208, 214, 217, 222, 358, 365, 372, 313, 341, 561, 586, 599, 603, 608, 690, 772
simplicity: II 447
sin: I 47, 132
suffering: I 187, 191, 205, 244, 353, 380, 571; II 35, 153, 165, 167, 181, 183, 202, 228, 267, 293, 299, 311, 523, 632, 638, 709, 741, 745
Sultan: I 603
temptation: I 408; II 165, 167, 183, 228–29, 714
watchfulness: I 67, 463, 448
weakness: II 409
whole: I 41, 159, 205, 221, 254, 339, 380, 439, 448, 460, 518; II 308
zeal: I 412, 473, 563, 579–80, 582, 606–07; II 144, 221, 347, 690, 687, 761

Sound: I 502; II 242, 410, 421, 657; III 157, 164, 388, 474, 487, 519, 596, 632, 774
arrow: I 797
bell: I 419
brass: III 487, 724
Clare: III 701
description: I 283, 300, 303, 320, 358, 360, 430, 481, 572, 607; II 91, 423, 482, 617, 656, 716, 804; III 619
Francis: I 194, 206, 256; II 536, 609; III 456, 595
heaven: I 538
horse: II 417
Jesus: I 256; II 609
Leo: III 456
lute: I 169
marching: I 464
Masseo: III 515
name of Jesus: I 256; II 609
Pacifico: III 691
praise: I 194, 219, 284; II 476
prayer: III 515, 595
Rule: III 406
Simon: III 691
trumpet: I 417; III 184, 871
voice: I 194; II 536; III 128, 595
Sour: I 206, 464–65
Sow: II 321, 590, 807; III 838, 851
Sowing: I 234, 236, 239, 396, 559, 589; II 134, 412, 601, 718, 792, 819; III 98
Spanish: II 466, 678; III 388
Speech: I 51, 72, 359, 439, 519, 546; II 289, 389, 401, 644, 650, 740, 812; III 175, 574
abbot of Mt. Subasio: III 120, 298
Assisi: II 313, 608
Augustine: II 389, 644, 716, 803; III 869
bishop of Assisi: II 313, 608
Francis: I 188, 220, 252, 359, 449, 505; II 69, 154, 261, 373, 546, 564, 622, 715, 791, 812–13; III 41, 119, 297, 865
gift: III 488, 526, 725
Gregory IX: I 295
humility: III 818
Innocent III: I 212
loss: I 306–07; II 416, 450–51, 453–55, 658, 673–74, 678, 813; III 45, 70, 72–73, 103, 345, 449, 580, 869
Mount Subasio: III 120, 298
Rule: III 834
Spirit. See also Divinity, Godhead, Father, Son, Trinity: I 75, 95, 99, 138, 144, 184–87, 193, 197–99, 205, 227, 249, 266, 276, 281, 296, 341, 346, 372, 375, 381, 390, 410, 412–13, 466, 487, 499, 517, 531, 546, 549–50, 554, 582, 584; II 42, 47, 54, 76, 79, 81, 97, 103, 121, 127–28, 137, 142, 144, 146, 153, 165–66, 172–73, 175, 181, 185–86, 189–92, 195, 206–07, 219, 227, 242, 248–50, 259, 273, 280, 284, 286, 293,

307–08, 313, 324–25, 329, 334, 337, 343, 352, 358–60, 363–64, 372, 405–06, 418, 420–21, 429, 432, 440, 475, 478, 523, 536, 548, 557, 561, 566–67, 570, 573, 588, 600, 618–19, 630, 640, 654–56, 662, 668, 673, 682, 700–01, 703–04, 714, 721, 724, 734–35, 737, 753–54, 762; III 33, 48, 87, 92, 173, 182, 184, 200, 248, 346–47, 398, 407, 421–22, 489, 600, 623, 635, 627, 848, 851, 889
  angelic: II 515, 522
  anger: II 367; III 573
  anointing: II 106, 329, 373, 532, 613, 685
  authority: III 203
  Bernard: III 439, 616
  binding: III 496–97
  bitterness: III 228
  body: I 131, 134, 165, 197, 390, 412, 466, 477; II 121, 127, 153, 165, 169, 175, 220, 267, 309, 332, 490, 522, 532, 562, 599, 640, 660, 662, 673, 714; III 192, 221, 227, 249, 268, 278, 356, 391, 421, 426, 552, 626, 653, 745, 838, 853, 868
  brave: II 640
  broken: II 519
  brother: II 42, 255, 700
  burning: II 561, 640
  charity: I 67, 93, 217, 247–48; III 38
  Christ: II 689; III 386, 391–92, 396–97, 403, 408, 418, 421–22
  Clare: III 515
  cleanliness: I 134
  compassion: III 800
  compunction: II 701
  consecrated: II 406
  consolation: I 380; II 169, 259, 544, 557; III 356, 364, 369, 371
  conviction: III 403
  crushing: III 59
  deceit: II 607
  demonstration: II 698
  desolation: II 267
  devil: III 199, 351
  devotion: I 102, 107, 219, 226
  devout: I 266; II 566, 674, 695
  dew: I 321
  distinguished: I 231
  disturbance: II 328
  divine: III 460, 695
  ecstasy: I 271; II 179
  enlightenment: II 763; III 460, 437
  envy: I 438
  equipment: I 437
  eternal: III 885
  evil: I 80, 241–43, 302, 323, 495, 599; II 223, 280, 628, 694; III 492–93, 547, 608, 858
  extinguish: III 45, 267
  extraordinary: II 75
  faith: II 712

Father: II 42; III 159, 384, 390, 800
fervor: I 202, 266, 542; II 83, 87, 119, 121, 180, 216, 560, 563, 603, 609, 624, 642, 694, 698, 714–15; III 135, 150, 159, 176, 220–21, 246, 256, 258, 271, 358, 369, 371, 396–97, 400, 418, 465, 469, 507, 540–42, 552, 583, 589, 596, 606, 623, 629, 656, 704, 707, 819
fire: I 245; II 178, 252
flame: I 460
flesh: I 67, 75, 90, 99, 128, 176, 266, 281, 412, 466, 542; II 165, 173, 245, 250, 273, 280, 325, 328, 358, 383–84, 499, 567, 600, 618, 640, 655, 688, 697, 701, 724; III 97, 182, 202, 352, 388, 394, 410, 730–31, 745, 839, 842, 868
Francis: I 263–64, 243, 277, 288, 323, 359, 377, 514, 517, 601; II 242, 252, 272, 308, 310, 316, 330, 332–33, 359, 371, 373, 383, 392, 402, 473, 490, 533, 599, 601, 605, 608–09, 615–16, 620, 630, 645, 656, 660, 697, 699–700, 703, 709, 714, 738; III 44, 56, 98, 149, 167, 181, 199–200, 202, 218, 220, 256, 258, 284, 288, 325, 348, 353, 364, 366, 369, 460, 458, 481, 616, 703, 707, 853, 863, 865
fulfillment: III 36
garment: II 734
general minister: II 371
gentleness: I 272; II 518
gift: I 475, 567; II 729; III 393, 524, 642
Giles: III 518, 564, 646
God: I 80, 88, 201, 209, 250, 262–63, 270, 351, 608; II 35–36, 53, 70, 89, 103, 129, 266, 273, 280–81, 301, 316, 328, 348, 369–70, 379, 445, 510, 528, 548, 557, 606, 618–19, 622, 686, 728–29, 734, 747–48, 759, 762; III 49, 202, 229, 393, 402, 404, 410, 469, 492, 550, 798, 852
good: II 38
Gospel: III 203
grace: I 117, 385, 548; II 89, 393, 520, 618, 626, 642, 702
greed: III 410
heavenly: I 258, 275, 282–83, 415; II 724
hierarchical: II 762
holiness: II 570
Holy: I 41, 45, 49, 51, 63, 73–74, 76, 78, 80, 82–83, 86, 88–91, 95, 116, 119, 127–28, 132, 141, 150, 160–61, 163, 182, 188, 205, 217, 224–25, 257, 284, 295, 321, 379, 385, 460, 464, 468, 475, 520, 537, 540, 553–54, 566, 595; II 35, 37, 51, 84, 87, 99, 105–06, 118–19, 126–27, 153, 165, 173, 185, 199–201, 203, 206–07, 217, 241, 248,

252, 256, 272–73, 278, 282, 301, 319, 349, 371, 378, 393, 477, 520, 532, 543–45, 548, 555, 558, 606, 613, 616, 618, 620, 626, 629, 685–86, 689, 717, 721–22, 729, 734, 737, 762, 764–65; III 93, 116–17, 119, 132, 135, 148–49, 163, 167–68, 173–74, 191, 196–98, 203, 216–18, 220, 226–27, 247, 257, 271, 274–75, 330, 347, 352, 354–55, 357–58, 369–70, 372, 381, 383, 398, 407–10, 435–37, 450, 453, 462–65, 468, 473, 476, 490, 492–93, 500, 516–17, 519, 525–26, 529, 539–40, 542, 550, 555–56, 566, 568, 581, 588–89, 596, 605, 615, 618, 631, 634–36, 646, 655–56, 704–05, 710, 712, 714, 721, 723, 740, 769, 828, 843, 863
hostility: I 231
human: III 181, 464, 718
humble: II 754–55; III 159
humility: I 262; II 570
imperturbable: II 714
impulse: I 231; II 686
inebriation: II 252, 598, 687; III 130, 656
inspiration: II 547, 555, 692, 793
instruction: I 461, 570; II 256, 536, 620, 629, 686
intensity: II 198, 206, 209
interior: I 75, 99
intoxication: I 230, 395; II 601
John: III 537, 642, 646
joy: I 390; II 45, 87, 103; II 229, 329–32, 361, 535, 545, 567, 626
joyful: I 40, 277; III 437, 445, 491, 507, 540–42, 552, 583, 653, 691
justice: I 226; III 96
kinship: I 542
lack: II 211; III 171, 414, 711
law: I 331; II 688
learning: II 99
letter: I 132
liberty: II 583
life: I 44–45, 67, 81, 88, 115, 125, 128–29; II 37, 352, 407, 428, 642; III 168, 202, 385, 390, 423, 476, 557, 647–48, 705
life–giving: I 128, 132
light: I 464
Lord: I 41–42, 47–49, 75, 90, 99, 105, 128–29, 133, 459, 533; II 51, 552, 625–26, 691, 704, 706, 762; III 174
malicious: II 607
melody: I 224, 296; II 331; III 340
ministry: I 41, 46, 67, 80, 88, 103, 125, 128, 131–32
new: I 260; II 47, 75
noble: I 254, 267
obedience: I 165, 404
obstinacy: II 575
Order: III 753, 777

outpouring: III 147
Paraclete: I 83, 119, 127, 163, 339
peace: I 76, 90, 134, 542
perfection: II 715, 763–64
perversity: II 426
piety: III 40, 364
pledge: I 553
poverty: I 133–34, 529, 535, 597, 582–83, 722, 736; II 534, 548; III 156, 159–60
power: I 215, 242, 335, 379, 408; II 37, 50, 84, 99, 543, 548, 553, 689, 691, 764; III 176, 408, 411, 545, 649, 821
prayer: I 102, 107; II 393
pride: II 522
prompting: I 261, 270, 282, 378, 536, 558
prophecy: I 205, 207, 328, 339, 380, 389, 413, 477, 542; II 83–84, 216, 241, 263–64, 526, 529, 614, 616, 620, 623, 629, 700–03, 717; III 79, 89, 93, 176, 182, 246, 349, 437, 443, 546, 568, 642, 892
prophet: II 543, 526, 617, 692, 700; III 96, 381, 81
prudence: II 335
pure: I 209; III 753, 777
purity: I 225
quiet: III 227
rapture: I 284
rebellion: II 575; II 245
religious: II 248; III 78
revelation: I 224; II 173, 623, 702; III 537, 863
riches: II 220
Rule: III 409, 418, 753, 777
saint: I 262
salvation: I 203
Satan: III 647
seraphic: II 632, 709
sight: I 128
silence: I 221
simplicity: I 222, 225
sober: I 253; III 865
sorrow: I 72, 91
strength: II 753
strong: I 321, 563, 566
submission: III 97
suggestion: II 301
supple: I 218
sweetness: III 506, 535, 588, 634, 653
temple: I 458
temptation: II 320; III 43, 346, 801
tepidity: III 267
threefold: II 764
truth: I 47, 207; II 542, 689; III 151, 176, 178, 394
unction: I 330
understanding: II 763
unity: I 223, 542; II 379, 389; III 41
unseemliness: I 80, 88, 242, 495; III 835

uplifting: II 762
vigor: I 214; III 741
visit: II 248, 310
weakness: II 321, 326, 563
willing: I 266; II 328, 384
wisdom: I 390; II 763; III 461, 585
word: I 44–45, 81, 88
world: I 182
working: II 118, 349; III 315, 421, 559
Spirituals: I 19, 524–25; II 13, 23, 116; III 15,
    20, 142, 145, 207, 318, 376–78, 380, 545,
    738, 767–68, 783–84, 813, 830, 878
Spit: I 536, 548; II 269, 369, 455, 619; III 632
Spleen: II 180, 183, 228, 311, 332, 609; III
    232, 283, 307, 339
Splendor
    Adam: I 537
    chariot: III 89
    Christ: III 643
    Clare: III 91
    clothing: I 586
    cross: I 281; II 545
    deeds: II 392, 526, 811
    fiery chariot: III 89
    Francis: I 499; III 175, 588, 665,
        869–70, 882–83
    heavenly: I 113, 344, 518; II 573, 606,
        721, 723, 744–45
    heavenly light: II 314, 612, 700, 707,
        728; III 86, 883
    holiness: II 338, 569
    John: III 643, 648, 649, 653
    knightly: II 70
    light: II 314, 612, 700, 707, 728; III 86,
        883
    miracle: I 603
    Peter and Paul: III 588
    place: III 648, 653
    poor: III 827
    Portiuncula: III 86
    poverty: I 534
    Rule: III 390
    seraph: III 451
    Sun: III 119
    understanding: I 570
    Virgin Mary: III 645
Spouse
    Christ: I 198, 536, 552; II 462, 482,
        675, 698–99, 772; III 88, 173, 188,
        193, 466, 478, 515, 517, 590, 598,
        626, 650
    figurative: I 456
    human: II 673
    Lady Poverty: III 162, 165
    Leah: III 87
    Spirit: I 42, 49, 141
Spring
    fountain: III 153, 463, 587, 876
    origin: I 283; II 410, 678, 793
    season: I 460; II 649
Square. See also Piazza: I 247; II 808; III 177,
    483, 500

Stain: II 36
    blood: I 264, 410; II 335, 388, 403, 473,
        476, 637, 697; III 560
    division: III 116
    sin: I 47, 226, 488; II 563, 586, 590,
        723; III 93, 175
Standard–bearer
    Francis: II 454, 460, 479–80, 651, 654,
        675, 681–82, 712; III 78, 185, 187,
        470, 670, 877
Star
    Bernard: II 280
    Francis: I 215, 255, 278, 288, 295, 323,
        332, 342, 344, 353, 385, 416, 568,
        603–04; II 107, 388, 475, 526, 554,
        644, 711, 716, 729, 784, 803; III 35,
        92, 678
    Gregory IX: I 499, 518
    Hugolino: I 499, 518
    Lucifer: I 488
Statue
    Nebuchadnezzar: III 486, 723
Stature
    Bernard: II 85
    Francis: I 519; II 105, 256
    poverty: I 534; II 301, 307
Steadfast: I 243–46; II 732
Stench
    fragrance: III 532, 651
    river: III 498, 612
    vice: I 585; III 389–90
    wound: II 466
Steward: I 93, 183, 456
Stigmata: I 308; II 630, 641, 650, 709, 715,
    727; III 346, 452, 457, 665, 866, 874, 876
    Christ: I 339, 416; II 58, 383, 402, 516,
        719; III 840
    Divine approval: II 513, 637, 722
    doubt: II 108, 404–05, 652, 654–55
    Francis: I 264, 280–81, 416; II 58, 108,
        401, 490, 514–15, 559, 634, 650,
        710–11, 719–20, 739, 742–43, 746, 780
    glory: III 499, 535, 653, 666, 668, 670
    Gregory IX: I 604
    hiding: I 265, 411; II 334–35, 633, 636,
        710–11; III 669
    like Christ: I 288; II 650, 713, 743; III
        728, 868
    mystery: I 408, 411; II 108, 401–02,
        490, 514, 634–35, 713; III 499, 535,
        653, 666, 668, 670, 867, 876
    portrait: II 404–05, 652, 654–55
    power: II 196, 287, 347, 408, 634–35,
        653–54, 712; III 131
    prediction: III 681
    symbol: I 281–82, 286; II 383, 727
    virginity: III 48, 99
    witness: II 514, 636, 719, 770; III 35,
        513, 670, 687, 870
Stimulus
    parent: II 669
    poverty: II 578

Stomach
    Francis: I 274, 514; II 161, 180, 183,
        228, 311, 332, 474, 609; III 232, 283,
        307, 334, 339
    gluttony: I 439, 587
    sickness: I 513; II 431
    vision: III 117, 393
Stone: I 397, 442, 454, 500, 504; II 69,
    428–30, 453, 570, 598, 642, 658, 660–62;
    III 463, 558, 733
    Bernard: III 33
    church repair: II 38–39, 81, 86–87, 319,
        540, 688
    Clare: I 197; II 378; III 845
    coins: I 70
    fire: I 288
    flint: III 558
    foundation: I 197, 325, 419, 529; II
        478, 642; III 836
    heart: I 281; III 505, 520, 618
    house: II 135, 157, 159, 285; III 172,
        259–60, 265
    living: II 378, 400
    pillow: I 277, 392, 552, 598; II 561,
        694; III 852
    precious: I 265, 494; II 168, 185, 328,
        478, 573, 723; III 96, 304
    Sultan: II 757
    tablet: II 634, 711
    throw stones: I 191, 320, 374; II 46, 78,
        93, 175, 292, 537, 751, 757
    tomb: I 518
    wine press: II 424
Storm
    devil: III 506, 619
    figurative: II 274, 280, 331, 534; III
        152, 506, 619, 648, 669
    weather: I 230, 394, 454, 483–84, 503;
        II 411, 415, 433–35, 601, 663–65,
        706–07, 783; III 856
Story: I 227, 231, 239, 300; II 141, 200, 436,
    480, 528, 666; III 61, 261, 334, 798–800
    Francis: I 231, 239, 258, 261, 287, 591;
        II 97, 158, 457; III 78, 721, 804
Stranger
    brother: I 103, 126, 597; II 47, 54, 94,
        102, 123, 160, 212, 294, 578; III 39
    Christ: I 70, 92, 145, 584
    Francis: I 165, 226, 269, 411, 530; II
        97, 146, 255, 258, 289, 366, 583, 760;
        III 288, 852, 864
    other: II 733
Straw: I 227, 344, 474; II 136, 157, 176, 288,
    290; III 153, 259–60, 271, 476, 525, 596
Street
    Assisi: I 191, 299; II 78–79, 751; III 800
    Babylon: I 184, 442, 444
    other: I 242, 530, 588; II 43, 221, 246,
        256, 463, 537, 687, 728; III 201
Strength: I 355, 434, 457, 536, 546, 553, 560;
    II 56, 266, 281, 393, 421, 433, 555, 562,

578, 628, 663, 692, 741, 753; III 43,
521–23, 548, 583, 622
    Divine: I 195, 224, 566; II 219, 248,
        347, 393, 555, 712; III 189, 248, 327,
        386, 395, 421, 479, 554, 598, 651,
        717, 846
    Francis: I 228, 263, 266, 275, 290, 371,
        392, 401, 414; II 71, 78, 81, 105, 143,
        219, 260, 323, 382, 384, 416, 436,
        474, 532, 566, 570, 603–04, 638, 685,
        698, 799; III 82, 85, 97, 152, 295,
        371–72; 383, 391, 408, 437, 492, 607,
        830
    God: I 49, 109–10, 352
    human: I 263; II 254; III 487–88,
        724–25
    John of Florence: II 363
    John of Lauds: III 125, 333
    limit: II 259–60, 325, 383–84; III 417,
        437
    Lucifer: III 411–12
    obedience: III 293
    observance of *Rule:* III 418
    physical: I 228, 272, 275, 371, 401; II
        81, 461, 474, 570, 685; III 371
    poverty: III 164
    privilege: III 154
    psalms: I 80, 146, 149, 151, 154–55,
        161; II 524
    Rule: III 418
Stretcher: I 300, 324; II 129, 455, 460, 702;
    III 70, 229
String: I 513; II 331, 373, 596
Struggle: I 493, 548; II 275, 406–07, 652,
    659; III 879
    devil: I 244, 263, 272, 408; II 248, 324,
        326, 343, 607, 640, 699, 714
    Francis: I 188, 193, 244, 263, 272, 408,
        414, 432, 515, 567; II 248, 252, 324,
        326, 384, 607, 622, 640, 697, 699,
        714; III 504, 868
    Jacob: II 753–54
    stigmata: II 652
Student
    Ancona: III 500, 615
    Bologna: III 614
    Christ: I 213
    Order: III 826
    Paris: II 719, 728
Stupidity
    brother: II 41, 89
    Francis: I 119, 166, 189, 194, 376; II
        106, 436, 539, 666, 739
    other: I 469, 530, 588
Style: II 68, 263, 370, 528, 809; III 78, 157,
    679
Subject
    brother: I 68, 74–75, 89–90, 93, 95,
        105, 125, 130, 207, 217, 222; II 94,
        125, 133, 162, 341, 345; III 38, 47,
        116, 171, 240, 297, 317, 336, 385,
        414, 419, 447, 711, 857, 859–60

Francis: I 45, 266, 489, 510; II 52, 101, 125, 143, 332, 340, 344, 695, 712, 739, 799; III 154–55, 191, 216, 225, 274, 287, 292, 733, 838, 849
  other: I 48, 119, 165, 182, 260, 291; II 200, 211, 246, 263, 518, 571–72, 724–25, 795; III 157, 186
  Rule: III 419
Sublimity: I 60, 587, 589; II 689
  cross: I 281
  Francis's sanctity: II 514, 521, 644, 647
  God: I 86, 119
  humility: I 118; III 397
  poverty: I 103, 329, 696; III 397
  Seraph: II 638, 713
Submission: I 106, 165, 236, 266, 270; II 261–62, 341; III 424, 853
Substance
  Divine: I 288, 487; III 380, 384, 397
  human: II 780; III 394, 424, 562–63, 593
Subtlety: I 253; II 228, 289, 320, 324, 370; III 63, 415, 567
Success: I 186, 189, 346, 371, 438, 465; II 87, 362, 441, 536, 772; III 74
Successor
  glory: I 438
  minister: I 104, 571, 574; II 393, 778; III 760
  Pope: I 292, 418; II 547, 558; III 93, 823
Suffering: I 260; II 177, 179, 222, 339, 370, 451, 523, 678; III 60, 115, 354, 476, 522, 722
  animal: I 256; II 711
  brother: I 585, 590; II 45, 92, 222, 225, 741; III 237, 312, 449–50, 524, 534, 580, 692, 864
  childbirth: I 256, 404; II 444, 668
  Christ: I 262, 264, 267, 288, 412, 540; II 142, 180, 311, 709, 729; III 188, 339–40, 382, 392, 598, 639, 740
  cross: I 131, 288
  Francis: I 187, 192, 236, 262, 276, 339, 374, 409, 414, 456, 601; II 75–76, 101–02, 146, 180, 184, 194, 197, 225, 297, 303, 311, 332, 367, 384, 410, 416, 474, 490, 512, 567, 609, 641–42, 694, 697, 704, 714–15, 761, 799, 806, 814, 816; III 188, 231, 288, 312, 339, 382, 398, 449, 476, 478, 598, 639–40, 668, 793
  Gregory IX: I 293
  illness: I 236, 275, 290, 299, 303, 305, 324, 403, 445, 494, 508, 513; II 146, 184, 192, 194, 197, 297, 311, 367, 432, 445, 447, 458, 555, 567, 609, 628, 681, 692; III 73, 91, 282, 608
  injury: I 236, 275, 290, 299, 303, 305, 324, 403, 445, 494, 508, 513; II 146, 184, 192, 194, 197, 297, 311, 367,

432, 445, 447, 458, 555, 567, 609, 628, 681, 692; III 73, 91, 282, 608
  joy: III 580
  Lady Poverty: I 548
  martyrdom: I 275, 339, 414
  other: I 159; II 101–02, 166, 303
  purgatory: III 522
  Saint Lawrence: III 534
  seraph: III 866
  shipwreck: I 483
  slight: III 479, 596
  women: I 239, 256, 404; II 192, 440, 444, 454, 668–69, 675
Sugar: II 122; III 222, 360
Suggestion
  Christ: II 686
  devil: I 129; II 153
  Francis: I 434
  other: I 383; II 431, 453, 616, 626, 664, 676; III 496, 611, 830
Sun: I 149, 295, 429, 452, 455, 463, 519, 503, 568; II 351, 419, 464, 482, 720, 745; III 149, 367, 494, 481, 551, 600, 628, 747, 800, 884, 887
  angel: II 527, 638, 714, 721, 735, 764
  Brother Sun: I 113; II 120–21, 184, 186–87; III 221, 349, 367, 371
  chalice: III 557, 647
  chariot: I 224, 321, 330, 389, 476; II 552; III 90, 815, 845
  Christ: III 815
  Francis: I 113, 250, 278, 322, 400; II 185, 388, 475, 691, 714, 784, 798, 803, 814; III 33, 35, 92, 152, 883
  John: III 558
  justice: III 367, 679
  Soldanerio: III 36
  stigmata: III 458
  wisdom: II 728, 814–15
Superior: I 575, 582–84, 587, 602; II 523, 695, 741, 777, 779, 817; III 389, 786, 828, 848
Superiority: II 752; III 828
Superstitious: I 594
Supper: I 343, 455; II 387, 803; III 567, 831
Supplication: I 459; II 57; III 55
Support: I 306, 450, 494, 541; II 213, 348, 372, 383, 673; III 45, 192, 813
  bishop: I 210; II 104
  bodily: I 102; II 298; III 747
  brother: I 48; III 758
  cane: I 185, 298, 371; II 479
  knowledge: III 173
  payment: I 102
  Pope: II 775
  practice: III 740
  world: III 46
Suppression: II 441; II 570
Surgeon: II 354–55, 408, 566, 798; III 861
Surname: II 154; III 120, 236, 331, 690

Swallow: I 235, 322, 397, 491; II 412,
   624–25, 783, 798, 801; III 104, 469, 504,
   550, 591, 593, 617, 684, 835, 860–61
Swamp: I 287, 513, 534; II 568
Sweat: I 46; II 83, 251, 297, 351, 792
Sweetness: I 216, 234, 358, 435; II 74, 149,
   313, 344, 356–57, 370, 372, 553, 631–32;
   III 447, 481, 506, 508, 531, 535, 543, 549,
   600, 610, 614, 616, 645–46, 649, 652, 653,
   656
   cross: II 682
   Divine: I 109, 111, 186, 205, 262, 431,
      568; II 246, 309, 312, 530, 536, 568,
      606, 609, 684, 757; III 87, 93, 103,
      339, 360, 388, 398, 426, 465, 528,
      534, 538–40, 619, 634, 637, 686, 841
   eternal: II 746
   Francis: I 124, 235, 325, 380, 399; II
      180–81, 186, 264, 310, 312, 589, 591,
      709, 756; III 193, 348, 549, 588, 616,
      688, 877
   love: III 193
   soul: I 124; III 103, 193, 549, 616
   voice: I 120, 256, 295
Swelling: I 274, 290, 437, 518; II 198, 352,
   460; III 55, 70, 272
Sword: I 246, 355, 470, 519, 539, 552, 585,
   606, 608; II 103, 118, 178, 346, 407–08,
   425, 451–52, 677; III 294
   bad example: II 348
   cross: I 411; II 632, 697, 709
   devil: I 355; II 317
   Francis: I 435; II 316, 556, 638, 693,
      697, 761, 798; III 482
   God: III 92, 404
   martyrdom: II 147, 604; III 323
   miraculous: II 407–08, 435, 797
   obedience: I 118, 346
   tongue: II 588; III 90
   violence: II 178, 270–71, 451–52; III
      422, 460, 585
   word of God: III 92, 404
Symbol: II 377, 556, 563, 681, 693, 727, 805;
   III 723, 845
Synagogue: I 423, 455; II 620; III 148

T

Table: I 534, 551; II 73, 77, 97, 149, 167, 171,
   175–76, 185, 200–01, 259, 276, 279, 287,
   295–96, 298, 361, 375, 389, 416–17, 420,
   427, 548, 582, 615, 757, 793–94, 802; III
   46, 49–51, 88, 94, 215–16, 243, 250, 259,
   270–75, 278, 303, 347, 359, 391, 463,
   466–67, 503, 516, 524, 539, 551, 560, 587,
   590–91, 597, 617, 624, 628, 634, 720, 777,
   792, 796, 801, 803, 847
   angels: I 529; III 160
   life: III 158
   Lord: I 125; II 247, 276; III 385, 388, 446
   Pope: II 255

Round: II 208, 208b; III 169, 320,
   320a, 705
Tablecloth: II 221; III 310, 463, 477, 587
Tablet: II 634, 712; III 792
Talent: I 43, 51, 348, 448–49, 600; II 633; III
   63, 103
Taste: I 46, 227, 262, 372, 398, 466, 493, 517,
   529; II 248, 273, 353, 410, 564, 567–68,
   598, 609, 704, 707, 757; III 91, 153, 162,
   244, 337, 388, 393, 503, 530, 549, 617,
   645–46, 852, 862, 876
Tau: II 317, 402, 458, 527, 556, 681, 693,
   735, 805; III 189, 805
Teacher
   apostle: I 540; II 763
   Bonaventure: III 149, 679
   Christ: I 141, 540; II 512, 522, 536,
      569, 572, 582, 613, 620, 623, 750; III
      160, 236, 298, 335, 357, 417, 464,
      607, 610, 719
   church: I 313
   Francis: I 155; II 509, 511–12, 516–17;
      III 67, 90, 502, 559, 890
   God: I 80–81, 88, 332
   human: I 338, 460–61, 606; II 141,
      314, 512, 522, 612, 763
   other: III 63, 150, 296, 698–99, 707,
      786, 836
   priest: I 321, 388
   spirit: I 460–61, 613
Teaching
   Anthony: III 519, 632, 694
   Bonaventure: III 78
   brother: II 148
   Christ: I 64, 81, 89, 196, 254, 259, 469,
      584; II 263, 343, 509–10, 516, 541,
      688, 745; III 87, 177, 196, 381–82,
      418, 421, 471, 680, 727, 731, 739–40,
      855
   church: I 568; III 849
   Francis: I 180, 205, 216, 259–60, 308,
      380, 386, 388, 406, 416, 487, 497; II
      42, 85, 146, 212, 332, 372, 381, 388,
      511–13, 526, 543, 551–52, 587, 613,
      625, 629, 689, 692–93, 717; III 33,
      49, 51, 53, 64, 133, 151–52, 160, 171,
      317, 323, 335, 400, 407, 414, 480,
      599, 611, 630, 636, 669, 727, 731,
      844–45
   Gospel: I 64, 81, 89, 196, 254, 259, 469,
      584; II 263, 343, 509–10, 516, 541,
      688, 745; III 87, 177, 196, 381–82, 418,
      421, 471, 680, 727, 731, 739–40, 855
   Holy Spirit: I 224, 553; II 620
   other 629;: III 289, 424, 522, 545, 559,
      586, 638, 640, 763, 770, 837
   pernicious: I 182, 593; II 255, 282
   saint: I 554; II 34, 369, 718; III 694, 837
   truth: I 259
Tears: I 40; II 284, 360, 364, 370, 695; III 57,
   62, 74, 151, 153, 178, 183, 221, 228–29,

231, 235, 325, 334, 350, 354, 371, 401, 450, 514, 524, 582, 635, 668, 697, 726, 876
compassion: II 250, 331, 515, 538, 577, 642, 686, 802; III 183, 306, 340, 452, 473, 489
cross: II 534, 536, 686; III 83, 94, 173, 874–75
grief: I 219, 245, 279, 286–87, 393, 402, 515, 538, 603; II 197, 226, 262, 274, 320, 369, 375, 464, 461, 476, 491, 657, 675, 817; III 577, 869–70
illness: II 695; III 97, 313, 861
joy: I 281, 292–93, 295–96, 342, 506, 568, 604; II 329–30, 403, 443, 477–78, 538, 651
prayer: I 191, 372, 374, 542; II 46–47, 54, 78, 93, 121, 165, 188, 250, 299, 309, 348, 405, 430, 432, 434, 446, 454, 463, 465, 467, 537, 577, 587, 607, 655, 664, 675, 679, 686, 699, 702, 744; III 40, 67, 73, 86, 102, 176, 222, 280, 346, 400, 437, 446, 464, 476, 501–02, 506, 513, 528, 530–31, 533, 538, 540, 549, 553, 555, 560–61, 576, 588, 596, 619, 630, 645, 650, 691, 719, 862
repentance: I 432; II 81, 174, 261, 267, 288, 320, 330, 334, 360, 375, 406, 448, 652, 672, 749, 817; III 43, 137, 319–20, 360–61, 451, 456, 493–94, 498, 500, 525, 608, 613, 615, 623, 651, 693, 801, 864
Temperance: I 110; III 176, 596
Temple
  body: III 728
  church: III 83, 331
  God: I 295, 406, 519, 604; II 599, 721, 731; III 191–94, 382, 421
  holy: I 151, 257, 329; II 309, 400
  inner: III 174, 189, 879
  spirit: I 73, 458
Temptation: I 193, 372, 374, 415, 540; II 118, 121, 127, 145, 166, 223, 280, 324–25 349; III 43–44, 221, 228, 233, 315, 342, 345–48, 446, 481, 497, 501–07, 539–40, 564, 577, 601, 611, 615–16, 712, 723, 801, 814, 863
  avarice: II 510, 722; III 60, 326
  Christ: I 131, 285
  devil: I 244, 608; II 79, 185, 223, 230, 264, 326–27, 793; III 227, 351, 354, 356, 370, 392, 546–48, 617–19, 633–35, 642, 722, 731, 739, 817, 842
  disturbance: I 214, 226, 390; II 145, 153, 227, 320, 329, 360, 365, 618, 701, 801–02; III 851
  flesh: I 165, 221, 386; II 732, 740, 562; 795; III 96, 853
  following Christ: I 131
  prayer: II 165–66, 324
  vainglory: III 797
Tendency: III 819

Tenderness. See also Compassion, Piety
  Francis: I 234–35, 250, 399, 406; II 72, 589, 697; III 173, 598
  God: I 287; II 72
Tepidity: II 138, 211, 795; III 98, 171, 267, 316, 390, 399, 414, 711
Territory: I 404, 546, 576; II 698; III 469, 490, 605, 855
Terror: I 408, 470; II 289, 322, 791; III 189, 324, 482, 498, 530, 613, 847–48, 791
Test
  probation: I 561; II 223, 337, 356, 512; III 351, 398, 583, 634, 798
  temptation: I 193; II 119, 127, 280, 349; III 136, 227, 315, 356, 723, 863
  tribulation: I 276; II 475
Testimony: II 136, 213, 288, 424, 434–35, 514, 527, 544, 558, 573, 636–38, 644, 659, 772; III 61–62, 150, 152, 198, 259, 303, 329, 693, 793, 804, 808
Thanksgiving. See also Gratitude: I 59, 81–86, 219–20, 413; II 100, 189, 466, 761; III 40, 338
Theft: I 79; II 130, 139, 304, 436, 464, 589, 665; III 123, 159, 280, 417
Theologian: I 125; II 207, 352; III 63, 168, 705, 738
Theology: I 107, 574; II 140–41, 315, 352, 358, 613, 778; III 31, 54, 58, 63, 78, 116, 296, 385, 409, 678, 714–15, 770, 813, 815, 828–30
Thief, See also Bandit, Brigand, Robber: I 69–70, 91, 228, 445, 466; II 124, 130, 139, 304, 312, 334, 571, 608; III 123, 158, 224, 265, 281, 291, 602, 820
Third Order. See also Penitent: III 64, 64b, 64d, 469, 591–594
Thirst: I 146, 227, 375, 505, 567, 582; II 45, 92, 278, 286, 409–10, 434, 525, 561, 578, 584, 664, 678, 694, 705, 793; III 101, 161, 308, 514, 524, 665, 818, 852–53, 855, 861
Thorn: I 184, 219, 566, 569, 576; III 40, 45, 81, 448, 497, 612, 739, 810
Throat: I 307, 505; II 407–08, 428, 453, 797; III 55, 73, 440, 511, 622
Throne: I 83, 129, 287–88, 296, 351, 534, 603; II 157, 168, 328, 345, 353, 455, 478, 481, 571, 573, 638, 674, 721, 725, 752–53, 764, 796; III 99, 122, 152, 201, 237, 243, 293, 300, 304–05, 420–21, 557, 647–48, 682, 692, 802, 808, 848, 878
Tile: II 157, 285; III 118, 260, 395
Title
  charity: I 598
  cross: II 700
  name: II 295, 338, 443, 582; III 471
  perfect: I 203
  Portiuncula: I 458
  poverty: I 198, 320, 594

Tonsure: II 51, 51c, 98, 98b, 549, 549a, 798,
    809; III 89, 466, 590
Tool: I 69; II 676–77
Torch: I 255, 292, 406, 417, 428, 458,
    505–06; III 90, 335
Torture: I 44, 231, 400, 403, 448, 486, 497; II
    439, 448, 458, 641, 668, 681, 714; III
    96–97, 383, 392, 493, 498, 509
Touch: III 32, 61, 82, 202, 247, 308, 417, 445,
    448, 452–53, 455, 460, 497, 501, 576, 584,
    669, 679, 741–42, 761, 789, 819, 874, 879
    angel: III 435, 498, 567, 612, 689
    animal: I 321, 489, 491; II 217, 357,
        414, 800
    coin: I 48; III 45, 266, 878
    cross: III 51, 87, 92, 161
    Francis: II 408, 461, 635, 653–54, 711;
        III 55, 102, 508, 513, 826, 835, 847
    Francis's clothes: I 235, 238, 240, 321,
        397, 402, 493; II 137, 800; III 82, 85,
        366, 469, 500, 593, 609, 621, 834,
        854, 860–62
    Francis's tomb: II 625, 646, 746, 808;
        III 70, 72–73, 835
    God: I 118; II 309–10, 608; III 34, 84,
        438, 551, 628–29, 651, 733
    head of God: I 118
    heaven: III 438, 569
    leper: I 74; III 303
    money: I 48; III 45, 266, 878
    place: III 48
    seraph: III 147
    spirit: III 437, 568, 615
    stigmata: I 411, 596; II 408, 635–36,
        653–54, 710; III 35, 509–10, 513,
        792, 804, 875
Tower: I 292; II 224, 326, 424–25, 437, 439,
    659, 667; III 231, 312–13
Town
    abandon: III 114, 215
    bishop: II 251
    boy: II 431
    building: II 286; III 133, 826
    burn: II 178, 270
    church: II 430
    citizen: I 403, 434; II 197, 808; III 230,
        363, 477, 482–83, 587, 593, 601–02,
        636, 833
    demon: II 795
    distance: I 436; II 540; III 463
    driven from: I 375
    fortified: II 172
    hall: II 808
    knight: II 198
    living in: II 167, 248, 428; III 405
    mission: III 269
    persecution: III 157
    preach: III 90
    street: II 246
    travel to: II 404, 552; I 416, 539, 606, 660,
        687; III 176, 441, 452, 469, 603, 795
    visit: II 43, 90, 103; III 272, 406, 453,
        488, 725
    woman: II 171–72, 430; III 359
Town–Crier. See also Cry: I 392
Trading: I 333, 442, 776; III 82
Transfer: II 345, 571, 776; III 60, 68, 537,
    644, 748
Transformation: III 87, 90, 187–88, 728
Transgression: I 117, 129, 187; II 75, 817; III
    151, 180, 197, 407, 423, 771
Translation
    Francis: I 419–20; II 424, 445, 658–59,
        673; III 67, 80
Travel: I 194, 221, 249, 266, 435, 564, 574,
    584, 595; II 41, 88, 94, 215, 434, 451, 664;
    III 55, 89, 223, 245, 283, 309, 441, 498,
    518, 520, 545, 572, 584, 685–87
    barefoot: I 594
    brother: I 574; II 41, 273, 619
    companion: I 249, 395, 400; II 174–75,
        194, 229, 571, 579, 799, 807; III 54,
        462, 512, 863
    Emperor Otto: I 221
    Francis: I 229–30, 234, 239, 249, 266,
        332, 395, 400, 434, 481, 499; II
        174–75, 194–95, 224, 271, 278, 292,
        307, 310–11, 358, 409, 413, 415, 559,
        571, 579, 606, 622, 757, 787, 793,
        799, 809–10; III 500, 523, 607, 826,
        854
    Francis's death: II 123; III 361
    hazardous: I 574; II 221, 778; III 98,
        310–11
    Otto: I 221
    pilgrim: I 286, 353, 578, 582
    poverty: II 554; III 751, 824
    preach: I 230, 289; II 104–05, 258, 599,
        622; III 284, 494
    simplicity: III 831
    supplies: I 446
    weariness: I 219, 481; II 180; III 40
    women: I 72
Treachery: II 562
Treasure
    alms: II 373, 596
    call: III 291
    canonization: I 293
    earth: III 347, 449, 479, 580, 598–99
    Francis: I 414, 420; II 474, 647, 673; III
        69, 471
    heaven: I 64, 188, 203, 266, 588; II 38,
        75, 86, 518; III 466, 524
    illness: II 185; III 347, 479, 598–99
    joy: II 40
    life: III 514, 623
    poverty: I 187–88, 333, 372; II 74, 88,
        284, 686, 696, 533, 577–78, 518; III
        159, 162, 463–64, 503, 587–88, 616,
        718–19, 781, 842, 874
    prayer: II 312, 608
    salvation: III 514

stigmata: I 285, 289; II 335, 418, 473, 636, 648; III 188
useless: I 446, 539, 588, 607; II 285, 384, 530, 684, 745
wisdom: II 681; III 589
Treasurer: I 68; II 776
Treatment: I 219, 267, 271, 274, 402, 478, 486, 503; II 158–59, 180, 184, 189, 307, 330, 386, 407, 426, 540, 627, 687; III 40, 79, 153, 238, 262, 339, 363
Tree: I 222, 429, 514, 519, 547; II 179, 283, 389, 410, 462, 466, 624, 678, 772; III 71, 449, 454–55, 469–70, 512–13, 530, 557, 593, 650, 693, 792
    allegory: I 183; II 746; III 158, 259, 557–59, 646–48, 678, 688, 708, 875
    branch: I 238, 284, 296, 322, 402, 417; II 129, 159, 210, 217, 647; III 229, 238, 261, 357, 454
    cricket: II 217, 357, 414, 593, 798
    cross: I 147
    cut down: II 192, 267, 354; III 354, 366
    dream: I 212–13, 383; II 98–99, 547
    knowledge: I 129
    life: II 499; III 398
    shade: II 460, 480
    vision: I 212–13, 383; II 98–99, 547
Tremor: I 432; II 421, 657
Trial: I 75, 79, 90, 152, 207, 263, 293, 322, 338, 476, 542; II 53, 56, 92, 127, 153, 165, 214, 216, 225, 227, 387, 489, 546, 550, 643, 741; III 115, 117, 129, 133, 152, 227, 231–32, 246, 261, 310, 313, 346, 355, 382, 388, 479, 488, 695, 712, 715, 723, 725, 731, 866, 869
Tribulation
    brother: III 129–30, 134–135, 156, 189, 390
    cross: I 463; III 450
    endure: I 95; II 45; III 391, 421, 530, 598, 650
    escape: I 80, 88
    fear: II 794
    fire: III 366, 488, 725
    flesh: II 329
    foretell: III 387, 706
    Francis: III 87, 651
    infirmity: I 147; II 187; III 349, 368
    patience: I 199; II 740–41
    perfection: II 385, 642
    persecution: I 79, 131; II 721
    rejoice: II 45, 92, 229–30, 688; III 39, 233, 342, 344
    saint: II 258; III 453
    sister: II 384, 641; III 868
    temptation: I 214–15; II 102, 325
    test: I 276; II 475, 643; III 392, 691
    time: II 149, 372, 378; III 129, 194, 314, 388–89, 409, 547, 643, 649, 706, 821, 869
Tribute: I 331; II 58, 600

Trinity. See also Divinity, Godhead, Father, Son, Spirit
    faith: II 601
    Francis: I 72, 78, 85, 91, 116, 121, 138
    mystery: III 689
    name: I 116; II 450, 627, 631; III 810
    order: III 655
    praise: I 72, 78, 91, 279, 296, 329, 519; II 86, 103, 544, 717
    question: III 533, 652
    sacrament: II 292
    witness: III 740
    word: III 79
    worship: I 72, 78, 91, 279, 296, 329, 519; II 86, 103, 544, 717
Triple: I 216, 460; II 541; III 469
Triumph: I 191, 357, 414, 416, 428, 436, 463, 465, 471, 485, 515, 568–69; II 266, 280, 384, 386, 600, 614, 681, 780–81, 811; III 191, 384, 601, 863, 876
Trouble: I 140, 142, 396, 433, 539; II 139, 305, 818; III 155, 186, 189, 231, 281, 346, 395, 417, 446, 522, 581, 614, 740, 788, 879
    anxiety: I 224, 226, 271, 390, 399; III 40
    conscience: II 93
    death of Francis: I 415, 432; II 226; III 533
    demon: I 241–42, 323; II 153, 280, 455, 574, 627; III 70, 524, 835, 863
    endure: II 158, 185; III 237
    evil: I 241–42, 323; II 153, 280, 455, 574, 627; III 70, 524, 835, 863
    Francis: I 248, 400, 447; II 185, 322, 336, 474, 625, 673, 704
    heart: I 226, 389
    husband: II 616
    illness: I 241, 370, 413, 416, 494; II 185, 188, 192–93, 410, 434, 443, 467, 474, 673, 675, 704; III 282, 337, 347, 598
    labor: I 279; III 78
    praise: I 580
    shame: II 125; III 225, 291
    stigmata: I 341, 346, 509; II 637
    temptation: II 127, 165, 329, 723, 740–41; III 227, 354, 356, 615, 650
Trough: II 327
Trumpet: I 284, 417, 419, 568, 585; II 522, 772, 811; III 130, 184, 476, 694, 871
Trust
    another: I 50; II 339; III 544, 553, 657
    brother: I 549; II 57, 107; III 194, 458, 537, 545
    Christ: I 50, 98, 177, 187; III 46, 418, 548, 720, 847
    Divine mercy: I 213, 245; II 605; III 855
    Francis: I 241; II 276, 435, 440, 465, 584, 653, 702; III 101, 127, 314, 353, 480, 553, 599, 710, 844

God: I 143, 152, 229, 395, 416, 446,
    472; II 89, 133, 170, 211, 221, 415,
    547, 600, 602, 667–68, 718; III 45,
    125, 163, 171, 250, 310, 314, 317,
    349, 352–53, 414, 552, 710, 712, 855
learn: III 117, 315, 712
Mary: II 598
mercy: I 213, 245; II 605; III 855
money: II 198, 298, 583, 722; III 272,
    751
oneself: I 214, 368; II 551; III 117, 315,
    712, 844
piety: I 213, 245; II 605; III 855
Truth
    charity: I 72; III 135, 147, 386, 419,
        448, 678, 721, 725
    Christ: I 42, 49, 81, 88, 128–29, 347,
        351, 448, 540; II 542, 720; III 151,
        333, 386, 421, 531, 541, 651, 655, 728
    discern: III 326, 573
    faith: I 188; II 551; III 386, 520, 857
    Francis: I 206, 215, 246, 259, 262, 265,
        281, 289, 293, 380, 385, 415, 460,
        476; II 67, 85, 99, 119, 121, 176, 193,
        216, 220, 223, 248, 251, 264, 307,
        339, 350, 383, 467, 489, 512, 532,
        543, 561, 569, 576, 626, 642, 645,
        689, 695, 748, 760, 763, 818; III 41,
        96, 98–99, 151, 154, 175, 218, 221,
        224, 246, 248, 271, 282, 310, 322,
        328, 350–51, 364, 370–71, 405–06,
        420, 426, 502, 665–66, 678, 718, 845,
        854, 864
    God: I 46, 143; II 511, 718; III 310,
        322, 372, 408, 718
    Gospel: II 542, 573, 582, 602, 613, 615,
        689, 691; III 203, 828
    humility: II 517, 725; III 136, 154, 320
    judgment: II 385
    Lesser Brother: I 585; II 545, 772; III
        41, 125, 147, 150, 203, 246, 271, 310,
        320, 322, 405, 517, 746, 786
    lies: I 228, 265, 393; III 408, 422–23,
        580
    life: I 115, 220; II 642, 693; III 41, 136,
        420
    light: II 701; III 520
    miracle: I 403, 603; II 108, 448, 467,
        610, 674; III 36, 805
    poverty: II 722; III 125, 136, 320, 333,
        372, 394, 746, 786, 817
    preach: I 600; II 85, 99, 512–13, 543,
        557, 587, 626, 689, 718; III 115, 135,
        150, 154, 271, 321, 845, 854
    priest: I 117, 476
    prophecy: I 206–07; II 614, 617–18; III
        96, 151, 388, 425, 502, 721, 728, 864
    spirit: I 46–47, 80, 88; III 176
    stigmata: II 108, 406, 527, 636, 638,
        647; III 665–66, 669, 870
    tell: I 228, 393, 606; II 124, 149, 151,
        188, 190, 198, 203, 216, 322, 325,

        344, 489, 570; III 150, 218, 224, 246,
        269, 290–91, 310, 350, 364, 370, 405,
        766, 805
    virtue: III 98, 175, 419, 814
    vision: I 206–07; II 614, 617–18; III 96,
        151, 388, 425, 502, 721, 728, 864
    way: I 262, 265, 415; II 475, 514, 587;
        III 321, 335, 394, 419, 520, 632
    write: I 180; II 528; III 332
Tumult: I 187, 372, 409, 562; III 384
Tunic. See also Capuche, Habit, Hood: II
    333, 351, 357, 413, 434, 462, 555, 664,
    692, 805; III 39, 45, 47, 91, 118, 130, 203,
    222–23, 234, 250, 360–61, 382, 480–81,
    508, 551, 560, 600–01, 628, 794
    Christ: I 146
    Francis: I 195, 202, 227, 234, 247, 249,
        264, 320, 334, 376, 379, 392, 396,
        399–401, 405, 410, 460, 489, 501; II
        84, 119, 122–23, 139, 149, 182–83,
        193–94, 218, 275, 285, 293, 304, 312,
        325, 332, 334–36, 386, 403, 411, 416,
        426, 473–74, 539, 561–62, 577, 624,
        633, 636–37, 642, 660, 696, 710, 771,
        782, 792, 809, 880; III 220, 247, 268,
        290, 307, 358, 456, 469, 497, 593,
        611, 810, 830, 833–34, 843, 847,
        849–50, 852, 860, 866
    give away: I 73, 89, 399; II 47, 94, 139,
        193–95, 281, 305, 312, 362–63, 373,
        590, 697, 795
    improper: II 267
    possess: I 64–65, 101, 125, 195,
        201–02, 218, 247, 249, 320, 379, 401,
        439, 459, 551, 583–84, 589; II 44, 46,
        84, 92, 138, 150, 193, 204, 206, 210,
        285, 293, 386, 542, 577, 642, 689; III
        166–67, 170, 183, 196, 255–56, 258,
        267, 279, 385, 702, 704, 708, 756,
        772, 774, 798
    strip off: II 221, 303, 363; III 249, 280,
        283–85, 305, 507, 510, 692
Turmoil: I 453, 469, 538
Turnip: I 220; II 99; III 38
Twig: II 274, 410, 615, 678; III 95, 456
Twin: I 400, 568; II 361, 442, 669; III 49, 687
Tyrant: II 273, 515, 604; III 523–526, 695

U

Ulcer: I 304, 476; II 167, 466–67, 481, 539,
    681, 688, 750; III 243, 303, 795
Uncle: II 427, 430
Unction
    anguish: I 431
    spirit: I 330
Understanding
    human: I 84, 197, 204, 251, 401, 530,
        570; II 79, 84, 207, 268, 312, 370,
        508, 552, 606, 633, 652, 699, 775; III
        344, 415, 416, 882

Rule: II 206; III 167, 256, 386, 406, 409, 704
scripture: II 510, 542, 612–13, 717; III 168, 319, 556, 705, 855
virtue: I 159, 190, 437, 499, 532, 587; II 273, 283, 314–15, 317, 402, 513, 547, 763; III 162, 388, 419, 421–22, 424, 503, 646, 684, 867
Uniformity: III 858–59
Unity
  brother: I 223, II 215, 260, 369–71, 723; III 41, 410
  composition: III 79
  God: I 78, 85, 91, 116, 121, 138, 284; III 330
  lover: I 289
  poor: I 542
  spirit: I 223; III 41
  virtue: II 723
  weak: II 268–69, 364
Universe
  Lord: I 118
  origin: I 487; II 384, 568
Uprightness
  brother: II 57, 156, 544, 644, 692; III 115, 121, 300, 402, 404, 408, 554
  Francis: I 85, 136, 192, 253, 267, 282, 339, 505; II 197, 227, 289, 697, 733–34, 749, 802, 811; III 196, 345, 381, 415, 665, 728
  God: I 85
  other: I 136, 204, 267, 349, 429, 455, 532; II 156, 169, 223, 405, 512, 514, 546, 652, 723, 764–65, 811, 815; III 33, 64, 69–71, 90, 121, 300, 351, 391, 397, 807–08
Utensil
  discard: II 570
  necessary: III 477, 597
  ownership: III 748–49, 785

V

Vacatio. See Leisure
Vagabond: I 370; III 886
Vainglory
  accuse: II 183, 333; III 147, 307
  avoid: I 75, 90, 105; II 332–33, 521, 734; III 448, 579, 585
  motive: I 185, 265; III 867
  temptation: II 183, 218, 333; III 307, 797
Valley: I 504, 554; II 520, 809; III 200, 366, 458, 495, 506, 593, 610
  misery: I 534; II 403, 491; III 153
  Spoleto: I 182, 213–14, 234, 370, 384, 396; II 68, 115, 167, 216, 411, 414, 450, 550, 684, 691, 706, 809; III 36, 120, 246, 298, 304, 310, 441, 452, 465, 571–74, 589, 596, 619, 860, 879
  tears: I 534; II 403, 491; III 153
Valor: I 338, 438, 441, 463

Value
  consideration: I 70, 91, 400, 473; II 72, 555, 777, 792; III 79, 134, 174, 266, 438, 487, 608, 708, 745, 756, 766, 778, 785–86
  instruction: II 136, 184, 288, 436, 449, 735; III 259, 339, 724
Vanity: I 70, 545–46; II 282, 563, 815
  age: I 182; II 81, 99; III 792
  avoid: I 229, 386, 583; II 301, 520, 523
  Francis: II 68–69, 782; III 840
  motive: I 185, 195, 209; II 169, 316–17, 327, 333, 337, 468; III 343, 382, 389, 410, 814
  world: I 182; II 81, 99; III 792
Variety: I 294, 552; II 192, 468, 556, 630, 681, 693, 729; III 274, 366, 470, 520, 593, 678, 685
Veil: I 510; II 295, 418, 637, 819; III 590
Veneration: I 47, 118–19, 180, 183, 227, 245, 270, 289–90, 295, 321, 565, 569, 600, 603; II 123, 146, 167, 169, 202, 215, 217, 224, 226, 257, 373, 381, 400, 404–05, 437, 449, 464, 477, 554–56, 637, 648, 666, 677, 693, 712, 717, 791; III 35, 67, 79, 98, 102, 187, 247, 452, 837, 871
Vestment: I 256, 256b, 294–95, 325, 406, 419, 579, 601, 604; II 109, 247, 389a, 425; III 66–67, 781
Vial: II 651
Viaticum: II 429, 662
Vicar
  Christ: I 213, 291, 293, 368, 384, 574; II 48, 95, 547–48, 629, 648, 690, 701, 785; III 326, 390, 415, 516–17, 519, 624, 748, 812
  Francis: II 131, 143, 264, 269, 291, 340, 363, 379, 387, 414, 418, 588, 619, 636; III 123, 127–28, 136, 197, 253, 261, 287, 442, 446, 573, 577, 684, 713, 783
  minister: II 775, 778; III 759, 829, 848
Vice
  confession: II 183
  cross: I 131
  detract: II 588
  Egypt: II 742
  flesh: I 202, 321, 567; II 563, 645; III 41, 95, 97, 411
  Francis: I 105, 179, 321, 386; II 221, 355, 511, 791; III 171, 317, 354, 392, 510, 621, 711, 747
  hatred: I 41, 567
  hypocrisy: II 364
  idleness: II 213
  ingratitude: II 616
  power: I 185, 259, 368, 386; II 351
  pride: II 800
  sin: I 41, 164
  singularity: II 253; III 700
  slander: II 363

temptation: III 307
virtue: I 105, 136, 164; II 46, 94, 800;
    III 747
world: II 399
Victory
    cross: II 720–21; III 190–91, 877
    devil: I 272; II 640, 714; III 181, 392,
        412, 446–47, 577
    follower: I 216; II 146, 209, 364, 541,
        560; III 190
    self: I 195, 357, 463, 533, 563, 540; II
        74, 266; III 508
    world: I 462, 596; III 257, 707
Vigil: I 532; II 423, 491, 681; III 497
    canonization: I 293
    Christmas: I 406
    death: I 284; II 476, 647
    feast: II 331, 432, 437–38, 442, 449,
        666–67, 671; III 533, 654
    Greccio: I 406
    Leo: III 512, 582
    John: III 533
    practice: II 169, 289, 330, 381, 558,
        567; III 196, 582
    prayer: I 50
Vigilance
    brother: I 54, 272, 284; II 202
    encouragement: I 80, 88; III 476
    Francis: I 205, 247, 254, 383–85; II 535
Vigor: I 214, 441, 446, 510, 514, 592; II 70,
    370, 449, 570, 616, 631, 634, 637, 641,
    645, 669, 711, 714, 717; III 38, 62, 66,
    83, 91, 164, 184, 189–90, 197, 741, 765,
    828
Vineyard: I 185, 246, 251, 270, 504, 563,
    565–67, 583, 589; II 34, 107, 152, 170,
    177, 179, 270, 357, 360, 413, 424, 450,
    466, 553, 593–94, 658, 672, 678, 706; III
    117, 190, 235, 280, 324, 352–54, 478–80,
    598–600, 712, 754–55, 777, 780, 858, 890
Vintage: II 170; III 353, 778
Violence: I 302, 307, 377, 429, 432, 435, 438,
    443, 449, 483, 486, 545, 568; II 270,
    324–25, 407, 411, 433, 435, 453, 575, 634,
    663, 665, III 389, 539
Violet: I 486
Virgin
    Christ: III 153, 176, 195, 381
    Clare: II 553, 623, 636, 647, 758; III 64,
        91, 176, 466, 690, 701
    Francis: III 47–48, 99, 680, 730, 842,
        879
    Mary: I 46, 129, 201, 295, 354, 378,
        387, 475, 506, 568; II 77, 100, 124,
        130, 155, 157, 196, 214, 226, 257–58,
        291, 375, 451, 457, 465, 477, 520,
        541–42, 555, 579, 591, 598, 653, 670,
        688–89, 692, 786, 802; III 42, 51, 53,
        57–58, 66, 72, 90–91, 121–22, 153,
        195, 224, 230, 236–37, 286, 291,
        299–300, 309, 330, 363, 372, 397,

474–75, 511–513, 526–28, 542–44,
    548–50, 555, 564, 566, 590, 594–95,
    607, 637, 639, 645–46, 656–58,
    694–95, 701, 740, 769, 810–11
    other: I 83–84, 138, 544, 554, II 54,
        323, 385, 450, 462, 533; III 54–55,
        67, 680, 689–90, 824
    Poor Ladies: I 197, 199, 285–86, 378,
        385, 417, 458; II 83, 103, 252, 378,
        533, 623, 647; III 64, 91
Virginity: I 198, 554; II 177; III 153, 564, 730
Virtue: I 164, 430–31, 497, 540, 575–76; II
    156, 419, 450, 779, 791; III 32, 79, 81, 83,
    137, 223, 331, 333–38, 421, 445, 522, 599,
    628, 724, 771, 814
    abstinence: I 198
    acquisition: II 510–11
    angel: II 364
    austerity: II 560–68; III 152–53, 237
    Bernard: III 501, 575, 577, 615
    brother: I 272, 384–86, 413, 462–63,
        468, 584; II 372, 255, 450, 514, 528,
        576, 652, 672; III 34–37, 41, 55, 63,
        89, 98–99, 133, 237, 333–38, 404,
        419, 421, 486–87, 489, 510, 568,
        621–22, 843
    cardinal: I 447, 497, 589; II 729
    charity: I 165, 198, 266, 440, 568, 588;
        II 143, 596–604, 698; III 173–175
    chastity: II 172
    Christ: III 195
    Cistercian: III 62
    Clare: III 91
    Conrad: III 183
    contemplation: III 185
    creature: I 440; III 580
    discernment: II 144, 259, 346, 564–65
    Elizabeth: II 242
    false: II 265
    fear of the Lord: I 437
    flesh: III 459, 853
    Francis: I 319, 342, 344, 351, 374, 442,
        498; II 105, 251, 256, 267, 300, 318,
        322, 349, 360, 385–86, 392, 526,
        559–69, 681, 684, 688, 694–98, 700,
        712, 716–17, 726, 730, 735; III 80,
        86, 96, 181, 267, 362, 401, 485, 566,
        585, 603, 621–22, 815, 843, 848, 852,
        868–67
    Friars Preacher: I 600
    Giles: II 544; III 184–85, 284
    Hugolino: II 289
    humility: I 165, 198, 217, 225, 321; II
        125, 142, 337–41, 519–24, 569–76,
        695, 732, 748–49, 752–53, 755,
        800–01; III 47, 98–99, 153–54,
        287–322, 325, 334, 385, 462, 464,
        583, 585–86, 615, 622–23, 848, 858
    integrity: III 342
    John: III 242
    joy: I 167
    Lady Jacoba: II 417

learn: II 147, 372; III 118, 389, 706, 724
Leo: III 513
Lord: I 529, 533
love: III 116
Masseo: III 461, 514
men: I 542
mirror: I 344
Monaldo: II 557; III 92
money: III 833
Nazarite: II 723
obedience: I 165, 564; II 125, 456, 575; III 154–59, 225, 444, 477, 596, 848–49
patience: I 191, 199, 219–20, 225, 440, 456; II 225, 740–41; III 40, 325
Pelligrino: III 501, 615
penance: II 740
Pica: II 242
piety: II 586–95, 697; III 81, 175, 325
Poor Ladies: II 378
Pope: II 106
Portiuncula: III 121, 237
poverty: I 103, 165, 466, 529–54; II 123, 378, 386, 577, 696, 756; III 159–73, 588
practice: II 510–11, 517–18, 704
prayer: II 605–11; III 342
preach: I 105; II 622–29
proposal: II 300, 579
purity: II 724, 740
Rufino: III 509
silence: I 198; II 564
simplicity: I 165, 225, 321, 503; II 144, 365, 696–97; III 325
spectrum: II 744
steps: I 567
theological: II 729
vice: I 442, 468; II 46, 94; III 744
words: II 318; III 389
world: II 255
zeal: III 175
Vision. See also Dream, Sight: I 450, 464, 567; II 271, 465, 566, 594, 654, 695, 746; III 54
    Anthony: I 225, 390, 874; II 557, 638, 700; III 92
    Apocalypse: III 151, 499–500
    arms: I 186, 371; II 70–71, 245, 532–33; III 873–74
    Augustine: II 389
    bishop: II 390, 644; III 869–70
    Bonaventure: III 557–59, 646–48
    book: III 130
    brother: I 336, 481, 550, 600–01, 627, 638–39
    chariot: I 224, 321, 389, 476; II 552, 620, 691–92, 743, 761, 783; III 388, 815
    Christ: III 83, 190, 475, 542, 595
    Cistercian: III 62
    Conrad: III 566, 638–39

cross: I 390; II 76–77, 87, 319–20, 545, 638, 692–93, 783; III 438, 569, 638
crucified: II 76–77, 638
death: I 323; II 203, 389–90, 644, 716, 784; III 218, 369, 869–70
Dominic: II 786–87
Emperor: III 56
entrance: III 41, 53–55, 62
eyesight: III 57, 805
fiery chariot: I 224, 321, 389, 476; II 552, 620, 691–92, 743, 761, 783; III 388, 815
God: I 154, 186, 194, 450; II 401, 746
hen: II 105, 260
host: III 534
James of Massa: III 557–59, 646–48
John: II 610
John of La Verna: III 534, 536, 655
John of Parma: III 557–59, 646–48
Lady Poverty: II 301
Leo: III 130–31, 550, 627
manger: I 256, 406; II 610
miracle: I 303; II 197, 408, 430, 433, 440, 452, 457, 464, 634–35, 711; III 71
Monado: I 225, 390, 874; II 638, 700; III 92
other: II 147, 197, 372, 634–35, 711; III 41, 53, 55, 58, 62, 475, 481, 595, 600–01, 835
Pacifico: II 168, 327–28, 573, 761, 796; III 304, 425, 682, 692, 838, 848
Pietro of Siena: III 701
Pope: II 97–98, 256, 548, 690, 785; III 682, 838, 844
Portiuncula: II 100, 258, 541; III 86, 486
preach: II 147, 372; III 315
reform: III 701
robber: III 609–14
saint: III 475, 595
small hen: II 105, 260
statue: III 486
stigmata: II 405, 635, 784
Sylvester: II 87–88, 319, 544–45, 638, 693; III 438, 569
Tau: II 405, 693
throne: II 168, 328, 752, 796; III 99, 243, 304, 682, 725, 838, 848
tree: I 210, 383–84; II 547; III 557–59, 646–48
Trinity: III 192, 655
Visit
    angel: III 443
    Assisi: I 305; II 421, 424, 447, 460, 465, 467, 480–81; III 70
    bishop: I 246
    brother: I 499; II 47, 54, 161, 288; III 39, 59, 239, 264, 271, 476, 557, 595, 647, 653
    Capua: III 71
    church: I 47

city: II 54, 103
custodian: I 62, 66, 105, 697
darkness: I 534
Elias: III 554, 630
Francis: I 329, 384, 458, 488, 514; II
    121–22, 152–53, 170, 192, 203–04,
    223, 276, 308, 312–13, 416, 452, 460,
    465, 467, 480–81, 556, 593, 656, 658,
    764, 787; III 66–67, 102, 137, 218,
    221–23, 255, 282, 311, 351–52,
    360–61, 370–71, 456, 702
Gargano: II 674
Giles: III 517, 625
hidden place: II 248
holy place: III 400, 501
Hugolino: II 224; III 311
La Verna: III 561
leper: II 74
minister: I 62, 66; III 697
other: I 329, 488, 534; II 103, 105, 460,
    656, 764, 787
Poggibonsi: II 452; III 72
Poor Ladies: I 292; II 188, 317, 379; III
    337
Portiuncula: I 275, 285, 458; II 47, 156,
    175–76
priest: I 246
Rome: I 213, 384, 472; II 224; III 83
Santiago: III 440, 686
Sultan: III 798
town: II 54, 103
Visitation
    God: II 309–10, 349, 566, 606, 608,
        761, 798; III 455, 463, 539, 541, 588,
        634, 649, 655
Visitator: II 54, 67, 103; III 690, 805
Vocation: II 207, 341, 543; III 58, 63, 81, 115,
    133, 168, 215, 319–20, 372, 380, 387–88,
    390, 404, 408, 705, 722
Voice
    angelic: I 538; III 595
    another: I 119–20, 144, 147, 151, 216,
        224, 242, 274, 342, 393, 489, 519,
        530, 537, 541, 550; II 100, 177, 215,
        258, 356, 391, 413, 425, 428, 434,
        455, 459–60, 480, 541, 594, 608,
        658–59, 662, 664, 676, 737, 742, 795,
        810–11; III 40, 67, 87, 96, 104, 128,
        200, 203, 275, 407, 417, 456, 463,
        475, 508, 515, 518, 521, 523, 541,
        563, 596, 598, 603, 633, 655–57, 760,
        811, 887–88
    Francis: I 194, 253, 256, 277, 284,
        295–96, 323, 332, 356, 381, 406, 415,
        489, 516, 551; II 40, 72, 76, 83, 87,
        202, 377, 388, 410, 444, 464, 475,
        539, 562, 574, 581; III 71, 181, 451,
        479, 493, 503, 573, 582, 728, 815
    God: I 116–17, 149, 489, 534, 538, 566,
        585; II 36, 76, 122, 132, 168, 381,
        401, 437, 510, 536, 558, 573, 638,
        643; III 43, 60, 84, 93, 124, 196, 223,

254, 304, 361, 418, 474, 476, 479,
512, 514, 570, 595, 599, 623, 713,
797, 809, 841–42, 848
Voluntary: I 183, 576, 598; II 736, 756, 772,
794; III 508, 550, 621
Vomit: I 130, 274, 307, 325, 513; II 147, 161,
177, 198, 219, 246, 264, 270, 274, 350,
451, 453, 455, 594, 615, 663, 702, 764–65,
793; III 49, 70, 72–73, 94, 240, 248, 322,
327, 334, 480, 718, 793
Vote: II 778; III 760, 782
Vow
    chastity: II 723
    continence: I 100
    crusader: I 601
    Francis: I 301, 303–05, 307; II 423,
        427–28, 430–37, 440–42, 444,
        446–47, 451–54, 460, 462, 465, 480,
        661, 663–64, 666–70, 675–76, 717;
        III 70, 70–74
    general: I 48d, 185, 300–04, 320, 329,
        394, 457, 460, 658, 691; III 57,
        70–74, 81, 91, 401, 412, 421, 514,
        623, 662
    God: I 301–03, 306, II 430, 450, 455,
        673–74
    Gospel: II 579; III 135, 198
    poverty: I 133a; II 579; III 777–79,
        781–82, 813
    profession: III 317, 712, 744, 771
    reception: III 55, 57–58, 92
    Rule: III 198
Vulgarity: II 246

W

Wafer–irons: II 215; III 245, 309
Wagon: I 434, 441
Wall: I 184, 194, 222, 243, 246, 273, 420,
457, 585; II 35, 70, 157, 161, 202, 224,
228, 292, 308, 311, 318, 361, 374, 402,
425, 427, 437–38, 478, 584, 605, 609, 659,
715; III 45, 67, 86, 101, 128, 231–32, 239,
260, 264, 341, 343, 369, 453, 499, 613,
769, 835, 888
War: I 144, 355, 377, 428, 438, 440, 462–63,
465–66, 469, 480, 485, 541; II 69, 178–79,
215, 243, 265, 270–71, 282, 318, 574, 602,
614, 720–21; III 90, 94, 133, 354, 389,
482, 864, 878, 884
Washing: I 130, 377; II 192, 197, 209, 464,
622, 740, 751; III 258, 469, 492, 592, 608,
707, 733
Water: II 185, 241, 355, 455, 647, 805; III
162, 235, 279, 347, 366, 381, 443, 449–50,
457, 479, 520, 532, 563, 574, 580, 588,
598, 613, 632, 691, 715, 769, 815, 834, 890
    ashes: I 392; II 561, 694; III 801
    bean: II 152
    blood: I 280

bread: I 547, 552; II 449, 558, 671; III 93, 197, 454, 497, 611
cure: I 405; II 634; III 493, 608
drink: I 227, 239, 301, 321; II 259, 278, 434, 561, 568, 628, 705, 716, 807; III 852
fire: II 740
fish: I 235–36; II 40, 88, 413, 562
flowing: I 146; II 359, 659
food: I 227; III 852
ice: II 562, 694
lake: II 625, 664
miracle: II 196–97, 409, 425–26, 434, 664, 705
Moses: II 585, 742
pitcher: I 582; II 279
rock: II 278, 409, 584–85, 705, 707; III 101, 733, 861
rose: II 127; III 227
sea: II 625, 664
Sister: I 114; III 368
spring: II 519–20, 660, 793
tear: II 309, 607, 699; III 176, 501
wash: I 551; II 192, 197, 411, 457, 634, 727
weather: I 454
well: II 519–20, 660, 793
wine: I 323; II 410, 567, 704, 707, 783, 799, 803; III 97–98, 153, 185, 733, 834, 862
Wax: I 146, 299, 303, 307; II 123, 436, 453, 723; III 69, 73, 190, 223, 361, 473, 529, 544, 649, 657, 875
Wayfarer. See also Pilgrim: II 688
Weakness
    Christ: II 632; III 250, 285, 745
    Francis: I 45, 119, 162, 369, 404, 412, 444, 514, 567, 606, 635, 798; III 124, 176, 250, 285, 334–35, 547
    human: I 118, 131, 134, 209, 268, 470, 570, 587; II 132, 153, 190, 221, 239, 326, 392, 442, 565, 578, 663; III 55, 254, 390, 393, 417, 713, 715, 745
    spirit: III 43
Wealth: I 43, 50–51, 185, 190, 338, 370–71, 375, 433, 435, 446, 583, 603; II 34, 47, 69–70, 284–85, 294, 405, 417, 512, 537, 577, 687, 696; III 44, 55, 80, 174, 215–16, 222, 273–74, 360, 436, 514, 739, 749, 778, 885
Weapon: I 244, 428, 435, 471, 546, 568; II 178, 246, 271, 343, 407, 614, 782; III 94, 353, 482
    charity: III 464, 588, 719
    heavenly: I 333, 440, 443; II 607; III 519
    humility: III 464, 588, 719
    iniquity: I 183, 566
    justice: I 462
    last resort: II 118, 346; III 293
    Lord: III 877

Wedding: II 738; III 692
Weeping: I 50, 191, 223, 228, 280, 285, 295, 416, 539; II 76, 78, 139, 142, 182, 208, 243, 250, 340, 388, 438, 467, 476, 511, 545, 565, 607, 646, 667, 695, 749; III 50, 56, 153, 169, 197, 281, 287, 335, 439, 446, 455, 472, 525, 530, 538, 541, 546, 570, 608, 621, 623, 641, 644, 650, 669, 706, 875
Weight: I 189, 325, 333, 357, 469–70, 482, 491, 502, 533; II 94, 109, 144, 229, 269, 337, 364, 424, 427–28, 438, 658, 661, 667, 671; III 164, 344, 398, 402, 527, 787, 815
Welfare
    brother: I 104; II 207, 700; III 257, 704, 754
    soul: II 207; III 168, 257, 704, 751
Wheat: II 129, 269, 375, 392, 594, 706
    bread: II 200, 807; III 216, 230, 274, 363
Whim: I 185; II 71, 148, 351, 562; III 322
Whip: I 319, 325; II 358, 371, 562, 564, 600, 602, 795; III 159, 266
Whisper: I 144, 440, 442; II 142, 175, 331; III 270, 340, 446–47
Wickedness: I 73, 143, 223, 273, 542, 566; II 141, 260, 273, 315, 364, 381, 515, 761; III 49–50, 81–82, 134, 165, 296, 416, 425, 489, 560, 610
Widow: I 456, 458, 533; II 103, 122, 405, 417, 460; III 51, 64, 70, 161, 222, 360, 569, 824
Wife: I 50, 64, 193, 241, 306, 373, 375, 403, 447, 495, 549, 567, 588; II 72, 79, 91, 97, 139, 141, 172, 272, 284, 305, 323, 325, 407, 425, 434, 436, 440–41, 443, 447, 450, 455–57, 464–65, 510, 537, 563, 616, 627, 653, 659, 669, 673, 680, 702, 795, 797; III 62, 74, 281, 334, 497, 612, 720, 809
Wind: I 114, 185, 229, 251, 394, 434, 452, 454–55, 458, 480, 482–85, 488, 503, 529, 546, 588; II 224, 415, 427, 433–34, 452, 600–01, 661, 663–65, 707, 732, 754, 756; III 117, 311, 320, 368, 392–93, 417, 648, 712
Window: I 191, 285, 373, 442, 449, 588; II 129, 173, 421, 463, 476, 653, 657, 782, 805; III 189, 229, 266, 352, 357
Windowsill: I 193; II 36, 47, 78, 137, 290, 537–38, 687; III 266
Wine: I 128–29, 227, 236, 250, 321, 323, 392, 398, 400, 435, 493, 518, 552, 589; II 170–71, 221–22, 259, 276, 323, 354, 360, 410, 416, 424, 466, 556, 561, 567, 658, 692, 694, 704, 783, 798–99, 803, 807; III 62, 91, 97, 117, 185, 250, 310–11, 352–53, 359, 477–80, 495–96, 531, 538, 541, 597, 598–600, 610, 644, 650, 712, 733, 777–78, 780, 803, 834, 852, 862, 890

Wing: I 143, 234, 263, 282–83, 359, 396, 410,
    482, 489–90, 503, 509, 570, 587; II 105,
    108, 260, 343, 374, 402, 411–12, 473, 594,
    607, 613, 624, 632, 706, 709, 743, 754,
    758, 772, 800; III 53–54, 104, 147, 176,
    454, 457, 470, 498–99, 593, 613, 668, 684,
    690, 859–60, 866, 874, 881
Winter: I 221, 250, 320, 386, 400–01, 452,
    503, 594; II 82, 138, 174, 182–83, 224,
    251, 304, 332, 354, 379, 561–62, 635, 694,
    723, 792, 798; III 58, 230, 280, 306, 311,
    449, 579, 678, 798, 853, 875
Wisdom
    Book of Wisdom: II 736, 815
    bride: I 188
    charity: I 136
    Divine: I 43, 50, 76, 90, 161, 190, 197,
        250, 259, 275, 291, 308, 334, 341,
        346, 349, 373, 400, 408, 447, 586; II
        42, 245, 301, 308, 314, 318, 322,
        367–68, 489, 511, 603, 681, 690, 694,
        700, 704, 728, 718, 735, 751, 819; III
        36, 176, 181, 188, 202, 330, 388, 395,
        421, 423, 436, 461, 486, 500, 505,
        518, 567, 585, 589, 618, 625, 652,
        697, 730, 769, 792, 844, 855, 882–83
    evangelical: III 159
    highest: I 131
    human: I 43, 50, 75, 90, 165, 215, 566;
        II 37, 81, 99, 113, 553, 578, 691, 809,
        813; III 125, 315, 320, 405, 409, 411,
        458, 529, 540, 545, 583, 640, 710,
        724, 844
    humility: II 575, 751
    Lady Poverty: I 550
    light: III 147, 190
    meaning: II 510, 813
    queen: I 164; II 368
    salt: I 560
    simplicity: II 367–68
    Solomon: I 125
Wish
    Bernard: III 436, 440, 568
    Bonaventure: III 238, 262
    brother: I 68, 93, 103, 106, 394, 401,
        773; II 38, 165, 173, 201, 210, 257,
        297; III 116, 132, 189, 196, 390, 419;
        III 159, 241, 245, 256, 403, 406, 409,
        419, 447, 466, 491, 508, 527, 534,
        546–47, 556, 563, 577, 636, 642, 696,
        702–03, 714, 756, 774, 799, 834, 837,
        864, 869
    carnal: I 165
    devil: I 79
    discipleship: II 511
    Dominic: II 149, 344; III 290
    evil: I 148; II 580
    feet: I 51; II 540
    fly: III 217, 275
    Francis: I 191, 205, 262, 265, 276, 353,
        414–15; II 53, 125, 130, 150, 153,

        156, 167, 169, 176, 183, 194, 204,
        212, 215, 275, 286, 319, 355, 360,
        369, 371, 386, 415–16, 474, 534, 574,
        576, 602–03, 642, 682, 690, 705, 715,
        798–99, 803–04; III 91, 96, 98, 100,
        121, 128, 137, 153, 155, 162, 166,
        234, 255, 279, 299–301, 329, 384,
        404, 440, 451, 551, 720, 809
    holy: I 46, 61, 76, 97, 100, 117, 130,
        137, 180, 206, 262, 278, 307, 393,
        409, 415, 434, 446, 532, 534; II 80,
        99, 164, 254, 273, 342, 451, 510, 537,
        544, 546, 579, 582, 780
    Hugolino: III 312
    kiss: I 51; II 540
    Lady Jacoba: III 474
    lamb: II 591
    Leo: III 797
    life: I 64
    marry: I 373
    mercy: I 47
    name: I 783
    novice: II 207
    Order's name: I 783
    Orlando: III 453
    other: III 491, 762, 886
    peace: I 58
    Pope: III 754–55, 766, 781–83, 789
    preach: I 397
    sinful: I 134–35
    salvation: I 46, 50, 67; II 772
    way of life: I 64
Witness: I 413, 460, 548; II 263, 286, 292,
    372, 383, 409, 557, 635, 637; III 102, 740,
    745, 802, 805–06
    apostle: III 392, 687
    brother: II 167, 199, 772; III 260, 273,
        279, 303, 416, 532
    charity: III 424
    Christ: I 117
    companion: II 126, 129, 150, 155, 170,
        188, 193, 212; III 121, 150, 172, 184,
        201, 215, 226, 230, 234, 236, 243,
        265, 282, 292, 299, 350, 353, 363,
        414, 418, 687, 703, 722
    conscience: I 393
    esteemed: I 180
    faithful: I 599
    false: I 79
    Francis: III 152, 159, 186, 383
    God: III 196
    grace: II 377; III 422, 424
    holiness: II 610
    indulgence: III 807
    innocence: I 28, 272
    kindness: III 424
    law: II 377; III 422, 424
    light: II 526, 607
    miracle: I 518, 569, 603; II 465, 648,
        651; III 836
    pardon: III 807
    people: I 351

preach: I 535; II 318, 355, 625, 629
reliable: I 225
religion: I 596
shepherd: III 458
stigmata: II 514, 734
trustworthy: I 180
truth: I 259, 289; II 647
virtue: II 618
wicked: I 145
wine: II 567
Wolf: I 192, 542; II 79, 807; III 104, 178, 399, 482–85, 489, 601–04
Woman. See also Female, Lady: I 41, 43, 203, 215, 238–39, 242, 290, 302, 323, 338, 405, 461, 579, 594; II 40–42, 103, 109, 122, 129, 155, 177–78, 199, 243, 418, 421–23, 480, 510, 628, 658, 665, 680, 735, 795, 808; III 73, 88, 95, 153, 334, 359, 498, 637, 699, 794, 822, 834–35, 878
  Apulia: III 72
  Arezzo: I 493; II 628; III 72
  betrothed: II 548
  birth: I 256, 283, 493–94, 507; II 359, 440–41, 444, 628, 668, 670, 716, 783
  blind: I 323; II 783
  Capua: II 480; III 70–71
  Citta' di Castello: II 628
  Clare: I 197, 285, 458; III 516–17, 624, 701, 794, 822
  Coccorano: I 300
  consecrated: I 294; II 177
  converse: I 106; II 322–23, 563–64
  demoniac: I 404
  desert: II 97, 255
  disease: II 192–93
  Eve: III 422
  eye disease: II 192–93
  Florence: II 44, 91; III 72
  Francis: I 494; II 50, 97, 255
  Francis's mother: II 242
  free: II 745
  give birth: I 256, 283, 493–94, 507; II 359, 440–41, 444, 628, 668, 670, 716, 783
  Gubbio: I 403, 323, II 627; III 72–73
  hunchback: II 75, 248
  Lady Jacoba: II 122; III 222, 561
  Limisiano: II 172
  lust: II 322, 141
  Machilone: II 306; III 282–83
  married: II 44, 91, 103, 172, 271–72, 616, 701–02
  Mary: I 141, 478
  Monte Marano: II 655
  Narni: I 403, 627; III 71
  noble: II 701
  old: II 139, 183, 304, 333
  Pisa: II 443
  Poggibonsi: III 72
  poor: I 285, 292; II 50, 83, 97, 138–39, 171, 183, 255, 276, 304, 306–07, 476,

580–81; III 46, 88, 161, 280, 282, 286, 307, 391, 720–21
  Poor Ladies: I 285–86; II 380, 476
  possessed: I 404, 783
  pregnant: I 328, 256, 404–05, 507; II 443–44, 783
  prophetic: II 242; III 152
  receive mantle: II 138–39, 304
  Rieti: II 171, 276
  Rome: II 122, 405, 652
  Samaritan: I 582
  seductive: III 491, 606
  Sibilla: III 71
  sick: I 494
  slave: II 745
  spiritual: II 122
  three: II 307, 580–81
  Vicalvi: III 70
  Volusiano: II 271–72
Womb: I 153, 291, 494, 507; II 196, 327, 360, 440, 523, 668–69, 735–36, 803; III 286, 436, 889
  Elizabeth: II 243; III 422
  Mary: I 46, 118, 475, 568; II 670; III 161, 740, 769
  Rachel: III 159
  Sarah: II 400
Wonder: I 209, 249, 461, 588, 591; II 211, 310, 511, 667; III 48, 171, 304, 413, 556, 647
  deed: I 342, 488, 512; II 168, 281, 401–04, 434, 651, 655, 664; III 391, 662
  state: I 202, 235, 306, 389, 491, 508; II 70, 158, 249, 375, 411, 417, 421, 424, 439, 451, 457, 481, 534, 573, 592, 598, 626, 654, 656, 674, 680, 730; III 73, 78, 99, 186, 401, 418, 426, 456, 465, 481, 486, 517, 530, 532, 543, 548, 555, 575, 600, 603, 636, 695, 723, 804, 875, 884–85
Wood: II 91, 124–25, 191–92, 198, 354, 425, 434, 450, 659, 664, 672, 676, 702, 711, 757, 813–14; III 67, 224, 291, 365–66
  building: II 135, 159, 161, 212, 285; III 45, 172, 238–39, 259, 261–62, 264–65, 792, 803, 819
  burden: I 248; II 222; III 251, 311, 850
  pillow: I 227, 392, 425, 561, 659, 694; III 476, 596, 852
  salvation: I 325, 419, 566; II 109, 250, 378, 401, 478, 538, 634, 720
Wool: I 249, 400, 451–52, 501, 583, 603; II 189, 335, 386; III 833, 867
Work: I 246, 602; II 118, 554; III 49, 52, 71, 80, 82,153, 248, 327, 329, 343–44, 850, 878
  alms: I 71, 92, 94
  beauty: I 419; III 67
  bee: II 202, 297
  brother: I 574; II 158, 161, 190

building: I 565; II 429–30, 443–44, 662
business: II 427, 530, 684
Creator: I 399; III 148
devil: II 323
devotion: I 75, 89, 93, 102; II 190, 208,
    546, 564; III 337
evil: II 109, 145, 169, 219
feast of Francis: II 442
God: I 117, 189, 209, 290, 294, 373,
    420, 435; II 297, 404, 430, 481, 642,
    688; III 850
Gospel: I 321, 582
hand: I 125, 204, 303, 403, 579, 587; II
    201, 222, 429, 433, 441–44, 524, 450,
    676; III 153, 169, 216–17, 219, 251,
    274
hard: I 510; II 81, 158, 253, 410, 441,
    450, 481, 546, 640, 662, 676, 714,
    782; III 153
idleness: I 69, 93; II 147, 161, 201, 213,
    229, 564; III 217, 239, 264
learn: I 68, 125
literature: I 319, 402, 407, 516; II 240,
    728; III 32, 78–80
manner: I 68
praise: I 516
preach: III 154, 169
repair: I 196, 377, 379; II 80–1, 83, 85,
    251, 253, 540, 689; III 843–44
salvation: II 300, 475, 772; III 47, 193
spirit: III 132
teach: III 51
wage: I 69, 436; II 133, 190, 341; III
    297, 326, 857
Worker: I 84, 484, 563, 565–66; II 34, 148,
    351, 424, 429, 482, 605, 658, 662; III 322,
    889
World: II 422, 522–23, 719, 735, 754, 760,
    818; III 58, 224, 522, 547, 550, 552, 557,
    627–28, 887, 889–90
    abandon: II 616, 621
    acclaim: III 31, 47, 178
    affection: III 175
    allurement: I 319, 370, 373, 541, 566,
        597; II 687; III 466, 579, 596
    ancient: II 399
    apostle: III 392, 435, 566
    author: II 696
    beast: III 175
    begin: I 82; III 542
    Bernard: II 253; III 227, 568–69, 576
    bishop of whole: II 57, 261; III 865
    bitterness: III 534, 596
    bodily need: III 311
    Bonaventure: III 78
    brother: I 97, 586; II 167, 169, 186; III
        46–47, 52, 129, 132, 217, 275, 290,
        386, 640
    brothers return: II 173, 223, 297; III
        130, 351–52, 480, 499, 600, 614, 801
    brothers leave: II 165, 182, 294, 299,
        359; III 55, 132, 155, 306, 437, 478,
        480, 500, 529, 615, 693, 834, 877
    brothers sent into: I 70, 73, 81, 89, 321,
        379, 381, 465, 580; II 98, 104, 295,
        376, 447, 554, 582, 670; III 79, 88,
        190, 231, 239, 295, 308, 444–45, 450,
        462, 478, 587, 594, 681, 834, 849
    care: I 79, 118, 165, 187, 543, 586; II
        46, 509, 686; III 57, 92
    Christ: I 46, 103, 248, 401, 535; II 82,
        151, 521, 622, 746, 756, 802; III 161,
        269, 381–82, 386, 496, 611, 730, 821
    churches throughout: I 42, 90, 125,
        222, 388; II 42, 90, 155, 258, 551; III
        121, 236, 299, 844
    Clare leaves: III 466
    cloister: I 552
    clothing: I 65, 195; III 57
    cold: I 593; II 399
    condemnation: III 393
    consolation: III 229
    contempt: I 277, 281, 292, 322, 381,
        547, 572, 582–83; II 533, 546,
        687–88, 698, 816; III 436, 476, 490,
        508, 552, 601, 605, 818, 843
    conversion: II 409; III 126, 251, 294
    creation: II 729; III 195, 471, 520, 799
    crucified: I 218, 328; III 203
    cross: II 402, 543, 692, 721, 727, 795;
        III 87, 470, 594
    darkness: II 684; III 147
    dead: I 285, 320; II 476; III 381, 383,
        465, 589, 634, 814, 831
    desert: I 260; II 255, 583; III 411, 818
    destruction: III 423
    disciple: I 42, 49, 547, 584, 553
    element: II 704
    Elias: III 630
    end: I 44, 51, 81, 120, 580, 582; II 135,
        162, 772; III 129, 194, 240, 244,
        335–36, 381, 868
    ends of: III 523
    error: II 399
    Eucharist: I 52
    example: III 46
    exchange: II 567; III 849–50
    exile: I 375
    eyes: II 201; III 164, 216
    flee: I 214, 230, 243, 292, 570, 579,
        592, 600
    flesh: I 43, 50, 567
    fragrance: III 532, 651
    Francis: I 195; II 47, 66, 81, 85, 133,
        150, 244, 250, 256, 260, 267, 294,
        311, 353, 400, 527, 530, 535, 538,
        567, 642, 686, 696, 725, 739, 750,
        752, 816; III 100, 124, 214, 231, 234,
        238, 269, 278, 281, 314, 337, 371,
        403, 448, 451, 457, 459, 492, 715,
        824, 846, 863

Francis as fool: II 133; III 124, 314, 403, 710
Francis leaves: I 124, 418; II 48, 72, 81, 121, 127, 151, 160, 162, 182, 263, 284, 289, 305, 309, 328, 339, 353, 383, 385, 390, 415, 467, 497, 631, 643–45, 647, 745; III 66, 84, 155, 193, 232, 239, 306, 345, 383, 395, 481, 500, 512, 567, 666, 669, 822, 838, 841–42, 869–70
Francis sent into: I 321, 381; II 546, 786; III 186, 215, 232, 273, 339, 341, 494, 500, 578, 599, 618, 878
Francis's fame throughout: II 199, 228, 241, 243, 252, 370, 390, 402, 406, 467, 477, 556, 626, 629, 647–49, 791; III 33, 80, 159, 175–76, 187, 191, 229, 268, 452, 458, 476, 500, 505, 583, 609, 618, 665, 696, 800, 841, 879, 883
Friars Preacher: II 811
freedom: I 214, 243, 292
Gentile: III 148
Giles: III 284, 685
God: I 52, 215, 260, 263; II 403–04, 418; III 82, 221, 242, 302, 318, 534, 608
goods: I 92, 94, 431, 586
grow cold: I 593; II 399
hidden: III 488, 725
house: II 159
involvement: III 46
John of La Verna: III 529, 649
Lady Poverty: II 577; III 162, 249
language: III 631
learning: III 405
leave: I 47, 71, 92, 94, 583; II 48, 71, 79, 81, 87, 124, 418; III 392, 466
light: I 278, 286, 288, 535, 585; II 148, 252, 342, 399; III 33, 36, 147, 182, 289, 318
little portion: II 256–57, 475
Mary: I 141
Masseo: III 514
misery: II 248; III 291
mission: III 190
Most High: I 52, 54
Mother Church: III 844
new: II 764
news: II 156; III 300
nothing of: I 289
Order: II 37, 39, 41–42, 53, 56, 70, 76, 87, 89, 96, 370, 387, 771; III 441, 486–87, 494, 572, 592, 609, 636, 724, 838
other: III 99, 173, 176, 508
Pacifico: II 316, 556; III 92, 792
papacy: I 213, 270, 291
peacemaker: I 134
Pellegrino: III 501
people: I 134, 136, 165, 265, 272, 547, 583; II 40, 100, 211, 216, 220, 279, 489, 546; III 48, 114, 263, 274, 310, 632, 852
persecution: III 163
Peter: III 33
pilgrim: I 103; III 128, 223, 386, 444, 492, 501, 545, 826
place: III 405, 492
planted: I 246
poor: II 300, 579; III 164
Poor Ladies: II 378
portion: II 256–57, 475
possession: I 92, 94, 431, 586; II 41, 74, 89, 94, 696; III 114, 215, 525
poverty: III 223, 249, 720, 724
power: III 171, 317, 414, 711, 855
preach: II 42, 226; III 215, 223, 273, 462, 592, 621, 727, 800
prelate: III 292
present: I 597, 600
priest: I 125
prince: II 205, 224, 266; III 114, 133, 219, 277, 423, 722, 876
prison: III 818
providence: III 882
province: I 582; III 669
punishment: III 171, 317, 414, 712
Redeemer: I 125, 288, 388, 599–600, 772; III 187, 799
religious: III 293
renewal: II 404; III 87, 157, 193, 678
renounce: II 578; III 33, 46, 100, 496
respect: II 199
Riccerio: III 502
rich: I 58, 247, 416; II 47, 94; III 39
robber: III 496
Roman: III 180
Rufino: III 511, 622
ruler: III 381
salvation: I 293, 601
shrine: III 625
sin: I 280, 331, 336, 346; II 562, 725, 739, 752; III 82, 96, 305, 451, 459, 547, 581, 643
standard: II 164
status: III 149, 157, 180, 197
struggle: I 596
Sylvester: II 319, 544, 692; III 592, 688
temptation: II 53, 88
things: I 105
vanity: I 50, 370; II 79, 88, 99; III 590
view: III 121
virginity: III 48
vomit: III 480
warn: II 400
way: II 136, 181, 287, 409; III 66
whole: I 45, 70, 73, 117–18, 164, 289–90, 412, 419, 545, 552, 580–81, 604; II 422
William: III 805
wisdom: I 75, 95, 165; III 269

Worm: I 43, 48, 51, 144, 250, 322, 400, 510,
    585; II 229, 311, 354, 466, 522, 609, 678,
    751, 798
Worship
    angel: II 519
    body: III 487, 724
    Christ: II 603
    Francis: II 243, 434, 664
    God: I 458; II 376, 534; III 83, 152–53,
        174, 381, 384, 424, 690, 723, 747, 797
Worshipper
    God: III 191
    Trinity: II 103
Wound: I 280, 304, 439; II 323, 404, 407,
    425, 431, 467, 654, 712, 797; III 450, 493,
    496, 504
    Christ: I 146, 281, 287, 331, 340, 366,
        395, 475, 510, 518, 540, 589, 601; II
        76, 249–50, 388, 490, 686, 784; III
        60, 161, 174, 176, 190, 193, 421, 423,
        426, 610, 665–66, 670, 700, 879
    cure: I 228, 475, 487; II 53, 102, 166,
        404–05, 407–08, 429, 431, 445, 450,
        467, 481, 654–55, 661–62, 672, 677,
        716, 797; III 89, 148, 152, 158, 530
    Francis: I 264, 287–88, 354, 411, 435,
        486; II 332, 335–36, 403, 634,
        636–37, 642, 780; III 43, 666,
        669–70, 792, 801
    heart: II 76, 249, 404
    leper: I 320; II 166, 539, 688, 716; III
        242, 303
    love: II 76, 758, 794
    stigmata: I 250, 264, 280, 288, 315,
        331, 335–36, 388, 410–11, 517, 589,
        600–01; II 76, 249–50, 332, 335–36,
        386, 388, 403, 474, 490, 514, 633–34,
        636–37, 642, 646, 651, 710–12, 715,
        719, 743, 758, 780, 784, 797, 807; III
        35, 187, 189–90, 424, 426, 489,
        509–10, 665, 688, 835, 866, 868, 871,
        875–76
    suffer: I 166
Writing
    Bonaventure: II 528, 701
    Companions: II 66, 403; III 268
    Francis: I 53, 55, 57, 59, 98, 120, 127,
        251–52, 469, 598; II 89, 106, 212,
        215, 352, 458, 530, 681, 684; III 199,
        418, 747
    John: III 149
    other: I 419, 504; II 636, 783; III 51,
        179–80, 473, 681

Y

Yoke
    another: II 344; III 849, 883
    Christ: I 46, 328, 347, 405, 446; II 597;
        III 395, 398, 410, 627
    devil: I 241
    discipline: III 834
    Emperor: I 480
    evil: III 136
    God: I 320
    obedience: I 48, 185, 236, 371; II 571,
        619, 688, 701; III 550
    youth: II 751
Youth: I 84, 152, 182, 184, 430, 458; II 155,
    422, 511, 684, 751; III 50–51, 73, 81, 391,
    442, 481, 529, 539, 559, 601, 715, 738, 833
    Francis: I 259, 319, 370, 431; II 39, 69,
        150, 511, 530, 685, 690; III 82, 234,
        833, 840, 884
    Lesser Brother: II 590, 593
    miracle: II 422–23, 428, 445, 450–51,
        453, 463, 657–58, 669, 673, 784; III
        522–23, 835

Z

Zeal: I 60, 145, 263, 462, 495, 542, 544, 547,
    579; II 85, 96, 360, 729, 755, 796; III 33,
    36, 40, 86, 150, 218, 323, 369, 455, 529,
    636, 638, 867, 890
    all: I 337, 385, 408
    apostolic life: III 41
    Christ: I 254, 323; II 712; III 169, 174
    faith: I 581; II 757, 759; III 490, 605
    Francis: III 692
    fraternal salvation: I 697, 700
    God: III 502, 527, 692
    humility: III 47, 413
    justice: I 242; II 702
    law of God: III 423
    perfection: III 323–24, 327–28, 333,
        337, 717–18, 774
    poor: I 401
    poverty: II 386, 642; III 45, 170, 173,
        316, 413, 476, 638, 710, 849
    prayer: II 612–13, 700; III 341–44
    preach: I 603; II 208; III 155, 169, 219,
        321, 415, 855
    profession of *Rule*: II 146, 380; III 323
    Rule: II 146, 380; III 323, 522, 697, 715
    salvation: I 697, 700
    silence: III 40
    soul: I 412; II 144, 347, 587, 598, 690,
        714, 761; III 62, 95, 103, 155, 178,
        295
    spirit: I 566, 608

Index of Names

of texts in *The Saint* (I), *The Founder* (II), and *The Prophet* (III)

A

Aaron: I 368; II 491, 558

Abate, Guiseppe: I 317–18; II 62, 65, 88; III 832

Abbate, Giuseppe. See Abate, Guiseppe

Abel: III 180, 422, 424

Abraham: I 539, 567; II 729; III 103, 182, 394, 422, 425

Accrocca, Felice: I 25, 27; II 116, 486–88; III 21, 113, 379–80, 389, 434, 526, 812, 817, 833

Accrocca, Francesco. See Accrocca, Felice

Accursio, Magno: III 831

Accurius: II 400

Adalbert de Vogue: III 853

Adam: I 129, 449, 455, 530, 538; II 491, 813; III 11, 84, 409, 422, 501

Adam Marsh. See Marsh, Adam

Adam of Saint Victor: I 318

Adelasia of Arezzo: II 444

Adjutus: II 400

Adnes, Pierre: III 147

Aegeas: III 684

Aegeatas: III 684

Aegidius: I 463

Aelius Donatus: III 892

Aelred of Rievaulx: I 61; II 372

Agathonice, St.: I 194

Ageno, Franca: III 873

Aglaia: I 440

Agnes, St.: I 286

Agnes of Assisi, St.: III 467, 517, 591, 624, 690

Agnes of Prague: III 442

Agnolo. See Angelo Tancredi of Rieti

Agostino: II 448, 671; III 820

Agostino da Stroncone: III 448

Ahab: II 519; III 117, 712

Ahasuerus: II 322; III 189

al-Adil al-Kamil: I 231

Alan of Auxerre: I 191, 219, 225, 266

Alan of Lille. See Allan of Lille

Alber, Erasmus: III 676

Albercius of Hierapolis: II 73

Alberic of Trois-Fontaines: I 601–02; II 122

Alberico: II 770

Albert of Assisi: III 695

Albert of Pisa: II 14, 233, 496; III 825, 828

Albert of Strade: III 696

Albert the Great: III 415

Albertino of Narni: I 301; II 452; III 72

Alberto: II 37, 48, 82

Alberto of Arezzo: II 437, 666

Alberzoni, Maria Pia: III 794

Albrizzi, J.B.: I 29

Aldebrandino of Florence: III 808

Aldigheri, Mainardo. See Mainardo Aldigheri

Alecto: I 440

Alessandri, Leto: III 433

Alessandro: II 431, 451, 678

Alessandro of Piazza: II 430

Alexander IV. See also Rainaldo, Rinaldo dei Conti de Segni: I 179, 558; II 19–20, 23, 472, 496, 508, 636, 660–01, 743, 779–80, 785, 814; III 661, 737, 829, 879

Alexander Maccabeus: II 743

Alexander of Alessandria: III 783–84

Alexander of Hales: I 317, 364, 477; II 23, 495–96; III 63, 699

Alexander the Great: I 426, 428

Alfred Angelicus de Sareshel: I 443

Allan of Lille: I 282, 480, 543

Aman: III 858

Amaryllis: I 453

Ambrose: II 54; III 35–36, 795

Ambrose, St.: I 163; II 252, 557, 565, 794, 801; III 93, 177, 698

Amelli, A.: I 179

Amman, Emil: III 112

Amyclas: III 884

Ananias: I 503

Anderson, John D.: II 505, 736

Andrea: II 807

Andrea del Prete: II 770

Andrea of Gagliano: III 430

Andrew, St.: II 693; III 683–84, 686

Angela of Foligno: III 880

Angelo: III 609, 809

Angelo (half brother of Francis of Assisi): II 83; III 680

Angelo (minister): III 808–09

Angelo (son of Siccolo): III 680

Angelo Clareno. See also Pietro of the Marche of Ancona: I 19, 29, 32, 66, 69, 74,

525–26, 528; II 18, 20, 26, 66, 116, 130; III 1, 3, 9, 12, 16–18, 22, 30, 110–11, 113, 126, 144, 373, 375–80, 383, 385, 389, 393, 396, 403, 405–06, 409–10, 412–13, 416, 419–20, 424, 430–31, 434, 526, 556–58, 675, 697, 699, 721, 812, 817–21, 832

Angelo da Borgo San Sepolcro. See Angelo of Borgo San Sepolcro

Angelo di Pietro of Assisi: II 83

Angelo of Borgo San Sepolcro: III 431, 495

Angelo of Clareno. See Angelo Clareno

Angelo of Rieti: II 67; III 183, 221, 810

Angelo of Todi: II 674

Angelo Tancredi of Rieti: I 15–16, 27, 272; II 15–16, 47, 62–63, 67, 113–14, 116, 121, 224, 475, 773; III 21, 27, 35, 56, 112, 114, 125, 183, 221, 312, 333, 371, 387, 454, 469, 495, 504, 592, 609, 681, 690, 699, 722

Angelus. See Angelo Tancredi

Anibaldi, Lord Trasmondo: I 465

Annas: III 142

Anselm of Canterbury, St.: I 69, 183–86, 191–92, 215–16, 224–25; II 753, 802; III 892

Antaeus: I 457

Anthony Gonsalvo: III 62

Anthony of Egypt, St. See also Anthony the Abbot, St.: II 252, 314, 448, 548

Anthony of Lisbon, St. See Anthony of Padua, St.

Anthony of Padua, St. See also Antony: I 7, 32, 107, 225, 364, 367, 390, 411, 477, 524, 527, 571; II 26, 270, 352, 400, 402, 448, 557, 638, 671, 700, 763, 782–83, 811; III 22, 35–36, 92, 376, 481, 519–21, 530, 601, 631–33, 694, 791, 824, 874

Anthony of the Desert. See Anthony the Abbot, St.

Anthony the Abbot, St. See also Anthony of Egypt, St.: II 763; III 345

Anthony the Hermit, St.: II 728

Antonio of Citta della Pieve: III 733

Antony. See also Anthony of Padua, St.: I 202, 229, 244; II 314, 317, 763; III 345

Aod: I 566

Apollo: I 443, 460, 463

Apostles: I 175, 262, 278, 342, 384, 468, 597; II 261, 426

Arachne: I 443

Archemorous: II 281

Archer, Marilyn: II 317

Aristotle: I 427, 432–34, 462, 464–65, 497, 503, 513; II 307, 346, 513

Arlotto of Tuscany: III 829–30

Armstrong, Regis J.: I 3, 5, 11, 28, 106, 179, 197, 199, 528, 575; II 3–5, 24, 83, 250, 560; III 3–5, 21, 515, 517, 795

Arnald of Sarano: III 673

Arnald of Sarrant. See Arnold of Sarrant

Arnald of Vallanova: III 377

Arnaud of Sarrant. See Arnold of Sarrant

Arnold of Arrant. See Arnold of Sarrant

Arnold of Bonval: I 203

Arnold of Sarrant: I 107; II 65, 503, 507, 548; III 1, 3, 17–18, 21, 25–27, 29–30, 35, 461, 661–63, 671, 673–78, 685–86, 694, 706, 714, 832

Arthur of the Round Table: II 208; III 320

Arturo a Monasterio: I 179

Asseldonk, Optatus van. See van Asseldonk, Optatus

Astell, Ann W.: II 245, 284

Athalia: III 158

Athanasius, St.: I 202, 229; II 252, 314, 763

Athene. See Pallas Athene

Atto of San Severino: I 305; II 453, 675

Audrey Marie: II 23

Augustine of Hippo, St.: I 71, 87, 120, 129, 182–83, 185, 252, 262, 266, 566, 578, 592; II 132–33, 148, 261, 334, 367, 372, 505, 520–21, 525, 561, 586, 662, 728, 751, 755, 763–74, 789, 794, 800, 818; III 11, 124, 185, 198, 208, 212, 314, 403, 692, 698, 709–10

Augustine of Terra di Lavoro: II 389, 448, 644, 671, 716, 803; III 36, 124, 869, 891

Aureliano, Ionae: I 69

Aurelius Clemens Prudentius: I 437

Aurelius Properitus: I 277, 429

Ausonians: I 481

Avicenna: I 432, 462, 510

Azarias: I 503

B

Baal: II 523

Bacchus: I 512

Bacon, Roger: III 415

Baglivi, Guiseppe: I 295, 590; II 24; III 30, 36, 55, 145, 405, 523, 698, 791

Baird, Joseph L.: I 295, 590; II 24; III 30, 36, 55, 145, 405, 523, 689, 791

Balaam: III 632

Balaam of Bosor: I 542; III 165

Balian II of Ibelin: I 605

Baliero: II 770

Balvina da Cocorano: III 515

Banarescu, Petru M.: III 236

Bandino dei Caetani: III 802

Barbaro: II 347; III 681

Barber, Malcom: III 452

Barnabas, St.: III 694–95

Barone, Giulia: II 472; III 554, 693

Barrett, Paul: I 5; II 5; III 5

Barrow, Julia: III 20

Bartholi della Rossa: III 682, 806

Bartholo of Perugia: III 808

Bartholomew, St.: III 691

Bartholomew of Arpino: II 453

Bartholomew of Assisi: III 804
Bartholomew of Ceperani: III 73
Bartholomew of Gaeta. See Bartolomeo of Gaeta
Bartholomew of Narni. See Bartolomeo of Narni
Bartholomew of Pisa: I 20, 25, 31, 366–67; III 17, 35, 37, 330, 433, 673, 675–77, 699
Bartholomew of Trent: II 472, 782
Bartolo (son of Lady Fantina): II 770
Bartolo of Gubbio: II 674
Bartolo of Massa Trabaria: III 411
Bartolomeo of Arpino: I 453
Bartolomeo of Corneto: II 427, 661
Bartolomeo of Gaeta: II 429, 481, 662
Bartolomeo of Narni: I 300; II 460, 480, 784; III 71
Baschi, Bonizio. See also Bonizzo of Bologna: III 416
Basil, St.: III 185, 682
Bathsheba: I 368; III 892
Beatrice of Florence: III 880–82
Beatrice of Rome: II 440, 668; III 882
Beaumont, Madeleine: II 506
Bede, St.: I 236; II 356
Beguin, Pierre: I 30; II 31–33, 36–37, 48
Belial: I 466, 542; II 260, 299; III 164, 324
Bell, Rudolph: I 199
Benedetta: II 773
Benedetto Gaetani. See also Boniface VIII: III 738
Benedict: I 319
Benedict XI: III 13, 15, 142, 663, 872
Benedict XII: III 662–63
Benedict of Arezzo: I 172; III 55, 807–08
Benedict of Nursia, St.: I 63, 66, 69, 102, 115, 120, 182, 185, 187, 201, 219, 221, 244, 592; II 11, 100, 132–33, 154, 268, 278, 297, 367, 723, 740; III 37, 60, 119, 124, 185, 236, 297, 314, 403, 709–10, 820, 853
Benedict of Piarocco. See Benedict of Pirato
Benedict of Piratio. See Benedict of Pirato
Benedict of Pirato: I 36; II 162; III 240, 335
Benedict of Prato. See Benedict of Pirato
Benjamin: III 144, 158–59, 383
Bentivenga da Todi: III 487
Bentivenga of Aquasparta: III 738
Bentivoglia: III 635
Bentivoglia Boni of San Severino: III 527, 636
Benvenuto: III 37, 677, 681
Benvenutus Bughetti. See Bughetti, Benvenutus
Benvenutus of Auxerre. See Benvenuto
Benvenutus of Gubbio. See Benvenuto
Benvenutus of Mantua. See Benvenuto
Benvenutus of Recanati. See Benvenuto
Berard: I 107; II 408
Bernard Barravi: III 813

Bernard of Besse: I 18, 32, 317, 367, 603; II 26, 448; III 1, 3, 7, 12, 18, 22–23, 25–26, 28–31, 33–34, 48, 53, 59, 64, 77, 141, 689, 697, 832
Bernard of Clairvaux, St.: I 14, 118, 190–91, 197–98, 203–04, 206, 217, 219, 221, 225, 229, 252–53, 256, 266, 284, 292, 543; II 11, 24, 132–33, 242, 303, 308, 346, 367, 372, 489, 498, 505, 519, 532, 565, 597, 732–33, 736, 739, 752, 800; III 124, 208, 314, 403, 533, 709–10
Bernard Prim: I 593–94
Bernard Quintavalle di Berardello: I 28, 203–04, 207–08, 272, 319, 461–62; II 32, 38–39, 43–44, 48, 64, 67, 85–87, 91, 95, 126–27, 132–33, 135, 235, 242, 253–54, 280, 319, 416, 472, 543–44, 554; III 25–29, 33, 35, 46, 86, 110, 114, 124–25, 226–28, 333, 336, 355–56, 376, 387, 419, 426, 430–31, 434–41, 443–47, 498–99, 501, 503–04, 511, 526, 567–72, 574–78, 613–17, 681, 683–84, 686, 810, 812, 839, 863, 884
Bernard the Treasurer: I 485, 607–08
Bernardi, Michele. See Michele Bernardi
Bernardini Senensis, St.: III 475
Bernardino of Copetrazzo: I 21
Bernardino of Gufaria: III 802
Bernardo (grand-nephew of Francis of Assisi): III 680
Bernardo de Vida. See Bernardo Vigalante
Bernardo Vigalante: III 681
Bernardone of Assisi: III 680
Bernardone, Pietro. See Pietro di Bernardone
Berthold of Regensburg: III 523–24
Bertrand de Got. See also Clement V: III 13
Beschin, Ignatio: I 179
Betterson, Henry: II 586
Betti, Umberto: III 487
Biagio of Tivoli: II 442
Bibi, Giorgio: III 360
Bice Portinari de' Bardi: III 880
Bigaroni, Marino: I 11, 17, 25, 28, 189; II 114–18, 136, 138; III 113, 212, 379–80, 389, 433, 435, 482, 495, 526, 561, 812
Bihel, Stephen: II 731; III 19
Bihl, Michael: I 179, 580, 591; II 24–25, 472, 503, 506–07, 770, 808
Birinus, St.: I 424
Birrell, Jean: II 419
Blanche of Castille: I 290
Blume, Clemens: III 531
Blume, Dieter: II 506
Blund, John: I 424, 427
Boccaccio: III 880
Boccali, Giovanni M.: I 31, 38, 115; II 65; III 31, 113, 212, 379–80, 389, 433, 435, 482, 495, 526, 561, 812

Boehmer, Henricus: I 38, 282, 317, 367; III 793

Boehner, Philotheus: II 505, 543, 631

Boethius: I 477; II 513

Bollard, Jean: II 32

Bollardists: I 29; II 62

Bonaccurso de Leto: II 770

Bonagratia of Bergamo: III 377, 768, 784

Bonagratia of San Giovanni in Persiceto: III 377, 738, 805, 829

Bonagrazia of San Giovanni. See Bonagratia of San Giovanni in Persiceto

Bonaparte: III 800

Bonaventure: II 435, 664; III 664

Bonaventure of Aresso: III 808

Bonaventure of Bagnorea: III 891

Bonaventure of Bagnoreggio, St.: I 11, 13, 17–19, 21, 23, 27, 29–32, 35, 37, 40, 256, 364, 524, 565, 582; II 1, 3, 9, 19–22, 24–26, 28, 62, 113, 117, 161, 264–65, 445, 471–72, 488, 493, 495–508, 513, 515, 517, 525–28, 530–32, 534, 536, 538–39, 541–45, 548–51, 555, 558, 560–66, 568–69, 574, 577–78, 581, 583, 586, 586–97, 599–600, 612–14, 616, 621, 624, 626, 630–33, 650, 646–47, 650, 653, 659–61, 677, 684, 689, 691, 693, 695–96, 708–10, 712, 717–18, 722, 731, 737, 739–40, 747–48, 761–62, 770, 773–74, 780, 788; III 11–13, 17–22, 25–27, 29–31, 34, 48, 53–54, 57–59, 63, 77–78, 81, 111–112, 141, 143, 145, 149, 153, 162, 199–200, 202, 207, 210, 376, 378–80, 399, 430, 436, 441, 455, 457, 468, 487, 490, 515, 558, 661, 674, 676, 679, 697–99, 730, 737–39, 745–747, 749, 758, 786–87, 791, 795–96, 798–99, 803, 806, 824–25, 829, 832, 837, 881, 883, 885, 887–88, 891–92

Bonaventure of Iseo: III 829

Bonaventure of Siena: III 238, 240, 262

Boncampagno of Signa: I 590; II 808

Boniface VIII. See also Benedetto Gaetani: III 13, 15, 142, 375, 377, 738, 768, 830, 871, 890–91

Bonizio of Bologna. See Bonizzo of Bologna

Bonizo of Bologna. See Bonizzo of Bologna

Bonizzo of Bologna. See also Baschi, Bonizio: I 36; II 19, 131, 471; III 123, 127, 253, 416, 713

Bontadoso: I 304; II 433

Bougerol, Jacques-Guy: II 507, 532, 583; III 737

Boulding, Maria: I 183; II 261

Boureau, A.: II 790

Bove, Gennard: II 506

Boving, Remigius: II 506

Boyle, John L.: III 147

Bracaloni, Leone: II 83; III 311

Bradley, Ritamary: II 257; III 212

Brady, G.: II 329

Brady, Ignatius C.: II 25, 51, 67, 241, 508, 532, 718, 731, 747

Braggadocio: I 437

Brentano, Robert: III 20

Brett, Edward T.: II 785

Brill, E.J.: I 189; II 447

Brinkley, Peter: I 427

Britt, Matthew: II 320

Brooke, Rosalind: I 11, 17, 28–29; II 21, 47, 65–67, 114–16, 128, 130–31, 264, 814; III 21, 110, 112–13, 123, 399, 415, 828

Brown, Raphael: II 51, 67, 241; III 213, 434

Brown, Stephen F.: II 505, 543, 631

Brufani, Stefano: I 28, 31, 317, 523–24, 526–27, 529; II 65, 398; III 31, 212, 214, 253

Bruning, Eliseus: I 318; III 530

Bruning, Elisio. See Bruning, Eliseus

Bughetti, Benvenutus: I 166; III 434, 449, 677, 681

Bughetti, P.B.: III 566

Bund, Konrad: I 427

Buonbarone, Elias. See Elias of Cortona

Buonuomo of Fano: I 306; II 454, 675

Buonromeo: III 377

Burchard of Ursperg. See Burchard of Urspurg

Burchard of Urspurg: I 68, 593–94

Burchard, Robert: I 32

Burkey, Blaine: II 5

Burr, David: III 21, 145, 162, 739, 764, 814–15

Butler, Salvator: I 28; II 116

Bynum, Carolyn Walker: I 196, 199; II 336

C

Cabassut, Andre: II 346

Cacanna, N.: III 448

Caeser, Julius: I 133, 235, 426, 428, 470; III 252, 884

Caeser of Heisterbach: I 594

Caeser of Speyer: I 36, 171, 525–28; II 265; III 110, 376, 409, 490–91, 676

Caiaphas: III 142

Cain: III 422

Calaroga: III 888

Cambell, Jacques: I 16, 28, 38; II 114, 116; III 110, 112–13, 432–33, 435, 558, 561

Cambio Catozzi of Chitignano: III 802

Canclias: III 808

Canedo, Lino Gomez: I 31

Cannarozzi, C.: III 832

Carbonell, Charles-Olivier: I 30

Cardinale, Clito: I 122

Cardini, Franco: III 257

Carney, Margaret: III 467

Caro of Arezzo: III 808

Carpenter, Charles: II 613

Carpus, St.: I 194
Carruthers, Mary J.: I 202; II 314
Casey, Michael: II 5
Cassian, John: I 37, 546; II 345, 362; III 837
Casteel, S.W.: II 196
Cataline: I 198
Cato: I 431, 466, 476; II 517
Causse, Maurice: II 24, 28, 62–63, 65
Cavanna, Nicola: III 448, 495
Celaschi, Nancy: I 41
Celestine IV: III 13
Celestine V: III 13, 141, 318, 375, 377, 816
Cenci, Cesare: II 21, 24, 488, 491, 505
Cencio Savelli. See Honorius III, Savelli, Cencio
Cermascoli, Guiseppe: III 212
Cesolo: III 183
Charlemagne: II 209; III 257, 707
Charles the Great. See Charlemagne
Charles I of Anjou: III 791
Chase, Wayland: II 517
Chatillon, Jean: I 582; II 506, 538, 541, 714
Chiappini, A.: II 409
Chiara (grand-niece of Francis of Assisi): III 680
Chilinski, David: I 5
Chiment, John: I 5; II 5; III 5
Chiment, Vicki: I 5; II 5; III 5
Chinicci, Joseph: I 5; II 5; III 5
Chiron: I 512
Christ, Jesus: I 20, 28–29, 41–46, 47–56, 63–64, 66, 68, 70–71, 74, 77–79, 82–83, 87, 89, 91–95, 102–03, 105–06, 108, 114, 116–22, 124–25, 128, 131–32, 134, 136, 142–44, 146–47, 152, 157, 159, 177–78, 189–90, 192–93, 196, 199, 201, 213–14, 216–17, 222, 225, 229–30, 239–40, 242–43, 248–49, 251, 254, 256–57, 259–60, 262, 266–67, 267–72, 278, 281, 283–85, 287–88, 291–92, 294, 298, 307, 314, 316, 322, 325, 328–29, 332, 334–35, 339–40, 342–43, 346–47, 349, 351, 353, 355–60, 366, 368–69, 376, 380, 383–84, 390, 392, 394–95, 398–401, 404–06, 409–10, 412–13, 416, 418, 428, 437, 441, 447–49, 452–53, 456–57, 459–60, 466, 471, 473, 475, 477, 479, 481–82, 485, 488, 493, 497, 500–01, 503, 506, 508–09, 514–20, 528, 533, 539, 544, 547, 553–54, 563–64, 567–69, 571–72, 576, 582–85, 589–90, 596–97, 608; II 20, 38, 42, 46, 48, 50, 52–53, 58, 66, 68, 72, 75–78, 83–85, 87, 90, 93–96, 102, 105, 107–08, 110, 120, 129, 131–32, 134, 142, 144–45, 148, 151, 154, 160, 167, 172, 177, 180, 182–83, 185, 188, 204, 207–09, 211, 214–15, 221, 226, 235–36, 239–40, 244–45, 247, 249–51, 253–58, 268, 272, 274, 278, 280, 282, 287, 289, 302–03, 306–08, 316, 319–20, 323, 329, 331, 334, 336–38, 343, 348, 358, 362, 365, 374–75, 378–80, 383–84, 386, 388–90, 393, 401, 403–06, 409, 411, 415–16, 419–22, 424, 430, 449–50, 452, 456–57, 462, 465, 468, 473, 476–77, 479–80, 486, 489–90, 497–99, 501–02, 504–05, 509–11, 513, 515–16, 521–22, 424–25, 527–28, 532–43, 545–48, 550–51, 553–57, 559–61, 565–66, 569–70, 572–73, 575, 578–80, 582–91, 594, 597–605, 607–10, 612–14, 616–19, 621–23, 625, 628–34, 637–49, 651, 654–55, 658, 663, 671, 678, 680–83, 685–91, 693–94, 696–99, 700, 704–05, 707–10, 712–15, 717, 719–22, 724, 726–30, 732–33, 738–39, 741–46, 748, 751, 753–54, 756–59, 764, 772–73, 781, 784–86, 792–93, 800, 802–03, 812, 814–19; III 11, 15–19, 25–26, 30, 33, 37, 39, 44, 46, 50–52, 57, 60, 63, 66–67, 71, 78–81, 83–84, 86, 88, 90–92, 97–98, 100, 103–04, 110, 114–20, 123–25, 127, 129, 131, 133–37, 141–44, 146–62, 164, 168–69, 171, 174–76, 181–82, 184–91, 193–94, 196–98, 200–02, 207–09, 211, 214, 220, 239, 245–46, 250, 253–54, 257, 263, 266, 269, 271, 285, 289–90, 295, 298, 309, 315, 318–19, 321, 326, 330, 333–36, 339–40, 357, 360, 372, 377–78, 380–81, 383, 385–88, 390–98, 401, 403, 405–06, 408–11, 415–26, 433, 435–40, 44–52, 454, 456, 458, 461–62, 464–66, 468–69, 471, 473, 477–86, 490–91, 494–96, 498, 500–01, 504, 507–12, 514–19, 521, 523–25, 528–38, 540–52, 554–56, 559, 561, 563–66, 568–69, 571, 573–76, 578–79, 581–83, 585–92, 594–602, 604–07, 609–11, 614, 616–24, 626–35, 637–41, 643–58, 666–70, 673, 675, 679–83, 682–83, 686–89, 692–95, 699, 701, 704–07, 709, 714–16, 719–22, 724–25, 727–28, 730–31, 739–40, 742–45, 747, 769–70, 773, 784–85, 789–90, 792, 794, 798–99, 805, 810–12, 814–18, 821–22, 826–27, 834, 838–42, 844, 846–47, 851, 854–55, 862–63, 865–71, 874–77, 884–85, 888–89
Christopher of Romagna: III 26, 28, 30, 36–37
Chrysologus, Peter. See Peter Chrysologus, St.
Chrysostom, John. See John Chrysostom, St.
Cicero: I 185, 266, 458, 461; II 49; III 843
Cirino, Andre: I 528; II 286, 361; III 468
Ciro da Pesaro. See Ciro Ortolani
Ciro Ortolani: II 167
Clare of Assisi, St.: I 11, 26, 31, 99, 106, 115, 137, 173–74, 176, 179–80, 197, 199, 203,

285, 290, 378, 417, 527, 575; II 24, 54, 66–67, 83, 128–29, 188, 250, 252, 322, 399, 476, 505, 623, 636, 647, 747, 750, 770, 773, 777, 812, 826; III 30, 35, 51, 64, 91, 176, 199, 228–29, 331, 337, 357, 434, 442, 466–68, 478–79, 504, 515–17, 564, 590–92, 598–99, 624, 626, 678, 689–90, 701, 794–95, 805, 821–22, 824, 840, 842, 845, 871, 874, 879, 898
Classen, Sophronius: I 25, 178; II 62, 65, 508, 718, 731; III 110, 112, 212
Clebsch, William A.: I 202; II 252, 314
Clement IV: III 738
Clement V. See also Bertrand de Got: I 16; II 113; III 13, 15, 21, 267, 375, 377, 699, 767–69, 776, 783–84, 881
Cochrane, Lydia G.: III 257
Coleti, S.: I 29
Colgrave, Bertram: I 190, 197, 236; II 356
Colin the Englishman: I 581
Comestor, Peter. See Peter Comestor
Compagno of Borgo: III 808
Condon, Veronica: III 663
Connors, Canisius F.: I 5, 31, 264; II 5, 770, 780; III 5, 677
Conrad: III 805
Conrad di Urslingen: III 696
Conrad of Falerone: III 430
Conrad of Offida: I 124; III 8, 16, 19, 22, 109–12, 127, 129–32, 134, 183, 194, 198, 210–11, 318, 522–23, 526, 528, 555–56, 635, 637–40, 694–95, 805
Constance, Empress: III 696
Constantine, Emperor: I 541; II 73, 720–21, 785
Constantine of Orvieto: II 784–85
Constantius: II 73
Constantius d'Medici: II 97
Conti dei Marsi: I 171
Cook, William R.: III 20, 663
Cooper, Eve Marie: II 51, 67, 241; III 664
Coradin: I 608
Cordova, Stephen: III 5
Corstanje, Auspicius van. See van Corstanje, Auspicius
Cosmas, St.: II 749, 750
Cosmo, Umberto: II 167
Costello, Hilary: III 853
Cothenet, Edouard: III 147
Cotton, B.L.: I 427
Coughlin, Edward: I 179
Cousins, Ewert H.: I 5, 27; II 5, 25, 237–38, 532, 599, 616; III 5
Cremascoli, Guiseppe: I 29, 31; II 65, 398; III 30–31, 212, 214, 253
Crescentius of Iesi: I 15–17, 28, 172, 179, 527; II 15–18, 23–24, 61, 63–64, 66, 113, 115, 233–34, 237, 239–40, 496, 774; III 12, 112, 144, 376, 791, 799, 825, 828

Crescentius of Jesi. See Crescentius of Iesi
Cristofani, Antonio: I 425, 427
Cromwell, Bruce: I 5
Cungio Dei Caetani: III 802
Cusato, Michael: I 5, 26, 28, 179, 525, 527–28; II 5
Cuthbert, St.: I 236; II 356
Cynthia: I 458

D

Dalarun, Jacques: I 24, 27–29, 31; II 28, 33, 36, 43, 63, 65, 117, 126, 237, 255, 322, 398
d'Alatri, Mariano: II 398
d'Alencon, Edouard: III 207, 212, 380, 832–33
d'Alerotto, Taddeo: III 889
Damian, St.: I 175, 189, 373; II 24, 36, 747, 749–50; III 845
Damiata, Marino: III 145–46
d'Angers, Octave: II 168
Daniel (brother): II 400
Daniel (prophet): II 301, 499, 522, 631, 754, 756; III 185, 378
Daniel, E. Randolph: II 771
Dante Aliegheri: I 20, 32; II 26; III 10, 22, 144, 146, 567, 880–85, 887, 890–92
David: I 71, 186, 247, 277, 368; II 181, 524, 597, 620, 720, 728, 736, 752; III 103, 177, 422, 758, 892
David Mary, Sr.: I 317
Davidsohn, Robert: III 880
Davis, Charles T.: III 145–46
De Beer, Francois: I 179; II 234, 237; III 21
De Col, Rossano Zas Friz: II 532
De La Marche, A. Lecoy: II 787
De Liney, Le Roux: II 298
De Robeck, Nesta: III 213, 434
De Thaon, Philippe: II 298
De Vinck, Jose: III 745, 799
Delcorno, C.: II 808
Della Porta, Maurizio: III 437
Delorme, Ferdinand: I 16–17, 23, 28–30, 367, 558; II 113–17, 119, 430, 507; III 25, 29, 210, 663, 673, 677–78, 791, 801
Delorme, Francois. See Delorme, Ferdinand
Delorme, Frederick. See Delorme, Ferdinand
Demus, Otto: III 681
Denifle, P.: III 832
Deodato: III 809
Desbonnets, Theophile: I 11, 23–25, 28–31; II 25, 28, 32, 43, 62, 65–66, 78, 116, 506, III 211–13
Desprez, Vincent: II 367
Diana: I 458, 512
Didacus of Palencia: III 677
Dietz, Margaret Mary: II 50
DiFonzo, Lorenzo: I 5, 11, 23–25, 30; II 5, 31–34, 36, 45; III 5, 145

Diocletian: III 54
Dionysius: III 815
Dioscorus: II 520, 755
Distelbrink, Baldwin: III 30
Doelle, Ferdinand: III 663–64
Dominic: III 115, 805
Dominic, St. See also Guzman, Dominic: I 18, 87, 364; II 97, 148–49, 242, 342–44, 466, 772, 782, 784–87, 797, 809, 811; III 47, 136, 144, 147–48, 185, 289–90, 391, 475, 477, 595–97, 661, 682, 749, 813, 823, 826, 883, 886–90, 892
Domino Leone. See also Leo of Assisi: III 35
Donatus: III 892
Doucet, V.: III 379
Douie, Decima: II 771; III 142, 145, 737
Doyle, Eric: I 27, 29; II 5; III 5
Dreves, Guido Maria: III 531, 665
Duby, George: I 190
DuCange,: I 196
DuCharme, Jerry: I 31
Dufeil, M.-M.: II 771
Duggan, Paul: I 30–31
Dulaey, Martin: I 186
Dunn, Charles W.: III 20
Duns Scotus: I 13
Dupre-Theisider, E.: III 880
Durand of Huesca: I 594

E

Eadmer of Canterbury: I 183–84, 186, 191–92, 215–16, 225
Ecclesiastes: II 718, 735, 815
Eccleston: II 744
Echo: III 887
Eddius Stephanus: I 197
Edmonds, Irene M.: II 308, 346, 565
Edouad d'Alencon: II 398
Eduardus Alenconiensis. See Edouad d'Alencon
Edward, St.: I 424
Egidio: III 685
Ehrenfeuchter, E.: III 791
Ehrle, Franz: I 29; II 13, 23, 116
Eleanor of Aquitaine: III 15
Electus: II 381
Eli: II 518
Elias: II 689, 692; III 381, 571–74
Elias of Assisi. See also Elias of Cortona: II 1, 3, 9, 483, 489
Elias Buonbarone of Cortona. See also Elias of Assisi: I 15, 20, 97, 116, 173–74, 242, 264, 267, 274, 276–77, 287, 381, 411–12, 414–15, 496, 508, 511, 514–15, 525, 528; II 13–14, 19, 21, 27, 51, 126, 131, 135, 184, 189, 202, 233, 264–65, 348, 387, 471–72, 474, 485–87, 489, 491, 496, 503, 558, 784; III 112, 117, 123–24, 127–28, 199–200, 202–03, 211, 217, 253–54, 336, 363–64,

369, 376, 381, 393, 399, 402, 410, 415–17, 431, 441–43, 446–47, 486, 490–91, 511, 553–54, 571–73, 577, 622, 629–31, 682, 692–94, 713, 825, 827–29, 830
Elijah: I 83, 224, 330; II 505, 519, 523, 526, 552, 617, 649, 761; III 11, 51, 90, 96, 144, 147, 421, 717, 815
Elisha: II 552, 585, 617; III 51, 90, 98, 101
Elizabeth, St.: II 242; III 33, 80
Elizabeth of Hungary: I 36, 594; II 242, 873
Elizabeth of Thuringia: III 824
Elm, Kaspar: I 30
Emden, Alfred B.: III 54, 500
Emicho of Mainz: I 480
Emmanuel: III 382
Emmerson, Richard: III 20
Engelbert, St.: I 594–95
Engels, O.: I 595
Englebert, Omer: II 51, 67, 241; III 664
Enoch. See also Henoch: I 83; II 649, 761; III 144, 147
Enrico of Pisa. See also Francesco of Pisa: II 443
Enrique of Castile: III 677
Eoin de Bhaldraithe: III 853
Eracles, Emperor: I 609
Erardus II: III 55
Ernoul: I 486–87, 605–07
Esau: II 299; III 422
Esser, Kajetan: I 11, 13, 24–25, 31, 38–41, 45, 54, 63, 66, 69, 74, 87, 91, 97, 108–12, 122–23, 134, 138, 140, 165–66, 527; II 23, 127, 129, 162, 361; III 191, 355, 449
Esther: II 64, 322, 505, 524, 746; III 858
Eubel, Conrado: III 739, 765
Euclid: I 484, 486
Eudes of Chateauroux: II 718, 811–12
Eudes Rigaud: I 317
Eugene III: I 292
Euphemia, St.: III 54–55
Euphrosyne: I 440
Eusebius: II 720
Eusebius Caesarea: III 688
Eustochium: II 362, 803
Eve: I 329, 488; III 423
Everhardus: II 472
Ezechiel: II 140–41, 330, 510, 735, 762; III 49
Ezra: II 385

F

Fabianus of Hungary: III 109
Fahey, Benan: III 213, 434
Faloci-Pulignani, Michele: I 22–23, 30, 122; II 806; III 207, 212
Fantina: II 770
Favre, L.: I 196
Federico Visconti of Pisa: II 808
Felder, Hilarin: I 317–18, 366, 586

Felice: III 889
Felicitas, St.: I 194
Felix: I 190; III 889
Ferguson, Everett: I 196
Ferranti, P.: III 434
Fierens, Alphonse: III 210, 212
Filippa: III 517
Filippo da Campello: II 88
Filippo di Majorca: III 832
Filippo Longo. See Phillip the Tall
Flavius Anicius: II 122
Fleming, John V.: I 527; III 145
Flood, David: I 24, 27, 63; III 201, 814
Folco Portinari: III 880
Fortini, Arnaldo: I 23, 30, 189, 193; II 39, 66–67, 69–70, 72, 79, 83, 85, 88, 131, 167, 178, 226, 298, 317, 770, 826; III 35, 123, 353, 452, 472–74, 506, 677, 680, 696, 800, 898
Fortini, Gemma: II 83
Fossier, Robert: III 20
Foster, K.: II 506
Francesca (daughter of Petruccio): III 674, 677, 680
Francesca (daughter of Siccolo): III 680
Francesca of Tolentino: II 443
Francesco (son of Petruccio): III 674, 677
Francesco (son of Siccolo): III 680
Francesco Bartholi Della Rossa: III 806–08
Francesco de Gonzaga: I 21, 58
Francesco of Assisi. See Francis of Assisi
Francesco of Pisa: II 443
Francesco of Tivoli: II 442
Francesco Pidino of Bologna: I 608
Francis of Assisi. See also John (Francis) of Assisi: I 1–3, 7–9, 11–33, 35–43, 45, 47, 49, 51–53, 56–58, 60–61, 63, 68–69, 72, 75, 78–79, 86–87, 93–94, 97–100, 102–03, 105, 107–08, 110, 113–16, 119–20, 122–30, 133, 137–41, 147, 157, 163–64, 166, 171–80, 182, 184–85, 187, 189–90, 192–94, 196, 201, 203–05, 207–17, 220–22, 224–27, 229–33, 235–43, 246–50, 253–61, 264, 266–72, 274, 277–79, 281–83, 287–88, 290, 293–96, 298–308, 311–19, 323–25, 327–33, 336–37, 339, 341–44, 346, 349, 351, 353, 355–61, 363–70, 372–73, 376, 379–81, 383–86, 388–92, 394, 396–99, 401–08, 410, 412–16, 418–21, 423–29, 432, 434–36, 440, 442, 445, 447, 449–51, 454–55, 457–59, 461–65, 468–69, 471–78, 480–84, 486–87, 492–96, 498–502, 504–08, 510, 512–17, 519, 521, 523, 525–32, 534–35, 549–51, 557–58, 560, 564–68, 570–71, 581, 589, 591, 595–606, 609, 613–16; II 1–4, 7–29, 31–43, 45, 47–58, 61–71, 73–76, 78–81, 83–107, 109–10, 113–136, 138–142, 144, 146, 148–55, 157–59,
161–85, 187–229, 231, 233–237, 239–260, 263–64, 266–68, 270, 272–74, 276–81, 283–84, 286, 290–91, 294–99, 301–08, 311, 313–15, 317–28, 330, 332, 334, 336–7, 339–40, 342–45, 348, 351, 355–56, 359, 361–65, 368–69, 371, 373, 375–76, 380–82, 389–91, 395, 397–99, 401–02, 404–16, 419–68, 471–75, 477–83, 485–87, 489–91, 493, 495–519, 524–37, 539–45, 548, 550–51, 553–54, 556–58, 560–62, 565–66, 571–77, 581, 583, 585–86, 592, 596–97, 599, 601–03, 605, 608–10, 612–14, 616, 618, 620–22, 625–27, 629–30, 632–34, 640, 644–45, 648, 652, 654–81, 683–87, 689, 691–95, 699, 702, 704–05, 707–09, 711–12, 714, 716–40, 742–57, 759–65, 769–74, 779, 782–84, 786–818, 823, 825–26; III 1–4, 7–23, 25–38, 41, 43, 45, 47–48, 50–54, 58, 60–62, 64–67, 69–75, 78, 80, 82, 84–96, 98, 101, 103, 105, 107, 109–117, 120–21, 123–37, 141–47, 149–54, 156–60, 162, 165–78, 180, 183–85, 187–97, 199–200, 202–03, 207–38, 240–58, 260–62, 264–70, 272–73, 275–76, 278–82, 284–92, 294–305, 307–16, 318, 321–25, 329, 333–34, 336–42, 345, 347, 349–55, 357–59, 361–65, 369–72, 375–81, 383, 385–87, 390–93, 395–400, 402–10, 412–13, 415–27, 429, 431–86, 489–517, 519, 522–23, 529, 535, 537–38, 550–55, 557–61, 564, 566–631, 633, 635–40, 643–44, 646–49, 652–55, 658–59, 661–71, 673–723, 726–28, 730–33, 740–41, 743, 757–58, 760–69, 771, 774, 785, 789, 792–821, 823–27, 831–33, 836–38, 840–46, 848–50, 852–54, 856–71, 873–77, 879, 881, 883–86, 888, 891–92, 895–98
Franciscus van Ortroy: I 367; II 31, 398
Frederick II, Emperor: I 185, 264, 292, 317, 424, 512, 564, 595; II 282, 316, 348, 472, 782; III 442, 553, 630, 693, 696
Friend, Albert: I 590–91
Fringillo: III 804
Frioli, D.: II 782
Froehlich, Karlfried: II 635
Froissant, Jean: III 20
Frugoni, Chiara: I 24, 31, 179
Fulcone of Toulouse: II 97
Fulgentius of Ruspe: I 114

G

Gabriel, Archangel: I 46, 83
Gaetani, Benedetto: III 738
Gaetani, James Tommasi: III 487
Gafaro: II 421
Gagnon, Dominique: II 284
Galenus: I 432
Gallus, Thomas. See Thomas Gallus

Gamboso, Vergilio: III 694
Garvin, J. N.: II 728
Gatti, Marcela: II 286; III 468
Gattucci, A.: II 116
Gaudentius, A.: II 808
Gaufredi, Raymond. See Raymond Gaufredi
Gaufridi, Raimondo. See Raymond Gaufredi
Geben of Erbach: I 595
Gedeon of Rieti. See Gedeone of Rieti
Gedeone of Rieti: II 197, 274, 615, 702; III 94, 839, 862
Genovesi, E.: III 437
Gentile: II 70
Gentile da Montefiore: III 487
Geoffrey of Auxerre: I 191, 203, 252
Geoffroi, Raymond. See Raymond Geoffroi
George, St.: I 203, 286, 294–95, 315, 363, 419, 424, 518; II 647; III 67, 835
Gerard de Frachet: II 786
Gerard Gilberti. See Gilberti, Gerard
Gerard of Abbeville: II 508; III 738, 787
Gerard of Clairaux: II 489
Gerard of Modena: I 571
Gerard Ruscinol: I 571
Gerardo of Borgo San Donnino: I 602; II 20, 174, 496, 771, 811; III 360
Gerardo of Zancato: II 448, 672
Gerken, Alexander: II 507
Gerlandino of Ragusa: II 424, 658
Germanus of Capua: I 278
Ghinato, Alberto: I 528; II 757
Ghisalberti, A. M.: II 779
Giacomo: III 653
Giacomo Colonna: III 376
Giacomo di Pellipario di Margarita of Nocera: II 771
Giacomo of Assisi: II 448, 671
Giacomo of Auxerre. See Giocomo of Auxerre
Giacomo of Fallerone. See also James of Fallerone: III 653
Giacomo of Iseo: II 445, 673
Giacomo of Massa. See Giocomo of Massa
Giacomo of Orte: I 461
Giacomo of Pioggibonsi: II 460; III 70
Giacomo of Rieti: II 434, 664
Giacomo of San Clemente: II 673
Giacomo of Tivoli: II 673
Gideon of Rieti. See also Geodeone of Rieti: III 94
Gieben, Servus: I 26; II 398; III 145, 379
Gilberti, Gerard: I 473; II 786
Giles of Assisi: I 15, 18, 28, 204, 207–08, 462–63; II 14, 18, 32–33, 39–40, 43, 47, 64, 67, 87–88, 126, 195, 498, 544, 814; III 33, 35, 87, 125, 183–84, 226, 284–85, 333, 355, 377, 387, 394, 431, 434–35, 441, 443, 447, 499, 504, 517–18, 526, 556, 561–64,

566, 574, 577–78, 613–14, 617, 625–26, 646, 681–82, 684–86, 799, 809–10, 885
Giles of Perugia. See Giles of Assisi
Giles of Trameggiana: III 802
Gineldo of Borgo: II 451
Giocomo of Auxerre: III 377
Giocomo of Massa: III 377
Giotto: II 705; III 12
Giovanna (great-grand-niece of Francis of Assisi): III 677, 680
Giovanna (mother of St. Dominic): III 889
Giovanni da Morrovalle: III 487
Giovanni de Colonna: I 210, 212
Giovanni de Settimo Pisano: III 529
Giovanni Deoteaiute: II 770
Giovanni di Fidanza: II 495
Giovanni di Guittolo: II 770
Giovanni di Magnolo: II 771
Giovanni Frigia Pennate: II 419
Giovanni of Greccio: II 770
Giovanni of Sora: II 447, 674; III 74
Giovanni (son of Angelo): II 770
Giovanni (son of Bernardo): III 677
Giovanni (son of Guarnerio): II 770
Giovanni (son of Siccolo): III 680
Giovanni (son of Simone): II 770
Girard Oddone: III 430, 661
Girolamo: II 770
Giuliana di Calvi: II 440, 669
Glare, P.G.W.: II 49
Glassberger, Nicholas: I 21, 367; III 677
Godet, Jean-Francois: I 11, 24, 31, 39; II 28; III 262–3
Godfrey of Amont: I 129
Godfrey of Auxerre: I 130
Goerres, Joseph: I 22, 30
Goetz, Walter: I 30, 38
Goldhammer, Arthur: I 194, 527, 545; III 20
Goliath: II 720; III 188
Golubovich, Giralomo: I 605, 608; II 25, 506
Gonsalvo. See Anthony Gonsalvo
Gonsalvo of Balboa: III 768, 783, 827
Gonsalvo of Santiago: III 830
Gonsalvo of Valboa. See Gonsalvo of Balboa
Gonzaga, Francisco: I 58
Good John of Arezzo: II 203; III 218, 370
Gottschalk, H.L.: I 231
Graese, Th.: II 790
Grant, Michael: II 281
Gratian of Assisi: I 71, 100, 424; II 251; III 804
Gratien Baden of Paris: III 20
Grau, Engelbert: I 25, 178; II 61, 64, 234–35, 237
Graziano: III 473
Gregg, Robert C.: I 202; II 252, 314, 763
Gregory IX. See also Hugo of Ostia, Hugolino dei Conti di Segne: I 14–15, 19, 28, 36, 100, 106, 124, 172–76, 178,

180–81, 199, 204, 215, 247, 259, 264, 287, 292–93, 295–97, 311–13, 316–18, 325, 327–29, 344, 347, 355, 365, 390, 413, 418–19, 423–26, 429, 499–500, 511, 513, 518, 525–28, 561–65, 568, 570, 575–76, 585, 595, 601–03; II 11–14, 16, 19–20, 23, 32, 57–58, 83, 107, 109, 132, 148, 174, 176, 233, 257, 262, 267, 282, 286, 288, 296, 348, 391, 400, 424, 437–38, 472, 477–78, 481, 485, 505, 572, 636, 648, 651, 658, 660, 667, 751, 763, 774–81, 784, 801, 809, 814, 819; III 13, 31, 34, 36, 53–54, 65, 67, 78, 109, 117, 120, 124, 179, 201, 271, 273, 298, 309, 393, 486, 519, 661, 674, 686, 697–99, 709, 714, 737, 740, 742, 744, 750, 758, 760–61, 777, 785, 802, 804, 819, 823–24, 828, 832, 834, 836, 859, 871
Gregory X: II 20, 496; III 738, 740, 803–04
Gregory XI: II 348; III 17
Gregory of Naples: II 489; III 399
Gregory of Nyssa, St.: I 196
Gregory of Tours: I 468, 541; II 557
Gregory the Great, St.: I 69, 72, 182, 185, 187, 194, 205, 219, 221, 225–26, 243, 261, 278, 282, 437, 459; II 249, 278, 282, 347, 386, 545, 647, 723, 727, 732, 739–40, 752–53, 762, 764, 801, 816; III 13, 530, 698, 841, 853
Grousset, Rene: III 492
Grout, P. B.: III 320
Grundmann, Herbert: I 570; II 133, 299; III 124
Gualfreduccio of Citta della Pieve: I 239, 405
Gualtiero of Arezzo: I 303; II 431
Guarnerio (father of Giovanni): II 770
Guerra, Jose Antonio: I 31
Guglielmo dei Caetani: III 802
Guglielmo of Rome: II 673
Guibertus of Novigneti: I 480
Guidalotto of San Gimignano: II 439, 667
Guido: II 44, 91
Guido of Arezzo: II 291; III 808
Guido of Rome: III 805, 808
Guido I of Assisi: I 193
Guido II of Assisi: I 176, 193, 210, 383, 470; II 32, 41, 49, 251, 390; III 14
Guidone: III 802
Gulubovich, Giralomo: III 526
Gunther of Brabant: III 60
Guthlac, St.: I 190–91, 224, 424
Guzman, Dominic. See also Dominic, St.: II 148

H

Habakkuk: II 720
Habig, Marion A.: I 28, 31, 527; II 116–17; III 213, 434
Hagenvoort, H.: I 189
Haggai: II 504, 731, 749; III 188

Hagman, Edward: I 5, 582; II 5; III 5
Halflants, M. Corneille: II 519, 733, 752; III 533
Hall, J. B.: III 320
Hallier, Amedee: II 372
Haman. See Aman
Hammond III, Jay: I 5; II 5: III 5
Hanes, Keith: II 695
Hardick, Lothar: I 367; II 371
Harkins, Conrad: I 5, 25; II 5; III 5, 677
Hase, K. See von Hase, Karl
Haugh, Eileen: I 5; III 5
Hayes, Zachary: I 179; II 506–07, 525, 527, 709; III 19
Haymo of Faversham: I 312–13, 317–18, 364, 367, 571; II 14–15, 21, 61–62, 66, 233, 237, 486–87, 496; III 53–54, 825, 827–28
Hazel, John: II 281
Healy, Emma Therese: II 506
Hefferman, Thomas: II 699
Heironimus, John Paul: I 427
Helen, St.: II 720
Hellmann, J. A. Wayne: I 3, 5, 11, 179; II 3–5; III 3–5
Henoch. See also Enoch: I 83; III 144, 147
Henri d'Avranches: I 1, 3, 9, 14, 23, 32, 35, 421, 423–30, 432, 435, 441–43, 448, 450, 453–54, 458–62, 471–75, 477–79, 481, 484–87, 494–98, 503–06, 508–11, 513, 515–18, 565; II 11–12, 26, 185; III 1, 3, 7, 12, 22, 75, 77–80, 141
Henri of Pisa: I 425
Henry, Hugh T.: II 320
Henry I, King of Cyprus: III 442
Henry III: I 424; II 812
Henry VI: II 316
Henry of Acre: I 581
Henry of Buford: II 23–24
Henry of Cologne: I 594
Henry of Susa: III 889
Herbert, Kevin: II 296, 334, 515, 715, 734
Hercules: I 457
Hermann, Placid: I 524, 527; II 23, 488; III 30, 213, 434, 553, 693, 824
Hermans, Vincentius: II 5, 54, 122
Herod: I 455, 546
Herzman, Ronald: III 20
Hester, Kevin: III 5
Hezekiah: II 762; III 422
Hildebert, St.: I 480
Hildegard: II 808–09
Hildegard of Bingen: I 595; II 808–09
Hill, Edmund: II 520, 728
Hinnebusch, William: I 580, 582, 584–85; II 786
Hippocrates: I 432; III 881
Hoeges, D.: II 806
Holder-Egger, O.: II 489; III 823, 825

Hollinger, Robert: III 880
Holvey, D. N.: III 345
Holzapel, Heribert: III 20
Homer: I 455
Homodeo of Arezzo: III 808
Honorius III. See also Savelli, Cencio: I 7, 15,
    45, 52, 55–56, 65, 68, 99–100, 117, 193,
    243, 245, 267, 270, 293, 311, 313, 317,
    327, 409, 413, 418, 498, 526, 558–63,
    578–80; II 56–57, 97, 105, 107, 148, 170,
    216, 233, 238, 261, 266, 339, 399, 558,
    763, 814; III 13–14, 79, 115, 135, 352, 400,
    418, 713, 807, 823–26, 859, 871, 885
Hopkins, Andrea: III 452
Horace. See also Horatius: I 426; II 267; III
    79
Horatius: I 452, 458, 466, 497, 505–06
Hostiensis: III 889
Houghton, Louise Seymour: I 30; II 65
Howard, Donald R.: II 50
Howard, Richard: I 190
Huber, Raphael: II 13, 23; III 20, 807
Hugh: II 20
Hugh of Digne: I 7, 32, 87, 92; II 26, 89; III
    22, 36, 142, 145, 201, 545, 817
Hugh of Saint Victor: I 252, 437, 497; II 296,
    334, 497, 515, 695, 734; III 27, 30, 208,
    212, 892
Hughes, Elizabeth: III 873
Hughes, Serge: I 5, 27; III 873
Hugo of Ostia. See also Gregory IX,
    Hugolino dei Conti di Segne: I 243, 245,
    513; II 261, 286; III 246, 259, 309, 390,
    859, 861, 864–65
Hugo of Saint Victor: I 437, 497
Hugolino dei Conti di Segne. See also Greg-
    ory IX, Hugo of Ostia: I 14, 36, 106,
    173–74, 180, 199, 243, 245, 247, 267, 270,
    413, 499–500, 513, 564; II 11, 55, 57,
    103–04, 107, 132, 148, 175, 184, 214, 216,
    224, 261–62, 286, 288, 636, 777, 781; III
    14, 112, 203, 246, 259, 309, 390, 402, 478,
    598, 794–95, 834, 839, 859, 861, 864–65
Hugolino of Monte Giorgio: I 20; III 110, 378
Hulsbusch, Werner: II 583
Humbert of Romans: I 18; II 771, 786
Humilis: III 537
Hurst, David: II 647, 727, 732, 753, 762
Hutton, Edward: III 396
Huygens, Constantijn: I 32, 580–81
Hyacinth: I 463
Hypsipyle: II 281

I

Iacoba De Roma: III 474
Ignatius of Antioch, St.: II 515
Ignatius of Loyola, St.: III 124
Illuminato of Acre: I 28, 605; II 63, 67, 265,
    602, 633, 672; III 490, 798–99, 891

Imperatore of Spello: I 304
Inguanez, M.: I 179
Inkey, Simone: III 147
Innocent III: I 16, 63, 74, 99–100, 174,
    179–80, 185, 189, 210, 212, 218, 238, 245,
    293, 295, 312–13, 317, 321, 327, 337,
    368–69, 383–84, 399, 418, 470, 473, 558,
    578–79, 592–93, 597–98, 602; II 50–51,
    56, 96, 99, 105, 205, 233, 254, 256, 317,
    321, 332, 547–48, 690, 697, 785, 792, 809,
    811; III 13–14, 276–77, 396, 680, 682,
    712, 720, 804, 823, 830–31, 844, 885
Innocent IV: I 295, 317; II 15, 17, 23–24,
    257, 399, 774–75, 777, 782; III 13, 29,
    109, 179, 434, 516, 661, 699, 737, 744,
    748, 750, 757, 759, 765, 777, 800, 806, 829
Ioannes de Castris: II 653
Ionae Aureliano. See Aureliano, Ionae:
Iriarte, Lazaro: I 24, 29; II 13, 17, 20,
    23–24; III 20, 145, 467
Iriarte de Aspurz, Lazaro. See Iriarte, Lazaro
Iris: III 887
Isaac: I 539; II 299; III 182, 394, 410, 422
Isaiah: I 42, 115, 178, 531; II 35, 505, 511,
    518, 562, 720–21, 732, 734, 748, 754–55,
    760, 817; III 435, 567, 689, 866
Ishmael: III 182, 394–95, 410, 422
Isidore of Seville. See Isidore of Spain, St.
Isidore of Spain, St.: I 329, 446, 459, 465,
    497, 513–14, 595; II 65, 116, 130, 255,
    727; III 111, 113, 126–27, 134, 207, 209,
    295, 333, 695
Isom, Gary: I 5, 26
Isom, John: II 4, 26; III 5
Israel: II 489–90, 504, 630, 692, 733, 753,
    757, 764; III 203, 410, 415

J

Jacapone da Todi: I 32; II 26; III 10, 22
Jachanan: I 568
Jacob: I 152, 174, 276, 323, 349, 414, 532,
    539, 544, 567–68; II 299, 319, 474, 486,
    489–90, 504, 630, 744, 753; III 422, 446,
    577, 868
Jacoba dei Settesoli. See Jacopa dei Settesoli
Jacoba Graziano dei Settesoli. See Jacopa
    dei Settesoli
Jacobi Vitriacensis: I 586
Jacobo: III 732
Jacobutio: III 809
Jacopa dei Settesoli: I 290; II 121–23, 126,
    197, 322, 397, 405, 417–19, 591; III
    66–67, 222–23, 355, 360–61, 431, 434,
    471–74, 481, 561, 686
Jacopo: II 770
Jacopo de Voragine: I 23; II 790
Jacopone da Todi: III 872–23
Jacques, St.: II 819

Jacques de Vitry: I 10, 485–87, 560, 578, 580–81, 585, 602, 605; II 375; III 794
James (father of Jude): III 692
James: III 35, 303, 646
James (soldier of Assisi): III 804
James Alpheus. See James the Lesser
James Coppoli of Perugia: III 809
James, Little: III 809
James Oddi di Perugia: III 495
James of Falerone: III 515, 533, 535–37, 623, 653–54
James of Florence: III 808
James of Guisia: II 485, 488
James of Massa: II 66; III 433, 458, 469, 526, 538, 556–67, 564, 593, 634, 646–48, 654
James of Rieti: II 805
James of San Clemente: III 805
James of Tivoli: III 805
James of Vitry: II 375
James of Voragine. See Jacopo of Voragine
James Tarlati: III 495
James the Greater, St.: I 77, 207; II 519, 730; III 151, 198, 441, 536, 571, 574, 654, 685–86, 740
James the Lesser, St.: III 688–89
James the Simple: II 166; III 242, 303
James Tommasi Gaetani: III 487
Jarmak, Claude: I 5; II 5; III 5
Jean de Cambrai: I 581
Jean of Brienne: III 55–57, 63
Jehoash: III 144
Jeremiah: I 589; II 771, 818
Jerome: II 770, 801, 803
Jerome, St.: I 69, 194, 197, 329, 498, 514, 582; II 242, 362, 530, 548, 733, 741, 801, 803; III 675, 683–85, 687–91, 693–95, 698, 892
Jerome, Sir: II 646–47
Jerome of Ascoli: II 548, 673, 680; III 12, 16, 25, 29, 377, 429, 487, 738, 803–06, 812, 816, 829
Jesse: I 251
Jesus. See Christ
Joachim of Fiore: I 56, 77, 469; II 20, 496, 525, 771; III 11, 19, 142, 145, 149, 203, 377, 674, 681, 814, 816, 892
Joash: III 158
Job: I 452; II 196, 505, 512, 521, 523, 530, 641, 714, 724, 729, 733–34, 736, 745, 749, 762, 764, 817; III 286, 853
Johanna: III 889
John. See Good John
John: I 28, 272; III 35–36, 240, 646
John XXI: III 769, 892
John XXII: I 19; III 15, 20–21, 141, 376–77, 680, 783–84, 786, 789, 815, 817
John Blund. See Blund, John
John Cassian. See Cassian, John

John Chrysostom, St.: II 720, 756, 764; III 892
John de Capella. See John of Capella
John de Laudibus. See also John of Lauds: III 28, 35
John de Schiacia. See John of Schiacia
John Damascene, St.: I 480
John (Francis) of Assisi. See also Francis of Assisi: II 68, 233, 241–42, 684, 790; III 33, 683
John Gonsalvo of Opta: III 677
John, King of England: III 830
John of Brienne: I 294; III 55–56
John of Campania: I 603
John of Campo: III 802
John of Capella: II 41, 63, 88; III 33–34, 431, 434–35, 511, 566, 622, 681, 693
John of Capello. See John of Capella
John of Celano: III 380, 388, 697, 832
John of Ceperano: III 832
John of England: III 58
John of Fermo. See also John of LaVerna: III 433, 529–37, 649
John of Florence: I 225, 390, 411; II 363
John of Greccio: I 254, 256, 405; II 228, 610; III 232
John of Kent: I 425
John of Komerow: III 793
John of LaRochelle: I 317, 364; II 23, 495; III 63
John of Lauds. See also John de Laudibus: III 35, 125, 333
John of LaVerna. See also John of Fermo: III 429–30, 540, 542–43, 649–57
John of Lerida: II 712
John of Murrovalle: III 13, 814, 830
John of Parma: I 172, 364, 524, 527; II 18–20, 25, 239, 397, 496, 506, 771–72, 774, 811; III 36, 112, 141, 150, 376–77, 379, 556–58, 646–48, 825, 827, 829
John of Penna: III 36, 544–47, 640–43
John of Perugia: I 15–16, 21, 28, 272; II 14–15, 23, 29, 32, 63–64, 67, 400; III 27, 556, 798
John of Piancarpino. See John of Pian di Carpine
John of Pian di Carpine: I 363; II 14
John of Reading: III 544
John of Rupescissa: III 20
John of Saint Paul: I 210, 383, 470–71; II 32, 49, 55, 96, 103–04, 547–49; III 196, 390
John of Salisbury: I 510, 543
John of San Costanzo: III 681
John of Schiacia: III 706
John of Ubeda: III 677
John Parenti. See Parenti, John
John Pecham of Canterbury: I 527; III 58
John Scotus Eurigena: I 329; II 526

John the Baptist, St.: I 83, 118, 171; II 486, 520, 526, 561, 696; III 11, 381, 474–75, 595
John the Evangelist, St.: I 21, 83, 266, 278, 415; II 97, 334, 387, 429, 475, 499–501, 503, 522, 527, 542, 577, 614, 643, 736, 751, 754, 764, 784, 815; III 144, 149–50, 152, 177, 191, 198, 474–75, 555, 567, 595, 639–40, 686–87, 692, 697–98, 745
John the German: II 343
John the Notary: III 808
John the Prothonotary: III 30–31, 697–98, 832, 833
John the Simple: II 163–64, 368–69; III 240–41, 301–02, 699
John the Teuton: II 784
John III Vatatzes: III 829
Johnson, Timothy: II 5, 531, 613; III 5
Jonadab: I 589
Jonah: III 521, 685
Jonathan: I 247, 743–44
Jonathan Maccabeus: II 743
Jordan of Giano: I 32, 173, 178, 317, 364, 367, 526, 559, 592, 594; II 14, 26, 38, 51, 265, 486, 488; III 22, 30, 36, 400, 490–91, 793, 825
Joseph: I 582; II 752; III 144, 158–59, 422, 875
Joseph of Nazareth, St.: III 695
Joseph the Just: III 692
Josiah: III 422
Juan of Llerda: II 653
Judah: I 155
Judas: I 117, 130; III 34, 431, 435, 566, 693, 745
Jude, St.: I 364; III 692
Judeans: I 536
Julian of Syria: I 197
Julian of Speyer. See also Julian the German: I 1, 3, 8, 11, 14–15, 18–19, 21, 23, 27, 32, 256, 311–18, 327–28, 330, 332, 337, 343, 361, 363–67, 369–70, 372–73, 376–81, 383–85, 388–92, 394, 399–402, 405–06, 408–11, 415–17, 419, 423, 425; II 11–12, 16, 21–22, 26, 28, 32, 48, 61, 270, 471, 500–02, 505, 531, 539, 551, 636; III 18, 22, 27, 29–31, 53, 697–98, 837
Julian the German. See also Julian of Speyer: I 367
Julius Caeser. See Caeser, Julius
Juniper: III 35–36, 125, 333, 526, 646
Juno: III 887
Justin, St.: III 103
Justinae Patavini: II 811
Juvenal: I 453, 460; II 358

K

Kaeppeli, Thomas: II 782, 785–787

Kane, John Robert: I 295; II 24; III 30, 36, 55, 145, 405, 523, 791
Katz, Steven T.: II 532
Katzenellenborgen, Adolph: II 712
Kedar, Benjamin: I 605–06
Keen, Maurice: III 452
Kehr, Paul Fridolin: III 529
Kennan, Elizabeth T.: II 505, 736
Kloos, Rudolph M.: III 681
Knowles, David: II 133; III 124

L

La Bande, E. R.: II 136
Labarge, Margaret Wade: III 518
Lachance, Paul: II 317
Lacombe, G.: II 728
Ladner, Gerhart: II 525
Lambert, Malcolm: II 774, 776; III 162, 739, 745, 764, 784, 786, 789
Lambertini, Roberto: III 737
Lancelot: III 320–21
Landini, Lawrence C.: I 29; II 23, 775; III 20, 145, 828
Langebeck, J.: III 826
Langeli, Attilio Bartoli: I 7, 24, 27, 31, 39, 110–12, 122–23
Langholm, Odd: III 20
Langton, Stephen: I 424
Lapsanski, Duane: I 39, 108–12; II 256
Laureille, Marie-Therese: II 23; III 30, 553, 693, 824
Lawler, Thomas Comerford: II 362
Lawrence, St.: II 376, 803; III 185, 533–34, 542, 656, 856
Lawrence of Beauvais: II 363
Lazzeri, Zepherinus: III 802
Leah: I 568; III 87
Leahy, E.: I 318
LeBreton, Marie-Madeleine: II 812
LeClercq, Jean: II 245, 253, 308, 597, 635, 800
Ledeur, Etienne: III 147
Legisima, Juan R.: I 31
LeGoff, Jacques: I 25; III 14–15, 20, 257
Lekai, Louis J.: II 268
Lemmens Leonard: I 37, 557, 581, 590, 592, 596, 602–03; II 116, 130, 400, 770, 773; III 1, 3, 8, 21, 111–12, 126, 205, 207–10, 212, 214, 253, 294, 802, 833
Lempp, Edward: III 554, 693
Lenghaus, C.: II 196
Leo of Assisi. See also Domino Leone: I 7–8, 15–19, 21, 27–28, 32, 36, 39, 108, 110, 112, 122–23, 166, 272; II 15–16, 26, 28, 47, 62–63, 66, 113–116, 121, 131, 134, 204, 280, 475, 773, 793; III 16, 19, 21–22, 27, 30, 35, 47, 109–115, 123, 125, 127, 129–31, 132–34, 142, 165–66, 168–70, 173, 183, 194, 197–99, 201, 207, 209–11,

214, 221, 230, 253, 295, 318, 333, 371,
380, 387, 397, 406, 416–18, 433, 449–52,
454–58, 473, 502, 504, 507, 511–14,
550–51, 579–82, 615, 620, 627, 686–87,
690, 697, 699, 701, 703, 705, 713, 721–22,
730, 797–98, 809–10, 814, 818, 820
Leo of Milan: I 571; III 28, 35
Leo of Santa Croce: II 224–26, 229, 326, 575,
796; III 230, 311
Leo XIII: I 122
Leonard di Giffoni: III 17, 674
Leonard of Assisi: II 266–67, 617, 793; III
839, 863–64
Leone, Domino: II 66
Leribert Rosweyde. See Rosweyde, Leribert
Lerner, Robert E.: II 133, 299, 737; III 124
Le Roux de Lincy. See De Liney, Le Roux
Liberatus: III 375
Liberius: I 201
Liebermann, F.: III 830
Little, Andrew G.: I 317, 425, 427, 505; III
29, 62, 112, 114, 127, 253, 433, 695, 805,
827
Little, Lester K.: I 190, 527, 530, 532–33, 552
Little James: III 809
Lodge, R. A.: III 320
Long, Michael: III 872
Lopez, Athanassio: III 804
Louis, Landgrave of Thuringia: III 824
Louis VIII: I 366
Louis IX, St.: I 290, 366, 424; II 811; III 431,
517–18, 625, 685
Lucanus: I 470, 485
Lucia of Collis, St.: III 809
Lucido: III 556, 646, 653
Lucido the Elder: III 526, 535, 636
Lucidus: III 125, 333
Lucifer: I 455, 488; II 168, 351, 751; III 186,
243, 304–05, 411–12, 422, 425, 524, 682
Lucius: I 593
Ludovici: III 434
Luibheid, Colm: I 282; II 635, 762
Luke, St.: I 21, 72; II 382, 497, 505–06,
509–10, 520, 560, 562, 626, 630, 688, 691,
696, 732, 747, 750; III 177, 697, 813
Luke of Bitanto: III 801
Luke of Tuy: I 595
Lull, Ramon. See Lull, Raymond
Lull, Raymond: III 415
Lunghi, Elvio: III 437
Lynch, Joseph: III 20

M

Maccabees. See also Alexander Macabeus,
Jonathan Maccabeus: II 743
Macharius: II 801
Macrobius: I 185, 266
MacVicar, Thaddeus: II 13, 23; III 145
Maggiani, V.: III 738

Magro, Pasquale: II 507
Maillieux, Georges: I 11, 24, 31, 39, 189; II
28; III 263
Mainardo Aldigheri: II 342
Maitana: III 809
Malachy the Irishman, St.: I 14, 190–91,
197, 203, 224–25
Maleczek, W.: I 593
Malherbe, Abraham: I 196
Malik al-Kamil: I 231, 486, 581, 605, 608; III
490, 492
Malik al-Mu'azzam. See also Coradin: I 608
Mancanella of Gaeta: II 432
Mancino: I 303
Mandelbaum, Allen: III 880–81
Mandonnet, Pierre: III 114, 127, 695
Mangenot, Eugene: II 23; III 112
Manselli, Raoul: I 23–24, 30; II 28, 55,
114–15, 117, 126, 157, 159, 212, 272, 779;
III 212, 262, 687
Mansueto: III 699
Marbodus of Rennes: I 494
Marcellinus: I 202; II 252, 314, 763
Marcianus: I 227
Marco of Citta della Pieve. See also Marco of
Mantino: I 306; II 450, 673
Marco of Montino. See also Marco of Citta
della Pieve: III 556, 646
Marconi, Luigi: III 434
Maria of Gagliano: II 409, 678
Marianus of Florence: I 138; III 676–77,
682, 832
Marie of Oignies: I 578
Marignolli, Giovanni: III 434
Marini, Alfonso: II 256
Mario of Sora: II 454, 675
Mark, St.: I 21; III 177, 697
Mark of Lisbon: I 21
Markey, Patrick: I 27
Markwald of Anweiler: I 185
Marsh, Adam: II 23
Marshal, William 1st Earl Pembroke: I 190,
423
Martha: I 61, 508; III 87, 184, 696, 795
Martial: I 446, 513
Martin IV: III 179, 294, 756, 764, 768–69,
776, 789
Martin V: III 769
Martin de Ramsey: I 519
Martin of Tours, St.: I 14, 180, 183, 195, 202,
221, 236, 244, 277, 285–86, 343; II 11,
182, 236, 244–45, 553, 557, 604; III 14,
93, 306, 840
Martino (owner of ox): II 464, 679
Martino (monk): II 249; III 841
Mary (sister of Martha): I 61; III 87, 696
Mary, Virgin Mother of God: I 46, 61, 82–83,
92, 108, 115, 118–19, 129, 139–44,
146–57, 159, 163–64, 175, 197, 201, 203,

295, 316, 330, 354, 378, 387, 462, 468, 475, 506, 519, 568; II 26, 77, 124, 130, 151, 157, 165, 196, 214, 226, 256–57, 374–75, 426, 451, 457, 465, 477, 520, 540, 542, 579, 591, 598, 670, 689, 692, 715, 738, 748, 753, 758, 760, 786; III 35, 42, 51, 53, 57–58, 72, 90, 120–22, 195, 224, 237, 285, 291, 299, 303, 313, 328, 330, 363, 381, 399, 434, 466, 474–75, 512, 526, 528, 542–44, 548–49, 555, 566, 590, 594–95, 607, 635, 637, 639, 645–46, 656–57, 658, 694–95, 701, 769, 810–12, 884

Mary, St. (Church of the Portuncula): I 76, 175, 195, 222, 249, 258, 274–75, 277, 329, 395, 415, 458, 515, 562, 597; II 17, 39, 41–42, 45, 47, 51, 76, 87–88, 93–94, 100, 104, 120, 125, 137, 154–55, 157–58, 166, 175–76, 180, 196, 198, 202, 208, 210, 212–13, 217, 256, 258, 285, 288, 290–91, 324, 350, 475, 540, 553, 557, 579, 591, 593, 642, 700; III 43, 110, 116–17, 119–21, 124, 131–32, 134, 169, 172, 210, 212, 220, 225, 236–37, 240, 242, 247, 258, 261, 264, 266, 271, 275, 286, 297–300, 330, 346, 360, 371–72, 399, 402, 434, 449, 458, 466–67, 472–73, 475, 486, 489, 579–80, 590–91, 595, 604, 708–09, 714, 799, 807–08, 810, 830, 843

Mary David: I 317

Mary Magdalene, St.: II 369, 656, 754, 763; III 222, 360, 383, 473, 531–32, 651

Massario of Arezzo: III 808

Masseo (son of Andrea del Prete): II 770

Masseo of Marignano: I 28; II 63, 67; III 125, 183, 333, 387, 431, 441–43, 454, 458–65, 468–71, 502, 505, 514–15, 527, 572–74, 583–89, 592–94, 615, 618, 622–23, 636, 691, 718–19, 807–08, 810, 812, 819

Mathias, St.: III 693–94

Mattea of Tolentino. See Francesca of Tolentino

Matteo: III 556, 647

Matteo d'Acquasparta: III 487

Matteo of Todi: I 302

Matteo of Tolentino: II 443

Matteo of Vicalvi: II 465, 663

Matteo the Elder of Monte Rubbiano: III 535, 547, 642–43, 653

Matthew, St.: I 21, 347, 369, 372–73, 376–78, 380–81, 383–84, 388–89, 392; II 38, 501, 508–09, 512, 517, 519, 732–34, 747, 762; III 177, 198, 690, 697, 699, 858, 867

Matthew of Acre: I 581

Matthew of Assisi: III 804

Matthew of Aquasparta: III 813, 830, 891

Matthew of Narni: III 399

Matthew of Paris: I 427, 552, 596–97, 601

Matthew of Vendome: III 77

Matthew Vind. See Vind, Matthew

Matthias, St.: I 201

Matura, Thades: I 27

Maxentius: II 720

McCarron, Charles: II 23; III 145

McGinn, Bernard: II 24, 238, 264, 301, 505–06, 526–27, 545; III 19–20, 149, 815

Mcguire, Brian Patrick: III 858

McMichael, Steven: II 136

Medici, Constantius: II 97; III 391

Megaera: I 440

Mehat, Andre: II 586

Melani, G,: III 529

Melchisedek: III 117, 410, 714

Melchiorri, Stanislao: I 21, 29

Melek el-Kamel. See Malik al-Kamil

Menard, Andre: II 583, 640

Menerchini, S.: III 802

Menesto, Enrico: I 31, 317, 527; II 65, 398; III 31, 212, 214, 253

Merlo, Grado G.: I 24, 31, 528

Merton, Thomas: II 306

Meyer, Robert: I 190

Micah: II 522

Miccoli, Giovanni: I 24, 27, 31; II 28

Michael: II 736

Michael Bernarducci: III 810, 819

Michael of Acre: I 581

Michael of Cesena: III 376, 784

Michael the Archangel: I 76, 83, 108, 138, 141, 301; II 51, 101, 226, 373–74, 390, 450, 454, 593, 598, 631, 634, 644, 674, 709, 711, 716, 736; III 454, 527, 635–37, 869

Michaels, Daniel: III 5

Michalczyk, Marian: III 673, 677–78, 680–81, 727

Michele Bernardi: III 693

Michelet, Jules: I 22, 30

Midianites: I 568

Mierow, Charles Christopher: II 362

Miles, Margaret: I 194

Minerva: I 428–29

Minos: I 512

Minotaur: I 512

Miramamolin: I 208, 230, 322, 395, 563, 601, 757, 783

Miramolin. See Miramamolin

Miskully, Jason. See Miskuly, Jason

Miskuly, Jason: I 5, 366–67

Mizael: I 503

Moak, Helen: I 30, 189, 193; II 178; III 35, 353, 696, 800

Mockler, Anthony: II 505

Modaldo of Le Marche: III 375, 874

Mohammed. See also Muhamed: I 584, 607; II 603

Mollat, Michel: I 194, 527, 545; III 20

Mombritius, B.: II 515

Monaldo: I 225, 390, 477; II 402, 557, 638, 783; III 51, 92, 805, 874
Monaldus. See Monaldo
Monasterio, Arthuro. See Arthuro a Monasterio
Mondonnet, Pierre: III 112
Monica, St.: II 565
Montefeltro: III 802
Monti, Dominic: I 5; II 5, 21, 24–25, 445, 488, 505, 507, 564, 613, 621, 774; III 5, 200, 699, 749–50, 758–59
Moorman, John R. H.: I 367; II 20, 23–24, 497, 505; III 20, 37, 109–113, 737, 764, 784, 789, 804, 827
Mordecai. See Moedechai
Mordechai: II 61, 505, 746
Morgan, M. R.: I 605
Morico the Short: II 41, 88, 374; III 34, 681
Morico (order of Crosiers): II 555, 692; III 34, 91
Mormando, Franco: I 5
Moses: I 55, 117, 196, 276, 368, 548; II 486, 491, 504, 519, 558, 732, 742, 745, 752, 772, 811; III 101, 111, 128–29, 399, 416–17, 424, 436, 456, 548, 567, 717, 815
Mousket, Philippe: II 806
Muhamed. See also Mohammed: I 480, 487
Muhammad al Nasir: I 230
Muller, Karl: I 22
Muratori: II 282, 465; III 434
Musa, Mark: III 880
Muscat, Noel: II 506

N

Nahash the Ammonite: II 733
Narcissus: III 887
Nardecchis, A.: III 434
Nardini, A.: III 479
Nathan: III 892
Nebuchadnezzar: II 301; III 486–89, 723–26
Nelson, Thomas: I 192
Nepotian: II 733
Niccolo (friend of Trasmondo Anibaldi): II 465
Niccolo da Clavi: III 516
Niccolo of Ceccano: II 446, 674
Niccolo of Ceprano: II 428, 662
Niccolo of Foligno. See Nicolo of Foligno
Nicholas of Assisi: III 35, 696, 800
Nicholas of Rome: I 580
Nicholas, St.: II 544
Nicholas. See also Nicolaus de Romanis: I 580; III 36
Nicholas III: III 13, 20, 29, 109, 179, 211, 267, 315, 487, 661, 699, 714, 737–41, 749–50, 756, 758, 761–62, 764–66, 772–77, 779–80, 784–86, 806, 816
Nicholas IV: II 548, 673; III 12–13, 64, 377, 661, 765, 806, 891

Nicholas of Carbio. See Bonaparte
Nicholas of Corbario. See Bonaparte
Nickels, Peter: I 5; II 5; III 5
Nicola di Giacomo: III 800
Nicolaus de Romanis: I 580
Nicolaus Magister: II 171
Nicolo of Foligno: I 299; II 458; III 69
Niermayer, Jan Frederik: II 23, 447
Nimmo, Duncan: I 25, 27, 29, 525, 528; II 13, 23, 25, 505; III 19–21, 110–113, 434, 764, 767
Noah: I 599; III 422, 470, 593, 887
Noone, Timothy: I 5; II 5; III 5
Notkero Balburo of Saint Gall: II 490
Noye, Irenee: I 189; II 586

O

Oakley, Chester: III 20
Oberman, Heiko Augustinus: III 20
Octave d'Angers: II 167
Octavian Ubaldi. See also Ottaviano degu Ubaldini di Mugello: I 519
Octavianus Ubaldi. See Octavian Ubaldi
Oddi, James. See James Oddi di Perugia
Oddone, Girard. See Girard Oddone
Odilo, St.: III 534
Odo of Cheriton: I 122, 590–91; II 50, 255, 543
Odo Rigaldi. See Odo Rigaldus
Odo Rigaldus: II 23, 495; III 63
Odoardi, Giovanni: I 178
Odonis, Gerald: III 113, 661
Odysseus. See Ulysses
Offreduccio: II 770
Oliger, Livarius: I 68–69; II 13, 23, 130; III 112, 434, 473, 545, 690, 696, 721, 792, 796, 832
Oliger, Remy: I 38
Oligny, Paul: I 28; II 116; III 213, 434
Oliver: II 209; III 257, 707
Oliverus: I 485
Olivi, Peter: I 124
Olschki, Leo S.: III 663
O' Meara, John: II 586
Opheltes: II 281
Origen: I 566; II 284
Orlando of Chiusi the Elder: III 453, 802–03
Orlando of Chiusi the Younger: III 802–03
Orlando of Tuscany: III 452–54
Orsini, Giovanni Gaetano: III 738
Orsini, Matteo Rosso: III 741
Orsini, Napoleone: III 141, 881
Ortolani, Ciro: II 167
Ortroy, Franceso van. See van Ortroy, Francesco
Ortulana: III 517, 624, 879
Ostian: III 889
Oswald, St.: I 424
Ot, Giral: III 661

Othon de Pavle: III 677
Ottaviani of Assisi: III 804
Ottaviano (Judge): II 673
Ottaviano degli Ubaldini di Mugello. See also Octavian Ubaldi: I 295
Otto: II 400
Otto (son of Ottaviani): III 804–05
Otto IV: I 58, 221, 386, 474; II 316; III 41
Ottoman of Assisi. See Ottaviani of Assisi
Ottone: II 673
Ovid: I 426, 429, 434, 436, 442–43, 445–48, 454, 460–73, 476–95, 497, 499–500, 502–05, 508–09, 512–17, 520; II 337; III 79
Ozanam, Frederic: I 22, 30

P

Paccioco, Roberto: I 25; II 398
Pachomius: III 124
Pacifica: II 128
Pacifico: I 559; II 167–68, 186, 216, 301, 316–17, 335–36, 402, 505, 556, 638, 693, 725, 752, 761; III 92, 246, 304–05, 310, 348, 425, 537, 643–44, 682, 691–92, 699, 792, 874
Paciocco, Roberto: II 398
Pagnani, Giacinto: III 434, 537
Pagnotti, F.: III 516
Pagoulatos, Gerasimos: I 5
Palaeologus, Michael. See Michael Palaeologus
Palazzo, Eric: II 506
Palazzolo, Juliiene: I 179
Pallas Athene: I 443
Panofsky, Eric: II 506
Paoli, Emore: I 31; II 65, 398; III 31, 212, 214, 253
Paolo of Spoleto: III 527
Papebroch, Daniel: I 21, 23; II 31–32
Papini, Niccolo: I 21, 29
Papylus, St.: I 194
Parenti, John: I 58, 60, 264, 287, 564, 571; II 496; III 828
Parr, Roger P.: III 77
Parsons, Wilfrid: II 521, 755, 764
Parthians: I 479, 481
Pasithea: I 440
Pasztor, Edith. See Paztor, Edith
Patten, Donald: III 5
Paul, Jacques: II 398
Paul the Deacon: II 291
Paul, St. See also Saul: I 53, 73, 83, 106, 122, 126, 182, 210, 219, 292, 295, 346, 368, 411, 455, 470, 472, 519, 531, 561–62, 565; II 245–46, 477, 499, 505, 510–13, 517–19, 522–23, 525, 575, 598, 714, 718, 720–21, 725–26, 731–32, 735–36, 743, 750–51, 755, 757–58, 760, 762, 764, 779, 815–17; III 41–42, 144, 158, 383, 431, 462, 464–65,

496, 562, 566, 587, 611, 694, 718–19, 740, 764, 767, 783, 790
Paul of Osimo. See Paul of the Marches of Ancona
Paul of the Marches of Ancona: I 248–49, 399–400, 411, 501
Paula, St.: I 197
Paztor, Edith: I 25; II 116; III 113, 123, 295, 333, 380
Pazzelli, Raffaele: I 24, 41; III 64, 110, 113
Peano, Pierre: III 791, 812
Peck, George T.: III 872
Pedro of Castile: III 677
Pegasus: I 460
Pelagius of Albano: I 605
Pelikan, Jaroslav: II 635
Pellegrini, Luigi: I 30–31; II 65, 398; III 31, 212, 214, 253
Pellegrino of Falerone: III 500–01, 615
Pennacchi, Francesco: I 179; II 770
Peregrine of Bologna: II 18; III 825, 827, 829
Peregrino of Falerone. See Pelligrino of Falerone
Peregrinus of Bononia. See Peregrine of Bologna
Perfetto: II 434, 663–64
Perotin: I 318
Perpetua, St.: I 194
Persius: I 437
Peter: I 239; II 32, 38–39, 86, 254, 400; III 33, 797
Peter, St. See also Simon Peter: I 83, 106, 175, 197, 213, 240, 292, 295, 329, 368, 455, 470, 472, 519, 561–62, 565, 614; II 73, 167, 235, 247, 437, 477, 481, 521, 523, 534, 540, 547, 598, 620, 627, 667, 735, 749, 756, 777, 779, 791; III 41–42, 83, 198, 425, 431, 462, 464–65, 587–88, 683–84, 686, 701, 718–19, 764, 767, 783, 790, 823, 896
Peter Alfonsus: I 480
Peter Bernadone. See Pietro di Bernadone
Peter Book-Devourer: III 892
Peter Cantanii. See Peter di Cantanio
Peter Cantor: I 220
Peter Chrysologus, St.: III 54
Peter Comestor: III 892
Peter Damian: I 543
Peter des Roches: I 424
Peter di Cantanio: I 97, 116, 174, 204, 239; II 32, 38–39, 85–86, 125, 142, 166–67, 182, 196, 254, 265, 291, 306, 340, 344, 363; III 33, 225, 243, 286–87, 303, 305–06, 434, 490–91, 681, 684, 686, 701, 810, 812
Peter di Guiduccio. See Peter di Cantanio
Peter Lombard: I 463, 543, 563; II 495, 497, 531; III 683
Peter of Alife. See Pietro of Alife
Peter of Assisi: I 36

Peter of Blois: II 491
Peter of Boreth: I 602
Peter of Bovaria, St.: III 243, 304
Peter of Brescia: I 571
Peter of Calabria: III 37
Peter of Cantanio. See Peter di Cantanio
Peter of England: III 397
Peter of John Olivi. See also Petrus Johannis
    Olivi: I 124; III 12–13, 15–17, 20, 141–43,
    145, 149, 162, 318, 376–77, 475, 545, 674,
    738–39, 749, 764, 784, 812–15, 817, 880
Peter of Monticello: III 635–37, 639–40
Peter of Narni. See also Pietro of Narni: I 403
Peter of Nemours: I 559
Peter of Nocera: II 421, 656
Peter of Portugal: I 74
Peter of San Damiano: II 36, 76
Peter of Sassoferrato: II 400
Peter of Spain: III 892
Peter of Tewkesbury: II 23
Peter of the March: III 639–40
Peter Rudolph a Tossiniano: III 832
Peter the Eater. See Peter Comestor
Peter Venerable: I 480
Peter Zalfani: III 808
Peterson, Ingrid: I 5, 197; II 5; III 5
Petrone, N.: I 178
Petruccio: III 677, 680
Petrus Johannis Olivi. See also Peter of John
    Olivi: III 20
Pharaoh: II 736, 752
Phillip, St.: I 128; III 689
Phillip: III 640–41
Phillip II: I 366
Phillip Nurbi: III 810
Phillip the Tall: I 28, 204, 207, 463; II 54, 63,
    67; III 33, 87, 435, 545, 566, 640–41, 681,
    689, 794–95, 810
Philippe de Thaon. See de Thaon, Philippe
Phinehas: II 760
Phoenix: I 512
Pica Bernadone: I 146; II 83; III 680, 682,
    696, 800
Picard, Marc: II 76
Picardo: III 680
Pickford, C. E.: III 320
Pierre, Dom: I 317
Pierre Dejean Olieu: III 20
Pietro della Spina, St.: I 201
Pietro di Bernardone: I 192, 203, 228, 393,
    479, 616; II 64, 79–80, 251, 570, 826; III
    440, 505–07, 571, 618–20, 680, 684, 885
Pietro Giovani of Capella: II 88
Pietro Mancanella: II 432; III 74
Pietro of Alife: II 438, 481, 667
Pietro of Foligno: I 301; II 454, 674
Pietro of Marcerrata: III 375
Pietro of Monticello. See Pietro of Monticulo
Pietro of Monticulo: III 527–28, 555–56

Pietro of Narni. See also Peter of Narni: I
    240; II 461
Pietro of the Marche of Ancona. See also
    Angelo Clareno: III 375
Pietro of Sicily: II 447, 674
Pietro Pettinario of Siena: III 710
Pietro Rainalducci: III 376
Pietro Ridolfi of Tossignano: I 21
Pietro Romano of Monte Gargano: II 450
Pietro Stacia: III 407
Pilate, Pontius: I 143, 546
Pipino, Francesco. See Francesco Pidino of
    Bologna
Pius V: I 315
Pius IX: III 37
Pius XI: III 807
Plato: II 346, 372
Plautus: I 430, 437
Pliny: I 429, 485, 512–13; II 272, 466
Podesta, Gian-Luca: III 379, 880–81
Polak, E. J.: I 590
Pompey: III 884
Pontius Pilate. See Pilate, Pontius
Portinari, Folco: III 880
Post, Gaines: I 571
Potesta, Gian Luga: III 379
Powell, James: I 605
Powicke, Frederick M.: III 500
Praepositivus of Cremona: II 728
Prassede: II 405, 462, 675
Pratesi, A.: I 122
Pressutti, P.: I 193
Price, R. M.: I 197
Prizer, William: III 872
Przewozny, Bernard: III 694
Pseudo-Anselmus: II 753
Pseudo-Augustine: II 753
Psuedo-Bernard of Cluny: I 118, 129–30
Pseudo-Dionysius: I 282, 329; II 354, 500,
    526, 635, 710, 762
Pseudo-Melito: I 468
Ptolemaeus: I 485
Ptolemy: I 429
Pulignani, Michele. See Faloci-Pulignani,
    Michele
Puzarelli, Simone: I 564
Python: I 443

Q

Quaglia, Armando: I 582; III 434
Quetif-echard: II 97
Quinn, John F.: II 718, 731
Quintilianus: I 429, 446, 472

R

Rabanus Maurus of Mainz: III 892
Rachel: I 568; III 87
Rahab: III 189

Rahner, Karl: II 566
Raimondo Gaufridi. See Raymond Gaufredi
Rainaldo: II 496
Rainaldo of Castiglione: III 808
Raineri: II 217
Ranieri Cappocci of Viterbo: I 14, 295, 311–12, 314–18, 338–39, 344, 519; II 636, 785; III 402–03, 698
Ranierio Cappocci. See Ranieri Cappocci of Viterbo
Rainerio of Gufaria: III 802
Rainerio (father of Tommaso): II 770
Rainerio of Mariano of Arezzo: III 807–08
Rainerus Sacconi: I 480
Raischl, Josef: I 528; II 286, 361; III 468
Ralph of Corbrigge: III 54
Ralph of Hereford. See Ralph of Maidstone
Ralph of Maidstone: III 53–54
Ralph of Rheims: II 61; III 54
Ramsey, Boniface: II 362
Ranier Cappocci: II 339
Rao: II 421, 657
Raphael, Archangel: I 83
Rashdall, Hastings: III 500
Ratzinger, Joseph: II 525, 527; III 19
Rauch, Winthir: II 506
Raymond: III 77, 105
Raymond Gaufredi: III 13, 375
Raymond Geoffrol: III 768, 806, 814, 830
Raymond of Carbone: III 37
Raymond of Provence: III 830
Raynald de Jenne: II 779, 781
Rayner: III 808
Rayner of Acre: I 580
Rayner of Viterbo: II 784
Raynerius: III 698
Ready, Gabriel: I 527
Rechab: I 589; III 117, 712
Reeves, Marjorie: II 771–72; III 19, 681
Reichert, Benedictus: II 97
Renan, Ernest: I 22, 30; II 764
Renaud of Le Simon: II 676
Retting, John: II 764
Riccardo degli Annibaldi: II 548; III 804
Riccardo di San Germano: II 282
Riccerio: I 226, 390, 411, 447, 477; II 204–05, 276; III 96, 165–67, 255, 500–02, 702–03, 819, 839, 864
Riccerio of Bologna: III 416
Riccerio of Muccia: III 165
Riccerius. See Riccerio
Ricci, Teobaldo: II 139; III 250, 495
Riccomagno of Volterrra: II 460; III 70
Richard of Saint Victor: I 282, 568; II 498, 506, 541, 714
Richard of San Germano: I 595
Richard the Lion Hearted: II 316
Richer of Sens: II 808
Riedlinger, H.: I 590

Rigg, A. G.: I 427
Riggs, Noel: I 5; II 5; III 5
Rinaldi, Stefano: I 21, 29; II 32
Rinaldo dei Conti de Segni. See also Alexander IV, Rainaldo: II 660
Rinaldo of Brunforte: III 537
Rinieri of the March of Ancona: III 615–16
Ritzler, Remigio: III 487
Riziero of Bologna: III 416
Rizzerio: III 165
Robert Courcon: I 559
Robert of Bascia: II 23
Robert of Bassee: I 317
Robert of England: II 472
Robert of Fondi: II 348
Roberto: II 447–48
Roberto of Naples: II 447–48, 670–71
Roberts, Alexander: I 183; II 244
Robson, Michael: II 41, 49
Roddy, Robert: I 5; II 5
Rodolfo of Rome: II 424, 659
Roest, Bert: III 792, 823
Rogatha of Sora: II 454, 675
Roger: III 34, 36, 125, 333
Roger Bacon. See Bacon, Roger
Roger of Wendover: I 74, 596–97, 601
Rogerio: III 34
Rogero of Apulia: II 797
Roland: II 209; III 257, 707
Rolfe, J. C.: I 235
Romano, Maria Antonietta: II 398
Roques, Rene: II 635
Rorem, Paul: II 762
Rosen, Cyprian: I 5; II 5; III 5
Ross, Patricia: I 29; II 23; III 20, 145
Rosweyde, Leribert: II 32
Rotelle, John: II 520, 728
Rouse, Mary A.: I 559
Rouse, Richard H.: I 559
Rowan, Steven: II 133, 299; III 124
Rubin, Miri: II 375
Ruf, Gerhard: III 20
Rufino: I 15–16, 27–28, 189, 195, 264–65, 272, 411; II 15–16, 19, 39, 47, 62–63, 65–66, 113–114, 116, 182, 241, 403, 471, 474; III 21, 27, 33, 35, 112, 125, 197, 333, 397, 416, 434, 436, 504–11, 567, 617–22, 681, 687–88, 812
Rufino Cipii: III 812
Rufino di Scipione di Offreduccio: III 35
Ruggero of Potenza: II 404, 654, 712
Rupert of Deutz: II 525
Russell, Josiah C.: I 427
Ryan, William Granger: II 790

S

Sabatelli, Giacomo: III 429, 433
Sabatier, Paul: I 22–23, 30, 38, 56; II 62, 65, 756; III 1, 3, 8, 21, 109–14, 127, 130, 134,

205, 207–12, 214, 253, 318, 431, 433, 474, 675–76, 682, 695, 806, 808
Sabbatino: II 41, 88; III 34, 681
Saladin: I 581, 605
Salimbene of Adam: I 287, 295, 316, 318, 425, 512, 590; II 20, 24, 66, 233, 237, 445; III 30, 36, 55, 145, 405, 415, 523–24, 526, 698, 791–92, 801, 825
Salimbene of Parma. See Salimbene of Adam
Sallust, Caius Crispus: I 198
Salvo: III 425
Samson: I 566; II 110
Samuel: II 733, 744; III 415
Sanguigna of Volterra: II 460
Saracen: I 74, 106, 229, 231, 394, 564, 581, 584, 600, 606, 608; II 146, 168, 381, 555, 600, 602, 726; III 37, 94, 119, 323, 383, 398, 605, 815–16, 855–56
Saraceno, Teobaldo: II 168
Sarah: II 400
Sassetti, A. Sacchetti: II 171
Satan: I 576; II 326; III 96, 100, 410, 647, 810
Saturn: I 512
Saul: II 752
Saul. See also Paul, St.: II 245–46
Savelli, Cencio. See also Honorius III: II 105
Sbaraglia, Giovanni G.: III 434
Sbaralea, Joanne H.: I 558; II 400; III 294, 677, 802
Scalla: II 770
Schmidt, Margo: II 257
Schmitz, Philibert: II 530
Schmucki, Oktavian: I 5, 24–25, 31, 115, 264; II 5, 55, 119, 161, 171, 180–81, 185, 189, 286, 303, 306, 317, 361, 539, 770, 780; III 5, 64, 338
Schroeder, Herbert J.: I 76; II 133
Seneca: I 182, 191, 214, 218
Sensi, Mario: II 54, 103
Serapion: II 306
Servadeo of Urbino: III 636
Seth: III 422
Seubert, Xavier John: I 178
Shamgar: I 566
Shanahan, Gregory: I 5, 427; II 5, III 5
Shealthiel: II 731
Sheba, Queen of: III 486, 724
Sheehan, Maurice: II 5
Sherley-Price, Leo: III 213, 434
Short, William J.: I 3, 5, 11; II 3–5; III 3–5
Sibilla: I 301; II 452; III 71
Siccolo: III 680
Sieben, Hermann Josef: I 427; II 308
Siger of Brabant: III 892
Silano, Giulio: III 872
Silvester: I 15
Simeon: III 528, 637, 694–95

Simon of Assisi: III 28, 35–36, 538–40, 633, 635
Simon Peter. See also Peter, St.: I 329, 364
Simon, St.: III 691–92
Simon the Englishman: I 363, 367
Simon the Just: I 295, 568; III 695
Simone: II 770
Simone De Bardi: III 880
Simone of the Countess: III 376
Simone Puzarelli. See Puzarelli, Simone
Sirach: I 124; II 509, 512, 517–20, 522, 524, 723, 726, 739–40, 755–56, 763, 813
Smith, Aloysius: III 212
Smith, Bradford P.: II 196
Soldanerio: III 28, 34–36
Solignac, Aime: II 586; III 147
Solomon: I 125, 511, 585; II 512, 734, 744, 746, 757–58; III 92, 385, 649, 769, 882
Solomon of the Marches: III 151
Solvi, Daniele: III 212, 318
Southern, Richard: I 192
Spaapen, Bernard: III 147
Spoelberch, Willliam: II 485–88
Stanislao da Campagnola: I 31; II 65, 398, 486, 488, 506–07; III 19, 31, 212, 214, 253
Stefano di Casa Nova: II 636
Stephen, St.: II 743; III 185, 793–96
Stephen Langton. See Langton, Stephen
Stephen of Bourbon: II 787–89
Stephen of Narbonne: III 37
Stephen of Saint-Thibery: III 37
Stevens, John: III 872
Stiegman, Emero: II 308, 346, 532
Strabo: I 429
Strayer, Joseph R.: I 318; III 872
Suetonius: I 235
Sulamite: I 548
Sulpicius Severus: I 14, 180, 183, 195, 202, 221, 236, 244, 277, 285–86; II 244–45, 553
Sumption, Jonathan: II 73, 136
Surius: II 763
Suyskens, Cornelius: I 21; II 32
Sybil: II 772
Sylvester: II 14, 32, 38–39, 86–87, 214–16, 256, 318–20, 401, 544–45, 574, 623, 638, 692–93, 795; III 33, 87, 176, 246, 431, 435–36, 438, 468–69, 567, 569, 591–94, 688–89, 874, 885

T

Taddeo d'Alderotto: III 889
Talar, C. J. T.: III 212
Tanner, Norman: III 741
Tassi, Luigi: III 434
Tebaldo of Arezzo: III 808
Teobaldo Saraceno: II 168
Terentius: I 430
Terracini, Benvenuto A.: III 210, 212
Terzi, Arduino: III 479

Thaddeus: III 692–93
Thode, Henry: I 22, 30
Theodore II: II 785
Theodore of Cyrus: I 197
Thomas, St.: I 424; II 646; III 687–88
Thomas a'Kempis: III 432
Thomas Aquinas, St.: II 25, 496; III 415, 786, 789, 881–82, 887, 890, 892
Thomas Becket, St.: I 424, 510; II 491
Thomas Gallus: II 500, 526
Thomas of Canterbury. See Thomas Becket, St.
Thomas of Capua: I 14, 311–12, 314–18, 331, 342, 344, 353; II 636; III 18, 698
Thomas of Celano: I 1, 3, 7–8, 11–12, 14–15, 17–19, 21, 23, 26–27, 29, 32, 35–36, 40, 58, 87, 95, 166, 169, 171–76, 178–80, 182–84, 187, 189–91, 196, 198, 201–04, 206–07, 209–10, 214–15, 218–19, 221, 230–31, 238, 243, 247, 251–53, 255–56, 258–59, 264, 270, 278, 282, 290, 292, 294–96, 311–14, 316–17, 319, 347, 356, 358, 363–67, 371–73, 375–78, 380–81, 383–84, 388–89, 392, 400, 406, 410, 413, 415–16, 423–26, 435, 449, 454, 461–62, 473, 484, 486, 500, 503–05, 514, 526–27, 565, 596; II 1, 3, 8, 11–12, 14–21, 24, 26–28, 32, 35, 38, 48, 61–64, 89, 114–15, 117–18, 129–30, 143, 231, 233–37, 242–43, 245–46, 248, 250–06, 264, 267–68, 270, 272, 277, 282, 284, 286–88, 290, 294–96, 298, 307–08, 318, 322, 330–01, 345, 382, 387–88, 395, 397–400, 403, 405–06, 408–10, 419, 427–28, 447, 467, 471–72, 475, 481, 485–86, 490, 497, 500, 502–03, 505, 528, 531, 539, 551, 554, 560–01, 563, 578, 596, 633, 647, 659–60, 686, 770, 782, 784–85, 837; III 13, 16, 18, 20–22, 27, 29–31, 34, 53, 58, 77, 112, 117, 137, 142–43, 207–08, 210, 214, 229, 253, 264, 277, 293, 376, 380, 393, 396, 408, 431, 441, 455, 462, 470, 472, 486, 510, 661, 675, 697, 727, 796, 802, 817, 821, 824, 832–33, 837
Thomas of Eccleston: I 32, 35, 317, 328; II 14–15, 18–19, 23, 26, 61, 64, 66, 471, 774; III 22, 54, 117, 393, 486, 796, 825, 827
Thomas of Pavia: III 791–93, 795–96
Thomas of Split: II 807; III 500
Thomas of Spoleto: II 265
Thomson, Williel R.: I 179, 558, 564
Tillard, Jean-Marie R.: II 345
Timothy: II 510, 513, 517–18, 735
Tinsley, Lucy: III 147
Tisiphone: I 440
Titus: II 525
Tobias: III 804
Tomassini, Giovanni: I 29
Tommaso: II 770

Tommaso of Pofi: II 425, 659
Toschi, Augusto: III 362
Tosi, Gianna: III 434
Towsend, David: I 427
Trajan: II 515
Trasmondo Anibaldi: II 465
Trexler, Richard C.: II 80, 83
Tristan: III 320
Trotemen: I 423
Tuchmann, Barbara: III 20, 345
Tugwell, Simon: II 785
Turk, James R.: II 196

U

Ubaldo of Gubbio: III 883
Ubertina of Poggibonsi: II 432
Ubertino da Casale. See also Umbertino of Cassale: I 526; II 26, 113, 116, 204; III 1, 3, 8, 12, 15–18, 22, 111, 139, 141–147, 156, 160, 162, 166, 183, 187, 193, 199, 201–03, 207, 266, 318, 376–77, 416, 422, 545, 557, 674, 768, 777–78, 815, 880–01, 884, 891–92
Ubertino of Rivarolo Canavese: II 680
Ugo: III 377
Ugolino: III 642
Ugolino Boniscambi of Montegiorgio: III 1, 3, 9, 16, 117, 393, 427, 430–34, 440, 455, 457–59, 462, 486, 491, 537–38, 540, 546, 558, 566
Ugolino Brunforte of Sarnano: III 434
Ugolino of Monte Santa Maria: III 430, 433
Ugono de Leto: II 770
Ulysses: I 455
Umbertino of Cassale. See also Ubertino da Casale: I 19, 29, 32, 116, 124
Umberto Cosmo: II 167
Umile: III 643–44
Urban IV: II 399, 747, 812; III 64, 824
Uriah: I 368; III 892
Uribe, Fernando: I 427

V

Vacant, Albert: II 23; III 112
Vagliani, A. Paravacini: II 779
van Asseldonk, Optatus: I 24
van Corstanje, Auspicius: I 124, 527
van den Ingh, T. S. G. A. M.: II 196
van Dijk, Stephen J. P.: I 317–18, 367
van Dijk, Willibroad: I 27
van Leeuwen, Bertulf P.: II 38
van Ortroy, Francesco: I 23, 30; II 62, 65; III 110, 113
van Slyke, Daniel: III 5
Varty, E. K. C.: III 320
Vauchez, Andre: I 25; II 24, 419, 472, 505, 770, 779–80; III 663
Vaughan, Richard: I 596

Vellekoop, K.: I 179
Venantius Fortunatus: I 294; II 320
Verde of Volterra: II 460
Vereecke, L.: III 54
Vergil: I 426–27, 429–30, 440, 442, 444–45, 453, 455, 461, 463, 470–71, 473, 482, 484–85, 488–89, 491, 503–04, 509, 512–13, 515, 517; II 253, 466; III 79
Veritas: III 51
Verlag, Patmos: II 507
Vian, Nello: I 28; II 116
Victor, St.: III 892
Victorinus, St.: II 72
Vidal, Jaime: I 5; II 5; III 5
Villa: I 307; II 453; III 73
Vincent, St.: III 185
Vincent the Donatist: II 794
Vind, Matthew: I 466
Virgil. See Vergil
von Aaw, Lidya: III 396
von Hase, Karl: I 22, 30
Voorvelt, Gebhard C. P.: II 38
Vorreux, Damien: I 28, 31

W

Wadding, Luke: I 21, 37, 58, 60, 287, 316, 318; II 41, 485, 487–88, 771; III 17, 25, 29, 34–35, 37, 54–55, 330, 448–49, 474, 519, 529, 663–64, 677, 741, 832
Wagner, F.: I 594
Waitz, G.: III 824
Walfried: I 494
Walker, J. Hazelden: I 317–18
Walsh, Kilian: II 308, 346, 519, 565, 597, 733, 752, 800; III 533
Walter of Brienne: I 185
Walter of Gisburn: III 830
Ward, Benedicta: II 259, 398, 419
Warner, Keith: I 5, 26; II 5; III 5

Weavers, Mark: II 5
Weis, J. E.: I 367
Welter, J. Th.: I 591
White, T. H.: II 315
Wilfrid, St.: I 197
William: III 36, 810
William Marshal. See Marshal, William
William of Bayonne: III 57
William of England: III 28, 62, 693–94
William of Middleton: II 495
William of Rome: III 805
William of Saint-Amour: I 524, 527; II 496, 508, 737
William of Saint Thierry: I 203; II 303
William of Tyre: I 605, 609
William the Great: I 226
Williams, Ann: III 19
Winters, William H.: II 5
Wolff, Ruth: II 507
Workman, Hyacinth: I 317
Wright, Frederick: II 733, 741

X

Xerxes: II 800

Y

Yates, Philippe: III 5

Z

Zachary: I 314, 337
Zas Friz de Col, Rossano: II 532
Zebedee: III 685
Zechariah: I 339; II 760
Zephaniah: II 518
Zerubbabel: II 504–05, 731, 749
Zimmerman, Odo John: I 185; II 278
Zinn, Grover A.: I 282, 568; II 506, 541
Ziolkowski, Jan: I 427

Index of Places

of texts in *The Saint* (I), *The Founder* (II), and *The Prophet* (III)

A

Abruzzi: I 171; III 663
Acquasparta. See also Aquasparta: III 891
Acre: I 580, 585
Adriatic Sea: I 229; III 88
Africa: I 230, 264; II 496
Akon: II 375
Albano: II 496; III 31
Alessandria: II 298, 802; III 50, 846
Alife: II 438, 481, 667
Allois, friary: III 25
Alps: I 76, 192, 499; II 56, 105, 122, 740; III 222, 559
Alviano: I 235, 397, 491; II 412, 624, 783, 801; III 860
Amandola: III 430
Amiens: II 244
Amiterno: II 456, 464, 679
Anagni: I 174, 575; II 448, 672, 781
Ancona, Custody: III 430, 528, 555, 637, 639
Ancona, Marche: I 229–30, 237, 248, 304–05, 394, 399–400, 411, 435, 473, 482, 484, 501–02; II 40, 66, 87, 167, 204, 237, 282, 300, 316–17, 415, 426, 435, 579, 600–01, 661, 663, 665, 707; III 34, 318, 375, 429, 432, 434, 494, 500, 502, 526–27, 545, 548, 615, 635–36, 702, 828
Antioch: II 515; III 682
Antrodoco: II 464, 679
Apennines: I 192
Apulia: I 185–88, 281, 301, 371–73, 434–36, 580; II 36, 70–71, 75, 245, 292, 404, 423, 430, 451, 466, 533, 579, 654, 656, 679, 712, 797, 801, 805; III 72, 100, 494, 801, 869
Aquasparta. See also Acquasparta: III 35
Aquila: I 171; II 456–57
Aquitaine: III 25–26, 30, 37, 57, 77, 105, 673, 676–78, 694, 715
Ara Coeli: II 496
Aragon: III 768
Arce: I 67; II 67
Arezzo: I 172, 238, 303, 404, 493; II 203, 214–15, 318, 431, 437, 444, 451–52, 574, 628, 666, 670, 783, 795; III 72, 218, 370, 459, 584, 792, 807, 808
Arles: II 557, 620, 700; III 694

Arno: III 885
Arpino: II 432; III 73
Ascesi. See also Assisi: III 567
Ascoli Piceno: I 236–37, 493; II 435, 665, 783; III 25, 29, 803, 812
Asia: I 264; II 496; III 150, 152
Assisi. See also Ascesi: I 26, 45, 110, 113, 172–73, 179, 182, 185, 187, 189, 192, 195, 197, 201, 203–04, 220, 228, 258, 264, 274, 277, 279, 284, 293–94, 297, 301, 312, 317, 319, 323, 329, 363, 370–71, 373, 378, 386, 392, 414, 416–19, 425, 429, 434, 442, 450, 452, 458, 461–62, 470, 478, 485, 501, 512, 514–15, 518, 564, 595, 597, 602–03; II 12, 34, 36–37, 39, 41, 43, 49, 66–71, 74–75, 78, 84–85, 88–90, 95, 99–100, 109, 114, 120, 128–29, 140, 154–55, 157, 178, 181, 183, 187, 243, 248, 252–53, 267, 273, 281, 285–86, 297–98, 319, 333, 347, 368, 388, 390–91, 403, 429, 436–37, 452, 455, 465, 474, 476–77, 503, 530–31, 533, 536–37, 540, 544, 551, 555, 570, 583, 623, 644, 646–48, 660, 673–74, 684, 691–92, 716–17, 770, 777, 782, 784, 791, 809–10; III 12, 16, 34–35, 38, 46, 51, 67, 70, 72, 84, 87, 91, 102, 119–20, 123, 132, 165, 183, 207, 217, 220, 228–29, 236, 239–40, 253, 255, 260, 263, 272, 275, 278, 297, 298, 300–01, 305, 307, 318, 349, 352–53, 357–58, 360, 369, 371–72, 404, 416, 429, 431, 436–37, 466–67, 471–72, 474, 476–77, 502, 504–05, 507–09, 511, 516, 554, 556, 561, 567, 575, 590–91, 595, 597, 615, 617, 620–21, 633, 646, 661, 663, 673, 676, 678, 680, 682, 694, 699, 702, 710, 713, 727, 733, 738, 741, 765, 768, 796, 800–01, 804, 806, 810, 813, 819, 823, 826–27, 830, 833, 835–36, 840, 863, 869, 871, 874, 883
Augsburg: I 593
Ausonia. See also Italy: I 481
Austria: II 819; III 112
Avignon: I 19, 37; III 12–13, 17, 109–10, 375–76, 662–63, 674, 768, 789–90, 819
Avranches: I 423

B

Babylon: II 504, 602; III 15, 151–52, 383, 398, 490, 605, 798
Bagnara: II 202
Baltimore: II 38
Barcelona: II 65, 76, 83, 107; III 111–12
Bari: II 292, 579; III 100
Barletta: II 433, 663
Bar-sur-Aube: I 192
Basilicata: III 376
Begnara: II 198; III 272
Belgium: I 37, 39; II 485; III 112, 145
Belvoir: I 596
Benevento: II 390, 419, 655; III 870
Besse: III 25
Bethlehem: I 196, 255–56, 405–06; II 14, 269, 411, 610
Bettona: II 178; III 353, 467, 591
Bevagna: I 234, 237, 396, 488; II 323, 411, 450, 624, 627, 706, 783; III 432, 469, 593, 795, 860
Beziers: III 812–13
Biscay, Bay: III 888
Bohemia: II 472
Bologna: I 171, 312, 590; II 131, 282, 286, 627, 807–08; III 35–36, 123, 253, 259, 406, 416, 444–45, 500, 575–76, 614, 694, 706, 713, 827, 829, 831, 889
Bominaco: III 663
Bordeaux: I 427; III 13
Borgo. See San Sepolcro and Casale, Monte
Borgo San Sepulcro. See San Sepolcro and Casale, Monte
Bosor: I 542; III 165
Bourges: I 427
Bovara: II 167; III 304
Brabant: III 60
Brescia: II 335
Britain See also England: I 435; II 23
Britany: III 419
Brittoni: III 35
Brunforte: III 430, 537, 540, 644
Burgundy: III 595, 694

C

Cahors: III 30, 37, 77, 105, 661, 663
Cairo: II 602
Calabria: III 37
Calaroga. See Caleruega
Caleruega: II 148; III 888
Calvi: II 440, 669
Calydon: I 512
Cambio Catozzi, church: III 802
Camerino: I 301; II 452; III 72, 150, 452, 558
Campagna. See also Campania, Terra di Lavoro: II 425, 442, 659
Campania. See also Campagna, Terra di Lavoro: II 442, 446, 449, 671, 677; III 891

Campiglia: II 307, 580
Campo: III 802
Cana: III 692
Canaan: III 144, 469
Cannara: III 469, 592–3
Canterbury: II 491; III 58
Capitanata: II 426
Capua: I 278, 324; II 422, 460, 480, 657; III 70
Carcassone, church: III 813
Carceri, hermitage: II 67, 286; III 505
Casa Gualdi: I 195
Casale: III 141, 891
Casale, Monte, hermitage. See also San Sepolcro: I 526; II 221, 376, 573; III 310, 431, 495, 609
Casamari, abbey: I 580
Caserta, province: II 438
Cassino, Monte: I 171
Castel San Gimigniano: II 430, 662
Castile: I 595; II 148, 407, 442, 466, 653, 797; III 677, 888
Castro dei Volsci: II 449, 671
Catalonia: II 653
Ceccano: II 446, 674
Celano: II 173, 178; II 138, 304, 409, 420, 660; III 94, 280, 380, 388, 408
"Celle" di Cortona. See also Cortona: I 274, 414; II 139, 198; III 281
Ceperani: III 73
Ceuta: II 400
Chalons-sur-Marne: I 601
Champagne: I 192, 194; II 442
Chartres: III 57
Chester: III 54
Chiascio, river: III 883
Chitignano: III 802
Chiusi: III 453, 802–03
Cibotella: III 431
Cibotolo, friary: III 111
Cibottola, hermitage: II 67
Cisterna: II 446, 647; III 74
Cisterna di Latina. See Cisterna
Città della Pieve: I 239, 306, 405, 494; II 450, 628, 673; III 73, 111
Città di Castello: I 242, 404, 496; II 437, 456, 462, 628; III 141
Coccorano: I 300
Collazzone, monastery: III 872
Colle. See Collestrada
Collestrada: II 69, 140; III 281
Collis: III 809
Cologne: I 171, 364, 594–95; III 61
Condigliano: II 218
Constantinople: II 429, 661, 785; III 25, 54–55, 804, 892
Cori: II 457, 681
Corneto: II 427, 661

Cortona. See also "Celle" di Cortona: I 235, 264, 514
Cosenza: II 431
Cosmedin: III 402
Couvent des Cordeliers: III 141
Crete: I 512
Crimea: I 513
Croatia: II 439, 807
Crowland Abbey: I 424
Cuenca: III 677
Cyprus: II 14, 347; III 295, 442

D

Dalmatia. See also Illyria, Slavonia: I 481; II 439, 707, 807; III 803
Damascus: I 608
Damietta: I 58, 231, 233, 482, 485–87, 580–81, 584, 605–06, 608–09; II 265, 602, 614; III 93, 839, 864
dell'Olmo, Monte: II 465, 679
Detroit: III 663
Dubrovnik: III 112

E

Egypt: I 204, 231, 329, 342, 344, 546, 580–81, 584, 605, 608–09; II 138, 180, 293, 602, 620, 682, 717, 735, 742, 752, 757; III 45, 189, 267, 397, 399, 410
Emmaus: II 582; III 186
Empyrean: III 885
England See also Britain: I 87, 166, 174, 328, 423–24, 519, 590, 596; II 14, 363, 812; III 15, 53–54, 58, 63, 145, 397, 429, 663, 693
Erycinum: II 431
Europe: I 585; II 295, 436, 496; III 11–12, 14–15, 888

F

Falerone: III 430, 500
Fano: I 299, 303, 306; II 432, 454, 459, 675; III 71, 73
Farfa, monastery: II 298
Fermo: III 318, 430, 529, 535, 540, 542, 544, 635, 649, 653
Firenze. See Florence
Flanders: I 435; III 54
Florence: I 246, 499, 590; II 43, 90, 214, 216, 452; III 14, 72, 134, 141, 212, 246, 309, 457, 459, 467, 584, 591, 663, 682, 764, 808, 813–14, 880–81, 891
Foggia: I 301
Foligno: I 189, 277, 299, 301, 373, 441, 508; II 36, 68, 77, 203, 454, 458, 536, 782, 784; III 69, 218, 243, 369, 472, 477, 597
Fondi: II 348
Fons Palumbae. See Palumma

Fonte Colombo. See also Palumma: II 131, 171, 189, 196, 226, 558; III 111, 197, 232, 313, 359, 363, 416
Fonte Columbo. See Fonte Colombo
Forano: III 526, 637
France: I 37, 166, 174, 246, 290, 363–64, 366, 499, 559, 579, 591; II 14, 23, 68, 182, 194, 214, 216, 281, 375, 442, 489, 556, 693, 725, 752, 782, 808–09, 811; III 15, 25, 29, 31, 34, 37, 109, 145, 246, 283, 309–10, 409, 431, 462–63, 465, 517–18, 587–89, 625, 677, 683, 685, 697, 764, 812, 890
Frankfurt am Main: I 363
Frascati: I 585; II 811
Fribourg: II 65, 76, 83

G

Gaeta: II 348, 429, 432, 481, 625, 662, 705
Gagliano. See Gagliano-Aterno
Gagliano-Aterno: II 409, 678
Galete: II 466
Galicia: III 572
Ganges: III 883
Gargano, Monte. See also Saint Michael the Archangel, shrine: I 301; II 101, 390, 430, 450, 644, 672, 716
Gembloux, abbey: III 141
Genoa: I 172–73; II 15, 61, 63, 65–66, 239, 471, 774, 790, 827
Germany: I 37, 171, 174, 178, 185, 264, 292, 324, 363–64, 526; II 14, 23, 56, 105, 424, 472, 658, 782, 808; III 36, 54, 112, 116, 145, 409, 419, 429, 714, 805, 837
Gers: III 677
Gisburn: III 830
Greccio: I 253–55, 307, 397, 405–06, 492, 526; II 174–75, 177, 227–28, 237, 269–70, 277, 287, 289, 355, 410, 412, 414, 592, 594, 610, 619, 706, 783, 793; III 104, 151, 232, 345, 558
Greece: I 172, 492, 512, 665; III 55, 375, 419, 782–83, 827, 829
Gualdo: III 883
Gubbio: I 195, 237, 240, 299–301, 304, 323, 376, 403, 456, 494; II 321, 432, 452, 459–61, 539, 590, 674, 782, 784; III 69–70, 72–73, 104, 432, 434, 482, 601, 603, 851, 883

H

Hades: I 517
Hales Owen: III 63
Halle: I 591
Hatay: III 682
Heaven: III 501, 514
Heisterbach, abbey: I 594
Hell: III 383

Hierapolis: II 73
Hill of Paradise. See also Paradise: III 67
Holland: I 37; III 112
Holy Land: I 232; II 136, 266, 282, 434, 602, 664; III 518, 686, 809
Hungary: II 56, 105, 819

I

Iberian peninusula: III 519
Ile-de-France: I 246; II 375
Illyria. See also Dalmatia, Solvonia: I 481
Imola: II 342, 574; III 154, 839, 857
Ireland: III 782–83
Iseo: II 445, 673; III 829
Island. See Place of the Island
Isola Maggiore: I 235; III 448
Israel: I 138, 147, 149, 151, 186, 262, 276, 341, 346, 372, 544, 566; II 129, 159, 189, 318, 399, 410, 415, 422, 757, 819; III 129, 203, 318, 343, 399, 410, 415
Italy. See also Ausonia: I 37, 56, 107, 171, 174, 229, 235, 292, 322, 378, 395, 436, 480–81, 578, 593, 599–600; II 23, 65, 101, 282, 390, 442, 471, 481, 707, 782, 811; III 13–14, 20, 29, 31, 82, 109, 127–28, 141, 145, 200, 362, 376, 431, 457, 491, 501, 663, 694, 697, 768, 793, 802, 825, 832, 872–73, 879

J

Jenne: II 779
Jericho: I 538; III 163
Jerusalem: I 197, 294, 351, 532, 538; II 14, 288, 317, 330, 347, 378, 720, 735; III 11, 55–56, 151, 163, 191, 201, 501, 686, 745

K

Kent: I 590

L

Lagny: I 192
Lago Trasimeno. See Trasimene, Lake
Lake Perugia. See Perugia, Lake
Languedoc: III 890
La Rochelle: III 63
La Sainte Chapelle: II 812
Lateran Basilica. See also Saint John Lateran: II 256, 266, 317, 342, 548, 690, 785–87; III 88, 682, 844
Lauterberg, abbey: I 591, 593
LaVerna, hermitage: I 36, 39, 108, 176–77, 238, 242, 263, 410, 526; II 108, 191, 226, 280, 472–73, 498, 530, 593, 618, 630, 634, 701, 709, 711; III 141, 193, 318, 346, 365, 433–34, 452–55, 529, 560–61, 649, 652–53, 655–56, 667, 687, 801–03, 866, 874, 885

Lazio: II 446; III 664
"Le Celle" di Cortona. See "Celle" di Cortona
Le Colonne: II 423, 658
Legnano: III 35
Le Mans: II 442, 677
Lemmos: II 281
Lentini: II 428, 661
Leon: I 595
Lerida. See also Llerda: II 653, 712
Le Simon: II 676
Lethe, river: I 517
Levant: II 602
Liège: I 578–79, 585
Limigiano. See Limisiano
Limisiano: II 172, 347
Limoges: II 786
Lisbon: I 107, 225; III 519
Llerda. See also Lerida: II 653
Lombardy: I 174, 580, 602–03; II 216, 286, 298, 568, 707, 781, 787–88, 802; III 50, 259, 402, 446, 576, 791, 825, 846
Lomousin, friary: III 25
London: III 764
Longhezza: III 872
Louvain: I 24; II 27
Lucca: II 173, 273; III 352
Lyons: I 593; II 18, 779, 787; III 738, 741, 803, 828–29

M

Maastricht: I 427
Macedonia: II 665
Macerata, province: III 527
Machilone: II 192, 306, 665; III 282
Maeos: I 513
Magdeburg: I 363, 367, 591–92
Manfredonia: II 430
Mansura: I 486
Mantua: III 37
Marano, Monte: II 419, 655
Marcerata, province: III 544
March of Treviso. See Treviso
Marche(s) of Ancona. See Ancona, Marche
Marches, province: II 61, 64; III 16, 36, 109–10, 150–51, 211, 377, 429, 433, 526, 535, 537–38, 540, 544–46, 555, 639–40, 642–43, 649, 803
Marignano: II 67; III 583, 691, 807, 810, 812
Marittima: II 446, 455, 674; III 74
Marro. See also Morro: III 636
Marseille: II 391, 481; III 36
Marsi: II 138, 304
Maryland: II 38
Massa: II 376, 451, 573, 677; III 411, 458, 536, 593, 653–54
Massa Fermana: III 430
Massa San Pietro. See also Massa Trabaria: II 436, 666

Massa Trabaria. See also Massa San Pietro: II 666; III 411
Mauritania. See Morocco
Mediterranean Sea: II 434; III 360
Mendesic branch of the Nile: I 486
Metz: I 172; II 19, 471, 774
Middle East: I 45, 56, 58
Milan: I 578–79; III 35, 132
Mogliano: III 430, 535–37, 542, 653–54, 656
Montagna Nera, monastery: III 682
Monte: II 431
Monte Canale. See Saint Francis in Monte Canale, chapel
Montecasale. See Casale, Monte
Monte Casale. See Casale, Monte
Monte Cassino. See Cassino, Monte
Montefeltro: III 452
Monte Gargano. See Gargano, Monte
Montelabate: III 664
Monte Marano. See Marano, Monte
Monte Mogliano. See Mogliano
Montenero: I 299; II 459, 479, 784; III 69
Montepulciano: II 756
Monte Rainerio. See Fonte Colombo
Monte Rubbiano. See Rubbiano, Monte
Monte San Giuliano. See San Giuliano, Monte
Monte Santa Maria: III 430, 433
Monte Sant'Angelo. See Gargano, Monte
Monte San Vicino. See San Vicino, Monte
Monte Subasio. See Subasio, Monte
Monticelli, monastery: III 591
Montino: III 556, 646
Montis Sereni. See Lauterberg, abbey
Montpellier: II 23; III 813
Mount La Verna. See LaVerna
Mount Parnassus: I 460
Mount Sinai: III 111, 128
Mount Subasio. See Subasio, Monte
Mount Subiaco: II 779
Morocco: I 225, 230, 322, 395, 484, 563; II 400, 416, 601, 757
Morro. See also Marro: III 527
Munchen: III 837

N

Naples: I 110; II 282, 348, 429, 431, 447, 670; III 430, 768, 791
Narbonne: I 17, 332; II 21, 24, 471–72, 495, 497, 503, 528, 774; III 377, 419, 750, 758–59, 765, 813
Narcia: II 455, 674
Narni: I 239–41, 298–303, 323, 403, 494; II 433, 450, 452, 454, 458, 460–61, 479–80, 627, 674, 783–84; III 71–72, 396
Navarre: II 442; III 62
Nazareth: I 390, 477; II 14, 700; III 411
Nettuno: II 427
New Haven: III 664

Nicosia: II 453; III 72
Nile River. See also Phatniticum channel, Mendesic branch: I 486; II 602
Nocera: II 198, 298, 421, 583, 656, 771, 804; III 272, 883
Norcia: II 455, 674; III 70
Notre Dame: I 318

O

Oberaltaich: III 837
Offida: III 127, 183, 430, 522, 637–38, 694
Ognisanti, friary: III 134, 212
Olignies: I 602
Olite: II 442, 677
Olomouc: II 472
Orient: II 265; III 883
Orte: I 213, 384; II 461, 627; III 50
Ortona: II 434
Orvieto: II 784–85; III 767
Osimo: I 248–49, 399
Osma: II 148
Ostia: I 127, 199, 243, 245, 267, 270, 413, 499, 513, 603; II 55–57, 83, 103–07, 148, 176, 184, 189, 200, 216, 224, 261, 286, 288, 296, 342, 344, 457, 572, 582, 626, 660, 681, 763, 797, 814; III 47, 114, 133, 155, 215, 259, 271, 273–74, 289, 309, 311, 313, 339, 363, 390, 476, 709, 722, 794, 801, 824, 834, 859, 861, 864
Outremer: II 434, 706; III 782–83
Oxford: III 54, 58, 113, 663

P

Padua: I 107; II 400, 811; III 25, 210, 519, 791, 804–05
Palazzo Veneto. See Veneto, Palazzo
Palencia: II 466, 679; III 677
Palestine: II 602
Palumma. See also Fonte Colombo: III 128
Panzo: I 220; III 680
Papal States: I 292; II 348, 779; III 13
Paradise. See also Hill of Paradise: III 581, 601, 609, 611, 641, 644, 653, 715, 769
Paris: I 13, 166, 195, 246, 290, 317, 363–65, 524, 526, 559, 578, 590; II 15, 18, 20, 22, 33, 472, 495–96, 498, 501, 504, 508, 517, 677, 718, 728, 731, 735, 747, 759, 771, 786–87, 811, 819; III 12, 19, 29, 31, 54, 58–59, 63, 78, 149, 376, 409, 544, 673, 678, 682, 685, 699, 727, 737, 796, 812–13, 816, 880
Parma: I 412, 456, 512; II 625; III 104, 150, 556, 647, 791
Parnassus. See Mount Parnassus
Pavia: III 791, 793
Penna. See Penna di San Giovanni
Penna di San Giovanni: III 430, 544, 548, 640, 643

Persiceto: III 738, 805, 829
Perugia: I 16, 166, 293, 307, 418, 565, 569,
    578–79, 595, 602, 604; II 28, 31, 56, 67,
    69–70, 105, 113–15, 118, 140, 143, 178,
    243, 270–71, 305, 313, 375, 391, 453, 477,
    608, 806; III 35, 73, 111–13, 183, 209–10,
    281, 353, 449, 476–77, 517–18, 561,
    578–79, 595–97, 625, 685–86, 709, 784,
    786, 807–09, 883
Perugia, Lake: I 235, 397; II 414, 592; III 448,
    578
Peschici: II 429–30
Peterborough Abbey: I 424, 519
Pharsalis: III 884
Phatniticum channel of the Nile: I 486
Philadelphia: III 156, 191
Phrygia: II 73
Piaroco. See Piratro
Piazza: II 430
Piazza Venezia. See Venezia, Piazza
Pietramala: II 466, 679
Piglio nella Campania: II 442, 677
Piratio. See Piratro
Piratro: II 162; III 830
Pisa: I 126; II 22, 348, 435, 443, 445, 503,
    808; III 676, 764, 825, 828
Place of the Island: III 579
Po River: II 568, 707; III 98
Pofi: II 425, 449, 659, 671
Poggibonsi: II 432; III 70, 72
Poggio Bustone: II 333
Poitiers: I 294; II 676
Poland: I 37
Pomarico: II 423, 656
Pomereto: II 805
Ponte della Trave: III 527
Ponte San Giovanni: II 69
Porta Sole: III 883
Portiuncula, see Saint Mary of the Angels
Portugal: I 107, 225; III 145, 519, 892
Postignano: II 178; III 353
Potenza: II 404–05, 654, 712
Prato. See Piratro
Provence: I 225, 390; II 20, 783, 786; III 36,
    109, 377, 545, 641, 694, 789, 830
Provins: I 192
Purgatory: III 396, 522, 534, 541, 547, 638,
    642, 652–53, 655, 715, 880

R

Ragusa: II 424, 658
Ravenna: III 880
Recanati: III 641
Red Sea: III 399
Rete: II 431
Rheims: I 578
Rhine Valley: I 363, 595
Riccardina: III 831

Rieti, city : I 267, 292, 413, 511, 558, 563–65;
    II 167–68, 170–71, 174, 189, 192, 197,
    218, 274, 276, 307, 330, 412, 416, 583,
    615, 702; III 94, 101, 128, 197, 199, 232,
    270, 282, 313, 352, 359–60, 363, 478–79,
    598–99, 810, 862
Rieti, diocese: II 461, 627
Rieti, Lake: I 235, 397; II 355, 412, 434, 592,
    665
Rieti, province: II 410, 634, 711, 727; III 268
Rieti Valley: I 204–05, 207
Rimini: III 520–21, 632–33
Rivarolo Canavese: II 680
Rivo Torto: I 195, 201, 220, 386; II 99, 149,
    195, 201; III 217, 235, 275, 278, 284
Rocca Campiglia: II 307
Rocca di Brizio: II 220; III 285
Rocca di Chiusi: III 803
Romagna: II 342; III 37, 452
Romania: I 172; II 14, 436, 665, 671, 436,
    449, 467, 665, 671; III 782–83, 807
Rome: I 204–05, 210–11, 213, 245, 292, 312,
    317, 383, 386, 470, 498, 585, 593,
    597–600, 603; II 14–15, 39, 48–49, 65, 73,
    95, 97–98, 101, 105, 116, 121–22, 136,
    148, 184, 224, 247, 261, 282, 311, 316,
    326, 417, 419, 421, 429, 438, 440, 481,
    496, 515, 591, 652, 657, 667–68, 675, 756,
    762, 786, 789, 791, 797, 805–06, 811; III
    13, 20, 35–36, 83, 85, 111–13, 133–34,
    207, 222, 289, 295, 311, 333, 360, 396,
    462, 464, 472–73, 588, 595, 666, 682, 686,
    719, 728, 792, 805–06, 813, 827–28, 839,
    844, 859
Rouen: III 63
Rubbiano, Monte: III 653

S

Sabina: I 210, 470; II 96, 547; III 196, 390
Sabino: II 463, 679
Sahagun: II 466
Saint Albans, monastery: I 596, 599
Saint Anthony, hospice: II 548
Saint Basil, abbey: III 682
Saint Benedict, monastery: II 100, 154; III
    119, 236, 297, 820
Saint Clare, basilica/monastery: I 203; II
    773, 812; III 64, 67, 199, 516–517, 590,
    624, 795
Saint Cosmas, monastery: I 603
Saint Damian, see San Damiano
Saint Eleuterio, hermitage: II 218
Saint Francis, basilica : II 88, 424, 430, 443,
    451, 660, 705, 714, 777; III 12, 35, 55, 62,
    66, 298, 474, 504, 515, 626, 765, 806
Saint Francis, hermitage. See Fonte Co-
    lombo
Saint Francis in Monte Canale, chapel: II
    409

Saint Gall: II 490
Saint George, church: I 27, 35, 203, 286, 294–95, 315, 363, 419, 424, 518; II 647; III 67, 835
Saint Isidore, friary: I 595; II 65, 116; III 113, 126, 134, 207, 209, 295, 333
Saint Jacques, church: II 819
Saint James, church: III 572
Saint James, shrine. See also Santiago de Compostella: III 685
Saint John Lateran. See also Lateran Basilica: II 97; III 721
Saint Mark, church: III 681
Saint Mary of the Angels, church of the Portiuncula: I 76, 175, 195, 201–22, 231, 242, 249, 258, 274–75, 277, 329, 366, 378, 387, 395, 415, 458, 515, 562, 597; II 17, 39, 41–42, 45, 47, 51, 67, 76, 87–88, 93–94, 100–01, 104, 120, 125, 132, 137, 142, 154–55, 157, 162, 165–66, 175–76, 180, 196, 198, 202, 208, 210, 212–14, 217, 235, 256–58, 285, 288, 290–91, 297, 313, 324, 350, 357, 414, 418, 475, 540, 553, 557, 579, 591, 593, 608, 642, 700, 715, 749, 782, 798; III 35, 43, 57, 66, 110, 116–17, 119–21, 124, 131–32, 134, 169, 172, 210, 212, 220, 225, 236–37, 240, 242, 244, 247, 258, 260–61, 264, 266, 271, 275, 286–87, 297–300, 303, 315, 318, 328–30, 339, 346, 360, 371–72, 397, 399, 402, 434, 449, 458, 466–67, 472–73, 475, 486, 489, 508, 561, 579–80, 583, 590–91, 595, 604, 621, 693, 708–09, 714, 732, 799, 806–10, 830, 843, 883
Saint Mary of the Angles of Cesi di Terni, chapel: I 138
Saint Michael, church: I 580
Saint Michael the Archangel, shrine. See also Gargano, Monte: I 301; II 390, 454, 644, 674, 716
Saint Nicholas, church: II 544
Saint Peter, church: II 73, 167, 175, 235, 247, 540; III 83, 243, 304, 462, 464, 588, 719
Saint Peter at Fermo. See San Pietro at Fermo
Saint Peter of Bovara, church. See also Bovara: III 304
Saints Cosmas and Damian, church: II 435, 749–50
Salerno: II 431
San Antonio, college: III 792
San Benedetto dei Marsi. See Santa Sabina in San Benedetto dei Marsi
San Clemente: II 673; III 805
San Damiano, church/monastery: I 40, 45, 106, 115, 174–75, 189, 196, 199, 220, 284–85, 373, 377, 417, 441, 527; II 36, 38, 76–78, 81, 83–84, 86, 128–29, 184, 188, 233, 235, 249, 252, 290, 379, 476, 536,

540, 647, 686, 688, 749, 760, 773–74, 782, 792; III 84, 131, 136, 228–29, 318, 338, 346, 357, 431, 466–67, 478, 515–16, 590–91, 598, 626, 680, 690, 794–95, 841, 843, 845
San Fabiano: II 170; III 352, 479
San Facondo: II 466, 678
San Francesco al Prato, friary: II 31
San Francesco in Camerino: III 558
San Francesco in Ravenna: III 880
San Gemini: I 241, 403; II 455, 627
San Gemino: I 495
San Gimignano: II 439, 667
San Gimigniano, Castel. See Castel San Gimigniano
San Giorgio. See Saint George, church
San Giovanni: III 548, 643, 738, 805, 829
San Giovanni di Val dei Varri, convent: I 173
San Giuliano, Monte: II 431
San Giustina, abbey: II 811
San Giustino: II 313, 608
San Lazaro, leper hospital: I 195
San Leo. See Montefeltro
San Liberato, friary: III 430
San Marco, church: II 421, 657
San Nicolo, church: II 85; III 431, 437
San Pietro della Spina, church: I 201
San Pietro at Fermo: III 529, 649
San Quirico: II 580
San Rufino, cathedral: II 39, 154, 182, 241, 761; III 119, 297, 305, 437
San Rufino dell'Arce, leper hospital: I 195
San Salvatore delle Mura, leper hospital: I 195
San Salvatore delle Parenti, leper hospital: III 472
San Salvatore di Copersito, monastery: II 317
San Savino: III 810
San Sepolcro. See also Casale, Monte: II 221, 312, 606; III 102, 250, 310, 495, 609, 801–02, 808, 847
San Sepulchro, Borgo. See San Sepolcro
San Severino: I 249, 305, 399, 501; II 317, 429, 453, 556, 661, 675, 693, 798; III 527, 539, 634, 636
Santa Croce, friary and school: III 457, 813, 880
Santa Croce in Gerusalemme: II 224, 326, 575; III 141, 311
Santa Lucia: II 224; III 311, 809
Santa Maria, church: III 402
Santa Maria D'Aspro: III 376
Santa Matia della Foresta. See San Fabiano
Santa Maria del Vescovada, pro-cathedral: II 241
Santa Maria Maggiore: III 437
Sant'Angelo, monastery: III 680
Sant'Antonio, church: III 112

Santa Sabina in San Benedetto dei Marsi, church: II 138, 783
Sant'Eleuterio: II 218
Santiago, province: III 830
Santiago de Compostela. See aslo St. James, shrine: I 207–08, 230; II 47, 136; III 440–41, 443, 572, 685, 806
Santo Stefano: III 544, 640
Sant'Urbano, hermitage. See also Speco di Sant'Urbano: I 236, 398, 410; II 704, 783; III 862
San Verecondo, monastery: I 195; II 321, 590, 806–07; III 851
San Vicino, Monte: III 527
Saragossa: I 60
Saran. See Sarrant
Sarnano: II 62, 65, 68, 78, 83, 107; III 482, 537
Sarranno. See Sarrant
Sarrant : III 677–78, 714
Sarteano: II 286, 324, 562
Satriano: II 298, 583
Saxony: III 19, 544
Scipio: II 347
Scopleto: II 464
Scoppito: II 456, 680
Sens: I 559; II 808
Septizonium: II 122
Serano. See Sarrant
Serignan: III 812
Serranno. See Sarrant
Sessa: I 324; II 423, 481, 658
Sheba: III 486, 724
Shropshire: III 63
Sicily: I 292, 324, 580, 595; II 122, 316, 424, 428, 430–31, 444, 447, 453–54, 658, 674; III 553–54, 630, 768
Siena: I 274, 414, 513; II 139–40, 159, 161–62, 198, 268, 304, 307, 315, 335, 350, 356, 413–14, 465, 474, 580, 589, 591, 593, 613, 617, 756; III 95, 238, 262, 280, 296, 432, 459–60, 482, 485, 584, 701, 764
Signa: I 590
Sinai: II 558
Sion: I 534
Siracusa: II 428
Sirolo: III 528, 637
Slavonia. See also Dalmatia, Illyria: I 229, 394, 415, 600, 668; II 415, 439, 600, 668; III 494
Soffiano, friary: III 429–30, 537, 548, 643–5
Sora: II 432, 447, 452–54, 675; III 71, 73–74
Spain: I 37, 45, 58–59, 171, 174, 207, 229–30, 264, 395, 563; II 14, 23, 266, 361, 407, 416, 601, 653, 757; III 17, 46, 49, 62, 145, 441, 631, 674, 677, 686, 694, 826, 888, 892
Spalato, See also Spilt: II 807
Speco di Sant'Urbano. See also Sant'Urbano: III 396

Spello: I 301, 304; II 446, 452, 674; III 72, 477, 597
Speyer: I 171, 363–64
Split. See also Spalato: II 807
Spoleto: I 122, 221, 268, 292; II 36, 71, 282, 464, 540; III 36, 85, 243, 402, 477, 597, 810
Spoleto Valley: I 138, 182, 213–14, 234, 370, 384, 396, 429, 472–73; II 68, 155, 167, 216, 411, 414, 450, 550, 684, 691, 706, 809; III 36, 120, 246, 298, 304, 310, 441, 452, 465, 477, 571–2, 589, 596–97, 810, 860, 879
Starkenburg: I 427
Strada Francesca: III 472
Subasio, Monte: I 201, 429; II 100, 154, 286, 298; III 236, 297, 431, 468, 505–06, 619, 688, 883
Subiaco: III 376, 664
Sulmona: II 409
Suessa: II 805
Susa: II 680
Switzerland: I 37
Syria: I 204, 229, 231, 322, 394–95, 479, 609; II 14, 415, 600, 602; III 689, 783, 793, 795, 826

T

Tagliacozzo: I 173
Tamarit: II 663
Tarquinia. See Corneto
Terni: I 138; II 124, 339, 471, 481; III 224, 291
Terra di Lavoro. See also Campagna, Campania: II 442, 803; III 511, 840
Thebes: II 449, 671
Thrace: II 665
Thuringia: III 824
Tiber: I 242; III 885
Tivoli: II 304, 438, 441, 667, 669, 673; III 667, 669, 805
Todi: I 302–03; II 431, 433; III 36, 872
Toledo: I 563; II 266; III 677
Topino, river: III 883
Toscanella: I 239, 402, 494; II 627, 783
Toulouse: II 67, 97; III 37, 61, 673
Tournai: II 806
Tours: II 182, 442
Trameggiano: III 802
Trapani: II 431
Trasimene, Lake: I 235; III 448
Trasimeno, friary: III 429
Trave Bonati: III 527, 636
Trebio, leper hospital. See also Trevi: III 243
Trent: II 782
Trevi. See also Trebio: II 167, 328; III 243, 304
Treviso: II 216, 568, 707; III 494
Tripoli: I 230

Trois-Fontaines, abbey: I 601
Troy: II 122
Troyes: I 192
Tunis: I 230; II 381
Turkey: III 682
Tuscanella: II 461
Tuscany: I 174, 246, 269, 323, 580, 602–03; II 216, 402, 444, 465, 781, 809; III 109, 111, 432, 452–53, 791, 793, 830, 833, 880–81, 891
Tusculum. See Frascati
Tuy: I 595
Tyrrhenian Sea: II 429

U

Umbria: I 13, 26, 220, 371; II 54, 103, 111, 401, 471–72; III 429, 503, 664, 765, 872
Upsala: III 113
Urbino: III 527, 636
Ursperg, abbey: I 593

V

Valaiano: III 537
Valenciennes, friary: II 485
Vallingegno: I 195
Vallodolid: II 442
Valva: II 409, 678
Varazze: II 790
Velletri: I 270, 413; II 446; III 74
Veneto, Palazzo: II 421
Venetzia, Piazza: II 421
Venice: II 216, 592; III 14, 681

Venosa: II 451; III 72
Vercelli: III 141
Verona: I 593; II 61, 286; III 880
Versailles: III 77
Via Lata: II 421
Via Salaria: II 101
Vicalvi: II 432, 460, 465, 663; III 70, 73
Vico Albo: II 452; III 71
Vienne: III 13, 55, 376, 768, 783
Villesilos: II 466, 678
Viterbo: I 55, 560–61, 577; II 51, 427, 441, 670; III 34–35, 402, 764
Vitry: I 578
Volterra: I 41, 56; II 460; III 70
Volturno River: II 422, 480, 657
Volusiano: II 321

W

Westminster Abbey: I 424
Winchester: I 424
Worcester Cathedral: I 87–88, 92; II 89
Worms: I 171, 363

Y

Yale: III 664
York: I 197
Yorkshire: III 830

Z

Zancato: II 448, 672

Index of Scripture

of texts in *The Saint* (I), *The Founder* (II), and *The Prophet* (III)

Old Testament

Genesis

1:2	II 434, 664
1:11	II 282, 729; III 678
1:14	I 260
1:16	II 342, 772
1:16–17	II 811
1:20,21	I 504
1:20–22	III 632
1:26	I 82, 131; II 813; III 147
1:26,27	II 812; III 483, 602
1:27–3:24	II 751
1:31	II 353
2:9	III 398
2:10	I 259
2:15	I 82
2:16,17	I 129
2:22	II 696
2:24	II 284, 577
2:25	I 537, 538
3:1	I 537
3:5,7	III 393
3:7	I 538
3:8	I 537, 538
3:9	I 277
3:9–10	I 538
3:12	III 422
3:12–13	I 132
3:14	II 141, 315, 613; III 296
3:15	I 468
3:17	II 321
3:18	II 723
3:19	I 539; II 351, 522
3:21	I 539; II 333
3:22	I 254
3:23	I 539
3:24	I 539
4:8	III 422
4:9	III 683
4:12	I 539
4:13	I 477; II 420
4:17	II 70, 245, 429, 662
4:25	III 180
5:4	III 681
5:24	II 649
5:29	II 140, 305; III 281
6–7	III 632
6:2	III 422
6:6	I 190, 248; III 248, :327, 417, 717
6:8	II 331
6:16	I 545
6:17	II 642; III 557, 558
7:3	III 593
8:3	I 206
8:9	I 539
8:15	I 306; II 450, 673
8:21	I 549
9:8–16	III 887
9:13	II 526
10:11	II 246
11:6	II 301
11:8,9	III 422
11:30	II 400
12:1	I 567; II 300, 579
12:2	I 206
12:3	III 383, 384
13:3	I 289
13:9	II 489
13:14	II 490
13:15	I 530
14:1–32	II 490
15:1	II 250, 329, 428
15:5	II 729
16:13	III 715
16:15	III 422
16:22	III 182
17:1	I 224
17:4	II 37
17:7,19	III 398
17:13	II 380
17:23	III 394
18:25	II 383
19:11	II 258, 541
19:16	I 265; II 403, 474
19:19	II 272, 616
19:26	I 549, 560
19:27	II 467
20:3	II 301

20:16	I 212
21:10–13	III 182
21:11	II 264
22:2	I 567
22:16–18	III 103
23:6	II 338
23:10	II 252
24:26	II 439, 667
24:45	I 226
24:54	II 301, 390, 465, 644; III 870
24:63	II 536, 686
25:23	II 359
26:1	II 282
27:4	I 515; III 446, 577
27:12	II 307, 419
27:27	I 279; II 361
27:27–28	I 127
27:29	III 383, 447, 577
27:34	II 299
27:36	I 446; II 312
27:38	II 271
27:40	I 185, 241, 371
27:41	III 422
28:1	II 319
28:2	II 280, 618
28:12	II 256, 267, 319, 421, 545, 630, 670, 690, 692, 744; III 88, 390, 398
28:12–13	II 353, 596
28:16	I 553
28:18	II 330
29	III 87
29:15	II 138, 293; III 267
30:25	II 254
31:4	II 327
31:10	I 304
31:24	I 304; II 468
32:2	I 272
32:8	I 390
32:9	II 36, 71, 245, 533
32:24–25	II 753
32:25	II 754
32:29	III 443, 574
32:30	III 221, 371
33:4	II 296
33:10	II 355, 408
33:12	II 307
33:14	II 393
35:1–15	I 567
35:29	I 381
37:2	I 547
37:4	I 530; II 258
37:14	III 557, 558
37:28,32	III 422
37:30	II 426, 660
38:18	II 246
39:10	II 333
39:11	II 290, 302; III 266
39:12	I 242, 582

41:10	II 436, 666
41:11	I 464
41:38	I 263; II 706, 710
41:46	I 266
41:52	II 557
42:8	II 280; III 228
42:30	I 551
42–46	III 158
43:21	II 248
43:30	II 370
44:30	III 158
45:1	III 426
45:3	II 438
45:4	III 158
46:32	II 393
47:29	I 58
48:7	II 258
48:10	II 715
48:14	I 276, 414; II 643, 715; III 226, 355, 426, 447, 577
48:14–15	I 323
48:14–22	II 387
48:17	III 244, 336
48:17,18	III 426
48:18	III 117, 410, 714
49	III 868
49:3	III 446, 577
49:23	III 425
49:26	I 270

Exodus

1:5	III 487, 724
1:14	I 344
3:1	I 343; II 742, 752
3:1,2	III 456
3:2	III 455, 456
3:5	I 202
3:12	III 189
3:17	I 539
3:22	I 329
2:5–7	II 742
2:10	II 742
2:12	I 344
4:10	III 175
4:12,15	III 383
4:15	III 256, 257, 263, 703, 704
4:18,19	III 400
4:21	II 265, 614
4:45	III 239
5:1	II 742
5:7	I 344
5:21	II 363
5:24	II 542
6:28	III 129
7:13,21	II 736
8:30	I 207
10:5	II 364
12:11	II 246
12:29	II 735

12:36	I 329
12:37	III 422
13:9	III 188
13:13	II 300
13:17	II 717
13:18	III 399
14:5	III 403
14:24	II 270
14:26–29	II 742
15	II 742
15:6–7	I 155
17:1ff	III 101
17:1–7	II 584, 585
17:11–13	II 359
18–24	II 742
19:1	II 634
19:3–6	II 742
21:19	I 408
22:12	I 456; II 305; III 281
24:9–10	II 723
24:18	III 253, 713
25:17–22	II 772
25:20	II 343
25:40	II 623; III 93
28:3	II 335
29:18	I 296; II 347, 587; III 295
30:1,27–28	II 599
30:23	III 769
31:18	III 417
32:9	II 291
32:17	III 416
32:27	I 585
33:3	II 291
33:10	I 280
33:11	II 742; III 435, 438, 567, 569, 689
33:19	II 735
38:23	I 216
40:13	I 294

Leviticus

1:9	I 216
1:13	II 363
2:9	III 447, 577
2:13	II 259
6:5,6	II 375
19:2	I 118
19:17	III 867
23:7	II 442, 444, 670

Numbers

5:19,23	II 305
6:24	I 97, 228
6:24–26	I 112
6:26	I 379; II 84; III 219, 276, 443, 493, 574, 608
6:27	I 112
7:89	II 638

10:2	II 772; II 811
11:4	I 262, 273; II 640
11:5	II 757
12:3	II 519
12:6	I 302
12:8	III 422
12:14	II 267, 617; III 863
12:17	II 732
14:2–4	II 138, 293; III 45, 267
14:5	II 426, 660
14:30	III 422
14:41	II 265
15:18	II 292
16:26	I 475
20:8–13	II 757
20:30	II 491
22:20–1	II 266
22:21–33	III 520
22:22–35	III 632
22:28–33	III 165
25:8	II 760
27:22	I 238; III 854
29:39	I 296
33:4	II 328

Deuteronomy

1:1	III 399
3:39	II 562
4:2	I 86; I 127
4:13	II 634
5:5	II 619
5:11	I 252
5:15	III 410
5:23	II 489
5–8	II 491
6:4,5	III 531
6:5	I 159; III 383, 651
7:12,13	I 212
7:25	I 531
8:3	III 404
8:16	III 318
8:17	II 521
9:9	II 558
9:10	I 436; II 634; III 417
9:11	III 226
10:3	II 558
10:4	II 558
10:18	I 584
11:24	I 533; III 161
12:7	I 531
12:12	II 275
12:32	I 86, 127
13:13	I 542; II 260; III 164
13:14	II 312
13:17	II 278; II 409
13:18	I 275
14:29	II 695
16:18	I 229; I 293
17:20	III 353

19:15	II 637
21:3	I 230
22:1	I 269
22:17	I 543
23:24	I 336
23:26	I 416
25:4	I 510
25:5	II 587
27:3	II 682, 717
28:56	II 271
30:1	III 65
31:6	III 391
31:11	I 278
31:12	II 271
31:21	III 188
32:6	II 355, 408
32:11	II 358
32:13	II 278, 409, 584, 705
32:15	I 547
32:18	I 538
32:27	II 522
32:35	II 133, 341; III 47, 297
32:40	II 369; III 242, 302
32:49	I 276; II 745
33:11	I 553
34:9	I 259

Joshua

1:5	III 391
1:9	II 296
2:16	II 278; II 409
2:18	III 189
3:3	I 285; II 476
3:13	II 382
6:20	I 284; II 476
7:15	II 299
8:20	I 278, 416; II 388, 475
8:34	I 248
9:2	I 225
11:3	II 489
13:1	II 460, 480; III 71
17:8	II 257
22:18	II 270, 282, 594
22:27	II 272, 616
22:33	III 119, 297
23:14	I 277; II 419
24:15	I 262
24:16	II 343

Judges

2:4	II 628
3:7	II 274, 615
3:31	I 566
7:18–22	I 568
9:15	II 364
9:54	II 383
11:34–35	I 567
13:6	I 252; II 261, 335, 339; III 859

13:6,8	II 292
13:16	I 235
14:18	II 299
15:18	II 428, 662
15:19	I 567
16:14	II 430
16:16	II 382
16:17	II 300
16:27	I 294
16:29	I 272
16:30	II 110
19:3	II 388
19:14	II 292, 580

Ruth

1:16	II 625
3:7–8	I 240, 461; III 43
3:10	II 446, 463, 675
3:18	II 280

1 Samuel

1:11	II 430, 437, 663, 676
1:28	II 295
2:5	II 208, 352, 375, 546, 587; III 321, 706
2:12	II 260
2:22–25	II 518
2:27	II 251, 252, 254, 271, 273, 302
2:30	II 755
2:35	III 381
3:8	II 324, 562
3:9	III 304
3:18	II 296
3:19	I 212
3:20	II 733
5:6	III 369
7:3	II 733
9:5	II 275, 416
9:6	II 401, 650
9:6, 10	I 243
9:7	II 318, 319
9:22	III 415
10:6	I 205; II 72, 312, 608; III 522, 842
10:9	III 403
11:2	II 733
11:5	I 295
12:19	I 294
12:23	II 383
13:1	II 277
13:14	I 566
14:13	II 744
14:27	II 410
14:36	III 275
15:23	I 549; III 416
16:11–12	II 620
16:12	II 490

16:18	II 269
17:26	I 186
17:40	III 188
17:41–51	II 720
17:42	II 490
17:45	I 186
18:1	I 247
18:9–12	III 422
18:27	III 390
20:13	II 307; III 282
20:34	II 375
24:11	I 291, 293, 294
24:17	II 422
25:17	II 260, 298; III 324
25:18	III 477, 597
25:28	I 263
26:25	II 383
27:4	II 258
29:7	II 332
30:6	II 602
30:13	II 325, 563
30:21–25	III 758

2 Samuel

3:7	II 282
4:5–12	III 117, 712
5:2	II 620
6:21–22	II 524, 736
6:22	I 252
7:3	III 275
7:12–17	III 103
7:14	III 384
12:3	I 235, 246
14:14	II 317
15:7	I 306
17:8	III 228
18:18	II 295
21:17	II 423
22:2	III 366
24:12	II 288
24:12,13	III 547
24:15	I 285; II 476
24:17	II 656

1 Kings

2:4	I 119; II 215
2:8	II 525
2:27	III 357
3:1	II 251
3:11	I 464
3:26	I 192, 249, 400, 551
4:7	II 555
4:9	II 414
4:9,16	II 456
4:30–31	I 125
4:33	I 458
5:4	II 260
5:9	III 385

5:13	III 449, 580
8:22,54	III 417
8:23	II 761
8:30	I 275
8:31	II 328
8:33	I 275
8:36	III 248, 317, 327, 414, 712, 717
8:63	I 406
9:6	I 240
10:1,4,7	III 486
10:3,4	I 213
10:6	I 319
11:28	I 306
13:1	II 260, 370
13:1,5,6	II 402
13:4	II 328
13:6	II 325
13:14,21	II 278, 409
13:29	II 298
13:31–32	II 280
14:6	III 388
17:22	III 51
18:16	II 491
18:44	I 416
18:45	II 426, 660
18:46	III 176
19:18	II 523
19:19	II 746; III 241
19:20	II 386, 642
21:29	II 519

2 Kings

1:8	I 355
1:9	II 294; III 46
1:10	II 298, 319, 320
2:4	II 265
2:9	I 389; II 490, 617; III 96
2:9,15	I 330; II 692
2:11	I 389, 476; II 526, 552, 649, 761; III 388, 421, 815
2:11,12	I 330
2:11–14	I 224; II 552; III 845
2:12	I 389; II 552, 692; III 90, 846
2:13	II 281
3:15	II 624; III 98, 176
4:1ff	III 101
4:9	I 470; II 357; III 416
4:26	I 293
4:31	I 530
4:37	III 51
4:42	II 285
5:8	II 308
5:14	II 312
6:9,10	II 36
6:17	II 552; III 90
6:32	III 388
8:10	II 265
10:30	II 261

13:4	I 259	20:4	I 251; II 642
13:13	I 242, 404, 532; II 456	20:22	II 441
13:14	II 363	20:27	II 652
13:17	I 280	21:5	II 264
14:2	II 524	21:6	II 313, 608
15:9	I 380; II 328, 330, 448, 463,	21:14	I 548
	573, 672, 676	21:15	II 800
15:17	II 322	21:24	II 270
		22:2	II 247
		22:29	II 521
		23:3	II 353

Job

		23:11	II 353, 596
1:1	I 182, 230, 254, 301, 462;	24:12	II 271; III 353
	II 410, 414, 415, 530, 600	24:18	II 321; III 851
1:1,8	I 339	26:11	I 274
1:2	II 749	26:13	II 729, 762
1:8	II 733, 749	28:11	II 399, 612, 613
1:18–19	III 117, 712	28:21	I 532
1:19	II 427, 661	28:23	I 532; II 310
1:21	II 523	29:3	I 541
2:3	I 204; II 298, 697; III 50	29:5	I 542
2:4	II 333	29:9	II 264
2:13	II 523	29:16	I 247, 248, 285, 339, 344;
3:5	II 448		II 275, 416, 583
3:19	I 294	30:2–4	I 547
3:21,22	II 440, 669	30:7–8	I 548
3:24–25	II 489	30:10	I 548
3:29	II 742	30:14	I 548
4:7	II 438, 439	31:1	II 694
4:12	II 142, 331; III 340	31:2	II 371
4:13	I 186; II 400	31:18	II 196, 530, 736; III 81, 286
4:18	I 549	31:23	II 337
5:7	II 351	31:36	II 325, 563
5:11	I 213	33:15	I 186
6:3	III 681	33:26	I 287
6:8	II 369	34:14	II 330, 369, 567
6:10	II 641	36:6	II 764
7:1	I 465; II 351	36:8	I 466
7:4	II 253	36:22	II 525, 745
7:15	II 762	37:19	II 283
7:16	II 383	38:7	I 296
9:20	II 817	38:14	II 734
9:26	II 315, 613	38:33	II 724
10:22	I 587	38:38	II 325
11:15	II 386, 642, 715	40:22	I 296; II 478
12:5	I 188	40:27	II 430, 437, 663
12:5,1	II 817	41:12	II 562
12:21	I 496	41:13	III 96
13:1	II 419	41:22	II 310
14:2	II 818		
15:8	II 531		
15:27	II 270	## Psalms	
16:6	III 864		
16:7	II 265, 614	1:1	I 446
16:16	II 293	1:3	II 278, 409
17:6	II 326	2:2	I 470
18:2	II 347	2:3	II 518
19:2	II 714	2:9	II 360
19:16	II 750	3:5	I 409
19:20	I 276; II 641	3:6	I 146
19:21–22	I 548	4:3	I 129; II 649

4:4–5	II 817	18:47	II 376, 574
4:9	III 536, 654	19:4	II 811
5:4	II 491	19:5	II 260, 266; III 382, 523
6:4	I 190	19:8	II 136, 288. 680; III 259, 708
6:7	II 511	19:11	I 225, 537; II 299, 374, 384
7:10	III 404	19:13	I 105
8:2	I 251	19:30	I 277; II 475
8:6	I 265, 288	20:2	I 152
8:7	II 746	20:3	I 152
9:9	I 152	20:4	I 152
9:10	I 152	20:5	I 152
9:19	II 294	20:6	I 152
10:2	I 395	20:7	I 152
10:4	II 721	21:3	II 281; III 551
10:5	II 721	21:4	I 534; II 530; III 388, 390, 538
10:6,11	III 499	21:4–5	I 347
10:7	III 413	22:5	III 266, 709
10:8	I 500	22:6	II 751
10:14	II 305, 491	22:7	I 48, 144, 250, 400; II 802; III
11:1	II 370; III 250, 310, 317, 349,		444, 455
	352	22:8	I 144
11:2	I 446; III 414, 712	22:10	I 142
11:4	II 270	22:11	I 142
11:6	II 433, 663	22:12	I 140, 276; II 147, 372; III 706
11:7	II 301	22:14	I 146
12:9	II 343	22:15	I 146; III 190, 529, 649
13:1	I 154	22:16	I 146
13:2	I 154	22:17	I 146
13:3	I 154	22:17–18	I 146
13:4	I 154	22:18–19	I 146
13:5	I 154	22:20	I 140, 144
13:6	I 154; II 331; III 472	22:24	I 138
13:7	I 105	23:1	I 448
14:1	I 196; II 72, 274, 370, 465, 663	23:4	II 360, 373, 602
14:3	II 817	24:3	I 532
14:4	III 408	24:10	I 529, 534
14:5	III 408	25:4	III 55
16:4	II 697	25:8	I 431; II 58
16:8	I 448	26:5	III 353
16:9	II 341	26:7	I 295; II 407
16:11	II 329; III 382	27:4	II 310
17:4	II 358, 600	27:12	II 294
17:7	III 502	27:13	II 333, 518, 570
17:8	II 374	28:31	II 716
17:8–9	II 607	29:2	III 372
17:13	I 446	29:3	I 278, 416; II 388, 475
17:26	II 509	29:4	II 374
18:3	III 366	29:10	I 261
18:7	I 151	30:9	I 277
18:8	II 261	30:10	I 492; II 270
18:15	II 554	30:11	I 194; II 80
18:16	I 416	30:12	II 570
18:18	I 143	30:21	I 261
18:20	I 270	31:4	II 641; III 366
18:21,25	II 336	31:5	I 109
18:39	II 354	31:6	III 398
18:43	I 191	31:10	III 531, 651
18:45–46	III 177	31:12	I 144
18:46	II 294	31:13	I 228, 256, 393; III 852

31:14	II 338, 569
31:16	I 374; II 537
31:20	I 431; II 284
31:21	II 260
31:23	III 411, 425, 843
32:2	II 328
32:4	I 47
32:5	II 818
32:6	I 192, 269; II 247, 439, 665
32:7	I 374; II 145, 365; III 325
32:11	II 297
33:1	I 349
33:3	I 296
33:5	III 531, 651
33:13	I 184
34:6	I 467
34:7	II 287
34:9	I 46, 262, 529
34:13	II 524
34:23	I 147
35:3	II 268
35:9	II 243
35:10	II 668
35:11	I 145
35:12	I 145
35:15	I 145
35:16	I 545; II 291; III 45
35:20	I 543
35:25	I 213
36:7	I 306; III 59
36:7–8	I 256
36:8	I 267
36:9	II 392, 645
36:10	III 487, 724
36:70	II 451
37:1	I 346
37:9	II 523
37:11	II 489, 518
37:30	I 334, 341
37:30–31	I 346, 349
37:31	I 335, 341
37:34	II 271
37:39	II 147, 372; III 314, 706
38:3	II 523
38:9	I 285, 432; II 476
38:10	I 330
38:11	I 541
38:12	I 140
38:14	I 334; III 436
38:21	I 145
38:23	I 140, 142, 144, 145
40:3	I 287, 534; II 448, 664, 671
40:13	II 296
40:18	II 275, 416
41:7	I 144; II 287
41:8	I 140, 144
41:9	I 144
41:14	I 141, 279
42:5	I 275; III 330
42:9	I 149, 156
43:2	I 109
43:15	II 789
43:20	II 489
43:22	II 800
44:5	I 142, 145
45:1	II 252
45:2	I 225; II 261, 282
45:3	III 528, 695, 728
45:8	II 329
45:10	I 294; II 510
45:12	I 534
45:14	III 533
45:16	I 286; II 477
46:2	I 285; II 145, 365
46:5	II 422, 480, 657
46:11	I 146
47:2	I 147, 156; II 449, 671
47:3	I 147, 156, 334
47:8	II 373
48:2	II 355, 408
48:3	I 194, 376
48:8	II 367
50:1	I 288
50:8	II 700, 704
50:14	II 437, 656
50:17	II 754
50:19	II 519
50:23	II 761
51	I 65
51:1	III 137
51:3	II 380; III 220, 372
51:6	II 607
51:10	I 135
51:12	I 205, 381; II 764
51:14	II 330; III 49, 343, 531, 651
51:17	I 491; II 817; III 454, 455
51:19	I 409, 432; II 359; III 744
51:20	II 313
52:10	I 260
53:3	III 400
53:6	II 327; III 408
55:6	I 570
55:9	I 538
55:17	II 258; II 541
55:23	I 191, 207, 337, 381; II 78, 546, 605; III 100, 476, 477, 715, 800
56:2	I 144
56:3	I 144
56:4	II 588
56:8–9	I 140
56:10	I 140
57:2	I 143
57:3	I 143
57:4	I 143
57:5	I 143
57:7	I 143; III 410
57:8	I 143

57:9	I 143		70:2	I 148
57:10	I 143		70:3	I 148
57:11	I 143		70:4	I 148
57:12	I 143, 148		70:5	I 148
58:5	III 424		70:6	I 148; III 531
58:9	II 745		70:7	I 148
59:7	I 585		70:15–16	II 578
59:17	I 152		71:1	I 152
59:18	I 152, 153		71:2	I 152
61:3	II 192, 354; III 366		71:3	I 152
62:9	I 118; II 530		71:5	I 109, 152
63:2	I 266; II 308, 332; III 853		71:6	I 153
63:3	I 535		71:8	I 153
63:7–8	II 754		71:10	I 140, 144
65:9	II 399		71:12	I 140; III 347
65:12	II 337		71:13	II 328
66	II 817		72:17	I 151
66:1–2	I 151		72:17,19	II 299
66:3	I 151		72:18	I 151
66:4	I 151		72:19	I 151, 287; II 393
66:8	I 151		72:24	II 754
66:12	I 515; II 740		73:1	I 262
66:15	II 310		73:7	II 303
66:16	I 151		73:17	I 296, 320; II 301
66:17	I 151		73:18	I 547
66:20	I 289; II 418, 439		73:24	I 146
67:6	II 489		73:25	I 146
67:8	II 717		73:28	I 261
68:8	II 682		74:12	I 147, 156, 529
68:9	II 719		75:5	II 815
68:17	II 296, 582		75:7	II 249
68:20	III 502		76:11	I 431; II 531
68:21	II 431		77:3	II 181, 281
68:33	I 149		77:4	II 253, 360; III 851
68:33–34	I 149		77:7	II 280
68:34	II 318		77:11	I 184, 236, 319, 332, 370;
68:34–35	I 149			III 552
68:36	I 149, 181		77:15	I 109
69:2	II 267		77:16	II 705
69:5	I 145		77:25	II 582
69:8	I 145		78:1	I 491
69:9	I 145; II 47, 94; III 39		78:8	III 183
69:10	I 145		78:8,40	III 425
69:14	II 376; III 531, 651		78:14	I 114; III 368
69:16	II 329		78:16	II 278, 409, 584, 585, 757
69:17	I 153		78:21,31	II 452, 677
69:18	I 153		78:24	II 757
69:19	I 142		78:25	III 100, 386
69:20	I 142		78:54	II 557
69:21	I 142; III 344		78:57	I 430; III 81
69:22	I 146		78:70–71	II 752
69:23	II 380		79:6	II 551
69:27	I 146		79:11	I 567
69:30–31	II 761		79:13	I 330
69:31	I 306, 489; II 376, 451		80:12	I 270; II 400
69:33	I 155; II 294		80:14	I 565
69:35	I 138, 155, 161		80:18	II 317
69:36	I 155		81:2	I 156
69:37	I 155		81:17	II 392

82:4	III 380
84:6–7	II 284
84:7	II 144, 364, 384; III 325
84:8	III 152
84:10	II 323
84:10, Vg	II 303
84:11	II 794
85:5	II 679
85:9	II 317, 531
85:11	III 439, 440
86:1	III 63
86:4	II 326
86:9	II 403
86:10	I 109
86:14	I 142
87:1	III 195
87:1–2	I 532
88:2	I 142
88:3	I 142
88:5–6	I 142
88:7	I 534
88:9	I 140
88:14	I 214
88:16	III 51
89:7	III 186
89:8	I 355
89:23	I 271, 453
89:25	I 347
89:27	I 156
89:28	I 156
89:36	II 403
89:50	II 348
90:15	II 490
91:4	II 596
91:5	II 695
91:6	I 261
91:13	III 482
91:14	III 266, 709
92:5	II 353, 637, 651
93:5	II 681; III 740
94:1	II 360
94:2	II 575
94:12	I 460
94:22	III 366
95:2	II 319
95:3	II 311
96:1	I 147, 156
96:2	I 489
96:4	I 147, 156
96:7–8	I 147, 149, 156
96:9–10	I 147
96:11	I 147
96:11–12	I 147, 149, 156
96:13	I 148
97:2	I 431
98:1	I 149
98:2	I 149
99:9	I 239
100:3	I 448; II 353, 521
100:4	I 529
101:3	II 310, 338
103:2–3	II 727
103:13	I 271
103:20	II 464
103:21	I 138
103:22	I 138
104:13,14	I 114; III 368
104:23	III 769
104:32	I 566
105:1	I 138
105:15	III 193
105:16	II 283
105:17,18	II 752
105:21	II 752
105:41	II 757
106:1	I 352, 551
106:21	II 270
106:30	II 813
106:35–36	II 509
106:35–37	III 180
107:4	II 343
107:6	II 329
107:8,15	II 308
107:23	I 585
107:24	II 601
107:26	II 265
107:27	I 43, 50
107:38	II 270
107:40	I 416
109:4	I 140
109:5	I 140
109:7	II 452, 677
109:17	I 519
109:28	II 251
109:31	II 537
110:1	I 355
110:3	I 270
110:4	III 117, 410, 533, 714
110:7	I 270, 535
111:1–2	II 268
111:4	I 370, 394, 500; II 489; III 421
111:5	II 814
111:7	II 385
111:8	II 339
112:1	I 489
112:3	I 534
112:6	II 475
112:7	I 281
112:9	I 567; II 300; III 33
113:1	I 138; II 717
113:1–2	III 275
113:2	I 236, 397
113:6	I 276
113:7	II 738
113:8	I 568
114:1	I 342; II 682; III 399
114:3	II 813
114:5	II 118, 349

114:6	II 519
115:1	III 220
115:3	II 803
115:4,6	II 732
115:5	I 209; III 723
115:12	II 392
115:15	III 86, 315
115:32	I 229
116:1	I 489
116:16	I 531; II 750
118:11	II 301
118:16	III 552
118:24	I 138, 149, 156
118:26,27	I 149
118:106	III 248
119:11	I 265, 411; II 474
119:21	I 43, 46, 58, 68; II 378
119:30	I 262, 415; II 296
119:32	I 418, 469, 514; II 385
119:37	II 335, 563
119:45	I 221, 386
119:62	II 46
119:64	III 531
119:96	I 260; II 385
119:100	II 763
119:106	III 328, 718
119:120	II 322
119:122,124	II 753
119:125	II 119, 350; III 322
119:127	I 448
119:132	I 308
119:140	I 223, 389
119:141	II 751
120:4	III 500, 615
120:5–6	III 546
120:7	I 203, 320
123:1	I 477
125:1	I 395
125:3	I 566
126:2	I 188, 293; II 307
126:6	I 331, 568
126:20	II 668
126:60	II 439
127:1	I 479; II 440, 669
127:5	I 231, 381, 395
128:1	III 248
128:2	I 68; III 237, 251, 311
128:5	I 228, 393
128:6	II 343
129:4	I 292
130	I 65
130:1	I 538; II 261
131:10	II 522
132:2	II 431, 444, 450, 673
133:1	I 472
135:1	I 551; II 297
135:13	II 717
136:1	I 117
136:2	I 109

136:4	II 464
136:11	I 248, 399
136:13	II 682
138:1	II 373
138:6	II 730
138:14	II 489
139:12	I 255
139:14	I 282
140:2	II 702
140:6	II 325
141:2	II 272
141:4	I 538
142	II 643; III 835
142:2	I 144, 516; II 643
142:2–8	I 277, 323, 415; II 388
142:3	I 144; II 328
142:4	I 144, 145
142:5	I 145
142:6	I 103; II 682
142:7	I 191; II 78, 537
143:2	I 538
143:4	I 264
143:8	III 55
143:10	I 187
144:1	I 153
144:12	I 246; II 260
144:18	II 679
145:10	I 331
145:12	I 368
145:14	I 368, 432; II 268, 360
145:15	I 270; II 291, 579
145:18	II 465
145:19	II 520
146:2	II 546
147:1	I 138; II 339
147:2	I 207; II 371
147:3	II 445; III 530
147:20	II 124, 339, 419; III 224, 291
148	II 597
148:3	I 113; III 367
148:4,5	I 114; III 368
148:11	II 391, 477
148:12	I 138
148:16,17	I 452
149:1	I 289
149:8	II 438
150:1	II 273, 455; III 275
150:6	I 138

Proverbs

1:17	II 380
1:27	II 147, 372; III 314, 706
2:5	II 315
3:12	III 231, 312
3:32	I 210; II 370, 620
4:25	I 549
5:22	I 468
6:16,19	II 736
6:26	II 301

6:28	II 322, 563
7:9	I 215; II 347
7:19–20	II 491
7:23	II 267
8:28	I 513
8:30	I 537
10:1	III 649
10:9	I 224
10:10	II 335
10:22	II 300
10:29	I 335; II 145, 366
11:5	I 335
11:12	I 509
11:13	I 252
12:25	II 523
13:16	I 560
13:20	II 509
13:24	II 360; III 851
14:26	I 193
14:29	I 189
15:4	I 253
15:4–1	I 218
15:5	II 520
15:13	II 329
15:24	I 497
16:1	II 748
16:2	III 59
16:4	II 663
16:7	I 484
16:16	I 190
16:24	II 374
16:29	II 436
17:17	II 740; III 48
18:19	II 268
18:21	II 564
18:24	II 268
20:6	II 747
20:7	I 222
20:15	II 418
20:27	II 445
21:31	II 265, 614
22:7	II 139, 304; III 280, 282
22:11	II 739
22:15	I 272
22:24–25	II 509
23:22	II 369
23:29	II 332
23:32	II 329, 347; III 295
23:35	II 816
24:27	I 255
25:14	II 313
25:27	II 631
26:11	I 130; II 246, 264, 270, 274, 594, 615, 764; III 94, 248, 327, 718
27:7	II 248, 249
27:17	II 268
28:13	II 817
28:23	II 291

28:27	II 326, 575
29:20	I 135; III 252
29:23	II 755
30:17	II 276, 417
30:24–28	I 586
31:19	I 229, 260; II 442, 677
31:20	I 320; II 670

Ecclesiastes

1:2	I 70, 545; II 815
1:8	II 377; III 422
1:17	III 413
2:3	II 694
2:11	II 815
2:14	II 141, 322; III 334
3:1	II 360
3:5	I 214
3:12,13	I 531
4:10	I 532; II 267
4:13	II 258
5:3	II 327
5:9	I 548
5:14	I 446
7:9	I 191
8:8	I 263
9:22	I 276; II 475
10:20	II 331
11:6	II 718
12:5	II 645
12:8	I 545
12:13	II 735
20:17	II 291
23:26	II 489
47:18	II 489

Song of Songs

1:3	I 532; II 392, 648
1:5	I 532
1:6	I 531
1:11	I 227, 534
1:12	II 597
1:13	II 303
2:1	III 366
2:5	I 531; III 173
2:7	II 361
2:9	II 361
2:12	I 255
2:14	I 206, 243, 253, 256
3:1–2	II 605
3:2	I 191, 530; II 79, 463; III 160
3:3	I 530
3:6	I 278; II 744
3:7	I 585
3:11	II 386, 642
4:2	I 568
4:5	II 772
4:9	II 758
4:11	II 318

5:2	II 715
5:4	II 309
5:6	II 250, 302, 310, 401, 534; III 549, 589
5:8	I 531; III 161
5:10	II 757
5:16	II 596
5:17	II 353, 596
6:4	III 476
6:4,10	III 520
6:9	I 278
7:1	I 548
7:8	II 746
7:9	II 310
8:6	I 536, 516, 734; III 381
8:6–7	II 631
8:7	II 512, 533, 686
8:11	III 858
8:13	II 361, 737

Wisdom

1:1	I 262; II 367, 512
1:3,4	I 447
1:4	II 511, 740
1:5	II 815
1:7	I 266
2:1	I 531; II 281
2:15	II 343
2:22	II 330
2:24	II 267
3:4	III 392
3:5	II 268
3:6	III 488, 726
3:13	II 341, 343; III 47, 289
4:3	II 300
4:10	I 254, 289
4:13	II 335
4:15	II 736
5:2	II 446, 447; III 74
5:4	II 251
5:4–5	II 58
5:9	II 815; III 525
5:10	II 584
5:11	II 308
6:3	I 403
6:7	I 58
6:13	I 532
6:16	I 532
6:24	II 316
7:8–9	II 512
7:9	II 384; III 347
7:13	II 512
7:22	I 253; II 310
7:23	I 253; II 384
7:24,27	II 620
7:25	II 270, 319
7:25,27	II 700
7:26	II 263, 283, 353, 740
7:29	III 494

8:2	I 535; II 284, 519
8:9	II 146, 380; III 323, 716
8:10–11	I 544
8:12	I 496
9:13	I 185
9:15	III 562, 563
9:18	II 338
10:4	I 566
10:10	I 341; II 37
10:12	II 343
10:17	III 320
10:21	II 812; III 466, 589
11:4	II 270
11:16	II 451, 678
12:13	III 100
14:1–7	II 538
15:11	II 407, 428
15:12	II 466
16:20	II 239, 757
16:24	II 567, 705
18:14–15	II 399
18:15	I 129, 534

Sirach

1:5	III 769
1:6	II 324
1:8,9	II 355, 408
1:11	I 283
1:13	II 735
1:16	II 735
1:28	II 735
2:8	II 608
3:4	I 429
3:19	I 265; II 518
3:20	II 520, 755
3:27	II 736
3:32	I 47
4:5	II 244
4:28	II 272
4:35	II 518
4:36	II 298
5:13	II 517
6:14	I 204
6:14–16	II 383
6:15	II 739
6:32	I 333
7:17	II 522
8:12	I 230, 245; II 261, 415
9:12	II 818
9:16	II 367
10:9	I 278; II 522
10:31	II 518
11:12–13	II 524
11:13	II 267
11:22	II 602
11:23	II 118, 349
11:27–28	II 385
11:33	II 364
13:1	II 509

13:17	II 468	41:15	II 335
13:24	II 756	41:16	I 520
15:3	III 388	43:1	II 723
15:5	II 763; III 36	43:12	II 726
16:24	II 338	43:22	II 301
17:1	II 813	43:29	II 377; III 422
17:4	II 702	44:1,2	II 370
17:11	II 308	44:14	III 35
17:24	II 274, 615	44:16	II 761
17:27	I 278	44:20	I 471
18:2	I 250; II 354	44:21	III 65
18:5	II 391, 552	44:22	I 471
18:6	I 266, 550	45:1	II 376, 489, 530; III 526
18:21	II 524	45:2	III 185
19:21	II 273	45:4	I 269, 351; II 736
19:23	II 519	45:6	II 489
20:8	II 295	45:13	I 294
23:19	II 813	45:14	I 294
23:22	I 202	45:23	II 760
24:4	II 755	45:31	II 308
24:8	II 726	46:8	II 266
24:11	I 539	46:14	II 649
24:12–34	I 544	46:22	II 733
24:19	I 251	47:10	II 284
24:20	I 519	47:13	I 351
24:21	II 490	48:1	III 90
24:23	I 216, 260; II 553	48:14	II 765
24:25	II 243	49:4	III 422
24:26–27	II 763	50:6	I 215, 278; II 388, 475, 526; III 678
24:29	III 769	50:6–7	I 295, 518, 568, 604
24:32	II 380	50:7	III 678
27:6	I 276; II 643	50:8	II 526, 646, 649
28:19,20	II 358	50:13	I 296
29:5	II 249	50:19	I 230, 243; II 416
29:9	III 284	50:22	I 296
29:28	I 552	51:26	II 344; III 834, 849
29:30	II 555	51:34	I 320
30:4	III 159		
31:8	II 530		
31:18	II 684	**Isaiah**	
33:9	II 261		
33:24	I 278	1:2	I 541
34:9	II 512	1:10	I 235
34:24–25	II 300, 579	1:15	I 296; II 478
34:30	II 740	1:16	II 511
35:4	I 124, 409; II 147, 372	2:3	I 532
35:10	II 334	2:10	I 279; I 520; II 374
35:17	II 520	3:2	II 324
35:21	I 463	3:8	I 187; II 147, 269, 381; III 323
36:5	III 421	4:2	I 294
36:6	I 282; II 270	4:4	II 252, 392
37:1	I 515	5:1,2	I 331
37:18	II 614	5:2,4	I 519
38:1	I 511	5:7	III 324, 480
38:4	I 267	5:8	I 222, 547
38:9	II 641	5:17	II 260
40:7	II 272	5:18	I 185; II 316
40:21	II 330, 567	5:19	II 303
40:25	I 261	6:1	I 296; II 455, 674

6:2	I 161, 251, 263, 283, 410, 509, 538; II 402; III 866
6:5	II 291
6:6,7	I 204; II 635; III 34, 435, 567
6:7	III 689
8:11	III 381
8:14	III 422
8:18	III 383
8:23	II 334
9:1	II 316
9:2	I 463; II 373
9:3	III 412
9:5	III 363
9:6	I 156; II 374
10:22	I 105
10:24	I 186, 433
10:33	II 491
11:1	I 251
11:2	I 41, 48, 207; II 552, 700
11:4	II 518
11:15	III 411
11:43	II 720
12:1	I 154
12:2	I 154
14:7	I 306
14:9–15	II 328, 573
14:12	III 422
14:12,13	III 425
14:14	I 535
16:3	I 288
16:6	I 554
16:14	II 244, 256
17:12	I 296
20:3	II 570
21:8	I 221, 386; II 562, 694
21:15	III 422
22:5	III 335
22:12	II 527
22:13	I 531
24:16	II 633
24:18	III 422
26:12	II 317, 521
26:20	I 538
28:8	II 246
28:19	II 267, 531
29:4	II 322
30:29	I 214
33:5	I 281
33:7	I 286; II 526
37:3	I 404
37:7	III 418
38:1	II 420, 615; III 94
38:15	I 72, 205, 380; II 371, 545, 762; III 843
38:17	I 541; II 313
39:2	II 400
40:3	II 526; III 381
40:4	II 325, 563
40:6	II 817
40:12	II 384
40:26	II 249, 410, 447, 653, 678
40:31	III 470
41:8	III 418
41:9–10	II 754; III 383
41:10	II 754
41:18	I 515
42:1	II 734, 747, 759
42:2	II 331
42:5	II 305
42:6	III 395
42:8	II 298
43:25	II 818
43:26	II 817
44:2	III 418
44:3	I 259
44:14	III 186
44:28	I 409
45:2	III 63
45:30,6	II 489
46:8	I 548; II 299; III 50, 847
48:9	I 184
48:10	II 736, 755
48:11	II 298
48:15	II 349, 588
48:21	II 278, 409; III 861
49:2	I 269
49:5	I 352
49:6	II 526
50:1	II 299
50:4	I 269; III 381
50:7	I 70, 92, 94
51:3	I 216, 219, 220, 386
51:6	III 287
51:9	I 552
51:16	III 239, 257, 263, 704
52:1	II 463, 675
52:7	I 335, 380; II 543
52:10	I 270
52:13	II 732
53:2–4, 4–5	II 490
53:3	II 256, 303, 339, 534
53:3–4	III 607
53:4	II 303, 522, 589; III 173, 250, 492
53:7	II 590; III 851
53:12	II 697
54:10	II 261
54:11	I 534
55:1	I 567
55:3	I 116
55:4	I 351
55:11	II 318; III 256, 703
56:8	III 400
56:10	I 580
57:19	I 335
58:1	I 585
58:7	II 35
58:10	II 35

58:13	I 261
60:8	I 533, 583
60:14	I 445, 536
61:1	II 625
61:3	III 384
61:6	II 331
61:9	I 534
61:10	I 294, 531, 535
62:3	I 294
62:4	II 760
62:6	I 585
63:1	II 812
63:14	II 378
65:14	II 427, 661
66:1–2	II 721
66:2	I 531, 271, 339, 525
66:8	I 552

Jeremiah

1:6	II 431
1:12	III 248
1:18	I 290
1:19	II 429, 662
1:52	II 818
2:21	I 246, 270
2:23	III 382
3:8	II 299
3:22	I 548
4:30	I 549
5:4	I 530
5:5	I 530
5:7	III 117
5:12	III 324
5:23	I 548
6:29	II 344, 571
7:3,5	I 285
7:5	I 269
7:11	I 437
7:16	I 549
8:5	I 549
8:11	II 270
9:3	I 547
9:20	III 41
9:21	III 97
12:7	I 534; II 510
13:1	I 548
13:23	II 511
14:5	II 282
14:8	III 739
15:2	II 270
15:19	II 339; III 224, 291, 423
17:1	I 386
17:5	I 50
17:7	I 446
19:1	II 491
19:11	II 491
20:10	I 548
20:17	II 440, 669
21:14	II 466, 679

22:28	II 695
23:9	II 252
25:10	I 294
28:17	II 270
29:13	I 275; III 330
31:3	II 284, 577, 696; III 248, 327, 717
31:22	I 416
32:19	III 722
32:27	II 474
35:6–7	I 589
35:19	I 589
44:27	III 857
45:3	I 539
46:10	II 270; III 857
48:10	I 117, 585
49:24	II 266
50:42	I 542; III 165

Lamentations

1:1	I 533; III 161
1:11	I 472
1:12	I 146
1:13	I 531
1:16	II 489
1:20	I 206
2:3	II 714
2:6	II 289
2:10	II 370
2:19	II 331
3:27	II 751
3:29,30	II 688
3:41	II 283
4:7	II 723
4:8	II 641, 714
4:17	II 336
4:20	I 533
5:3	I 277; II 489, 491
5:7	II 348
5:15	I 279, 416; II 430, 663
5:21	I 436; II 392

Baruch

2:11	I 343
3:2	II 441
3:13	I 259
3:30	III 502
3:35	I 286; II 477
3:38	I 535; III 844
4:27	II 369
5:1	II 221, 303; III 249

Ezekiel

1:1	I 263
1:3	I 184; II 531, 556, 685, 693; III 469, 522, 552
1:5ff	I 410

8:2	I 410
8:26	II 328; III 305
8:27	II 260
9:18	II 393
9:23	I 319
9:24	II 637
9:25	I 259, 272, 298
10:7	II 260
10:15	II 322
10:19	II 460, 480; III 71
12:13	III 388, 390, 395, 397
13:42	III 781
13:52	II 260
13:60	II 439, 667
14:22	II 544
14:36	II 356
14:37	I 276; II 475

Hosea

1:6	II 457
2:6	I 184
2:7	I 550
4:6	II 392
6:6	III 234, 278
9:7	II 315, 372, 379; III 314, 706
10:2	II 343
11:4	I 269, 533
13:14	I 242

Joel

2:2	I 215
2:12	I 191; II 78
2:13	I 262

Amos

1:5	III 424
5:10	II 351
8:11	II 282

Micah

1:7	III 117
4:2	I 532
5:7	I 279
5:7,8	II 403
6:14	II 522

Nahum

3:6	II 298
3:15	III 94

Habakkuk

1:8	III 436, 567
2:1	I 386
2:3	II 330
3:11	II 720
4:12	III 90

11:33–38	II 258

Zephaniah

1:14–15	III 335
2:3	II 518
3:16	I 534

Haggai

2:23	II 731, 734, 749; III 188, 248
2:24	II 219; III 327, 717

Zechariah

1:13	II 386, 643
4:3,14	II 772
4:14	I 205, 380
5:7–8	II 269
6:8	III 417
8:12	I 216
9:5	II 489
12:10	I 286, 417; II 393
13:7	II 350

Malachi

1:6	II 750
1:7	II 276, 416
1:11	III 397, 424
2:2	I 117
3:1	I 535
3:20	III 367
4:6	II 399

1 Maccabees

2:26,58	I 334
3:47	II 380
3:58	I 533
4:4	II 360
4–21	II 491
5:50	I 272, 413
5:54	I 207
6:29–30	II 491
6:34	III 189
8:16	II 343
10:20	II 743
13:5	II 360
14:31	I 292
14:45	II 404
15:32	II 282

2 Maccabees

3:12	II 343
3:20	I 295; II 391, 477
3:22	I 296
3:26	II 255
4:1	I 183
4:15	II 368
5:5	II 305

8:18	I 245	14:15	II 343
9:28	I 336	14:20	II 240
10:4	II 347	14:34	II 258, 348
11:6	III 400	14:35	I 271
12:22	II 378	14:45	II 654
12:44	II 491	15:16	I 249
13:13	II 280		

New Testament

Matthew

1:20	II 267, 329, 381, 440, 447, 617, 651, 669; III 71, 393
1:23	II 440, 669
1:24	II 260
2:1,2	I 255; III 223
2:10	I 204, 273; II 640; III 446, 492, 577, 607
2:11	I 247
2:12	I 238; II 390
2:13	II 448, 454, 460, 480, 672
2:13,19	II 651
2:13,23	III 397
3:2	I 78, 274; III 508, 621
3:3	I 331
3:4	III 406
3:4–5	III 704
3:5	I 279; II 403, 476
3:8	II 594, 706; III 388
3:10	I 514
3:11	II 378; III 383
3:12	I 336, 416
3:15	I 459; II 520, 695
4:1	I 209, 270; II 249
4:1–2	II 286
4:1–11	II 597
4:2	I 101; III 262, 381, 448, 579
4:3	II 296
4:4	I 219; II 316, 402; III 49, 855
4:8	III 497, 611
4:10	II 325
4:17	I 202; III 382
4:20	III 683
4:21	III 685
4:23	III 398
4:24	I 343
5–9	II 260
5:1	III 177, 253, 713
5:2	III 521
5:3	I 133, 275, 339, 529, 530, 535; II 582, 722, 736; III 329
5:3,10	III 387
5:5	II 518
5:8	I 134; III 159
5:9	I 133, 134; II 242; III 324
5:10	I 74, 105, 541; II 537
5:11	I 74, 75
5:12	I 75, 452; II 297
5:13	I 585
5:14	I 543, 585; II 352; III 318
5:15	I 278, 569; III 834
5:15–16	II 347
5:16	I 42, 49
5:17	I 329
5:18	I 328
5:19	II 512; III 392
5:20	II 455
5:22	I 72, 94; II 273, 296, 619
5:23–24	II 374
5:25	II 384
5:26	I 336, 380; II 754
5:28	I 73, 89
5:29	III 799
5:31	II 299
5:39	I 73, 89, 134
5:40	III 799
5:40–41	I 539
5:42	I 196
5:44	I 48, 79, 87, 105, 132; II 45
5:45	I 42, 49; II 548; III 628
5:48	III 198
6:2	I 75, 90; II 287
6:2,16	I 135; III 252
6:4	II 309
6:6	I 187, 372; II 75, 405, 652
6:9	I 47, 80, 88, 158, 222, 224, 388; II 80, 251, 538; III 695
6:9–13	I 65, 125, 475
6:10	I 158
6:11	I 159
6:12	I 114, 159
6:13	I 159, 160; II 393, 436, 666
6:14	I 78, 262
6:16	I 65, 478; II 364
6:18	I 265
6:19	I 265
6:19,21	II 745
6:19–20	I 539
6:20	I 137
6:21	II 380

6:22   I 217, 253; II 734
6:22–23   I 282
6:24   II 368, 510, 733
6:26   I 396, 400; III 780
6:31   I 539
6:31,34   II 159; III 238, 262
6:33   I 61; III 190
6:34   I 337, 539; II 152; III 235, 270
7:1   I 72
7:3   I 72
7:6   II 555
7:8   II 294
7:12   I 48, 66, 68, 98, 103, 134, 329
7:13   I 416, 567; III 316, 711
7:14   I 72, 336, 416, 533; III 821
7:15   I 549; II 260; III 399, 488, 725
7:24   III 223, 236, 290, 298
7:24–25   III 159
7:25   I 529
8:4   II 426
8:8   III 479, 599
8:9   II 337
8:11   I 289
8:12   II 818; III 524
8:14–15   II 627
8:16   III 382
8:17   II 303, 589; III 173
8:20   I 535, 583; II 159, 285, 328,
            578, 802, 815; III 262, 382
8:22   I 80, 88
8:23   III 386
8:24   II 434, 664
8:26   II 434, 664, 665; III 364
8:34   I 279; II 403, 476
9:1–8   III 607
9:2   I 240, 302; II 431
9:8   II 412, 624
9:9   III 383
9:10–13   II 247
9:11   III 495, 610
9:12   I 67, 98
9:12,13   III 495, 610
9:13   II 360; III 278
9:20   I 325, 454, 675
9:20–21   I 402
9:21   I 238; II 254
9:22   II 426
9:24   II 72
9:26   II 410, 678
9:35   I 214, 215, 236, 338, 385, 402,
            412; II 99, 256, 553; III 398
9:36   III 335
9:37   III 853
9:38   II 34
10:1   I 242
10:2   III 435, 566
10:3   III 685, 686
10:5   I 459
10:9   II 37, 542, 733

10:9–10   I 201, 379, 459, 539, 583, 589;
            II 84, 689; III 196, 833
10:10   I 73, 89, 335; III 824, 843
10:12   II 543
10:14   II 430
10:16   I 74, 321, 458, 462; II 602,
            613, 728; III 44
            III 800
10:19–20   I 499, 537; II 42, 762
10:20   I 499, 537; II 42, 762
10:22   I 75, 105, 276, 415; II 386;
            III 382, 397
10:23   I 74, 95, 126; III 157
10:24   II 522
10:28   I 75; II 750; III 484, 603
10:32   I 74; III 452
10:34–35   II 54
10:36   III 425
10:37   III 60
10:39   I 515
10:40   III 383, 384, 408
10:41   II 615
11:4   III 449, 580
11:5   I 290, 518; III 382, 827
11:8   I 65; II 293, 561
11:11   II 243
11:12   I 436, 465, 568; III 389
11:18   I 303; II 431
11:25   I 81, 109, 140, 154; II 446,
            513, 620, 682, 732; III 74
11:25–26   I 531
11:29   I 248, 542, 256; II 338, 508;
            III 384, 398
11:29,30   III 395
11:30   I 46, 328, 446; II 269; III 398,
            410
11:39   III 730
12:4   I 71
12:7   III 278
12:13   I 240, 403; II 430
12:18   II 353
12:31   III 422
12:33   III 259, 708
12:34   I 283
12:35   II 350
12:35,36   II 350
12:36   I 44, 53, 55, 59, 67; II 258,
            340; III 121, 249, 287, 299,
            328, 414, 718
12:37   II 564
12:38   I 235
12:39   II 490
12:43   I 80, 88
12:44   I 80, 437
12:45   I 383, 543; II 274, 280, 615,
            616; III 95
12:50   I 42, 49
13:3   I 230; II 255; III 739
13:8,23   II 320
13:11   III 422

13:12	I 58; III 248
13:18–23	III 739
13:19	I 79, 386
13:20	I 79
13:21	I 79
13:22	I 69, 79, 105
13:23	I 80
13:24	II 256, 295
13:25	III 740
13:25,28	III 388
13:32	III 158
13:44	I 188, 266, 333; II 578, 636; III 159
13:44,45	II 686; III 188
13:44–46	I 203, 319, 372; II 533, 620; III 842
13:45	III 849
13:45–46	II 284, 577
13:46	I 187, 203
13:47	III 390
13:47–48	I 206; II 620
13:48	III 390
13:52	II 491
14:15	I 213, 384
14:15–21	II 247
14:17,18	II 387
14:19–21	I 483
14:23	II 247
14:25	III 186
14:27	II 255; III 46, 88
14:31	II 328, 355, 409; III 359, 861
14:36	I 493
15:6	III 158
15:14	I 445; III 321
15:18–19	I 48
15:19	I 43, 50, 79
15:20	I 79
15:22	I 241, 403; II 455
15:23	I 242; II 456
15:27	I 529; II 279
15:30	II 320; III 43, 285, 350
15:32	I 336, 416
15:32–37	III 632
15:36	I 380
15:36–37	II 295
16:7	II 281
16:16	II 490
16:17	II 118, 345, 349, 370; III 267, 293, 315, 723
16:18	III 224
16:19	I 530
16:23	II 370
16:24	I 48, 64, 582; II 38, 86, 254, 534, 544, 685; III 83, 381, 438, 568
16:26	II 145; II 365; III 325
17:1	I 329
17:2	I 330
17:4	I 329
17:5	I 82
17:6	III 686
17:7	II 255, 427; III 46
17:9	II 711
17:14	III 228, 401
17:19	II 166, 324; III 346
17:20	III 43, 415
17:23–26	III 632
18:3	II 517
18:6	II 269, 434, 664
18:8	I 78
18:15–17	I 67
18:16	II 292, 514
18:18	I 78
18:19	I 86
18:20	I 81, 88
18:22	II 509
18:23	I 80
18:26	I 532
18:27	II 665
18:31	I 239
18:32	II 322
19:5	II 284
19:8	I 435
19:12	II 723
19:21	I 64, 100, 203, 319, 333, 462; II 296, 300, 368, 510, 544, 579; III 227, 242, 302, 355, 393, 422, 438, 568
19:21,29	II 319
19:24	II 722
19:26	III 391
19:27	I 70, 553; II 288, 338; III 418, 435, 566
19:28	II 548, 764
19:29	I 64, 450, 584; II 252, 285
19:30	II 399
20:1	II 365
20:1–7	I 565
20:6	I 545; III 250, 296, 311
20:8	II 426
20:14	II 307; III 282
20:15	I 132; II 516, 655
20:16	II 370, 399; III 99, 388, 425
20:20	II 333
20:21	I 42, 49, 81, 89; II 324; III 853
20:25	I 67
20:25–26	I 93
20:26	I 67; II 148, 343, 572; III 289, 699
20:26–2	II 572
20:26–27	I 48
20:27	I 67, 68
20:28	I 66, 130
20:32	II 276, 416
21:8	I 284, 296, 322, 417; II 647
21:13	I 437
21:19	II 298
21:21	II 435

21:33	II 489
22:11	I 65
22:14	III 388, 393, 425
22:16	II 223, 264, 618; III 351
22:21	I 133, 250; II 376, 434; III 252
22:30	I 554
22:34	II 412
22:37	I 282; II 247; III 372
22:37, 39	I 46
22:39	I 41, 47
22:40	I 329
22:43	II 248
23:3	I 540; II 817
23:4	II 205; III 167, 255, 703
23:5–7	III 256
23:8	I 68
23:8–9	I 88
23:8–10	I 81; I 88
23:9–10	II 203; III 218, 370
23:10	III 471
23:11	III 858
23:12	II 573
23:14	II 328
23:27–28	II 282
23:31,17	III 422
23:37	II 260
23:38	II 271
24:4	I 224
24:6	I 75
24:4,11	III 817
24:12	I 576; II 515; III 425, 721
24:13	I 51, 75; III 393, 397, 489, 726
24:14	III 398
24:22,24	III 135
24:24	II 321
24:25	I 550
24:28	III 470
24:29	III 388, 389
24:30	II 718, 719
24:45	I 136, 239, 270; II 283, 631, 733, 747; III 494
24:46	I 132, 134, 135; II 733
25:4	III 355
25:5	I 190, 274, 300, 414, 508; II 445, 537, 542
25:8	I 544
25:10	I 286; II 476
25:14	III 227
25:16,17	II 338
25:18	I 134
25:19	I 204, 230
25:20	I 348
25:21	I 263; II 208, 733; III 320, 706
25:25	II 633
25:25–44	I 456
25:29	III 248, 319, 327, 717
25:30	I 544; II 734; III 321
25:34	I 82, 207
25:34–40	II 815

25:36,42	II 666
25:40	II 205, 295, 582; III 166, 276, 699, 845, 867
25:41	I 78
25:41–46	II 815
25:45	II 572; III 849
25:46	I 74; III 119
26:7	III 295
26:20	II 387
26:20–25	III 693
26:24	II 349; III 248
26:26	I 46; II 387; III 244, 336, 542, 543, 544, 656
26:28	I 46
26:39	I 46; II 701
26:41	I 266; II 328, 384; III 731
26:42	I 46
26:45	III 489, 605
26:48	II 389
26:50	I 79, 87
26:52	III 94
26:63	II 490
26:70	II 307; III 282
26:75	II 328
26:75,58	II 342, 574
27:1	II 254, 544
27:3	I 195; II 441
27:4	I 194
27:5	III 435, 566, 680, 683
27:6	III 382
27:24	III 842
27:25	I 296
27:39	III 384
27:43	III 272
27:46	II 444
27:51	I 429; II 584
27:59	I 286
28:16	I 532
28:18	III 733
28:19	III 699
28:20	I 81, 88, 129

Mark

1:4	I 207, 215; II 546
1:11	III 418
1:12–13	II 286, 597
1:13	III 415
1:14–15	II 489
1:23	III 381
1:24	I 255, 274; II 356, 357, 405, 414, 655; III 411
1:34	II 410
1:35	I 343; II 327
2:14	III 383
2:17	I 67, 98
2:26	I 71
3:13	I 276, 414; II 474
3:14	I 335
3:35	I 49

4:1	III 381
4:11	II 209; III 169
4:15	I 79
4:16	I 79
4:17	I 79
4:18	I 79
4:19	I 79, 80, 88
4:25	I 43, 51, 58; III 409
4:34	II 509
4:39	III 186
5:4	I 502
5:8	I 243
5:15	II 404, 655
5:22	II 339; III 224
5:26	I 271
5:28	I 402
5:30	II 439, 667
6:6	I 266
6:7	I 336; III 309
6:8	I 337, 381; II 733
6:8–9	I 379, 459
6:12	I 201; II 428, 662
6:13	I 496
6:20	I 231
6:31	III 177
6:33–44	II 247
6:41	I 202
6:47	II 462
6:48	I 230, 480; II 415; III 186
6:49	II 429
7:13	II 278
7:21	I 43, 50, 79, 87
7:21–22	I 79
7:23	I 48, 79
7:28	II 279; III 160
7:34	II 271
7:37	I 324; II 812
8:33	II 273
8:34	I 48
8:36	I 68, 93
9:5	I 186; III 686
9:19	I 241, 494, 496
9:20	I 403; II 428, 467
9:22	III 392
9:24	I 495
9:27	II 463, 675
9:28	I 65; III 415
9:37	II 324
10:7	II 284, 577, 696
10:18	I 49
10:21	I 100; II 38, 86
10:29	I 64
10:43–44	I 48
11:25	I 78, 80, 88
12:1	III 399
12:30	I 41, 84; II 449, 671
12:30–33	I 84
12:42	II 599
13:1	II 400

13:20,22	III 135
13:24	III 389
14:3	III 228
14:9	II 489
14:13	I 213
14:17–21	III 693
14:22,24	I 129
14:33	I 261; II 328
14:35	II 294; III 46
14:45	I 195, 377
14:52	II 268
14:68	II 325
14:70	II 426
15:39	II 473
16:2	II 327
16:6	II 42
16:9	II 321, 411
16:18	I 325, 465; II 663
16:20	I 203, 320, 377, 383, 540; II 399, 468, 513, 626, 691; III 177, 223, 229, 382 397

Luke

1:10	I 274
1:11	II 760
1:13	III 464, 588, 719
1:14	I 209; II 428
1:15	III 422
1:17	I 335; II 489, 526, 692; III 381
1:25	I 537
1:27	III 397
1:28	I 138, 475; II 760
1:30	II 463, 520, 675
1:31	II 443
1:32	I 116, 284
1:35	I 195, 259, 403, 420; II 649; III 862
1:37	III 391
1:38	II 324; III 44, 346
1:41	II 243, 489
1:41–45,60	III 80
1:42	I 475
1:44	I 534
1:47	I 201; II 181, 316
1:48	II 257, 520
1:51	II 371
1:52	II 573
1:52,53	II 753
1:56	II 449, 671
1:57	II 441, 443, 669
1:57–63	II 242
1:58	I 238
1:60	II 443, 684
1:66	II 242; III 176
1:67	II 526
1:68	I 147, 531; II 309, 312, 568, 608
1:75	II 550
1:76	III 381

1:76,79	II 526	5:10	II 447
1:77	III 381	5:11	I 380; III 100
1:78	II 489, 547	5:19	II 285
1:79	II 489, 526, 714, 772	5:26	II 355, 409, 566; III 862
1:79,78	I 534	5:29–32	II 247
2:1	II 267	5:31	I 98
2:7	I 156, 255, 535; II 815; III 230, 363, 381, 397	5:32	III 395
		6:8	II 463, 675
2:7,12	III 381	6:12	I 262; III 177, 382
2:8	I 224; III 458	6:14	III 686
2:10	II 408, 490	6:18	I 323
2:11	II 468, 490; III 363	6:20	III 539, 635
2:13	I 279, 296, 416; II 446, 677; III 74, 870	6:22	I 74, 75
		6:23	I 75, 452
2:13,20	II 403	6:27	I 48; III 422
2:14	I 156	6:29	I 73, 89; II 44, 92
2:15	II 388, 476	6:30	I 73, 89; II 47, 73, 94, 300, 530; III 438
2:19	I 284		
2:19,51	I 135, 137	6:31	I 48, 98
2:20	II 325, 388, 426, 476	6:34	II 139, 304, 306; III 280, 282
2:25	I 226	6:38	I 78
2:26	II 662	6:41	I 72
2:28	III 528, 637, 696	6:44	III 259, 708
2:28ff	III 695	6:48	III 236
2:29	II 361; III 49	7:4	II 245; III 466
2:35	II 632, 638, 709	7:11–12	I 212
2:40	II 445	7:12	I 228, 239, 246, 402; II 461; III 51
2:44	I 189; III 501		
2:45	II 277, 619	7:13	II 423, 656; III 235
2:46	III 397	7:15	I 245
2:47	I 321	7:16	II 295, 568
2:51	II 405	7:22	I 324
2:52	II 466	7:25	I 65; II 326, 561, 575
3:3	II 546	7:32	III 186
3:5	II 707	7:33	I 404
3:8	I 47, 78; II 270, 568; III 388	7:36–50	II 754
3:9	I 514	7:37–51	III 651
3:16	II 265; III 383	7:38	II 339
3:22	III 418	7:38,44	II 267, 617
4:1	II 278	7:39	II 266, 617
4:1–13	II 597	7:44	II 420
4:2	I 101; II 286	7:44–45	III 473
4:2,5	III 862	7:47	I 282; II 754
4:4	I 283	7:48	II 511
4:15	I 228, 322, 393; II 264	7:49	I 195
4:18	I 48; II 373, 625, 704, 712; III 174, 514	8:1	I 266, 403; II 455, 640, 714
		8:2	I 323
4:22	III 401, 859	8:5	I 79, 88
4:25	II 149, 344, 355, 409; III 290	8:10	III 258, 409, 708, 814
4:30	I 234, 396, 545	8:11	I 79, 88, 266
4:33	II 456	8:12	I 79
4:34	I 203, 226; II 278, 319, 326, 356, 376, 409, 411, 413; III 411	8:13	I 79
		8:14	I 79
		8:15	I 80, 88
4:37	I 195	8:18	I 43, 58, 134; III 409
4:43	I 239, 241; III 843	8:21	I 49
5:1	I 320	8:24	III 186
5:6	I 206	8:28	I 240
5:9	II 408	8:42	II 267

8:44	III 508, 621
9:1–3	I 583, 589
9:1–6	II 206; III 256, 704
9:1–16	III 704
9:2	I 201; II 626
9:3	I 73, 89, 379, 539; II 38, 84, 86, 254, 400, 544; III 196, 382, 438, 568, 715
9:5	I 508
9:6	I 267
9:10	II 264
9:12–17	II 247
9:23	I 48, 130; II 254, 640; III 381, 438
9:24	I 74, 95; II 305; III 119
9:26	I 74
9:28	I 261
9:32	III 686
9:33	I 300
9:35	III 418
9:39	II 389, 644, 716; III 869
9:48	I 519; II 256; III 408
9:55	II 271
9:58	II 159, 285, 578; III 262
9:59	III 383
9:60	II 553, 691
9:62	I 65, 101, 130, 537; II 754; III 390
10:1	I 207, 321, 336, 465; III 245, 269, 309, 462, 587
10:1–4	I 583, 589
10:3	III 523
10:4	I 73, 89, 379; II 84, 400; III 196, 382
10:5	I 73, 102, 461; II 543
10:6	I 203, 320; II 133, 341; III 297, 857
10:7	I 73, 392, 583; II 561
10:7–8	I 227; III 573
10:8	I 66, 102; II 298; III 50, 442, 846
10:11	I 261, 409, 508; II 622
10:16	III 383, 384, 403, 408, 418
10:17	I 212; II 297
10:20	I 75, 90
10:21	II 682
10:24	III 443, 574
10:27	I 84, 159, 325; II 247; III 383, 384, 531, 651
10:30	I 376, 538; II 326, 428, 575, 654; III 163
10:30–37	II 539
10:34	I 435, 500; II 360, 464, 679
10:35	II 340, 382
10:38–42	I 61; III 696
10:40	I 541
10:42	III 87
11:1	I 222
11:2	I 80, 88, 388; II 551
11:2–4	I 475
11:8,13	III 391
11:10	II 294
11:15	II 626
11:20	III 833
11:21	I 137, 186
11:21–22	I 568
11:24	I 80
11:25	I 437
11:26	I 80, 88; II 274
11:28	II 271, 454, 549, 675
11:41	II 306
11:52	III 423
11:54	II 273
12:1	I 236
12:4	I 75, 95, 549; II 412
12:4–5	II 265
12:8,9	II 490
12:12	II 256; III 247, 308
12:15	I 69, 105, 548; III 294
12:17	I 185; II 281
12:20	II 816
12:22	II 159; III 262, 238
12:24	I 234; II 400; III 296, 470, 593, 860
12:32	I 380; I 382; II 42, 205, 260, 359, 392, 553, 690; III 166, 276, 391, 702, 865
12:35	II 732
12:37	I 271; II 732
12:42	I 246, 350; II 747
12:47	II 623, 750
12:49	I 247
13:7	II 466
13:10	III 382
13:12	II 447
13:24	I 72
13:25	II 276, 416
13:34	II 260
14:9	II 276, 307, 416
14:10	II 737
14:11	III 452, 582
14:15–20	I 567
14:19	II 521
14:26	I 64; II 510
14:27	I 131, 147, 157, 471; II 756
14:30	II 382
14:32	I 203, 269
14:33	I 130, 539, 582; II 509, 756
15:2	II 247
15:4	II 145; III 325
15:4,6	II 365
15:4–7	III 630
15:5	II 489
15:6	I 190
15:8	II 405
15:9	I 374
15:12	II 368
15:13	II 271, 273, 619; III 351

15:16	II 246
15:17	I 380; II 313
15:18	III 502
15:24	II 429
16:2	I 74; III 414
16:3	I 545
16:4	II 364, 370
16:8	II 330
16:9	II 615
16:14	II 72
16:15	II 569, 736
16:16,31	I 329
16:23	I 235, 397
17:4	I 477
17:10	I 72, 83, 209; II 133, 341, 521; III 297, 857
17:12	III 417
17:16	III 401
17:32	I 549
17:34–35	I 587
18:1	I 47, 80, 88
18:3	II 168, 328; III 304, 513
18:4	II 118, 346; III 294
18:11	II 361, 641
18:13	I 205, 308; II 312, 363, 588; III 455
18:19	I 49, 76, 85, 162; II 203; III 218, 370
18:22	I 64, 100; II 296; III 301, 393, 404, 426
18:24	I 530
18:30	I 64
18:43	I 296; II 339, 478
19:3	II 268
19:8	III 526
19:12	II 489
19:13	I 337, 384
19:14	II 217, 341; III 247, 308
19:15	II 250
19:17	I 263
19:20	I 183
19:36	II 531
19:47	III 382
20:25	III 252
20:36	II 242
21:8	III 405
21:9	II 282
21:15	II 603
21:17	III 382
21:19	I 75
21:20	III 425
21:28	II 414
21:30	II 466
21:34	I 69; III 403
21:34–35	I 71
21:36	I 80, 88
21:37	III 382
22:10	II 416
22:15	III 336

22:19	I 78, 117
22:20	III 382
22:21–2	III 693
22:23	I 224, 239; II 444
22:24	II 342
22:26	I 48, 67, 68
22:28	II 325; III 382
22:31	II 326
22:41	II 277, 292
22:42	I 46, 436
22:43	II 384; III 868
22:44	I 46; III 393
22:45	I 262, 409; III 861
22:62	II 676
23:26	II 489
23:28	I 515
23:33	III 422
23:35	II 72
23:39	III 382, 383
23:42	I 158; II 343
23:45	I 288
23:46	III 398
23:47	I 203, 235; II 439, 667
24:13	II 582
24:14	III 186
24:17	I 213
24:18	II 287
24:29	II 687
24:32	II 288
24:39	II 651
24:41–43	III 632
24:45	I 225
24:46	III 397
24:47	II 526
24:49	I 585; II 293; III 176, 267, 467
24:52,53	I 296; III 272
24:53	I 235, 261; II 278; III 275, 484, 603

John

1:1–5	II 729
1:3	I 46; III 471
1:6	II 347; III 295
1:6:7	I 259
1:7	II 526, 557, 644; III 381
1:8,9	II 489
1:9	I 286; II 672
1:10	II 371
1:11	III 387, 395, 408
1:14	II 542
1:15	II 387, 445; III 244
1:17	II 377; III 422
1:17,45	I 329
1:18	I 128, 129, 539; II 622
1:40	III 683
1:42	III 426
1:43	II 299
1:47	II 359, 552
2:1–11	III 632

2:2	III 692	7:43	I 543
2:3	I 339, 552	8:11	I 98
2:9	I 323	8:12	II 316
2:11	III 692	8:16	II 368
2:12	I 374	8:29	II 760
3:5	I 47, 74, 95; II 241, 370; III 381	8:39	III 425
		8:41	I 43, 50, 78
3:11	II 282, 403	8:47	I 119
3:13	I 282	8:50,54	III 730
3:16	II 376	8:56	I 255
3:18	II 358, 599	8:59	I 191
3:19	I 46	9:1	I 306; II 450, 672, 673
3:29	I 291; II 527, 596; III 173	9:24	I 304, 306; II 334
3:31	I 282; II 376; III 856	9:27	I 460; II 276, 416
3:34	II 315	9:32	II 249, 490, 552
4:6	I 551; II 266, 278, 292, 409	9:34	II 522
4:10	II 520	9:35	I 129
4:13	II 298	9:38	II 434, 664
4:14	I 567	10:3	III 399
4:17	II 272	10:10	III 248
4:21	II 325, 388; III 43	10:11	I 88; II 464, 679; III 510, 511
4:23	I 46, 80, 88	10:12	III 399
4:24	I 47, 80, 88, 128	10:14	III 510, 621
4:28	I 582	10:14–15	I 80
4:35,36	I 331	10:15	I 42, 49, 88; III 382
4:36	I 515	10:16	III 90
4:42	II 603	10:18	I 79, 87
5:4	II 410	10:19	I 543
5:24	II 490	10:28	II 367, 420; III 288
5:25	II 287	11:6	II 274
5:31	II 383	11:9	I 272
5:32	II 223, 264; III 351	11:27	I 70, 92, 94; II 634
5:33	I 289; II 636	11:28	II 283
5:33–34	III 638	11:39	III 163
5:35	I 269, 428; II 315; III 50, 90, 526, 636	11:47	I 496
		11:52	I 381
5:41	I 544	12:1	I 278
5:44	III 408	12:3	II 347, 587
6:5	II 312	12:3–8	III 651
6:5–13	II 247	12:6	I 70, 130; II 139, 300, 304, 579; III 281, 406
6:10–13	I 483		
6:12	I 472; II 528; III 93	12:12	II 299
6:15	II 247; III 177	12:13	I 284, 417; II 647; III 854
6:31	III 318	12:15	I 534
6:33	III 548	12:19	I 545; III 458, 583
6:38	III 157	12:23	I 138
6:41	I 336, 416	12:28	I 81; III 479, 598
6:54	I 57, 78	12:31	III 423
6:54,57	I 47	12:32	I 291; III 739
6:55	I 129	12:36	III 383
6:63	I 44, 45, 81, 88, 125, 128	12:40	I 506; II 265, 614
6:64	II 352; III 385	12:44	III 870
6:68	II 384	13:1	I 278, 415, 516; II 385, 386, 387, 475, 583, 631, 643, 715
6:69	I 553		
7:12	I 487, 543	13:13	II 522
7:15	I 204	13:13–16	II 750
7:26	II 389	13:14	I 68
7:34	II 294	13:15	II 287, 379, 522
7:38	III 532	13:16	II 733

13:18	III 505, 618
13:19	II 251
13:21	II 328
13:21–6	III 693
13:27	III 232
13:29	II 579; III 406
13:34	III 335, 447
13:37–38	III 382
14:6	I 81, 88, 448; III 408, 421, 541, 655
14:6–9	I 128
14:8	III 689
14:10	III 384
14:14	III 43
14:18	I 415; III 335
14:23	I 41, 48, 80, 88
14:26	I 338; II 301, 307; III 274
14:30	III 382, 423
15:2,8	II 148, 343, 572; III 289
15:4,5	III 384
15:5	III 395
15:7	I 81, 88
15:10	III 384
15:12	I 72; III 335
15:13	I 130; III 382
15:14	II 320
15:14–15	II 358
15:15	II 291
15:16	II 736
15:19	II 256; III 382
15:20	I 74; III 395
15:22	II 295
15:26	II 316; III 49, 855
16:2	III 424, 723
16:12	I 458, 550; II 259
16:13	II 271
16:23	II 620
16:25	I 550
16:28	II 390, 644
16:33	I 331; III 382
17:1	II 340, 703; III 398, 539, 635
17:1	I 81
17:3	II 603
17:6	I 42, 49, 81, 89
17:8	I 42, 49; II 321
17:8–10	I 81
17:9	I 42, 49
17:10	III 382
17:10–12	II 247
17:11	I 42, 49, 81, 109, 140, 144, 145, 146
17:11	I 81
17:11,16	II 353
17:13–15	I 81
17:14	III 382
17:15	I 458
17:16	III 382
17:17	I 42, 49, 115
17:17,19	III 382
17:17–20	I 81
17:19	I 42, 49
17:20	I 42
17:21	III 384
17:23	I 42, 81
17:24	I 42, 49, 81, 89
17:26	I 81, 82
18:9	III 357, 382
18:16	II 273, 287
18:29	II 273, 446
18:36	I 536; III 382
19:11	I 165, 276, 414
19:17	I 147, 157, 471
19:18	III 382, 383, 422
19:19	I 225, 390, 477; II 557, 700; III 92
19:20	II 282
19:28	II 640
19:30	II 420; III 857
19:31	II 490
19:34	I 280
19:35	II 286; III 303, 687
19:40	I 242
20:2	III 686
20:4	I 255; II 386
20:11	I 242; II 456
20:11–18	III 651
20:21	III 71
20:25	I 410, 416; II 406, 490, 652
20:25–29	III 687
20:27	II 406, 646; III 688
20:30	I 484; II 468
21:1–14	III 632
21:4	I 284, 417; II 328, 476, 533, 647
21:7	II 623
21:7,20	III 686
21:15	II 620
21:17	II 601
21:19	III 383
21:24	II 286; III 121, 260, 273, 299, 303, 414
21:25	II 185

Acts of the Apostles

1:1	I 180, 323; II 368, 550; III 321, 462, 587, 731
1:3	I 207, 381
1:5	II 271
1:8	II 764
1:9	II 746; III 732
1:16	III 358
1:24	II 408
1:26	II 466; III 693
2:4	I 459; III 519
2:4–13	III 631
2:5	I 206, 380
2:6	I 284
2:7,8	III 519, 631

2:11	I 279; II 347, 388, 476, 552; III 295
2:13,15	II 252
2:14	I 116
2:17	II 525
2:28	II 329; III 382
2:34	I 278
2:37	I 228, 245, 249
2:41	I 209, 234
2:44	I 272; III 259
2:44,47	I 540
2:45	I 540
2:46	II 259
2:47	I 206, 210, 322, 545; III 260
3:2	II 138, 304, 306; III 280
3:4	II 273; III 426
3:5	II 248
3:6	I 540; II 456
3:7	I 240; II 328, 627
3:8	II 627
3:10	I 306; II 370, 412, 624
3:14	I 271
4:6–7	I 403
4:8	III 426
4:10	I 403; II 274, 299
4:13	I 204, 245; II 341, 370, 620, 763; III 327, 717
4:19	I 240
4:26–27	I 546
4:32	I 579; II 46; III 259, 528, 637
5:3	III 352
5:3–4	II 273
5:4	I 196; II 72
5:7	I 300
5:9	III 388
5:11	I 270
5:12	II 698
5:17	II 347
5:29	II 265, 614
5:35	III 403
5:36	I 246
5:38–39	III 850
5:41	I 334, 456; III 842
6:4	II 343, 371
6:7	I 473, 486; III 119, 120, 297, 298, 316, 393, 414, 711
6:10	II 626
6:14	II 352
6:15	I 280; III 870
7:3	II 300
7:5	II 682, 717
7:55	I 477; II 322, 386
7:58	II 743
7:59	II 475; III 398
7:60	I 278, 323, 415; II 420, 644, 656, 715
8:10	II 406, 652
8:21	II 273
8:37	II 421
8:39	I 234
9:4	I 300; II 328, 437, 460, 480, 573, 676; III 304
9:5	III 200
9:6	II 36, 71, 245, 533
9:7	II 71
9:9	I 303; II 431
9:15	II 243, 757; III 631
9:28	I 215, 385
9:31	I 205, 225, 380; II 259, 387; III 256
9:34	I 242
10:1	II 446
10:1–2	II 455
10:2	I 239, 241
10:4	II 441, 670
10:10	I 464; III 411
10:16	I 473
10:25	I 247; III 224, 291
10:27	II 251
10:31	III 546, 549, 645
10:36	I 207, 215
10:44	II 272, 616
11:5	II 313, 463; III 411, 425
11:7	II 464
11:12	III 248
11:17	II 421
11:21	II 289
11:28	II 370
12:5	II 258
12:6	I 334
12:7	II 407, 437, 667
12:9	II 463, 676
12:10	II 437, 667
12:11	II 268, 328, 355, 412, 463, 573; III 492, 607
13:5	I 244, 298, 299
13:9	I 270; II 620; III 426
13:10	I 445
13:16	I 487
13:26	II 255
13:48	I 71, 91, 96; II 146, 360; III 288
14:3	II 368
14:11	I 278; III 869
14:15	II 409
14:21	I 263
14:22	III 227
15:11	II 468
15:13	III 403
15:36	I 248; I 479
15:39	II 149; II 344; III 290
16:17	I 190; II 295, 321, 325, 375; III 43
16:18	I 242; III 483, 602
17:3	II 270
17:13	II 352
17:19–20	I 530
17:31	II 421, 657

18:9	I 303; II 319	4:11	II 735
18:25	I 266; II 400; III 391, 400	4:18	II 400, 466
19:19	III 406	4:19	II 400
20:19	III 227	4:20	I 304, 306
20:24	II 280; III 863	4:25	I 567
20:28	II 250, 536, 686; III 239	5:2	II 324
20:29	III 488, 725	5:5	II 762, 814
20:31	III 400	5:10	III 392
20:32	I 209	5:12–7	III 876
20:34	I 125	5:15	II 411
21:4	II 273, 619	5:20	I 293
21:14	II 313	6:5	I 510
21:30	I 279, 416; II 388, 403, 476; III 870	6:6	I 567; II 732
		6:7	I 259
22:16	I 234, 397; II 422, 480	6:10	III 381
23:4	II 389, 644, 716; III 869	6:11	III 388
23:9	II 256	6:13	I 183
23:11	III 390	6:19	II 266, 617, 732
24:3	I 214	6:20	I 183
25:13	II 256	7:6	I 466
26:8	II 421	7:22	II 261, 311, 380
26:16	I 248, 99	7:24	II 401, 650
27:10	III 411	7:25	I 331
27:35	I 213, 234, 249, 305; II 148, 344, 390; III 289	8:4	I 67, 79, 87
		8:5	II 313, 608
28:6	I 238; II 444	8:6	1:75; 1:90; III 388, 393, 399, 410
28:15	I 242, 299		
28:25	III 358	8:6–7	I 466
30:9–10	III 684	8:8	II 815
31	III 688	8:9	II 250
		8:11	I 266; III 397

Romans

		8:12	III 850
		8:13	I 331
1:1	I 227; II 256; III 844	8:14	II 273
1:5	III 388	8:17	I 449, 515, 516; II 255, 295; III 46, 88
1:7	II 468		
1:8	III 391	8:18	II 645
1:9	II 372	8:21	I 251
1:19	I 277	8:22,26	III 321
1:20	III 257, 274, 317, 397, 414, 704, 712	8:24	III 392
		8:26	II 534; III 415, 514, 530
1:22	II 755	8:33	I 275; III 329
1:25	I 76, 90, 116; III 220, 372, 517, 518, 535, 563, 564, 565	8:35	II 393
		8:38–39	I 449
1:29	II 343	9:5	I 279; II 299; III 438, 569
1:29–30	I 72	9:6	III 395
1:30	II 363	9:8	III 425
1:32	III 392	9:11	II 350
2:1	III 397	9:12	II 359
2:3	II 271	9:16	III 540
2:5	I 133; I 538	9:27	III 395
2:7	II 300	9:28	I 105; II 322, 370; III 398
2:11	II 144, 365, 371	9:33	I 448
2:15	II 314	10:11	I 448
2:29	I 197; II 337	10:15	I 587; II 526
3:4	II 511	10:18	III 382
3:5	III 715	11:5	III 395
3:8	III 857	11:23	I 553
3:12	I 132	11:31	III 438
4:2	I 273		

11:33	I 86; III 421
12:1	I 275, 554; II 326, 600, 698; III 231, 232, 312, 393, 398
12:2	II 240, 760; III 393, 852
12:3	I 265, 274, 323; II 473; III 867
12:5	III 542
12:10	II 376
12:11,12	I 542
12:12	I 207, 273
12:14	I 207
12:16	III 389
12:17	II 339, 373
12:18	II 133, 341; III 47, 296, 297
12:19	I 190, 333, 374; II 537
12:21	I 76
13:7	II 247
13:12	II 348
13:14	III 174, 422
14:3	I 71
14:10	I 44
14:13	II 273, 619
15:5	III 410
15:13	I 335, 408
15:13,19	I 242; III 397
15:14	II 343
15:15	II 254
15:18,19	I 540
15:23	I 266
16:9	II 358
16:16	I 278
16:27	I 282, 308, 420; II 649, 717; III 382
21:27	III 715

1 Corinthians

1:1	I 271, 413
1:2	I 212
1:5	I 547
1:13	II 691
1:21	I 259
1:22	I 260
1:23	II 393; III 694
1:24	II 603, 625, 690, 704
1:24,30	II 622
1:25	II 400
1:26	I 48, 118, 543; II 296; III 388, 406
1:26–27	II 736
1:27	I 291, 566; III 188, 381
1:27–29	III 459
1:28	I 291; III 388
1:29	II 357, 414; III 459
1:31	II 332; III 583
2:1–2,4–5	II 318
2:2	I 284; II 316
2:4	I 215; II 37, 50, 99, 369, 698; III 176
2:4–5	I 566
2:4,13	II 553; III 545

2:5	II 320
2:6	I 165
2:9	II 308; III 397
2:10	II 280, 618, 701; III 404
2:14	I 53, 54; II 300, 301, 510, 579; III 163, 219, 277
2:15	II 364
2:16	III 403
3:3	II 297
3:8	II 133, 341; III 47, 297, 857
3:11	I 196
3:13	I 479
3:15	III 392
3:17	I 73
4:3	I 479; II 265, 468, 614; III 864
4:5	I 479
4:7	III 581
4:12	I 578; II 351, 404
4:15	II 690
4:16	II 386
4:21	II 518
5:2	II 491
5:3	I 390; II 308, 552; III 388
5:4–5	I 73
6:11	II 390
6:17	II 389
6:19	I 73
6:20	I 42, 49; III 250, 382
7:2	I 452
7:5	II 264, 324, 325, 562, 563, 618
7:11	II 441
7:14	II 272
7:20	II 343, 573
7:20,24	II 147, 372; III 314
7:24	I 69, 93
7:28	II 329
7:31	II 815
7:32	I 244
7:33	I 194. 214
7:33–34	II 289, 290
7:34	I 185
7:40	I 262; II 301, 316; III 49, 852
8:1	I 588; II 209; III 118, 258, 314, 315, 320, 394, 408, 707
8:6	III 471
9:9	I 510
9:14	III 850
9:19	II 731; II 750
9:19,22	I 479
9:27	I 266; II 751, 817; III 691, 854
10:4	II 354, 798
10:12	III 693
10:13	III 502
10:27,28	III 407
11:20	I 209, 224
11:23	III 386
11:24	I 117
11:27	I 117

11:29	I 47, 117, 129, 265
12:3	I 132
12:6	I 308; II 303, 354, 389
12:9,10	I 477
12:11	I 243; II 379, 729; III 421
12:12	II 404, 655
12:28	I 131
12:28–31	III 862
12:31	I 260; II 324, 681
13	I 447
13:1	I 529; III 487, 724
13:1–3	II 358, 600
13:2	I 131; III 449, 580
13:3	II 300; III 562
13:4	I 532
13:5	II 282
13:6	I 516
13:7	I 480
13:12	I 450; II 141, 322; III 221
14:3	II 282
14:25	I 224, 225, 251, 321, 389; II 263, 614
14:37	II 364
15:8	II 327
15:16	II 297
15:32	I 531
15:33	III 392
15:41	I 278
15:45	III 393
15:58	II 297
16:7	II 310
16:9	II 288

2 Corinthians

1:1	I 413
1:3	I 262, 282; II 360, 587; III 220, 451, 582
1:4	II 330, 491
1:5	I 285
1:8	II 641
1:12	II 387, 403
2:3	III 504, 618
2:4	II 336
2:5,19	III 730
2:7	II 329
2:14	I 251
2:15	II 261, 319, 361; III 324
2:16	II 295
3:2	II 314
3:3	II 528
3:6	I 132; III 423
3:18	II 334, 634, 637, 710
4:6	III 410
4:7	I 339; II 694; III 464, 588, 718
4:16	I 266; III 868
4:17	II 384
5:6	II 308; III 181
5:6,8	II 605
5:8	II 272; III 392

5:10	II 314; III 320
5:13	I 199, 271, 284; II 361, 695
5:14	I 270; II 358, 599, 607, 699
5:15	I 214; II 551; III 388, 392
5:17	II 645
5:19	I 280
5:20	II 399
6:1	II 310, 606
6:2	II 272
6:3	I 159
6:4	I 385
6:5	II 57; III 381
6:6	I 534
6:10	I 222, 520; II 333; III 46, 394
6:13,18	II 339
6:15	I 466
7:4	I 202, 292, 553; II 249, 534, 688
7:5	I 266
7:6	I 274
7:6–7	II 489
7:8	II 261; III 324
7:9	I 265, 323
7:15	III 388
8:2	I 292; II 257, 378, 722; III 386
8:5	II 266
8:7	I 228
8:9	I 46, 103, 248, 298, 567; II 151, 295, 296, 582; III 269, 274, 386
8:14	I 247
8:19	I 230
9:15	III 391
10:7	I 265
10:10	II 378
10:13	III 421
11:3	I 488; II 329
11:6	II 315, 613, 622
11:13–15	II 282
11:14	I 569
11:23–29	II 258
11:27	I 220; II 259, 561; III 121, 234, 237, 279, 299, 381
11:29	II 53; III 44
11:31	III 220, 372, 569
12:1–4	II 743
12:2	I 435; III 435, 566
12:2,3	III 516
12:2–4	III 304
12:4	I 463; II 633
12:5	I 131
12:7	I 445; II 575; III 312
12:8	II 119, 269; III 322, 350
12:9	II 143, 340; III 288, 369
12:10	III 392
12:12	I 343; II 147, 381
12:13	II 258
12:14	I 544
12:15	II 697

13:11	III 410
13:13	I 298

Galatians

1:1,12	III 391
1:4	II 379
1:8	II 376; III 856
1:10	I 260, 265; II 732; III 408
1:11–12	II 511
1:12	II 324; III 383
1:14	I 183
1:16	III 267
1:19	III 689
1:20	I 308
2:5	I 540; II 284, 324, 407
2:11	I 230; III 198
2:14	II 321; III 851
2:19	II 640, 714
2:19–20	II 383
2:20	I 278, 479, 567; II 362, 430, 474, 758
3:1	II 683; III 867
3:16	III 394
3:27	II 401, 531, 650; III 174, 422
4:2	II 374
4:15	II 294; III 46
4:19	II 359; III 175, 335
4:22	II 745
4:22–3	III 182
4:23,29	III 422
4:28,29	III 422
4:29	III 410
4:29–30	III 182
4:30	III 394, 422
4:31	II 260; III 324
5:4	II 340
5:13	I 68; II 750
5:15	II 343; III 389
5:16	II 274, 702; III 862
5:17	III 202
5:22	II 329
5:24	I 202, 567; II 560, 645, 694, 720; III 96, 392, 411
5:26	I 185, 247, 541; II 332
6:2	I 134
6:3	III 561
6:10	I 446, 545; II 358
6:14	I 218, 328; II 377, 383, 401, 682, 758; III 203, 422, 450, 581
6:16	I 341; II 682; III 189
6:17	I 267, 281, 308, 412; II 490, 37, 654, 682, 719, 743, 816; III 189, 426, 740, 868, 877
6:17,18	I 341
6:18	II 682
6:28	III 250

Ephesians

1:3	I 271; III 447, 577
1:4	II 735
1:9	III 416
1:10	III 385
1:18	I 275
1:21	II 312
1:22	II 404, 655
2:1–2	III 876
2:2	I 554
2:3	II 241; III 306
2:4	II 632
2:8	I 448
2:15	II 399
2:17	I 335; II 489
2:18	II 284, 348
2:19	I 286; III 545, 683
2:20	I 217; II 272; III 148
2:20–21	II 257
2:22	I 217, 221; III 330
3:1	III 381
3:7	I 188
3:8	III 158, 383
3:8–9	III 158
3:14	I 335; III 391
3:16	II 261
3:17	III 39, 424
3:18	I 158; III 542
3:19	III 542
4:1	II 341
4:2	II 272
4:3	II 260, 261, 369; III 324
4:3–5	I 223
4:4,5	I 542
4:6	I 276; II 354, 474
4:8	I 568
4:13	II 246
4:14	II 360
4:18	III 416
4:21	II 386, 642
4:22	III 58
4:24	I 542; II 401, 650; III 165, 695
4:28	I 578; III 311
5:3	II 215; III 245, 309
5:5	I 548; II 384, 733
5:8	II 347, 672
5:14	II 817
5:19	I 263
5:20	I 414; III 347
5:26	II 622
5:32	I 261
6:6	I 117; III 408
6:10	I 205, 381, 385, 533; II 248, 545
6:11	II 329, 404, 655; III 876
6:12	I 567; II 343, 353; III 381, 411
6:14–16	I 462
6:16	I 191, 584
6:16–17	I 355

Philippians

1:11	II 393, 490
1:19	II 294
1:21	II 251, 601
1:22	I 180, 250, 289; II 300, 435
1:23	I 243, 267, 322, 412; II 764; III 392, 855
1:24	I 274
1:29	II 378
2:2	III 410
2:3	II 523
2:4,21	III 39
2:5–7	I 586
2:5,8	II 522
2:5–11	III 876
2:6,7	II 732
2:7	I 244; II 751; III 765
2:8	I 120, 129, 536; II 344, 726; III 392, 821
2:10	II 58
2:11	III 382
2:12	II 349; III 388
2:13	III 865
2:21	I 273, 568, 576; II 293; III 267, 408, 410
2:23	II 268
3:1	I 205; II 545
3:6	II 148, 343, 572; III 289
3:8	I 529, 544; II 145, 251, 365; III 174, 325, 382, 862
3:9	III 487
3:10	I 288; III 382, 871
3:10,21	II 401, 650
3:13	I 273, 533, 583, 589
3:14	I 567; II 254, 715
3:16	III 410
3:18	I 269
3:19	II 336; III 724
3:20	III 230, 362
4:1	II 281, 296
4:2	III 410
4:3	III 549
4:4	I 69, 91; II 545; III 342, 371
4:7	III 397
4:8	I 254; III 408
4:8–9	I 209
4:10	I 210
4:11	II 512
4:15	II 314
4:18	II 345; III 293
4:19	I 279
4:20	III 372

Colossians

1:9	II 278, 409
1:10	I 306
1:11	I 306
1:12	III 393
1:15	I 83
1:20	I 117
1:24	I 267, 412; III 867
1:26	II 314, 612; III 855
2:2	II 247
2:2–3	II 245
2:3	II 681
2:4,8	III 403
2:5	II 379; III 388
2:18	II 260, 293, 519
2:19	II 260; III 324
3:1	III 563
3:1–2	III 382
3:1–3	II 314; III 855
3:5	III 393
3:9–10	II 567
3:10	III 695
3:12	I 194; II 80, 306, 564, 735
3:14	II 261, 343; III 324, 786
3:16	II 215; III 245, 309
3:17	I 86, 207, 249; II 347; III 295, 846, 867
3:20	II 383
3:22	I 117
3:24	II 380, 383, 715
4:3	I 225; II 388
4:6	III 436, 453

1 Thessalonians

1:9	I 57, 109, 141
2:4	III 403
2:7	I 71, 103
2:13	II 258
2:16	III 422
3:1	II 737
4:1	I 537
4:4	II 694
4:5	III 351
4:11	II 351; III 321
5:5	II 407, 452, 677; III 383
5:8	I 355; II 380; III 323
5:14	I 336; II 355, 409
5:15	I 159
5:17	II 258, 699, 605; III 125, 333
5:18	I 78, 96, 271; II 146, 359; III 288
5:19	II 137, 293; III 45, 267
5:23	II 416
5:25	II 325

2 Thessalonians

1:3	I 273
2:4	III 421
2:11	I 265
3:10	I 69
3:16	I 126, 203, 379; II 84; III 219

1 Timothy

1:5	II 271; III 384, 401
1:15	I 295, 519; II 347, 588, 639, 725; III 295, 611
1:17	I 420; III 224, 291, 383, 459
2:3	II 406; III 857
2:7	I 188
2:10	II 251, 402
3:7	III 779
3:16	II 377; III 422
3:17	II 403, 413
4:1	I 469
4:5	I 119; II 215
4:6	II 393
4:7	II 417
4:8	II 586, 595, 735; III 175
4:9	II 639
4:12	II 315; III 50
6:3	II 420
6:5	I 542; III 165
6:7	II 523
6:7–8	I 531
6:8	I 70, 91, 545; III 550, 627
6:9	II 510, 722
6:10	III 329
6:15	II 578, 813; III 100
6:16	I 128

2 Timothy

1:7	I 253; III 865
2:3	I 189, 428; II 75, 258, 533
2:4	II 681
2:11	III 90, 95
2:14	I 72, 74, 102
2:15	II 282
2:19	I 401
2:24	II 517
3:6–7	II 510
3:10	II 603
3:14,39	II 513
3:16	I 270
3:17	II 350, 356
4:2	II 718
4:3	II 258
4:6	II 285
4:7	I 418, 515; II 280; III 863
4:8	I 568; II 386
4:18	II 310, 436, 666

Titus

1:12	II 371
2:7	II 145, 322, 342, 366
2:7,8	I 469; III 91
2:8	II 637; III 324
2:11	I 391; II 277, 525, 684
2:12	I 204; II 305, 325, 525
2:13	II 525
2:14	I 257; III 230, 363

3:1	III 343
3:2	I 72, 74, 254; III 865
3:5	I 370

Philemon

1:21	I 479
12	II 440

Hebrews

1:1	III 421
1:2	II 525; III 769
1:3	I 288
2:2	I 276; II 475
2:7,9	III 382
2:10	I 85
3:1	II 543
4:12	II 317; III 397, 404
5:5	II 491
5:7	II 273, 360, 371
5:8	II 289, 404, 512
5:9	I 243
5:14	II 763
6:1	II 338
6:6	III 867
6:9	I 549; II 339
7:3	II 284; III 175
9:9	I 277
9:14	II 299
9:15	II 358
9:19	I 295; II 391, 477
10:23	I 553
10:28	I 117
10:28–29	I 548
10:29	I 117; II 642
10:31	I 67
10:32	I 548; III 392
10:36	I 553; II 384
10:38	III 856
10:39	I 548
11:6	I 479; II 370; III 392, 403
11:12	I 465
11:13	I 515; II 267
11:14	I 446
11:26	III 384
11:37	II 324; III 43
11:37–38	III 392
12:1	I 532, 553
12:2	I 553; III 392
12:5	III 312
12:6,7	III 231
12:7	I 117
12:14	I 219
12:17	I 293
12:22	I 279; III 842
13:5	III 391
13:12	III 382; III 422
13:14	III 125, 333
13:20	III 323

James

1:2	I 75, 90
1:4	II 641
1:6	III 392
1:7	III 392
1:9	II 521
1:12	II 119, 322, 349; III 315, 723
1:17	I 282; II 314; III 383, 740, 765, 855
1:19	I 253
1:21	III 740
1:23	I 460
1:25	II 335, 512
1:27	I 188; III 740
2:2	I 448
2:5	I 103; II 295, 296, 300, 736; III 381
2:10	I 164
2:13	I 47
2:18	I 72
3:1	II 252
3:2	II 800; III 198
3:8	II 363; III 411
3:17	I 219
4:1	II 343
4:6	II 519, 520, 730
4:9	II 443
4:10	I 118
4:13	II 324, 416
5:16	I 77, 78, 98
5:17	I 260
8:31	II 256

1 Peter

1:5	I 259
1:9	II 341, 358, 410, 445; III 47, 116, 118, 297, 387, 394, 403, 408, 412, 419, 420
1:12	I 118; II 312
1:14	III 517, 624
1:17	I 382
1:19	I 280, 281; II 375, 598
1:20	III 867
1:21	II 682
1:22	I 68, 130; II 258
2:1	II 302; III 849
2:3	I 529
2:5	I 217; II 133, 341, 378, 400; III 297
2:9	II 735
2:10	II 598
2:11	I 103, 126; II 54, 160, 578, 583; III 163, 223, 239, 263, 383, 384, 386, 444, 492, 545, 575, 826
2:13	I 48, 68, 74, 89, 95; III 47
2:13–15	I 68

2:21	I 46, 79, 87, 147, 157, 259, 307; II 145, 148, 306, 343, 366, 390, 477, 802; III 288, 289
2:25	I 80; I 88
4:1	I 323
4:2	I 289
4:9	I 69, 91, 93
4:13	III 392
4:14	I 239, 404
5:2	II 620
5:3	II 245
5:5	II 523
5:6	I 118; II 349, 521
5:7	I 214
5:8	I 80, 88; III 539
5:8,9	III 876
5:10	III 382
9	II 133

2 Peter

1:4	I 230; II 247
1:7	I 542
1:10	III 388
1:11	II 548; III 381
1:14	II 641, 715
1:17–18	II 381
2:8	II 348, 588
2:15	I 542; III 165
2:17	II 320
2:20	I 543
2:22	I 130; II 264, 270, 594; III 94, 248, 327, 718

1 John

1:1	I 264, 293; II 376, 406, 419, 646, 648, 652; III 286
1:1–2	III 804
1:1,4	II 403
1:5	I 158
1:8	III 198
1:9	II 270
1:15	III 382
2:1	II 754
2:8	I 277
2:15	I 243, 541; II 319
2:16	III 481, 601
2:17	II 815
2:18	II 295, 339, 348, 582; III 224, 276, 291, 384, 388, 397, 422, 702, 849
2:19	I 542; III 164
2:20	II 613
2:27	I 537; III 274
3:10	I 78
3:14	I 52, 54
3:15–16	I 130
3:16	I 515

3:17	II 145, 365
3:18	I 72, 89, 220
4:1	I 549; II 337
4:9	I 147, 152
4:16	I 44, 51, 75, 80, 88, 89
4:17–18	III 384
4:18	I 165; II 600
4:21	II 358
5:4,5	I 428
5:5	III 155
5:13	I 267
7:44	II 420, 615
9:32	II 406

2 John

3	I 115
4	I 115
9	III 400
12	II 280; III 414

Jude

6:19	I 306
11	II 348
12	II 427
14:6	II 706
18	I 469; II 347; III 295
19,12	I 547

Revelation

1:5	I 116, 280, 281; III 381
1:7	II 720
1:8	II 140, 305; III 281, 423
1:9	II 404, 655; III 310
1:16	II 697
2:5	I 274
2:7	I 537, 553
2:9	I 542; III 164
2:10	II 268
2:11	I 114; III 368
2:17	I 520; II 309
2:23	III 404
3:5	II 380; III 323, 715
3:8	III 156
3:9	I 542; III 164
3:12	III 156, 191, 192, 193, 194
3:16	II 147, 350; III 49, 322
3:17	II 523, 728
3:19	I 72, 91, 96; II 146, 360; III 289
3:20	I 514
4:1–2	II 328, 573
4:5	III 122, 237, 300
4:6	II 301
4:6,8	III 412
4:8	I 161
4:9	I 141, 326, 554
4:9,11	I 113; III 367

4:11	I 138, 161; III 383
4:12	II 168
5:7	I 262
5:8	I 262
5:9	I 554; II 599; III 836
5:12	I 138, 161, 162; II 375, 604; III 383
5:12,9,2	II 728
5:12,13	I 339
5:13	I 49, 161, 282, 308; III 291
6:12	II 527; III 188, 191
6:13	II 280
7:2	II 527, 559, 638, 714, 717, 721, 735; III 149, 816
7:2–3	I 540
7:2,4	II 764
7:3	I 536; II 714
7:9	I 84, 206, 480; II 560
7:12	III 382
7:15	III 122, 237, 300
8:7	II 270
9:1	II 280
9:3	III 230, 312
9:6	II 294
10:1–3	III 815
10:3	II 349, 588
10:6	II 683
10:8	III 347
10:9	I 520
10:10	III 381
11:3	II 772
11:11	III 557, 558, 647
11:15	I 326; II 393, 683
12:1	III 422, 499, 614
12:3	I 355
12:4	I 370
12:7	II 573
12:9	II 290, 324; III 424, 740
12:12	I 554
12:14	I 531
13:1	I 355
13:1–10	III 816
13:4	III 421
13:5,7	III 312
13:7	I 270
13:8	III 549, 715
13:11–8	III 879
13:11–18	III 816
14:3	II 57
14:4	I 554
14:7	I 138
14:14	I 278, 294, 323, 416; II 388, 475, 644
16:13	I 355
16:14	I 286, 326; II 441
17:1	III 152
17:3	III 152
18:19	I 547
19:1	II 440, 668

Index of Textual References

for Primary Sources in Inner Margins

of texts in *The Saint* (I), *The Founder* (II), and *The Prophet* (III)

Francis of Assisi: Early Documents I, The Saint

The Writings of Francis of Assisi

Earlier Exhortation to the Brothers and Sisters of Penance (The First Version of the Letter to the Faithful) (1LtF): II 303, 311, 375; III 382

Later Admonition and Exhortation to the Brothers and Sisters of Penance (Second Version of the Letter to the Faithful) (2LtF): III 382

Exhortations to the Clergy (Letters to the Clergy)—Earlier Edition (1LtCl): I 251; II 376

Exhortation to the Clergy (Letters to the Clergy)—Later Edition (2LtCl): II 376

The First Letter to the Custodians (1LtCus): I 251, 376

A Rule for the Hermitages (RH): II 361, 564; III 696

The Earlier Rule (*Regula non bullata*) (ER): I 63, 92–96, 209, 218, 227, 273, 583; II 44, 46–48, 51–52, 89, 92–93, 98, 100–01, 125, 142, 146–47, 151, 287, 290, 291, 293, 295, 298, 300, 303, 323, 331–32, 340, 345, 359, 362, 375, 380, 622, 561, 563–64, 572, 579; III 49, 50, 59, 119, 154, 225, 235, 287–88, 293, 301, 322, 382–83, 393, 406, 442, 456, 550, 699, 858, 878

The Later Rule (*Regula bullata*) (LR): I 206–07, 210, 218, 227, 248, 385, 572–75; II 44–45, 50, 52, 56, 93, 98, 101, 123, 143, 147, 151, 267, 287, 290, 293, 295–96, 298, 300, 322, 332, 340, 342, 345, 362, 368, 561, 564, 577–79, 582–3, 600, 775–79; III 45, 50, 59, 64, 119, 128, 135, 148, 153, 157, 160, 162–63, 197, 223, 256, 269, 283, 287, 290, 293, 301, 322, 381, 384, 386, 391, 393, 406, 419, 442, 444, 456, 462, 492, 526, 545, 699, 702, 705, 709, 712, 742–44, 747, 756–58, 760, 769–77, 785, 826, 858–59

A Letter to Brother Anthony of Padua (LtAnt): II 352; III 519

The Praises of God (PrsG): II 280, 618

The Canticle of the Creatures (CtC): I 250, 401, 415; II 121, 186,187, 385; III 221, 348–49, 367, 371

The Canticle of Exhortation for the Ladies of San Damiano (CtExh): II 188; III 337–38

A Letter to the Entire Order (LtOrd): I 251; II 214, 287

The Testament (Test): I 195, 217–18, 222, 251, 379, 388, 571; II 42, 46, 52, 54, 74, 84, 86, 90, 93, 147, 160, 205, 207, 212, 247, 249, 253, 267, 276, 285, 287, 315, 332, 340, 344, 351–52, 376, 380, 416, 543, 750; III 128, 154, 157, 162–63, 172, 183, 203, 219, 239, 265, 270, 276, 322, 384–86, 395, 405, 420, 443, 493, 761, 877

The Admonitions (Adm)
  Adm 1: II 52
  Adm 3: I 222; II 46
  Adm 4: I 273; II 300, 579
  Adm 5: I 228; II 334
  Adm 6: II 209; III 707
  Adm 7: I 228
  Adm 8: I 228
  Adm 9: III 156
  Adm 11: III 252
  Adm 19: II 569
  Adm 20: I 228; II 753; III 343
  Adm 21: II 312; III 252, 878
  Adm 22: II 564
  Adm 23: I 228; II 52
  Adm 24: I 228
  Adm 26: II 52
  Adm 28: II 312; III 878

A Prayer Inspired by the Our Father (PrOF): III 383

A Salutation of the Virtues (SalV): II 328, 368

True and Perfect Joy (TPJ): II 341

The Life of Saint Francis by Thomas of Celano (1C)

1C 1: I 319, 370, 429, 431; II 34, 68, 684, 530
1C 2: I 319, 370, 430; II 69, 242, 246, 530, 531
1C 3: I 319, 370, 421; II 530, 532
1C 4: I 320, 371, 433, 443; II 70, 72, 531, 569
1C 5: I 371; II 245, 281, 509, 532, 638
1C 6: I 333, 371–372, 436; II 71, 72, 74, 75, 309, 248, 249, 533
1C 7: I 372; II 75, 272; III 833
1C 8: I 319, 373, 441; II 36, 76, 77, 249, 399, 536; III 833
1C 9: I 319, 373, 441; II 36, 77, 290, 536; III 833
1C 10: I 333, 373, 443; II 78, 251, 537
1C 11: I 320, 333, 374; II 37, 78, 265, 537
1C 12: I 319, 374, 445; II 79, 537; III 833
1C 13: I 334, 374–75, 447; II 37, 79, 537–38; III 833
1C 14: I 334, 375, 449; II 37, 251, 538
1C 15: I 375, 449; II 80, 538; III 695
1C 16: I 320, 334, 376, 452; II 535, 539
1C 17: I 320, 335, 376, 456; II 34, 47, 69, 72, 74, 244, 248, 373, 524, 530, 532, 534; III 492, 834
1C 18: I 291, 377, 457; II 83, 250, 540
1C 19: I 458; II 540
1C 20: II 83, 541; III 871
1C 21: I 222, 378–79, 458, 475; II 257, 540, 542, 689; III 871
1C 22: I 320, 379, 459; II 132, 399, 401, 530
1C 23: I 234, 320, 335, 379, 460; II 54, 84, 543, 625; III 443, 493
1C 24: I 320, 335, 462; II 280, 253–54, 543; III 436, 683
1C 25: I 461; II 544; III 435
1C 26: I 262, 320, 335, 380, 463, 816; II 41, 89, 263, 545; III 87
1C 27: I 321, 380, 408, 464; II 42, 545; III 388
1C 28: I 464; II 40
1C 29: I 321, 381, 465; II 41–42, 546; III 834
1C 30: I 381, 468; II 45, 264, 546; III 440, 834
1C 31: I 337, 382, 469
1C 32: I 321, 337, 383, 469; II 95, 254, 380, 547; III 390, 834
1C 33: I 383–84, 470; II 96, 248, 256, 547; III 390
1C 34: I 384, 472; II 276, 550; III 391
1C 35: I 337, 384; II 550, 623
1C 36: I 321, 338, 385, 473; II 37, 99, 255, 347, 400, 553, 626; III 90, 176, 415
1C 37: I 320, 385; II 99, 260, 399, 541, 553–54; III 834
1C 38: I 321, 338, 385, 473; II 46, 256, 572; III 38, 47, 699
1C 39: I 46, 257, 554; III 39, 492
1C 40: II 53, 56, 259, 551, 554; III 40, 234
1C 41: II 46, 555; III 39–41
1C 42: I 386, 474; II 99, 551, 662; III 38, 41, 89

1C 43: I 321, 386; II 563; III 41, 855
1C 44: I 386; II 99, 257; III 46, 89
1C 45: I 388, 475; II 42, 90, 401, 551, 609; III 41, 89
1C 46: I 388, 476; II 320; III 40–41, 694
1C 47: I 321, 389, 476; II 552; III 388, 421, 834
1C 48: I 321, 389, 390, 477; II 263, 552, 557, 618; III 49, 92, 834, 863
1C 49: I 390, 477; II 276, 617; III 469, 863–64
1C 50: I 390; II 617; III 864
1C 51: I 321, 389, 392; II 560; III 41, 45, 834
1C 52: I 321, 392, 478; II 333, 561, 570; III 305, 834
1C 53: I 321–22, 393, 478; II 52, 569–70
1C 54: II 570
1C 55: I 322, 393–94, 479, 482; II 309, 415, 584, 600; III 667, 855–56
1C 56: I 394, 484; II 416, 603; III 667
1C 57: I 320, 322, 395, 485; II 265, 602–03; III 44, 398, 490, 667, 856
1C 58: I 321, 338, 343, 396–97, 488, 491–92; II 321, 353, 411, 519, 624, 813; III 469, 834, 860
1C 59: I 322, 397, 491; II 412, 624, 798; III 834, 860
1C 60: I 322, 397, 492; II 414, 592
1C 61: I 323, 397–98, 492; II 410, 567, 665; III 396, 834, 862
1C 62: I 321, 388, 402; II 52, 256, 551; III 854, 856–57
1C 63: I 322, 323, 404–05, 493; II 411, 628; III 50, 834, 862
1C 64: I 404–05, 494; II 628; III 43, 862
1C 65: I 402, 494; II 461, 627
1C 66: I 166, 323, 403; II 461; III 834
1C 67: I 412, 403; II 450, 627; III 834
1C 68: I 323, 403, 494; II 467, 628
1C 69: I 323, 403, 494–95; II 627
1C 70: I 404, 496; II 67, 456, 628; III 834
1C 71: I 408; II 476, 605–06
1C 72: I 408, 496; II 606, 699; III 854
1C 73: I 409, 494; II 261, 511, 626; III 855
1C 74: I 499; II 260, 475, 696; III 871
1C 75: I 500
1C 76: I 339, 401, 500; II 275, 302, 577, 589–90
1C 77: I 322, 398–99, 401, 501, 504; II 321, 354, 590
1C 78: I 399, 501
1C 79: I 322, 501; II 590
1C 80: I 322, 400, 503; II 353, 551, 590, 798; III 834, 859
1C 81: I 322, 396, 401, 504; II 590, 798; III 834
1C 82: I 322, 401, 504; II 609; III 415
1C 83: I 504–05; II 256; III 728, 865

1C 84: I 323, 405, 506; II 269, 374, 411, 610; III 855
1C 85: I 406, 506; II 610
1C 86: I 406, 506; II 610
1C 87: I 406, 506; II 411, 610
1C 88: I 277, 325, 418; II 107, 390, 477, 647; III 425
1C 89: II 399, 685
1C 90: I 323; II 263, 650; III 867
1C 91: I 409, 508; II 263, 539, 623, 630; III 855, 865
1C 92: I 409, 509; II 544, 631; III 667, 865–66
1C 93: I 409, 509, 514; II 631; III 865
1C 94: I 323, 410, 509, 596; II 250, 402, 473, 630, 632; III 423, 688, 866
1C 95: I 323, 410, 510; II 108, 334, 336, 402, 473–74, 636, 645; III 423, 668, 688, 866–67
1C 96: I 323, 411, 473; II 308; III 867
1C 97: I 323, 412, 498; II 332, 640; III 867
1C 98: I 412, 510; II 354, 640; III 867–68
1C 99: I 413, 511–12; II 274
1C 100: I 413; II 57, 261, 814; III 476, 834, 864
1C 101: I 413, 511, 513; II 651
1C 102: I 413; III 868
1C 103: I 414; II 640; III 492, 868
1C 104: I 414
1C 105: I 414, 513–14; II 474, 641
1C 106: I 415; II 257, 540, 642; III 329
1C 107: I 339, 414; II 474, 641; III 868
1C 108: I 323, 414; II 281, 387–88, 474–75, 641; III 868–69
1C 109: I 323, 415, 418, 508, 514; II 388, 475, 641; III 682, 868
1C 110: I 323, 415–16, 516; II 107, 386–88, 475, 644; III 868–69
1C 112: I 323, 517; II 401, 645–46; III 665–66, 668, 870
1C 113: I 324, 416; II 108, 403, 646; III 666, 668, 866, 870
1C 114: I 517; III 668
1C 115: III 666
1C 116: I 324, 417, 518; II 476, 647; III 871
1C 117: I 417; II 476, 647; III 67, 871
1C 118: II 477, 647; III 871
1C 119: III 871
1C 120: II 110, 241, 411, 648; III 50, 80
1C 121: I 325, 518; II 648; III 871
1C 123: I 325, 418, 518; III 871
1C 124: II 648
1C 125: I 518; II 477
1C 126: I 519; II 109, 477–78, 648
1C 127: I 324; II 458, 479; III 69
1C 128: II 458; III 71
1C 129: II 458; III 69
1C 130: II 459; III 69
1C 131: II 459; III 71
1C 132: II 459; III 69
1C 133: II 459, 479; III 69
1C 134: II 460; III 70
1C 135: II 460; III 71
1C 136: II 452; III 71–72
1C 137: II 454
1C 138: II 454
1C 139: II 431
1C 140: II 431
1C 141: II 432
1C 142: II 432; III 73
1C 143: II 467
1C 144: II 446
1C 145: II 467
1C 146: II 453–54
1C 147: II 450; III 73
1C 148: III 73
1C 149: II 453; III 73
1C 150: II 453; III 73

The Legend for Use In the Choir by Thomas of Celano (LCh)

LCh 2: II 791–92
LCh 3: II 792
LCh 4: II 792
LCh 7: I 396–96; II 798; III 826
LCh 8: III 398, 826
LCh 9: I 409; II 399, 803
LCh 10: II 250, 803
LCh 11: II 796; III 826
LCh 13: I 416
LCh 14: II 479
LCh 15: I 407; II 422–24; III 827
LCh 16: II 454, 465
LCh 17: I 419; II 109, 478; III 425, 826, 836

The Divine Office of Saint Francis by Julian of Speyer (Off)

Off 1: I 388, 397, 400, 405, 413, 418
Off 5: I 389
Off 9: I 370–72
Off 11: I 372–74
Off 12: I 374–75
Off 14: I 376, 378–79
Off 15: I 379–80
Off 17: I 381–82, 384, 416
Off 18: I 385, 396–97, 401
Off 21: I 410

The Life of Saint Francis by Julian of Speyer (LJS)

LJS 1: III 842
LJS 2: II 532

LJS 3: I 371; II 245, 509, 532–33
LJS 4: II 248
LJS 6: II 249, 536
LJS 7: II 251
LJS 8: II 537; III 842
LJS 9: II 251, 687; III 435, 842
LJS 10: II 538
LJS 11: II 539
LJS 12: II 534
LJS 13: II 250; III 843
LJS 15: II 84, 542, 689
LJS 16: II 84, 543
LJS 17: II 85, 543
LJS 18: II 545; III 388, 843
LJS 19: II 546
LJS 20: II 546
LJS 21: II 254, 533, 547–48, 690
LJS 22: II 542, 550; II 391
LJS 23: II 550–51, 553; III 845
LJS 24: II 562
LJS 27: II 551
LJS 28: II 248; III 40
LJS 29: II 552; III 388
LJS 31: II 276, 561; III 864
LJS 33: II 569–570
LJS 34: II 585, 600–01; III 855
LJS 35: II 601
LJS 36: II 265, 603; III 398, 856
LJS 37: II 519, 624; III 860

LJS 38: II 412; III 861
LJS 39: III 846
LJS 40: III 396, 862
LJS 41: II 551
LJS 44: III 415
LJS 48: II 627
LJS 49: II 628
LJS 50: II 627
LJS 51: II 628
LJS 52: II 628
LJS 54: II 610
LJS 55: II 611
LJS 56: III 871
LJS 58: II 511, 626
LJS 61: II 473, 630; III 866
LJS 62: II 473; III 669, 867
LJS 63: II 403, 474
LJS 64: II 567, 640
LJS 65: II 572
LJS 67: II 474
LJS 68: II 257, 474–75
LJS 69: II 475, 642
LJS 71: II 476, 646; III 871
LJS 72: II 477, 647
LJS 73: II 647; III 425
LJS 74: II 478, 648; III 66, 871
LJS 75: II 478, 648; III 67
LJS 76: II 478, 648–49; III 67, 836

The Sacred Exchange between Saint Francis and Lady Poverty (ScEx)

ScEx 5: III 160
ScEx 13: III 160
ScEx 28: III 163
ScEx 33: III 876

ScEx 36: III 162
ScEx 38: III 164
ScEx 45: III 878

Francis of Assisi: Early Documents II, The Founder

The Beginning or Founding of the Order and the Deeds of Those Lesser Brothers Who Were the First Companions of Blessed Francis in Religion (The Anonymous of Perugia) by John of Perugia (AP)

AP 3: II 69
AP 4: II 69
AP 5: II 70, 245
AP 6: II 71, 245
AP 7: II 71
AP 8: II 78, 79, 80, 81, 251
AP 9: II 81, 82, 251; III 695
AP 10: II 85, 254
AP 11: II 86, 254; III 406, 436
AP 12: II 86, 319
AP 13: II 87
AP 14: II 86, 87; III 684, 686
AP 15: II 87; III 39
AP 16: II 88
AP 17: II 88; III 46
AP 18: II 58, 89, 90
AP 19: II 90
AP 20: II 90
AP 21: II 91
AP 22: II 91
AP 23: II 92
AP 24: II 92
AP 25: II 93

AP 26: II 93; III 39
AP 27: II 93; III 39
AP 28: II 94
AP 29: II 94; III 39
AP 30: II 94
AP 31: II 95; III 390
AP 32: II 95, 96
AP 33: II 96
AP 34: II 96; III 45, 720
AP 35: II 97, 255; III 46
AP 36: II 98, 99, 100; III 38, 721
AP 37: II 101; III 44, 47
AP 38: II 101; III 44
AP 39: II 102; III 40
AP 40: II 102; III 39
AP 41: II 103; III 39
AP 42: II 103
AP 43: II 104, 261; III 475, 709
AP 44: II 104
AP 45: II 106, 107, 261
AP 46: II 107, 108
AP 47: II 109

The Legend of the Three Companions (L3C)

L3C 1: III 682, 683
L3C 2: II 242
L3C 3: II 244
L3C 4: II 243
L3C 5: II 245, 246
L3C 6: II 244, 245; III 695
L3C 7: II 246
L3C 8: II 247
L3C 10: II 247
L3C 11: II 248, 249, 253
L3C 12: II 248
L3C 13: II 249, 250
L3C 14: II 249, 250
L3C 15: II 375
L3C 19: II 251
L3C 20: II 251
L3C 21: II 251
L3C 22: II 253
L3C 23: II 251; III 695
L3C 24: II 250, 252
L3C 26: III 443
L3C 27: II 253; III 436
L3C 28: II 254
L3C 29: II 254; III 406
L3C 30: II 319

L3C 31: II 319
L3C 35: III 46
L3C 42: III 39
L3C 43: III 39
L3C 45: II 290; : III 39
L3C 46: III 390
L3C 47: III 390
L3C 48: III 390
L3C 49: II 256; III 390
L3C 50: II 255; III 46, 390, 720
L3C 51: II 256; III 390
L3C 52: III 38, 390
L3C 54: III 415
L3C 55: III 38
L3C 56: II 258
L3C 57: III 44, 47
L3C 58: III 40, 44
L3C 59: III 39
L3C 60: III 39
L3C 61: III 709
L3C 63: II 260
L3C 64: II 261
L3C 65: II 261
L3C 68: III 425

The Assisi Compilation (AC)

AC 1: II 346; III 293
AC 2: II 349; III 389, 723
AC 3: II 350
AC 4: III 220, 358
AC 5: III 220, 371
AC 6: III 221
AC 7: III 221, 370
AC 8: II 417; III 66, 222, 360, 472
AC 9: III 223, 290
AC 10: II 333, 339; III 224, 291
AC 11: II 340, 344; III 225, 226, 292, 413, 687
AC 12: II 280; III 226, 355, 426
AC 13: III 228, 357
AC 14: II 375; III 229, 362, 363, 687
AC 15: III 123
AC 16: III 123, 708
AC 17: III 123; III 127, 253, 416, 713
AC 18: III 124, 402, 403, 414, 709
AC 19: II 341; III 47, 296
AC 20: III 126, 251, 294
AC 21: III 125, 295, 687
AC 22: III 386, 387; III 244, 336
AC 23: II 285, 286; III 45
AC 24: II 287
AC 25: II 288; III 45, 406, 708
AC 26: II 288
AC 27: II 290
AC 28: II 293
AC 29: II 293
AC 30: II 293
AC 31: II 304; III 280
AC 32: II 304; III 280
AC 33: II 305; III 281
AC 34: II 305; III 281
AC 35: II 315; III 296;
AC 36: III 296
AC 37: II 322, 323; III 334
AC 38: II 331; III 340
AC 39: II 340; III 225, 287
AC 40: II 340; III 226, 287
AC 41: II 347; III 295, 408
AC 42: II 364; III 324
AC 43: II 365; III 325
AC 44: II 366; III 288
AC 45: II 359; III 288
AC 46: II 380; III 323, 398
AC 47: II 372; III 118, 394, 706
AC 48: II 350; III 49
AC 49: II 342, 344; III 47, 155, 289, 402
AC 50: II 258, 259; III 47, 234, 278, 687
AC 51: II 296; III 234
AC 52: III 235
AC 53: II 360; III 235, 279
AC 54: II 313
AC 55: II 329; III 354
AC 56: II 256; III 119, 236, 237, 297, 390, 687
AC 57: II 286; III 238, 687
AC 58: III 238, 384

AC 59: III 240, 334, 425
AC 60: III 240, 300
AC 61: II 368; III 241, 301
AC 62: II 300
AC 63: II 324; III 43, 346
AC 64: III 242, 303
AC 65: II 327, 328; III 47, 243, 304, 425, 682
AC 66: II 330
AC 67: II 188; III 352, 687
AC 68: II 276; III 359
AC 69: II 271
AC 70: II 273; III 352
AC 71: III 360
AC 72: II 266
AC 73: II 277
AC 74: II 269, 270, 287, 288
AC 75: II 270; III 353
AC 76: II 313
AC 77: III 339
AC 78: II 250; III 339
AC 79: II 316
AC 80: III 305, 684
AC 81: II 332, 333; III 306
AC 82: II 333; III 307, 687
AC 83: II 385; III 339, 346, 367, 478
AC 84: III 349, 687
AC 85: III 337, 479
AC 86: II 355; III 337, 363, 365, 687
AC 87: II 365
AC 88: II 354; III 366
AC 89: II 306; III 282, 687
AC 90: II 362; III 283
AC 91: II 373; III 284
AC 92: III 284
AC 93: II 306; III 286
AC 94: III 733
AC 95: II 274
AC 96: II 297; III 214, 385
AC 97: II 296, 297; III 215, 217
AC 98: II 297
AC 99: III 217, 369
AC 100: III 218, 370
AC 101: III 166, 219, 255, 384, 702, 703, 687
AC 102: II 288; III 167, 406, 704
AC 103: II 352; III 169, 219, 408, 409, 705, 707
AC 104: II 372; III 169, 258, 409, 707
AC 105: III 169, 258, 409, 708
AC 106: III 170, 413, 414, 703, 710, 687
AC 107: II 350; III 244, 329
AC 108: II 318, 376; III 245, 462
AC 109: II 340; III 247, 307
AC 110: II 357
AC 111: III 247, 687
AC 112: II 349; III 248, 327, 395, 717
AC 113: II 302; III 249
AC 114: II 303; III 249, 285
AC 115: III 250, 495

AC 116: II 264; III 350
AC 117: II 326; III 230, 687
AC 118: III 232, 346

AC 119: II 289, 311, 326; III 232, 341, 345
AC 120: II 311, 329, 331; III 233, 341, 342, 344

The Remembrance of the Desire of a Soul (The Second Life of Saint Francis)
by Thomas of Celano (2C)

2C 3: II 684, 790, 791; III 33, 80, 682, 683, 695, 840
2C 4: II 531; III 841
2C 5: II 530, 532; III 840
2C 6: II 532, 533
2C 7: II 530
2C 8: II 589, 791
2C 9: II 253, 524, 533, 534, 791; III 841
2C 10: II 401, 406, 534, 536, 792; III 555, 841, 842
2C 11: II 401, 534, 536, 607, 792; III 339, 842
2C 12: II 538, 792; III 695, 842
2C 13: II 540, 790
2C 14: II 540; III 289, 700
2C 15: II 543; III 406, 436, 683
2C 16: II 547, 548; III 46, 88, 390, 720
2C 17: II 548, 550, 792; III 88, 390, 682, 844
2C 18: II 541; III 236, 843
2C 21: II 565; III 234, 852
2C 22: II 564; III 278
2C 23: III 858
2C 24: III 44, 324, 859
2C 25: III 859
2C 26: II 569, 645
2C 27: II 614
2C 28: II 618, 792; III 350, 700
2C 30: II 309, 614, 864
2C 31: II 614, 617, 793; III 863
2C 34: II 619
2C 35: II 594
2C 36: II 594
2C 37: III 353
2C 38: II 616, 793
2C 39: II 619
2C 40: III 352
2C 41: II 416, 615; III 862
2C 43: II 416
2C 44: II 416, 583; III 359, 864
2C 45: II 619
2C 46: II 409, 793; III 861
2C 47: III 94
2C 48: III 227, 356, 863
2C 49: II 618, 801
2C 50: II 802
2C 51: III 292
2C 52: II 793; III 498, 512
2C 53: II 793; III 512
2C 55: II 577, 578; III 849
2C 56: II 135, 578; III 259
2C 57: III 260
2C 58: III 259; 406
2C 59: II 136, 578; III 261, 262

2C 60: II 136; III 259
2C 61: II 582, 793; III 270
2C 62: II 136; III 45, 259, 406, 708
2C 63: II 136; III 259, 271, 475, 476
2C 64: II 562; III 232, 345, 852
2C 65: II 137; III 266
2C 66: III 45
2C 67: II 579; III 684
2C 68: II 801
2C 69: II 137, 138; III 45, 267
2C 70: II 794; III 46, 849
2C 71: II 582; III 849
2C 72: II 581, 582
2C 73: II 582; III 215, 273
2C 74: III 269, 849
2C 75: II 564; III 217, 275
2C 77: II 583, 589; III 272, 385
2C 78: II 579, 802; III 50, 846
2C 79: II 802; III 846
2C 80: II 578
2C 81: II 579
2C 82: III 117, 393, 486
2C 83: II 303, 375. 581, 589, 794, 849, 850
2C 84: II 581, 794; III 249, 268
2C 85: II 589, 795; III 249
2C 86: II 138
2C 87: II 139, 589, 850
2C 88: II 139
2C 89: II 140
2C 93: II 580, 795
2C 94: II 605, 608
2C 95: II 606, 607
2C 96: II 609; III 232, 233, 341
2C 97: II 609
2C 98: II 606; III 847
2C 99: II 607, 608
2C 100: II 608
2C 101: II 608
2C 102: II 612, 613; III 855
2C 103: II 140, 141, 613; III 49, 296
2C 104: III 49, 855
2C 106: II 402, 556, 798; III 692
2C 108: II 574, 795; III 245
2C 109: II 401, 544, 554, 795; III 468
2C 110: III 43
2C 111: II 590; III 851
2C 112: II 563
2C 113: II 141, 564; III 334
2C 114: II 142, 563; III 334
2C 115: III 43, 346
2C 116: II 332, 383, 562, 795; III 853
2C 117: II 563, 643, 795; III 43

2C 118: III 43, 853
2C 119: II 575, 796; III 230
2C 120: II 796; III 230, 414
2C 122: II 573, 607, 796; III 304, 847, 848
2C 123: II 573, 796; III 47, 304, 425, 682, 848
2C 124: III 354
2C 125: III 49
2C 126: II 567
2C 127: II 142; III 340
2C 129: II 383, 564
2C 130: III 306
2C 131: III 306
2C 132: III 307
2C 133: II 570; III 224, 291, 848
2C 134: II 571
2C 135: II 633, 634, 636
2C 136: II 636; III 867
2C 137: III 792
2C 138: II 403, 636
2C 140: II 569, 578; III 47, 848
2C 141: III 224, 291
2C 143: II 142; III 67, 225, 287, 292, 413, 684, 848
2C 144: II 143; III 226, 287, 848
2C 145: II 572; III 247, 307
2C 146: II 133; III 47, 296, 856, 857
2C 147: II 574; III 154, 857
2C 148: II 148, 572, 797; III 47, 155, 402
2C 150: II 148; III 47, 289
2C 151: II 571; III 225, 292, 848
2C 152: II 571; III 293
2C 153: II 118; III 293
2C 154: II 576, 799
2C 155: II 143, 587; III 295, 408
2C 156: II 588; III 408
2C 157: II 118, 588; III 315, 389, 723
2C 158: III 327, 395, 717, 850
2C 159: II 119; III 322, 852, 854
2C 160: II 564; III 329
2C 161: II 147, 564, 645; III 49, 322, 852
2C 164: II 587; III 409
2C 165: II 596, 798; III 173, 366, 851, 860
2C 166: II 408, 411, 566, 798, 813, 860, 861

2C 167: II 813
2C 168: II 413, 813
2C 169: II 414, 813
2C 170: II 413, 593, 813
2C 171: II 414, 798, 813
2C 172: II 587, 599
2C 173: II 599
2C 175: II 146; III 44, 288, 850
2C 176: III 235, 279
2C 177: III 851
2C 178: III 49
2C 182: II 588
2C 184: II 144; III 324
2C 185: II 144, 145; III 325
2C 186: II 145; III 326
2C 188: II 145; III 288
2C 190: III 241, 301
2C 191: III 476, 858
2C 193: II 798
2C 194: II 578
2C 195: II 147; III 118, 314, 394
2C 196: II 531, 596; III 846
2C 197: II 598
2C 198: II 542, 598
2C 200: II 577, 802; III 230, 363
2C 201: II 598, 803; III 245, 309, 856
2C 202: II 573
2C 203: II 401; III 422, 424, 867
2C 207: III 136
2C 208: II 146; III 323, 398, 715
2C 209: II 558, 640
2C 212: II 641; III 868
2C 213: II 641; III 348, 868
2C 214: II 539, 642, 803, 868
2C 215: II 642
2C 216: II 475, 642, 643, 803; III 244, 868, 869
2C 217: II 403, 475, 476, 643, 803; III 244, 336, 868, 869
2C 218: II 644, 803; III 869
2C 219: III 66
2C 220: II 477, 644; III 66, 425, 869

The Treatise on the Miracles of Saint Francis by Thomas of Celano (3C)

3C 2: II 534, 536, 638, 650
3C 3: II 638, 651; III 733
3C 4: II 473, 632, 633; III 457, 688
3C 5: II 636, 637, 645; III 666
3C 6: II 654, 797; III 669
3C 7: II 797; III 669
3C 8: II 652
3C 9: II 652
3C 10: II 652
3C 11: II 653, 797
3C 12: II 653, 797
3C 13: II 654, 797
3C 15: II 584; III 733
3C 16: II 678

3C 17: II 567; III 396
3C 18: II 634
3C 19: II 628; III 50
3C 20: II 592, 624; III 469
3C 21: II 624; III 469
3C 22: II 625
3C 23: II 592
3C 24: II 592
3C 25: II 593
3C 26: II 593
3C 27: II 593
3C 29: II 592
3C 30: II 592
3C 31: II 591

3C 32: II 644; III 229
3C 34: III 46
3C 37: III 66, 472
3C 38: III 66, 472
3C 39: III 66, 472
3C 40: II 655, 804
3C 41: II 614
3C 42: II 657
3C 43: II 656, 804
3C 44: II 480, 657
3C 45: II 481, 658
3C 46: II 656
3C 47: II 658
3C 48: II 658
3C 49: II 659
3C 50: II 659
3C 51: II 660
3C 52: II 663
3C 54: II 661
3C 56: II 662
3C 57: II 661
3C 58: II 661
3C 59: II 662
3C 61: II 662
3C 70: III 73
3C 71: III 73
3C 72: III 73
3C 73: III 74
3C 75: III 74
3C 80: III 71
3C 81: II 663
3C 82: II 664
3C 83: II 664
3C 84: II 665
3C 85: II 665
3C 86: II 664
3C 88: II 665
3C 89: II 666, 804
3C 91: II 666
3C 93: II 667
3C 94: II 667
3C 95: II 668
3C 96: II 668
3C 97: II 669
3C 98: II 670
3C 99: II 669
3C 100: II 677
3C 101: II 677
3C 102: II 677
3C 103: II 677
3C 106: II 670
3C 108: II 628
3C 109: II 673
3C 110: II 674
3C 111: II 674; III 72
3C 112: II 674
3C 113: II 674
3C 114: II 674; III 72
3C 115: II 674

3C 116: II 670
3C 117: II 672
3C 118: II 671
3C 119: II 671
3C 120: II 671
3C 122: II 672
3C 123: I 672
3C 124: II 627
3C 125: II 673
3C 126: III 72
3C 127: III 72
3C 128: II 678
3C 129: II 677, 804
3C 130: III 71
3C 131: III 71
3C 132: III 72
3C 133: III 72
3C 134: III 72
3C 135: III 72
3C 136: III 72
3C 137: III 72
3C 138: III 67, 72
3C 139: III 72
3C 140: III 73
3C 141: III 73
3C 142: III 73
3C 143: III 73
3C 145: III 72
3C 146: II 675
3C 147: II 675
3C 148: II 675
3C 149: II 654, 675
3C 150: II 674
3C 151: II 674
3C 152: II 674
3C 153: II 674; III 70
3C 154: II 674
3C 158: II 680
3C 159: II 681, 805
3C 160: II 479; III 69
3C 161: II 479; III 71
3C 162: III 69
3C 163: III 69
3C 164: III 71
3C 165: III 69
3C 166: II 479; III 69
3C 167: III 70
3C 168: III 70
3C 169: III 70
3C 170: III 70
3C 171: III 70
3C 172: II 480; III 70
3C 173: II 480; III 71
3C 174: II 627
3C 175: II 627
3C 176: II 627
3C 177: II 627
3C 178: II 627
3C 179: III 50

3C 181: II 675
3C 182: II 679
3C 183: II 679
3C 184: II 679
3C 185: II 679
3C 186: II 679
3C 187: II 663

3C 189: II 678
3C 190: II 678
3C 191: II 679
3C 192: II 679
3C 195: II 628
3C 196: II 481

The Major Legend of Saint Francis by Bonaventure of Bagnoregio (LMj)

LMj Prologue
  1: II 684
  2: II 556; III 423
  3: II 717
LMj Chapter I
  1: II 684, 685; III 80, 81, 682, 683, 730
  2: II 685; III 82, 840
  3: II 685; III 873
  4: II 685
  5: II 685; III 82, 83, 841
  6: II 732, 791; : III 83
LMj Chapter II
  1: II 685, 686, 760; III 84, 841, 842, 874
  2: II 687, 751
  3: II 687
  4: II 687, 751,792; III 84, 85, 695, 842
  5: II 685, 687, 792
  6: II 688, 732, 750; III 85
  7: II 725, 749
  8: II 725, 749; III 66, 85
LMj Chapter III
  1: III 86, 195
  2: III 443
  3: III 86, 196, 406, 436
  4: II 814; III 87, 435
  5: II 623, 795; III 87, 468, 874
  6: II 754; III 87
  7: II 749; III 435, 844
  8: II 742, 762; III 196
  9: III 88, 195, 196, 390, 844
  10: III 38, 88, 195, 390; III 682
LMj Chapter IV
  1: III 391
  2: III 90, 844, 878
  3: III 38, 89
  4: II 620, 743, 761; III 89, 388, 421, 815
  5: III 90, 415
  6: II 750; III 91
  7: III 90; III 91
  8: III 90; III 91
  9: II 725, 752, 761, 798; III 92, 692,
      792, 874
  10: II 620; III 92, 694, 874
  11: II 722, 742; III 93, 196, 416
LMj Chapter V
  1: III 98
  3: II 723, 732, 739, 740
  4: II 740, 795; III 96
  5: III 97, 98
  6: III 97
  8: II 798; III 153, 439, 861

  9: II 798, 803; III 97, 153, 861
  10: II 799; III 97, 153, 185, 396, 862
  11: III 98, 153
  12: II 708; III 98, 153
LMj Chapter VI
  1: II 753, 799; III 99
  2: II 752
  4: II 750, 799
  5: III 155, 402
  6: II 725, 752, 796; III 99, 425, 682
  8: III 154
  10: II 796
  11: II 799
LMj Chapter VII
  1: II 722, 733, 745; III 100, 160, 163
  2: II 722, 733, 745; III 163, 164, 202
  3: II 722, 733, 745
  4: II 745
  5: II 745, 801; III 100
  6: II 745, 795
  9: III 100
  10: III 385
  11: III 101
  12: III 101, 773
  13: III 101
LMj Chapter VIII
  1: III 103, 175
  2: III 409, 706
  3: II 726; III 103, 395, 408
  5: II 795
  6: III 175
  7: III 175
  8: III 175
  9: II 799; III 104, 175
  10: III 175
  11: III 104, 175
LMj Chapter IX
  1: III 173, 174, 846
  2: III 174
  3: III 174
  4: III 103
  5: II 726, 741; III 104, 174
  6: II 726, 741, 757
  7: II 726, 741, 757; III 398
  8: II 726, 741, 757; III 490
  9: III 856
LMj Chapter X
  1: II 744; III 181
  2: II 744; III 102
  3: II 744; III 102, 181, 848
  4: II 744, 749; III 181

5: II 761; III 102
7: II 757
15: II 757
LMj Chapter XI
  1: II 760, 763
  2: II 745, 760, 763
  3: II 728, 760; III 93, 96, 176, 182, 864
  4: II 728, 760, 799; III 94, 182
  5: II 728, 760, 764; III 94, 182
  6: II 728, 760; III 95, 96, 182
  7: II 728, 760; III 95, 182
  8: II 728, 760; III 182
  9: II 728, 760, 801; III 182
  10: II 728, 792; III 182
  11: II 728; III 182
  12: II 728; III 181, 182
  13: II 728; III 182
  14: II 728; III 182
LMj Chapter XII
  1: II 709; III 175
  2: III 175, 176, 468, 689
  3: II 714, 800; III 860
  4: II 801; III 469, 861
  5: III 104
  6: III 176, 185
  7: II 763
  12: II 717
LMj Chapter XIII
  1: II 709, 727, 734
  2: II 734; III 865, 866, 874
  3: II 709, 710, 719, 727, 734, 738, 742,
    743, 758; III 457, 668, 866, 874
  4: II 710, 727, 734
  5: II 711, 727, 734
  6: II 711, 727, 734; III 733
  7: II 711, 734; III 733
  8: II 710, 719, 734, 743
  9: II 734

10: II 734; III 873, 874
LMj Chapter XIV
  1: II 714; III 176, 665
  2: II 714, 715
  3: II 715, 745
  4: II 715, 745, 758; III 670
  5: II 715, 745
  6: II 715, 716, 803
LMj Chapter XV
  1: II 746; III 870
  2: II 719, 746, 758; III 866, 875
  3: II 746; III 875
  4: II 746
  5: II 746; III 67, 874
  6: II 746; III 425
  7: II 746
  8: II 746;
  9: II 716, 745, 746;

LMj Miracles

Chapter I
  2: III 666
  5: II 711
Chapter II
  2: II 805
  4: II 805
  6: II 805
Chapter V
  3: II 805
  6: III 669
Chapter VI
  1: II 712
Chapter VII: III 185
Chapter VIII: III 185
Chapter X
  9: II 717

The Minor Legend of Saint Francis by Bonaventure of Bagnoregio (LMn)

LMn Chapter II
  4: III 38, 390
  5: III 38
  6: III 388, 421
  9: III 692

LMn Chapter III
  9: III 398
LMn Chapter IV
  4: III 694
LMn Chapter V
  2: III 396

Francis of Assisi: Early Documents III, The Prophet

A Book of the Praises of Saint Francis by Bernard of Besse (BPr)

BPr Intro: III 78, 697
BPr 1: III 86, 388, 435, 693, 698
BPr 5: III 289

BPr 6: III 341
BPr 7: III 91, 380
BPr 8: III 360, 425

A Mirror of the Perfection, Rule, Profession, Life, and True Calling of a Lesser Brother (The Lemmens Edition, 1901) (1MP)

1MP 1: III 272, 385
1MP 2: III 273
1MP 3: III 275
1MP 4: III 369
1MP 5: III 370
1MP 6: III 276; 702
1MP 7: III 321
1MP 8: III 358
1MP 9: III 371
1MP 11: III 360
1MP 12: III 290
1MP 14: III 287; 413
1MP 16: III 287
1MP 17: III 355, 426
1MP 18: III 357
1MP 19: III 363
1MP 20: III 312, 414
1MP 21: III 346
1MP 22: III 341

1MP 24: III 278
1MP 25: III 341, 344
1MP 29: III 261
1MP 30: III 262, 334, 384, 425
1MP 31: III 300–01
1MP 32: III 303
1MP 33: III 425
1MP 34: III 336
1MP 35: III 329
1MP 36: III 309
1MP 37: III 308–09
1MP 38: III 307
1MP 39: III 268
1MP 40: III 327, 395, 717
1MP 41: III 268
1MP 42: III 285
1MP 43: III 310
1MP 44: III 294

A Mirror of the Perfection of the Status *of a Lesser Brother* (The Sabatier Edition, 1928) (2MP)

2MP 1: III 416, 713
2MP 2: III 702
2MP 3: III 406, 704
2MP 4: III 409, 707
2MP 5: III 406
2MP 6: III 406
2MP 8: III 237
2MP 9: III 238
2MP 10: III 238, 384
2MP 11: III 414, 703
2MP 13: III 708
2MP 14: III 290
2MP 16: III 247
2MP 17: III 249
2MP 18: III 234
2MP 19: III 235
2MP 22: III 214, 385
2MP 23: III 215
2MP 24: III 217
2MP 26: III 219, 384, 702
2MP 27: III 234
2MP 28: III 235
2MP 37: III 249
2MP 39: III 225, 413

2MP 40: III 226
2MP 43: III 402
2MP 44: III 223
2MP 45: III 224
2MP 46: III 225–26
2MP 50: III 251
2MP 51: III 408
2MP 55: III 236, 390
2MP 56: III 240
2MP 57: III 241
2MP 58: III 242
2MP 59: III 243
2MP 60: III 425
2MP 64: III 257
2MP 65: III 245
2MP 66: III 250, 495
2MP 67: III 230, 414
2MP 68: III 402–03, 709
2MP 69: III 394, 706
2MP 70: III 389, 723
2MP 71: III 129, 413, 710
2MP 72: III 408–09, 705
2MP 73: III 219
2MP 76: III 398, 715

2MP 81: III 248, 395, 717
2MP 82: III 244
2MP 85: II 686, 690
2MP 87: III 240, 425
2MP 88: III 244
2MP 94: III 232
2MP 95: III 233
2MP 97: III 233
2MP 98: III 232
2MP 99: III 232

2MP 107: III 226, 426
2MP 108: III 228
2MP 109: III 220
2MP 112: III 222
2MP 113: III 229
2MP 114: III 230
2MP 121: III 217
2MP 122: III 218
2MP 123: III 221
2MP 124: III 220, 425

The Deeds of Blessed Francis and His Companions by Ugolino Boniscambi of Montegiorgio
(DBF)

DBF 1: III 566–67
DBF 2: III 570
DBF 7: III 686
DBF 8: III 513, 686
DBF 9: III 512–13, 686–87
DBF 10: III 459
DBF 11: III 584
DBF 12: III 587
DBF 13: III 718
DBF 14: III 589
DBF 15: III 590
DBF 16: III 591, 689
DBF 19: III 512, 594
DBF 20: III 595
DBF 21: III 598
DBF 22: III 600, 686
DBF 23: III 601
DBF 24: III 604
DBF 25: III 723
DBF 26: III 604
DBF 28: III 605, 607
DBF 29: III 609
DBF 30: III 614
DBF 31: III 688
DBF 32: III 616, 684

DBF 33: III 617
DBF 34: III 620, 688
DBF 37: III 621
DBF 40: III 622, 691
DBF 41: III 626
DBF 42: III 624
DBF 43: III 625
DBF 44: III 631
DBF 45: III 632
DBF 46: III 638
DBF 48: III 635, 694
DBF 49: III 640, 649
DBF 51: III 652
DBF 52: III 653
DBF 53: III 643, 686
DBF 55: III 633
DBF 56: III 655
DBF 57: III 656
DBF 59: III 645
DBF 60: III 627
DBF 61: III 627
DBF 62: III 629
DBF 63: III 639
DBF 64: III 646

Bibliography

Francis of Assisi: Early Documents I, The Saint

The Writings of Francis of Assisi (1205/06–1226)

Kajetan Esser, *Die Opuscula des hl. Franziskus von Assisi* (Grottaferrata-Rome: Editiones Collegii S. Bonaventurae ad Aquas Claras, 1976); *Opuscula Sancti Patris Francisci Assisiensis,* 2nd rev. ed., (Grottaferrata-Rome: Editiones Collegii S. Bonaventurae ad Aquas Claras, 1978); *Die Opuscula des hl. Franziskus von Assisi:* Neue textkritische Edition. Spicilegium Bonaventurianum XIII. Zweite, erweiterte und verbesserte Ausflage besorgt von Engelbert Grau (Grottaferrata-Rome: Editiones Collegii S. Bonaventurae ad Aquas Claras, 1989).

Attilio Bartoli Langeli, "Gli scritti da Francesco. L'autografo di un *'illiteratus,' " Frate Francesco d'Assisi: Atti del XXI Convegno internazionale* Assisi: 14–16 ottobre 1993. (Spoleto: Atti dei Convegni della Società internazionale di studi francescani e del Centro, 1994).

Giovanni Boccali, "Parole di esortazione alle 'poverelle' di San Damiano," *Forma Sororum* 14 (1977): 54–70; and "Canto di esortazione di San Francesco per le 'poverelle' di San Damiano," *CF* 48 (1978): 5–29.

Thomas of Celano, *The Life of Saint Francis* (1228–1229)

Thomae de Celano, *"Vita prima s. Francisci," Analecta Franciscana sive Chronica Aliaque Varia Documenta ad Historiam Fratrum Minorum* X, ed. Patres Collegii S. Bonaventurae (Ad Claras Aquas, Quaracchi: Collegium S. Bonaventuarae, 1926–1941), 1–117; *Fontes Francescani,* ed. Enrico Menestò, Stefano Brufani, Giuseppe Cremascoli, Emore Paoli, Luigi Pellegrini, Stanislao da Campagnola (S. Maria degli Angeli, Assisi: Edizioni Porziuncola, 1995), 273–424.

The Liturgical Texts (1230–1234)

Thomas of Celano, *The Legend for Use in the Choir* (1230–1232)

Thomae de Celano *Legenda ad usum chori, Analecta Franciscana sive Chronica Aliaque Varia Documenta ad Historiam Fratrum Minorum* X, ed. Patres Collegii S. Bonaventurae (Ad Claras Aquas, Quaracchi: Collegium S. Bonaventuarae, 1926–1941), 119–126; *Fontes Francescani,* ed. Enrico Menestò, Stefano Brufani, Giuseppe Cremascoli, Emore Paoli, Luigi Pellegrini, Stanislao da Campagnola (S. Maria degli Angeli, Assisi: Edizioni Porziuncola, 1995), 427–439.

Julian of Speyer and Others, *The Divine Office of Saint Francis* (1228–1232)

Iuliani de Spira, *Officium rhythmicum s. Francisci, Analecta Franciscana sive Chronica Aliaque Varia Documenta ad Historiam Fratrum Minorum* X, ed. Patres Collegii S. Bonaventurae (Ad Claras Aquas, Quaracchi: Collegium S. Bonaventuarae, 1926–1941), 375–388; *Fontes Francescani,* ed. Enrico Menestò, Stefano Brufani, Giuseppe Cremascoli, Emore Paoli, Luigi Pellegrini, Stanislao da Campagnola (S. Maria degli Angeli, Assisi: Edizioni Porziuncola, 1995), 1105–1121.

Masses in Honor of Saint Francis

Analecta Franciscana sive Chronica Aliaque Varia Documenta ad Historiam Fratrum Minorum X, ed. Patres Collegii S. Bonaventurae (Ad Claras Aquas, Quaracchi: Collegium S. Bonaventuarae, 1926–1941), 389–396.

Sequences in Honor of Saint Francis

Analecta Franciscana sive Chronica Aliaque Varia Documenta ad Historiam Fratrum Minorum X, ed. Patres Collegii S. Bonaventurae (Ad Claras Aquas, Quaracchi: Collegium S. Bonaventuarae, 1926–1941), 400–404.

Julian of Speyer, *The Life of Saint Francis* (1232–1235)

Iuliani de Spira, *Vita sancti Francisci, Analecta Franciscana sive Chronica Aliaque Varia Documenta ad Historiam Fratrum Minorum* X, ed. Patres Collegii S. Bonaventurae (Ad Claras Aquas, Quaracchi: Collegium S. Bonaventuarae, 1926–1941), 333–71; *Fontes Francescani,* ed. Enrico Menestò, Stefano Brufani, Giuseppe Cremascoli, Emore Paoli, Luigi Pellegrini, Stanislao da Campagnola (S. Maria degli Angeli, Assisi: Edizioni Porziuncola, 1995), 1025–1096.

Henri d'Avranches, *The Versified Life of Saint Francis* (1232–1239)

Henrici Abrincensis *Legenda s. Francisci versificata, Analecta Franciscana sive Chronica Aliaque Varia Documenta ad Historiam Fratrum Minorum* X, ed. Patres Collegii S. Bonaventurae (Ad Claras Aquas, Quaracchi: Collegium S. Bonaventuarae, 1926–1941), 405–521; *Fontes Francescani,* ed. Enrico Menestò, Stefano Brufani, Giuseppe Cremascoli, Emore Paoli, Luigi Pellegrini, Stanislao da Campagnola (S. Maria degli Angeli, Assisi: Edizioni Porziuncola, 1995), 1131–1206.

The Sacred Exchange between Saint Francis and Lady Poverty (1237–1239)

Sacrum commercium sancti Francisci cum domina Paupertate. Medioeva francescano 1. ed. Stefano Brufani, (S. Maria degli Angeli: Edizioni Porziuncola, 1990); *Fontes Francescani,* ed. Enrico Menestò, Stefano Brufani, Giuseppe Cremascoli, Emore Paoli, Luigi Pellegrini, Stanislao da Campagnola (S. Maria degli Angeli, Assisi: Edizioni Porziuncola, 1995), 1705–1732.

Related Documents (1215–1237)

Papal Documents

Pope Honorius III (1216–1227)
> *Cum dilecti* (1219)
>> *Bullarium Franciscanum* I, ed. Johanne Hyacinthe Sbaralea. (Rome, n.p., 1759–68): 2, n. 2.
>
> *Pro dilectis* (1220)
>> *Bullarium Franciscanum* I, ed. Johanne Hyacinthe Sbaralea. (Rome, n.p., 1759–68): 5, n. 4.
>
> *Cum secundum* (1220)
>> *Bullarium Franciscanum* I, ed. Johanne Hyacinthe Sbaralea. (Rome, n.p., 1759–68): 6, n. 5.
>
> *Solet annuere* (1223)
>> *Bullarium Franciscanum* I, ed. Johanne Hyacinthe Sbaralea. (Rome, n.p., 1759–68): 15–19, n. 14.
>
> *Quia populares* (1224)
>> *Bullarium Franciscanum* I, ed. Johanne Hyacinthe Sbaralea. (Rome, n.p., 1759–68): 20, n.17.
>
> *Vineae Domini* (1225)
>> *Bullarium Franciscanum* I, ed. Johanne Hyacinthe Sbaralea. (Rome, n.p., 1759–68): 24, n. 23.

Pope Gregory IX (1227–1238)
> *Recolentes qualiter* (1228)
>> *Bullarium Franciscanum* I, ed. Johanne Hyacinthe Sbaralea. (Rome, n.p., 1759–68): 40–41, n. 31.

Mira circa nos (1228)
  Bullarium Franciscanum I, ed. Johanne Hyacinthe Sbaralea. (Rome, n.p.,
  1759–68): 42–44, n. 25.
Quo elongati (1230)
  Bullarium Franciscanum I, ed. Johanne Hyacinthe Sbaralea. (Rome, n.p.,
  1759–68): 68–70, n. 56; Herbert Grundmann, "Die Bulle 'Quo elongati' Papst
  Gregors IX," *Archivum Franciscanum Historicum* 54 (1961): 1–25.
Quoniam abundavit (1237)
  Bullarium Franciscanum I, ed. Johanne Hyacinthe Sbaralea. (Rome, n.p.,
  1759–68): 214–15, n. 224.

Writings of Jacques de Vitry

Letter I (1216)
  R. B. C. Huygens, *Lettres de Jacques de Vitry (1160/1170–1240), Évêque de Saint-Jean
  d'Acre* (Leiden: E.J. Brill, 1960), 72–76.

Letter VI (1220)
  R. B. C. Huygens, *Lettres de Jacques de Vitry (1160/1170–1240), Évêque de Saint-Jean
  d'Acre* (Leiden: E.J. Brill, 1960), 131–33.

Historia Occidentalis (c. 1221/25)
  John Frederick Hinnebusch, *The* Historia occidentalis *of Jacques de Vitry* (Fribourg:
  The University Press, 1972), 158–63.

Sermon I to the Lesser Brothers (1229/40); Sermon II to the Lesser Brothers
(1229/40)
  Hilarin Felder, "Jacobi Vitriacensis (1180–1240): Sermones ad Fratres Minores,"
  Analecta Ordinis Fratrum Minorum Capuchinorum 19 (1903): 22–23; 114–122;
  149–158.

Other Chronicles and References

Boncompagno of Signa (c. 1215/20)
  Testimonia minora saeculi XIII de S. Francisco Assisiensis, ed. Leonard Lemmens
  (Quaracchi: Collegium S. Bonaventurae, 1926), 92.

Odo of Cheriton (1219/47)
  Michael Bihl, "S. Francisci parabola in sermonibus Odonis de Ceritona an. 1219
  conscriptis," *Archivum Franciscanum Historicum* 22 (1929): 584–96.

Chronicle of Lauterberg (c. 1224)
  Testimonia minora saeculi XIII de S. Francisco Assisiensis, ed. Leonard Lemmens
  (Quaracchi: Collegium S. Bonaventurae, 1926), 18–19.

Burchard of Ursperg (c. 1228/30)
  Testimonia minora saeculi XIII de S. Francisco Assisiensis, ed. Leonard Lemmens
  (Quaracchi: Collegium S. Bonaventurae, 1926), 17–18.

Caesar of Heisterbach (c. 1225–1235)
  Acta Sanctorum Vol. 3:. Société des Bollandistes. (Antwerp, n.p., 1643): November,
  650.

Richard of San Germano (1228)
  Testimonia minora saeculi XIII de S. Francisco Assisiensis, ed. Leonard Lemmens
  (Quaracchi: Collegium S. Bonaventurae, 1926), 15–16.

Luke of Túy (1231–1234)
  Testimonia minora saeculi XIII de S. Francisco Assisiensis, ed. Leonard Lemmens
  (Quaracchi: Collegium S. Bonaventurae, 1926), 92–93.

Roger of Wendover (c. 1225–1235)
  Rerum Britannicarum Medii Aevi (Rolls Series), no. 84, Vol. 2; 35–36; 328–333;
  Testimonia minora saeculi XIII de S. Francisco Assisiensis, ed. Leonard Lemmens
  (Quaracchi: Collegium S. Bonaventurae, 1926), 26–32 (partial edition);
  Monumenta Germaniae Historica 28:128.

Alberic of Trois-Fontaines (c. 1227–1235)
Monumenta Germaniae Historica Scriptores 13: 887–888; 918, 922; *Testimonia minora saeculi XIII de S. Francisco Assisiensis,* ed. Leonard Lemmens (Quaracchi: Collegium S. Bonaventurae, 1926), 19–20.

The Life of Pope Gregory IX (c. 1240)
Testimonia minora saeculi XIII de S. Francisco Assisiensis, ed. Leonard Lemmens (Quaracchi: Collegium S. Bonaventurae, 1926), 11–14.

Chroniclers of the Fifth Crusade

Chronicle of Ernoul (1227/29)
Girolama Golubovich, *Biblioteca Biobibliografica della Terra Santa e dell'Oriente Francescano,* Vol. 1 (Ad Claras Aquas, Quaracchi: Collegium S. Bonaventurae, 1906), 10–13.

Bernard the Treasurer (1229/30)
Girolama Golubovich, *Biblioteca Biobibliografica della Terra Santa e dell'Oriente Francescano,* Vol. 1 (Ad Claras Aquas, Quaracchi: Collegium S. Bonaventurae, 1906), 13–14.

The History of the Emperor Eracles (1229/31)
Girolama Golubovich, *Biblioteca Biobibliografica della Terra Santa e dell'Oriente Francescano,* Vol. 1 (Ad Claras Aquas, Quaracchi: Collegium S. Bonaventurae, 1906), 14.

Francis of Assisi: Early Documents II, The Founder

John of Perugia, *The Beginning of Founding of the Order and the Deeds of Those Lesser Brothers Who Were the First Companions of Blessed Francis in Religion* (The Anonymous of Perugia) (1240–1241)

Lorenzo di Fonzo, "L'Anonimo Perugino tra le Fonti del secolo XIII: Rapporti letterari e testo critico," *Miscellanea Francescana* 72 (1972): 435–65; *Fontes Francescani,* ed. Enrico Menestò, Stefano Brufani, Giuseppe Cremascoli, Emore Paoli, Luigi Pellegrini, Stanislao da Campagnola (S. Maria degli Angeli, Assisi: Edizioni Porziuncola, 1995), 1311–1351.

The Legend of the Three Companions (1241–1247)

Théophile Desbonnets, "Legenda Trium Sociorum: Edition Critique," *Archivum Franciscanum Historicum* 67 (1974): 38–144; *Fontes Francescani,* ed. Enrico Menestò, Stefano Brufani, Giuseppe Cremascoli, Emore Paoli, Luigi Pellegrini, Stanislao da Campagnola (S. Maria degli Angeli, Assisi: Edizioni Porziuncola, 1995), 1373–1445.

The Assisi Compilation (1244–1260)

Compilatio Assisiensis dagli Scritti di fr. Leone e Compagni su S. Francesco d'Assisi. Dal Ms. 1046 di Perugia. II edizione integrale riveduta e corretta con versione italiana a fronte e variazioni, ed. Marino Bigaroni (Assisi: Pubblicazioni della Biblioteca Francescana Chiesa Nuova, 1992); *Fontes Francescani,* ed. Enrico Menestò, Stefano Brufani, Giuseppe Cremascoli, Emore Paoli, Luigi Pellegrini, Stanislao da Campagnola (S. Maria degli Angeli, Assisi: Edizioni Porziuncola, 1995), 1471–1690.

Thomas of Celano

The Remembrance of the Desire of a Soul (1245–1247)

Thomae de Celano, *Vita secunda s. Francisci, Analecta Franciscana sive Chronica Aliaque Varia Documenta ad Historiam Fratrum Minorum* X, ed. Patres Collegii S. Bonaventurae (Ad Claras Aquas, Quaracchi: Collegium S. Bonaventuarae, 1926–1941), 127–268; *Fontes Francescani*, ed. Enrico Menestò, Stefano Brufani, Giuseppe Cremascoli, Emore Paoli, Luigi Pellegrini, Stanislao da Campagnola (S. Maria degli Angeli, Assisi: Edizioni Porziuncola, 1995), 443–639.

The Treatise on the Miracles of Saint Francis (1250–1252)

Thomae de Celano, *Tractatus de miraculis b. Francisci, Analecta Franciscana sive Chronica Aliaque Varia Documenta ad Historiam Fratrum Minorum* X, ed. Patres Collegii S. Bonaventurae (Ad Claras Aquas, Quaracchi: Collegium S. Bonaventuarae, 1926–1941), 269–331; *Fontes Francescani*, ed. Enrico Menestò, Stefano Brufani, Giuseppe Cremascoli, Emore Paoli, Luigi Pellegrini, Stanislao da Campagnola (S. Maria degli Angeli, Assisi: Edizioni Porziuncola, 1995), 641–754.

An Umbrian Choir Legend (1253–1259)

Analecta Franciscana sive Chronica Aliaque Varia Documenta ad Historiam Fratrum Minorum X, ed. Patres Collegii S. Bonaventurae (Ad Claras Aquas, Quaracchi: Collegium S. Bonaventuarae, 1926–1941), 543–554.

A Letter on the Passing of Saint Francis Attributed to Elias of Assisi (After 1253)

William Spoelberch, *Speculum vitae b. Francisci et sociorum ejus* II (Antwerp: 1620); Luke Wadding, *Annales Minorum ad annum 1226,* n. 45, T. II (Ad Claras Aquas, Quaracchi: 1931), 167–169; *Epistola encyclica de transitu s. Francisci a fr. Helia tunc Ordinis Vicario generali ad omnes provincias Ordinis missa, Analecta Franciscana sive Chronica Aliaque Varia Documenta ad Historiam Fratrum Minorum* X, ed. Patres Collegii S. Bonaventurae (Ad Claras Aquas, Quaracchi: Collegium S. Bonaventuarae, 1926–1941), 523–8; *Fontes Francescani,* ed. Enrico Menestò, Stefano Brufani, Giuseppe Cremascoli, Emore Paoli, Luigi Pellegrini, Stanislao da Campagnola (S. Maria degli Angeli, Assisi: Edizioni Porziuncola, 1995), 253–55.

Bonaventure of Bagnoregio

The Morning Sermon on Saint Francis (Paris, October 4, 1255)

Opera Omnia Doctoris Seraphici S. Bonaventurae, IX, ed. Patres Collegii S. Bonaventurae (Ad Claras Aquas, Quaracchi: Collegium S. Bonaventuarae, 1882–1902), 590–594.

The Evening Sermon on Saint Francis (Paris, October 4, 1255)

Opera Omnia Doctoris Seraphici S. Bonaventurae, IX, ed. Patres Collegii S. Bonaventurae (Ad Claras Aquas, Quaracchi: Collegium S. Bonaventuarae, 1882–1902), 594–597.

The Major Legend of Saint Francis (1260–1263)

"Legenda maior s. Francisci," Analecta Franciscana sive Chronica Aliaque Varia Documenta ad Historiam Fratrum Minorum X, ed. Patres Collegii S. Bonaventurae (Ad Claras Aquas, Quaracchi: Collegium S. Bonaventuarae, 1926–1941), 555–652; *Fontes Francescani,* ed. Enrico Menestò, Stefano Brufani, Giuseppe Cremascoli, Emore Paoli, Luigi Pellegrini, Stanislao da Campagnola (S. Maria degli Angeli, Assisi: Edizioni Porziuncola, 1995), 777–961.

The Minor Legend of Saint Francis (1260–1266)

"Legenda minor s. Francisci," Analecta Franciscana sive Chronica Aliaque Varia Documenta ad Historiam Fratrum Minorum X, ed. Patres Collegii S. Bonaventurae (Ad Claras Aquas, Quaracchi: Collegium S. Bonaventuarae, 1926–1941), 653–78; *Fontes Francescani,* ed.

Enrico Menestò, Stefano Brufani, Giuseppe Cremascoli, Emore Paoli, Luigi Pellegrini, Stanislao da Campagnola (S. Maria degli Angeli, Assisi: Edizioni Porziuncola, 1995), 965–1013.

The Evening Sermon on Saint Francis (Paris, October 4, 1262)

Opera Omnia Doctoris Seraphici S. Bonaventurae, IX, ed. Patres Collegii S. Bonaventurae (Ad Claras Aquas, Quaracchi: Collegium S. Bonaventurae, 1882–1902), 585–590.

Sermon on Saint Francis (Paris, October 4, 1266)

Opera Omnia Doctoris Seraphici S. Bonaventurae, IX, ed. Patres Collegii S. Bonaventurae (Ad Claras Aquas, Quaracchi: Collegium S. Bonaventurae, 1882–1902), 573–575.

Sermon on the Feast of the Transferal of the Body of Saint Francis (probably Paris, May 25, 1267)

Opera Omnia Doctoris Seraphici S. Bonaventurae, IX, ed. Patres Collegii S. Bonaventurae (Ad Claras Aquas, Quaracchi: Collegium S. Bonaventurae, 1882–1902), 534–535; R. E. Lerner, "A Collection of Sermons Given in Paris c. 1267, including a new text by Saint Bonaventure on the Life of Saint Francis," *Speculum* 49 (1974), 466–498.

The Morning Sermon on Saint Francis (Paris, October 4, 1267)

Opera Omnia Doctoris Seraphici S. Bonaventurae, IX, ed. Patres Collegii S. Bonaventurae (Ad Claras Aquas, Quaracchi: Collegium S. Bonaventurae, 1882–1902), 575–580.

The Evening Sermon on Saint Francis (Paris, October 4, 1267)

Opera Omnia Doctoris Seraphici S. Bonaventurae, IX, ed. Patres Collegii S. Bonaventurae (Ad Claras Aquas, Quaracchi: Collegium S. Bonaventurae, 1882–1902), 580–582.

Related Documents (1237–1272)

Miscellaneous Franciscan Sources

Witnesses to the Stigmata (1237–1250)
Testimonia minora saeculi XIII de S. Francisco Assisiensis, ed. Leonard Lemmens (Quaracchi: Collegium S. Bonaventurae, 1926), 41.

Encyclical Letter of John of Parma and Humbert of Romans (1255)
Luke Wadding, *Annales Minorum,* Vol. 3 (Ad Claras Aquas, Quaracchi: Collegium S. Bonaventurae, 1931–51), 380–381.

Inscription of Brother Leo (1257–1260)
Testimonia minora saeculi XIII de S. Francisco Assisiensis, ed. Leonard Lemmens (Quaracchi: Collegium S. Bonaventurae, 1926), 61.

Papal Documents

Pope Innocent IV
Ordinem vestrum (1245)
Bullarium Franciscanum I, ed. Johanne Hyacinthe Sbaralea. (Rome, n.p., 1759–68): 400–402, n. 104.

Pope Alexander IV
Benigna operatio (1255)
Bullarium Franciscanum 2, ed. Johanne Hyacinthe Sbaralea. (Rome, n.p., 1759–68): 85–87, n. 120.

Dominican Hagiography and Sermons

Bartholomew of Trent (c. 1240–1245)
Testimonia minora saeculi XIII de S. Francisco Assisiensis, ed. Leonard Lemmens (Quaracchi: Collegium S. Bonaventurae, 1926), 63–65; 67–68; 70; Thomas Kaeppeli, *Scriptores Ordinis Praedicatorum Medii Aevi* I (Rome: Istituto Storico Domenicano, 1970–93), 172–74; 292–94.

Constantine of Orvieto (1246–48)
Testimonia minora saeculi XIII de S. Francisco Assisiensis, ed. Leonard Lemmens (Quaracchi: Collegium S. Bonaventurae, 1926), 67–68; Thomas Kaeppeli, *Scriptores Ordinis Praedicatorum Medii Aevi* I (Rome: Istituto Storico Domenicano, 1970–93), 292–94.

Gerard de Frachet (1257–1260)
Testimonia minora saeculi XIII de S. Francisco Assisiensis, ed. Leonard Lemmens (Quaracchi: Collegium S. Bonaventurae, 1926), 70–71; Thomas Kaeppeli, *Scriptores Ordinis Praedicatorum Medii Aevi* I (Rome: Istituto Storico Domenicano, 1970–93), 35–38.

Stephen of Bourbon (1250–1261)
Testimonia minora saeculi XIII de S. Francisco Assisiensis, ed. Leonard Lemmens (Quaracchi: Collegium S. Bonaventurae, 1926), 93–95; Thomas Kaeppeli, *Scriptores Ordinis Praedicatorum Medii Aevi* I (Rome: Istituto Storico Domenicano, 1970–93), 354–55.

Jacopo de Voragine (c. 1255–1267)
Legenda Aurea, ed. Johann G. Theodor Grässe (Leipzig: Librariae Arnoldianae, 1846), 662–674.

Chronicles

Philippe Mousket (c. 1238–1243)
"Historia Regum Francorum," *Monumenta Germaniae Historica, Scriptores* 26 (Hanover: Hahn, 1897): 816.

Passion of San Verecondo (1250–70)
Testimonia minora saeculi XIII de S. Francisco Assisiensis, ed. Leonard Lemmens (Quaracchi: Collegium S. Bonaventurae, 1926), 70–71.

Thomas of Split (1250–1265)
"Historia Pontificia Salonitanorum et Spalatensium," in *Monumenta Germaniae Historica* 29 (Hanover: Hahn, 1897): 580; *Testimonia minora saeculi XIII de S. Francisco Assisiensis,* ed. Leonard Lemmens (Quaracchi: Collegium S. Bonaventurae, 1926), 10.

Richard of Sens (1255–1264)
"Gesta Senonensis Ecclesiae," *Monumenta Germaniae Historica, Scriptores* 24 (Hanover: Hahn, 1897): 306–307; *Testimonia minora saeculi XIII de S. Francisco Assisiensis,* ed. Leonard Lemmens (Quaracchi: Collegium S. Bonaventurae, 1926), 32–33.

Annals of Santa Giustina (1260–1270)
"Annales S. Justinae Patavini," *Monumenta Germaniae Historica, Scriptores* 15 (Hanover: Hahn, 1897): 151–154.

Eudes of Châteauroux (Paris, October 4, 1262)
Opera Omnia Doctoris Seraphici S. Bonaventurae, IX, ed. Patres Collegii S. Bonaventurae (Ad Claras Aquas, Quaracchi: Collegium S. Bonaventurae, 1882–1902), IX: 582–585.

Rhymed Austrian Chronicle (1268–1272)
"Anonymi Chronicon Rhytmicum Austriacum," *Monumenta Germaniae Historica, Scriptores* 25 (Hanover: Hahn, 1897): 357–58.

Francis of Assisi: Early Documents III, The Prophet

Bernard of Besse, A Book of the Praises of Saint Francis (1277–1283)

Analecta Franciscana sive Chronica Aliaque Varia Documenta ad Historiam Fratrum Minorum III, ed. Patres Collegii S. Bonaventurae (Ad Claras Aquas, Quaracchi: Collegium S. Bonaventuarae, 1926–1941), 666–92; *Fontes Francescani,* ed. Enrico Menestò, Stefano Brufani, Giuseppe Cremascoli, Emore Paoli, Luigi Pellegrini, Stanislao da Campagnola (S. Maria degli Angeli, Assisi: Edizioni Porziuncola, 1995), 1253–96.

Henri d'Avranches, The Versified Life of Saint Francis: Additions, Amplications in Light of The Major Legend (after 1283)

Analecta Franciscana sive Chronica Aliaque Varia Documenta ad Historiam Fratrum Minorum X, ed. Patres Collegii S. Bonaventurae (Ad Claras Aquas, Quaracchi: Collegium S. Bonaventuarae, 1926–1941), 489–521; *Fontes Francescani,* ed. Enrico Menestò, Stefano Brufani, Giuseppe Cremascoli, Emore Paoli, Luigi Pellegrini, Stanislao da Campagnola (S. Maria degli Angeli, Assisi: Edizioni Porziuncola, 1995), 1210–42.

A Collection of Sayings of the Companions of Blessed Francis (Late 13th– Early 14th Century)

An Old Legend (*Legenda Vetus*)

Paul Sabatier, ed., "S. Francisci legendae veteris fragmenta quaedam ou de qualques chapitres de la compilation franciscaine connue sous le nom de Legenda Antiqua (circa 1322) qui paraissent provenir de la Legenda Vetus (circa 1246)," Andrew G. Little, Pierre Mandonnet, Paul Sabatier, *Opuscules de critique historique:* Tome I (Paris: Fischbacher, 1903), 87–109.

The Words of Saint Francis

Edith Pásztor, "Il manoscritto Isidoriano 1/73 e gli scritti leonine su S. Francesco," *Cultura e società nell'Italia medievale. Studi per Paolo Brezzi.* Studi Storici, fasc. 188–192 (Rome: n.p., 1988), 661–3.

The Words of Brother Conrad

"Verba Fr. Conradi. Extrait de Ms. 1/25 de S. Isidore," Andrew G. Little, Pierre Mandonnet, Paul Sabatier, *Opuscules de critique historique:* Tome I (Paris: Fischbacher, 1903).

Ubertino da Casale, The Tree of the Crucified Life of Jesus, Book Five (Excerpts) (1305)

Arbor Vitae Crucifixae Jesu (Venice: n.p., 1485). Monumenta Politica et Philosophica Rariora, Series I, Numerus 4, fascismile edition with page numbering added, Introduction and bibliography, by Charles T. David. (Turin: Bottega d'Erasmo, 1961), 421–449.

A Mirror of the Perfection, Rule, Profession, Life and True Calling of a Lesser Brother (The Lemmens Edition, 1901)

Documenta Antiqua Franciscana, pars II, ed. Leonard Lemmens (Ad Claras Aquas, Quaracchi: Collegium S. Bonaventurae, 1901), 23–84; *Fontes Francescani,* ed. Enrico Menestò, Stefano Brufani, Giuseppe Cremascoli, Emore Paoli, Luigi Pellegrini, Stanislao da Campagnola (S. Maria degli Angeli, Assisi: Edizioni Porziuncola, 1995), 1745–1825.

A Mirror of the Perfection of the Status of a Lesser Brother (The Sabatier Edition, 1928)

> *Le Speculum Perfectionis ou Mémoires de frère Léon sur la seconde partie de la vie de Saint François d'Assisi,* 2 vols, eds. Paul Sabatier, George Little (Manchester: British Society of Franciscan Studies 13, 1928), 1–350; *Fontes Francescani,* ed. Enrico Menestò, Stefano Brufani, Giuseppe Cremascoli, Emore Paoli, Luigi Pellegrini, Stanislao da Campagnola (S. Maria degli Angeli, Assisi: Edizioni Porziuncola, 1995), 1849–2053.

Angelo Clareno, The Book of Chronicles or of the Tribulations of the Order of Lesser Ones (Prologue and the First Tribulation) (1323–1325-6)

> Angelo Clareno, *Liber Chronicarum sive Tribulationum Ordinis Minorum,* ed. Giovanni Boccali, with introduction by Felice Accrocca; Italian trans. Marino Bigaroni (Santa Maria degli Angeli, Assisi: Edizioni Porziuncola, 1998).

Ugolino Boniscambi of Montegiorgio, The Deeds of Blessed Francis and His Companions (1328–1337)

> *Actus beati Francisci et Sociorum Eius: Nuova Edizione Postuma di Jacques Cambell,* eds. Jacques Cambell, Marino Bigaroni, Giovanni Boccali (Santa Maria degli Angeli, Assisi: Tipografia Porziuncola, 1988); *Fontes Francescani,* ed. Enrico Menestò, Stefano Brufani, Giuseppe Cremascoli, Emore Paoli, Luigi Pellegrini, Stanislao da Campagnola (S. Maria degli Angeli, Assisi: Edizioni Porziuncola, 1995), 2085–2219.

Anonymous, The Little Flowers of Saint Francis (A Translation and Re-editing of The Deeds of Saint Francis and His Companions) (After 1337)

> " 'I Fioretti di San Francesco,' Riveduti su un Nuova Codice da P. B. Bughetti (Quaracchi: Collegio San Bonaventura, 1926),"*Fonti Francescane* (Assisi: Movimento Francescano, 1977), 1441–1624.

Arnald of Sarrant, The Kinship of Saint Francis (1365)

> Ferdinand Delorme, "Pages inédites sur S. François: Ecrites vers 1365 par Arnaud de Sarrant, Min. Prov. d'Aquitaine," *Miscellanea Franciscana* 42 (1942): 103–31; Marian Michalczyk, "Une Compilation Parisienne des Sources Primitives Franciscaines, Paris, Nationale, Ms. La. 12707," *Archivum Franciscanum Historicum* 74 (1981): 3–32, 401–55; 76 (1983): 3–97.

Related Documents (1261–1323)

> Papal Documents
>
> Pope Nicholas III
> *Exiit Qui Seminat* (1279)
> > *Bullarium Franciscanum* III, ed. Johanne Hyacinthe Sbaralea. (Rome, n.p., 1759–68): 404–416, n. 127; *Bullarii Franciscani Epitome,* ed. Conrado Eubel (Ad Claras Aquas, Quaracchi: Collgium S. Bonaventurae, 1905) 290–300.
>
> Pope Martin IV
> *Exultantes in Domino* (1283)
> > *Bullarium Franciscanum* V, ed. Johanne Hyacinthe Sbaralea. (Rome, n.p., 1759–68): 501, n. 40; *Bullarii Franciscani Epitome,* ed. Conrado Eubel (Ad Claras Aquas, Quaracchi: Collgium S. Bonaventurae, 1905), 301.
>
> Pope Clement V
> *Exivi de Paradiso* (1312)
> > *Bullarium Franciscanum* V, ed. Johanne Hyacinthe Sbaralea. (Rome, n.p., 1759–68): 195; *Seraphicae legislationis textus originales* (Ad Claras Aquas, Quaracchi: Collegium S. Bonaventurae, 1897), 229–260.

Pope John XXII
Ad Conditorem (1322)
Bullarium Franciscanum V, ed. Johanne Hyacinthe Sbaralea. (Rome, n.p., 1759–68): 233, n. 5; 235b–237a.
Cum inter nonnullos (1323)
Bullarium Franciscanum V, ed. Johanne Hyacinthe Sbaralea. (Rome, n.p., 1759–68): 256–259, n. 317.

Miscellaneous Franciscan Sources

Thomas of Pavia (c. 1272–1280)
"Gesta Imperatorum et Pontificium," ed. E. Ehrenfeuchter, *Monumenta Germaniae Historica, Scriptores* 22 (Hanover: Hahn, 1897): 483–528; Livarius Oliger, "Descriptio codicis Sancti Antonii de urbe unacum appendice textuum de Santo Francisco," *Archivum Franciscanum Historicum* 12 (1919) 382–384, n. 59.

A Book of Exemplary Stories (c. 1280–1310)
Livarius Oliger, "Liber exemplorum Fratrum Minorum Saeculi XIII," *Antonianum* 2 (1927): 203–276.

Donation of La Verna (1274)
Testimonia minora saeculi XIII de S. Francisco Assisiensis, ed. Leonard Lemmens (Quaracchi: Collegium S. Bonaventurae, 1926), 36–37.

Jerome of Ascoli (1276)
Athanasio Lopez, ed., "Litterae ineditae fr. Hieronymi ab Asculo," *Archivum Franciscanum Historicum* 1 (1908): 85–87; *Testimonia minora saeculi XIII de S. Francisco Assisiensis,* ed. Leonard Lemmens (Quaracchi: Collegium S. Bonaventurae, 1926), 90–1; Andrew George Little, "Definitiones Capitolorum Generalium Ordinis Fratrum Minorum 1260–1282," *Archivum Franciscanum Historicum* 7 (1914): 681.

Documents Concerning the Portiuncula Indulgence (1277–1300)
1. Francesco Bartholi della Rossa, *Tractatus de Indulgentia S. Mariae de Portiuncula,* ed. Paul Sabatier, (Paris: Fischbacher, 1900), 44; *Testimonia minora saeculi XIII de S. Francisco Assisiensis,* ed. Leonard Lemmens (Quaracchi: Collegium S. Bonaventurae, 1926), 42–43.
2. Bartholi della Rossa, 54; *Testimonia minora saeculi XIII de S. Francisco Assisiensis,* ed. Leonard Lemmens (Quaracchi: Collegium S. Bonaventurae, 1926), 43–44.
3. Bartholi della Rossa, 135; *Testimonia minora saeculi XIII de S. Francisco Assisiensis,* ed. Leonard Lemmens (Quaracchi: Collegium S. Bonaventurae, 1926), 44–45.
4. *Analecta Franciscana sive Chronica Aliaque Varia Documenta ad Historiam Fratrum Minorum* III, ed. Patres Collegii S. Bonaventurae (Ad Claras Aquas, Quaracchi: Collegium S. Bonaventuarae, 1926–1941), 632–33.

Peter of John Olivi (c. 1272–1297)
Lectura on Luke
Testimonia minora saeculi XIII de S. Francisco Assisiensis, ed. Leonard Lemmens (Quaracchi: Collegium S. Bonaventurae, 1926), 97–8.
Commentary on the Rule of the Lesser Brothers
Peter Olivi's Rule Commentary, ed. David Flood, (Wiesbaden: F. Steiner, 1972), 189.
Commentary on the Book of Revelation
Bernard McGinn, *Visions of the End: Traditions in the Middle Ages* (rev. ed.) (New York: Columbia University Press, 1998), 208–11.

Angelo Clareno
Exposition on the Rule of the Lesser Brothers (1321–1322)
Felice Accrocca, "Angelo Clareno, Testimone di S. Francesco. Testi sulla Vita del Santo e dei Primi Frati Contenuti nell' 'Expositio Regulae Fratrum Minorum,' e Sconosciuti alle Primitive Fonti Francescane," *Archivum Franciscanum Historicum* 81 (1988), 225–53.

Chronicles
  Chronicle of Erfurt (c. 1275)
    "Chronica Minor Auctore Minorita Erphordinse," ed. O. Holder-Egger, *Monumenta Germaniae Historica, Scriptores* 24 (Hanover: Hahn, 1897): 172–215.
  List of the General Ministers (c. 1261–1264)
    "Series Magistrorum Generalium Ordinis Fratrum Minorum," ed. G. Waitx, *Monumenta Germaniae Historica, Scriptores* 24 (Hanover: Hahn, 1897): 514; *Testimonia minora saeculi XIII de S. Francisco Assisiensis,* ed. Leonard Lemmens (Quaracchi: Collegium S. Bonaventurae, 1926), 20–21.
  Norman Chronicle (1269–1272)
    "Chronicon Normannii or Annales Normanici," ed. O. Holder-Egger, *Monumenta Germaniae Historica, Scriptores* 24 (Hanover: Hahn, 1897): 514.
  Danish Chronicle (c. 1275–1285)
    "Chronica Danorum et praecipue Sialandiae," ed. J. Langebeck, *Scriptores Rerum Danicarum* 2 (1772), 626; *Testimonia minora saeculi XIII de S. Francisco Assisiensis,* ed. Leonard Lemmens (Quaracchi: Collegium S. Bonaventurae, 1926), 22–23.
  An Abbreviated Chronicle of the Succession of General Ministers by Peregrine of Bologna (c. 1305)
    Tractatus Thomae vulgo dicti de Eccleston, De Adventu Fratrum Minorum in Angliam. Collection d'Études d'Histoire Religieuse et Littéraire du Moyen Âge 7. ed. Andrew G. Little (Paris: Fischbacher, 1909), 141–145.
  Chronicle of Walter of Gisburn (1305–1313)
    "Chronica de gestis regum Angliae," ed. F. Liebermann, *Monumenta Germaniae Historica, Scriptores* 28 (Hanover: Hahn, 1897): 631–632; Lemmens, 23–24.

A Liturgical Legend in the Tradition of the Friars Preacher (1268)
  Testimonia minora saeculi XIII de S. Francisco Assisiensis, ed. Leonard Lemmens (Quaracchi: Collegium S. Bonaventurae, 1926), 259–262; *Analecta Franciscana sive Chronica Aliaque Varia Documenta ad Historiam Fratrum Minorum* X, ed. Patres Collegii S. Bonaventurae (Ad Claras Aquas, Quaracchi: Collegium S. Bonaventuarae, 1926–1941), 533–535.

A Life of Saint Francis by an Anonymous Monk of a German Monastery (c. 1275)
  Analecta Franciscana sive Chronica Aliaque Varia Documenta ad Historiam Fratrum Minorum X, ed. Patres Collegii S. Bonaventurae (Ad Claras Aquas, Quaracchi: Collegium S. Bonaventuarae, 1926–1941), 653–78; 694–719.

Vernacular Poetry
  Jacopone of Todi (1278–1293)
    Jacopone da Todi: Laudi, Tratte e Detti, ed. Franca Ageno, (Florence: Le Monnier, 1953); *Jacopone of Todi, The Lauds,* trans. Serge and Elizabeth Hughes, (New York: Paulist Press, 1982).
  Dante Alighieri (1315–1318)
    The Divine Comedy of Dante Alighieri, Paradiso, trans. Allen Mandelbaum, (Berkeley: University of California Press, 1984).